Contributions to Management Science

More information about this series at http://www.springer.com/series/1505

Hasan Dincer • Ümit Hacioglu • Serhat Yüksel
Editors

Strategic Design and Innovative Thinking in Business Operations

The Role of Business Culture and Risk Management

 Springer

Editors
Hasan Dincer
Istanbul Medipol University
Istanbul, Turkey

Ümit Hacioglu
Istanbul Medipol University
Istanbul, Turkey

Serhat Yüksel
Istanbul Medipol University
Istanbul, Turkey

ISSN 1431-1941   ISSN 2197-716X (electronic)
Contributions to Management Science
ISBN 978-3-319-77621-7   ISBN 978-3-319-77622-4 (eBook)
https://doi.org/10.1007/978-3-319-77622-4

Library of Congress Control Number: 2018940270

Printed on acid-free paper

This Springer imprint is published by the registered company Springer International Publishing AG part of Springer Nature.
The registered company address is: Gewerbestrasse 11, 6330 Cham, Switzerland

Preface

Competition increased almost in all sectors all over the world especially in the last years. This situation caused significant threats for the companies. Therefore, it becomes necessary for these companies to take some actions. Otherwise, it cannot be possible for them to survive in such a competitive environment. Hence, it is understood that companies should take strategic actions in order to be different from its competitors, such as generating new products or services. Owing to this issue, it can be preferred by many different customers.

Within this framework, strategic decisions taken by top managers play a very key role. The main reason behind this situation is that their decisions have an influence on many different parties. It can be said that top mangers should consider many different factors at the same time while developing new strategies. For this issue, top managers should design future with innovation and potential risks should also be taken into consideration in this process. With the help of this condition, companies can increase their competitive power in the market.

Similarly, the main purpose of this book is to provide a unique approach to strategic issues in management with innovative thinking and strategic design. Within the scope of this book, authors of contributory chapters develop innovative insights on supportive business culture, innovation, and strategy for competitive business operations. The main novelty of this book is to identify such a significant factor of the companies by considering different aspects. Therefore, it is believed that this study has an important contribution to the literature.

The book mainly consists of four different parts, which are business and organizational environment, strategic design on business operations, innovative thinking, and risk management activities in business operations. With respect to the business and organizational environment, some studies emphasized the effects of competition. In addition to this situation, the importance of customer selection is also underlined in this category. Moreover, the effects of the globalization are also underlined in this part.

On the other side, the part of strategic design on business operations focuses on mainly the actions taken by the companies in order to survive in competitive environment. Within this framework, there is a study that focuses on the relationship between strategic design and financial performance. Additionally, the effects of strategic design on business operations are also analyzed in this part. Moreover, in the category of innovative thinking, some studies regarding the product and service development are taken into account. In addition to them, there are also some studies related to the know-how and incremental innovation. The importance of disruptive innovation is also emphasized in this category.

In addition to them, regarding the risk management category, different kinds of risks for the companies are taken into consideration. For example, some studies focus on market risk which shows the risk of the companies in case of any changes in the market. Moreover, political risk is also emphasized in some different studies. Additionally, document risk in international trade is underlined in this category.

We believe this premier reference book will have a major role in the literature of business and strategy with its pioneering effects on strategy development process for competitive business environment.

Beykoz Istanbul, Turkey   Hasan Dincer
Beykoz Istanbul, Turkey   Ümit Hacioglu
Istanbul, Turkey   Serhat Yüksel

Contents

Part I
The Importance of Business and Organizational Environment

The Effects of Companies' Reverse Logistics Motivations on Their Reverse Logistics Networks

Metehan Feridun Sorkun and Meltem Onay

Abstract The aim of this paper is to show how the differences in the motivations of companies to implement reverse logistics affect their reverse logistics networks. Effective reverse logistics management facilitates the accomplishment of many goals for companies, such as reducing operational costs, increasing customer satisfaction, boosting brand value, and meeting the requirements of environmental regulations. However, the prominence of these motivations may vary according to sector. In some sectors, the strict government regulations in force may compel companies to implement reverse logistics, while in others, consumers may be highly conscious of the environmental-friendly production, encouraging companies to engage into reverse logistics activities. This situation calls for studies that analyse the differences in companies' motivations to implement reverse logistics, and explain in turn how these differences shape their reverse logistics networks. Hence, this study has adopted a multiple-case study analysing reverse logistics activities of four companies each representing one of the following sectors: textile, battery, building materials, and food. Such cross-sectoral analysis enables an examination of the reverse logistics network design according to different motivation factors. The results reveal that different RL motivations have an impact on three reverse logistics design issues: the collection of returns, the location to inspect returns, and forward/backward integration on RL networks. This study explicates the theoretical and practical implications of these results as well.

M. F. Sorkun (✉)
Department of Business Administration, İzmir University of Economics, İzmir, Turkey
e-mail: metehan.sorkun@izmirekonomi.edu.tr

M. Onay
Manisa Celal Bayar University, Manisa, Turkey

3

1   Introduction

Managing reverse product flows effectively provides many benefits to companies, which has recently put a spotlight on reverse logistics (RL). The companies having effective RL program are able to benefit from greater competitive, operational, environmental, and financial gains (Jayaraman and Luo 2007). First, RL directly affects customer service level. For example, the rapid repair and return of a customer's product increases customer satisfaction (Daugherty et al. 2002). Similarly, the source reduction in production via the reuse of the product parts and via the recycling of materials provides low-cost inputs to the company's production (Jack et al. 2010). Good RL management may also enable companies to capture more revenue by reselling on secondary markets those products, which could not be sold on primary markets (Ye et al. 2013). Alternatively, the collection and proper disposal of end-of-life products may arouse a feeling in consumers that a company executes its operations in an environmental-friendly way, boosting the company's brand value (Kumar and Christodoulopoulou 2014). In the same vein, when there is either government regulation or incentive with respect to the disposal and recovery of the returned products, the companies having effective RL activities can more easily satisfy these regulations and more frequently benefit from the incentives (Demirel et al. 2016).

Not all the above-mentioned motivation factors encouraging companies to adopt RL are equally significant in all sectors. The critical factor in one sector might be irrelevant in others. Therefore, the significances of the RL motivation factors largely depend on the sectoral characteristics and contingencies (e.g., customers' acceptance of used products, the importance for the customers of companies' having environment friendly operations etc.). For instance, whereas the government regulations for the recovery of products mainly drive the RL activities of electric-electronic and battery sectors in Turkey, such regulations are not binding in many other sectors. Nonetheless, that is not to say that RL is unimportant for other sectors. However, its importance may derive from distinct motivating factors. As an example, despite lack of binding regulation in textile sector in Turkey, RL is still important for the management of unsold products because fashion trends may quickly change. Similarly, the opportunity of recovering some valuable materials (e.g. lead in battery sector) from end-of-life products to feed the production of new original products can become major motivation to implement RL.

The companies' major motivation, partly influenced by sectoral factors, may significantly determine their RL network designs. Assuming that customer satisfaction is more important for a company than its cost reduction objectives, in this case, its RL network should be designed to keep the customer service level high. This requires the set of supporting RL network design decisions. Accordingly, many collection points should be available close to customers. In case the returned product needs to repaired and returned to the customer, partial shipments and fast transportation modes should be preferred for quick delivery despite their effects on costs. Similarly, the location where the condition of returned product is examined should be close to customers in order not to prolong the process. After this examination, if it is understood that resolving the problem takes time, the product ought to be replaced, but it should also be sent from the distribution centre close to the customer for quick delivery. This is just one example how the dominant reverse logistics motivation factor (customer satisfaction in this case) plays a significant role in the design of RL network. If the dominant motivating factor exemplified was cost minimization, then the above-mentioned network design decisions would be made to exploit the scales economy for higher efficiency. In that case, the centralized RL might be more favourable, in which RL activities (e.g. collection, inspection and processing) would await until the returns reach the sufficient amount to achieve economies of scale.

The aim of this paper is to show the dynamics of companies' RL networks with respect to their major motivations for implementing RL. Accordingly, a multiple-case study is adopted, in which the RL activities of four companies are examined. The case companies are selected from different sectors (textile, battery, building materials, and frozen food sectors) to increase the likelihood that they have different motivations for implementing their RL activities, since each operates within its own idiosyncratic context. Such cross-sectoral analysis makes a theoretical contribution by highlighting the relationship between RL motivation factors and RL network design. Similarly, the findings of this study provide useful managerial insights, guiding practitioners to design their RL networks with respect to their companies' main RL motivation.

The structure of this study is as follows. Section 2 first introduces the term "reverse logistics" and the related RL activities, and also provides information on RL motivation factors and RL network design. Section 3 explains the research design and methodology applied. Section 4 examines the case companies' RL activities and their RL networks. Section 5 makes cross-case analysis that enables the identification of the linkages between RL motivation factors and RL network design. Last, Sect. 6 concludes the study by discussing the theoretical and practical implications of the research results.

2 Literature Review

This section starts with the definition of the term "reverse logistics", and introduces related activities. Subsequently, it lists the most common motivations that may draw companies' attention to RL. Finally, it covers fundamental issues about RL network design.

2.1   Reverse Logistics Activities

The product flows across supply chain can be divided with respect to their directions: (i) forward flows, and (ii) reverse flows. The forward flow, which has long been the focus of scholars, refers to the forward movement of materials, parts, and products from upstream to the downstream supply chain stages. In contrast, the reverse flow refers to the movement of materials, parts, and products in the opposite direction. Recently, the necessity for the systematic management of reverse product flows for sustainable competitiveness has become well understood (Agrawal et al. 2015).

Rogers and Tibben-Lembke (1999) define reverse logistics as: "[T]he process of planning, implementing, and controlling the efficient, cost effective flow of raw materials, in process inventory, finished goods and related information from the point of consumption to the point of origin for the purpose of recapturing value or proper disposal". Das and Chowdhury (2012) list the reasons for the reverse flows across supply chain as follows:

- After use (end of life or before end of life);
- Returned under warranty;
- Defective;
- Obsolete products returned by the retailer (obsolescence due to emergence of new model or new technology)
- Products returned by consumers under exchange programs.

RL activities start with the collection of product returns, mainly for the reasons listed above. The condition of returns is then assessed, which provides an input to the disposition decision that aims to maximize the value recaptured from returned product, while carefully considering its proper disposal. Three main disposition alternatives for the decision makers are: (i) direct recovery, (ii) reprocessing, and (iii) final disposal, as shown below in Fig. 1 (Silva et al. 2013). Whereas it is possible to recapture value via the first two (i.e. direct use and reprocessing), the third aims to ensure the appropriate disposal of the returned products through incineration or landfilling.

Direct recovery is the disposition alternative, referring to recapturing value without processing the returned products. That is to say, the returned product can directly be resold at secondary markets, or its working parts can be re-used in other products without additional processes. Another disposition alternative is to reprocess the returned products. Depending on their conditions, value can be recaptured through different reprocessing operations—repairing, remanufacturing, and recycling. Thierry et al. (1995) makes the distinction between these three reprocessing operations in their study. Accordingly, the repairing involves fixing or replacing parts in order to return products to working order. The remanufacturing disassembles the product for testing, inspecting, and replacing all worn-out parts to restore the quality of returned product to the level of a new product. The recycling recovers the materials (e.g. plastic, glass, paper) from returned products to use them in the production of new original products. Figure 2 shows the supply chain stages at which each RL activity is usually implemented.

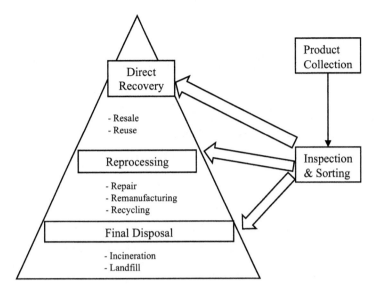

Fig. 1 Reverse logistics activities. Source: Silva et al. (2013, p. 379)

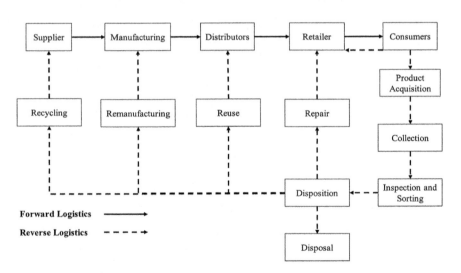

Fig. 2 Reverse logistics activities and supply chain stages. Source: Agrawal et al. (2015, p. 78)

2.2 Reverse Logistics Motivation Factors

Many incentives are available to motivate companies to adopt RL practices. These cover wide range of topics, such as marketing, competition, environment, social, and legislation. Nikolaou et al. (2013) classify these motivation factors either proactive or reactive. The factors within proactive group refer to the willingness of companies to apply RL to obtain benefits such as cost saving, retaining customers, improving company image, and increasing environmental performance. Factors, classified as reactive, imply that companies are compelled to adopt RL practices to meet the legislative requirements.

In a similar classification, the investigation of Ye et al. (2013) reveals three institutional pressures on managers to implement RL programs: government, customer, and competitor. Accordingly, government pressure encompasses the laws, regulations, and standards that enforce the production, collection and disposal of products in an environmentally friendly way. The customer pressure represents the expectations of the downstream supply chain members and end-consumers. Supply chain partners expect to be able to return the products back if they cannot sell. Similarly, in case end-consumers have problems after-sale, they demand a repair or replacement. The last pressure identified by Ye et al. (2013) is competitor pressure, which indicates the obligation of companies to implement RL due to competition. Any superiority of the company's rivals in terms of green actions, cost reduction and customer service via RL may cause a company to lose its customers, and thus decrease its profits.

As seen above, the studies categorize the drivers of RL in different ways; thus, each categorization may lack some RL motivations factors at micro level. Sorkun (2018) synthesises the categorizations available in literature, and then, extracts the RL motivations at micro-level in order to rank them hierarchically. Table 1 lists the companies' RL motivations identified by Sorkun (2018).

Table 1 Companies' reverse logistics motivations	
	• Boosting the repurchasing behaviour of customers
	• Creating good corporate social image
	• Exploting financial opportunities (e.g. second-hand market sales or extracting valuable items like gold)
	• Meeting government requirements
	• The preferential subsidy and tax policy
	• Reducing raw material cost
	• Reducing inventory
	• Reducing transportation costs
	• Increasing product quality
	• Reducing supply chain carbon footprint

2.3   Reverse Logistics Network Design

Logistics network design encompasses the set of strategic decisions given on the configuration of supply chain, such as the number of facilities, their locations, capacities, integration, roles, and the quantities of flow between them (Pishvaee et al. 2010). Since these decisions significantly affect companies' costs and customer service levels, the logistics network design has long been a focus of studies (Ramezani et al. 2013; Ghayebloo et al. 2015). The synthesis of these studies indicate that the logistics network design should be in accordance with the companies' objectives, such as quality level, responsiveness, and efficiency.

Logistics network design consists of the forward and reverse logistics network designs. Forward logistics network represents the roles, numbers, locations, capacities, and links (transportation and information) of facilities utilized to manage the product flows towards end-customers, such as supplier facilities, manufacturing plants, distribution centres, and retailer stores. The RL network similarly represents the roles, numbers, locations, capacities and links (transportation and information) of facilities; however, the facilities considered in RL network handle reverse flows, such as collection points, inspection points, remanufacturing site, recycling centre and disposal centres (Pishvaee et al. 2010). The RL network is usually not designed from scratch, but based on the forward logistics network (Srivastava 2008). For example, the facility, a part of forward logistics network (e.g. to store products), can also be used for inspection of the returned products in RL network.

RL network design decisions usually have contrary effects on costs (facility, distribution, and inventory costs) and customer service elements (e.g. quality, flexibility, responsiveness) (Shen and Daskin 2005). For instance, whereas the increase in the number of collection points means less distance for customers to travel to return products (Srivastava 2008), it is likely to raise the facility and distribution costs. Similarly, the use of same facility for both reverse and forward product flows may provide a saving in facility and distribution costs, although, such integration can increase inventory and information costs (Chopra 2003). The functions of facilities in network design are also important; remanufacturing centres requires higher investment than repair centres (Srivastava 2008) but their resulting lower production costs might outweigh this expense. On the other hand, repair centres are critical to customer satisfaction. The existence of such trade-offs shows the necessity of considering companies' priorities, and operational contexts while designing their RL networks (Fleischmann et al. 2004).

3   Research Design and Methodology

The research design of this study aims to illustrate how companies' RL motivations affect their RL network design. This cause-effect relationship requires a research methodology that provides rich and in-depth information, due to many variables involved in the research constructs of this study: RL motivations and RL network design. Therefore, a case study, as a qualitative research, is an appropriate methodology, since it supports the exploratory and descriptive purposes of this study (Yin 1994). Hence, in order to better explain the effect of RL motivation factors on RL network design, the multiple-case study was found appropriate (Miles and Huberman 1994) because it covers the analysis of distinct sectors across which the dominant RL motivation factor is likely to vary.

Two considerations are important while sampling in multiple-case study research, according to Seawright and Gerring (2008): (i) the sampled cases should represent the population of interest, and (ii) they should allow exploration of the variation in theoretical interest. With respect to the studies' positions along these two considerations, Seawright and Gerring (2008) list seven sampling methods: typical, typical, diverse, extreme, deviant, influential, most similar, and most different. The current sampling methodology can be categorized in "diverse", because this study examines how different motivations to implement RL affect companies' RL network designs. As motivations of RL activities vary across the sectors, four companies were selected, representing textile, building materials, battery, and food sectors. One difference is the shelve life of products, short in textile sector, but long in the building materials sector. Alternatively, while the recovery of products in battery sector provides low cost input, the recovery of frozen food provides no substantial gain to companies. These types of variations across sectors are assumed to have impact on the RL designs of the case companies. Therefore, this sampling allows this research examine the effect of the variations in RL motivation factors on RL network design.

The unit of analysis adopted in this multiple-case study is a company with substantial RL activities. For data collection, the semi-structured interview method was used to examine the RL activities of the following companies: (i) Jimmy Key, in textile sector, (ii) AKG Gazbeton, in building materials sector, (iii) İnci GS Yuasa, in battery sector, and (iv) Feast, in frozen food sector. The companies' senior managers with control and knowledge on their companies' RL activities were contacted for interviews. After getting necessary permissions from the companies for them to participate in this study, the list of open questions planned to structure interviews was e-mailed to the respective managers (interviewees) to allow them to prepare for interviews. These questions were developed after a comprehensive literature review by the authors of this study. Before the interviews, the authors also examined the company documents and company news, to guide question development. The interviews lasted for about two hours on average. In the meetings on the RL activities of Jimmy Key and Feast, there was one interviewee, the supply chain managers of their respective companies. In the meetings where the RL activities of AKG Gazbeton and İnci GS Yuasa were examined, multiple interviewees were available. For AKG Gazbeton, these were the director and deputy general manager, and for İnci GS Yuasa, these were the quality manager, purchasing manager, and sales manager. In all meetings, both authors of this study were present and individually took notes related to the research questions. In addition to interview notes, the companies provided their written answers to the questions e-mailed to them before interviews.

For data analysis, this study followed the structure of Eisenhardt (1989) which suggests a two-phase-analysis. First, the authors examined each company's RL activities and RL networks to become familiar with them and understand the unique patterns of each. In the second phase, a cross-case search was made between the case companies to compare their patterns (i.e. their similarities and differences). Here, the tactic followed was to make pairwise comparisons between the companies' RL motivation factors, and then to identify the similar and/or different effects on companies' RL network designs. To increase the reliability of analysis, the authors exchanged notes, and coded them with respect to this study's research questions.

4 Case Study: The RL Activities of the Case Companies

This section gives basic information on the case companies, and conveys their RL activities within their sectoral boundaries.

4.1 Jimmy Key

Jimmy Key, established in 1997, operates in the textile sector. Jimmy Key sells causal and comfortable clothing products, such as dresses, t-shirts, trousers, and skirts, procuring most of its products from Sun Tekstil. The company has a very strong relationship with Sun Tekstil, which are the members of the same holding company (Sun Holding). The company's manufacturing facility and the distribution centre are located at the same site in İzmir, Turkey. The number of Jimmy Key employees is around 90. The number of stores exclusively selling Jimmy Key products is 18, mostly on the coastal regions of Turkey, but the company also has two stores abroad in Ukraine and Azerbaijan. In addition, Jimmy Key products reach to final consumers through nearly 40 dealer stores, which sell other brands' products.

Sun Tekstil not only manufactures textile products but also sells products' design to big retailers such as Zara and Marks & Spencer. For these products, Jimmy Key is not the producer; instead, it procures products and designs from its sister company, Sun Tekstil, or supplies them from contract manufacturers, again through Sun Tekstil. However, Sun Tekstil is not involved in Jimmy Key's supply of the accessories. Jimmy Key directly procures the accessories for its products from various accessory suppliers. The company outsources its transportation activities to UPS for outbound logistics, and to local transportation firms for inbound logistics.

The reasons for the product returns in the Jimmy Key supply chain are mainly quality problems and unsold products. Most quality problems are identified with the arrival of products at the Sun Tekstil warehouse. These problems are generally related to product packaging, labelling, or size. In these circumstances, products are rejected and returned back suppliers.

The seasonality of demand in textile sector is another major reason for product returns. The products that cannot be sold in season are returned. Similarly, keeping products on shelves for a long time can cause product defects (e.g. hanging a t-shirt for a long time may create a defect). In these cases, returned products are sold in Jimmy Key outlet stores which sell second quality products at lower prices. If the defects are at a reasonable level, Jimmy Key takes one of the following three actions: (i) selling them to wholesalers, (ii) donating them, and (iii) upcycling to design new products.

End-consumers may return their products to Jimmy Key stores after-sale. The return policy of the company is very flexible, and most consumers are pacified by offers of product exchange, gift card, and reimbursement. However, if the problem with the product becomes widespread, it is withdrawn. Since the disposition decision on the returned products does not require any technical knowledge, the head of the Jimmy Key warehouse can make rapid disposition decisions. Note that Jimmy Key does not ship the products returned from consumers immediately to its distribution centre, makes monthly deliveries to allow the returns reaching a certain level for higher operational efficiency.

4.2   AKG Gazbeton

AKG Gazbeton, operating in building materials sector, produces autoclaved aerated concrete (AAC) blocks that are heat-insulated, light, non-combustible block, as well as, reinforced products with earthquake safety and Minepor Insulating Board. AKG Gazbeton has currently 472 employees, and has the production capacity of 1,713,960 m^3/year, with its three manufacturing facilities in the Turkish cities of Kırıkkale, İzmir, and Çorum. The company's manufacturing facility in Çorum had the world's largest capacity in its sector by the time it was established. Raw materials (e.g. aluminium, lime and cements), consumable material, and pallets are the main supply categories of the company. AKG Gazbeton sells its products to building firms' construction sites, dealers in specific regions, and retailers from which households purchase building materials.

The product fracture is the main cause of returns to AKG Gazbeton from its customers. In these instances, the company's quality team visits the customer's site to examine the case instead of returning these products to AKG Gazbeton's facility, to avoid the excessive transportation costs (note that the company outsources all transportation activities to various transportation companies). After the quality team's examination, if the customer is found right, the product is replaced. Another purpose of the quality team's visits is to educate customers since most product fractures are due to the inappropriate treatment of their workers.

The reuse of materials in the production of ACC is possible and the product shelve life of the products is very long. These properties diminish the amount of efforts made for waste management. Nevertheless, it is necessary to carefully handle potentially dangerous material, including aluminium and some oils. AKG Gazbeton accumulates these materials during production up to a certain level and then sends them in certain quantities to the disposal centre authorized by government in return for a fee. On the other hand, AKG Gazbeton can generate extra profit by selling the surplus production materials. While metals can be sold to scrap dealers, wooden pallets can be sold to employees at an affordable price as firewood.

AKG Gazbeton's product selling price includes the cost of pallet used to transport the product. If these pallets are returned from customers in good condition, AKG Gazbeton reimburses the cost of the pallets. These pallets can be made of wood or plastic. Although the cost of plastic pallets is currently higher than the cost of wooden pallets, AKG Gazbeton has implemented an EU funded project (Horizon 2020 programme) to increase the use of plastic pallets owing to their many advantages. First, the high robustness of plastic pallets enables multiple use. Besides, the assessment criteria for the condition of the returned plastic pallets are more objective, eliminating the disputes with customers. Moreover, there is little risk of theft for plastic pallets because their use for other purposes is limited in contrast to wooden pallets (e.g. wood is used for heating). Plastic pallets also weigh less, lowering transportation costs and improving job safety. Last, the use of plastic pallets has positive environmental effects, eliminating the need to cut trees for wooden pallets.

4.3 İnci GS Yuasa

İnci GS Yuasa was established in 2015, as the joint venture of İnci Akü and GS Yuasa. The company operates in the battery sector, and has over 700 employees. İnci GS Yuasa has the highest level of battery export in Turkey and the second largest market share in Turkish domestic market. İnci GS Yuasa has two factories in Manisa (Turkey) where it produces industrial and starter batteries. For the production of these batteries, İnci GS Yuasa purchases lead, plastic, chemicals, battery terminal, separator and other materials from suppliers. To increase the value generated along the supply chain, the parent company, İnci Akü, sometimes becomes the second-tier supplier of İnci GS Yuasa, supplying plastic and battery terminals to the first-tier suppliers of İnci GS Yuasa.

İnci GS Yuasa sells its products directly to major automotive OEMs (original equipment manufacturers) and also to these giant manufacturers' OESs (original equipment services), such as Fiat, Ford, Mercedes Benz, Hyundai, Cat, and Peugeot. For the after-market, generally consisting of individual users replacing their vehicle batteries, İnci GS Yuasa has 60 main dealers dedicated to selling the products of İnci GS Yuasa. Alternatively, these main dealers may get the batteries to the individual end consumers through sub dealers spread all over Turkey.

The product life of batteries ranges between 2 and 5 years. It is also noteworthy that after the battery is produced, it starts depleting even if unused. Thereby, İnci GS Yuasa operates the built-to-order production system. That is to say, the company's production activities start in response to customer demand. İnci GS Yuasa's production system is designed to produce a high volume and low variety products.

Therefore, the efficiency in production, avoiding the stoppage of the production lines is crucial. If it occurs because of the supplier's failure, both the related components are shipped back to the respective supplier, and that supplier is compelled to compensate for the loss incurred due to the stoppage. The returns from individual end-consumers through dealers is another cause of reverse flow on the İnci GS Yuasa's RL network. The customer service team examines these returned batteries. Unless the problem is obviously due the consumer, actions are taken to increase customer satisfaction, even if guarantee period (generally 2 years) has expired.

If manufacturing defects occur due to the operations of İnci GS Yuasa, these defective products are kept first in the company's waste unit. As they reach up to certain level (usually once a month), the defective products are shipped to the recycling centre. Similarly, the company's policy to collect returns from dealers aims to strike a balance between costs and the customer service level provided to dealers. İnci GS Yuasa's frequent collection of the returns from its dealers increases its transportation costs, but on the other hand, long waits disadvantage its dealers, because the low collection frequency increases their holding costs.

The recovery of lead constitutes the important part of İnci GS Yuasa's RL activities. After the batteries are returned due to manufacturing defects, product problems, and completed lifecycles, they are broken down to recover the lead. This reuse option is profitable for the company when it is less costly than the price of imported lead which is determined by the lead commodity exchange market based in London. Another important driver of the company's RL activities is the government regulations enforcing battery manufacturers to collect 90% of the batteries produced. İnci GS Yuasa needs to pay the battery owners, even if the battery lifecycle has ended because the reusability of materials in batteries (e.g. lead) gives them commercial value. At this point, coping with scrappers who are competing for the end-of-life batteries from owners is a challenge for İnci GS Yuasa.

The collection of end-of-life batteries is carried out by the company's sister company, İnci Logistics. Since a battery contains materials such as lead and poly-propylene, it is categorized as dangerous cargo, and requires the preparation of specific transportation document (ADR). After the end-of-life batteries are collected, they are sent to an authorized recycling centre. Based on the results of the chemical analysis made in this centre, İnci GS Yuasa decides how much lead recovered from returned batteries should be used in the final mix, in which high quality pure imported lead and recovered lead are mixed for the production of new batteries.

4.4 Feast

Feast, a company operating in the frozen food sector, was established in 2000. The company has around 1300 employees, and has a plant covering around 85,000 m^2 in İzmir, Turkey. This plant, having 100,000 tons annual capacity, is used to produce potato products, fruit and vegetables, coated and pastry products. In addition, Feast has six warehouses, one of which is the one of largest in its kind within Europe. This warehouse is equiped with computerized technology that can keep up to 30,000 tons of products at either $-25\,°C$ or $0–4\,°C$.

Feast claims its products (frozen foods) are fresher than the foods reaching the consumers through traditional channels because the company freezes the products just after harvest. In contrast, the foods delivery to retailer stores over traditional distribution channels takes much longer, since they have to pass through various wholesale market locations. Therefore, Feast works closely with its farmers to provide the freshness promised, and to increase its production productivity. Likewise, to capture higher productivity, Feast makes R&D on the seed production and procures some of the imported seeds through its sister company, Öztar. After Feast completes its production processes (e.g. collecting food, sorting them, and packaging), the products are directed to the company's cold storage warehouse until shipment to customers. For transportation, Feast works with transportation companies that have special refrigerated vehicles.

Feast mainly has three types of customers: supermarkets, chain stores, and local grocery stores. Feast has collaborative relationship with its supermarket customers such as Migros and Bim, cooperating on aggregate production planning and product customization (e.g. sizes, packaging etc.) with respect to the supermarket customer needs. Feast also sells its products to chain stores such as Burger King and McDonalds. Additionally, the company has regional dealers through which its products are delivered to the local grocery stores.

The reasons for the reverse product flows on the Feast's RL network are mainly due to packaging problems, the sensorial complaints of consumers about foods, and the visual distortions on foods perceived by consumers. Packaging problems are the major cause of product returns. Improper handling of products, the overturns and falls of products from shelfs, and the shocks and vibration during transportation are the main causes of packaging problems. These are usually identified by the Feast's customers (by other supply chain members) before they reach to the end-consumers. In these cases, Feast sales personnel go to the customer's site and send photos of the problematic product to their quality department. If no customer fault is found, the products are returned on trucks on their return journeys if there is enough capacity to deliver the damaged products back to Feast's facility. This integration between reverse and forward transportation is necessary because the transportation of frozen food is costly, requiring considerable energy (fuel) to keep the foods at the predetermined temperature. After the products are returned to the site of Feast, the examinations are made to see if the damage to the packaging has caused any harm to the food. If not, the product is repackaged, and alternative markets are sought for these products.

The returns due to the sensual and visual complaints of end-consumers are handled differently because they concern the important issues of the company's image, and human health. For this reason, in the case that Feast suspects any risk to products might be incurred, the company has the policy of recalling all respective products. Even if this problem has not yet happened in the company's history, the managers take this issue very seriously. The visual and sensory complaints of consumers are assessed by the company's food engineers to check if the company

Table 2 The major RL motivations of the case companies	Jimmy Key	• Increasing customer satisfaction • Reselling unsold products
	AKG Gazbeton	• Reducing transportation costs • Reducing supply chain carbon footprint
	İnci GS Yuasa	• Meeting government regulations • Reducing raw material cost
	Feast	• Maintaining good corporate image • Reducing transportation costs

has any fault. If there is any risk (i.e. even there is a slight probability that the consumers are right), Feast takes all necessary actions to eliminate the problem, because these issues are closely related to human health and corporate image.

The foods delivered from farmers might also create quality problems for Feast. In these cases, the company separates the parts of food that can be used, and returns the rest to the farmers. On the other hand, the waste caused by the production processes of Feast is held for disposal in amounts of 100 tons. If the waste (food) sorting is possible, it is used to feed animals, if not, it is incinerated.

5   The RL Motivations as the Dynamics of RL Network Design

The previous section has depicted the case companies' RL activities shaped by their RL program goals. Based on their RL activities, this section aims to explain the role of RL motivations in companies' RL network design decisions. For this purpose, the authors have made cross-case analysis and identified key differences and similarities across cases, considering the companies' major RL motivation factors, as illustrated in Table 2. This analysis allows making propositions on the following three RL network design issues: (i) the collection of returns, (ii) the location of product inspection, (iii) forward and backward integration for RL activities.

The method of collecting returns is the first critical design decision for RL networks. Among the four case companies, the results show that İnci GS Yuasa is the only company that is proactive and willing to collect returns. The other three case firms aim to handle returns efficiently but do not look motivated to initiate the collection process. Therefore, they are reactive in collecting returns because their product returns usually occur due to problems. The main reason for Jimmy Key usually taking products back is failure to sell because of seasonality factors. AKG Gazbeton have returns due to the product fractures. Likewise, Feast receives the products back when there are packaging problems. In contrast, İnci GS Yuasa acts proactively in order to meet government regulations, enforcing battery manufacturers to collect back the 90% of the batteries produced. Besides, the returned batteries, even if they complete their lifetimes, enable them to reduce their raw material cost by reusing the recovered lead for new original battery production.

Proposition 1 *The RL motivations of meeting regulations and reducing raw material costs make companies act proactive in collecting product returns from their customers.*

Another important RL network design issue is a choice of location where product inspection is made to assess the condition of returns. Some differences exist between the case companies in this parameter of RL network design. Feast and AKG Gazbeton inspect the returned products at the customer-site to avoid an extra shipment to their own facility that would incur a large transportation cost. For İnci GS Yuasa and Jimmy Key, transportation costs are also significant, but they are able to delay the returns to the some extents, allowing them exploit a scales economy in transportation. In addition, Jimmy Key and İnci GS Yuasa have the opportunity to recover value from the returns. In contrast, the value that can be recovered from the product returns of AKG Gazbeton and Feast are very limited.

Proposition 2 *The RL motivation of reducing transportation cost makes companies to inspect the returns on customer-sites.*

Proposition 3 *The RL motivation of recovering value from returns allow companies to make inspection at their own facilities.*

There are variations in supply chain stages with which the case companies integrate for RL activities. The analysis results indicate that the respective forward/backward integration of the case companies depends on the purpose (motivation) of their RL activities. To begin with, there is forward integration on Jimmy Key's RL network. The company's distribution centre highly integrates with other aspects of the business, since the products have high seasonality, thus, the company has to find ways of reselling unsold products. Moreover, to keep the customer satisfaction level high, Jimmy Key establishes close relationships with its stores to find solutions to the problems of returned products.

Proposition 4 *The RL motivations of increasing customer satisfaction and reselling unsold products lead to forward integration on RL network.*

When RL network of İnci GS Yuasa is examined, backward integration draws attention. Two main motivations of İnci GS Yuasa's RL activities are collecting end-of-life batteries, and reusing lead for new original battery production. For collection, İnci GS Yuasa works with its sister transportation company, İnci Lojistik. To recover lead, İnci GS Yuasa has a strong relationship with the authorized recycling centre that carries out the chemical analysis of returned batteries and reports the reusability of lead for new original product production. Similarly, Feast integrates backward with its suppliers (farmers), because the food health is very important for maintaining its corporate image. In order to prevent incurring a risk from food supplies, Feast carefully selects and trains its farmers.

Proposition 5 *The RL motivations of reducing raw material cost and maintaining good corporate image lead to backward integration on RL network.*

A final distinctive point is how AKG Gazbeton's aim to reduce supply chain carbon footprint results in both forward and backward integration on its RL network. In parallel to this goal, the company focuses on decreasing the number of returns by educating customers rather than handling returns efficiently and effectively. Similarly, the AKG Gazbeton's plastic pallet project, which aims to increase the reusability of pallets, helps company reduce carbon footprint. However, this project requires company to make R&D on material technology, enforcing AKG Gazbeton to work closely with the producers of materials used in plastic pallets (i.e. with its suppliers).

Proposition 6 *The RL motivation of reducing carbon footprint results in both forward and backward integration on RL network.*

6 Conclusion

The prior research has attempted to reveal the dynamics of RL networks with various variables such as the demand level for used products (Mutha and Pokharel 2009), product modularity (Sorkun and Onay 2016), uncertainty (Lee and Dong 2009), and retailer competition (Savaskan and Wassenhove 2006). This study contributes to this line of research by showing possible ways that companies' RL motivations influence their RL network designs. The multiple case study conducted for this purpose illustrates that the collection of returns, the location to inspect returns, and forward/backward integration on RL networks are the three RL network design issues that vary with respect to companies' RL implementation motivations. These findings have a number of important theoretical and practical implications, providing insights on the nature of relationship between the companies' RL motivations and RL networks.

First, the findings imply that whether companies should act proactively or reactively to collect their returns depends on companies' expectations from RL activities. Different from other case companies analysed, only İnci GS Yuasa was found to act proactively. The main reason for this is that the increase in the number of product returns helps İnci GS Yuasa accomplish its goals of meeting of government regulations and the reduction in raw material costs. Nonetheless, when the main RL motivation is the reduction of negative consequences of product returns (e.g., loss of reputation, cost), it is important to take managerial actions to reduce the number of returns, because no return means no RL cost and no customer complaints. Therefore, companies that expect to reduce negative consequences of returns via RL activities, do not waste their efforts in collecting higher number of returns, instead, their consideration is to manage effectively the after-customer return process.

This study also reveals that the location choice for inspecting returns on RL network, where the condition of returns are assessed, is influenced by the companies' motivations to implement RL activities. For this choice, two factors play a major role in companies' decisions: transportation costs and the recovered value obtained from the returned product. According to results, as the recovered value is high and the transportation cost of returns is negligible, companies prefer inspecting their returns at their own facilities. However, when the transportation cost is high and the recovered value is limited, the companies choose to inspect their returns on customer-site or close to the collection points, to decrease transportation costs. If there is high (low) transportation costs and high (low) value that can be recovered from returns, practitioners should make cost-benefit analysis and then should determine the optimal inspection location for company.

The results suggest that the companies' RL motivations, at least partly, determine the level of forward or backward integration on RL network. The findings indicate that the market-oriented motivation factors (i.e. increasing customer satisfaction and reselling unsold products) encourage companies to integrate forward on their RL networks. As companies are able to increase the level of coordination and collaboration with their stores and distribution centres, they are able to better address customer complaints, and find profitable ways of selling their unsold products. On the other hand, the results demonstrate that when the RL motivation is focused on keeping costs low and improving corporate image, companies rely on close relationships with their suppliers, and keep control on them. Such control mechanism causes a backward integration on companies' RL network. Finally, it is noteworthy to state that carbon footprint reduction requires both forward and backward integration.

This study has a number of limitations that might guide future research to explore further factors relevant to the relationship between RL motivation factors and RL network design. The number of companies that this study has examined is limited to four. Therefore, this study's cross-analysis on these companies' RL activities may not be sufficient to explore all factors involved in the cause-effect relationship between companies' RL motivations and RL network designs. Thus, future research may use a larger company sample, which will allow more precise conclusions. This further research endeavour will also help test the validity of the propositions in this study. Another possibility for future research is using different case selection techniques. This study's research design was planned to select the case companies from different sectors to ensure the diversity of RL motivations, hence, it will be possible to observe their distinct effects on RL network design. Nevertheless, other case selection techniques might also be useful to shed further light on this study's research questions. For example, selecting companies within same sector and with the same RL motivations will allow a comparison of their RL networks. Such research design could help testing the significance of the proposed relationship between RL motivations and RL network designs.

References

Agrawal, S., Singh, R. K., & Murtaza, Q. (2015). A literature review and perspectives in reverse logistics. *Resources, Conservation and Recycling, 97*, 76–92.

Chopra, S. (2003). Designing the distribution network in a supply chain. *Transportation Research Part E: Logistics and Transportation Review, 39*(2), 123–140.

Das, K., & Chowdhury, A. H. (2012). Designing a reverse logistics network for optimal collection, recovery and quality-based product-mix planning. *International Journal of Production Economics, 135*(1), 209–221.

Daugherty, P. J., Myers, M. B., & Richey, R. G. (2002). Information support for reverse logistics: the influence of relationship commitment. *Journal of Business Logistics, 23*(1), 85–106.

Demirel, E., Demirel, N., & ve Gökçen, H. (2016). A mixed integer linear programming model to optimize reverse logistics activities of end-of-life vehicles in Turkey. *Journal of Cleaner Production, 112*, 2101–2113.

Eisenhardt, K. M. (1989). Building theories from case study research. *Academy of Management Review, 14*(4), 532–550.

Fleischmann, M., Bloemhof-Ruwaard, J. M., Beullens, P., & Dekker, R. (2004). Reverse logistics network design. In R. Dekker, M. Fleischmann, K. Inderfurth, & L. N. Van Wassenhove (Eds.), *Reverse logistics* (pp. 65–94). Berlin: Springer.

Ghayebloo, S., Tarokh, M. J., Venkatadri, U., & Diallo, C. (2015). Developing a bi-objective model of the closed-loop supply chain network with green supplier selection and disassembly of products: the impact of parts reliability and product greenness on the recovery network. *Journal of Manufacturing Systems, 36*, 76–86.

Jack, E. P., Powers, T. L., & Skinner, L. (2010). Reverse logistics capabilities: Antecedents and cost savings. *International Journal of Physical Distribution & Logistics Management, 40*(3), 228–246.

Jayaraman, V., & Luo, Y. (2007). Creating competitive advantages through new value creation: A reverse logistics perspective. *The Academy of Management Perspectives, 21*(2), 56–73.

Kumar, V., & Christodoulopoulou, A. (2014). Sustainability and branding: An integrated perspective. *Industrial Marketing Management, 43*(1), 6–15.

Lee, D. H., & Dong, M. (2009). Dynamic network design for reverse logistics operations under uncertainty. *Transportation Research Part E: Logistics and Transportation Review, 45*(1), 61–71.

Miles, M. B., & Huberman, A. M. (1994). *Qualitative data analysis: An expanded sourcebook.* Thousand Oaks, CA: Sage.

Mutha, A., & Pokharel, S. (2009). Strategic network design for reverse logistics and remanufacturing using new and old product modules. *Computers & Industrial Engineering, 56*(1), 334–346.

Nikolaou, I. E., Evangelinos, K. I., & Allan, S. (2013). A reverse logistics social responsibility evaluation framework based on the triple bottom line approach. *Journal of Cleaner Production, 56*, 173–184.

Pishvaee, M. S., Farahani, R. Z., & Dullaert, W. (2010). A memetic algorithm for bi-objective integrated forward/reverse logistics network design. *Computers & Operations Research, 37*(6), 1100–1112.

Ramezani, M., Bashiri, M., & Tavakkoli-Moghaddam, R. (2013). A new multi-objective stochastic model for a forward/reverse logistic network design with responsiveness and quality level. *Applied Mathematical Modelling, 37*(1), 328–344.

Rogers, D. S., & Tibben-Lembke, R. S. (1999). *Going backwards: Reverse logistics trends and practices.* Pittsburgh, PA: RLEC Press.

Savaskan, R. C., & Van Wassenhove, L. N. (2006). Reverse channel design: The case of competing retailers. *Management Science, 52*(1), 1–14.

Seawright, J., & Gerring, J. (2008). Case selection techniques in case study research: A menu of qualitative and quantitative options. *Political Research Quarterly, 61*(2), 294–308.

Shen, Z. J. M., & Daskin, M. S. (2005). Trade-offs between customer service and cost in integrated supply chain design. *Manufacturing & Service Operations Management, 7*(3), 188–207.

Silva, D. A. L., Renó, G. W. S., Sevegnani, G., Sevegnani, T. B., & Truzzi, O. M. S. (2013). Comparison of disposable and returnable packaging: A case study of reverse logistics in Brazil. *Journal of Cleaner Production, 47*, 377–387.

Sorkun, M. F. (2018). The hierarchy of motivations turning manufacturers' attention to reverse logistics. *Ege Academic Review, 18*(2). https://doi.org/10.21121/eab.2018237353.

Sorkun, M. F., & Onay, M. (2016). Ürün modülerliğinin ters lojistik süreçleri üzerinden tedarik zinciri stratejilerine etkisi. *Sosyal Ve Beşeri Bilimler Dergisi, 8*(2), 41–57.

Srivastava, S. K. (2008). Network design for reverse logistics. *Omega, 36*(4), 535–548.

Thierry, M., Salomon, M., Van Nunen, J., & Van Wassenhove, L. (1995). Strategic issues in product recovery management. *California Management Review, 37*(2), 114–135.

Ye, F., Zhao, X., Prahinski, C., & Li, Y. (2013). The impact of institutional pressures, top managers' posture and reverse logistics on performance—Evidence from China. *International Journal of Production Economics, 143*(1), 132–143.

Yin, R. (1994). *Case study research: Design and methods*. Beverly Hills, CA: Sage.

Business Performance, Corporate Structure and Competitiveness in Mexico

José G. Vargas-Hernández and Martha Lizbeth Bautista Ramírez

Abstract This paper aims to analyze the structure, characteristics and business performance in the 32 States of Mexico, to determine their levels of competitiveness. It follows a previous study by Unger, Flores and Ibarra (*Productividad y capital humano: fuentes complementarias de la competitividad de los estados mexicanos*, 2013), in which a model is applied to measure business competitiveness. The variables that are taken are the salary and the value added in the model to measure competitiveness. The research results confirm the hypothesis that the competitiveness of States can be determined by the business structure, productivity and therefore higher wage advantage.

1 Introduction

The objective of this research is to determine the structure, characteristics and business performance of MSMEs and the large company (LC) within 32 States of the Mexican Republic, in order to observe that States are competitive or noncompetitive. It departs from a previous study by Unger et al. (2013), in which a model is applied to measure the competitiveness of States, creating two sub-groups. The first includes the competitive States and the second noncompetitive States. The application of this model will be for all States classifying MSMEs and LC to meet corporate behavior and show whether or not these States are competitive.

For purposes of this paper, it presents an analysis of each of the economic activities of the States of Mexico that is done by selecting the total industrial branches. In addition, the variables of interest in the study that were selected are

J. G. Vargas-Hernández (✉)
University Center for Economic and Managerial Sciences, University of Guadalajara, Guadalajara, México

M. L. B. Ramírez
Centro Universitario de Ciencias Económico Administrativas, Universidad de Guadalajara, Guadalajara, México

© Springer International Publishing AG, part of Springer Nature 2018
H. Dincer et al. (eds.), *Strategic Design and Innovative Thinking in Business Operations*, Contributions to Management Science,
https://doi.org/10.1007/978-3-319-77622-4_2

23

economic units, total personnel employed, total remunerated personnel, total remunerations, total gross output, gross value added census, gross fixed capital formation, total investment, total stock of fixed assets and total depreciation of fixed assets.

They are proposed as specific targets.

A. Describe competitiveness in terms of wages and value added.

Therefore, in this investigation it arises to describe the relationship between company performance and competitiveness of States, establishing the following assumptions:

1. H0 the performance of companies determines the level of competitiveness of States.
2. H1 The competitiveness of States is measured through the MSME business structure.

2   The Business Structure

In Mexico the overview of studies on the business structure, business, merchant, etc., presents very heterogeneous characteristics (Romero 2003, p. 805). This paper focuses on the classification of companies by size, since the behavior of MSMEs and LC described to identify which States of the Mexican Republic are competitive (SCIAN, 2013). Likewise, competitiveness is described in terms of wages and the value added generated in each State.

From the results of the Economic Census 2009, the National Institute of Statistics and Geography (INEGI), allows stratification of establishments by employed personnel. Companies can be classified depending on their sector, as these may be commercial, industrial or service. Also, companies are classified as micro, small, medium or large by the number of employees working within the volume of production and sales measured in annual minimum wage.

In many regions, the SME is the only source of employment and economic renewal SMEs go through major changes due to globalization and economic liberalization that has experienced the country as they are a key to economic development. They are an important part of the national economy by trade agreements that Mexico has had in recent years, contributing to a high rate of productivity, competitiveness and sustainability, as well as increased market participation within a framework of increasing production chains that generate greater domestic value added.

3 Competitiveness

The concept of competitiveness is very broad because there is a widespread use made of it and the abundant literature on the subject. There is ambiguity in the meaning that is given. For this paper, competitiveness is associated with profitability, productivity, costs; value added, market share, exports, technological innovations, among others (McFetridge 1995). Unger et al. (2013) measure the competitiveness of States through two key economic indicators, labor productivity and wages. Each of these indicators is associated with the economic activities of each State and in this way classifies and groups the States according to their competitiveness to guide policy measures.

This work is based on the study of labor productivity and average wages as explanatory variables of States revealed competitiveness, making parallel an observation about the specializations that entities have in their respective industries. Add to this, the revealed competitiveness index focused on company size and economic activity is calculated. Likewise, the level of industrial concentration and Herfindahl-Hirschman index (HHI) and Dominance Index (DI) shall be calculated.

4 Methods

Competitiveness analysis is done in consideration of two key economic indicators, labor productivity and wages in order is to distinguish the States in terms of two criteria:

A. By type of State under competitive conditions—competitive and noncompetitive.
B. By sub-groups in each State reflects their conditions of productivity and wages.

The variable used is the gross value added Census (Thousand Pesos).

Plan information processing indices are developed to measure competitiveness, in terms of wages and added value and competitiveness by State and stratum (MSMEs - LC).

A. **Estimated advantage for labor productivity and wage advantage**.

The study of regional competitiveness begins with labor productivity, but it has to go beyond the description of the result. It is necessary to study other characteristic dimensions of any territory (Martin and Sunley 2003). This paper delves into the version of competitiveness of activities and entities. The estimate is to integrate two key elements of economic competitiveness: labor productivity on the country (revealed advantage by productivity), and the wage level relative is associated as an employment indicator of labor with better qualification (salary revealed advantage).

Selected variables for estimating advantage for labor productivity and wage advantage compared to 2009 economic census are:

  a. Gross value added census.
  b. Paid staff
  c. Total remuneration.

To estimate labor productivity of each economic activity by State it is divided "VA" (Gross Value Added Census) between "L" (paid staff). To estimate wage advantage of every State and every economic activity, it was divided "W" (total remuneration) between "L" (paid staff).

B. Relative Index Competitiveness or Unveiled (ICR).

With data of variables INEGI Economic Census (2009) (total gross value added census, paid staff and total salaries) are calculated separately each of the revealed advantage benefits. First, the product is obtained by working for the state $\left(\frac{VA}{L} state\right)$ and is divided for the same reason but nationally $\left(\frac{VA}{L}\right)$ *country*. The same is true for average wages $\left(\frac{W}{L}\right)$ *state* between $\left(\frac{W}{L}\right)$ *country*. Both measures together bring us closer to the relative competitiveness or "revealed" C ** activity in the State.

In other words the competitiveness of activities in each entity can be seen in comparing each activity on two factors:

(a) The estimate of labor productivity of each activity in the State with respect thereto nationally (VA/L)
(b) The comparison of the average salary of the activity in the State to the national average wage of such activity (W/L).

The following formula expresses the sum of both advantages in relation to the activities of each state
Formula 1

$$C^{**}_{act} = \left(\frac{VA}{L}\right) + \left[\left(\frac{W}{L}\right) - 1\right] = \left[\left(\frac{\frac{VA}{L_{edo}}}{\frac{VA}{L_{país}}}\right)\right] + \left[\left(\frac{\frac{W}{L_{edo}}}{\frac{W}{L_{país}}}\right) - 1\right]$$

1. Analysis of the results obtained.

Below are observed the rates by productivity advantage, wage and relative competitiveness to each of the states of the Republic for fiscal 2009 census (INEGI 2009a, b). See Table 1.

The relative competitiveness index is obtained through data of productivity advantage and wage advantage. Queretaro is the State with the highest relieved competitiveness, followed by Nuevo Leon, Tamaulipas, Sonora, Mexico City, Baja California Sur, Baja California, Mexico and Jalisco are kept at pair, followed by Chihuahua and Coahuila finally.

Figure 1 shows the behavior of added value/personal paid nationally and in Nuevo Leon, Mexico City, Baja California, Queretaro, Sonora, Baja California Sur, Coahuila, Chihuahua, State of Mexico, Jalisco and Tamaulipas. The City of

Table 1 Productivity advantage index—wage and relative competitiveness by Federal entity of the competitive states

Entity	Productivity advantage (VA/L*)	Advantage by salary (W/L*)	Relative competitiveness (C**)
Nuevo León	1.10129116	1.12002702	1.221318184
Mexico City	1.364488434	0.44693109	0.811419521
Baja California	1.012005606	0.36235269	0.374358298
Querétaro	1.124042443	1.11073543	1.23477787
Sonora	0.940678309	1.01921129	0.959889597
Baja California Sur	1.171728391	0.37230465	0.544033042
Coahuila	0.740608869	0.3327698	0.073378671
Chihuahua	0.874791711	0.3341344	0.208926115
México	0.949551927	0.2932799	0.242831828
Jalisco	0.914535955	0.32997744	0.244513398
Tamaulipas	1.016609742	0.97542984	0.992039579

Source: Own elaboration based on data from the 2009 Economic Census, INEGI

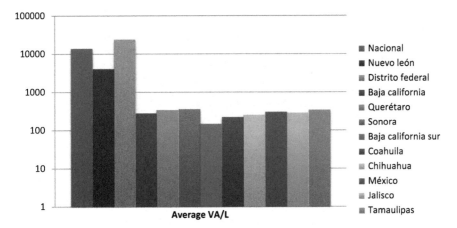

Fig. 1 Total Average value added/personal paid (2009). Source: Based on data from the 2009 Economic Census, INEGI

Mexico has a higher competitive level of value added, followed by the national average, followed by Nuevo Leon, Sonora, Tamaulipas, Queretaro, State of Mexico, Jalisco, Baja California, Chihuahua, Coahuila and finally the State of Baja California Sur (Table 2).

The Fig. 2 shows a comparison of the value added/staff paid between MSMEs and the large company (LC) of Nuevo Leon, Mexico City, Baja California, Queretaro, Sonora, Baja California Sur, Coahuila, Chihuahua, State of Mexico, Jalisco and Tamaulipas. It can be seen that the VA/L of MSMEs is superior in

Table 2 Comparison of added value between personal paid (2009)

Average of VA/L			
Entity	SMEs	Large	Total general
National	17999.62	950.45	13796.80
Nuevo Leon	4966.72	430.51	4059.48
Mexico City	31918.07	738.54	24161.97
Baja California	237.88	507.77	280.89
Querétaro	348.77	311.77	342.81
Sonora	281.27	733.98	360.43
Baja California Sur	122.73	380.01	147.16
Coahuila	195.23	391.29	223.24
Chihuahua	251.89	264.49	254.16
México	268.07	456.79	303.64
Jalisco	268.36	367.66	286.79
Tamaulipas	298.72	601.78	344.18

Source: Own elaboration based on data from the 2009 Economic Census, INEGI

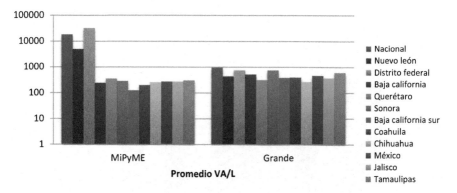

Fig. 2 Comparison of Added Value/Personal Paid (VA/L) between MSMEs and LC (2009). Source: Based on data from the 2009 Economic Census, INEGI

National, Nuevo Leon and Mexico City; while LC in the rest of the States has a higher value (Table 3).

Figure 3 shows the comparison of the wage advantage of MSMEs. The State of Queretaro shows greater wage remuneration followed the State of Nuevo Leon, Sonora, Tamaulipas, National, Mexico City, Baja California Sur, Baja California, Jalisco, Coahuila and Chihuahua remain the same and finally State of Mexico.

The Fig. 4 shows the comparison of the wage advantage of LC. The State of Nuevo Leon showing greater wage remuneration followed by Queretaro, National, Sonora, Mexico City, Baja California, Mexico, Coahuila and Tamaulipas remain the same, Chihuahua, Baja California Sur and finally Jalisco.

This Fig. 5 shows the comparison of the wage advantage between MSMEs and LC. LC in Nuevo Leon shows greater wage remuneration, followed by Queretaro, National, Sonora México City, Baja California, State of Mexico, Coahuila and

Table 3 Comparison of the wage advantage among MSMEs, LC and general total (2009)

Wage advantage			
Entity	MSMEs	LC	Total general
National	0.99	0.98	0.99
Nuevo Leon	13.96	2.20	1.12
Mexico City	0.44	0.48	0.45
Baja California	0.36	0.37	0.36
Querétaro	36.65	1.37	1.11
Sonora	10.06	0.89	1.02
Baja California Sur	0.38	0.32	0.37
Coahuila	0.33	0.35	0.33
Chihuahua	0.33	0.33	0.33
México	0.28	0.36	0.29
Jalisco	0.34	0.27	0.33
Tamaulipas	9.61	0.35	0.98

Source: Own elaboration based on data from the 2009 Economic Census, INEGI

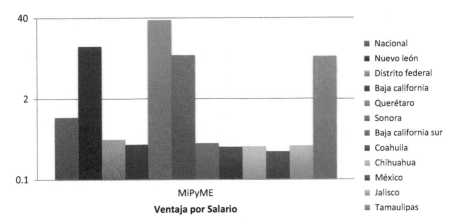

Fig. 3 Wages advantage of MSMEs (2009). Source: Own elaboration based on data from the 2009 Economic Census, INEGI

Tamaulipas remain the same, Chihuahua, Baja California Sur and finally Jalisco, while in the MSME the first place is obtained by the State of Queretaro followed by Nuevo Leon, Sonora, Tamaulipas, National, Mexico City, Baja California Sur, Baja California, Jalisco, Coahuila and Chihuahua remain the same and finally State of Mexico.

The Fig. 6 shows the wage advantage nationwide and Nuevo Leon, Mexico City, Baja California, Queretaro, Sonora, Baja California Sur, Coahuila, Chihuahua, Mexico, Jalisco and Tamaulipas.

As shown in the Fig. 6, the State of Nuevo Leon has the higher wage level, followed by Queretaro, Sonora, National, Tamaulipas, Mexico City, Baja California

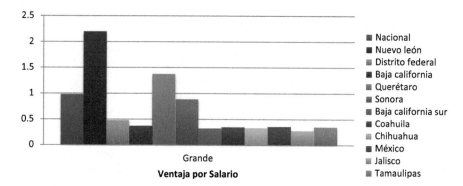

Fig. 4 Wage advantage of the LC (2009). Source: Own elaboration based on data from the 2009 Economic Census, INEGI

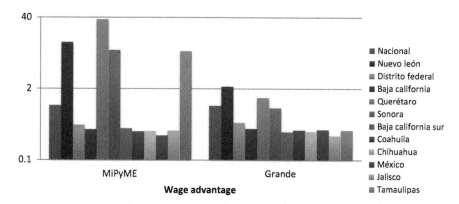

Fig. 5 Comparison of the wage advantage between MSMEs and LC (2009). Source: Own elaboration based on data from the 2009 Economic Census, INEGI

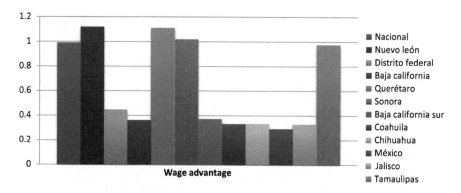

Fig. 6 Wage advantage by federal entity and national (2009). Source: Own elaboration based on data from the 2009 Economic Census, INEGI

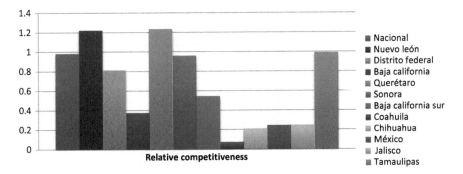

Fig. 7 Relative competitiveness index by federal entity and national (2009). Source: Own elaboration based on data from the 2009 Economic Census, INEGI

Table 4 Comparison of productivity-wage advantages and relative competitiveness of the micro enterprise (2009)

Micro Entity	Advantage by productivity	Wage advantage	Relative competitiveness
Nuevo Leon	1.26	36.27	36.52
Mexico City	1.78	0.35	1.13
Baja California	0.94	0.32	0.26
Querétaro	1.25	61.20	61.45
Sonora	1.06	20.41	20.47
Baja California Sur	1.06	0.32	0.38
Coahuila	0.75	0.30	0.06
Chihuahua	0.90	0.30	0.20
México	0.84	0.22	0.06
Jalisco	0.98	0.27	0.25
Tamaulipas	0.96	15.78	15.74

Source: Own elaboration based on data from the 2009 Economic Census, INEGI

Sur, Baja California, Jalisco, Chihuahua and Coahuila are maintained with the same competitive wage level and finally the State of Mexico.

In Fig. 7 is shown the relative competitiveness index. This index is obtained through data of productivity advantage and wage advantage. Queretaro is the State with the highest relative competitiveness, followed by Nuevo Leon, Tamaulipas, National, Sonora, Mexico City, Baja California Sur, Baja California, Jalisco, State of Mexico, Chihuahua, and finally Coahuila (Table 4).

The Fig. 8 shows the indexes prepared by productivity advantage, the advantage for wages and the relative competitiveness of the micro enterprise for Nuevo Leon, Mexico City, Baja California, Queretaro, Sonora, Baja California Sur, Coahuila, Chihuahua, State of Mexico, Jalisco and Tamaulipas. It can be seen that Queretaro has higher index and competitive wage level. While productivity advantage in the México City, is the most competitive (Table 5).

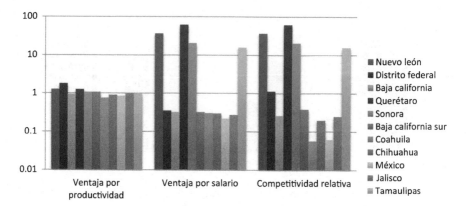

Fig. 8 Productivity-wage advantage and relative competitiveness of the Micro Enterprise (2009).
Source: Own elaboration with data of Economic Census 2009, INEGI

Table 5 Comparison of Indexes of productivity-wage advantage and relative competitiveness of
SMEs (2009)

SMEs			
Entity	Advantage by productivity	Advantage by wage	Relative competitiveness
Nuevo Leon	1.13	13.96	14.09
Mexico City	1.43	0.44	0.87
Baja California	0.99	0.36	0.35
Querétaro	1.19	36.65	36.85
Sonora	0.99	10.06	10.05
Baja California Sur	1.19	0.38	0.57
Coahuila	0.75	0.33	0.08
Chihuahua	0.96	0.33	0.29
México	0.94	0.28	0.21
Jalisco	0.96	0.34	0.30
Tamaulipas	1.06	9.61	9.66

Source: Own elaboration based on data from the 2009 Economic Census, INEGI

The Fig. 9 shows the indexes prepared by productivity advantage, the advantage
for wages and the relative competitiveness of SMEs for Nuevo Leon, Mexico City,
Baja California, Queretaro, Sonora, Baja California Sur, Coahuila, Chihuahua, State
of Mexico, Jalisco and Tamaulipas. Mexico City has a higher level in the productivity advantage, while Queretaro stands out a lot in the wage advantage; also it
shows higher performance in relative competitiveness (Table 6).

The Fig. 10 shows the indexes prepared by productivity advantage, the advantage
for wages and the relative competitiveness of large companies for Nuevo Leon,
México City, Baja California, Queretaro, Sonora, Baja California Sur, Coahuila,
Chihuahua, State of Mexico, Jalisco and Tamaulipas. This figure highlights the

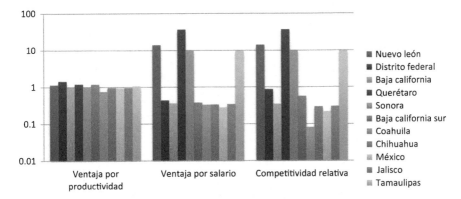

Fig. 9 Indexes of productivity-wage advantage and relative competitiveness of SMEs (2009). Source: Own elaboration based on data from the Economic Census 2009, INEGI

Table 6 Comparison of Indexes of productivity-wage advantage and relative competitiveness of large companies (2009)

Large			
Entity	Advantage of productivity	Advantage by wages	Relative competitiveness
Nuevo Leon	0.97	2.20	2.17
Mexico City	1.15	0.48	0.63
Baja California	1.15	0.37	0.52
Querétaro	0.76	1.37	1.13
Sonora	0.69	0.89	0.57
Baja California Sur	0.99	0.32	0.32
Coahuila	0.68	0.35	0.04
Chihuahua	0.50	0.33	−0.17
México	1.01	0.36	0.37
Jalisco	0.73	0.27	0.01
Tamaulipas	0.79	0.35	0.14

Source: Own elaboration based on data from the 2009 Economic Census, INEGI

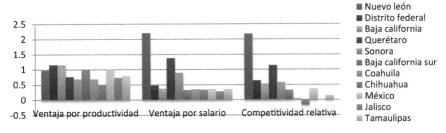

Fig. 10 Indexes of productivity-wage advantage and relative competitiveness of large companies (2009). Source: Own elaboration based on data from the 2009 Economic Census, INEGI

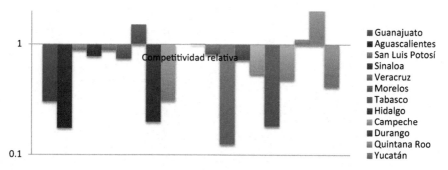

Fig. 11 Comparison of Relieved Competitiveness Index between noncompetitive States (2009). Source: Own elaboration based on data from the 2009 Economic Census, INEGI

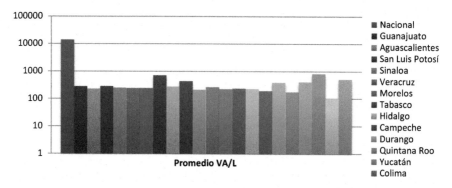

Fig. 12 Total average added value/paid personnel (2009). Source: Own elaboration based on data from the 2009 Economic Census, INEGI

index of wage advantage and relative competitiveness of Nuevo Leon being 2.20 and 2.17 respectively, with a very high index in comparison of other entities.

The following Fig. 11 shows the relative competitiveness index. This index is obtained through data of advantage for productivity and wage advantage. Michoacan is the State with the highest relieved competitiveness, followed by, Tabasco, Guerrero, Nayarit, Quintana Roo, San Luis Potosi, Veracruz, Yucatan, Sinaloa, Morelos, Puebla, Tlaxcala, Zacatecas, Oaxaca, Campeche, Guanajuato, Hidalgo, Chiapas, Aguascalientes, Colima and finally Durango. The State of Michoacan, Tabasco, Nayarit and Quintana Roo are below 3.16 and the rest of the States are greater than −0.15.

The Fig. 12 shows the behavior of added value/paid personnel from the national average, Aguascalientes, Campeche, Chiapas, Colima, Durango, Guanajuato, Guerrero, Hidalgo, Michoacan, Morelos, Nayarit, Oaxaca, Puebla, Quintana Roo, San Luis Potosi, Sinaloa Value, Tabasco, Tlaxcala, Veracruz, Yucatan and Zacatecas (Table 7).

Table 7 Comparison between value added and paid personnel (2009)

VA/L average			
Entity	SMES	Large	General total
National	17999.62	950.45	13796.80
Guanajuato	231.57	541.79	282.42
Aguascalientes	218.88	343.05	231.07
San Luis Potosí	264.81	428.93	285.20
Sinaloa	249.66	260.04	251.28
Veracruz	108.52	924.57	245.26
Morelos	225.22	397.13	244.66
Tabasco	608.18	1369.73	715.06
Hidalgo	206.34	796.18	276.56
Campeche	162.02	2279.67	437.69
Durango	182.64	418.81	214.04
Quintana Roo	252.87	358.47	268.13
Yucatán	229.21	221.35	228.06
Colima	237.96	250.81	239.07
Puebla	204.48	381.03	232.10
Tlaxcala	169.80	687.63	195.15
Chiapas	233.89	1548.09	390.34
Zacatecas	108.96	1018.96	179.42
Nayarit	401.74	535.86	413.47
Michoacán	355.97	4232.74	823.86
Oaxaca	103.94	70.10	101.89
Guerrero	543.62	316.79	519.46

Source: Based on data from the 2009 Economic Census, INEGI

The national average has a higher competitive level of added value, followed by the average Michoacan, Tabasco, Guerrero, Campeche, Nayarit, Chiapas, San Luis Potosi, Hidalgo, Quintana Roo, Sinaloa, Veracruz, Morelos, Colima, Puebla, Aguascalientes, Yucatán, Durango, Tlaxcala, Zacatecas and finally the State of Oaxaca.

The Fig. 13 shows a comparison of the value added/staff paid between MSMEs and the large companies of the national average, Aguascalientes, Campeche, Chiapas, Colima, Durango, Guanajuato, Guerrero, Hidalgo, Michoacan, Morelos, Nayarit, Oaxaca, Puebla, Quintana Roo, San Luis Potosi, Sinaloa, Tabasco, Tlaxcala, Veracruz, Yucatan and Zacatecas. It can be seen that the VA/L of large companies is greater than the MSMEs except the national average.

The following Fig. 14 shows the behavior of total remuneration/Paid personnel nationwide, Aguascalientes, Campeche, Chiapas, Colima, Durango, Guanajuato, Guerrero, Hidalgo, Michoacan, Morelos, Nayarit, Oaxaca, Puebla, Quintana Roo, San Luis Potosi, Sinaloa, Tabasco, Tlaxcala, Veracruz, Yucatan and Zacatecas. As shown in Fig. 14 Tabasco presents a more competitive wage advantage, followed by the national average, Guanajuato, Campeche, Durango, Quintana Roo, San Luis Potosi, Veracruz, Puebla, Aguascalientes, Zacatecas, Morelos, Sinaloa, Hidalgo,

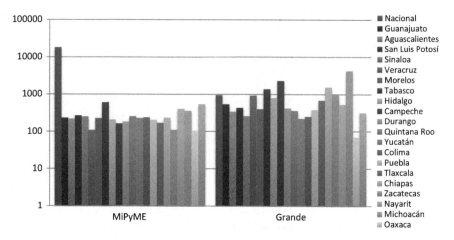

Fig. 13 Comparison of added value/paid personnel between MSMEs and LC (2009). Source: Own elaboration based on data from the 2009 Economic Census, INEGI

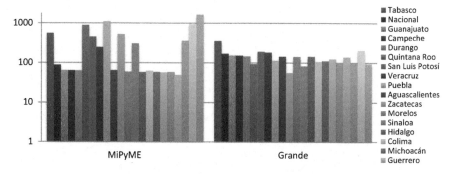

Fig. 14 Comparison of total remuneration/paid personnel between MSMEs and LC (2009). Source: Own elaboration based on data from the 2009 Economic Census, INEGI

Colima, Michoacan, Guerrero, Nayarit, Chiapas, Yucatan, Oaxaca and finally Tlaxcala.

This figure shows the overall comparison of remunerations/paid staff of MSMEs and large companies. MSMEs show higher wages in the States of Quintana Roo, San Luis Potosi, Puebla, Zacatecas, Sinaloa, Yucatan, Oaxaca and Tlaxcala in the LC while the rest of the States are maintained with lower wage pay than LC (Table 8).

This Fig. 15 shows the comparison of the wage advantage of MSMEs. The State of Puebla showing greater wage remuneration followed by the States of Oaxaca, Quintana Roo, Tlaxcala, San Luis Potosi, Zacatecas, Tabasco, Yucatan, Sinaloa, Veracruz, National average, Morelos, Nayarit, Aguascalientes, Guanajuato, Colima, Campeche, Hidalgo, Guerrero, Michoacan, Durango and Chiapas (Fig. 16).

This figure shows the comparison of the wage advantage of LC. The State of Tabasco shows greater wage remuneration followed by Veracruz, Tlaxcala, San Luis

Table 8 Comparison of the wage advantage among MSMEs, LC and general total (2009)

Advantage by wage			
Entity	MSMEs	Large	Total general
National	0.99	0.98	0.99
Guanajuato	0.29	0.37	0.30
Aguascalientes	0.29	0.42	0.31
San Luis Potosí	11.41	1.13	0.95
Sinaloa	7.06	0.72	0.91
Veracruz	5.21	2.35	0.84
Morelos	0.86	1.05	0.88
Tabasco	8.20	5.52	1.11
Hidalgo	0.28	0.33	0.28
Campeche	0.28	0.39	0.29
Durango	0.26	0.33	0.27
Quintana Roo	21.41	0.56	1.01
Yucatán	7.56	0.93	0.80
Colima	0.29	0.26	0.29
Puebla	30.34	0.93	0.84
Tlaxcala	20.05	1.98	0.77
Chiapas	0.23	0.30	0.24
Zacatecas	10.13	0.53	0.89
Nayarit	0.86	0.82	0.85
Michoacán	0.27	0.30	0.28
Oaxaca	26.84	0.73	0.74
Guerrero	0.27	0.38	0.29

Source: Own elaboration based on data from the 2009 Economic Census, INEGI

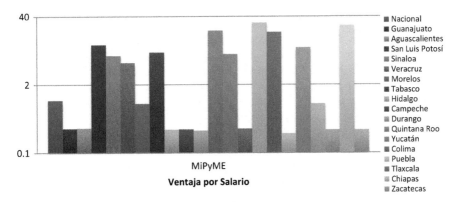

Fig. 15 Advantage for wages of MSMEs (2009). Source: Own elaboration based on data from the 2009 Economic Census, INEGI

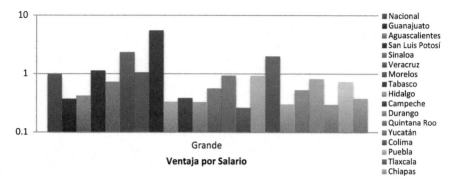

Fig. 16 Advantage for wage of LC (2009). Source: Own elaboration based on data from the 2009 Economic Census, INEGI

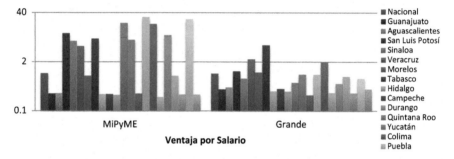

Fig. 17 Comparison of advantage by salary between MSMEs and LC (2009). Source: Own elaboration based on data from the 2009 Economic Census, INEGI

Potosi, Morelos, National average, Yucatan, Puebla, Nayarit, Oaxaca, Sinaloa, Quintana Roo, Zacatecas, Aguascalientes, Campeche, Guerrero, Guanajuato, Hidalgo, Durango, Chiapas, Michoacan and finally Colima (Fig. 17).

This figure shows the comparison of the wage advantage between MSMEs and LC. It can be seen that the State with the highest pay remuneration of MSMEs is the State of Puebla and Tabasco in LC is the best paid State. The MSME has States better paid than the LC. The salaries are less than 30.3 and greater than 0.2. While at LC remuneration it is greater than 0.2 and less than 5.5 (Fig. 18).

The following figure shows the wage advantage of National average, Aguascalientes, Campeche, Chiapas, Colima, Durango, Guanajuato, Guerrero, Hidalgo, Michoacan, Morelos, Nayarit, Oaxaca, Puebla, Quintana Roo, San Luis Potosi, Sinaloa, Tabasco, Tlaxcala, Veracruz, Yucatan and Zacatecas. As shown in the figure, the State of Tabasco, followed by the State of Quintana Roo, National Average, San Luis Potosi, Sinaloa, Zacatecas, Morelos, Nayarit, Veracruz, Puebla, Yucatan, Tlaxcala, Oaxaca, Aguascalientes, Guanajuato, Campeche, Colima, Guerrero, Hidalgo, Michoacan, Durango and finally Chiapas.

The following figure shows the relative competitiveness index. This index is obtained through data of advantage for productivity and wage advantage. Michoacan

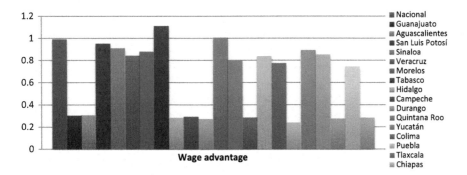

Fig. 18 Wage advantage for federal entities and national (2009). Source: Own elaboration based on data from the 2009 Economic Census, INEGI

Table 9 Comparison of productivity-wage advantage index and relative competitiveness of the micro enterprise (2009)

Micro			
Entity	Productivity advantage	Wage advantage	Relative competitiveness
Guanajuato	0.86	0.27	0.14
Aguascalientes	0.98	0.25	0.23
San Luis Potosí	0.80	23.88	23.68
Sinaloa	1.06	15.62	15.68
Veracruz	0.89	11.05	10.94
Morelos	0.78	0.88	0.66
Tabasco	0.95	9.00	8.95
Hidalgo	0.69	0.22	−0.09
Campeche	0.70	0.23	−0.07
Durango	0.25	0.24	−0.51
Quintana Roo	0.93	15.59	15.52
Yucatán	1.54	14.54	15.08
Colima	0.90	0.28	0.18
Puebla	1.00	59.64	59.64
Tlaxcala	0.63	33.98	33.61
Chiapas	0.92	0.19	0.11
Zacatecas	0.75	18.14	17.89
Nayarit	2.22	0.93	2.15
Michoacán	0.90	0.24	0.14
Oaxaca	0.73	18.71	18.44
Guerrero	1.16	0.23	0.39

Source: Own elaboration based on data from the 2009 Economic Census, INEGI

is the State with the highest relative competitiveness, followed by Tabasco, Guerrero, Nayarit, Quintana Roo, National average, San Luis Potosi, Veracruz, Yucatan, Sinaloa, Morelos, Puebla, Tlaxcala, Zacatecas, Oaxaca, Campeche, Hidalgo, Chiapas, Aguascalientes, Guanajuato, Colima and finally Durango (Table 9).

Fig. 19 Productivity-wage advantage and relative competitiveness index of the Micro Enterprise (2009). Source: Own elaboration based on data from the 2009 Economic Census, INEGI

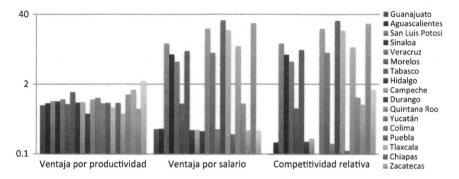

Fig. 20 Productivity advantage, wage advantage and relative competitiveness indexes. Source: Own elaboration based on data from the 2009 Economic Census, INEGI

The Fig. 19 shows the indexes made of the advantage for productivity, the advantage for wages and the relative competitiveness of the micro enterprise to Aguascalientes, Campeche, Chiapas, Colima, Durango, Guanajuato, Guerrero, Hidalgo, Michoacan, Morelos, Nayarit, Oaxaca, Puebla, Quintana Roo, San Luis Potosi, Sinaloa, Tabasco, Tlaxcala, Veracruz, Yucatan and Zacatecas. It can be seen that Puebla has higher indexes at wage and competitive level. While in productivity advantage Nayarit is the most competitive (Fig. 20 and Table 10).

This figure shows the indexes made of the advantage for productivity, the advantage for wages and the relative competitiveness of SMEs to Aguascalientes, Campeche, Chiapas, Colima, Durango, Guanajuato, Guerrero, Hidalgo, Michoacan, Morelos, Nayarit, Oaxaca, Puebla, Quintana Roo, San Luis Potosi, Sinaloa, Tabasco, Tlaxcala, Veracruz, Yucatan and Zacatecas. The State of Guerrero has a higher level in the productivity advantage, while Puebla stands out a lot in the wage advantage; also it shows higher performance in relative competitiveness (Table 11).

This Fig. 21 shows the indexes made of the advantage for productivity, the advantage for wages and the relative competitiveness of the large company to Aguascalientes, Campeche, Chiapas, Colima, Durango, Guanajuato, Guerrero, Hidalgo, Michoacan, Morelos, Nayarit, Oaxaca, Puebla, Quintana Roo, San Luis Potosi, Sinaloa, Tabasco, Tlaxcala, Veracruz, Yucatan and Zacatecas. This Fig. 21

Table 10 Comparison of Indexes of productivity-wage advantage and relative competitiveness of MSMEs (2009)

MSMEs			
Entity	Productivity advantage	Wage advantage	Relative competitiveness
Guanajuato	0.80	0.29	0.09
Aguascalientes	0.87	0.29	0.16
San Luis Potosí	0.96	11.41	11.37
Sinaloa	0.94	7.06	7.00
Veracruz	1.03	5.21	5.24
Morelos	0.84	0.86	0.70
Tabasco	1.40	8.20	8.61
Hidalgo	0.89	0.28	0.17
Campeche	0.91	0.28	0.19
Durango	0.56	0.26	-0.18
Quintana Roo	1.03	21.41	21.43
Yucatán	1.09	7.56	7.66
Colima	0.87	0.29	0.16
Puebla	0.89	30.34	30.23
Tlaxcala	0.72	20.05	19.77
Chiapas	0.88	0.23	0.12
Zacatecas	0.56	10.13	9.69
Nayarit	1.26	0.86	1.12
Michoacán	1.55	0.27	0.82
Oaxaca	0.69	26.84	26.53
Guerrero	2.30	0.27	1.57

Source: Own elaboration based on data from the 2009 Economic Census, INEGI

highlights the relative productivity and competitiveness advantage of Michoacan being 20.8 and 20.1 respectively, with a very high index in comparison of other entities, while in the wage advantage Tabasco State is the best paid (Table 12).

As shown in the Table 13 it is observed the position in which every State of Mexico was placed in comparison of competitiveness, productivity and wages of total general, where 1 means that it is the most competitive and 32 the least competitive State.

Also, the correlations range were calculated of general total of states; in the case of C** and (VA/L)*: 0.25626; and (VA/L)* Y (W/L)*: 0.013703; as the value approaches 0 means that no linear correlation in the case of C** and (W/L)*: 0.891544 there is a positive correlation.

As shown in the above in Table 14, it is observed the position in which was placed every State of Mexico in comparison of competitiveness, productivity and wages of MSMEs, where 1 means that it is the most competitive and 32 the least competitive State. Also it was calculated the correlations range of general total of the States; in the case of C** and (VA/L)*: 0.313085; and (VA/L)* Y (W/L)*: 0.093332; as the value approaches 0 means that no linear correlation in the case of C** and (W/L)*: 0.903075 there is a positive correlation.

Table 11 Comparison of Indexes of productivity-wage advantage and relative competitiveness of large companies (2009)

Large	Productivity advantage	Wage advantage	Relative competitiveness
Guanajuato	0.95	0.37	0.33
Aguascalientes	0.86	0.42	0.28
San Luis Potosí	0.79	1.13	0.93
Sinaloa	0.49	0.72	0.21
Veracruz	1.09	2.35	2.44
Morelos	1.07	1.05	1.12
Tabasco	1.33	5.52	5.85
Hidalgo	1.10	0.33	0.43
Campeche	1.71	0.39	1.10
Durango	0.65	0.33	−0.02
Quintana Roo	0.88	0.56	0.45
Yucatán	0.55	0.93	0.48
Colima	0.53	0.26	−0.20
Puebla	0.87	0.93	0.80
Tlaxcala	1.55	1.98	2.53
Chiapas	1.37	0.30	0.67
Zacatecas	0.88	0.53	0.41
Nayarit	1.29	0.82	1.11
Michoacán	20.90	0.30	20.20
Oaxaca	0.40	0.73	0.14
Guerrero	0.80	0.38	0.18

Source: Own elaboration based on data from the 2009 Economic Census, INEGI

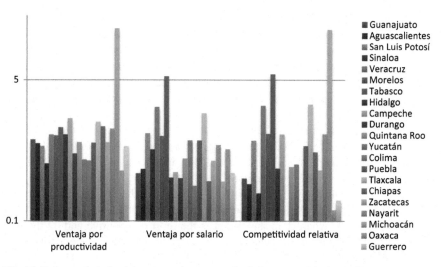

Fig. 21 Indexes of productivity-wage advantage and relative competitiveness of large companies (2009). Source: Own elaboration based on data from the 2009 Economic Census, INEGI

Table 12 Indexes of productivity-wage advantage and relative competitiveness of Guanajuato (2009)

Guanajuato	Productivity advantage	Wage advantage	Relative competitiveness
Micro	0.863540519	0.272550159	0.136090678
SMEs	0.800179017	0.289495156	0.089674173
Large	0.950981386	0.374265123	0.325246509

Source: Own elaboration based on data from the 2009 Economic Census, INEGI

As shown in the above Table 15, the position in which it was placed every State of Mexico in comparison of competitiveness, productivity and wages of MSMEs, where 1 means that it is the most competitive State and 32 the least competitive State. Also, correlations range of general total States were calculated; in the case of C** and (VA/L)*: 0.71; and C** and (W/L)*: 0.65625 exists a positive correlation as values approaching 1. In the case of (VA/L)* Y (W/L)*: 0.11; as the value is closer to 0 means that there is no linear correlation.

5 Conclusions and Future Extensions

The intent of this research work has been to analyze business performance through the relative competitiveness of the 32 States of the country. For this purpose, it was chosen 18 of 20 branches of economic activity. MSMEs and large companies were classified and it was highlighted the importance of activities on productivity, employment and wages for each State of the Mexican Republic including the national level.

The importance of stratification of companies in Mexico that informs the official Journal of the Federation (Diario Oficial de la Federación, DOF) in June 2009, is very important, because depending on the number of range of workers are classified businesses as micro, small, medium or large. This stratification is applied to the corresponding period in 2009 economic census.

In Mexico, SMEs with micro represent more than 99% of all businesses; out of which 4,877,070 they are micro, 214,956 are small and 42,415 medium enterprises, while 9615 are large companies. In addition to being majority, they represent an important part of employment in Mexico and constitute 78.5% of employment by MSMEs and 21.5% of LC. Coupled with that, SME occupies 78.5% of the workforce and contributes 52% of national GDP, while the large company occupies 21.5% of job creation and contributes 48% of national GDP.

It is noteworthy that although MSMEs are an important part of the employment generated in Mexico and its contribution to GDP is higher than LC, SMEs do not have many of the resources needed to develop in full and there are in the country major problems that greatly affect them. Calculating the structure by size and business sector in Mexico, where industrial, commercial and service micro-enterprise activities represent a total 3,534,526 (94.98%), small 142,653 (3.83%), medium was obtained 37,186 (1.00%) and large with 7055 (0.19%).

Table 13 Planning competitiveness, productivity and wages: total correlations range of States

State	C**	ORDEN of C**	(VA/L)*	ORDEN of (VA/L)*	(W/L)*	ORDEN of (W/L)
Querétaro	31.09	1	1.12	7	30.97	1
Puebla	25.63	2	0.89	21	25.74	2
Oaxaca	24.93	3	0.67	30	25.26	3
Tlaxcala	18.93	4	0.76	28	19.17	4
Quintana Roo	18.40	5	1.01	14	18.39	5
Nuevo León	11.71	6	1.10	8	11.61	6
San Luis Potosí	10.07	7	0.94	18	10.13	7
Zacatecas	8.97	8	0.59	31	9.39	8
Sonora	8.39	9	0.94	17	8.45	9
Tamaulipas	8.23	10	1.02	11	8.22	10
Tabasco	8.22	11	1.39	3	7.83	11
Yucatán	6.61	12	1.02	12	6.59	12
Sinaloa	5.94	13	0.87	23	6.07	13
Veracruz	4.77	14	1.04	9	4.73	14
Michoacán	3.16	15	3.89	1	0.28	30
Guerrero	1.42	16	2.14	2	0.29	28
Nayarit	1.12	17	1.27	5	0.85	16
Mexico City	0.81	18	1.36	4	0.45	17
Morelos	0.74	19	0.86	25	0.88	15
Baja California Sur	0.54	20	1.17	6	0.37	18
Baja California	0.37	21	1.01	13	0.36	19
Campeche	0.31	22	1.02	10	0.29	25
Jalisco	0.24	23	0.91	20	0.33	22
México	0.24	24	0.95	15	0.29	26
Colima	0.21	25	0.87	22	0.33	20
Hidalgo	0.20	26	0.92	19	0.28	29
Coahuila	0.18	27	0.94	16	0.24	32
Aguascalientes	0.18	28	0.87	24	0.31	23
Guanajuato	0.13	29	0.82	27	0.30	24
Chihuahua	0.12	30	0.84	26	0.29	27
Chiapas	0.07	31	0.74	29	0.33	21
Durango	−0.16	32	0.57	32	0.27	31
Correlación De Rango (Sperman)						
C** y (VA/L)*: **0.256267**			(VA/L)* Y (W/L)*: **0.013703**		C** y (W/L)*: **0.891544**	

Source: Own elaboration based on data from the 2009 Economic Census, INEGI

The first result was observed comparing the State ranking of Mexican Institute for Competitiveness (IMCO Instituto Mexicano para la Competitividad 2008) and relieved competitiveness of the Economic Census 2009. Ranking the relieved competitiveness of the overall total, MSME and large enterprise, where the position

Table 14 Planning competitiveness, productivity and wages: correlations range of MSMEs of States

State	C**	ORDEN of C**	(VA/L) *	ORDEN of (VA/L)*	(W/L) *	ORDEN of (W/L)
Querétaro	36.85	1	1.19	6	36.65	1
Puebla	30.23	2	0.89	22	30.34	2
Oaxaca	26.53	3	0.69	30	26.84	3
Quintana Roo	21.43	4	1.03	12	21.41	4
Tlaxcala	19.77	5	0.72	29	20.05	5
Nuevo León	14.09	6	1.13	8	13.96	6
San Luis Potosí	11.37	7	0.96	15	11.41	7
Sonora	10.05	8	0.99	13	10.06	9
Zacatecas	9.69	9	0.56	31	10.13	8
Tamaulipas	9.66	10	1.06	10	9.61	10
Tabasco	8.61	11	1.40	4	8.20	11
Yucatán	7.66	12	1.09	9	7.56	12
Sinaloa	7.00	13	0.94	18	7.06	13
Veracruz	5.24	14	1.03	11	5.21	14
Guerrero	1.57	15	2.30	1	0.27	29
Nayarit	1.12	16	1.26	5	0.86	16
Mexico City	0.87	17	1.43	3	0.44	17
Michoacán	0.82	18	1.55	2	0.27	30
Morelos	0.70	19	0.84	26	0.86	15
Baja California Sur	0.57	20	1.19	7	0.38	18
Baja California	0.35	21	0.99	14	0.36	19
Jalisco	0.30	22	0.96	17	0.34	20
Colima	0.29	23	0.96	16	0.33	21
México	0.21	24	0.94	19	0.28	27
Campeche	0.19	25	0.91	20	0.28	26
Hidalgo	0.17	26	0.89	21	0.28	28
Aguascalientes	0.16	27	0.87	24	0.29	23
Chihuahua	0.16	28	0.87	25	0.29	25
Coahuila	0.12	29	0.88	23	0.23	32
Guanajuato	0.09	30	0.80	27	0.29	24
Chiapas	0.08	31	0.75	28	0.33	22
Durango	−0.18	32	0.56	32	0.26	31
Correlation of range (Sperman)						
C** y (VA/L)*: **0.313085**		(VA/L)* Y (W/L)*: **0.093332**			C** y (W/L)*: **0.903075**	

Source: Own elaboration based on data from the 2009 Economic Census, INEGI

Table 15 Planning competitiveness, productivity and wages: correlations range of large companies of the States

State	C**	ORDEN of C** (VA/L)*	(VA/L)*	ORDEN of (VA/L)*	(W/L)*	ORDEN of (W/L)
Nuevo Leon	5.85	1	0.97	14	2.20	3
Quintana Roo	2.53	2	0.88	16	0.56	14
Oaxaca	2.44	3	0.40	32	0.73	12
Veracruz	2.17	4	1.09	10	2.35	2
Tabasco	1.13	5	1.33	5	5.52	1
Nayarit	1.12	6	1.29	6	0.82	11
Guerrero	1.11	7	0.80	20	0.38	19
Colima	1.10	8	0.53	29	0.26	32
Durango	0.96	9	0.65	27	0.33	27
Zacatecas	0.93	10	0.88	17	0.53	15
Yucatán	0.80	11	0.55	28	0.93	8
Campeche	0.67	12	1.71	2	0.39	18
Chihuahua	0.63	13	0.50	30	0.33	26
San Luis Potosi	0.57	14	0.79	21	1.13	6
Guanajuato	0.52	15	0.95	15	0.37	20
Puebla	0.48	16	0.87	18	0.93	9
Tamaulipas	0.45	17	0.79	22	0.35	24
Morelos	0.43	18	1.07	11	1.05	7
Querétaro	0.41	19	0.76	23	1.37	5
Mexico City	0.37	20	1.15	7	0.48	16
Baja California	0.33	21	1.15	8	0.37	21
Chiapas	0.32	22	1.37	4	0.30	29
Coahuila	0.28	23	0.68	26	0.35	23
Sonora	0.21	24	0.69	25	0.89	10
Baja California Sur	0.18	25	0.99	13	0.32	28
Tlaxcala	0.14	26	1.55	3	1.98	4
Sinaloa	0.14	27	0.49	31	0.72	13
Aguascalientes	0.04	28	0.86	19	0.42	17
Michoacán	0.01	29	20.90	1	0.30	30
Jalisco	−0.02	30	0.73	24	0.27	31
México	−0.17	31	1.01	12	0.36	22
Hidalgo	−0.20	32	1.10	9	0.33	25
Correlation of range (Sperman)						
C** y (VA/L)*: **0.71**			(VA/L)* Y (W/L)*: **0.11**		C** y (W/L)*: **0.65625**	

Source: Own elaboration based on data from the 2009 Economic Census, INEGI

placed is shown in each State of Mexico in which 1 means that it is the least competitive and 32 the most competitive State.

Relative competitiveness is constructed from the sum of the estimates of advantage for productivity and wage advantage by State; resulting in a group of competitive States significantly above another group of lower competitiveness. In the case of Ranking IMCO (2008), the overall relative competitiveness, and relative competitiveness MSMEs and competitiveness of large company's results were mixed, since the competitive States are characterized with much higher production levels and wages.

On one hand, the anticipated confirmation of anticipated hypothesis where the competitiveness of the country's States is measured through the corporate structure of MSMEs, as the most competitive States, either is the case of MSMEs or LC have a business structure, productivity and therefore higher wage advantage, while the less competitive States depend on few activities and have lower productivity and wages indexes Thus the performance of companies determines the level of competitiveness of States.

On the other hand, it is observed that in those States, the competitive salaries vary depending on the position of the State. For example, in the case of general total, the same competitive States meet except Yucatan State, since the State of Tlaxcala has increased wage and productive competitiveness. In the MSMEs, the best and most favorable terms of productivity and high wage level meet; Queretaro is the State with the highest pay remuneration with 36.6%; and in large companies Tabasco ranks first as the State with the highest pay remuneration 5.5, followed by the State of Veracruz, Nuevo Leon, Tlaxcala, Queretaro, San Luis Potosi, Morelos, National average, Yucatan, Puebla and Sonora.

In the case of the productivity advantage of general total State with greater competitiveness is Michoacan, followed by the States of Guerrero, Tabasco, Mexico City, Nayarit, Baja California Sur, Queretaro, Nuevo Leon, Veracruz, Campeche and Tamaulipas. In MSMEs, Guerrero is the State with more productive competitiveness followed by the State of Michoacan, Mexico City, Tabasco, Nayarit, Querétaro, Baja California Sur, Nuevo Leon, Yucatan, Tamaulipas and Veracruz. In the large company sector, Michoacan is the State most productive competitiveness, followed by the State of Campeche, Tlaxcala, Coahuila, Tabasco, Nayarit, Mexico City, Baja California, Hidalgo, Veracruz and Morelos.

Given the IHH and ID indexes for general total and MSMEs, the States of Baja California, Coahuila, Colima, Chihuahua, Morelos, Nayarit, Puebla, Sinaloa and Yucatán are the States with monopoly control, since the results will be 10,000, while the rest of the States have a competitive structure. In the case of the large company, the States of Chihuahua and Sinaloa are States with monopoly control, since the results will be 10,000 while other States have a competitive structure.

Future research should consider the relevant economic census for the period 2014 at just made official the INEGI, for further analysis. Also to integrate economic census 2014 to see how it has changed over this period of time and see whether the hypotheses are still compliance or rejected.

Key Concepts and Words

Business performance The accomplishment of a given business strategic goals measured against preset known analytic processes, standards and indexes supported by technology to involve data analysis and consolidation from various sources to determine best practices for better reaching the goals. Business performance entails reviewing aggregate available information and data on the business as a whole to determine the firm's position, how the business can better reach its goals by the alignment of strategic and operational objectives and the business' set of operations, functions and activities.

Competitiveness The set of institutions, policies and factors that determine the level of productivity of a firm or country that enable the ability to meet quality life standards at competitive prices while providing adequate returns on resources consumed. For this paper, competitiveness is associated with profitability, productivity, costs; value added, market share, exports, technological innovations, among others (McFetridge 1995).

Corporate structure The overall makeup of an organization or firm as a unit formed by the way it is organized as a system and interrelated between each other organizational sub-units, divisions, departments, etc. depending of the level of complexity to share tasks, responsibilities, work processes, etc. that contribute to the accomplishment of the common goals of the firm.

México A country, nation and state located in the Western Hemisphere, south of the United States Border and North of Guatemala Border, in a geographic area covered by the south of North America and North of Central America. It has extensive coastlines on the Gulf of Mexico and the Pacific Ocean. The estimated population is about 127,000,000 Mexicans. Spanish is the main and official language.

MSMEs It is an acronymic that stands for Micro, small and medium enterprises. What defines if an enterprise is Micro, Small and Medium are number of employees, the investment in plant and machinery, excluding land and buildings for those engaged in manufacturing or production, processing or preservation of goods and on the investment in equipment for enterprises engaged in providing or rendering of services.

References

IMCO Instituto Mexicano para la Competitividad. (2008). *Índice de competitividad estatal 2008: Aspiraciones y realidad; las aGEndas del futuro*, México DF. [Online] http://goo.gl/bGLJcZ

INEGI Instituto Nacional de Estadística y GEografía. (2009a). *Micro, pequeña, mediana y gran empresa: estratificación de los establecimientos: Censos económicos 2009*. México: INEGI, c2011. [Online] http://goo.gl/Xpnk7Z

INEGI Instituto Nacional de Estadística y GEografía. (2009b). *Censo Económico 2009*. Consultado Junio 2014. [Online] http://www.inegi.org.mx/, http://goo.gl/lDpQGR

Martin, R., & Sunley, P. (2003). Deconstructing cluster: Chaotic concept or policy panacea? *Cambridge Journal of Economic Geography, 3*, 5–35.

McFetridge, D. (1995). *Competitiveness concepts and measures*. Gouvernement du Canada – Industrial Organization 5, Gouvernement du Canada – Industry Canada.

Romero Ibarra, M. E. (2003). *La Historia Empresarial*. *Historia Mexicana*. El Colegio de México A.C., Mexico City, México. Vol. LII, Núm. 3, enero-marzo (pp. 806–829).

SCIAN. (2013). Instituto Nacional de Estadística y GEografía. Sistema de Clasificación Industrial de América del Norte, México, SCIAN, 2013.

Unger, K., Flores, D. E., & Ibarra, J. E. (2013). Productividad y capital humano: fuentes complementarias de la competitividad de los estados mexicanos En cide.edu, julio 2013, Número 554.

Leadership, Personal Values and Organizational Culture

Oznur Gulen Ertosun and Zafer Adiguzel

Abstract Organizational culture creates a sense of identity and belonging for employees and also has importance in desired organizational behaviors by overlapping organizational values with individual values (Smircich, Administrative Science Quarterly, 28, 339–358, 1983). On the other hand, the individual values, beliefs, anticipations, attitudes, behaviors and actions that employees have are considered important factors in shaping and adopting organizational culture (Daft, Organizational theory and design. West Publishing, 1986). Values are immensely substantial with regard to influencing organizational dynamics, especially at a management level (Chusmir and Parker, Journal of Social Psychology, 132, 87–100, 1992). Personal values set standards about thought and sense unclear besides shaping the decisions and behaviors of managers thus constituting an ideology and consequently an organizational culture (Russell, Leadership & Organization Development Journal, 22, 76–84, 2001).

Because of the mentioned critical importance, this study aims to holistically examine the association among culture, leadership, and values. For that purpose, this chapter continues in the following manner; (i) The importance of organizational culture and effect on the decisions and behaviors in an organization (ii) Elements contributing to organizational culture (iii) Personal values and importance within management (iv) Leadership and association with organizational culture, and finally, (v) The effects of a leader's personal value on organizational culture.

1 Introduction

In order to understand organizational life, we need to examine the concept of culture. Social culture defines the acceptable and unacceptable behaviours either consciously or unconsciously. Culture also ensures that the needs of the individuals and the

O. G. Ertosun (✉) · Z. Adiguzel
School of Business and Management Sciences, Istanbul Medipol University, Istanbul, Turkey
e-mail: ogertosun@medipol.edu.tr; zadiguzel@medipol.edu.tr

© Springer International Publishing AG, part of Springer Nature 2018
H. Dincer et al. (eds.), *Strategic Design and Innovative Thinking in Business Operations*, Contributions to Management Science,
https://doi.org/10.1007/978-3-319-77622-4_3

community are in line with each other, providing guidance and creating norms of behaviour (Hofstede 1980; Smircich 1983).

It is possible to explain the concept of organizational culture with two different approaches. According to the first one, culture is regarded as a subsystem within the organization that allows individuals to adapt to their environment. This is an explanatory approach and accepts that every organisation has a culture, and it is usually enough to make a list of some characteristics of the organization. The second approach regards the organisational culture as an information system within which each member can interpret themselves. This approach allows the social system to have a dynamic structure in all its complexity and then leads to the concept of corporate identity (Koźmiński and Obłój 1989, p. 202).

Organizational culture regulates the behaviours of the participants within the organization and plays an important role in ensuring, in extreme cases, that the organisation acts as a whole. If the organization operates in a similar and steady way for a period of time, gaining goals and achievements, the members of the organisation learn certain behavioural styles and accept some successfully accepted standards. For this reason, organizational culture also means the "idealization of a common experience" (Daft 1986). Organizational culture can, therefore, effectively support or hinder collaboration, information exchange, experience and ideas. For example, the culture that promotes the creativity and participation of all team members provides a favourable environment for employees to be effective in their initiative (Schein 1983).

Similarly, values have a very important role in forming organisational culture and determining an employee's behaviour and judgment. The interactions between values, attitudes, beliefs and behaviours are stated in many studies in literature. A value system can be considered as a relatively permanent frame of perception that shapes and influences the general nature of an individual's behaviour. Values are similar to attitudes, but they are more naturally rooted, permanent, and stable. Furthermore, a value appears to be more general and less connected to any particular object. Values are closer to ideology or philosophy rather than attitude. At a more concrete level, the values are principles that direct an individual's desires, feelings, and actions (Bernthal 1962; Shah 1985).

Also, values predict most of the behaviours at a particular level. But, if the values are not based on prior cultural learning, they can be seen as merely advocated values and do not reflect on employees' behaviours. If the accepted values are logically compatible with the basic assumptions, these values can then be transformed into philosophy, which can bring the group together, establishing an identity and creating basic tasks (Ouchi 1981). Values start at the individual level, thus, the values of a few individuals constitute the values of the group, and the values of a group constitute the values of the organisation (Harrison 1975).

An organizational culture, as well as its values and leadership, are frequently mentioned in the literature as closely related concepts. One of the most known theories is Schein's (2004) culture and leadership theory, which emphasizes the role of leaders in creating, sustaining, and modifying the content of an organizational culture. Schein's theory states that cultural content starts with the decisions taken by the leaders. In this context, the leader is the one who can create more effects on his/her followers rather than how they influence him/her.

Leadership is extremely important for the organizations in terms of achieving certain common goals because the leaders have a strong influence on the behaviours and performance of individuals and groups. In addition, the aims of the group are also the targets that are approved or requested by the leader (Şimşek 1997). As a result, the leader has an important role in acquiring a new corporate identity during the re-institutionalization processes by supporting certain approaches, attitudes, under-standings, values, and behaviours (Merih 2002). Otherwise, if the conflicts of values emerge, it may cause the re-examination of the organizational values, or the establish-ment of new mechanisms for harmonization, or a change in leadership style.

Additionally, as specified by Schein, the cultural characteristics can be modified according to needs- like behavioural patterns. In the case of strategic conflicts in values, norms, philosophy, organizational rules and organizational culture, the need for the organizational renewal may arise (Schein 1984). It is believed that this study will contribute to the literature by summarizing the critical relationship between these elements and clarifying the conceptual framework.

2   Organizational Culture

Individuals constitute societies who are trying to satisfy their needs and expectations and to find solutions to the problems they are experiencing. As a result, the individuals living in the society jointly create ideas, traditions, and rules to regulate their relationships with each other. This phenomenon, consisting of all these factors, is called culture (Erdoğan 1994).

Culture reflects the lifestyles of the societies and therefore different communities have different cultural characteristics (Baymur 1994). Culture does not differ only among societies. Organizations operate in the same social systems and are also influenced by the values, traditions, customs and beliefs of their communities (Apulgan 1996). Organizations try to survive like any living creature and not only for a certain limited period of time. In line with this, organizations form a culture mosaic consisting of individuals with different beliefs and traditions (Ersen 1997). The existence of "culture" in organizations is a binding element for communication and interactions between employees. Naturally, individuals who participate in a particular culture bring along their own beliefs and traditions (March and Simon 1958).

Although organizational culture is an abstract concept, it affects the employees and organizational processes and plays a significant role in companies. A positive culture is not only a factor for the success or failure of a business, but also can bring significant competitive advantage.

Organizational culture studies began in the USA during the nineteenth century. And, specifically, in the book titled "Institutional Cultures: Rituals in the Life of the Institution", the concept and understanding of positive organizational culture was widely presented (Deal and Kennedy 1982). Since then, organizational culture has become an integral part of much research, especially in the context of studying business strategies of institutions. It is clear that organizational culture has become an important element for the senior managers; therefore, discussions were carried out regarding the continuity of organizational culture and leadership, notably about leadership and communication methods.

2.1 Definition of Organizational Culture

Organizational culture is a difficult term characterizing the quality of the social climate within an organization that determines the working conditions of all employees. Clearly, it represents a phenomenon related to emotions rather than the rational minds of an observer (Mohelska and Pitra 2012). In addition, the individuals and societies are continuously influenced by their environment and time unclear, and it directly affects concepts of culture thereby making it difficult to define culture within a single expression (Erdoğan 1994).

Yet, it is possible to define organizational culture as a kind of genetic code which leads to the reproducibility of both individual and collective behaviours, images, emotions and attitudes. But, also, it can be defined as a set of symbols, ceremonies, and myths which help members of an organization to understand organizational assumptions and values (Koźmiński and Obłój 1989).

According to Weis and Wiest, organizational culture consists of a system that includes typical values, norms, and symbols of a company. An organisational culture develops over a long period, as a result of the best practices of the whole social group, creating a hierarchy of certain values (West 2000).

Zbiegień-Maciąg (1994) describes organisational culture as a way of perceptions, thoughts, feelings, and reactions that are shared by company employees and often stay deeply hidden and unrecognized in the human mind. It emphasizes what they have in common, what unites them, and what reduces uncertainty. It is accepted as the product of the way employee's live together, interact, and cooperate.

An organizational culture is formulated by Schein (1990) and defined as the whole of basic assumptions that a particular group learnt, discovered, and developed while adapting to their environment or solving problems during internal integration.

Although a culture has various definitions and is difficult to make a joint description about, there are some common characteristics shared by communities. O'Reilly et al. stated seven different characteristics which drive members of an organisation to collectively pursue the aims of an organization (O'Reilly et al. 1991).

1. Innovation and Risk Taking: The level of the incentives provided to help the organizational members to take risks and create innovation within an organization.
2. Attention to detail: The level of importance given to details by the employees when fulfilling their responsibilities, as well as their ability to analyse.
3. Result-Oriented: If the management of the organisation is result-oriented, they will focus on the level of realization and the final result, rather than on how the duties are performed.

4. People-Oriented: The level of importance given to how the decisions of the management will affect the members of an organisation
5. Team-Oriented: The level of the importance attached to tasks that are organised as team-based, rather than individually-based.
6. Aggression: The level of how aggressive the competitive aspects of the members of the organization are, rather than on members having submissive behaviour.
7. Stability: The level of stability of the activities carried out in the organisation, rather than continuous development.

2.2 The Factors that Constitute Organizational Culture

Schein (1990) explains the formation of the organization culture by dividing the organization culture into three layers. The top layer consists of observable objects that can be felt by five senses and are the most openly accessible. The second layer contains norms and values. This part is generally described as a foundation stone and reflects the philosophy, functioning, general aims, and ideals of the organization showing itself in the behaviours of its members. The last layer consists of assumptions. According to Schein (1990), assumptions constitute the core of an organizational culture. This factor is abstract and more difficult to observe, often including perceptions of organizational members about functional problems and solutions.

Organizational culture includes visible cultural items: ceremonies, parades, rituals, stories, myths, symbols, slogans, language, leaders and heroes (Güçlü 2003). It is accepted that common beliefs and assumptions are the invisible dimension of the organisational culture lying at the heart of an organization; however, symbols, heroes, language, and symbols are actually the visible dimension of organisational culture, which are more presentable (Schermerhorn et al. 2000).

The organizational culture is shaped under the influence of very different variables and these variables are categorized in different dimensions in the related literature (Pettigrew 1979; Berberoğlu 1991). In our study, the effects of values and leadership on the formation of culture are examined, and other factors of culture formation are briefly explained as they are frequently discussed in the literature.

2.2.1 Values

Values provides a framework for understanding the beliefs, goals, attitudes, ethics, self-concept, behaviour, and other elements of the individual system; additionally they also help to evaluate the dynamics of an organizational culture (Bernthal 1962).

Past studies define the organizational values in various forms. For example, O'Reilly et al. (1991) describe the values of an organization as "the elements that revolve around norms, symbols, rituals, and other cultural activities." Johnson and Jackson (2009) describe organizational values as the standards that determine member behaviours and organizational success.

Organizational values are based on the ability of directing and influencing the preferences, priorities, actions, and attitudes of an institution and its members (Toh et al. 2008). Chatman (1989) states that the values of an organisation provide a detailed and general justification for the activities and functions of a system and for the appropriate behaviours of its members.

Shared values are the primary focus of organizational culture research, and it is thought that they facilitate effective interaction between members and provide integration. In the literature, there are cultural values that are believed to represent organizational culture. Organizational culture theorists argue that organizations have a relatively narrow set of values and certain values are useful in understanding organizational processes (Meglino and Ravlin 1998).

2.2.2 Leadership

A leader is the person who brings his/her followers together and directs them towards their desired goals. The leader may have an innate ability to influence others or may have charismatic aspects generated by a number of personal characteristics that are highly valuable for his/her followers (Bingöl 2006). It is also possible that the authority is legal (formal).

It can be said that leadership is the most common concept among the factors that constitute culture. In the literature, it is accepted that the organizational culture and leadership have reciprocal effects on each other; therefore they are considered highly related concepts in organizational life (Schein 2004). It is also believed that senior leaders have a primary influence on the creation and development of an organizational culture (Schein 2004; Trice and Beyer 1993).

2.2.3 Other Factors

The level of culture in an organisation is the ultimate determinant of perceptions, language, opinions, emotions, accepted values, and the behaviours of a group. If a group has a common past, they may also have a common culture and therefore many subcultures form within an organization. When we examine the organizational symbols, stories, legends, and other factors of these subcultures, we should know how they relate to fundamental assumptions, and we should be aware of the fact that we might make incorrect deductions (Pondy et al. 1983, 1988; Wilkins 1983) because the meaning of an organizational culture is closely related to the meaning of these factors. Although different studies have had different titles in the literature, they include many factors (rituals, symbols, stories and legends, material symbols, language and metaphors, architectural characteristics and organizational identity, organization history, environment, technology, size) when providing meaning for an organisational culture.

Ceremonies and Symbols

In the literature, ceremony is accepted as the expressions for a planned event or object that is meaningful and special for a certain group of people (Varol 1989). They are the significant key activities of organisation that enable its members to identify themselves with the organization (Kamoche 1995). Symbols are also considered to be indicative of cultures (such as ceremonies, slogans, logos, emblems, and mascots) and are accepted as symbols used to represent culture.

Also, cultural structures have their own symbols and ceremonies. Flags and religions are considered effective unifying symbols for individuals forming a society (Dönmezer 1994). Each culture has its own unique symbols, but the degrees of importance given to the symbols are different for each culture. For this reason, the effect of symbols on a culture changes accordingly. Therefore, it is very important that leaders use symbols effectively in order to be successful in the process of creating and changing cultures (Kamoche 1995).

Ceremonies and symbols can be listed as the meetings and dinners arranged by an organisation; greeting styles of the employees; uniforms or a dress code; events organised to celebrate a foundation day or the founder of the organization; events organised for retiring personnel; the title attached to special moments; the pennants and badges representing the organization; social signs to determine the distance between senior management; and, employees within the organization (Varol 1989).

Stories and Legends

Since the establishment of organizations, stories and myths as culture bearers emerge as a result of the recounting of the past events with exaggerated expressions used to influence employees. The most important feature of stories and legends is that the heroes and symbols serve as a cultural bridge contributing to the adoption of symbols and values among employees (Daniel and Robert 1978). The stories and myths, usually include sections from the life of founders of the organisation, stories of those who break the rules in the organization, those who start from the lower level and reach the top of the hierarchy, or those who started in poverty but become rich (Boje 1991; Deutsch 1991; Seiling 2003).

Language

The most important part of a culture is the "language" that helps to carry the culture among the individuals. Culture that is carried through language between individuals is transferred from generation to the generation and helps the continuation of social relations between individuals (Eroğlu 1996). From the moment that an organization is established, the individuals and sub-units who join organisations begin to use a common language that indicates that they accept and adopt the organisational culture and are, hence, integrated into the culture. This common language covers the terms used by employees in relation to work (Robbins and Judge 2013).

As the languages used by societies are made up of signs and voices, the concept of "language" falls within symbols (Robbins and Judge 2013). However, the impact on culture must be addressed separately because the language used within the organization is meaningful for individuals working within the organization. Naturally, each organization has its own "special" language that makes sense to them. For this reason, the language used within the organization does not make sense to the external individuals and organizations.

Customs and Manners

Customs and manners are described as the rules affecting the daily lives, attitudes, behaviours, and lifestyles of the individuals generated by the influence of the environment. People may obey those rules, rules which appear or disappear instinctively (Dönmezer 1994).

Manners are the behaviours that are constantly repeated for a period of time, but the majority of the population does not feel obligated to implement. Yet, customs, unlike manners, include punishments if people do not obey and follow the rules. Since the opposition to customs is only moderately tolerated, rules are stricter than manners (Köse et al. 2001).

Schein (1983) points out that an organizations' existing customs and manners largely depend on both what was done before and the success achieved in this way. This leads us to the ultimate source of the organization culture: Founders of the Organization. There are many ways to create a culture, but the most basic beginning is the beliefs of the founders of the organization and those employees who come after them. It is evident that the personalities of the founders are reflected in the organizational culture in terms of training of the employees and their adaptation to customs and manners.

Norms

Norms are defined as orders and rules that individuals, who have adopted a specific role in the organization, must comply with (Erdoğan 1994). Norms constitute the general culture of the communities; therefore, executives who are involved in the formation of organizational norms have an important task. They must create principles and rules of management according to the cultural norms of their employees (Özkalp 1995).

Additionally, norms represents the information that should be obeyed by individuals. It is certain that everybody is informed about the norms through communication between people- sooner or later, directly or indirectly. The norms have an influence on the actions of the participating members and if the norms of organization are known, it would be clearer what information is needed by the employees or groups and what they can do to forward this information to others (Stamper and Liu 1994).

In organizations, a constant change of norms depends on the mutual interaction between employees: employees observe their environment and reflect, diversify, and change the norms. Norms, in turn, are used to improve the learning ability of organizations as an organizational concept, especially in transforming organizations (Andersen 1995).

It would be possible to obtain very detailed information about organizational change and organizational learning if we had sufficient information about the norm structure of the organisations and the process of creating and changing norms (Stamper et al. 2000).

Socializing is carried out with an aim to help new employees blend into an organisation and adapt to the organisational culture (Cable and Parsons 2001). The basic philosophy of organizational socialization is to ensure that employees become a member that embraces and sustains the organisational culture (Can 1997). Especially important, senior management, due to their position in decision-making mechanism, should spend more time and effort to organise socialization activities for employees.

Socialization is examined in three stages, with the main purpose of each stage examining how long it will take the members to settle into the organisation or how long it will take them to leave (Robbins and Judge 2013). The first stage is called the pre-accession stage. Pre-access refers to the fact that new recruits join the organisation with a number of expectations (Collins 2007). It is possible to predict the attitudes and behaviours of the employees by referring to the attitudes and behaviours they have shown in the past. Therefore, it is necessary give significant importance to the socialization process for pre-accession (Wangm et al. 2011). The Encounter is the stage of clarification between the expectations of the new employees and the organisational environment. If the expectations are met, the individuals socialize faster in the organization (Morrison 2002). Transformation is the stage that employees willingly go through while adapting to the organisation, and specifically, if they realise that the organisation does not comply with their expectations (Bauer et al. 2007).

3 Personal Values

Values are the primary elements that enable individuals to control themselves and the community to control individuals. Consequently, values are influential in determining the status of the individuals within the community. Through these values, an individual can communicate effectively with other people and create a suitable infrastructure for the determination of his/her social position. According to Rokeach (1973), values are the determinants of all important behaviours: social activity, attitudes, ideology, evaluation, moral judgment, and legalization (Cheng and Fleischmann 2010).

Socio-psychological values are important factors and the key predictors for human and social dynamics in explaining individual decisions. In fact, in various fields, the importance of values for describing individual and organizational behaviour has been emphasized. In the literature of personality, it is stated that values are related to personality (Allport 1961). According to Giberson et al. (2009), personal values are the dimension of personal characteristics—the same as personality traits. In related literature, it specifically states that values are an element t governing and motivating one's behaviour (Locke 1976) and managing strong individual differences—such as personality (McClelland 1985; Giberson et al. 2009). In sociology, values are seen as significant variables in defining community consciousness (Durkheim 1960). In the organizational behavioural field, it is stated that values affect strategic organizational decisions and organizational commitments. In political science, personal values are the factor that influences governments, laws, parties, and also institutions (Schwartz 2006; Cheng and Fleischmann 2010).

New social arrangements emerge as an inevitable consequence of socio-economic developments, and it is important that new arrangements should be compatible with the values of the individuals in order to ensure healthy functioning. Accordingly, values should be examined in detail to understand communities better and to achieve social and political success (Kağıtçıbaşı and Kuşdil 2000; Çetin 2004).

3.1 Definition of Personal Values

Indeed, the concept of value is a difficult issue. Values add different characteristics to different people, so it is appropriate to start the analysis of this concept with a few meaningful definitions. Values are accepted as normative standards influenced by the choices of individuals, individuals who selected from several perceptions of alternative actions (Bernthal 1962). Values can thus be seen as an open or implicit understanding of the choice of actions of an individual, group or organization selected from existing alternative modes (Harrison 1975).

"Value" as a term, refers to our standards and principles that constitute our judgment for objects, people, ideas, situations, and actions—such as good, bad, desirable, undesirable (Halstead and Taylor 2000).

Values are the principles that guide human behaviours (Gutman 1982), as well as the tendencies to behave in certain ways according to individual preferences (Grey 2005). Also, values are preferences or standards of each individual (Ramos 2006), and the belief that individuals prefer certain situations to others (Choi 2005), beliefs regarding desirability or undesirability (Byrd 2002).

More broadly, value is defined as beliefs that are long-lasting causing certain behaviours and goals to be preferable to others (Solomon 1996). Rokeach defines value as a constant personal or social belief compelling the preference of particular behaviours or purposes to others (Cheng and Fleischmann 2010). According to Rokeach, each individual has constant values that he/she prefers more than others thereby affecting his/her behaviours. The total value of each person is called a "values system". S value system is a set of persistent beliefs that are related to one's purpose of existence or preferred behaviours (Rokeach 1973). Kluckhohn (1951) states that values are not rooted from simple desires but from desires that are possible to reach; in other words, they are not just something we want, but things we feel are right and appropriate to desire for ourselves and others (Silah 2005). In literature, the emphasis is put on definitions of how values differ; in contrast, Rokeach and Schwartz say a value is defined as "a constant belief". At the same time, Kluckhohn, Guth and Tagiuri define values as an "understanding", Braithwaite and Blamey define a value as "principles" (Cheng and Fleischmann 2010).

Values are one of the core elements of identity (Schwartz 2000; Hitlin 2003), a key part in a continuing process of presentation that includes consciously designing targets (Bilsky and Schwartz 1994), which, in turn affect an individual's behaviour (Debatts and Bartelds 2006; Lipponen 2004). Values are social representatives of purposes; they act as guiding principles and motivate people (Rokeach 1973; Schwartz 1992; Rohan 2000). These guiding principles can be expressed as an individual's choice of actions, his/her evaluation criteria of other individuals and events, and methods of explaining their own assessments (Schwartz and Sagiv 2000; Gandal and Roccas 2002; Altıntaş 2006).

Hofstede (2001) stated that values are standards of belief related to the right-wrong distinction of individuals. In this sense, values have an impact on the positive or negative attitudes and behaviours of individuals in relation to certain events or results (Rokeach 1973; Mayton et al. 1994; Feather 1995).

Due to the relation between the beliefs and emotions of individuals (Hansson 2001), Wiener (1988) defined values as "internalized normative beliefs". Similarly, Özen (1996) stated that values are the "special state" of beliefs, and this particular state gives value the potential to influence the selection of a certain behaviour towards particular people, objects or events—due to the its normative patterns.

Whiteley (1995) described values as thoughts and emotions deeply related to a particular subject. He also indicated that behaviours are observable but values are not, rather they guide behaviours that are not observable. Therefore, values are concepts that are accepted by individuals in the form of behaviours (Guth and Taguiri 1965; Ericson 1969; Elizur et al. 1991; Schwartz 1990). Accordingly, the values represent the "ideal targets" that are desired, not the easily possible targets. The preference of a target is determined by the benefits presented by the subjects or events in the individual's environment (Bozkurt 1997; Altıntaş 2006).

Organizational values play a critical role in influencing a members' behaviours and actions (Newnam et al. 2008; Robert and Wasti 2002). As Williams (2002) points out, organizational values shape every action and decision made by employees; also, empirical studies show that employees easily adapt rewarded values within their organizations (Chatman 1989). Studies suggest that a value-oriented approach should be adopted to understand organizational behaviour better (Voss et al. 2000).

3.2   Components and Characteristics of Values

The elements, emphasised by the leading scientists who study the distinctive features of values (Rokeach 1973; Chusmir and Parker 1991; Zhao 1998) are:

1. Value is a preference: Value is a preference or request for a particular behavioural rule. As a selective system, values select between behaviours and behavioural systems and put forward some normative regulations.
2. A value is permanent: Values are permanent beliefs. However, they are not completely stable.
3. Values are open to change. The priorities of values can change over time, in order to meet new and emerging needs (Schwartz and Bilsky 1987).
4. A value is a belief: Values, like all beliefs, have cognitive, emotional and behavioural dimensions. If we say that an individual has a value, it means that he/she cognizes that he/she is correct, and he/she holds a characteristic that can cause him/her to behave in a certain way.
5. Value is a form of behaviour or the ultimate state of being: in a way, a value is the main purpose of human life. The possession of a value means that he/she has beliefs about the desirable behaviours or the final result of the situation.
6. Values are related to the goals of the individual (such as equality) and to behaviours performed in order to achieve these goals (being fair, being charitable).
7. Values are above specific actions and situations. For example, the value of obedience is valid at home, at work, at school, and in all of our relationships with people we do not know.
8. Values serve as standards that guide the selection or change of behaviours, people, and events.
9. Values are sorted among themselves according to their level of priority, creating a ranking system that determines the priorities of values. Cultures and individuals can be described by their value priority systems, and different societies may have the same value but the level of importance given to those values can be different. It is the element that separates people and societies from each other and distinguishes values from norms and attitudes (Schwartz 2005).
10. Values shape the perspective of the individual about his/her environment and also are very influential elements of culture that hold the members of a society together (Altıntaş 2006).
11. A value is a mode of personally or socially choosing a preferable behaviour or an eternal belief of the ultimate state of existence (Pang 1996).
12. A value is a great tendency to prefer certain relationships to others (Hofstede 1980).
13. A value is form of selective tendency indicating preferences, interests, motivations, needs, desires, goals, behaviours, and attitudes (Van and Scarbrough 1995).
14. A value is the rule-maker that differentiates results for the individual and others (Carling 1999).

15. It is the standard that helps people to choose between actions and behaviours and motivates ideal behaviour (Kilby 1993).
16. A value functions as a positive situation or object that an individual tries to acquire, apply, honour, proclaim, voluntarily consume, or bear the cost of (Herriot 1976), therefore it influences the level of cooperation, selective perception, and informative comments of the individual.
17. Values limit the field of vision, play an important role in selecting between alternatives, and serve as a plan or basis for decision-making, solving problem and conflicts (Russell 2001).

4 Leadership

Studies about leadership theories include research about what characteristics leaders possess, what they see as important, what actions they take against problems, how their decision-making processes are, how they respond to needs and requests during organisational activities, and how effective they are in affecting individuals and groups (Turhan 2007).

4.1 Definition of Leadership Concept

It is difficult to generate one clear definition of the concept of "leadership" from literature because leadership is a social, universal, and human phenomenon: a concept that is enriched by the fact that individuals have different characteristics and each characteristics carry different meanings (Bolat et al. 2008).

Leadership is the process of interacting with individuals, leading them in the direction of the goals and objectives of the organization by influenced communication. In other words, if individuals freely follow a leader, creating their targets under the influence of the leader, it can be said that is "leadership". We can summarize the concept of leadership as the ability to influence individuals and groups. Otherwise, we can talk about "managerialism" but not the concept of "leadership" (Yulk 2013). Krausz describes leadership as the power to influence the movements of individuals who follow him/her (Krauzs 2003). According to a definition based on the relation between leader and viewers, "a leader is the person who manages the process of social interaction that affects the behaviours of viewers" (Dasborough and Ashkanasy 2002). Another definition states that leadership is a state of being superior to other members of the group as a result of having certain characteristics—such as charisma, intelligence, and talent (Fielder 2005).

4.2 Leadership Theories

Although the act of leadership has existed for ages, the scientific research on this speculative subject only began to be published at the beginning of the twentieth

Fig. 1 The characteristics
that leaders should possess

century. Leadership types are popular fields of interest in literature and nearly a new type of leadership is proposed every day. There is no consensus in the literature on classifying types of leadership, but it can be addressed under different approaches according to its focus points. Leadership approaches are summarized below, taking into account the classification preferred by Yukl (1994) in his book.

4.2.1 Theory of Characteristics

Accepted as the first approach developed in relation to the concept of leadership, the characteristics of a leader that influence the leadership process are considered the most important factor. In other words, if an individual emerges as a leader, it means that his/her personal characteristics influence his/her followers and give him power to manage them. The leader, with these characteristics, has a different personality from those who follow him (Koçel 2001). The main philosophy of this theory is based on identifying and distinguishing successful and unsuccessful personality traits of such an individual (Owens 1976).

In literature, one opinion is that "there is no school of leadership", and it explains that leader possesses some innate qualities and attributes that cannot be gained through education. This is a way of summarising the Theory of Characteristics. This theory is also called 'the Great People Approach', and it aims at distinguishing characteristics of leaders from non-leaders—as the researchers make an effort to explain leadership (Buono and Bowditch 1990).

The studies about theory of characteristics summarise the features that leaders should possess as follows (Fig. 1).

4.2.2 Behavioural Leadership Theories

The behavioural approach emphasizes how a leader behaves. It separates the qualitative approach that highlights the leader's personal characteristics from the skills approach that highlights the leader's talents. The behavioural approach focuses only on what leaders do and how they behave. Researchers examining the behavioural approach state that leadership is composed of two general types of behaviour: Task Behaviours and Relationship Behaviours. Task behaviours help group members to achieve their goals, while relationship behaviours help subordinates to feel comfortable in communicating with their supervisors and colleagues. The main purpose of the behavioural approach explains the reasons a leader's behaviour influences subordinates and helps achieve their aims (Northouse 2013).

In the behavioural leadership style, the leader has mutual communication with his/her subordinates. This communication requires that the leader fulfil the wishes of his/her subordinates in order to fulfil his/her own wishes. In other words, there is a relation of mutual dependency. According to the behavioural approach, the relationships are divided into two groups: low quality relations and high quality relations. Low quality behaviours are based on rights (salary increase, social and personal rights) between leader and subordinates, while high quality behaviours depend on reciprocity between the leader and the subordinates (reward system) (Kuhnert and Lewis 1987, p. 649).

Many studies have been conducted to investigate the behavioural approach. Stogdill (1948) carried out research at Ohio State University, in the late 1940s, which emphasized the importance of the characteristics of leaders in leadership research. At the same time, another group of researchers at the University of Michigan conducted a series of studies that investigate how leadership affects small groups. A third research series was initiated by Blake and Mouton at the beginning of the 1960s and studied how managers use task and relationship behaviours in the organizational environment (Blake and Mouton 1964).

While many studies can be categorized under the heading of Behavioural Approach, the Ohio State studies, Michigan studies, and studies by Blake and Mouton (1964, 1978, 1985) strongly represent ideas in this approach (Blake and Mouton 1985).

4.2.3 Situational Contingency Theory

One of the more widely accepted approaches of leadership is the situational approach introduced by Hersey and Blanchard (1969a, b), which is based on Reddin's (1967) three-dimensional management style theory. As the title implies, situational leadership focuses on the leadership of the situations (Blanchard et al. 1993). The priority of the theory is that different situations demand different leadership. In this sense, an effective leader should customise his or her style according to the demands of different situations (Hersey and Blanchard 1977, 1988).

Situational leadership emphasizes that leadership has both a procedural and a supportive dimension and that each must be applied appropriately for certain situations (Blanchard et al. 1985). To identify what is needed in any situation, a leader must evaluate his employees to decide how competent and determined they are to perform a particular task. Situational leadership—based on the assumption that employees' skills and motivations change over time—suggests that leaders must change to the degree necessary to meet the changing needs of subordinates (Blanchard 1985). In short, the core of situational leadership is that leaders must determine their style according to the ability and commitment of their subordinates. Effective leaders are people who can identify what their employees need and set their own style to meet these needs (Hersey and Blanchard 1969a, b).

4.2.4 Power/Influence Approach

This approach explains leadership through two aspects. The Power relations period emphasizes the source, the amount of power, and how they used this power. In todays' organizations, a leaders dictatorial and authoritarian characteristics are considered ineffective; however, it is prevalent to experience such managers in organizations. The second aspect is the persuasion period. Instead of cooperation and mutual interaction between the leader and the employee, a structural antagonism emerges which is led by the leader of the employees. The biggest drawback of this aspect is that an employee's competency or ability to take initiative remains undeveloped (Seters and Field 1990).

4.2.5 Modern Leadership Approach

Recently, researchers tried to define new types of leadership ethical, servant, spiritual, and authentic leadership that are centered on different components. They suggested that these types of leadership are more effective in meeting the demands of the new business world and the current needs of employees. Leadership theorists have studied integrative leadership theories containing multiple components: traits, behaviors, influence processes, situational variables, and outcomes. However, new leadership concepts are also insufficient to define all aspects and all required properties of leadership (Yulk 2013).

5   The Relationship Between Leadership, Personal Values and Organizational Culture

Everybody judges situations they encounter differently, which results in different behaviours. The degree of importance given to values differs from person to person, also affecting attitudes in business life (Cohen 2009). In this context, values also have great importance at the management level in terms of organizational effectiveness. Giberson and others carried out a study on the personalities of CEOs and stated that their values not only affected their behaviours and decisions but also the social environment of the organisation (for example, culture). They argue that the personalities of senior managers affect the new or existing members of the organisation and the relationship between the members as a result of making decisions or approving or disapproving of members' behaviours (Giberson et al. 2009).

Personal values bring certain standards to the thoughts and feelings of the managers within the organizational culture and shape the behaviours and decisions, thus creating an ideology for the organization. The concept of value is highly influential in a managers' decisions about their work, managerial success, and other relationships (Russell 2001; Naktiyok 2002). Again, research on this subject states that personal values influence strategies and behaviours such as selection and reward system, organizational responsibility, adaptation to the job, superior-subordinate relationship, amount of risk, decision style, productivity, service quality, group behaviour, communication, and leadership and conflict level (Burke 1997; Russell 2001). In addition, theorists on this subject state that value is related to leadership types and managerial decision mechanisms (Altıntaş 2006). Life values are considered to be the most important elements of economic, social, and political theories in communities experiencing a rapid development process. When we take into account the above mentioned effects of life values, it is clear that the satisfaction of work life depends on the results of values because behaviours such as election and reward system, organizational responsibility, adaptation to work, superior-subordinate relationship, decision making style, group behaviour, communication, leadership and conflict level are influenced by values and elements of job satisfaction (Naktiyok 2002).

Organizational values constitute the framework of all other strategic decisions. It shapes the professional roles and responsibilities of employees, as well as shaping the company's performance evaluations, training programs, business organization, and key business decisions (Howard 1990, p. 143). Values contribute to the formation of organizational culture through these elements.

Studies have shown that the human resources department within an organization is influenced by the core values of the organization. Toh et al. (2008) found that organizational values are associated with the innovation, human orientation, and the stability of the human resource practices adopted by an organization. Accordingly, reformist organizations give importance to the employees' risk taking, competitiveness, and ability to take advantage of potential opportunities. People-oriented organizations place emphasis on cooperation, support, information sharing, flexibility, respect and tolerance. Lastly, stable institutions take notice of predictability and continuity.

Multidimensional studies have been carried out on leadership and culture relations in literature. Some researchers have found relationships between the personal characteristics of leaders and structural characteristics indicators of companies (Miller 1986). Likewise, it has been pointed out in related literature that the behaviours of senior leaders who aim to improve performance or establish an institution should also form the organizational processes and structural characteristics to strengthen organizational cultures (Tsui et al. 2006). However, in addition to the theoretical studies on the joint subject of culture and leadership, when these subjects were considered separately, it is evident that leaders play an important role in creating and sustaining the culture in organisations (Schein 1992). Furthermore, it is important to both understand the culture and have the ability to perform success-fully in this culture in order to increase the effectiveness of leadership (Hennessey 1998; Bakan 2009).

Organisational culture is a subject that interests researchers of leaderships, man-agement consultants, and company managers. Organizational culture is also described as the reason behind the failure of mergers and acquisitions and as a management tool to create a competitive advantage and provide a base (Bennis and Nanus 1985; Trice and Beyer 1993; Donahue 2001). The senior managers should manage complex relationship in order to create a successful organizational culture (Schein 2004; Trice and Beyer 1993). Although, there are a number of theories that show that leaders are influential in their organizations, there are only a few studies that examine the individual differences of the leaders, and their organizational characteristics and achievements.

The research about leadership characteristics and organizational structures, espe-cially with organizational culture, might be difficult due to the complications in measuring and assessing psychological attributes such as individual personality characteristics of leaders. In 1968, research conducted by L. K. Williams stated that different disciplines have different interests at micro-levels as well as macro levels e.g. personality traits. Williams notes that it is important to study the person-ality, structure, and functioning of the organizational system concurrently in order to understand organizational behaviours.

Schneider, Goldstein, and Smith (1995) state that organizational goals are gen-erally generated from the personality characteristics of their executive leaders. Thus, top-tier leaders, and especially founders, mirror their own characteristics onto organisations by emplacing their own aims (Schneider 1987). In other words, the content of organisational culture is not randomly formed but is formed by the key strategic and operational decisions of the senior executives, which is a reflection of the characteristics of senior executives. These decisions form the basis of shared values and assumptions that have become the culture of the institution. For this reason, there is a relationship between personal characteristics of senior managers and cultures that emerge in their organizations.

Schein (2004) states that managers consciously and unconsciously place their tendencies and preferences in their organizations through various mechanisms, such as the criteria used to allocate rewards or personnel decisions. Leaders interact with the individuals of the organisation and determine how the organization will reach its targets; meanwhile, leaders also create cultural forms by behaving sensibly on how the organization will work. Leaders further strengthen cultural content through explanation or empowerment mechanisms such as stories, legends and official statements—particularly during the decision process of organizational design.

Researchers who present their views on the causes of relationships between organizational culture and leadership consider culture as a complementary part of an organisation and argue that a leader has a significant influence on organizational cultures since his/her emotions, thoughts and reactions shape the culture (Bass and Avolio 1994; Schein 1992). In addition, Richard Hendrickson, in his 1989 study on culture and leadership, notes that leadership is, in fact, a cultural expression. Both findings of empirical and theoretical studies and predictions show that these variables have complex relationships, thereby shaping one another.

As a result of these findings, it is understood that the personal values and leadership are inevitably influential in the formation of an organizational culture, which leads to the achievement of desired aims by determining common understanding and behaviours in an organization. For this reason, it is vital for an organization to use these tools effectively in order to achieve positive outputs, competition superiority, and ensure sustainability and continuity, which are the basic principles of an organisation.

References

Allport, G. W. (1961). *Pattern and growth in personality*. New York: Holt, Rinehart & Winston.

Altıntaş, F. Ç. (2006). Bireysel Değerlerin Örgütsel Adalet ve Sonuçları İlişkisinde Yönlendirici Etkisi: Akademik Personel Üzerinde Bir Analiz. *İşletme Fakültesi Dergisi, 7*(2), 19–40.

Andersen, P. B. (1995). *Organisational semiotics and the theory of autopoesis, colloquium on organisational semiotics*. Enschede: Twente University.

Apulgan, O. (1996). *İşletme Bilimine Giriş* (Vol. 73). Trabzon: Derya Kitabevi.

Bakan, İ. (2009). Liderlik tarzları ile örgüt kültürü türleri arasındaki ilişkiler: Bir alan çalışması. *TISK Academy/TISK Akademi, 4*(7), 138–172.

Bass, B. M., & Avolio, B. J. (1994). Transformational leadership and organizational culture. *International Journal of Public Administration, 17*(3–4), 541–554.

Bauer, T. N., Bodner, T., Erdogan, B., Truxillo, D. M., & Tucker, J. S. (2007). Newcomer adjustment during organizational socialization: A metaanalytic review of antecedents, outcomes, and methods. *Journal of Applied Psychology, 92*(3), 707–721.

Baymur, F. (1994). *Genel Psikoloji*. İstanbul: İnkilâp Kitabevi.

Baymur. (1994). Genel Psikoloji, İnkilâp Kitabevi, İstanbul.

Bennis, W., & Nanus, B. (1985). *Leaders: The strategies for taking charge*. New York: Harper & Row.

Berberoğlu, G. (1991). *Karşılaştırmalı Yönetim*. Eskişehir: Anadolu Üniversitesi İİBF Yayınları.

Bernthal, W. (1962). Value perspectives in management decisions. *Academy of Management Journal, 5*, 190–196.

Bingöl, D. (2006). *İnsan Kaynakları Yönetimi*. İstanbul: Arıkan Basım Yayım Dağıtım Ltd. Şti.

Blake, R. R., & Mouton, J. S. (1964). *The managerial grid*. Houston, TX: Gulf Publishing.

Blake, R. R., & Mouton, J. S. (1978). *The new managerial grid*. Houston, TX: Gulf Publishing.

Blake, R. R., & Mouton, J. S. (1985). *The managerial grid III*. Houston, TX: Gulf Publishing.

Blanchard, K. H. (1985). *SLII: A situational approach to managing people*. Escondido, CA: Blanchard Training and Development.

Blanchard, K., Zigarmi, P., & Zigarmi, D. (1985). *Leadership and the one minute manager: Increasing effectiveness through situational leadership*. New York: William Morrow.

Blanchard, K., Zigarmi, D., & Nelson, R. (1993). Situational leadership after 25 years: A retrospective. *Journal of Leadership Studies, 1*(1), 22–36.

Boje, D. M. (1991). The storytelling organization: A study of story performance in an office-supply firm. *Administrative Science Quarterly, 36*, 106–126.

Bolat, T., Seymen, A. O., Bolat İnci, O., & Erdem, B. (2008). *Yönetim ve Organizasyon* (p. 54). Ankara: Detay Yayıncılık.

Bozkurt, T. (1997). In S. Tevrüz (Ed.), *İşletme Kültürü, Endüstri ve Örgüt Psikolojisi içinde*. Ankara: Türk Psikologlar Derneği ve Kalite Derneği Yayını.

Buono, A. F., & Bowditch, J. L. (1990). *The human side of mergers and acquisitions.* San Francisco, CA: Jossey-Bass.

Burke, W. W. (1997). What human resource practitioners need to know for the twenty-first century. *Human Resource Management, 36*(1), 71–79.

Byrd, R. R. (2002). *Exploring internet survey techniques: A study of personal values-leadership style congruence.* University of Louisville, Phd dissertation, USA. UMI.

Cable, D. M., & Parsons, C. K. (2001). Socialization tactics and person-organization fit. *Personnel Psychology, 54,* 1–23.

Can, V. (1997). *Okul Kültürü ve Yönetim.* Ankara: Önder Matbaacılık.

Carling, A. (1999). Marxism today: What can we learn from yesterday? *Science & Society, 63*(1), 89–97.

Çetin, M. Ö. (2004). *Örgüt Kültürü ve Örgütsel Bağlılık.* Ankara: Nobel Yayın Dağıtım.

Chatman, J. A. (1989). Improving interactional organizational research: A model of person–organization fit. *Academy of Management Review, 14,* 333–349.

Cheng, A.-S., & Fleischmann, K. R. (2010). Developing a meta-inventory of human values. *Proceedings of the American Society for Information Science and Technology, 47*(1), 1–10.

Choi, C. C. (2005). *Cultural values in context: Implications for behavioral intentions.* University of Illinois, Phd dissertation, USA. UMI.

Chusmir, L. H., & Parker, B. (1991). Effects of generation and sex on dimensions of life success. *Psychological Reports, 68*(1), 335–338.

Chusmir, L. H., & Parker, B. (1992). Success strivings and their relationship to affective work behaviors: Gender differences. *Journal of Social Psychology, 132,* 87–100.

Cohen, A. B. (2009). Many forms of culture. *American Psychologist, 64*(3), 194–204.

Collins, C. J. (2007). The interactive effects of recruitment practices and product awareness on job seekers' employer knowledge and application behaviors. *Journal of Applied Psychology, 92*(1), 180–190.

Daft, R. (1986). *Organizational theory and design.* St. Paul, MN: West Publishing.

Daniel, K., & Robert, L. K. (1978). *The social psychology of organizations* (2nd ed.). New York: Wiley.

Dasborough, M. T., & Ashkanasy, N. M. (2002). Emotion and attribution of intentionality in leader-member relationships. *The Leadership Quarterly, 13,* 615–634.

Deal, T. E., & Kennedy, A. A. (1982). *Corporate cultures: The rites and results of corporate life.* Reading MA: Addison-Wesley.

Debats, D. L., & Bartelds, B. F. (2006). *The structure of human values: A principal components analysis of the Rokeach Value Survey.* http://www.Ub.Rug.Nl/Eldoc/Dis/Ppsw/D.L.H.M. Debats/C5.pdf.

Deutsch, C. H. (1991). The parables of corporate culture. *New York Times, 25.*

Dönmezer, S. (1994). *Toplum bilim* (p. 99). İstanbul: Beta Basım Yayım Dağıtım A.Ş.

Donahue, L. M., & Webber, S. S. (2001). Impact of highly and less job-related diversity on work group cohesion and performance: A meta-analysis. *Journal of Management, 27*(2), 141–162.

Durkheim, E. (1960). *The division of labor in society.* New York: Free Press.

Elizur, D., Borg, I., Hunt, R., & Beck, I. M. (1991). The structure of work values: A cross cultural comparison. *Journal of Organizational Behavior, 12*(1), 21–38.

Erdoğan, İ. (1994). *İşletmelerde Davranış* (p. 111). İstanbul: Beta Basım Yayım Dağıtım A.Ş.

Ericson, R. F. (1969). The impact of cybernetic information technology on management value systems. *Management Science, 16*(2), 40–60.

Eroğlu, F. (1996). *Davranış Bilimleri* (p. 109). İstanbul: Beta Basım Yayım Dağıtım A.Ş.

Ersen, H. (1997). *Toplam Kalite ve İnsan Kaynaları Yönetimi İlişkisi* (p. 42). İstanbul: Sim Mabaacılık.

Feather, N. T. (1995). Values, valences. and choice: The influence of values on the perceived attractiveness and choice of alternatives. *Journal of Personality and Social Psychology, 68,* 1135–1151.

Fielder, R. (2005). ESAs and leadership development: History, research, and one agency's experience. *A Journal of Research and Opinion About Educational Service Agencies, 11*, 1–11.

Gandal, N., & Roccas, S. (2002). *Good neighbors/bad citizens: Personal value priorities of economists* (Working Paper, No. 3660). Center for Economic Policy Research (CEPR).

Giberson, J. R., Dickson, W., Mitchelson, K., Randall, R., & Clark, A. (2009). Leadership and organizational culture: Linking CEO characteristics to cultural values. *Journal of Business and Psychology, 24*(2), 123–137.

Grey, C. A. K. (2005). *Managerial ethics: A quantitative, correlational study of values and leadership styles of veterinary managers.* University of Phoenix, Phd dissertation, USA. UMI.

Güçlü, N. (2003). Örgüt Kültürü. *Gazi Üniversitesi Sosyal Bilimler Dergisi, 23*(2), 61–85.

Guth, W. D., & Tagiuri, R. (1965). Personal values and corporate strategy. *Harvard Business Review, 43*(5), 123–132.

Gutman, J. (1982). A means-end chain model based on consumer categorization processes. *Journal of Marketing, 46*(2), 60.

Halstead, J. M., & Taylor, M. J. (2000). Learning and teaching about values: A review of recent research. *Cambridge Journal of Education, 30*, 169–202.

Hansson, S. O. (2001). *Structure of values and norms.* West Nyack, NY: Cambridge University Press.

Harrison, E. F. (1975). *The managerial decision making process.* Boston: Houghton Mifflin.

Hennessey, T. (1998). "Reinventing" government: Does leadership make the difference? *Public Administration Review, 58*(6), 522.

Herriot, P. (1976). *Essential psychology: Values, attitudes and behavior change.* New York: Methuen Co. Ltd..

Hersey, P., & Blanchard, K. H. (1969a). Life-cycle theory of leadership. *Training and Development Journal, 23*, 26–34.

Hersey, P., & Blanchard, K. H. (1969b). *Management of organizational behavior: Utilizing human resources.* Englewood Cliffs, NJ: Prentice Hall.

Hersey, P., & Blanchard, K. H. (1977). *Management of organizational behavior: Utilizing human resources* (3rd ed.). Englewood Cliffs, NJ: Prentice Hall.

Hersey, P., & Blanchard, K. H. (1988). *Management and organizational behavior.* Englewood Cliffs, NJ: Prentice-Hall.

Hitlin, S. (2003). Values as the core of personal identity: Drawing links between two theories of self. *Social Psychology Quarterly, 66*(2), 118.

Hofstede, G. (1980). Culture and organizations. *Journal International Studies of Management & Organization, 10*(4), 15–41.

Hofstede, G. (2001). *Culture consequences: Comparing values, behaviors, institutions and organizations accross nations* (2nd ed.). Thousand Oaks, CA: Sage.

Howard, R. (1990). Values make the company: An interview with Robert Haas. *Harvard Business Review, 68*, 132–144.

Johnson, R. E., & Jackson, E. M. (2009). Appeal of organizational values is in the eye of the beholder: The moderating role of employee identity. *Journal of Occupational and Organizational Psychology, 82*, 915–933.

Kağıtçıbaşı, Ç., & Kuşdil, E. M. (2000). Türk Öğretmenlerin Değer Yönelimleri ve Schwartz Değer Kuramı. *Türk Psikoloji Dergisi, 15*(45), 59–76.

Kamoche, K. (1995). Rhetoric, ritualism and totemism in human resource management. *Human Relations, 48*(4), 367–385.

Kilby, R. W. (1993). *The study of human values.* Lanham: University Press of America, Inc.

Kluckhohn, C. (1951). Values and value-orientations in the theory of action: An exploration in definition and classification. In T. Parsons & E. Shils (Eds.), *Toward a general theory of action* (pp. 388–433). Cambridge, MA: Harvard University Press.

Koçel, T. (2001). *İşletme Yöneticiliği, 8.* İstanbul: Bası, Beta Basım Yayım Dağıtım A.Ş.

Köse, S., Tetik, S., & Ercan, C. (2001). Örgüt Kültürünü Oluşturan Faktörler. *Yönetim ve Ekonomi, C.B.Ü. İ.İ.B.F. Dergisi, 7*(1).

Koźmiński, A. K., & Obłój, K. (1989). *Zarys teorii równowagi organizacyjnej*. Warszawa: PWE.

Krauzs, R. (2003). Power and leadership in organizations. *Transactional Analysis Journal, 16* (Akt; Arıkan, S. (2003). "Kadın Yöneticilerin Liderlik Davranışları ve Bankacılık Sektöründe Bir Uygulama", G.Ü. İ.İ.B.F.Dergisi, 1(2), 2).

Kuhnert, K. W., & Lewis, P. (1987). Transactional and transformational leadership: A constructive developmental analysis. *Academy of Management Review, 12*, 648–657.

Lipponen, J. (2004). Perceived procedural justice and employee responses to an organizational merger. *European Journal of Work and Organizational Psychology, 13*(3), 391–413. https://doi.org/10.1080/13594320444000146.

Locke, E. A. (1976). The nature and causes of job satisfaction. In M. D. Dunnette (Ed.), *Handbook of industrial and organizational psychology* (pp. 1297–1349). Chicago: Rand McNally.

March, J. G., & Simon, H. A. (1958). *Organizations* (p. 84). New York: Wiley.

Mayton, D. M., Ball-Rokeach, S. J., & Loges, W. E. (1994). Human values and social issues: An introduction. *Journal of Social Issues, 50*(4), 1–8. https://doi.org/10.1111/j.1540-4560.1994.tb01194.x.

McClelland, D. C. (1985). *Human motivation*. Glenview, IL: Scott, Foresman.

Meglino, B. M., & Ravlin, E. C. (1998). Individual values in organizations: Concepts, controversies, and research. *Journal of Management, 24*, 351–389.

Merih, K. (2002). *Network Yapılarda Yönetim*. www.eylem.com

Miller, J. (1986). *Pathways in the workplace: The effects of gender and race on access to organizational resources*. London: Cambridge University Press.

Mohelska, H., & Pitra, Z. (2012). *Manařerskй metody* (1st ed.). Praha: Professional Publishing.

Morrison, E. W. (2002). Newcomers' relationships: The role of social network ties during socialization. *Academy of Management Journal, 45*, 1149–1160.

Naktiyok, A. (2002). Motivasyonel Değerler ve İş Tatmini: Yöneticiler Üzerinde Bir Uygulama. *Atatürk Üniversitesi İktisadi ve İdari Bilimler Dergisi, 16*(3–4), 166–195.

Newnam, S., Griffin, M. A., & Mason, C. (2008). Safety in work vehicles: A multilevel study linking safety vehicles and individual predictors to workrelated driving crashes. *Journal of Applied Psychology, 93*, 632–644.

Northouse, P. G. (2013). *Leadership theory and practice* (6th ed.p. 75). Thousand Oaks, CA: Sage.

O'Reilly, C. A., Chatman, J. A., & Caldwell, D. F. (1991). People and organizational culture: A profile comparison approach to assessing person–organization fit. *Academy of Management Journal, 34*, 487–516.

Ouchi, W. G. (1981). *Theory Z*. Reading, MA: Addison-Wesley.

Owens, W. A. (1976). Background data. In M. D. Dunnette (Ed.), *Handbook of industrial and organizational psychology* (pp. 609–644). Chicago: Rand McNally.

Özen, Ş. (1996). *Bürokratik Kültür 1, Yönetsel Değerlerin Toplumsal Temelleri* (p. 272). Ankara: Türkiye ve Orta Doğu Amme İdaresi Enstitüsü.

Özkalp, E. (1995). *Örgütlerde Davranış* (p. 116). Eskişehir: Anadolu Üniversitesi Yayınları.

Pang, N. S. K. (1996). School values and teachers' feelings: A LISREL model. *Journal of Educational Administration, 34*(2), 64–83.

Pettigrew, A. M. (1979). On studying organizational cultures, qualitative methodology. *Administrative Science Quarterly, 24*(4), 570–581.

Pondy, L. R., Frost, P. J., Morgan, G., & Dandridge, T. C. (Eds.). (1983). *Organizational symbolism*. Greenwich, CT: JAI Press.

Pondy, L. R., Boland, R. J., & Thomas, H. (1988). *Managing ambiguity and change*. New York: Wiley.

Ramos, A. (2006). Social values dynamics and socio-economic development. *Portuguese Journal Of Social Science, 5*(1), 35–64.

Reddin, W. J. (1967). The 3-D management style theory. *Training and Development Journal, 21* (4), 8–17.

Robbins, S. P., & Judge, T. A. (2013). *Organizational behavior* (15th ed.pp. 511–543). New York: Pearson.

Robert, C., & Wasti, S. A. (2002). Organizational individualism and collectivism: Theoretical development and an empirical test of a measure. *Journal of Management, 28*, 544–566.

Rohan, M. J. (2000). A rose by any name? The values construct. *Personality and Social Psychology Review, 4*(3), 255–277.

Rokeach, M. (1973). *The nature of human values*. New York: Free Press.

Russell, R. F. (2001). The role of values in servant leadership. *Leadership & Organization Development Journal, 22*(2), 76–84.

Schein, E. H. (1983). The role of the founder in creating organizational culture. *Organizational Dynamics, 12*, 13–28.

Schein, E. H. (1984). Coming to a new awareness of organizational culture. *Sloan Management Review, 25*(2), 3.

Schein, E. H. (1990). Organizational culture. *American Psychologist, 45*(2), 109–119. https://doi.org/10.1037/0003-066X.45.2.109.

Schein, E. H. (1992). The role of the CEO in the management of change. In T. A. Kochan & M. Useem (Eds.), *Transforming organizations*. New York: Oxford University Press.

Schein, E. H. (2004). *Organizational culture and leadership*. San Francisco, CA: Jossey-Bass.

Schein. (2016). Learning when and how to lie. Human Relations, 57(3), 259-273.

Schermerhorn, J., Hunt, J., & Osborn, R. (2000). *Organizational Behaviour* (7th ed.). New York: Wiley.

Schneider, B. (1987). The people make the place. *Personnel Psychology, 40*, 437–453.

Schneider, B., Goldstein, H. W., & Smith, D. B. (1995). The ASA framework: An update. *Personnel Psychology, 48*, 747–773.

Schwartz, S. H. (1990). Individualism-collectivism: Critique and proposed refinements. *Journal of Cross-Cultural Psychology, 21*(2), 139–157.

Schwartz, S. H. (1992). Universals in the content and structure of values: Theoretical advances and empirical tests in 20 countries. In M. P. Zanna (Ed.), *Advances in experimental social psychology* (Vol. 25, pp. 1–65). New York: Academic Press.

Schwartz, S. H. (1994). Are there universal asects in the content and structure of values? *Journal of Social Issues, 50*, 19–45.

Schwartz, S. H. (2000). Worries and values. *Journal of Personality, 68*, 309–346.

Schwartz, S. H. (2005). Basic human values: Their content and structure across countries. In A. Tamayo & J. B. Porto (Eds.), *Valores e comportamento nas organizações* [Values and behavior in organizations] (pp. 21–55). Petrópolis: Vozes.

Schwartz, S. H. (2006). *Basic human values: An overview*. Unpublished manuscript. Accessed August 20, 2013, from http://151.97.110.134/Allegati/convegno%207-8-10-05/Schwartzpaper.pdf

Schwartz. (2016). Individualism-Collectivism. Journal of Cross-Cultural Psychology, 21(2), 139-157.

Schwartz, S. H., & Bilsky, W. (1987). *The structure and importance of personal values in six societies*. Manuscript in preparation.

Schwartz, S. H., & Sagiv, L. (2000). Value priorities and subjective well-being: Direct relations and congruity effects. *European Journal of Social Psychology, 30*(2), 177–198.

Seiling, J. G. (2003). Language, metaphors and stories: Catalysts for meaning making in organizations. *Organization Development Journal, 21*(4), 33–43.

Shah, S. (1985). In V. Gokak Chandana (Ed.), *Education in human values: A medicine for a modern epidemic*. Puttarparthi: Prasanthi Nilayam.

Silah, M. (2005). *Endüstride Çalışma Psikolojisi, 2.Baskı*. Ankara: Seçkin Yayınevi.

Şimşek, H. (1997). *Paradigmalar Savaşı*. İstanbul: Sistem Yayıncılık.

Smircich, L. (1983). Concepts of culture and organizational analysis. *Administrative Science Quarterly, 28*, 339–358.

Solomon, M. R. (1996). *Consumer behavior: Buying, having and being* (3rd ed.). Upper Saddle River, NJ: Prentice Hall International Editions.

Stamper, R. K., & Liu, K. L. (1994). Organisational dynamics, social norms and information systems, in Proc. HICSS-27. *Los Alamitos (IEEE Computer Society Press), 6*, 645–654.

Stamper, R., Liu, K. L., Hafkamp, M., & Ades, Y. (2000). Understanding the roles of signs and norms in organizations, a semiotic approach to information design. *Journal of Behaviour and Information Technology, 19*(1), 15–27.

Stogdill, R. M. (1948). Personal factors associated with leadership: A survey of the literature. *The Journal of Psychology, 25*(1), 35–71.

Toh, S. M., Morgeson, F. P., & Campion, M. A. (2008). Human resource configurations: Investigating fit with the organizational context. *Journal of Applied Psychology, 93*, 864–882.

Trice, H. M., & Beyer, J. M. (1993). *The cultures of work organizations.* Englewood Cliffs, NJ: Prentice-Hall.

Tsui, A. S., Zhang, Z. X., Wang, H., Xin, K. R., & Wu, J. B. (2006). Unpacking the relationship between CEO leadership behavior and organizational culture. *The Leadership Quarterly, 17*(2), 113–137.

Turhan, M. (2007). *Genel ve Mesleki Lise Yöneticilerinin Etik Liderlik Davranışlarının Okullardaki Sosyal Adalet Üzerindeki Etkisi* (p. 34).

Van Seters, D. A., & Field, R. H. (1990). The evolution of leadership theory. *Journal of Organizational Change Management, 3*(3), 29–45.

Van, J. D., & Scarbrough, E. (1995). *The impact of values.* New York: Oxford University Press.

Varol, M. (1989). *Örgüt Kültürü ve Verimlilik.* Verimlilik Dergisi, MPM Yayını.

Voss, G. B., Cable, D. M., & Voss, Z. G. (2000). Linking organizational values to relationships with external constituents: A study of nonprofit professional theatres. *Organization Science, 11*, 330–347.

Wangm, M. Y. Z., McCune, E., & Truxillo, D. (2011). Understanding newcomers' adaptability and work-related outcomes: Testing the mediating roles of perceived P-E fit variables. *Personnel Psychology, 64*(1), 163–189.

West, M. A. (2000). *Rozwijanie kreatywności wewnątrz organizacji.* Warszawa: PWN.

Whiteley, A. (1995). *Managing change: A core values approach.* Melbourne, VIC: Macmillan Education.

Wiener, Y. (1988). Forms of value systems: A focus on organizational effectiveness and cultural change and maintenance. *Academy of Management Review, 13*(4), 534–545.

Wilkins, A. L. (1983). Organizational stories as symbols which control the organization. In L. R. Pondy, P. J. Frost, G. Morgan, & T. C. Dandridge (Eds.), *Organizational symbolism* (pp. 81–91). Greenwich, CT: JAI Press.

Williams, S. L. (2002). Strategic planning and organizational values: Links to alignment. *Human Resource Development International, 5*, 217–233.

Yukl, G. (1994). *Leadership in organizations* (3rd ed.). Englewood Cliffs, NJ: Prentice Hall.

Yulk, G. (2013). *Leadership in organizations* (5th ed.p. 18). Upper Saddle River, NJ: Prentice Hall.

Zbiegień-Maciąg, L. (1994). Duch przedsiębiorstwa, czyli budowanie corporate identity w polskich firmach. *Przegląd Organizacji, 11.*

Zhao, Y. (1998). *Media, market, and democracy in China: Between the party line and the bottom line.* Urbana, IL: University of Illinois Press.

Is It Possible to Define Globalization in One Definition?

Fulya Kıvılcım

Abstract When approximately past 50 years of past experience considered; it can be defined as a period where bipolar system that dominates the world collapsed and instead, monopole system established and thus, depending on the development of communication and transportation technologies of capitalism, economic, political and cultural dimensions of the relations are changed and intensified among the societies. This period has led to the differentiation in the ways of perceiving the world and in the lifestyles of the societies. In this context, time-space perceptions of societies and the processes of meaning the world began to develop and differ. Thus, globalization emerged where the contrast between far-near is removed and dimension of cross-border interaction developed and the nation states which are important actors of the past periods left their power to local cities and regions. As it can be seen from this, the past time has been subject to a social transformation.

Therefore, the concept of globalization has been formed where the contrast between far-near is removed and dimension of cross-border interaction developed. Definition of the concept of globalization in its simplest form is; convergence of countries and people by ignoring the distance between the distant and nearby places and having economic and social interaction with each other.

An important element in the definition of globalization is; decisions taken at the local level and adopted policies has the power to pass other nations and influence them. Especially when the last three decades considered; the mankind history felt the power of globalization and it will continue to be felt more effective in the coming years due to the circumstances of the current period.

Within this rapid change and development process; supranational organizations that are competitive in global market conditions have taken their place in the process as global actors with their areas of activity they are dominant, organizational structures, understanding of management, forms of competition and capital structures they have.

F. Kıvılcım (✉)
Beykoz University, Istanbul, Turkey

© Springer International Publishing AG, part of Springer Nature 2018
H. Dincer et al. (eds.), *Strategic Design and Innovative Thinking in Business Operations*, Contributions to Management Science,
https://doi.org/10.1007/978-3-319-77622-4_4

In this study; access to the definition of globalization concept and its evaluation for the last five decades targeted within the framework of approaches to the concept of globalization by emphasizing rapid and radical change.

Field Definition International economic order, Economic integration and globalization, International economics

1 Introduction

There is a change-transformation process in which almost every field can experience the effect which began in the last quarter of the twentieth century and reached to peak in the 1990s. Today's conditions are also shaped as the result of this change-transformation process. The key concept of this change process is globalization. With globalization, the discourse that the world turns into a "global village" often repeated. The borders have removed in this global village; companies, human relationships, living conditions, clothes, foods, ideas began to have no limits. The globalization process, which has gained great momentum; affects life economically, socially, politically and technologically, and reorganize the structure and function of the state and its institutions which are the main actors of international relations.

The mankind studied the development of economic theories and will continue to study. This case began to give fruit in the twentieth century and the economic policies of states have been questioned as a result of economic research. As it is known, Classical Economics Theory which is about economic fluctuations are a temporary phenomenon, the economy will always be self-sustaining in full employment, and therefore based on the assumption that the state should not intervene in the economy was insufficient to explain the crisis of 1929. Keynesian influence of thought began to be dominant from the 1930s. In fact, while Keynes Revolution continued to dominate from the mid-1950s until the 1970s, it was also subjected to reinterpretations of Neoclassical Economics and turned into Neoclassical Synthesis. In this case, it can be thought that many of the suggested economic theories aimed at regulating the current economic situation. But this evolved into the globalization.

The main purpose of this study is to evaluate the globalization process conceptually within the scope of historical development and actors of the process, and verify whether there is a single definition of globalization within the framework of approaches to the process.

This study is composed of three parts including the introduction. The first part of the study tries to define the globalization process and give a place to the historical development of the process, and the actors. The second part of the study discusses the approaches to the globalization process and it is aimed to define the globalization process within the framework of these approaches. The existing approaches discussed within the study with the following order: Excessive Globalization

Approach, Moderate Globalization Supporters (Transformists) and Globalization Resisters (Traditionalist Approach). The element that can be expressed in the simplest terms about the purpose of the study and the second part of the globalization process is; there is no single definition of the current concept, it is a multidimensional concept and its influence is broad.

In summary; this study tries to state that the definition of the concept, historical development, actors and basic approaches reviewed in the last part are evaluated in three parts within the framework of a general overview of the concept of globalization. Within these evaluations, it was emphasized that it is not possible to make a single definition of the concept of globalization and the concept has a different meaning and importance for everyone.

2 Defining the Globalization. . .

2.1 Definition of Globalization

Despite it is a new word, its richness in literature and interest of the academic circles, it is not possible to have a sole definition of "globalization" which is describing an old process (Ellwood 2002) and the key term that refers to the explanation of the world's period of change. Also, it can be observed that there is a quite controversial situation about the definition (Aydemir and Kaya 2007). Mostly, differences in political and social opinions, interests of those who study globalization and often considering some dimensions of globalization in efforts to define globalization with the ignorance of some dimensions are the main reasons of this controversial situation but in addition to these, globalization has been perceived by a different point of view in developed countries than the developing countries (Aslan 2005). It is also a fact that, globalization is a dynamic process which makes it difficult to define it. This means, the fact that globalization is an ongoing process that did not end and up-to-date, leads to the continual emergence of new definitions of globalization and continue the debated over the definition. One of the reasons why globalization is still a controversial concept is that, the absence of a consensus among researchers about which social processes constitute the essence. Besides, by stating that concrete facts of globalization are a hidden concept, it is emphasized that especially the negative aspects of globalization are invisible (Timur 2004).

Different or opposite views on the definitions making it almost impossible to create a single definition that everyone will agree on globalization. Differences in the definition of globalization which are quite complicated and a multidimensional and dynamic process are in the focus of the globalization research of today (David Held 2008). According to Zengingönül, the common feature of the definition of globalization is the fact that it is not possible to agree on a common definition (Zengingönül 2004). A definition will be attempted in this study by considering the common concepts used in the context of globalization. Although it is not easy to give a clear definition of globalization, it can be explained as increased communication and interaction between society and states living in different parts of the world and become interdependent in the process of national economies becoming involved in world markets and cross-border economic integration as a result of increased mobility in goods, services, and capital.

The concept of globalization was first used in a paper on the distribution and use of resources in the world written by the British economist W. Foster in 1833, and then it took place in The Economist magazine later on April 4, 1959. The fact that globalization becomes effective today is based on the study of Garett Hardin wrote in 1968 about the share and use of resources (Karabıçak 2002). According to Joseph Stiglitz, globalization is the integration period of countries and world societies. The obstacles in front of goods, capital, services, and information will be lifted along with globalization, however, new actors are also included in the international arena apart from the existing institutions (Giddens 2000).

The globalization is seen as an economic concept by many researchers. For example, globalization; is defined as the integration of the world economies with trade, financial flows, technology change by knowledge and mobility of the workforce (Aktan and Şen 1999). Another definition that sees globalization as an economic basis is as follows: "In today's world, an integration process began with the increasing interdependence in intercontinental interaction and economic relations and this tendency are called 'globalization'" (Aslan 2005). The common point of those who define globalization as an economic basis is, "the integration of world economies into one another and economic life is defined in a structure where common and non-state actors are included in almost world-wide." However, it makes it difficult to understand globalization only on an economic basis. Because it is seen that social, cultural and political aspects of this process are also important and globalization is not just an economic process. For example, Anthony Giddens stated that no any conversation can be expressed fully without mentioning globalization (Giddens 2000). Therefore, the concept of globalization with economic, political and cultural structures which is multidimensional and whose domain is very broad is now a trend term (Thompson 2007).

Each period is defined with the dominant thought of that time. The current period is represented with "globalization". Globalization is a very controversial concept that refers a world with standardized, different and subjectified values, thoughts and knowledge (Ekşi 2004). Globalization can affect the concept of security with different dimensions. Today, globalization process has begun to build a structure that narrows the domain of the nation-state. New non-national actors emerging in this process also disturbs the notion of the sovereignty of the nation-state. Chomsky's the transnational state institutions refers to other great masters such as the typical state power; emphasizing criticisms of the globalization process namely, financial and other services, the emergence of transnational corporations in the fields of manufacturing, media, and communication, the internal work serves the institutions of superior power, which is totalitarian, totally irresponsible (Chomsky et al. 2000).

Although no definitive and structural reconciliation can be reached on the concept of globalization, it is a process that primarily explains the transformations that have taken place in recent years in the world. Innovations that can be counted as a revolution in communication technologies are the only element that fosters globalization. Because, if it were not for the convenience provided by technology, we were not able to talk about a global economic or social world today. Thanks to technological innovations (many innovations related to internet, Telecom and similar IT sector) distances are not an obstacle anymore.

"Globalization is defined as the political, economic and social phenomenon of the new millennium, and it affects all countries as an inevitable phenomenon. As much as those who adopt the trend of globalization, there are also those who oppose to this tendency" (Aktaş 2004). Pros and cons on the effect of globalization on the transformation of the world system still exist for both sides of the political or ideological views. Some common values spread worldwide by crossing local and national boundaries in economic, political, social and cultural fields with globalization. The economic system adopted both in developed and developing countries in the economic field and the applied economic policies are increasingly getting similar. With the collapse of real socialism, the liberal economic order in the world, i.e., free market economy is increasingly being global and the limitation of the state are gaining importance (Aktaş 2004).

As can be seen from the above evaluations, the concept of globalization is the most controversial issue in recent years. The real reason of this can be explained as the effect of the global system can be seen almost every field. Of course, giving place to discussions and solutions about globalization will exceed the limitations of this debate. However, there are two separate views on globalization. Mentioning these interpretations on globalization is a lack of subject when assessed within the context of globalization. Interpretations on globalization are divided into two, the first one is the globalization is beneficial for the society and it is a view that treats globalization as highly positive as this process has developed naturally. Another existing view of globalization is; it is the negative approach that predicts that globalization is not generally equally beneficial to everyone.

According to this approach; globalization is not a naturally developing process. It is a conscious and fictional process aimed at making the rich richer. Habermas supports the negative direction of globalization as follows (Habermas 2002):

> The consequences of a policy that seeks to abolish the social state and persistently high unemployment to compete internationally can be seen in OECD countries. In this context, the resources of solidarity of the society are dissolved. These developments bring a new lower class to the scene. From this extraordinary situation, sociologists refer those who are disconnected from other parts of the society as marginal groups. Those who belong to low classes are the impoverished groups, left to themselves when they cannot change their social institutions with their own efforts. As a result, it is not possible to avoid three outcomes in the long run. The lower class will create social tensions. These tensions will lead to self-destructive and irrational riots and can only be controlled by repressive methods. In this case, the construction of prisons and the organization of internal security, in general, will become a growth industry. In addition, social pollution and physical poverty will not be classified as regionally. Unfortunately, ghettos will be in the infrastructure within the city, and even reach to regions and embed it into the cells of the whole community.

As a result, although some of the positive results compared to some of the negative results of globalization, it can be seen that it will continue to influence world order with all its dimensions.

2.2 Historical Development of Globalization

With significant developments in the navigation field, the West began to explore beyond the seas after 1490. According to Oran, the reason for this was the desire of the Absolute Monarchy to seize precious metals and merchandise in overseas countries which began to be adopted in Western Europe. This was also accepted as the beginning of Mercantilist policy which reached its peak between sixteenth and eighteenth centuries (Oran 2001). As a result of these discoveries, Noam Chomsky also considers that invading America by as foreign culture was due to this and it was the beginning of the globalization. According to some, this process leads to widespread colonialism which was accompanied by Westerners' discovering of Cape of Good Hope and leading to the emergence of capitalism with capital accumulation and industrialization which continued until today's globalization (Atasoy 2005).

As a result of this first Western expansion that was the result of navigation developments, the economic system of Western Europe has been determined as an economic system based on colony economies. Classical colonial economy structure, where the raw materials and intermediate materials obtained from these colonies are converted into finished goods and sold again to neighboring countries, adopted during this period. This process was a period where intensive labor and capital flow realized and this, the foundation of world economic integration began (Oran 2001).

In this period, which began with the discovery of America by Columbus in 1492–1800, recorded as the power that the leading countries have (human, horsepower, steam power) (Yılmaz 2007). In short, the first wave of globalization, which the World Bank pointed out that it took place between 1870 and 1914, is the result of my extensive accumulation. This accumulation mainly lead to navigation advancements, development of the railway, cheaper telecommunication such as the invention of the telegraph and the telephone and emergence of new markets such as Canada, Argentina, Australia, New Zealand, Russia, and China and ultimately leading to the rapid development and expansion of the world economy. The largest share was in England and France in these developments and expansion of foreign trade. Some researchers relate the increase in economic relations between countries to capitalism which the first globalization took place between 1870 and 1914. According to this, "capitalism" that is the basis of the economic system of the West which began and continued to develop between 1870 and 1914, has become an important tool in the realization of globalization (Aktan and Şen 1999). As a result, basic dynamics of globalization was "change" and "spread" and the reason was the economy. As a result of developments in navigation in the first globalization, the telegraph's invention and advancements on the railway has provided an opportunity for West for the spread of political, military and commercial influence in overseas countries (Oran 2001). Moreover, the intensification of competition in international trade in this new period leads to specialization in production. According to Yılmaz; the technological field has reached advanced levels of development, connections that connect nations and societies increased. Just like similar to the collapse of the traditional society and form the modern industrial society, new technological developments collapsed industrial society and form a new postmodern society and lead to the second way of the globalization (Yılmaz 2007).

The second globalization coincides with the second spread of the West after 1870. According to Oran, these spreading opportunities are tremendous technological possibilities created by the industrial revolution which had created a great disproportion between the West and other parts of the world. In other words, there is industrial revolution behind this expansion (Oran 2001). This globalization will affect the social life quite positively (Atasoy 2005). While providing steam machines, sea and rail transportation prevalence at first and then distance problems were lifted in communication, telegraph, telephone, PC, satellite, optical cables and maritime transportation (Yılmaz 2007).

In fact, the second globalization "was an answer to new and specific economic and financial repression coming from within Europe". "At the end of the nineteenth century, capitalism has faced the necessity of restructuring. The second spread ensures this and has allowed the system to reproduce itself. Therefore, a new game was given to this concept which was known as "colonialism" in that time; Imperialism." As a result, the second Western expansion, Imperialism settled strongly in these overseas territories, and according to Oran, in contrast to the first globalization, it has infused its own infrastructure in a very radical way (Oran 2001).

Between 1914 and 1945 was the time globalization, i.e., the Second Globalization was in the period of stagnation. The outbreak of World War I in 1914, the beginning of the Great Depression in 1929 and then the beginning of World War II has slowed down the globalization process very much (Aktan and Şen 1999). In other words, wars and the resulting crises prevented globalization from continuing and different periods of globalization emerged.

After two great wars and depressions, the Second Globalization continued from where it left off after 1945. The next period is also seen as the revitalization of the capitalist economy by many researchers. However, the effect of the problems causing the stagnation is negative. After World War II, Europe has lost great power and has been economically destroyed. Aslan summarizes the process of re-emerging globalization after World War II as follows: "While Europe's production capacity is being destroyed during World War II, US began to their re-liberalization trends again as being the dominant economic and social power of the world. Thus, the effort to develop international cooperation has intensified and in this context, efforts have been made to establish international organizations to orient the world economy. As known, decisions are taken on the establishment of IMF and International Bank for Reconstruction and Development (IBRD) at the 1944 Bretton Woods Conference and decreasing the regulations preventing international trade" (Aslan 2005).

When we check the period after World War II, it can be seen that many countries subjected their international capital circulation to solid supervision and the idea of the IMF and the World Bank designed to provide opportunities for international trade and investments in an environment where private capital circulation is limited, restrictions on capital circulation were lifted over time and international capital movements have also accelerated during the time of Reagan and M. Thatcher in the early 1980s, and the financial markets have started to become truly global especially at the beginning of the 1990s with the collapse of the Soviets. Indeed the importance of international institutions such as IMF, the World Bank, the GATT and the Organization for Economic Cooperation and Development (OECD) are great in the acceleration of the globalization process. Such international organizations which almost all of them were established in the second half of the 1940s created under US patronage and a new wave of globalization emerged in the 1950s and 1960s with the contribution of these institutions. "A turning point for the second globalization took place in the 1970s: fixed exchange rate system abandoned with the collapse of the Bretton Woods System in August 1971 and the developed countries, especially USA, Germany, England and Japan, abolished restrictions on capital movements in succession. The abolition of restrictions on capital movements in these countries has gained an extraordinary momentum with financial globalization" (Aktan and Şen 1999).

The third globalization is the product of globalization accumulations and forms the dynamics of the later periods. Globalization is not a single process, however a series of processes that occur at the same time and at various levels, irregularly and in various dimensions. In other words, globalization is a structure that contains distinctions between historical processes but blends the accumulation of each other. In this sense, the third globalization has the distinctions of some differences, as much as the continuation, follower, and conclusion of the first and second globalizations. It is the period of the third globalization in terms of the history of globalization since 1980. The third globalization is a complex, multi-dimensional period quite different from the others. Fast-growing technologies affect a wide range of technologies, from human life to environment.

The post-1980 globalization was basically the stage of the following developments and became evident: "The activities of companies concentrated in the industrial field are the fast market changes, dizzying developments in product and manufacturing technology and the high competition. After 1990, this process was summarized with the economic and political collapse of the former Eastern Bloc countries. These countries, which are dominated by the planned economy, have started to approach the Western countries economically and politically in time" (Aktan and Şen 1999). Most researchers claim that the rising wave of globalization, especially after the 1990s, is based on the environment that arises from the fact that the bipolar military equilibrium in the world has been lifted.

The tool of the third globalization is the advancements in science and technology where researchers could reach common ground. For this reason, the third period of globalization is also called Information Age. Oran explains the following three

Table 1 Globalization stages

	First globalization	Second globalization	Third globalization
Driving force	Navigation developments, Mercantilism	Industrialization and requirements	1. Multinational Companies in the 1970s 2. Communication Revolution in the 1980s 3. The collapse of the USSR and the rival left for West
Method	First explorations, then military occupation	First missionaries, then discoveries, then the trading companies, then occupy	Cultural-ideological influence
Right opinion	Bringing the religion of God to Pagans	"Civilization task", racist theories	The highest level of civilization The will of the international community The secret hand of the market Globalization is beneficial to all
Consequence	Colonialism	Imperialism	Globalization

Source: Oran (2001)

events that took place in succession for decades to come to the Third Globalization (Oran 2001):

- Multinational corporations dominate the world economy starting from the 1970s;
- The Communication Revolution that the West created in the 1980s by introducing technological inventions such as optical cables, communication satellites, computers, and the internet;
- The disintegration of the USSR in the 1990s has left the power balance unchanged, and the West has become the only power again.

One of the basic dynamics of the third globalization is communication and one of the basic symbols is the internet. The Internet, a revolution in the field of communication, is now widely and cheaply used all over the world. The Internet plays a crucial role in the realization of globalization by creating the World Wide Web (www), which connects billions of people, private organizations and governments (Aktan and Şen 1999).

To summarize the historical development of globalization, the development of this process generally takes place in three stages. The first stage is the period from 1490 to 1914, the second is the period from 1914 to 1950 and the third is the period from 1950 to 1950 and the period until the end of the 1980s. The stages in which globalization has taken place are expressed in table form (Table 1).

When evaluations on the relevant table are carried out, it can be seen that the first globalization phase differs from the others and the second and third globalization phases are spreading within the economic, political and socio-cultural development processes of the West. The main reason why the first globalization phase differs from the second and third stages is that the West has not yet matured in this period due to economic, political and socio-cultural developments.

2.3   Globalization Process Actors

In the global economy, the internationalization of production (i.e., the completion of a product's production stages in different countries), the intertwining of financial markets and national economies, and the development of communication and transport possibilities through technological innovations come to mind.

Besides this, while the concept of international economy has been used in the past (Seyidoğlu 2003), the global economy concept has taken its place today. This is due to the size of the surplus and relations of actors and activities in the globalization process.

For instance, while inter-state economic relations in the past have been explained by concepts such as foreign trade and are considered as a transnational economy, actors such as multinational corporations, international organizations, International NGOs takes place in these economic relations. As the international economy evokes inter-state relations and borders, it describes a process in which the effects of global economic borders are diminishing and even inter-individual relations are intense. For this reason, almost every segment of the global economy, today, countries, businesses, and individuals, is concerned and influenced.

Here, within the global system of economic, political, cultural and technological dimensions, enterprises try to adapt themselves to the rules of this game. Almost every field is affected by the global economy from investments to production relations, marketing activities to public relations efforts of the companies.

2.3.1   Multinational Companies

The International business administration is all kinds of business activities organized by businesses and carried out outside the national borders. Even on an increasingly shrinking scale, some international business activities are still being carried out by the states for political and strategic purposes. In addition to this, International business activities are mainly undertaken by private enterprises (Özalp 2004).

It can be said that the most important reason for this is private companies can take action more quickly than state institutions and can be adapt to changes in global markets and technological changes more quickly. In addition, private companies, have started to operate in different countries much more rapidly since they have a more flexible structure due to the absence of bureaucracy and partnership structures are shaped in different ways according to the nature of the work done.

It is any kind of business activity within or between two or more independent countries.

In other words, international business administration is defined as the intervention of the sectoral enterprises covering the resources, goods, services and similar movements between the borders of various countries by private or public sector initiatives (Mutlu 1999).

International Management is named as the process of reaching global goals by providing the protection of the dynamic equilibrium state in the global environment by effectively coordinating the supply, distribution and use of material and human resources (Mutlu 1999). International Company is the company that tries to enter and settle in other countries by taking advantage of a centralized management after a strong settlement in the country (Taşlıca 1999).

These companies (enterprises) usually come from developed countries and expand towards a market of some similar countries through a horizontal transition after entering the market of developing or underdeveloped countries. Or sometimes the opposite is the case, i.e., companies from a developing country are similarly expanding towards a similar market. Finally, the Multinational Company which have emerged as a result of their activities with their partners in foreign countries is one of the most important economic events of our time.

The multinational company is a worldwide enterprise. As a definition of multinational enterprises, they are the partnership that is deployed around the world but is based in a national state in terms of nationality and senior management which divide their partnership resources without regard to national boundaries. Multinational companies are internationally known companies that undertake private investments in accordance with the legislation governing foreign capital in the country in the form of direct investment and show integrity in organizational structure, decision-making and supervisory (Yüksel 1999). For example, companies like Nokia or Coca-Cola are multinational companies. When you look at the turnover of multinational companies, you can see that they have a high income, and sometimes the turnover of multinational companies are greater rate than GNP of the countries.

The activities and event of the Multinational Companies in the world economy are quite high, and when they are evaluated in terms of the effects of the nation-state on the globalization process they threaten the domain of the nation-state thanks to their economic power on the world economy.

Global Company is the business managed by world citizen managers which use advanced technology, carrying out global product, price, etc. policies to continue their activities around the world (Mutlu 1999). In addition to these, there are definitions such as Transnational Corporation and Supranational Corporation in the literature. Transnational Corporation is the company with a multinational character with expert management staff from different countries in senior management with ownership and people who are citizens of different countries are partners in property (Taşlıca 1999).

Since old times, international works were full of wars, political conflicts, piracy, economic changes and cultural quotas. On the contrary, without a doubt, human desire and the desire to earn money supported the development of internationalization by going beyond the limits of international trade (Taggart and McDermott 1993).

Although today, international business administration activities have been reached to a large volume, its foundations date back thousands of years. Commercial relationships among societies have a history of 4000 years. There were trade relations between Mesopotamia, Asia and North Africa and Mediterranean was the trade center. During this period, clothes, spices, and olive oil were products subject to commercialization. Later trade developed under the control of the Roman Empire. The return of this period was securing commercial activities with the regulation of trade routes, the advanced legal system, and strong authority. China has begun exporting silk to India and Europe and important trade routes were established during this period (Yüksel 1999).

When the international trade considered, it was under the authority of the states until the industrial revolution. It allowed the companies to enter into the far markets during the Global Expansion years and the problem of communication has been removed to a great extent. US businesses, which are relatively passive compared to European businesses until this period in the field of international business, began to operate in other countries especially in the 1950s and 1960s and internationalization have become a US phenomenon in almost the world. US businesses, which have gone through technological progress in Europe over these years and are the most technology-transferring countries in the world, tried to merge their marketing, management and financial superiority in their overseas workforce with lower wages and they have achieved great successes and profits (Özalp 2004).

This phenomenon is still present in the form of producing some products in the lowest cost countries in the name of alternative cost and then merging them. For example, although Nokia is a Finnish company, they produce some of the parts in China or similar low-cost countries and present them to the final customer after they merge these parts. In fact, this type of production is also called global production.

2.3.2 International Organizations

Integration has been important for those interested in international politics in two respects. First, there are a lot of international and supranational organizations in today's system, and new ones are added to them day by day. Secondly, the fact that national governments are now insufficient to fulfill most of their basic responsibilities, particularly peace and security, to their own people, has increased the importance of such global structures and higher institutionalization in achieving these goals.

Integration is a concept of change and it is used to refer a "political community" or an "integrated society". Integrations are the elements in which the elements of violence diminish among them, and the concepts of interdependence, mutual benefit, and cooperation take place (Arı 2002).

Integration concept constitutes one of the important issues of international relations with the definition and attributed features. In this context, the diversity in the content and number of international relations issues have also affected the theories of EU integration. Different approaches such as functionalism, neo-functionalism, doctrinairism, which is an extension connected with the discussion of idealism-realism in international relations were dominant in theoretical work in the first 20 years of EU integration. Especially, current discussions up to the year 1990, qualifications of the relationship between the member countries and implemented policies (Arı 2002).

By its simplest definition, the European Union is a regional integration project with economic and political objectives. It is possible to classify the economic integration forms under the five headings as Free Trade Area, Customs Union, Common Market, Monetary Union and the Economic Union in general. The customs barriers in the area of free trade and the circulation of goods and services between member countries have been abolished.

Along with the disadvantages of globalization, the emergence of the failure of traditional downward development policies led to the questioning of ongoing development approaches. As a result, a series of policies and strategies have begun to be produced within the framework of the local economic development approach. In this context, international organizations such as the European Union (EU), the International Labor Organization (ILO), the Organization for Economic Cooperation and Development (OECD), the United Nations Development Program (UNDP) and the United Nations Project Services Office (UNOPS) support local development practices in many developed and developing countries.

2.3.3 International Non-governmental Organizations

In the modern sense, civil society is a term that expresses the society that is apart from the state domain, i.e., political domain (Erözden 2001). In a broader sense, it is possible to define it as a network of social relations that cannot be subjected to central control and hierarchy (Doğan 2002). The concept of civil society is so flexible that, there is no definition that everyone agrees on. However, there are common expressions used in definitions. The concept of civil society has reached today's modern meaning through many transformations in the history of social thought. Therefore it is required to examine the different meanings and contents of the term in social thought history in order to better understand the concept. Non-Governmental Organizations are the organizations which engaged in activities aimed at the goals of their members or entirely for the interests of its members. These organizations, operating in the economic, political, cultural and social fields of social life have very different goals. The activities and events of mentioned organizations targeted education, culture, arts, religion, social work, economic and professional solidarity, social solidarity (philanthropy), mental solidarity, city club, health, sports, hobby (Tosun 2001b).

According to Savran, Ferguson, one of the most important representatives of Scottish enlightenment provides the first signs of the civil society and state identity separation. Savran describes human history as an evolution that advances from primitive to civil on An Essay on the History of Civil Society 1767. After Ferguson, the first thinker to make the state meaningful in an instrumental sense is Locke.

Locke foresees a political structure that protects his own property (life, freedom, and property), not a political authority in which they will disappear (Savran 1987).

According to Savran, Hegel defines the civil society as the protection of income, personal happiness and person's status that represent the non-state institutions and life processes as opposed to political society while she defines the civil society as the area beyond the political community. Civil society is a mosaic composed of private persons, classes, groups and institutions organized by civilized law and whose qualities are not directly related to the political state itself (Savran 1987). According to Cevizci, the element that determines Marx's relationship in civil society is the property relations. For instance, when talking about freedoms, property freedoms are understood. A Civil society which has a broader meaning also includes the bourgeois society. Detailed discussions on civil society in the Marxist literature have been put forward by the Italian thinker Antonio Gramsci and today the positive approaches to civil society in the Marxist societies are derived from this thought (Cevizci 1997).

Again, according to Cevizci, Gramsci, who laid out a more detailed framework of civil society understanding locates it between the economic area that comes from the production with the state's mandatory actions and interventions. According to this, civil society is an area of social life that emerges as a private citizen and an individual attestation area (Cevizci 1997). According to Tosun, unlike Marx, Gramsci believes that civil society is forming an upper structural area, not a sub-structural area. In this sense, Gramsci took his notion of civil society not from Marx but from Hegel. While accepting the concept of civil society as the cultural face of the hegemony of a social group on society, he argued that civil society is the whole of special relations (institutions) that ensures the function of so-called hegemony (Tosun 2001a).

The state and civil society need to interact in the process of democratization. It does not mean that the fact that civil society is autonomous from the state does not mean that it is against it. The basic concept referred in civil society debates is the public domain. While the concept of the public area is defined, it is sometimes defined separately from the state, sometimes defined as the realization of activities of civil society, individuals and the state. Also thinking the public area separately from private life is in the capitalist structure that is the result of industrialization. There must be the public area in order to let the non-governmental organizations operate. The public area is understood as the field of activity of civil society (Çaha 2008).

The concept of globalization makes the distances and borders meaningless and make the world a global village, it also leads to the formation of an increasingly homogeneous world society by bringing universal values to almost every corner of the world through the spread communication network (Çaha 2008).

In fact, the globalization is "melting process of various socio-political elements economically and politically in a wider formation". The foundation of the globalization is the acceptance of cultural, religious and language differences mutually. In this sense, the number and success of internationally active NGOs in the globalizing world have reached a level not to be underestimated. Non-governmental organizations working in a very wide variety of areas from prevention conflict processes to the end of existing conflicts and early warning against violence. They try to create a dialogue between conflicting groups, act as direct intermediaries, and are engaged in initiating democratic processes in countries that are subject to violence (Çaha 2008). In the light of all these developments, the activities of NGOs worldwide are increasing rapidly and these organizations feel responsible for the solution of human, social and educational problems. In recent years, thousands of non-governmental organizations operating in many countries of the world have been established.

In summary, globalization has strengthened the system of independent states in Europe and in world by contributing to the increase of the diversity among institutions. But each of these organizations has served as a cradle for new autonomy and diversity. However, the fact is, this process significantly affected the strength of the nations and thus, affected the political development and its future (David Held 2008).

3   Basic Approaches to the Concept of Globalization

In its broadest sense, globalization can be referred as the tendency of the domain of influence of production relations to expand by internal and external processes in the economy. From an economic point of view, globalization can be defined as "the spreading of the influence of capital and commodity movements to the world level in increasing intensity" (Kara 2004). With the positive and negative consequences, it has created on the country's economies globalization became one of the most discussed concepts in the field of business and economics. This concept, which expresses free circulation of goods, services, capital, information, and technology, is a way of applying neo-liberal economics in the world. In the 1980s and 1990s, the international economic integration accelerated and more efficient production, investment, trade value adapted by removing the country borders. Globalization is not only a system based on profitable market economics but also a major change project including political and socio-cultural fields (Ayşe Çelikel Danışoğlu 2004).

According to Bauman, globalization has its own unique nature, especially in the cultural sense. There is no dominant control mechanism controlled from a specific center. Globalization is the "new world irregularity" (Bauman 1999). The hope of establishing the order of the basic concepts such as development, civilization, universalization in modern thought and unlike the intention of the concept of globalization uncertainty and the unplanned emphasis is said to stand out.

According to this opinion, globalization can be regarded as a fact that weakens the social nature of the state, reviews the social consensus as a process predicting the withdrawal of the state from economic life with international capital and multinational companies (Bulut 2003).

Approaches related to globalization are separated into three. One of these approaches is anti-globalization approach that globalization advocating that nation is under the sovereignty of international capital and it weakened and destroyed nation-state and nationality. The second approach is the approach in which globalization is an inevitable outcome for the world's future and that there are extreme globalizations that support the necessity of global new world order. The third and last approach to globalization is based on the position of the nation-state in the face of globalization, which follows a cautious approach towards neither acceptance nor objection to globalization, is the approach of moderate globalization supporters that rejects the theses of the other two approaches (Bozkurt 2006).

3.1 Excessive Globalization Approach

Other names of extreme globalizers are radicals and according to their belief, the nation-state has now lost its significance together with the globalization process. According to extreme globalization/radicals, nation states have begun to struggle to control their national borders. In this context, while global and regional governments are demanding a greater role the autonomy and sovereignty of states are also eroded. In addition, extreme globalization claims that the international cooperation is easier and that the people of different countries are more aware of the common interests of the people of different countries thanks to the increasing telecommunication infra-structure, and as a result, there is a common ground for the birth of a global civilization. According to extreme globalization supporters, nation-states weakened and markets have become more powerful (Kazgan 2009).

According to the opinions of the radicals, they emphasize that international markets are working more rationally than national governments and politicians have begun to lose their importance and place today. In summary, extreme globalizers think that national policies remain effective only at the local and national scale and that they are powerless to influence the movements of the global economy (Esgin 2001).

Radicals (extreme globalizers), i.e., those who claim that globalization is a positive process usually on the right-wing. Like researchers determined, these are liberals.

According to the globalization supporters, the market mechanism is taking place of politics since it works more rationally than the governments. Politics do not have the power to influence the movements of the global economy, even if they are still effective at the local or national scale. As a result of this, nation-state, a product of industrial societies has lost its importance in relation to the globalization process. Thus, markets have become more powerful than state mechanisms and processes. The country also states that radical globalizers claim that globalization leads to the national economies' departure from nationality through the establishment of inter-national networks of production, trade, and finance (Kır 2002).

The alternative that emerges with the loss of the importance of the nation-state is the tendency towards the understanding of world society. Here, the notion of citizenship is now transcending nationality and world citizenship is emerging. World society understanding takes the place of traditional state understanding and thus, new forms of social organization are beginning to emerge (Timur 2004).

Indeed, globalization for many neo-liberal is regarded as the first true herald of the global civilization. "From an over-globalist point of view, the rise of the global economy is interpreted as a manifestation of radical new-world order, a cultural mix at the global level, the emergence of institutions of global expansion and global governance, deeply rooted evidence of new world order, and the death of the nation-state. Besides this, international cooperation among countries has become easier; with the increasing global communication infrastructure, the peoples of different countries are more conscious of their common interests and as a result of this, they claim that there is a common ground for the birth of a global civilization" (Kır 2002).

As a result, general theses of those who support globalization reflect the traces of an ideological view based on the understanding that globalization is a natural and inevitable process and with little to no opposition to globalization in addition to the creation of a world-wide union.

According to the neo-liberal approach, the nation-state, which is a product of industrial civilization, lost its importance parallel to the globalization process. Now the global market is taking the place of politics; because the market mechanism is more rational than the governments.

Although the policies are still effective at the local or national level they do not have the power to influence the movements of the global economy. In this sense, in the majority of the world's countries, the citizens are less interested in politics, or the politicians are more disappointed with the citizens (Lipson 2003).

Positive discourse on globalization developed by neo-liberalism (Sarıbay and Keyman 2000):

A. Emphasizes the source of inequalities in society is not individual but structural as far as individual/group achievements. Thus, for example, unemployment is not seen as a structural consequence of economic processes, but as a problem faced by individuals who cannot adapt to change.
B. Therefore, it is emphasized that the distribution of justice for individuals who cannot adapt to the globalizing world is obstructing economic entrepreneurship and founded on a problematic concept of justice to the extent that it defends "welfare rights" which the citizens do not deserve.
C. Ultimately it is suggested that it may be democratic when the nation isolates itself from state's social and economic life and as long as it minimizes its movement area in an individual morality structure based on equal opportunity.

Essentially the thing recommended in these three articles is to abolish the welfare state with the globalization = free market equation, to develop a new "individualism/ freedom understanding" by taking basic criteria of individual morality and to identify democratization with a minimal state.

"The main proposal of neoliberalism on the concept of globalization usually due to an ending and a preliminary recognition of a new beginning. Liberalism is presented as the bearer of the "new" beginning while the subject of the end is Marxism. In fact, it can be stated as the final declaration that it is no longer unrivaled for the prosperity of the world idealized with the face of liberalism (liberal ideology) already available following the World War II. Because it is based on the acceptance of an absolute truth in an open or closed form: 'the end of history'" (Coşar 2000).

In other words, according to the supporters of globalization, markets are now stronger than states. This decline in state authority can be seen as an extension of associations with other institutions and local/regional authorities. The globalization supporters believe that world society is taking the place of (or will take) traditional nation-states and new forms of social organization have begun to take shape. However, those in this group do not have a homogeneous presence.

For example, while neo-liberals, welcoming the success of the market and individual autonomy over the state power, neomarkists who are in the same group with them consider the contemporary globalization as repressive representatives of global capitalism. However, despite the differences in these ideological approaches, they share the view that there is an increasingly integrated global economy today (Vegin 2003; Sandıklı 2006).

Those who think positively about the globalization process believe that the economy creates winners as well as losers ones. A "new global division of labor" takes the place of the traditional center-periphery structure; and on the other hand, there is an "increasing anachronism" between the South and the North. Despite this background, the states have to "manage" the social consequences of globalization. Globalization is able to link the polarization between winner and loser in the global economic order. At least according to the neoliberal movement, it is not possible to find global economic competitiveness in "zero-sum" production. Almost all countries have a comparative advantage in the production of certain goods, even if the status of certain groups in the economy deteriorates in the face of global competition.

There is no such "optimistic approach" for Neo-Marxists. According to them, global capitalism creates inequality for both between the nations and in the nations.

However, they agree with neo-liberals in terms of it makes it difficult to maintain the traditional welfare state path in social protection and it getting increasingly old.

For many neo-liberals, globalization is considered as the first true herald of the global civilization. According to this point of view, the rise of the global economy can be interpreted as a proof of radical new world order, the birth of cultural mixture at the global level (hypredization), global governance institutions and global governance institutions can be interpreted as the evidence of a new world order in a deeply rooted way and the death of the nation-state. They are now beginning to struggle to control the borders of the national government. While global and regional governments demand greater roles, autonomy and sovereignty of states are also more abused. Besides this, international cooperation among countries has become easier; the peoples of different countries are more aware of their common interests thanks to the increasing global communication infrastructure and thus, they claim to have a common ground for the birth of a global civilization (Sim 2006; Bilgiç and Göksu 2004).

3.2 Moderate Globalization Supporters (Transformists)

According to the moderate globalization supporters, the globalization is the basic power behind the social, political and economic change and development which is restructuring modern societies and world order. Moderate globalization supporters; accept that the globalization process and the nation-state are restructuring, they reject both the claims of extreme globalization by "the end of the sovereign nation-state" and the "anti-globalization" skeptics saying "nothing has changed". Moderate globalization supporters are following a view that is close to extreme globalization supporters more than the opposers of globalization about the globalization. According to Bozkurt, who supports the moderate globalization; Giddens emphasizes the following view of the new role of nation-states (Bozkurt 2006).

> Do nation states and, political leaders are still strong managers or they cannot make anything against the forces shaping the world? Nation states are in fact still strong, and political leaders have a major role to play in the world. At the same time, no one can deny the process of reforming the nation-state in front of our eyes. National economic policy can no longer be as effective as its predecessor. More importantly, they have to rethink their national identities according to the old forms of geopolitics.

3.3 Globalization Resisters (Traditionalist Approach)

Globalization resisters place themselves in opposition of globalization supporters and they are called as skeptics since they are skeptical about every aspect of globalization. Globalization is only an ideological discourse, according to the suspicions of those who emphasize the negative aspects of globalization. The skeptics claim that the ideological discourse called globalization strengthen the dominance of international capital and free market over the world and therefore, it is needed to be opposed. Also, skeptics criticize globalization for creating a single world dominated by western culture and lifestyle. Another criticism of skeptics towards globalization is that globalization is considered as an irresistible and an inevitable process, thus it leads people to not resist to international capital movements and encourage minimal state understanding (Balay 2004).

Another of the most important arguments that globalization resisters use is that the poor countries are getting poorer, and the wealthy countries are getting richer. Researchers unite on the idea that anti-globalization is right in this thesis, which is also an important topic of the world economic agenda. This is mainly due to inequalities besides the ruthless competitiveness that appears with globalization.

The collapse of the nation-state and international institutions are starting to become stronger than states are the claims of globalization resisters. According to this, one or two global corporations use their economic power to control and utilize the interests of the state machinery that manages millions of people.

Sometimes there are interesting similarities in globalization resisters among the arguments of globalization resisters in developed countries or countries which

Table 2 Three approaches in concept of globalization

	Extreme globalization supporters	Moderate globalization supporters	Globalization resisters
What is new?	A global era	Historically unique global interdependence	Trade blocks
			Weaker joe-governance than the past periods
Major features	Global capitalism	Intensive and deep globalization	The world is less connected than it was in the 1890s
	Global governance		
	Global civil society		
Power of national governments	Being regressed and wear down	Being rebuilt	Getting stronger and multiplies
		Restructured	
Driving force of globalization	Capitalism and technology	The unifying powers of modernity	Nation and markets
Stratification	Wear of old hierarchies	New architecture of world order	Gradually increasing marginalization of the South
Dominant Motif	McDonald's, Madonna, etc.	Transformation of the political community	National interests
Conceptualization of globalization	With the rearrangement of the framework of human-itarian action	By rearranging actions at a certain distance and interregional relations	Internationalization and regionalization
Historical circle	Global civilization	Mutual dependence: global integration and fragmentation	Regional blocks
			Civilization conflict
Summary	End of the nation state	Globalization trans-forms the power of the state and world politics	Internationalization depends on the adop-tion and support of the state

Source: Bozkurt (2006)

cannot benefit from globalization or can benefit from globalization with the less developed countries. For example, some European nationalist parties present an economic nationalism that emphasizes national solidarity in the face of globalization like the East (Vural 2005).

Even sometimes globalization is even seen as a threat. A French Nationalist Party, FN states in their program that globalization leaves the laborers unemployed and on the other hand, the ethnic/cultural harmony of the community is being broke down. They also refer to their opposition to globalization as evaluating the globalization of Anglo-American neoliberalism and its hegemony as a process of dissemination (Vural 2005). It can be seen as an opposite situation at the first glance. Because in less developed countries, skepticism is perceived as the occupation of the West. But once again, it is seen how complex the process of globalization is when it examines the opposition to globalization.

When approaches related to the concept of globalization assessed on the basis, the amount divided as it was summarized in Table 2 and when assessed in the context of the existing questions mentioned in the study, it is expressed as extremism. This is the globalist approach and the sustainable power in the essence; it emphasizes that any power can affect global economic movements and it is now indisputable reality that globalization is inevitable.

4 Conclusion

The definition of the phenomenon of globalization in its simplest form can be stated as the closeness of the country and the people, and the economic and social interaction with each other.

Although globalization process is perceived as a new process, it began with the emergence of the capitalist process and revealed with its scattered logic. Globalization is the most advanced stage we have reached today in capitalism. Therefore, the subject must be reviewed from this point of view while assessing globalization and nation-state relationship. Today, globalization it is not just the flow of goods, information, and people. Globalization is also a dialectical process which is becoming widespread in the world such as poverty, terror, fear, insecurity, inequality, and chaos. An important element in the definition of globalization is the ability of decisions taken at the local level to go beyond the boundaries of the policies pursued and the ability to enter and intervene in other countries.

Especially when you look at the last three decades of the process; the mankind history felt this power of globalization in every dimension and it will continue to be felt more effective due to the conditions of the present age in the coming years. Globalization after 1980 has become the mainstream of the following developments: the activities of the companies concentrated in the industry, rapid changes in the market, dizzying competition in competition for product and production technology, and fierce competition. This process peaked with the economic and political collapse of the former Eastern Bloc countries after 1990. In time, these countries, where the planned economy dominated have begun to get closer the Western countries economically and politically. It is believed that the wave of globalization, especially after 1990 is due to the bipolar military equilibrium in the world removed. Therefore, this period is called Information Age.

Within the framework of a general overview of the concept of globalization; definition of the concept, historical development, actors and the basic approaches to the concept discussed in the last part are evaluated in three parts. The answer to the problem of globalization is multiple within the scope of these evaluations. In essence, globalization (David Held 2008); emphasizes accelerated interconnection, remote action, time and space constraints (such as global warming) and global dependence, the expansion, deepening and accelerating of global interdependence in addition to this concept (Keohane 1990; Giddens 1990; Harvey 1989).

In summary, from this perspective, the social relations and processes that are evaluated in terms of volume, intensity, speed, and effectiveness can be expressed as a process or process that transforms the space organization (David Held 2008).

Intraregional and interregional activities create flows and networks with interaction, and maybe one of the most important features of the concept is, it is not possible to make a single definition of the concept of globalization in the context of speed and uncontrollability; dimensions and concept reached in this framework has a different meaning and importance for everyone.

References

Aktan, C., & Şen, H. (1999). *Globalleşme, Ekonomik Kriz ve Türkiye.* Ankara: TOSYÖV Yayını.
Aktaş, F. K. M. (2004). Küreselleşme ve Küreselleşmenin Türkiye Üzerindeki Etkileri, "2004 Türkiye İktisat Kongresi Tebliğ sunuşları": Küreselleşme ve Türkiyenin Dış Ekonomik İlişkileri. *Paper presented at the Devlet Planlama Teşkilatı,* İzmir.
Arı, T. (2002). *Uluslararası İlişkiler Teorileri.* İstanbul: Alfa Yayınları.
Aslan, N. (2005). Dünya Ekonomisinde Gelişmeler: Küreselleşme. In O. Küçükahmetoğlu, S. Tüylüoğlu, & H. Çestepe (Eds.), *Ekonomik Entegrasyon: Küresel ve Bölgesel Yaklaşım.* Bursa: Ekin Yayinevi.
Atasoy, F. (2005). *Küreselleşme Ve Milliyetçilik.* İstanbul: Ötüken Yayınları.
Aydemir, C., & Kaya, Ö. G. D. M. (2007). Küreselleşme Kavrami Ve Ekonomik Yönü. *Elektronik Sosyal Bilimler Dergisi, 20*(20).
Balay, R. (2004). Küreselleşme, Bilgi Toplumu ve Eğitim. *Ankara Üniversitesi Eğitim Bilimleri Fakültesi Dergisi, 37*(2), 61–82.
Bauman, Z. (1999). *Küreselleşme.* İstanbul: Ayrıntı Yayınları.
Bilgiç, V., & Göksu, T. (2004). *Yeni Gelişmeler Işığında Türkiye'de Kamu Yönetimi ve Yereleşme Eğilimleri.* Paper presented at the Türkiye İktisat Kongresi, İzmir.
Bozkurt, V. (2006). Küreselleşme Kavram, Gelişim Yaklaşımlar. *İşüç Elekronik Dergi, 3*(2).
Bulut, N. (2003). Küreselleşme: Sosyal Devletin Sonu mu? *Ankara Üniversitesi Hukuk Fakültesi Dergisi, 52*(2), 173–197.
Çaha, Ö. (2008). *Sivil Toplum, Aydınlar ve Demokrasi.* İstanbul: Plato Film Yayınları.
Cevizci, A. (1997). *Felsefe Sözlüğü.* Ankara: Ekin Yayınları.
Chomsky, N., Çakıroğlu, A., & Birkan, T. (2000). *Dünya düzeni: eskisi yenisi.* Metis.
Coşar, S. (2000). *Küreselin Neo-Liberal Görüntüleri, Global Yerel Eksende Türkiye.* İstanbul: Alfa Yayınları.
Danışoğlu, A. Ç. (2004). Küreselleşmenin Gelir Eşitsizliği ve Yoksulluk Üzerindeki Etkisi. *İstanbul Ticaret Üniversitesi Dergisi, 3*(5), 215–216.
David Held, A. M. (2008). *Küresel Dönüşümler.* Ankara: Phoenix.
Doğan, İ. (2002). *Sivil Toplum.* İstanbul: Alfa Yayınları.
Ekşi, H. (2004). Kamu Yönetiminde Değişim Dinamikleri ve Değişimin Yönü. *Türkiye İktisat Kongresi Proceedings.*
Ellwood, W. (2002). *Küreselleşmeyi Anlama Kılavuzu (Çev. Betül Dilan Genç).* İstanbul: Metis Yayıncılık.
Erözden, O. (2001). Sivil Toplum Kuruluşları ve Hukuki Çerçevede Yenilik Talepleri Üzerine Notlar. In T. Ulaş (Ed.), *Merhaba Sivil Toplum* (p. 13): Helsinki Yurttaşlar Derneği Yayınları.
Esgin, A. (2001, Aralık). Ulus Devlet ve Küreselleşmeye İlişkin Bazı Yaklaşımlar. *Cumhuriyet Üniversitesi Dergisi, 25*(2), 185–192.
Giddens, A. (1990). *The consequences of modernity.* Cambrigre Polity.
Giddens, A. (2000). *Elimizden Kaçıp Giden Dünya.* İstanbul: Alfa Yayınları.
Habermas, J. (2002). *Öteki Olmak ve Ötekiyle Yaşamak (İ. Aka, Trans. Vol. 2).* İstanbul: Yapı Kredi Yayınları.
Harvey, D. (1989). *The condition of postmodernity.* Oxford: Blackwell.
Kara, U. (2004). *Sosyal Devletin Yükselişi ve Düşüşü.* Ankara: Özgür Üniversite Kitaplığı.

Karabıçak, M. (2002). *Küreselleşme Sürecinde Gelişmekte Olan Ülke Ekonomilerinde Ortaya Çıkan Yönelim ve Tepkiler*. *Süleyman Demirel Üniversitesi İktisadi ve İdari Bilimler Fakültesi Dergisi, 7*(1).

Kazgan, G. (2009). *Küreselleşme ve Yeni Ekonomik Düzen* (Vol. 5). İstanbul: İstanbul Bilgi Üniversitesi.

Keohane, O. (1990). *The borderless world*. London: Collins.

Kır, A. (2002). *Küreselleşme Ulus Devletin Sonu mu?* Ankara: Eylül Yayınları.

Lipson, L. (2003). *Uygarlığın Ahlaki Bunalımları: Manevi Bir Erime mi? Yoksa İlerleme mi?* İstanbul: Türkiye İş Bankası Yayınları.

Mutlu, E. C. (1999). *Uluslararası İşletmecilik*. İstanbul: Beta Yayınları.

Oran, B. (2001). *Küreselleşme ve Azınlıklar*. Ankara: İmaj Yayınları.

Özalp, İ. (2004). *Uluslararası İşletmecilik*. Anadolu Üniversitesi Yayını.

Sandıklı, A. (2006). Uluslararası Politik Ekonomi. *Stratejik Öngörü Dergisi, 9*, 17.

Sarıbay, A. Y., & Keyman, F. K. (2000). *Globalleşme Söylemleri ve Kimlik Talepleri: Türban Sorununu Anlamak Global Yerel Eksende Türkiye*. İstanbul: Alfa Yayınları.

Savran, G. (1987). *Sivil Toplum ve Ötesi*. İstanbul: Alfa Yayınları.

Seyidoğlu, H. (2003). *Uluslararası İkitisat Teori Politika ve Uygulama*. İstanbul: Güzem Can Yayınları.

Sim, S. (2006). *Post Modern Düşüncenin Eleştirel Sözlüğü* (M. E.-A. Utku, Trans.). İstanbul: Babil Yayınları.

Taggart, J. H., & McDermott, M. C. (1993). *The essence of international business*. New York: Prentice Hall.

Taşlıca, A. O. (1999). Uluslararası İşletmecilik (Seçme Yazılar II). In İ. Özalp (Ed.), *Çok Uluslu İşletmeler ve Türkiye* (pp. 123–124, 197). Eskişehir: Anadolu Üniversitesi, İİBF Yayınları.

Thompson, P. H. G. (2007). *Küreselleşme Sorgulanıyor* (Ç. E. v. E. Yücel, Trans.). Ankara: Dost Kitabevi.

Timur, T. (2004). *Türkiye Nasıl Küreselleşti?* Imge Kitabevi.

Tosun, G. E. (2001a). *Demokratikleşme Perspektifinden Devlet-Sivil Toplum İlişkisi*. İstanbul: Alfa Yayınları.

Tosun, G. E. (2001b). *Hak Örgütleri ve Halkla İlişkiler, Medyada Görünür Olmak*. İstanbul: İletişim Yayınları.

Vegin, N. (2003). *Siyasetin Sosyolojisi*. İstanbul: Bağlam Yayınları.

Vural, H. S. (2005). *Avrupa'da Radikal Sağın Yükselişi*. İstanbul: İletişim Yayınları.

Yılmaz, A. (2007). *Romantizmden Gerçeğe Küreselleşme*. Ankara: Minima Yayıncılık.

Yüksel, B. (1999). *Uluslararası İşletme Yönetimi ve Türkiye Uygulamaları*. Gazi Kitapevi.

Zengingönül, O. (2004). *Yoksulluk Gelişmişlik Ve İşgücü Piyasaları Ekseninde Küreselleşme*. Ankara: Adres Yayınları.

Part II
The Effects of Strategic Design
on Business Operations

Strategic Design and High-Growth Firms: A Case from Turkey

Aytug Sozuer and Tuba Bozaykut-Buk

Abstract This chapter focuses on the elements of entrepreneurship and high firm growth phenomenon through a case analysis. The study first defines the fundamental concepts of entrepreneurship and its use as a strategy to yield above average returns in the middle term. Then, the relevance of entrepreneurship for emerging economies as wells as how high growth firms are explained in literature are discussed. Drawing on an actual case in the pasta market, the study analyses the strategy design that works successfully. Based on the effectuation theory, the chapter aims to unfold the entrepreneurial activity and operating mechanisms in a firm, which tripled its sales within 5 years and has become one of the fastest growing firms in Turkey. The inferences of the study would have valuable implications for small and medium-sized enterprises that pursue market expansion in competitive industries.

1 Introduction

As a driver mechanism for innovation, strategic design stands as a critical topic both for high-growth firms and entrepreneurs. The rationale behind the statement is that strategically designed products and services are closer to satisfy customer needs, meet turbulent environmental changes and overcome uncertainties (de Mello Freire 2017; Meroni 2008). Thereby, strategic design is a valuable tool for high-growth firms (HGFs) and entrepreneurs in creating unique firm identity and strategies for competitive advantage (Deserti 2009) and long-term sustainability (de Mello Freire 2017).

A. Sozuer (✉)
University of Yalova, Yalova, Turkey
e-mail: aytug.sozuer@yalova.edu.tr

T. Bozaykut-Buk
Istanbul Medipol University, Istanbul, Turkey
e-mail: tbozaykut@medipol.edu.tr

Meroni (2008, p. 31) describes strategic design as an "activity concerning the product-system; the integrated body of products, services and communication strategies that either an actor or networks of actors (be they companies, institutions or non-profit organizations etc.) conceive and develop so as to obtain a set of specific strategic results". In line with the definition, Meroni (2008) proposes that strategic design process comprises setting new problems to be solved, creating social innovations, developing visionary scenarios, co-designing through collaborative and strategic networking and dialoguing.

From the perspective of strategic design, entrepreneurs can also be called as "designers" as they are the innovative individuals who take risks in exploring new opportunities in markets (Schreyer 2000). Additionally, entrepreneurs' ability to combine production factors differently and design effective institutional and competitive strategies that would energize the markets has been evaluated as critical to economic growth. In this respect, entrepreneurial activities and their value in creating strategic designs can be more valuable and present more opportunities for developing country economies.

In an emerging country context, entrepreneurship is mostly associated with small and medium sized enterprises (SMEs) in Turkey (Karadeniz and Ozdemir 2009). SMEs have a critical role in Turkish economy as they constitute 99.8% of the total Turkish enterprises and 73.5% of total employment in 2014 (TUIK 2016). Based on World Economic Forum classification of economies, Turkey is listed among the efficiency-driven economies with a focus on efficient production processes and increased product quality in the latest Global Entrepreneurship Monitor's report (GEM 2017). The report assumes that there are "connections between entrepreneurial ecosystem and societal values and entrepreneurial potential on the individual level" (p. 21). The report additionally points out a positive perception related with entrepreneurship in Turkish society and indicates that Turkish people see entrepreneurship as a good career choice and an important source for job creation.

Because of its' potential of creating jobs and economic development, HFGs has been the subject of many empirical studies (Brown et al. 2017; Coad et al. 2014a, b). However the studies on the developing countries' HGFs are scarce as most of the empirical research on HGFs is conducted in North America and Europe (Brown et al. 2017). Therefore, it seems that the literature on HGFs is mainly focused on labor market consequences and geographically focused on the developed countries (Aggarwal and Sato 2015).

Although the literature on Turkish entrepreneurship is vast (e.g. Altuntaş and Dömez 2010; Çetinkaya Bozkurt et al. 2012; Gürbüz and Aykol 2009; Karadeniz and Ozdemir 2009; Sönmez and Toksoy 2014; Ocak and Basim 2017), HGFs are rarely studied and there is limited empirical study focusing on the link between strategic design, HGFs and entrepreneurship as far as to the researchers' knowledge.

In line with these given aims, the paper continues with relevant knowledge on HGFs and entrepreneurship. Following literature, a case study of Oba Macaroni is presented and possible implications are discussed.

2 High-Growth Firm: Definitions and Drivers

High-growth firms are critical for nations in terms of economic development (Anokhin et al. 2008; OECD 2006; Wong et al. 2005), labor market (Coad et al. 2014a; Krasniqi and Desai 2016; Schreyer 2000), innovation and knowledge creation (Colombelli et al. 2013; Hölzl 2009; Wong et al. 2005), firm internationalization (Castaño et al. 2016; Keen and Etemad 2012) and industry growth (Bos and Stam 2013; Du and Temouri 2015). Further, the studies of HGFs have significantly contributed to the knowledge of strategic management in explaining the reasons behind firm growth by showing HGFs potential of preserving positive outcomes to stakeholders (Demir et al. 2017).

The literature provides various definitions for HGFs since the debate on the nature and measures of high growth is still unresolved (Brown et al. 2017; Coad et al. 2014a, b; Demir et al. 2017). For instance, Delmar and Davidsson (1998) contribute to the discussion with four measures [the indicator of growth, measurement of growth (relative vs. absolute change), the period studied, the process of growth] and depending on these measures Coad et al. (2014b, p. 95) define HGFs as "firms growing at or above a particular pace, measured either in terms of growth between a start and end year, or as annualized growth over a specific number of years". Another reference for the concept, OECD (2007, p. 61) takes employment and turnover as measures and defines HGFs as "all enterprises with average annualized growth greater than twenty percent per annum, over a 3-year period, and with ten or more employees at the beginning of the observation period". Further to these definitions, many other studies use increase in sales (Chan et al. 2006; Coad et al. 2014a, b; Gundry and Welsch 2001; Nicholls-Nixon 2005; Parker et al. 2010; Siegel et al. 1993) and/or increase in employees (Baum and Bird 2010; Fischer and Reuber 2003; Lee 2014; Littunen and Tohmo 2003; Sims and O'Regan 2006; Stam and Wennberg 2009) as the main criterion for HGF definitions. The increase in productivity is also taken as a measure of high growth during a special time period (Demir et al. 2017; Du and Temouri 2015).

Although HGFs have examples in all sizes in every industry making generalizations difficult for the concept (Brown et al. 2017), the literature still shows evidence that small size and medium sized enterprises are higher in HGF population (Demir et al. 2017; Schreyer 2000). Similarly, HGFs are also identified as being younger than the average (Goedhuys and Sleuwaegen 2010). They also found out to be oriented on research and development activities and are "partly or wholly owned by others" (Schreyer 2000, p. 3). Moreover, HGFs can be classified in terms of their growth processes. Those that grow through entrepreneurial activity by creating new jobs and new methods of doing business are set to have an "organic growth" whereas the growth achieved through acquisitions is classified as "acquired growth" (Davidsson and Henrekson 2002; Delmar et al. 2003; Penrose 1959). This differentiation also has some implications in terms of job creation as the location of the acquired firms can be either in the local home or in another country (Brown et al. 2017).

The previous studies empirically proved that HGFs are exporters and innovators (Coad and Rao 2008; Feeser and Willard 1990; Goedhuys and Sleuwaegen 2010; Hölzl 2009). Moreover, HGFs are found out to be strategically oriented to growth and invest in R&D activities (Barringer et al. 2005; Gundry and Welsch 2001; O'Regan et al. 2006; Stam and Wennberg 2009). Similarly, they have high awareness of the importance of strategic planning, networks and relationships (Demir et al. 2017; Gundry and Welsch 2001; Nicholls-Nixon 2005; Sims and O'Regan 2006; Shuman et al. 1985). Further, HGFs differs in their strategic goal setting plans and they are found out to focus more on a single product rather than product diversification searching for new markets for that specific product (Demir et al. 2017).

In line with the given studies, the practices of human resources management and strategic orientation of the firm are identified as the foremost growth drivers for HGFs (Barringer et al. 2005; Coad et al. 2014b; Demir et al. 2017; Fischer et al. 1997; Fombrun and Wally 1989; Littunen and Tohmo 2003; Lopez-Garcia and Puente 2012; Siegel et al. 1993). Also, having team-based designs and managers with industry experience are among other literary proposed growth determinants of HGFs (Brüderl and Preisendörfer 2000; Gundry and Welsch 2001; Siegel et al. 1993; Stam and Wennberg 2009).

Additionally, the link between entrepreneurship and high growth comes to the fore as another critic topic for HGF studies (Delmar et al. 2003). That's to say, the entrepreneurial activities that succeed in the market can lead to high-growth. Similarly, the importance of the entrepreneurial experience of founders-managers for high growth (Florin et al. 2003; Shuman et al. 1985; Stam and Wennberg 2009) has been discussed by many researchers. To exemplify, Mason and Brown (2013) indicate that policy-makers should be careful in designing entrepreneurial environment and initiatives for high growth. Correspondingly, Schreyer (2000) in his analysis of HGFs in OECD countries comes to the conclusion that HGFs are also successful entrepreneurs in their industry. Based on the given studies, the current study aims to unfold the interaction between entrepreneurship and HGFs through analyzing a Turkish case.

3 The Entrepreneurship and Competitiveness in Emerging Economies

Since Schumpeter (1934), entrepreneurs are described as innovators and as the numbers of innovators increases in a society so does economic growth. Entrepreneurship is not only one of the production factors but also creates economic growth by combining other production factors in unusual ways (Stam et al. 2011). Therefore innovation can't be confined into the boundaries of entrepreneurship, but entrepreneurship is strongly associated with innovation.

Although the link between entrepreneurship and high growth is in need for a bulk of research for developing countries (Naudé 2010), a variety of studies associates entrepreneurship with high growth (Davidsson and Henrekson 2002; Goedhuys and Sleuwaegen 2010). In their literary review, Carree and Thurik (2003) emphasize that entrepreneurship is a trigger for economic growth through innovation, creating change and competition. Similarly, to Stam et al. (2011), entrepreneurs' successful local operations are one of the most critical means for economic growth of low-income countries. Besides economic growth, as Naudé (2009, 2010) points out entrepreneurship has positive outcomes on the structure of the national economy and labor market; and consequently on the life quality in developing countries. From the entrepreneurship perspective, developing countries not only have a high demand for entrepreneurship (Leff 1979; Naudé 2009) but also offer an a more encouraging atmosphere regarding the low costs of economic activities (Naudé 2010).

As the entrepreneurial activity is a critical trigger for high growth, the institutional framework that would provide the infrastructure for entrepreneurs also plays a significant role in determining the proliferation of entrepreneurial activities (Baumol 1990; Davidsson and Henrekson 2002; Stam et al. 2011). At the institutional level, for instance equity financing or incentives for wealth accumulation, high rates of taxation for production sources or entrepreneurial income (Davidsson and Henrekson 2002) can be examples of infrastructural elements that can encourage or inhibit the entrepreneurial activities in that given industry.

Besides entrepreneurial competence and institutional factors, the strategic design process can also be a significant indicator for a HGF. Following the growth strategy, organizational and financial structures, R&D and marketing strategies are to be designed respectively taking into consideration the customer requirements and environmental dynamics. How this strategic design is undertaken by entrepreneurs will be discussed in light of the of the effectuation theory in the following part.

4 The Effectual Logic

Effectuation theory (Sarasvathy 2001, 2008) identifies two sorts of new venture creation processes as causation and effectuation. These distinct logics are differentiated in terms of choice sets and defined as: "...choosing between means to create a particular effect, versus choosing between many possible effects using a particular set of means" (Sarasvathy 2001, p. 245). One of the typical examples on these processes is asking a chef to cook a given menu (causation) in contrast to giving the chef a variety of ingredients and utensils and let the chef cook whatever he or she desires (effectuation). Although the flow between means and ends is different in the causation-effectuation dichotomy, the ultimate aim is to be successful. For a given set of action, the causal models suggest defining and evaluating the alternatives first in order to make the rational choice. However, the effectual reasoning proposes that it is neither possible nor practical to forecast expected returns based on formulas in the context of environmental uncertainty. Therefore, the steps are taken based on the affordability of the venture and network connections are reinforced to hedge the undertaking (Chandler et al. 2011). Effectual reasoning is characterized by five heuristic principles of expert entrepreneurs (Dew et al. 2009; Sarasvathy 2008):

- *Non-predictive as opposed to predictive control (Pilot-in-the-Plane Principle)*: Entrepreneurs understand that their actions can shape the future, so they do not accept the notion that it is totally uncontrollable.

- *Means-driven as opposed to goal-driven action (Bird in Hand Principle)*: To build up a new venture, entrepreneurs first consider what their capabilities are and who they can reach and then undertake the experiment based on these means.
- *Affordable loss as opposed to expected return (Affordable Loss Principle)*: Entrepreneurs assess the affordability of the new project in case of its failure and limit their risks throughout the phases of implementation.
- *Partnerships as opposed to competitive analysis (Crazy Quilt Principle)*: In order to lessen uncertainty, entrepreneurs are keen on engaging key stakeholders and forming new alliances starting from the early stages of the undertaking.
- *Leveraging as opposed to avoiding contingencies (Lemonade Principle)*: Entrepreneurs do not avoid unexpected incidents and they rather perceive all critical changes as opportunities to exploit.

In their meta-analytic review, Read et al. (2009) find empirical support for a positive relationship between the effectual approach and strategic design as well as business performance. Besides, the operationalization of the causation and effectuation constructs are being refined (Chandler et al. 2011). Furthermore, despite being criticized in several ways, the potential of effectuation to become a solid theory in entrepreneurship is recognized by scholars (Arend et al. 2015; Perry et al. 2011). Effectuation theory is also found applicable in various entrepreneurship contexts such as angel investing (Wiltbank et al. 2009), internationalization (Kalinic et al. 2014), high-growth firms (Chidakwa 2015), and family start-ups (Jones and Li 2017).

After this brief description of the effectuation perspective, its principles will be associated with a high-growth firm case in the following part.

5 A Case of High-Growth Firm in Turkey: Oba Macaroni

Originating from Italy, pasta is now a popular dish worldwide, as one of the most accessible and nutrient-dense foods. It's typically made from unleavened dough of durum wheat flour combined with water or eggs. In the market, pasta product is available in various shapes, distributed through stable channels, and has long shelf life, which have most probably driven its increasing consumption so far. Moreover, the trend of manufacturing pasta in newer varieties is expected to expand the market in the coming years. In 2016, the market is estimated at more than USD11 billion value with an average annual growth rate at 4% and the forecast by 2022 is that it will reach to USD14 billion (IMARC 2017).

In terms of production volume, over 14 million tons of pasta are produced worldwide and Turkey (1.3 tones) is the third largest manufacturer after Italy (3.2 tones) and US (2 tones) (UNAFPA 2015). Turkey is also the third biggest pasta exporter at a value of USD422 million after Italy (USD2.6 billion) and China (USD838 million) in 2016 (ITC 2017). On the other hand, over one third of Turkey's pasta exports is realized through only four partners, namely Benin, Angola, Japan, and Iraq, although it is exported to more than 140 countries (TCEB 2017). One of the reasons of this concentration into Africa and Asia is the import tariffs and quota applied by US and EU to restrict free entry of selected items in their markets, which include pasta.

Turkey's domestic pasta market is competitive as in 20 producers, employing almost 30,000 people and has a total revenue estimated at USD1 billion (TMSD 2016). Despite being one of the leader manufacturers and exporters, the pasta consumption per capita in Turkey is 7.5 kg and ranking as 15th in the world (UNAFPA 2015). This is probably due to the domestic preference of substitute foods such as rice and bulgur. On the other hand, the pasta consumption shows an increasing trend when compared with 6 kg level in 2010 (TCEB 2014).

OBA Macaroni (hereinafter Oba) is one of the biggest players in Turkish pasta market. It is distinguished in respect to its consistent high growth rates especially after 2010. Located in Gaziantep, a major city in the southeast of Turkey, Oba is a reputable national brand, which was founded in 1966. In 2005, it was acquired by Ozguclu Family, who has been in the livestock feed industry. Since then, significant capital investments have been carried out in Oba and the firm has gained a prominent position in the pasta market.

Oba's remarkable growth is well recognized in two separate reports by The Union of Chambers and Commodity Exchanges of Turkey (TOBB 2016) and Turkish Enterprise and Business Confederation (TURKONFED 2017) as being one of the top 100 highest growing firms in Turkey. Specifically, between years 2012 and 2016, Oba has increased its sales by 212%, assets by 103% and the number of employees by 87% (ISO 2017). This is about three-fold of the overall development in Turkish economy (TUIK 2017). As of 2016, Oba is the number two producer in the pasta industry in Turkey with USD230 million in revenues of which approximately USD100 million is export sales and has around 600 employees (ISO 2017; TIM 2017).

In this study, the strategic design and transition of Oba into a high-growth firm will be analyzed in light of the effectuation perspective. All inferences below are based on news and reports that are publicly available on the internet.

- *Pilot-in-the-Plane Principle*: Oba pays special attention to children. It is probable that likeability of a product and awareness of a brand are easier to create at early ages. Thus, Oba occasionally visits elementary schools with food trucks and treats pasta to kids. Another project is organizing games at nursery schools to paint and sculpt butterflies with pasta. At national level, Oba introduced the pasta boxed with toys to increase appeal. Moreover, Oba sometimes hosts children in the factory to show them around and make them have enjoyable time. Site visits are not limited to children. Oba also welcomes university students from nearby regions to increase public knowledge and arranges training sessions for students of nutrition sciences. These can be examples of deliberate actions to create positive attitude of young people towards pasta consumption and the company itself. There are projects for adults as well. Within the advertising campaigns, Oba often delivers new dish recipes that include pasta. Besides, cooking workshops are organized with celebrities to engage people in preparing different food with pasta. With this communication, Oba tries to popularize the pasta consumption among adults. On the other hand, Oba aims to expand in challenging markets such as Japan. To keep up with the competition in Japan, it is required to be innovative even for an uncomplicated product like pasta. That's why; Oba invests in new production technologies and R&D, recognizing that it is the strategic way to sustain in the long term.

- *Bird in Hand Principle*: As remarked previously, Oba was acquired by Ozguclu Family in 2005. They have been in feed mill business since 1988 and were a customer of Oba for industrial purchases. When operations started going bad for Oba in the beginning of 2000s, the family decided to buy the renowned company. They could undertake this because they were already in the agriculture sector in the same region and they were familiar with the raw material. After several years of adaptation to the pasta market, they invested about USD65 million to renew the factory between 2010 and 2012. Step by step, they increased the export market entries and they tripled the export sales figure from 2011 until 2015. Meanwhile, they also paid attention to the domestic market. Built on the brand name, they spared a significant budget for advertising, introduced new product varieties, and reinforced the distribution channels to increase the market share. Furthermore, they made a nation-wide research named *pasta map* of Turkey. Data is collected in regard to pasta consumption in the country such as eating habits, cooking styles, shape and sauce preferences, and demographics. With this information, they could design marketing programs specifically for different regions. These show that, Oba strengthens a function based on available resources and then it is stretched further to achieve more.
- *Affordable Loss Principle*: Oba was eager to make additional capital investments. They were looking for sites in the region to build a new plant. Eventually, they ended up buying a working factory in the northwest of Turkey from one of the competitors. Instead of constructing a new plant in the same area, they preferred the takeover opportunity at a distant location. It looked feasible because they could start operations immediately, they became closer to the most populated region of the country, and they could also diversify since the plant had facilities for *flour* production. Oba also followed the gradual internationalization strategy, which is the conventional way. They first entered Africa and the Middle East and tried to hold on as many markets as possible. Then they targeted more competitive markets such as the Far East, Europe, and North America. That means Oba moves along the learning curve and takes judicious actions in the sense of globalizing. Furthermore, Oba values governance and innovation culture in the organization. They pursue to remain updated by business process improvements, market research, third party counseling, and investment on R&D in order to keep up with the quality regulations, market dynamics and changing technologies worldwide. These examples reveal that Oba is quite prudent in planning and implementing new endeavors.
- *Crazy Quilt Principle*: Oba extensively participates to food fairs and exhibitions in Turkey and abroad to extend their networks. They regularly take place in big international events like in Lebanon, UAE, Japan and France. They want to increase awareness and availability of the brand in world markets, so they tailor promotion and distribution strategies particular to each country by working closely with channel partners. They also follow public tenders to close substantial deals. For example, in 2015 they invited Iraqi government representatives to the factory and held a meeting to develop the relationships. In addition, Oba sees

community as a vital stakeholder and often sponsors social events. Some of them are fashion shows, local food festivals, fast-breaking meals in Ramadan, parties at nursing homes, and giving presents to children who fight serious illnesses, all of which help Oba to increase reputation within the society.

- *Lemonade Principle*: Oba tries to cope with the general apprehension in public that pasta causes weight gain. In their marketing communication, Oba underlines that pasta is actually a good choice for diets but high calorie intake through sauces or other types of carbohydrates may be the reasons of unwanted weight. Nevertheless, they also introduce *healthier* pasta options such as whole-wheat and vegetable or vitamin added versions. Besides, they often share new recipes in media to motivate more use of pasta in the kitchens. Oba exploits special days by exclusive advertising as well. For example, they remind that pasta is a very practical meal while fasting in Ramadan or in Valentine's Day; they treat flowers and pasta on streets mentioning the bond between food and love. Another move by Oba was, when the Turkish government advised business people not to avoid investments during hard times in the economy and called them to increase employment, Oba responded this by announcing additional investments worth of USD10 million to support the action. Naturally, this is appraised by public and the political elite, which favored Oba's image. These signal that, even in undesirable circumstances, Oba attempts to benefit from the underlying opportunities.

To sum up, the above case illustrates that effectuation is an applicable logic in understanding high growth, particularly in an emerging market setting.

6 Conclusion

As strategic designers, entrepreneurs play a critical role in the formation of HGFs. Similarly, high-growth oriented firms require entrepreneurial activities or orientation for being competitive and sustainable. In line with this perspective, this study aims to understand the strategic design and high-growth firms phenomena through entrepreneurship framework. Relying on a case analysis, it is emphasized that a firm's effectual logic as a strategy can yield exceptional outcomes. Instead of setting goals and trying to configure the organization accordingly (causation), effectuation denotes that expert entrepreneurs take action based on the available means, consider the affordability of the undertaking, and pursue extending the network connections. In the described case, the firm runs in line with the capabilities first at hand and as they learn and develop the competencies, they move one step ahead.

Oba bears some common points with the previously studied HGFs and their strategic designs. For instance, Oba stands on the same line with the studies that describe HGFs as being growth-oriented, innovative and exporter. Moreover, Oba's emphasis on R&D and marketing strategies supported by strategic alliances indicates Oba's success in formulating a new strategic design concerning the production, sales and marketing strategies though it is one of the oldest pasta producers in Turkey. Through its tremendously increased sales, Oba has also played a significant role in enlarging Turkish pasta market and the employability in that given market. This situation is also in line with the studies discussing HGFs' high potential of creating industry growth.

What Oba did in terms of business functions can also have managerial implications for particular contexts. (1) In the production side, they made remarkable capital investments to increase the capacity. They were keen on using state-of-the-art technology and being innovative through R&D. (2) Internationalization was actually the spring board for the firm. The more markets they entered the more confident they became to introduce themselves to the global arena. (3) They were mindful of the market intelligence. They conducted surveys to understand the consumer tendencies and adapt themselves to changing dynamics. (4) In marketing, the distinct intentions were (a) to promote the brand by thematic advertising and (b) to increase the popularity of product consumption. Hence, the communication is blended for both short-term and long-term objectives. (5) For public relations, they focused on the socially responsible activities. They especially supported projects involving children and local community. That characterized the firm cared for its existing space as well as the future. Finally, it required strong determination and persistence of the family members to scale up the company; however, it would be the next challenge to sustain position and progress.

Therefore, the current study calls the attention of both academics and policy makers to the role of entrepreneurship in the development of HGFs and their strategic designs. The policy makers' efforts in encouraging entrepreneurial activity would provide positive results both in national and global economies in terms of job creation and innovation. Further, the literature requires more empirical studies in explaining the entrepreneurial efforts on the strategic design of HGFs. In conclusion, it is expected from future studies to overcome this deficit by studying diverse industries of the developing countries.

References

Aggarwal, A., & Sato, T. (2015). *Identifying high growth firms in India: An alternative approach.* Research Institute for Economics and Business Administration, Kobe University.

Altuntaş, G., & Dömez, D. (2010). Girişimcilik yönelimi ve örgütsel performans ilişkisi: Çanakkale bölgesinde faaliyet gösteren otel işletmelerinde bir araştırma. *Istanbul University Journal of the School of Business Administration, 39*(1), 50–74.

Anokhin, S., Grichnik, D., & Hisrich, R. D. (2008). The journey from novice to serial entrepreneurship in China and Germany: Are the drivers the same? *Managing Global Transitions, 6*(2), 117–142.

Arend, R. J., Sarooghi, H., & Burkemper, A. (2015). Effectuation as ineffectual? Applying the 3e theory-assessment framework to a proposed new theory of entrepreneurship. *Academy of Management Review, 40*(4), 630–651.

Barringer, B. R., Jones, F. F., & Neubaum, D. O. (2005). A quantitative content analysis of the characteristics of rapid-growth firms and their founders. *Journal of Business Venturing, 20*(5), 663–687.

Baum, J. R., & Bird, B. J. (2010). The successful intelligence of high-growth entrepreneurs: Links to new venture growth. *Organization Science, 21*(2), 397–412.

Baumol, W. J. (1990). Entrepreneurship: Productive, unproductive, and destructive. *Journal of Political Economy, 98*(5), 893–921.

Bos, J. W., & Stam, E. (2013). Gazelles and industry growth: A study of young high-growth firms in the Netherlands. *Industrial and Corporate Change, 23*(1), 145–169.

Brown, R., Mawson, S., & Mason, C. (2017). Myth-busting and entrepreneurship policy: The case of high growth firms. *Entrepreneurship & Regional Development, 29*(5–6), 414–443.

Brüderl, J., & Preisendörfer, P. (2000). Fast-growing businesses: Empirical evidence from a German study. *International Journal of Sociology, 30*(3), 45–70.

Carree, M. A., & Thurik, R. (2003). The impact of entrepreneurship on economic growth. In D. B. Audretsch & Z. J. Acs (Eds.), *Handbook of entrepreneurship research* (pp. 437–471). Boston/ Dordrecht: Kluwer/Academic Publishers.

Castaño, M. S., Méndez, M. T., & Galindo, M. Á. (2016). Innovation, internationalization and business-growth expectations among entrepreneurs in the services sector. *Journal of Business Research, 69*(5), 1690–1695.

Çetinkaya Bozkurt, Ö., Kalkan, A., Koyuncu, O., & Alparslan, A. M. (2012). Türkiye'de Girişimciliğin Gelişimi: Girişimciler Üzerinde Nitel Bir Araştırma. *Journal of Suleyman Demirel University Institute of Social Sciences, 15*(1), 229–247.

Chan, Y. E., Bhargava, N., & Street, C. T. (2006). Having arrived: The homogeneity of high-growth small firms. *Journal of Small Business Management, 44*(3), 426–440.

Chandler, G. N., DeTienne, D. R., McKelvie, A., & Mumford, T. V. (2011). Causation and effectuation processes: A validation study. *Journal of Business Venturing, 26*, 375–390.

Chidakwa, A. M. (2015). *Causation and effectuation in Zimbabwe's high growth firms.* Dissertation, University of the Witwatersrand.

Coad, A., & Rao, R. (2008). Innovation and firm growth in high-tech sectors: A quantile regression approach. *Research Policy, 37*, 633–648.

Coad, A., Daunfeldt, S.-O., Hölzl, W., Johansson, D., & Nightingale, P. (2014a). High-growth firms: Introduction to the special section. *Industrial and Corporate Change, 23*, 91–112.

Coad, A., Daunfeldt, S.-O., Johansson, D., & Wennberg, K. (2014b). Whom do high-growth firms hire? *Industrial and Corporate Change, 23*, 293–327.

Colombelli, A., Krafft, J., & Quatraro, F. (2013). High-growth firms and technological knowledge: Do gazelles follow exploration or exploitation strategies? *Industrial and Corporate Change, 23* (1), 261–291.

Davidsson, P., & Henrekson, M. (2002). Determinants of the prevalence of start-ups and high-growth firms. *Small Business Economics, 19*(2), 81–104.

de Mello Freire, K. (2017). From strategic planning to the designing of strategies: A change in favor of strategic design. *Strategic Design Research Journal, 10*(2), 91.

Delmar, F., & Davidsson, P. (1998). A taxonomy of high-growth firms. In P. D. Reynolds & W. D. Bygrave (Eds.), *Frontiers of entrepreneurship research* (pp. 399–413). Wellesley: Babson College.

Delmar, F., Davidsson, P., & Gartner, W. B. (2003). Arriving at the high-growth firm. *Journal of Business Venturing, 18*(2), 189–216.

Demir, R., Wennberg, K., & McKelvie, A. (2017). The strategic management of high-growth firms: A review and theoretical conceptualization. *Long Range Planning, 50*(4), 431–456.

Deserti, A. (2009). The strategic role of design: The Italian case. *Strategic Design Research Journal, 2*(2), 64–68.

Dew, N., Read, S., Sarasvathy, S. D., & Wiltbank, R. (2009). Effectual versus predictive logics in entrepreneurial decision-making: Differences between experts and novices. *Journal of Business Venturing, 24*, 287–309.

Du, J., & Temouri, Y. (2015). High-growth firms and productivity: Evidence from the United Kingdom. *Small Business Economics, 44*(1), 123–143.

Feeser, H. R., & Willard, G. E. (1990). Founding strategy and performance: A comparison of high and low growth high tech firms. *Strategic Management Journal, 11*(2), 87–98.

Fischer, E., & Reuber, A. R. (2003). Support for rapid-growth firms: A comparison of the views of founders, government policymakers, and private sector resource providers. *Journal of Small Business Management, 41*(4), 346–365.

Fischer, E., Reuber, A. R., Hababou, M., Johnson, W., & Lee, S. (1997). The role of socially constructed temporal perspectives in the emergence of rapid-growth firms. *Entrepreneurship: Theory and Practice, 22*(2), 13–14.

Florin, J., Lubatkin, M., & Schulze, W. (2003). A social capital model of high-growth ventures. *Academy of Management Journal, 46*(3), 374–384.

Fombrun, C. J., & Wally, S. (1989). Structuring small firms for rapid growth. *Journal of Business Venturing, 4*(2), 107–122.

Global Entrepreneurship Monitor (GEM). (2017). *Global report 2016/2017.* London: Global Entrepreneurship Research Association, London Business School.

Goedhuys, M., & Sleuwaegen, L. (2010). High-growth entrepreneurial firms in Africa: A quantile regression approach. *Small Business Economics, 34*(1), 31–51.

Gundry, L. K., & Welsch, H. P. (2001). The ambitious entrepreneur: High growth strategies of women-owned enterprises. *Journal of Business Venturing, 16*(5), 453–470.

Gürbüz, G., & Aykol, S. (2009). Entrepreneurial management, entrepreneurial orientation and Turkish small firm growth. *Management Research News, 32*(4), 321–336.

Hölzl, W. (2009). Is the R&D behaviour of fast-growing SMEs different? Evidence from CIS III data for 16 countries. *Small Business Economics, 33*(1), 59–75.

IMARC. (2017). *Pasta market: Global industry trends, share, size, growth, opportunity and forecast 2017–2022.* Accessed December 20, 2017, from http://www.imarcgroup.com/pasta-market

ISO (Istanbul Chamber of Industry). (2017). *Turkiye'nin 500 buyuk sanayi kurulusu.* Accessed December 21, 2017, from http://www.iso500.org.tr/iso-500-hakkinda/gecmis-yil-verileri

ITC. (2017). *International trade statistics.* Accessed December 20, 2017, from https://www.trademap.org/tradestat/Country_SelProduct_TS.aspx?nvpm=1||||1902|||4|1|1|2|2|1|2|1|1

Jones, O., & Li, H. (2017). Effectual entrepreneuring: Sensemaking in a family-based start-up. *Entrepreneurship & Regional Development, 29*, 2–33.

Kalinic, I., Sarasvathy, S. D., & Forza, C. (2014). Expect the unexpected: Implications of effectual logic on the internationalization process. *International Business Review, 23*, 635–647.

Karadeniz, E., & Ozdemir, O. (2009). Entrepreneurship in Turkey and developing countries: A comparison of activities, characteristics, motivation and environment for entrepreneurship. *Mibes Transactions, 3*(1), 30–45.

Keen, C., & Etemad, H. (2012). Rapid growth and rapid internationalization: The case of smaller enterprises from Canada. *Management Decision, 50*, 569–590.

Krasniqi, B. A., & Desai, S. (2016). Institutional drivers of high-growth firms: Country-level evidence from 26 transition economies. *Small Business Economics, 47*(4), 1075–1094.

Lee, N. (2014). What holds back high-growth firms? Evidence from UK SMEs. *Small Business Economics, 43*(1), 183–195.

Leff, N. (1979). Entrepreneurship and economic development: The problem revisited. *Journal of Economic Literature, 17*(1), 46–64.

Littunen, H., & Tohmo, T. (2003). The high growth in new metal-based manufacturing and business service firms in Finland. *Small Business Economics, 21*(2), 187–200.

Lopez-Garcia, P., & Puente, S. (2012). What makes a high-growth firm? A dynamic probit analysis using Spanish firm-level data. *Small Business Economics, 39*(4), 1029–1041.

Mason, C., & Brown, R. (2013). Creating good public policy to support high-growth firms. *Small Business Economics, 40*(2), 211–225.

Meroni, A. (2008). Strategic design: Where are we now? Reflection around the foundations of a recent discipline. *Strategic Design Research Journal, 1*(1), 31–28.

Naudé, W. A. (2009). *Out with the sleaze, in with the ease: Insufficient for entrepreneurial development?* UNUWIDER research paper no. 2009/01. Helsinki: United Nations University.

Naudé, W. A. (2010). Entrepreneurship, developing countries, and development economics: New approaches and insights. *Small Business Economics, 34*(1), 1–12.

Nicholls-Nixon, C. L. (2005). Rapid growth and high performance: The entrepreneur's "impossible dream?". *Academy of Management Executive, 19,* 77–89.

O'Regan, N., Ghobadian, A., & Gallear, D. (2006). In search of the drivers of high growth in manufacturing SMEs. *Technovation, 26*(1), 30–41.

Ocak, M., & Basim, H. N. (2017). An empirical research on the antecedents and consequences of corporate entrepreneurship in Turkish industry companies. *Business and Economics Research Journal, 8*(1), 131.

OECD. (2006). *Understanding entrepreneurship: Developing indicators for international comparisons and assessments.* Paris: OECD.

OECD. (2007). *Eurostat-OECD manual on business demography statistics.* Paris: OECD.

Parker, S. C., Storey, D. J., & Witteloostuijn, A. (2010). What happens to gazelles? The importance of dynamic management strategy. *Small Business Economics, 35*(2), 203–226.

Perry, J. T., Chandler, G. N., & Markova, G. (2011, January). Entrepreneurial effectuation: A review and suggestions for future research. *Entrepreneurship Theory and Practice,* 1–25.

Read, S., Song, M., & Smit, W. (2009). A meta-analytic review of effectuation and venture performance. *Journal of Business Venturing, 24,* 573–587.

Sarasvathy, S. D. (2001). Causation and effectuation: Toward a theoretical shift from economic inevitability to entrepreneurial contingency. *Academy of Management Review, 26*(2), 243–263.

Sarasvathy, S. D. (2008). *Effectuation: Elements of entrepreneurial expertise.* Cheltenham: Edward Elgar Publishing.

Schreyer, P. (2000). *High-growth firms and employment* (OECD Science, Technology and Industry Working Papers 2000/03). Paris: OECD Publishing.

Schumpeter, J. A. (1934). *The theory of economic development.* Cambridge, MA: Harvard University Press.

Shuman, J. C., Shaw, J. J., & Sussman, G. (1985). Strategic planning in smaller rapid growth companies. *Long Range Planning, 18*(6), 48–53.

Siegel, R., Siegel, E., & Macmillan, I. C. (1993). Characteristics distinguishing high-growth ventures. *Journal of Business Venturing, 8*(2), 169–180.

Sims, M. A., & O'Regan, N. (2006). In search of gazelles using a research DNA model. *Technovation, 26*(8), 943–954.

Sönmez, A., & Toksoy, A. (2014). Türkiye'de Girişimcilik ve Türk Girişimci Profili Üzerine Bir Analiz. *Yönetim ve Ekonomi, 21*(2), 41–58.

Stam, E., & Wennberg, K. (2009). The roles of R&D in new firm growth. *Small Business Economics, 33*(1), 77–89.

Stam, E., Hartog, C., Van Stel, A., & Thurik, R. (2011) *Ambitious entrepreneurship, high-growth firms and macroeconomic growth.* The Dynamics of Entrepreneurship: Evidence from Global Entrepreneurship Monitor Data, 231–249.

TCEB (Republic of Turkey Ministry of Economy). (2014). *Sektör raporları.* Accessed December 21, 2017, from https://www.gtb.org.tr/dosya/pdf/makarna-sektor-raporu-1.pdf

TCEB (Republic of Turkey Ministry of Economy). (2017). *Sektör raporları.* Accessed December 21, 2017, from https://www.ekonomi.gov.tr/portal/content/conn/UCM/uuid/dDocName:EK-051173

TIM (Turkish Exporters' Assembly). (2017). *Ilk 1000 ihracatci arastırması.* Accessed December 21, 2017, from http://www.tim.org.tr/tr/ihracat-arastirma-raporlari-ilk-1000-ihracatci-arastirmasi.html

TMSD (Association of Pasta Producers Turkey). (2016). *Un ve unlu mamuller.* Accessed December 21, 2017, from http://www.makarna.org.tr/images_upload/files/Unlu%20mamuller%20sekt%C3%B6r%20haberi.pdf

TOBB (The Union of Chambers and Commodity Exchanges of Turkey). (2016). *Turkiye'nin hizli buyuyen sirketleri.* Accessed December 21, 2017, from https://mobil.tobb.org.tr/MansetResimleri/21749-37.pdf

TUIK (Turkish Statistical Institute). (2016). *Küçük ve Orta Büyüklükteki Girişim İstatistikleri, 2016.* Accessed November 19, 2017, from http://www.tuik.gov.tr/PreHaberBultenleri.do?id=21540

TUIK (Turkish Statistical Institute). (2017). *Temel istatistikler.* Accessed December 21, 2017, from http://www.tuik.gov.tr/UstMenu.do?metod=temelist

TURKONFED (Turkish Enterprise and Business Confederation). (2017). *Turkiye'nin yukselen liderleri.* Accessed December 21, 2017, from http://www.turkonfed.org/Files/ContentFile/turkonfed-turkiyenin-yukselen-liderleri-bb-111017.pdf

UNAFPA. (2015). *Statistics.* Accessed December 20, 2017, from http://www.pasta-unafpa.org/ingstatistics5.htm

Wiltbank, R., Read, S., Dew, N., & Sarasvathy, S. D. (2009). Prediction and control under uncertainty: Outcomes in angel investing. *Journal of Business Venturing, 24*, 116–133.

Wong, P. K., Ho, Y. P., & Autio, E. (2005). Entrepreneurship, innovation and economic growth: Evidence from GEM data. *Small Business Economics, 24*(3), 335–350.

The Effects of Strategic Design on Business Operations

Fatih Pınarbaşı

Abstract Organizations are structures that are constantly progressing, interacting with their external environment. During these interactions a lot of decision-making and selection processes take place. Some of the decision-making processes are short-term, some are medium term, others are long term.

Long-term decision-making processes naturally involve a broader planning process. Long-term decisions are more complex and have different conditions. This planning process is discussed together with strategy concept in business literature. This study is a study that focuses on the concepts related to strategy and strategy, and focuses on strategic design. While the concepts related to the strategy are discussed, the processes involved in the organizations, and the academic studies in which these processes are used together with the strategic design are included.

This study mainly consists of three parts and answers three basic questions. (i) What are the concepts of strategy, strategic management, strategic planning and strategic design? (ii) What are the types of business operations and functions? (iii) how was strategic design used in business operations in academic literature?

With a brief examination of third part of this study, it can be seen that most of the studies focused on long-term process planning.

1 Introduction

This study mainly consists of two subjects. Strategic design and operations of enterprises. Accordingly, a section consisting of three sections has been prepared.

In the first part, strategic design will be mentioned. Strategic design process begins with strategy. If the etymological root will be mentioned before the concept of strategy starts, "strategy" word derived from Greek to English and its original version was "strategos"/which means "commander in chief". According to Bratton

F. Pınarbaşı (✉)
School of Business and Management, Istanbul Medipol University, Beykoz, Istanbul, Turkey
e-mail: fpinarbasi@medipol.edu.tr

© Springer International Publishing AG, part of Springer Nature 2018   115
H. Dincer et al. (eds.), *Strategic Design and Innovative Thinking in Business Operations*, Contributions to Management Science,
https://doi.org/10.1007/978-3-319-77622-4_6

and Gold (2012), this word was first used in English language in 1656 and it could be composed from two words. First one is stratos/army, second one is agein/to lead. In the first part, concepts such as strategy, strategic management and strategic planning will be addressed in order to better understand strategic design.

In the second part, in order to better understand business operations, the classification of Porter's value chain and business functions will be given firstly. Then, today's business functions will be explained one by one. Business processes consist of short, medium and long term processes. While strategic design is generally concerned with long-term processes, it is useful to know other short- and medium-term processes of operation.

The third and final part of the study will include academic studies on how strategic design takes place in the work of the various departments of the enterprises. The academic studies examined in this section mainly involve strategic design studies on distribution channels and production systems. Strategic design approach is especially found in processes that require long-term planning, such as distribution processes.

2 Strategy and Strategic Design

Strategy, strategic management, strategic planning and strategic design are closely related. Therefore, this section will start with the definitions of these topics.

2.1 What Is strategy?

Chandler (1990) defines strategy as the determination process of elemental long-term goals of a company. After this determination acception follows and for reaching goals, resource allocation process is included in strategy. Hill et al. (2014) use management perspective in their study and define strategy as series of associated actions which managers use their company's achievement. Mintzberg (1978) defines strategy as a pattern in decisions sets/series. According to him, just after a series of decisions happens, the strategy will be formed.

Strategy can be defined as a match between the sources of organization and the elements of external environment, comprehensively. The elements can be both opportunities, threats or risks. So strategy is an important key link that connects objectives of organizations with policies to achieve these objectives (Bowman and Asch 1987).

In Chaffee's (1985) study, three models for strategy are revealed. These are;

1. Linear Strategy
2. Adaptive Strategy
3. Interpretive Strategy

In linear strategy, the "strategy" consists of decisions, plans and actions in integrated way to reach organizational goals. So goals and the tools of them are consequences of strategic decision. Organizations improve/changes their links with environment, by using of product-market change. Strategic planning, formulation and implementation are related to this linear model.

Adaptive model is based on the adaptability to environmental conditions. Changes for the environment is simultaneous and ongoing function in this model. Adaptive model focuses on manager's attention on tools and therefore the goal of the organization is coalignment process between organization and its environment.

Lastly interpretive model is about directing metaphors/references for stakeholders to understand organization and its environment. Interpretive strategy sees organization and the environment of the organization as open system. The different part of interpretive strategy is about outputs. Leaders of organizations formalize the attitudes toward organizations and outputs, but they don't make any physical modification in outputs.

In sum, linear strategy focuses on dealing with competitors about organization's goals, adaptive strategy focuses on organization itself and its parts to change according to consumer preferences, lastly interpretive strategy focuses on stakeholders to motivate for the favor of organization.

Mintzberg and Waters (1989) studied how strategies form in organizations in their study. They studied eight types of strategies and these are planned, entrepreneurial, ideological, umbrella, process, unconnected, consensus and imposed. *Planned strategy* derives from formal plans, central strategy has effect in it. *Entrepreneurial strategy* is derived from central vision, leader has an effect as personal control on organization. *Ideological strategy* arise from shared beliefs, there is a collective vision. *Umbrella strategy* derives from restrictions, leaders have partial control in organizations. *Process strategy* arise from its name, leaders have controls of only strategy aspects. *Unconnected strategy* arise from enclaves, actors do not attach to rest of organization much. *Consensus strategy* originates in its name, mutual adjustment is in the center. Finally *imposed strategy* derives from environment, environment has a dominant side in this strategy.

2.2   What Is Strategic Management?

There are many different definitions in the academic literature on the definition of strategic management. These descriptions have been the subject of research (Nag et al. 2007). According to Jemison (1981), strategic management is the process which general managers in complex organizations implement to create a strategy which makes organizations align their competences to constraints in environment.

According to Bratton and Gold (2012), strategic management process has five steps in itself. These steps are;

1. Mission and goals

2. Analysis of environment
3. Formulation of strategy
4. Implementation of strategy
5. Evaluation of strategy

2.3   What Is Strategic Plan?

Shrader et al. (1989) discuss strategic plan as a written long-range plan includes corporate mission and statement of objectives.

According to Kudla (1980), strategic planning is a systematic process about determining organization's goals/objectives for the future, which he approaches it as "at least 3 years". Strategic planning is also about developing strategies to use resource in order to reach objectives.

2.4   What Is Strategic Design?

According to Meroni (2008), strategic design is about a whole body/system of rules, values and beliefs for one's identity to deal with external variables. It includes tools to evolve and maintain its identity. He examined the strategic design in terms of Product-Service Systems (PSS) in his study. As an activity, Strategic design;

- Must conceive collective values and interest,
- Defines the actions by going step by step, after implementing orientation from scenarios,
- Revolves around learning to deal with environment, rather than learning procedures.

At this stage, it is worth mentioning the definition of Product-Service Systems. According to Mont (2002), product-service system is a system consists of product-service and related networks and infrastructure. This system provides being competitive and satisfying customer needs. Also this system has lower impact to environment than traditional business model.

Burkhardt (2009) approaches to strategic design in terms of education. He defines the strategic design as in concern with the overall structure consists of product set and the way that structure relating to user-system. He remarks some of components which strategic design includes. Some of them are;

- Identification of opportunities that lead to improvement,
- Selection of goals to improvement,
- Designing the complete structure of tools that can forward.

Montuori (2003) discusses the strategic design with strategic plan in a transition and historical view. He examines scope of strategy with strategic planning and includes some critiques of strategic planning. He approaches to strategic design in terms of design. According to him, design is a method of questioning. It helps people about;

- Exploring their current position,
- Featurizing their ideals about future,
- Having an understanding about values and assumptions,
- Developing a model to reach future state.

In summary, the concept of strategy refers to the long term thinking and decision making, strategic management is the general process in which this thinking and decision process is applied, strategic planning is the design phase of this application, and strategic design is the whole system in the process of interacting with the environment. After that, strategic design has three elements, firstly organization itself, secondly environment of the organization and internal elements of organization. It's an overall process and usually long-term period.

Following section will provide information about business functions and business operations, which are the second part of the chapter.

3   Business Functions and Operations

Porter (1998) sees competition as the center for business performance, success or failure. In his study, he included different competitive strategies for organizations in competitive situations. It is mentioned that organizations must be examined as a whole in order to fully understand and resolve competition. Therefore Porter mentions a concept named "value chain" when it includes competitive strategies in its work. Basically value chain is a basic tool for investigate activities of organizations. In value chain, activities divided into two main categories; primary activities and support activities. Primary activities include;

- Inbound Logistics
- Operations
- Outbound Logistics
- Marketing and Sales
- Service

Inbound logistics focus on input part of product, for example receiving and storing. It contains warehousing, controlling of inventory, scheduling of transportation. *Operations* focus on "processing" part of business which includes transforming input to final version. It contains producing, packaging, testing. *Outbound logistics* focus on output part of product which includes storing and distributing. It contains delivering of goods, warehousing and order processing. *Marketing and Sales* focus on making buyers purchase products, these activities include advertising, quoting, sales force and channel related operations. *Service* focus on supplying service to enhance or maintain product value. It contains repairing, supplying parts, installation.

Support activities include;

- Firm Infrastructure
- Human Resource Management
- Technology Development
- Procurement

Firm infrastructure focuses on supporting entire chain not only individual activities and includes general management, finance, accounting and quality management. *Human resource management* focuses on personnel side of organizations. It includes starting stage activity like recruiting, and inside organization activity like training and development. Human resource management activities have impact to competitiveness of any firm. *Technology development* includes activities improving both product and process. "Research and development" terms is not used, because author thinks that R&D has narrow meaning to most managers. *Procurement* focuses on purchasing process not purchased inputs. Items that fall under the scope of purchase can be supplies, raw materials and assets like laboratory equipments, machinery.

After Porter's classification, some functions have come to the forefront, some of the functions have become less important, and some functions have become more prominent, as the business world and circumstances have changed. When a classification is made with a more general approach, a summarizing function list is obtained. These new functions are; management, production, marketing, finance, accounting, human resources, public relations and lastly research and development.

Management Management is about the reaching to goals with using people and other business resources effectively. After this definition a new question may come to mind, what are the resources and who are these people? Resources could be money the organization use for its processes, equipment to produce the goods. People of course would be personnel who work in organization (Burrow et al. 2008).

There is a "holistic" nature in management function. All the other functions (marketing, human resources, finance etc.) are leaded by this function, so there is a hierarchy in operations, by dominance of management function.

The management function has four functions in itself. These functions are planning, organizing, implementing and controlling. *Planning* consists of processing the information and concluding about process. *Organizing* deals with how much plan need to be done. *Implementing* is action of plan stage and it relates with performing the plan and helping to workers. Finally, controlling is assessment of results to check whether objectives are reached or not (Burrow et al. 2008).

Strategic design and the management function are directly related because the management function has its own planning function. In addition, the management function is also a function that is empowered to make long-term decisions.

Production Production function plays an important role in the nature of the business structure of the output of the inputs. Production is a process about goods and services that contains creating, manufacturing or improving (Brown and Clow 2008).

Product development is about creating product/service or improving them. Today, products/services are changing consistently and organizations have to take action against market trends (Burrow et al. 2008).

Marketing Marketing means processes with product/services, including creating, promoting or offering. It aims to answer the need/wants of consumers (Brown and Clow 2008).

Marketing, in simple terms, can be defined as producing value for customers and third parties. This value producing process includes both creating the value and other processes like communication, delivering and exchanging (American Marketing Association 2017).

Marketing management, according to Kotler and Keller (2012), is the science and art that choose target markets, reach to customers and increase the customers by using customer value.

Widespread marketing activities are buying, selling, storing, transporting, researching, financing. Buying is relating to acquiring of products, selling is providing these products to appropriate consumers. Storing is relating to stocking products before selling, transporting is moving products to consumers at right time. Researching is studying consumer intentions, financing is about supplying necessary funds for marketing activities (Burrow et al. 2008).

Marketing involves a wide range of processes from planning the production of the product or service to communicating to the consumer and after-sales service. Therefore, planning in a wide frame, thinking long term and developing strategies accordingly takes place at the center of marketing management.

Finance Finance means, in general, the management, creation and studying of financial systems which consist of money, credit, investment, assets/liabilities (Investopedia 2017a, b).

In the beginning stage of organization or ongoing basis, managers evaluate the conditions if they are financially practicable. Financial plans can be used for this purpose. Financial plans are the document sets that outline general situation of financial state. They guide organizations and managers through to future (Brown and Clow 2008).Therefore, financial management contains financial data analyses, after that it involves fund decisions like obtaining and using (Madura 2007).

Accounting Accounting is about financial condition of an organization and it summarizes and analyse that condition. Financial statements which produced in accounting process give information about organization's financial performance and current condition. Management function can benefit from these financial statements in the decision-making process (Madura 2007). It is a process works in systematically and includes both recording and reporting. Financial transactions are important for organizations, because they affect operations of them. The system of accounting gathers, records and reports these financial transactions (Brown and Clow 2008).

The accounting function is important in the strategic design and strategic thinking system, in terms of control utility. It is important for organizations to check and observe the existing situation at certain periods during long-term plans and decision making processes.

Human Resources Management Employees are at the center of organizations, therefore managing relations with them is necessary for all organizations to work efficiently.

"Human resources" refers to people who work in a business, these people contribute to organizations by skills, experience, knowledge. Thereby, human resources management refers to find, choose, coach and evaluate these people (Brown and Clow 2008).

Human resources management has sub-processes inside. Acquisition of new employees, developing current employees inside organizations and answering them are these sub-processes (Burrow et al. 2008).

Public Relations Harlow (1976) studied many definitions of public relations to conclude a final definition. In his study, hundreds of definitions were collected from journals and other publications, researched the environment influences to these definitions. The time interval for definitions collected in the survey is 1906–1976. According to final definition, public relations is a characteristic management function, helping to connection between organization and its publics. This connection contains communication, acceptance, cooperation and understanding. Also public relations help to management by informing the public interest. Lastly, public relations researches and warn organizations to anticipate trends.

Hutton (1999) studied definitions of public relations and examined a number of definitions to illustrate a new definition. The result of that study is a short definition which consists of three words. It was "managing strategic relationships". The strategy part of this definition can be associated with strategic thinking and decision making, and therefore with strategic design. Public relations are a long-term and strategic function that needs strategic thinking aligning with objectives of organizations.

Research and Development R&D relates to investigation activities of organization to improve current products or develop new products (Investopedia 2017a, b). Djellal et al. (2003) studied current definitions of research and development and formulated a new definition from them. According to their new definition, R&D expresses creative work in systematic basis. This creative work means to increase knowledge, and use this knowledge to invent new applications.

As is seen, strategic thinking and strategic design have direct and indirect influences and relationships on the functions and operations of the organizations. In the next section, studies in the academic literature that focus on strategic design in various areas of the business will be examined.

4 Strategic Design Applications in Business Operations

Realff et al. (2000) studied reverse production systems in sustainability context. They worked on reverse production systems by design side and formulated an integer linear program. They employed a strong optimization framework. That framework has objective of minimization the maximum deviation which comes from network performance.

In their study, they presented that strategic reverse production system has five decisions.

1. Collection/Processing number and size
2. Feature allocation
3. Product/Material Routes
4. Transportation Modes
5. Material Amount for allocating

Number and size means the amount of collecting and processing sites. *Feature allocation* means function allocations to geographic places. *Product/material routes* refer to task network that materials use. *Transportation modes* refer to modes that connect physical sites. Finally, *material amount* means the amount of allocation to potential end-use.

Their hypotheses are about features shaping structure of reverse production system. These features consist of two variables, first one is product retirement frequency; in terms of average and variability, and second one is complexity in manufacture and materials. For the first hypothesis, they conceived that if the frequency of product retirement increases, length of use will increase, circulation numbers will decrease. For the second hypothesis, they conceived that strategic design of reverse production system will be impacted by complexity in manufacture and materials. If complexity in manufacturing is high, value of product will be implicit, so it would be preserved to reuse, so more complexity means more intention to reuse. On the other side if complexity is low but value of material is high, efficient recycling will be new goal.

After formulating a model, they studied on a robust case study to illustrate use of model. At the end of their study, they found that robust approach suits to design of reverse production systems. The systems mentioned in study were in high uncertain conditions and difficult to change. Also it's hard to formulate stochastic approach, because there is not enough information. So with that approach, they concluded that it can be developed new insights about reverse production systems in alternative conditions.

Manzini and Bindi (2009) studied strategic design in distribution context. They proposed that logistic networks design is important in supply chain management topic. According to them, there are not any models for strategic design of distribution and therefore they developed a framework as a contribution. Their goal was illustrating a framework for multilevel distribution system.

Their conclusion of previous studies was that they were usually focusing on only some part of all systems, like production, transportation, procurement. They classified logistic decisions by planning types (strategic/tactical/operational) and process types (purchase and production/distribution/supply). For example concepts in the field of intersection of strategic design and purchase and production were,

- Selection of suppliers
- Production plants capacity
- Location of production facilities

Concepts in the field of intersection of strategic design and distribution were,

- Distribution network configuration
- Transportation modes

Concepts in the field of intersection of strategic design and supply were,

- Selection of channels
- Single or multi sourcing
- Strategic sales
- Planning of forecasting

In methodology stage, they implemented three different strategies for their study. Following this, they included a multi-period mixed programming model, short time planning and trips organization. For strategic design, they presented a section as a case study of strategic design.

For example, Model 1 included some hypotheses in itself, including single period, single product, multi-level, single sourcing and single channel. For that case study authors presented a comparative table that includes current cost contributions and expected cost contributions. According to new configuration, total cost can be decreased 11%, if fixed costs reduced significantly.

As the result of this study, authors concluded that 11% percent advantage would be thousands of dollars for a year in a large-scale economy. With integration of logistics services, new methods and applications would help to organizations and managers. Using complex distribution systems with effective integrated tools would support decision-making process of managers and minimize management costs.

Rezapour and Farahani (2010) included strategic design in their study as a design tool for centralized supply chain networks. These supply chain networks have rival chain and they are in markets with price-depended demand conditions. Two chain in the study have products in retail markets and they are competitive to each other.

They, studied modelling of behaviours in chains, attained conditions of equilibrium, formulated finite-dimensional variational inequality and figured out it by a modified projection method. They produced properties of equilibrium pattern as existence and uniqueness dimensions. From strategic point of view, their models includes decisions of strategic facility locations, which effect tactical inventory and transporting decisions.

They discussed sensitivity analysis of some parameters. These parameters included market shares, total income, total cost and equilibrium prices. They also studied the total profits of chains resulting from several marketing decisions.

As the conditions and environment of chains, they included;

1. Facility specifications
2. Market demands
3. Networks' cost functions
4. Chains' competitions

After that they formulated a mathematical model and included equilibrium condition, qualitative properties, algorithm and numerical example.

As the result stage of study, they demonstrate a model with numerical example and discuss how financial terms behave according to marketing activities. These financial terms refer to cost, income, price and profits; and the marketing activities refer to brand loyalty, brand positioning and advertising. Their conclusion was, if market share increases, managers in both chains should try reducing self-price effect using brand loyalty and should use marketing activities to have more continual brand switching. This reducing activity of self-price effect with increasing crosspiece effect together contribute to more profit, in a condition that income increasing rate is greater than total cost increasing rate.

Their suggestions for following research were; adapting their models to different random demands, and extending their models to multi-criteria.

Lin et al. (2006) researched distribution systems in terms of strategic design in a economy of scale context. Their formulation and analyze were based on multi-echelon, multi-product distribution systems and a strategic design model was for-mulated. Their target in this study were formulating a strategic design model for multi-level distribution systems.

Design decisions are related to total cost and service level. From strategic point of view, decisions are long-term decisions which include inventory levels, investment of facilities and transport channel selections.

Some of decisions were included in this study, some of them are;

• Distribution center amount and places,
• Consolidation center amount and places,
• Products' inventory levels at distribution centers,
• Shipment routes from plants to distribution centers.

According to the authors' previous findings, studies in the literature are concen-trated in four basic areas.

1. Location Models of Facilities which are uncapacitated
2. Covering Models aims to maximal stage
3. Uncertain demands conditions and strategic production/distribution design
4. Concave-cost network flow problem

The aim of their study to research determining;

- Location of distribution and consolidation centers regionally,
- Transportation option for products from plant to retail outlets.
- Inventory level of each required product for each distribution center.

After they presented their problem, they formulated a model with some decision variables, sets, subscripts and input parameters. Decisions variables refer to, stages of consolidation and distribution centers, transported product volumes and product stock levels. Sets and subscripts are; plants, distribution centers, retailers, products. Lastly input parameters refer to, distances (between plants, distribution centers and consolidation centers), shipping cost, fixed cost etc.

In addition to their model, they presented an illustrative example in their study that show their overall distribution system.

Results of this study included a solution procedure. One of the elements of that procedure was a repeated use of greedy heuristic approach for distribution and consolidation center locations. The solution procedure was also tested to evaluate quality of that procedure, therefore some problems were solved. For all problems the optimal solutions were found and the procedure has valuable potential for solving large problems.

Lin and Yang (2011) studied strategic design subject with public bicycle systems in terms of service level considerations. They proposed a model that aims to find out bike station related concepts (amount and locations), bike paths connecting stations and their network structure, travel paths for users. In this find out process, they also considered users' and investors' interests. Similar to previous studies, they set an example to illustrate the proposed models. Finally a sensitivity analysis was implemented, to have better insights about how parameters affect the system design.

Authors firstly indicated that there were few studies about strategic design of public bicycle systems and the motivation of them is that fewness. Their study had a mathematical formula that had integrated approach.

The contributions of this study can be summarized in three main headings:

1. Previous studies on bicycle systems had a safety related approach. Authors did not find any studies about network design and location determination. So this study had a new approach and developed a mathematical model.
2. The model in study was designed by a practical approach, not only for user but also for investors. User side had parameters like bike availability at stations, travel costs and demand coverage level. Investors side had parameters like bike station setup costs, bike lanes setup costs and bike inventory costs.
3. Study has a part consisting of example and sensitivity analysis.

Their suggestions for future research were firstly approaching to network structure by existing street structure. Because their models did not consider it currently. This approach could be practical. Secondly, demand variation could be an important for evaluation. Demand for travel changes day by day and this changement influence system design, also choices of routes. Thirdly, inventory level for rental stations is not good enough, as reusing not accounted. Including reusing calculations would result more accurate prediction.

Tuzkaya et al. (2011) researched strategic design subject in terms of reverse logistic networks, they also examined application of this in white goods industry for Turkey country. Environment problems were increasing and actions had to be taken in regard to these problems and concerns of customers, governments and companies, therefore reverse logistics was an interesting subject to research. In their study, they used a multi-objective model and presented a new methodology. Their new methodology had two stages, first one for centralised return center, second one for reverse logistics network design. As in previous studies examined in this chapter, they implemented their methodology to a white goods industry case in Turkey.

Their methodology consisted of five phases and phase 1 was the process which initialisation process took place. General data for network was collected and RLN design model was presented. Phase 2 was the process which utilisation of methodology process took place. In phase 3, an algorithm was formed for solving RLN design problem, with data summed in phase 1 and phase 2. They analysed the results in phase 4, and results were proposed, in phase 5.

Their suggestion for future research was investigating of maximising utilisation of resources integratedly. Another point they discussed was uncertainty. Reverse logistics systems had uncertain nature itself and this uncertainty was related to return volumes, return qualities and return times. They also indicated that some type of uncertainties could be studied with sensitivity analysis.

Vila et al. (2009) investigated strategic design in terms of supply chain in the forest industry. More specifically, the production-distribution networks in lumber industry have been examined in a market-oriented approach. In their methodology, they had a sample average approximation (SAA) method which is used with Monte Carlo sampling. Results showed that their approach performs better than deterministic models which rely on averages. At the end of the study, their decision system implemented as a demonstration to see how it could help to cope with strategic issues. The implementation area was East-Canada and sector was lumber industry.

The methodology used in this study could indicate relationship between opportunities took place in market and resources of production-distribution. Previous studies in literature focused on optimizing supply chain in regards to future demand expectations. Their stochastic programming model take into account different market environments and try to capture profitable situations by prepositioning company.

Their findings presented that their approach had advantage over deterministic models which are relying on averages.

References

American Marketing Association, A. (2017). *Definition of marketing*. Retrieved November 2017, from https://www.ama.org/AboutAMA/Pages/Definition-of-Marketing.aspx

Bowman, C., & Asch, D. (1987). *Strategic management*. London: Macmillan Education.

Bratton, J., & Gold, J. (2012). *Human resource management: Theory and practice*. Basingstoke: Palgrave Macmillan.

Brown, B. J., & Clow, J. E. (2008). *Introduction to business*. Woodland Hills, CA: McGraw Hill.

Burkhardt, H. (2009). On strategic design. *Educational Designer*, 1–49.
Burrow, J. L., Kleindl, B., & Everard, K. E. (2008). *Business principles and management* (12th ed.). Mason, OH: Thomson.
Chaffee, E. E. (1985). Three models of strategy. *Academy of Management Review, 10*(1), 89–98.
Chandler, A. D. (1990). *Strategy and structure: Chapters in the history of the industrial enterprise* (Vol. 120). Cambridge: MIT Press.
Djellal, F., Francoz, D., Gallouj, C., Gallouj, F., & Jacquin, Y. (2003). Revising the definition of research and development in the light of the specificities of services. *Science and Public Policy, 30*(6), 415–429.
Harlow, R. F. (1976). Building a public relations definition. *Public Relations Review, 2*(4), 34–42.
Hill, C. W., Jones, G. R., & Schilling, M. A. (2014). *Strategic management: Theory: An integrated approach*. Boston, MA: Cengage Learning.
Hutton, J. G. (1999). The definition, dimensions, and domain of public relations. *Public Relations Review, 25*(2), 199–214.
Investopedia. (2017a). *Finance*. Retrieved November 2017, from https://www.investopedia.com/terms/f/finance.asp
Investopedia. (2017b). *Research and development – R&D*. Retrieved November 2017, from https://www.investopedia.com/terms/r/randd.asp
Jemison, D. B. (1981). The contributions of administrative behavior to strategic management. *Academy of Management Review, 6*(4), 633–642.
Kotler, P., & Keller, K. L. (2012). *Marketing management* (14th ed.). London: Pearson.
Kudla, R. J. (1980). The effects of strategic planning on common stock returns. *Academy of Management Journal, 23*(1), 5–20.
Lin, J. R., & Yang, T. H. (2011). Strategic design of public bicycle sharing systems with service level constraints. *Transportation Research Part E: Logistics and Transportation Review, 47*(2), 284–294.
Lin, J. R., Nozick, L. K., & Turnquist, M. A. (2006). Strategic design of distribution systems with economies of scale in transportation. *Annals of Operations Research, 144*(1), 161–180.
Madura, J. (2007). *Introduction to business*. Boca Raton, FL: Florida Atlantic University.
Manzini, R., & Bindi, F. (2009). Strategic design and operational management optimization of a multi stage physical distribution system. *Transportation Research Part E: Logistics and Transportation Review, 45*(6), 915–936.
Meroni, A. (2008). Strategic design: Where are we now? Reflection around the foundations of a recent discipline. *Strategic Design Research Journal, 1*(1), 31–38.
Mintzberg, H. (1978). Patterns in strategy formation. *Management Science, 24*(9), 934–948.
Mintzberg, H., & Waters, J. A. (1989). Of strategies, deliberate and emergent. In *Readings in strategic management* (pp. 4–19). Basingstoke: Macmillan Education.
Mont, O. K. (2002). Clarifying the concept of product–service system. *Journal of Cleaner Production, 10*(3), 237–245.
Montuori, A. (2003). From strategic planning to strategic design: Reconceptualizing the future of strategy in organizations. *World Futures: The Journal of General Evolution, 59*(1), 3–20.
Nag, R., Hambrick, D. C., & Chen, M. J. (2007). What is strategic management, really? Inductive derivation of a consensus definition of the field. *Strategic Management Journal, 28*(9), 935–955.
Porter, M. E. (1998). *Competitive advantage: Creating and sustaining superior performance with a new introduction*. New York: The Free Press.
Realff, M. J., Ammons, J. C., & Newton, D. (2000). Strategic design of reverse production systems. *Computers & Chemical Engineering, 24*(2), 991–996.
Rezapour, S., & Farahani, R. Z. (2010). Strategic design of competing centralized supply chain networks for markets with deterministic demands. *Advances in Engineering Software, 41*(5), 810–822.

Shrader, C. B., Mulford, C. L., & Blackburn, V. L. (1989). Strategic and operational planning, uncertainty, and performance in small firms. *Journal of Small Business Management, 27*(4), 45–60.

Tuzkaya, G., Gülsün, B., & Önsel, Ş. (2011). A methodology for the strategic design of reverse logistics networks and its application in the Turkish white goods industry. *International Journal of Production Research, 49*(15), 4543–4571.

Vila, D., Beauregard, R., & Martel, A. (2009). The strategic design of forest industry supply chains. *INFOR: Information Systems and Operational Research, 47*(3), 185–202.

Strategic Packaging and Labelling Policies Affecting Purchase Intention Towards Harmful Products

Murat Aktan

Abstract Characteristics of effective health warning labels (HWLs) were determined strategically by the collaboration of variety of stakeholders such as international, governmental and non-governmental organizations. As one of the important stakeholders Health Ministry of Turkey requires cigarette companies to put HWLs on cigarette packs in addition to other anti-smoking measures. Yet, Turkey still ranks 10th in smoking prevalence in Europe. In this respect, this research aims to understand whether strategic packaging and labelling regulations are effective and the determinant of effective HWLs on Turkish sample. This study explores the influence of believability levels of HWLs on individuals' perceived health and social risks associated with smoking. Furthermore, total effect of these variables on the effectiveness of HWLs was assessed. Relations within the model were analysed with Partial Least Square Structural Equation Modelling (PLS-SEM) software WarpPLS. In data collection, survey link was administered online and 432 valid responses were obtained from non-smokers (210) and smokers (212). Findings revealed that the believability of the HWLs' content is an essential element to boost perceived health and social risks of smoking as well as increasing the intention to abstain from smoking regardless of participants' smoking status. Surprisingly, for both subsamples perceived health risks of smoking was found to have no influence on smoking intentions. But social risk perceptions positively encouraged individuals to abstain from smoking. Therefore, to discourage smoking, social costs of smoking such as peer disapproval, yellow teeth and bad breath etc. should be emphasized on cigarette packs rather than relying on only health risks. In addition, the structural model exhibited that relations between two paths (believability levels of the HWLs' content → effectiveness of HWLs; the perceived social risks of smoking → effectiveness of HWLs) were stronger for the smokers' subsample. Therefore, designing convincing warnings in addition to emphasizing social risks of smoking are more effective to motivate smokers than non-smokers. Hence, health promoters must make sure that health warnings are perceived as credible prior to implementation. They should also

M. Aktan (✉)
Nevsehir Hacı Bektaş Veli University, Nevsehir, Turkey
e-mail: murat.aktan@nevsehir.edu.tr

© Springer International Publishing AG, part of Springer Nature 2018

131

H. Dincer et al. (eds.), *Strategic Design and Innovative Thinking in Business Operations*, Contributions to Management Science,
https://doi.org/10.1007/978-3-319-77622-4_7

take smoking status into account rather than pursuing a mass communication strategy targeting the whole population.

1 Introduction

The tobacco industry has very high profit levels in comparison with other industries worldwide. To be more precise, total profits of the top six transnational tobacco companies outweighed the combined profits of the Coca-Cola Company, Walt Disney, FedEx, Google, McDonald's and Starbucks in 2013. In addition, top cigarette companies account for the sales over 85% of all cigarettes smoked globally. Each cigarette company also creates gross revenues which are comparable to the GDP of a small country (Eriksen et al. 2015). However, smoking has serious health consequences to individuals in addition to making an important burden on economy due to health expenditures caused by smoking.

According to "World Health Organization" (2015) smoking is the cause of about six million deaths every year. It is also estimated that by 2020 eight million people will have died globally from health problems caused by smoking (Murray and Lopez 1997). While smoking is a dangerous habit with long term losses to individual's health, it also negatively affects economy since increased health expenditures make an important burden. Ekpu and Brown (2015) reported that 15% of health care costs are due to diseases caused by tobacco products in high-income countries. Therefore, to diminish harms of smoking on individuals and the economy, governments worldwide have been taking serious steps to reduce smoking prevalence.

The Turkish Health Ministry has been implementing several measures to diminish smoking rates in Turkey since 2004. Turkish government has passed numerous legislations such as the bans on cigarette advertising and smoking in closed public areas as well as increased taxes on tobacco products. While there has been a decrease in the number of cigarettes sold in Turkey, it has not dropped at a desirable rate. In 2004, over 108 billion packs were sold. As of 2015, according to Turkish Tobacco and Alcohol Market Regulatory Authority, Turkey is still selling over 103 billion packs a year (Tapdk 2015). Therefore, smoking is still prevalent problem in Turkey, which ranks 10th in smoking prevalence in Europe. In addition, 24% of individuals aged 15 years and over are daily cigarette consumers (OECD 2014). To reduce smoking prevalence, cigarette companies have been entailed to place health warning labels (HWLs) on cigarette packs since 2010. In this respect, there are 14 different HWLs presently on use that elicit the health consequences of smoking. However, there is still a lack of research investigating the efficacy of these HWLs on the smoking habits of Turkish people.

Smoking problem is of interest to marketing and health communication scholars as designing an effective HWL requires careful communication strategy. In other words, adopting marketing theory to health promotion is believed to help to address the right health messages to the right targeted population. Although there are numerous research about smoking behaviour the majority of these studies were mostly conducted in high income countries, and research on high income countries illustrated that pictorial health warning encourages individuals to abstain from smoking. Yet there is a need of research focusing middle-and low-income countries as individuals risk perception tend to vary with socioeconomic factors (Siahpush et al. 2006). Therefore this research aims to explore the effectiveness levels of HWLs in general and determinants of an effective HWL in an upper-middle income country, Turkey.

2   Strategic Design of HWLs

In the context of profit oriented manufacturing firms, strategic design refers to including stakeholders in the process of generating, providing and delivering solutions, thereby enabling firms to have sustainable profitable growth under changing market conditions. Hence, strategic design establishes system of tools, rules and beliefs facilitating firms to adapt the changes in external environment, helping them operate in a sustainable manner (Meroni 2008). When it comes to non-profit institutions, strategic design ensures that actions serving for public interests or the needy people are planned systematically through the collaboration of all stakeholders for the purpose of improving individuals' live and society.

The World Health Organization's (WHO) Framework Convention on Tobacco Control (FCTC) was first coined by Ruth Roemer and Allyn Taylor in 1993 to develop international conventions to advance global health. The FCTC treaty entered into force in 2005. Since then, it has required partnerships between WHO (World Health Organization), UN (United Nations), bodies, governments, NGOs and academia (Jackson et al. 2007). The treaty also has entailed concurrent restrictions on advertising, sponsorship, and promotion and implements strong packaging and labelling requirements. Therefore, FCTC opens the way for partnerships across governmental and non-governmental organizations (NGOs) and even the tobacco companies, which results in a combination of integrated actions. In other words, variety of entities employ health promotion strategies at multiple levels, serving for the same goal (Center for Disease Control and Prevention 2017). Therefore, HWLs represent one of the important pillars of this integrated health promotion strategy in addition to other measures as high tax on cigarette prices, bans on smoking in public areas, and compulsory broadcasting of informative ads depicting harms of smoking etc.

Packaging and labelling regulations of cigarette packs were determined after extensive research to ensure that warnings on packages are effective in smoking abstinence. Article 11 of FCTC which was ratified by more than 175 countries dictated that warnings cover 50% or more, but no less than 30% of the principal display areas of the pack and include pictures. It also provides guidance on other design elements such as the warning size, language, rotation of the warnings, message content and location (WHO 2018). In this respect, characteristics of HWLs were not designed by individual efforts of any country and organization, but were reached systematically through the collaboration of variety of stakeholders. Only in that way, HWLs align with other preventive measures for the purpose of preventing smoking behaviour. But still, the question whether strategic design of cigarette packs is really effective in terms of smoking abstinence remains not completely answered. Although, there is extensive research investigating the effectiveness of HWLs, they offer controversial results.

2.1 Effectiveness of HWLs

Effectiveness of HWLs has recently attracted researchers' interest especially after governments entailed cigarette companies to place HWLs on cigarette packs as a part of their strategic packaging policies. The first research on the effectiveness of HWLs appeared in early 2000s and up to recently much has been done, but the available literature seems not to reach a consensus on whether HWLs are really effective to abstain from smoking. In their pioneering research, Hammond, Fong, McDonald, Brown and Cameron (2004) illustrated that nearly half of their research subjects tend to ignore on-pack warnings. Another important study examining HWLs' effectiveness revealed that although individuals reported that they perceived on-pack HWLs as effective, it did not represent reality. Applying fMRI (Functional Magnetic Resonance Imaging) and SST (Steady-State Typography) techniques, researchers found out that HWLs increased the desire to smoke (Lindstrom and Underhill 2010). In this respect, some previous international researches suggest that it is hard to determine whether HWLs are indeed effective in smoking prevention (Bhatti 2004; Glock et al. 2012; Cheron 2015; Andreeva and Konstantin 2011). On the other hand, there is also some research illustrating that HWLs eliciting serious health consequences give rise to negative intentions towards smoking (Willemsen 2005; Peters et al. 2007), and HWLs raise awareness of smoking health harms and quitting benefits (Veer and Rank 2012). A recent study by Mazlum and Mazlum (2014) also depicted that HWLs were effective on university students to prevent smoking, thus had to be continued.

Considering controversial findings in previous research the real impact of HWLs is still under question since there are other tobacco control measures as well such as tax increases and smoking bans (Ruiter and Kok 2005). Therefore, the decrease in smoking can be attributed to other measures rather than only HWLs, and it is hard to distinguish the real impact of HWLs on smoking behaviour. Hence, it is off great importance to describe the determinants of effective HWL.

The first constituent of an affective advertisement is its believability. An advertisement is not judged as "believable" unless it leaves the individuals with that attitude, belief, or intention toward the product which was intended in the first place by the advertiser. As everyone has pre-existing beliefs, advertisement contents seeking to change individuals attitude is sure to run into a conflict. Therefore, it is prerequisite to have convincing and credible content to affect individuals' intention favourably (Maloney 1963). On-pack warnings are made up of textual warnings and visual images which aim to change individuals' perception of smoking. Thus, health promoters wouldn't disagree with the statement that "HWL is an advertisement that promotes healthy behaviour, and they must be believable in the first place to make the desired impact against smoking." In addition, previous research has shown that once one believes that smoking behavior is unhealthy, unwise and unattractive, these beliefs deter them from smoking (Ajzen and Fishbein 1980). Therefore, as a prerequisite, HWLs posing health consequences must be believable to increase negative attitudes towards smoking (Beltramini 1988; Bansal-Travers et al. 2011). In other words, when HWLs' credibility suffers their effectiveness is hampered (Kees et al. 2006). Following these discussions, the first hypothesis of the research is established.

H_1: Believability of HWLs increases the effectiveness of HWLs.

Risk perception has been widely studied by many scholars. A noteworthy study by Fischhoff et al. (1978) developed a model showing that risk can be characterized in two factors. In their study, the first dimension of risk is termed tread which relates scale of the risk and the degree to which it harms innocent individuals. The second dimension is termed knowledge as it pertains to the degree to which the risk is understood and how observable its consequences are. These two dimensions jointly determine how individuals react when they encounter with a risky situation. In this respect, no one would disagree with the statement that consequences of any risk factors should be explained properly to change behaviour. Therefore, a careful risk communication strategy is needed to enlighten individuals about harm and scale of the risks involved in smoking. In its original definition, risk communication refers to any purposeful exchange of information about health or environmental risks between interested parties (Covello et al. 1986). Although that definition seems to limit the scope of risk communication to health and environmental issues, this limitation refers to only what is being communicated. Therefore, social consequences of risks are still crucial elements when communicating risk (Renn and Levine 1991). In addition, for those who communicate risk, credibility is a precious commodity since it affects the way people process information and subsequently perceive risk (Trumbo and McComas 2003). Therefore, the fact that health warning messages are perceived as plausible is believed to be important to persuade individuals about the health and social risks of smoking. Hammond (2011) illustrated that increases in risk perceptions are associated with believability of cigarette HWLs. In addition, adolescents reporting the cigar warnings to be very believable are less likely to be susceptible to using cigarettes as they perceive smoking as risky (Kowitt et al. 2016). Hence, credibility and believability of a message is off great importance in the formation of individuals' risk perceptions toward smoking.

H_2: Believability of HWLs increases negative health risk perceptions of smoking.
H_3: Believability of HWLs increases negative social risk perceptions of smoking.

People's evaluations of any behaviour as risky form negative attitude towards it. Hence, risk perceptions of smoking is expected to encourage reduction in smoking. Previous research revealed that HWLs posing serious health risks are more effective in persuading individuals not to smoke (Cameron and Williams 2015) and smokers who perceive greater health risks of smoking are more likely to quit smoking successfully (Nourjah et al. 1994). Followingly, hypothesis 4 is established.

H_4: Perceived health risks of smoking positively influence the effectiveness of HWLs.

On the contrary, literature also suggests that HWLs may not always result in behavior change as individuals' positive reactions to self-reported questionnaires evaluating HWLs do not necessarily mean that they will display the same positive reactions (Ruiter and Kok 2005). Furthermore, this research only concentrates on how smoking intentions can be reduced as actual behavior change may be attributed to different factors such as smoking bans; therefore, the following hypothesis is formed.

In addition to health risks, social risks of smoking such as repelling others with bad breath, having yellow teeth and disapproval from peers and social environment can deter individuals from smoking (Dalton et al. 1999; Kim 2006). In Turkey, there has been a negative atmosphere toward smoking for quite a while and smoking is only allowed in designated places, within public spaces. Therefore, smokers at present have to bear more social risks in addition to health risks since smoking has become socially more stigmatized (Chuang and Huang 2012). Considering the discussion above, the following hypothesis is designed:

H_5: Perceived social risks of smoking positively influence the effectiveness of HWLs.

Finally, it is also believed that relations between believability perceptions of warnings, perceived risks of smoking and effectiveness of HWL would depend on smoking frequency. Based on terror management theory, death is an inevitable end and when individuals are faced with their own mortality, they develop variety of mechanisms to protect themselves from anxiety (Veer and Rank 2012). In this respect, some individuals are inclined to engage in a particular dangerous behaviour despite the mortality risk associated with that behaviour. By this way, they relieve anxiety and manage distress by bolstering their self-esteem (Hansen et al. 2010; Veer and Rank 2012). This behavioural phenomenon has the potential to help our understanding of why smokers and non-smokers possibly pursue different reactions when they both are exposed to same warning label. In fact, it is believed that smokers are more likely base their self-esteem on smoking than non-smokers. A study on U.S. university students illustrated that when individuals were stimulated with same cigarette health warning labels, smokers showed higher levels of anxiety in comparison to non-smokers (Moore et al. 2011). Hence, it is not surprising if one can expect that smokers would display more defensive behaviours than non-smokers to relieve their distress. In line with that, previous research found that heavy smokers were less likely to consider on-pack health warnings influential compared to non-smokers (Hammond and Parkinson 2009). Thus smoking increases their self-esteem. Other than terror management theory, another possible explanation to this defensive behaviour comes from cognitive dissonance theory. According to cognitive dissonance theory, dissonance or discomfort occurs when an individual acts in a way that is inconsistent with her beliefs and attitudes. One alternative to resolve this inconsistency is to change perception of action. In other words, one thinks about her action in a different context so that it no longer appears to be inconsistent with her beliefs and attitudes (Schiffman et al. 2008). In smoking terms, when smokers have negative attitude towards smoking but still continue smoking, they feel discomfort. Unless they quit smoking, the only way to resolve this problem is to change how they perceive smoking behaviour. In fact, smokers tend to perceive the warnings depicting health consequences as exaggerated and unconvincing, thus changing their perception of smoking. Also not surprisingly, smokers in general do not perceive smoking as much risky as non-smokers. Some of them even believe that their likelihood of developing lung cancer is no more than an average smoker (Weinstein et al. 2005). In other words, smokers are not willing to admit that smoking is very risky to them, thus reflecting defensive optimism (Hahn and Renner 1998), and smokers are in an attempt to reduce their cognitive dissonance to rationalize their unhealthy behaviour (Hammond and Parkinson 2009). Finally, Elaboration Likelihood Model can also provide an important clue to prevent smoking. According to Elaboration Model, attitude change depends on the importance of the message to the receiver. If the message relates to an important issue for the receiver, information is processed rationally. On the other hand, peripheral route will be pursued if the message content is perceived as irrelevant for the receiver. In this respect, HWLs containing vivid and visual images may more likely attract non-smokers who will follow peripheral route. In contrast, smokers are expected to pursue the central route which requires an elaboration to process the message content (O'Hegarty et al. 2006).

To sum up, theories such as Elaboration Likelihood Model, Terror Management Theory and Cognitive Dissonance Theory can be useful to understand the differences between the attitude of smokers and nonsmokers. Whilst, it is beyond the scope of this research to discuss these theories in a detailed manner, these theories still suggest that reactions to HWLs can change according to smoking status. Therefore, one can expect that smoking status must moderate the strength of the relationships between believability of HWLs, perceived health and social risks of smoking and the effectiveness of HWLs.

3   Objective of the Chapter

This research proposes an inclusive model integrating different constructs where the independent variables consist of believability levels of HWLs, health and social risks associated with smoking. The dependent variable of the model is the effectiveness of health warnings. In addition, smoking status is also included into the model to examine whether there are any differences in the relations between constructs across smokers and non-smokers. To put it differently, this study treats smoking status as a moderator variable and offers two models explaining HWLs' effectiveness for

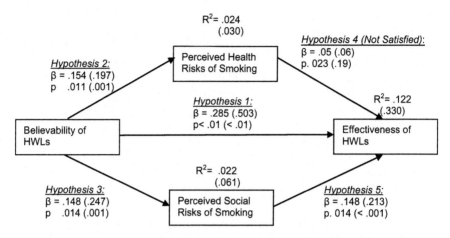

Fig. 1 Structural models for smokers and nonsmokers' subsamples with path coefficients, significance levels and explanatory powers. *Note*: Values for the nonsmokers's (smokers) subsample are outside (within) the brackets

smokers and non-smokers. Hence, this study examines whether the relations between constructs differ according to smoking status (See Fig. 1).

The fact that mainstream research on HWLs effectiveness were conducted in high income countries there is still a need of research focusing middle-and low-income countries. Individuals risk perception tend to vary with socioeconomic factors (Siahpush et al. 2006), therefore country specific differences on the risk perceptions of smoking will be expected. From this point of view, this research aims to explore the effectiveness levels of HWLs in general and determinants of an effective HWL in an upper-middle income country, Turkey.

4 Data and Methodology

4.1 Participants

Ethic approval was obtained prior to data collection from the Ethics Committee of Nevşehir Hacı Bektaş Veli University on 2 Dec. 2016 with an approval number of 84902927. Then the survey link was administered through a Turkish website that concentrates on higher educational issues (www.akademikpersonel.org). Participation in the research was on a voluntary basis and informed consent was obtained prior to data collection.

A total of 432 responses were obtained after the elimination of incomplete questionnaires. Both females and males constituted 50% of the sample, 48% were non-smokers and 52% were smokers. In terms of age, the largest number of respondents fell within the 17–22 year age interval (35%). Finally, participants

Table 1 Demographic characteristics for each subsample

Characteristics	Nonsmokers ($n = 210$)	Smokers ($n = 222$)
Age, n (%)		
17–22	79 (18%)	73 (17%)
23–28	63 (14%)	60 (14%)
29–34	35 (8%)	56 (13%)
35+	33 (8%)	33 (8%)
Gender, n (%)		
Female	113 (26%)	102 (24%)
Male	97 (22%)	120 (28%)
Education, n (%)		
High school or less	9 (2%)	12 (3%)
Bachelor or equivalent	118 (27%)	131 (31%)
Post-graduate	83 (19%)	79 (18%)

having bachelor or equivalent education levels constituted the largest population in the sample with 249 respondents (58%). Demographics data of the participants are shown in Table 1.

In addition, several Chi-square analyses were applied to ensure that smoker and non-smokers' subsamples are homogenous in terms of their characteristics. Results revealed that frequencies of age (χ^2: 4.827/df: 3; p. 0.185), gender (χ^2: 2.669 / df: 1; p. 0.123) and education levels (χ^2: 0.873 / df: 2; p. 0.646) do not vary with smoking status, which provided that comparisons can be made across smokers and non--smokers' subsample.

4.2 Measures

In the questionnaire, 14 HWLs which are presently on use in Turkey were firstly shown to participants. Afterwards, thanks to a four part questionnaire, variables in the model were measured. Participants were firstly asked to indicate the extent to which they perceive HWLs as believable in general. Hence, respondents were asked to use the semantic differential scale comprised of 5 bi-polar adjectives. Items derived from previous literature were as follows: (1) believable–unbelievable, (2) convincing–unconvincing, (3) reasonable–unreasonable, (4) easy to understand– hard to understand, (5) informative–uninformative (Beltramini 1988).

Effectiveness of HWLs was measured in part two of the questionnaire using 1 item semantic differential scale. Respondents were asked to respond a five-point scale question which was tailored to their smoking status, thus, non-smokers evaluated whether "HWLs reduce their curiosity and desire to try smoking", whereas smokers indicated whether "HWLs motivate them quit smoking".

In part three of the questionnaire, health and social risk perceptions of smoking were assessed with five statements. In this context, the five-point Likert scale was used and participants were asked to indicate their level of agreement with the given statements. Health risk perceptions of smoking were assessed with following statements: Smoking makes me "(1) contract various diseases, and (2) become addicted". Social risk perceptions of smoking were evaluated with three statements as follows: "Smoking makes me look (1) stupid and (2) filthy (Kim 2006)".

Final part of the questionnaire firstly measured respondents' smoking status, and participants were asked to indicate whether they smoke or not. Besides, characteristics of the respondents namely age, gender and education levels were also measured to ensure that smokers' and nonsmokers' subsamples are homogenous.

5 Results

This research adopts structural equation modelling (SEM). SEM is a very general statistical modelling technique and can be viewed as a combination of factor analysis and regression analysis. SEM is widely used in social behaviour research since it allows handling complex models which have different constructs affecting each other (Hox and Bechger 2007). This research, as mentioned earlier, aims to understand the interrelations between perceived health and social risks of smoking, believability of HWLs and perceived effectiveness of HWLs in general. Therefore, structural equation modelling was adopted in this study due to the complexity of the research model. In addition, as an alternative method to covariance based SEM (CB-SEM), Partial Least Square-SEM (PLS-SEM) was adopted. One of the strength of PLS-SEM over CB-SEM comes from its precise estimation ability of parameters at complex paths. In other words, PLS-SEM has greater statistical power than traditional CB-SEM. Therefore, with PLS-SEM, it is more likely to render a specific relationship significant when it is in fact significant in the population (Hair et al. 2016). PLS-SEM also does not require normal distribution and accounts for presence of skewness in distribution of variables (Kock and Lynn 2012). As seen in Table 2, perceived health risk scale had skewness and kurtosis values higher than 2 in absolute values for each subsample, thus signalling non-normal distributions (Field 2013). Therefore, PLS was considered appropriate method also to handle this non-normality issue. During analysis, PLS-SEM software WarpPLS 5.0 was used.

5.1 Measurement Models

After having examined the subsamples in terms of their demographics, the author assessed the measurement model through standardized factor loadings, convergent and discriminant validity. In this respect, he firstly implemented exploratory factor

Table 2 Measurement scale characteristics for each subsample

		BE	HR	SR	E
Nonsmokers' sample					
Square roots of AVE & Correlation between latent constructs	Believability (BE)	*0.885*	0.125	0.081	0.289
	Health Risks (HR)	0.125	*0.889*	0.356	0.000
	Social Risks (SR)	0.081	0.356	*0.843*	0.041
	Effectiveness (E)	0.289	0.000	0.041	*1.000*[b]
Composite reliabilities, block VIF and other measurement scale characteristics	Mean Score	2.752	4.685	4.131	2.897
	Standard Deviation	1.037	0.662	0.970	1.578
	Skewness	0.116	−2.976	−1.058	0.054
	Kurtosis	−0.537	10.845	0.499	−1.559
	Block VIF	1.051	1.004	1.052	n.a[a]
	Composite Reliability	0.878	0.883	0.831	1.000[b]
Smokers' sample					
Square roots of AVE & Correlation between latent constructs	Believability (BE)	*0.880*	0.189	0.182	0.521
	Health Risks (HR)	0.189	*0.876*	0.278	0.102
	Social Risks (SR)	0.182	0.278	*0.835*	0.294
	Effectiveness (E)	0.521	0.102	0.294	*1.000*[b]
Composite reliabilities, block VIF and other measurement scale characteristics	Mean Score	2.695	4.331	3.272	2.263
	Standard Deviation	1.010	0.962	1.146	1.270
	Skewness	0.092	−1.912	−0.260	0.756
	Kurtosis	−0.638	3.556	−0.820	−0.521
	Block VIF	1.069	1.061	1.040	n.a[a]
	Composite Reliability	0.873	0.869	0.822	1.000[b]

Notes: Square roots of AVEs are italic and shown in the diagonal
[a]Non applicable as the construct includes single indicator
[b]Square roots of AVE and composite reliabilities are equal to 1 as there is one indicator

analysis (EFA) to make sure that all items of believability were loading at least with 0.5 for each subsample. Results illustrated that the item "easy to understand" loaded weakly for both subsamples (smokers: 0.25; nonsmokers: 0.39), and it was eliminated. Subsequently, items namely "reasonable" and "informative" were also cancelled out as their factor loadings were "0.41" and "0.46" only for the nonsmokers'

Table 3 Loadings of indicators on their latent constructs for each subsample

	Believability factor	Health risk factor	Social risk factor	Effectiveness
Indicators for Nonsmokers' Sample				
Believability	*0.847*	0.043	0.012	0.086
Convincing	*0.922*	−0.043	−0.012	−0.086
Disease	0.029	*0.865*	0.049	0.030
Addiction	−0.029	*0.913*	−0.049	−0.030
Filthy	0.050	−0.039	*0.854*	−0.023
Stupid	−0.050	0.039	*0.832*	0.023
Effectiveness	0.000	−0.000	0.000	*1.000*
Indicators for Smokers' Sample				
Believability	*0.872*	0.048	0.044	−0.140
Convincing	*0.852*	−0.055	−0.050	0.161
Disease	0.079	*0.917*	0.060	−0.004
Addiction	−0.073	*0.965*	−0.055	0.004
Filthy	−0.173	−0.032	*0.956*	0.233
Stupid	0.163	0.031	*0.961*	−0.220
Effectiveness	0.000	0.000	0.000	*1.000*

sample. After these adjustments, believability scale was ended in two items: "believ-ability" and "convincing". Then reliability scores of the scales were evaluated for each subsample. Results revealed that believability and health risk scales achieved equal or slightly more than 0.7 Cronbach's α scores. Nevertheless, reliability scores of the two-item social risks scales were around 0.6 α levels for each subsample. As "α" will get lower values with the decrease in the number of items on the scale, reliability levels for social risk scales across subsamples were considered sufficient (Field 2013).

After having evaluated the scales, thanks to WarpPLS, the author firstly assessed the assumptions of PLS-SEM. Variance inflation factors (VIFs) are well below the recommended 3.30 criterion, hence, vertical and lateral collinearity assumptions were met (Kock and Lynn 2012). Afterwards, he evaluated convergent and discrim-inant validity of latent constructs. Discriminant validity was achieved as the square roots of AVE (average variance extracted) scores were higher than any correlation of that factor with another measure (Fornell and Larcker 1981). For each subsample, composite reliabilities of all factors were greater than 0.8 (See Table 2), and indicators loaded with more than 0.5 to their latent constructs (See Table 3 for items' loadings on their constructs), thus, all scales in the model achieved conver-gent validity for each subsample.

5.2 Structural Models

Having verified that the scales were valid, the author subsequently assessed the amount of variance explained by the independent variables, the path coefficients, and the overall explanatory power of the structural models. To test the hypotheses, two different structural models were developed as the first one represented smokers' sample and the second was for nonsmokers. The results of nonsmokers' sample suggest that the model explained 12% variation in effectiveness of HWLs, thus suggesting that the structural model provided a low explanatory power. However, this result can be attributed to other factors influencing the effectiveness of HWLs such as age, gender and cigarette prices since getting high explanatory power is not always easy in complex behavioral research. Besides, the nonsmokers' model still shows that all paths were significant except the one between effectiveness of HWL and health risks ($\beta = 0.05$, $p = 0.23$). Other paths' coefficients and significance levels were as follows: believability of HWL and perceived health risks ($\beta = 0.154$, $p = 0.011$), believability of HWL and perceived social risks ($\beta = 0.148$, $p = 0.014$), believability of HWL and effectiveness of HWL ($\beta = 0.285$, $p < 0.01$), perceived social risks and effectiveness of HWL ($\beta = 0.148$, $p = 0.014$) (See Fig. 1).

In contrary to nonsmokers, smokers' samples model explained 33% variation in effectiveness of HWL, thus providing that the structural model had an adequate explanatory power for smokers' subsample. As it was the case in the nonsmokers' sample, the path between "effectiveness of HWL and health risks" was also not significant for the smokers' subsample ($\beta = 0.06, p = 0.19$), thus being omitted from the structural model. In addition, path coefficients and significance levels attained in the smokers' subsample were relatively better as follows: believability of HWL and perceived health risks ($\beta = 0.197, p = 0.001$), believability of HWL and perceived social risks ($\beta = 0.247, p < 0.001$), believability of HWL and effectiveness of HWL ($\beta = 0.503, p < 0.001$), perceived social risks and effectiveness of HWL ($\beta = 0.213$, $p < 0.001$). For illustration purposes, the author depicted two structural models for each subsample showing the set of relationships (See Fig. 1).

6 Discussion

This study examined the constituents of effective HWLs namely, believability of HWLs, perceived health and social risks of smoking. In addition, it sheds light on how independent constructs interact with each other and affect effectiveness perception of HWLs. Findings of PLS-SEM support the proposed model to a great extent as only one hypothesis had to be rejected. For each subsample perceived health risks of smoking does not significantly affect the intention to abstain from smoking (H_4 rejected), which is partially consistent with some previous literature suggesting that individuals are barely provoked by health risks. In other words, HWLs eliciting fearful consequences of smoking can be considered exaggerating and result in defensive responses, thus not always motivating individuals against smoking (Glock et al. 2012).

In addition, this research displays that focusing on social risks rather than health risks caused by smoking has a wider potential to deter smoking behavior as perceived social risks significantly affects smoking behavior for each subsample (H_5 accepted). Hence, it is believed that this finding makes an important contribution to health promotion literature. HWLs which are currently on use have little or no message content eliciting social consequences of smoking. Therefore, the author of this study believes that important potential to abstain smoking is neglected by health promoters and public policy makers. In this respect, developing new HWLs which highlight the social cost of smoking is believed to contribute in health promotion efforts.

Findings also revealed that believability of HWLs is the most critical element in terms for provoking negative behavioral intention towards smoking (H_1 accepted). As for each subsample, the more believable the message is the more negative feelings toward smoking is created, which shows how essential is to design plausible, convincing messages to promote healthy behavior. In addition, smokers are more influenced when they consider the message believable than nonsmokers as the path between believability and effectiveness of HWLs is stronger for the smokers' subsample. Hence, health promoters should pay attention to whether HWLs are perceived as credible especially when they design messages to smokers. In this respect, elaborating health messages in terms of believability and persuasiveness prior to implementation should be a preliminary part of a successful health message design.

In the structural models, despite having lower coefficients, regression between believability and health/social risk perceptions are still significant for both subsamples, thus providing that H_2 and H_3 are valid hypotheses for both subsamples. Also note that, believability of HWLs is regressed weakly on perceived health and social risks across nonsmokers whereas these relations are stronger for the smokers, suggesting that smokers' risk perceptions are more influenced with the believability perceptions than the nonsmokers. From this point of view, believability of the HWLs is a more crucial element for smokers than nonsmokers in enlightening individuals on social and health risks of smoking. Back to Cognitive Dissonance Theory, discomfort can occur when there is incongruence between one's attitude toward smoking and his real behaviour. The only solution to resolve this incongruence is to change one's negative perceptions about smoking, unless he/she is capable to quit smoking. Since it is not always easy to change behaviour and quit smoking, smokers are inclined to perceive HWLs as exaggerated and unconvincing, thus changing their attitudes toward smoking and HWLs. In this way, attitude and behaviour become congruent and discomfort problem is resolved. For instance, smokers can commence to believe that smoking is not as dangerous as it is depicted in HWLs. In addition to Cognitive Dissonance Theory, Elaboration Likelihood Model can also explain why believability of HWLs' content is found to be more important for the smokers' sample. As the theory suggests, the extent that the information contained in the message is related to one's self, receivers are more likely to make efforts to process the message content. This means that the receivers will use the central route and evaluate the message content systematically and in a rational way when the content relates to them. In contrast, when the message content is irrelevant, the receivers do not spend much time and effort to figure out what the message is about. Therefore, believability of any advertisement is assumed to gain more importance when the content is relevant to the receiver. When it comes to smoking behavior, since smokers are the ones who will bear the health and social risks of smoking, an advertisement depicting harm of smoking is related to their personal selves. Therefore, it is not surprising that they may seek believability in the first place more than nonsmokers since they tend to process HWLs' content systematically and rationally.

7   Conclusion

Based on strategic design perspective, contributions of all stakeholders should be considered prior to selecting and implementing HWLs. In this respect, research conducted in different country settings should be incorporated so that relevant and effective HWLs can be accessed for different populations. In contrast to mainstream research held in developed countries, this research is conducted in a less developed country where smoking prevalence is high especially at younger population. Therefore, this study is believed to provide some useful insights about HWLs for decision makers at international, governmental and non-governmental organizations.

This research revealed three important conclusions: (1) believability of HWLs is an important element in the development of health and social risks perceptions, along with the intention to avoid smoking (2) perceived health risks do not affect peoples' intention to abstain from smoking regardless of their smoking status and (3) influence of believability and perceived social risks on the intentions to abstain from smoking is stronger in the smokers than the nonsmokers sample.

Health promoters should ascertain the believability of the health warnings before implementation, thereby creating more effective HWLs against smoking. Although some previous research has suggested that perceived health risks have an influence on the intentions to avoid smoking, this study produced disapproving results and displayed that perceived health risks is ineffective to abstain individuals from smoking. Contrarily, perceived social risks proved to be of great importance for encouraging negative intention towards smoking behaviour. Therefore, social costs of smoking, such as repelling others or an individual's reduced self-esteem due to unhealthy physical appearance should also be emphasized in health promotion practices. Finally, this research concluded that using social risk perceptions along with the believability of HWLs are more relevant for smokers than nonsmokers in changing people's intentions to abstain from smoking. Hence, efforts should be made to design specific HWLs for promoting health to different populations with different backgrounds. In this respect, individuals can be clustered into groups according to their demographics and smoking status etc. Furthermore, identifying preferred brands of these clusters will enable communicating right anti-smoking messages to the right population. Thus, this study suggests that future research examine the impact of aforementioned or similar variables in their contribution to the formation of negative intention towards smoking. This will allow for a more comprehensive understanding of smoking behaviour.

To the extent of author's knowledge, strategic design perspective has not yet been fully adopted in smoking prevention literature. Rather, research in the field mainly concentrated on the effectiveness of HWLs but not the effects of other anti-smoking promotion campaigns and practices. Therefore, for future research, it is advised to investigate relative effects of other smoking preventive measures such as smoking bans in public areas, tax increases etc. In this respect, strategic design perspective which requires collaboration of all stakeholders should be adopted in future research.

Key Words Definitions

Health promotion Health promotion is the process of enabling people to increase control over, and to improve, their health. It moves beyond a focus on individual behaviour towards a wide range of social and environmental interventions.

Health warning labels Health warning labels are textual-and-pictorial warnings on cigarette packages concerning health effects of smoking.

Believability Capable of eliciting belief or trust.

Social marketing Social marketing is applying marketing principles and techniques to influence target audience behaviors that benefit society as well as the target audience.

Social risks Degree of the likelihood that one will be rejected by his peer group and lack his friends' support due to his behavior.

Health risks Degree of the likelihood that something could cause harm to people's health

Strategic design Strategic design refers to the use of and considering all stakeholders as partners in the process of generating, providing and delivering sustainable solutions.

References

Ajzen, I., & Fishbein, M. (1980). *Understanding attitudes and predicting social behavior*. Englewood Cliffs, NJ: Prentice Hall.

Andreeva, T. I., & Konstantin, S. K. (2011). Recall of tobacco pack health warnings by the population in Ukraine and its association with the perceived tobacco health hazard. *International Journal of Public Health, 56*(3), 253–262.

Bansal-Travers, M., Hammond, D., Smith, P., & Cummings, K. M. (2011). The impact of cigarette pack design, descriptors, and warning labels on risk perception in the U.S. *American Journal of Preventive Medicine, 40*(6), 674–682.

Beltramini, R. F. (1988). Perceived believability of warning label information presented in cigarette advertising. *Journal of Advertising, 17*(2), 26–32.

Bhatti, J. (2004). European smokers snuff out cigarette-package warnings. *Wall Street Journal*, https://www.wsj.com/articles/SB107652900146827150. Accessed 03.08.2017.

Cameron, L. D., & Williams, B. (2015). Which images and features in graphic cigarette warnings predict their perceived effectiveness? Findings from an online survey of residents in the UK. *Annals of Behavioral Medicine, 49*, 639–649.

Center for Disease Control and Prevention. (2017). Chapter 1. Engage stakeholders. https://www.cdc.gov/tobacco/stateandcommunity/tobacco_control_programs/surveillance_evaluation/evaluation_manual/pdfs/chapter1.pdf. Accessed 05.09.2017.

Cheron, E. (2015). Effect of graphic images in cigarette health warning: a call for stricter packaging regulation in Japan. *Journal of International Consumer Marketing, 27*(2), 137–151.

Chuang, S. H., & Huang, S. L. (2012). Changes in smoking behavior among college students following implementation of a strict campus smoking policy in Taiwan. *International Journal of Public Health, 57*(1), 199–205.

Covello, V. T., Von Winterfeldt, D., & Slovic, P. (1986). Communicating risk information to the public. *Risk Abstracts, 3*(4), 1–14.

Dalton, M. A., Sargent, J. D., Beach, M. L., Bernhardt, A. M., & Stevens, M. (1999). Positive and negative outcome expectations of smoking: implications for prevention. *Preventive Medicine, 29*(6), 460–465.

Ekpu, V., & Brown, A. (2015). The economic impact of smoking and of reducing prevalence: review of evidence. *Tobacco Use Insights, 8*(1), 1–35.

Eriksen, M., Mackay, J., Schluger, N., Gomeshtapeh, F., & Drope, J. (2015). *The tobacco atlas* (5th ed.). Atlanta, GA: American Cancer Society.

Field, A. (2013). *Discovering statistics using IBM SPSS statistics*. London: Sage.

Fischhoff, B., Slovic, P., Lichtenstein, S., Read, S., & Combs, B. (1978). How safe is safe enough? A psychometric study of attitudes toward technological risks and benefits. *Policy Sciences, 9*, 127–152.

Fornell, C., & Larcker, D. F. (1981). Structural equation models with unobservable variables and measurement error: Algebra and statistic. *Journal of Marketing Research, 18*(3), 382–388.

Glock, S., Müller, B. C., & Ritter, S. (2012). Warning labels formulated as questions positively influence smoking-related risk perception. *Journal of Health Psychology, 18*(2), 252–262.

Hahn, A., & Renner, B. (1998). Perception of health risks: How smoker status affects defensive optimism. *Anxiety, Stress and Coping, 11*(2), 93–112.

Hair, J. F., Jr., Hult, G. T. M., Ringle, C., & Sarstedt, M. (2016). *A primer on partial least squares structural equation modeling (PLS-SEM)*. Thousand Oaks, CA: Sage.

Hammond, D. (2011). Health warning messages on tobacco products: A review. *Tobacco Control, 20*(5), 327–337.

Hammond, D., & Parkinson, C. (2009). The impact of cigarette package design on perceptions of risk. *Journal of Public Health, 31*(3), 345–353.

Hammond, D., Fong, G. T., McDonald, P. W., Brown, K. S., & Cameron, R. (2004). Graphic Canadian cigarette warning labels and adverse outcomes: Evidence from Canadian smokers. *American Journal of Public Health, 94*(8), 1442–1445.

Hansen, J., Winzeler, S., & Topolinski, S. (2010). When the death makes you smoke: A terror management perspective on the effectiveness of cigarette on-pack warnings. *Journal of Experimental Social Psychology, 46*(1), 226–228.

Hox, J. J., & Bechger, T. M. (2007). An introduction to structural equation modeling. *Family Science Review, 11*, 354–373.

Jackson, S. F., Perkins, F., Khandor, E., Cordwell, L., Hamann, S., & Buasai, S. (2007). Integrated health promotion strategies: A contribution to tackling current and future health challenges. *Health Promotion International, 21*(suppl_1), 75–83.

Kees, J., Burton, S., Andrews, J. C., & Kozup, J. (2006). Tests of graphic visuals and cigarette package warning combinations: Implications for the framework convention on tobacco control. *Journal of Public Policy and Marketing, 25*, 212–223.

Kim, Y. (2006). The role of regulatory focus in message framing in antismoking advertisements for adolescents. *Journal of Advertising, 35*(1), 143–151.

Kock, N., & Lynn, G. S. (2012). Lateral collinearity and misleading results in variance-based SEM: An illustration and recommendations. *Journal of the Association for Information Systems, 13* (7), 546–580.

Kowitt, S. D., Jarman, K., Ranney, L. M., & Goldstein, A. O. (2016). Believability of cigar warning labels among adolescents. *Journal of Adolescent Health, 60*(3), 299–305.

Lindstrom, M., & Underhill, P. (2010). *Buyology: Truth and lies about why we buy.* New York: Crown, Double Day.

Maloney, J. (1963). Is advertising believability really important? *Journal of Marketing, 27*(4), 1–8.

Mazlum, F. S., & Mazlum, Ö. (2014). Sigara Paketlerinin Üzerindeki Görsel ve Sözel Uyarı Mesajlarının Üniversite Öğrencileri Üzerindeki Etkisinin İncelenmesi ve Yeni Öneriler. *E-Journal of New World Sciences Academy, 9*(1), 12–32.

Meroni, A. (2008). Strategic design: where are we now? Reflection around the foundations of a recent discipline. *Strategic Design Research Journal, 1*(1), 31–28.

Moore, J., Thorson, E., & Leshner, G. (2011). Terror management theory and anti-tobacco advertising: An experimental examination of influence of death explicit anti-tobacco messages on young adults. *Journal of Health & Mass Communication, 3*, 1–4.

Murray, C. J., & Lopez, A. D. (1997). Alternative projections of mortality and disability by cause 1990-2020: Global burden of disease study. *Lancet, 349*, 1498–1504.

Nourjah, P., Wagener, D. K., Eberhardt, M., & Horowitz, A. M. (1994). Knowledge of risk factors and risk behaviors related to coronary heart disease among blue and white collar males. *Journal of Public Health Policy, 15*(4), 443–459.

OECD. (2014). Health statistic how does Turkey compare? http://www.oecd.org/els/health-sys tems/Briefing-Note-TURKEY-2014.pdf. Accessed 03.04.2017.

O'Hegarty, M., Pederson, L. L., Nelson, D. E., Mowery, P., Gable, J. M., & Wortley, P. (2006). Reactions of young adult smokers to warning labels on cigarette packages. *American Journal of Preventive Medicine, 30*(6), 467–473.

Peters, E., Romer, D., Slovic, P., Jamieson, K. H., Wharfield, L., Mertz, C. K., & Carpenter, S. M. (2007). The impact and acceptability of Canadian-style cigarette warnings among U.S. smokers and nonsmokers. *Nicotine and Tobacco Research, 9*, 473–481.

Renn, O., & Levine, D. (1991). Credibility and trust in risk communication. In R. E. Kasperson & P. M. Stallen (Eds.), *Communicating risks to the public: International perspectives.* Dordrecht: Springer.

Ruiter, R. A. C., & Kok, G. (2005). Saying is not (always) doing: Cigarette warning labels are useless. *European Journal of Public Health, 15*, 329–330.

Schiffman, L. G., Kanuk, L. L., & Hansen, H. (2008). *Consumer behavior—An European outlook.* New York: Prentice Hall.

Siahpush, M., McNeill, A., Borland, R., & Fong, G. T. (2006). Socioeconomic variations in nicotine dependence, self-efficacy, and intention to quit across four countries: Findings from the International Tobacco Control (ITC) Four Country Survey. *Tobacco Control, 15*(suppl 3), iii71–iii75.

Tapdk. (2015). Yearly cigarette sales report of Turkey. http://www.tapdk.gov.tr/tr/piyasa-duzenlemeleri/tutun-mamulleri-piyasasi/tutun-mamulleri-istatistikleri.aspx. Accessed 03.04.2017.

Trumbo, C. W., & McComas, K. A. (2003). The function of credibility in information processing for risk perception. *Risk Analysis, 23*(2), 343–353.

Veer, E., & Rank, T. (2012). Warning! The following packet contains shocking images: The impact of mortality salience on the effectiveness of graphic cigarette warning labels. *Journal of Consumer Behaviour, 11*(3), 225–233.

Weinstein, N. D., Marcus, S. E., & Moser, R. P. (2005). Smokers' unrealistic optimism about their risk. *Tobacco Control, 14*(1), 55–59.

Willemsen, M. C. (2005). The new EU cigarette health warnings benefit smokers who want to quit the habit: Results from the Dutch continuous survey of smoking habits. *European Journal of Public Health, 15*, 389–392.

World Health Organization (WHO). (2015). Tobacco Fact Sheet. http://www.who.int/mediacentre/factsheets/fs339/en/. Accessed 03.04.2017.

World Health Organization (WHO). (2018). Guidelines for implementation of Article 11 of the WHO Framework Convention on Tobacco Control (Packaging and Labelling of Tobacco Products). http://www.who.int/fctc/guidelines/article_11.pdf?ua=1. Accessed 20.12.2017.

Mainstream Politics and the South African SOEs Dynamics

Mavhungu Abel Mafukata and Mavhungu Elias Musitha

Abstract State Owned Enterprises (SOEs) in South Africa are thought to be vulnerable to debt burdens, underinvestment, depreciation of assets, weak corporate governance and systems, and are characterised by massive corruption which render SOEs effectively unprofitable, inefficient and ineffective as development facilitator tool in the economy. This article used literature review, document analysis and Key Informant Interviews (KIIs) to investigate the role of party and state politics in the affairs of SOEs in post-apartheid South Africa. Mainstream politics have effect on the affairs of SOEs. Transformation of SOEs should begin by regularising mainstream politics and its influence in SOEs environment.

1 Introduction and Background to This Chapter

> When secretive evil deeds are covered in darkness they prosper. This work shines a light, revealing many uncomfortable truths
> Thuli Madonsela—former Public Protector (RSA) (Van Vuuren 2017).

State Owned Enterprises (SOEs) have evolved into universal tool to attain economic growth in global economics (Sungkar 2008). Governments all over the world have therefore been highly involved in the formation of SOEs in order to participate in active business in what Musacchio and Lazzarini (2012) call "state capitalism", "state corporatism" or "state entrepreneurship" (Radygin et al. 2015). South Africa also has a growing SOEs sector. The importance of SOEs in South Africa is demonstrated by the South African government's National Development Plan 2030 policy which has identified SOEs a critical and major driving

M. A. Mafukata (✉)
Vhutali Leadership and Management Institute, Limpopo, South Africa
e-mail: drmafukata@gmail.com

M. E. Musitha
Limpopo Tourism Agency, Polokwane, South Africa

© Springer International Publishing AG, part of Springer Nature 2018
H. Dincer et al. (eds.), *Strategic Design and Innovative Thinking in Business Operations*, Contributions to Management Science,
https://doi.org/10.1007/978-3-319-77622-4_8

151

force for the post-apartheid economy to meet its public service delivery and structural development imperatives and expectations (Chilenga 2016). Fourie (2014) mentions that "these enterprises were initially given a mandate to strengthen import-substitution industries and operated as exclusive franchises" to "ensure the country's [economic] sustainability and self-sufficiency". Gumede (2016) on the one hand reasoned that post-apartheid South Africa had sought to use SOEs in the redistribution of wealth to the formerly disadvantaged designated groups to achieve equitable redress of the socio-economic injustices meted out by apartheid on black people in particular. The African National Congress (ANC) also believed in a strong SOE economy to redress the effects of socio-economic inequalities between black South Africans and their white counterparts. Together with its tripartite alliance partners; the South African Communist Party (SACP) and Congress of South African Trade Unions (COSATU), the ANC had sought to achieve the objective firstly by nationalisation of the SOEs sector (Gumede 2016). Unforeseen multiple pressure factors however emerged to push the ANC to change its original position of intense state involvement in the SOEs sector to (full and partial) privatisation and promotion of state capitalism. The ANC's about turn was very much against the targets of COSATU and the SACP. The ANC, COSATU and SACP were expected to continue their long held "common history and core ideological persuasions which has been articulated as the National Democratic Revolution (NDR)" from since struggle days against apartheid into post-apartheid South Africa; that is, from 27 April 1994 at South Africa's first black-led democratic government which had replaced white apartheid minority rule of the National Party (NP) (Kuye and Cedras 2011). The COSATU and the SACP opined that the ANC has instead diverted to adopt what they called "the ANC government's adoption of the conservative macro-economic development programme; Growth Employment and Redistribution—GEAR" controversial policy which COSATU and the SACP thought was Thabo Mbeki's "neo-liberal orthodoxy" approach to the economy meant to be anti-workers and the poor (Beresford 2009). Privatisation has since been highly contentious in the tripartite alliance to the point of nearly tearing the alliance apart (Beresford 2009; Mfuku 2006). Views of the relevance and ability of privatisation in addressing the post-apartheid state's socio-economic challenges affecting in particular the majority of poor black population remain unresolved to date (Beresford 2009; Mfuku 2006). On many occasions COSATU has had several protests against the ANC government's insistence on privatisation—especially during President Thabo Mbeki's term of office, because Mbaki had apparently become too powerful through a centralised political power model around him and a weakened parliament (Klippenstein 2009). Privatisation was even duped "the new apartheid" in South Africa by various pressure groups such as workers and civic organisations (Mfuku 2006) and individuals such as Julius Malema who was the president of the African National Congress Youth League (ANCYL) and Zwelinzima Vavi who was the General Secretary of COSATU (Beresford 2009; Crowell 2012) for example. Julius Malema and Zwelinzima Vavi vehemently disdained Thabo Mbeki and his neo-liberal political and economic policies, and the two supported Jacob Zuma to become the president of the ANC and subsequently that of the country post-Polokwane 2007 ANC conference. Popular hypothesis amongst the ANC partners, and certain powerful individuals was that Jacob Zuma unlike Thabo Mbeki would be sympathetic and understanding to the block's anti-privatisation sentiments. From the Polokwane conference, signs were there that SOEs in South Africa would provide serious economic and political battle field. As it would reveal in this article, it has become increasingly hard to dismiss the influence of SOEs in the dynamics of mainstream politics and state administration, and in reverse the influence of the latter in the dynamics of SOEs in modern post-apartheid South Africa. To access the other, one needs the other. This assertion could be observed in the work of Karodia et al. (2017) in which the multi-pronged roles of business, political and state institutions are laid bare. Currently, the politics of SOEs, state administration, state security agencies, media houses, South African Reserve Bank (SARB), South African Revenue Services (SARS), mainstream Banking institutions such as ABSA, audit firms such as KPMG, office of the Public Protector, parliament, the courts, political parties and civic pressure groups such as AfriForum and so forth are at critical phase of wanting to dominate the political-economic space in what could be described as the battle for the sole of the South African public resources and state capture. Others want to exploit the system for access to resources while others want to protect the resources. Resultantly, this battle only produced South Africa's worst political-economic environments since apartheid. The country suffered the famous technical economic recession and downgrading by global ratings agencies (Karodia et al. 2017). The next section details the design of this chapter.

2 Structure of This Chapter

Although the battle for the soul of the economic resources in South Africa is fundamentally broad, this article only investigates these issues as they pertained to SOEs. In its discourse, the article would reveal and demonstrate how mainstream (party and state) politics were calculatively used by the political and business elite to influence, exacerbate and entrench a corrupt and poisoned SOEs environment leading to a systematic decline of performance and output of the SOEs sector. This article first and foremost begins its discourse by reviewing appropriate literature on several aspects of SOEs. Considering that the crisis affecting SOEs in South Africa has been new and most recent, empirical literature covering this aspect of the SOEs is scares and rare to come by, the review would therefore include substantial public media material and data. Print and electronic media always post some usable excerpts on these entities from time to time which this article also considered authentic and reliable for use in its discourse. First and foremost is to shed light on the nature of this article. This article does not attempt to be predictive in the same way as "predictive" literature are known to be. The article is neither "prophetic"; that is, trying to "predict" what would the future be in the SOEs in South Africa using empirical evidence or "prophesy"; that is, "predicting" without empirical evidence. Having looked into the weaknesses of predictive approach in socio-economic disciplines, this article shuns away from adopting this line because of the tendency of predictive literature's weakness of "creating over-zealousness and over-expectations at times" (Mafukata 2016). The volatility of the unfolding issues in the South African SOEs might provide impetus for predictive approach where catastrophic demises of SOEs might be opined as the impending end. Despite the mounting challenges in the sector, this article's discourse still expresses optimism; that is the SOEs in South Africa might be experiencing multiple complexities, but those complexities might still be correctable. Therefore, this article instead presents a documentary of the state of the SOEs in South Africa while trying to show what needs to be done to provide solutions to the complexities the sector currently faces. That there are complexities affecting the sector is therefore undebatable; the only issue is to determine the extent of the complexities. This article observes and examines the issues as they unfold in the SOEs, and as the issues unfold through current public debate. This article recognises the fact that South Africa has approximately 717 SOEs, and to therefore focus on all of them would be unrealistic and over ambitious. However, this article covers a number of SOEs with special focus on those which are currently on public scrutiny and debate such as Denel, Eskom, SABC, SAA, Transnet for example. This approach is a departure from (Chilenga 2016; Sadiki 2015) who adopt one entity case studies on the SAA and Eskom for example to analyse similar factors on SOEs competence in South Africa. In addition, for this article, data sourced from the case study entities were limited to data already in public use because, for example, most information on state assistance to the SOEs would be closely guarded and therefore not easily obtainable in public sources such as published literature such as papers and books for instance. Sadiki (2015) found that any such information is often confidential and secret. This article therefore used data collected from media sources; print and electronic amongst others. To clarify identified complex areas of reference in the article, especially on political paradigms, some key informants were purposively identified to assist with construction of meaning. In its discourse, this article however shies away from popular approach of wanting to display the "corruption is the cause" of every complexity affecting governance in post-colonial Sub-Saharan Africa (SSA) mostly common in literture on state and State Owned Enterprises (SOEs) governance and administration. In some cases, proponents of "corrupt Africa" trajectory lack authentic and verifiable evidence therefore displaying the shortcomings of Western-orientated literature on Africa and its issues. Western-orientated approaches usually play the man (Africa) and not the game (African issues). This article concludes its discourse by suggesting a policy framework for successful reforms which need to be effected in the SOEs in South Africa. Before "jumping" into the politics of SOEs in South Africa, it is imperative to follow the chronicle of global SOEs for its trends remain something of global attention.

3   Global State Owned Enterprises (GSOEs) Trends

For the sake of this chapter, these trends are categorised into general global trends and trends as they unfold in the South African SOEs.

3.1   State Owned Enterprises (SOEs) in Global Economics

Globally, state capitalism has seen the sudden rise of powerful global entities driven by state initiatives which are even listed amongst highly competitive global enterprises. Amongst the best known and highly rated enterprises are Brazil's Petroleo Brasileo S.A. (Petrobas) which is rated 28th in the Fortune Global 500 list of companies (Reddy 2016), Japan's Post Holdings, Sinopec, China National Petroleum and State Grid which have been listed in the top ten list of influential and highly revenued enterprises by the same Fortune Global 100. Fortune Global 100 rates companies according to their revenue strength. State Owned Enterprises (SOEs) have become so influential that global economic interest groups such as the World Bank (WB) and International Monetary Fund (IMF) for instance have all been advocating for governments to establish these entities to improve development imperatives (Sungkar 2008). These development advocacy groups opine that SOEs could become pillars of development—especially for developing regions as these entities provide governments with that critical role to play in the direction of economic systems of their respective economies (Sungkar 2008). The involvement of the state in the economy through SOEs would promote and protect public interests because the economy would have been placed "in the hands of the government" (Sungkar 2008). It is crucial to note however that this assertion would emerge to have notable critiques who would argue that state capitalism rather becomes a negative of the market because it could be exploited to produce a political outcome which threatens market capitalism—especially where governments used SOEs such as Development Banks for instance to influence the market (Musacchio and Lazzarini 2012). On the other hand, proponents of SOEs and state capitalism argued that the same provide governmental capital for states to actively participate in local and global economy in the interest of the citizenry for developmental imperatives (Musacchio and Lazzarini 2012). In addition, state capitalism through SOEs balances public interests with those of business because there are incidences where animosities against private business have been evident in societies around the world—especially where such animosities were demonstrated by intense political opposition on privatizations (Musacchio and Lazzarini 2012). Whilst SOEs have been highly regarded for their economic growth contributions in many regions of the world which have seen sudden expansion of these entities, these entities have for some reasons thought to be faced with weak and poor entity governance and management characterised by threat to viability, profitability, sustainability and efficiency. In most regions of the world- especially in developing economies, SOEs are poorly run, vulnerable to increased debt burdens, exposed to underinvestment, perpetual depreciation of assets, weak corporate governance structures and systems characterised by massive endemic corruption which render these entities irrelevant and ineffective as development facilitator tool of the particular economy. Muzapu et al. (2016) bring to the fore a sensitive issue affecting SOEs. Muzapu et al. (2016) postulates that SOEs contend with corrupt business executives such as CEOs, politicians and company employees who plunder company resources "by awarding themselves unjustifiably hefty salaries and allowances, flouting tender procedures, and diverting organizational property for private benefit" for instance.

While Muzapu et al. (2016) dealt with issues in the Zimbabwean SOEs, the South African situation is no different. The next section details trends in the South African SOEs environment.

3.2 State Owned Enterprises (SOEs) in South Africa

Chilenga (2016) opines that SOEs in South Africa are currently in public scrutiny mainly as a result of the strain they are going through—especially as it regards their unprofitability and massive losses they seem to be amassing for the state. Loss-making SOEs would always be burdensome to the state and public service (Sungkar 2008). Chilenga (2016) furthermore contends that major SOEs in South Africa are currently economically uncompetitive almost to dysfunctionality, insolvency and disintegration. Some are only surviving because the state is always providing huge bail-outs budgets to these entities. For example, Chilenga (2016) reveals that the South African Airways (SAA) for far too long has been relying on state bail-out budgets to keep its commercial competence and functionality alive. At some point, SAA has had debts amounting to approximately R ($1.5) billion with a bail-out of approximately 6.5 billion rands ($560 million). The national carrier has had some considerable state bail-out and guarantees assistance in January 2015 and September 2016 (Mhlanga et al. 2017). It has been revealed that SAA had in the past already received bail-out amounting to some R14billion (News24). The SAA is known for dubious spending. For example, a former CEO Mr Coleman Andrews has received R232million in settlements for his discontinued employment contract, Khaya Ngqula received R9.3 million while Andre Viljoen received R7million (News24) for similar labour practices of contract termination. The entity has, in a period of 11 years to date employed eight CEOs who have been paid huge sums of monies in salaries and settlements for terminated employment contracts. The SAA has a demonstrable unstable business environment characterised by poor and weak business decisions. In fact the entity has been facing possible liquidation for a long time (Chilenga 2016). What remains challenging however is the fact that despite the complexities SAA seems to be undergoing the company has failed in fact "to develop and implement necessary organisational and sustainable strategic changes" needed to float its business (Mhlanga et al. 2017). In the failures of these SOEs, these "frustrate the state's intentions to achieve growth and development objectives" (Kanyane and Sausi 2015). This article investigates the state of State Owned Enterprises (SOEs) in South Africa while observing the factors affecting their profitability and relevance to post-apartheid South Africa's economic development imperatives. The paralysis of SOEs has in fact been linked to the failure of post-colonial African states' failure and struggles to move the region towards meaningful economic development and subsequent attainment of social justice through redistribution of wealth or otherwise as most post-colonial political elite had intended to achieve (Gumede 2016; Edoun 2015).

This article notes that whereas a plethora of existing information points to the complexities affecting the current state of the SOEs as being mainly organisational; malfeasance, inept leadership and mismanagement characterised by lack of proper organisational oversight, accountability and transparency (Chilenga 2016; Edoun 2015; Makhado 2016; Sadiki 2015) for example, pointers are that these complexities could be informed by deep-rooted intertwined (unknown) factors within and without these entities. These entities continue to fail despite useful and extensive tools such as legislative acts and frameworks which governments put in place to guide their discourses. Critically, Makhado (2016) reveals the shortcomings of SOEs despite useful and what could be critical tools to properly manage SOEs business practices. For example, Sections 55(2) and 114(2) of the Constitution of the Republic of South Africa (1996), the National Assembly and Provincial Legislatures for example have been given powers to "conduct oversight and hold the executive accountable on how" the entities conducted their businesses—especially with regard resource usage (Makhado 2016). The failure of SOEs to be entrepreneurially competent, economically and developmentally relevant in South Africa for example would not translate into a unique post-apartheid South African product because that SOEs could at times not be entrepreneurially competent, economically and developmentally relevant has been an experience of global economy for decades. Such unprofitabilities are said to have cost governments huge sums of public money elsewhere in the world (Frank 2013). To illustrate trends in the South African SOEs, some SOEs were purposively selected from the bigger SOEs pool for this study.

4 Selected SOES Which Recently Received State Bailouts in South Africa

Figure 1 reveals that there have been numerous SOEs in South Africa who have received large sums of bailouts over extended period. Figure 1 shows that Eskom (1), Denel (2), Land Bank (3), SAA (4), PebbleBedModular Reactor (5), SABC (6),

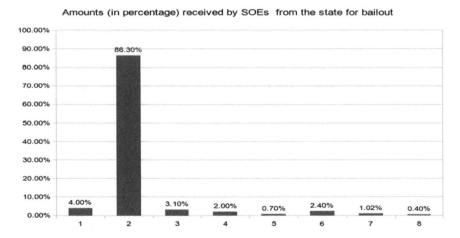

Fig. 1 State bail-out received by SOEs as percentage of total (n = 218.533 billion). Source: DA Website

SA Post Office (7) and Sentech (8) for example were leading SOEs in receiving state bailouts by 2009. For example, The SABC has received approximately 2.24 billion in four consecutive years (2005, 2006, 2007 and 2009). This is despite the poor organisational performance of this entity. It is on record that higher company spending in the SABC was also exacerbated by huge salaries and bonuses paid out to executives including the Board, and also reckless spending. Between 2005/06 and 2008/09, Denel received between R260 million and R2 billion of unconditional transfers, guarantees and loans between 2005/06 and 2008/09 financial years. All in all, the 717 SOEs in South Africa have received approximately R461.1 billion at least by 2012 financial year. By 2012, the total company value of the 717 SOEs in South Africa was approximated at R364 billion, and for these entities to be spending this way presents a complexity worth investigation.

5   Political Influence and Interference in the Affairs of SOEs

Politics has had notable role in the affairs of mainstream business for decades the world over. Faccio et al. (2006) demonstrated this insinuation in their study on political connected firms and non-politically connected firms from 35 countries around the world. Faccio et al. (2006) concluded that politics would influence corporate practices such as bail-out which often would favour politically connected firms than the non-politically connected firms. On the one hand, political influence in SOEs has been listed as a factor with negative influence on organisational perfor-mance (Mbo and Adjasi n.d; Thomas 2012). In fact, Thomas (2012) found strong relational connections of politics and SOEs in South Africa in particular. This section of the article analyses the role of politics – political influence in particular in SOEs performance and output in South Africa. This section concurs with the findings reported by Mbo and Adjasi (n.d) who concluded that organisational performance improved with less political influence. Mbo and Adjasi (n.d) concurred with public choice theorists who contend that it is common for politicians to meddle in SOEs using public interest assumptions whereas in most cases such meddling is driven by the politician's personal interest than public interest. In addition, where political interference in the direction of SOEs increases, it is often driven by the desire of the politician to achieve socio-political goals rather than financial targets and performance of SOEs (Mbo and Adjasi n.d). This factor was discovered and listed as one of the major complexities of SOEs growth and development in China, and the government's transformation of the sector therefore sought to minimise political influence and interference in SOEs operations (Mbo and Adjasi n.d).

Political interference has been cited in several other government-economic inter-actions in South Africa. For example, it has been reported as a factor in the Black Economic Empowerment (BEE) deals—especially in the mining sector where its influence has been the source of corporate governance transgressions characterised by acts of violation of applicable legal frameworks meant to support the BEE instrument, nepotism, cronyism, fraud, fronting, corruption and corporate mismanagement (Thomas 2014). It is regrettable that such violations threaten the broader attempts by the post-apartheid government to transform and improve the socio-economic paradigm of the historically disadvantaged South Africans—especially the Blacks and other designated groups such as Indians and Coloureds for instance (Thomas 2014). These violations slow-down the pace of socio-economic transformation of the South African society which should facilitate redistribution of resources in the country while growing the economy at the same time (Thomas 2014). In other words, the integrative attempts by the post-apartheid South African government that would have seen the development of a non-racial economy in South Africa where the formerly disadvantaged groups also participate unhindered in mainstream formal economy remain increasingly compromised. Political interference has unintended consequences of perpetuating South Africa's "glaring [socio-economic] disparity between rich and poor" (Thomas 2014) where Black people remain trapped in abject poverty for example.

Political interference in this regard is categorised in terms of the role played by government and political elite in the SOEs sector. First and foremost, the role of government is specified according to the type of government in relation to its mission. For example, benevolent and malevolent government. Filippo Beloc (n.d) describes malevolent government as government whose elected politicians, non-elected public administrators, bureaucrats such as enterprise managers tended to demonstrate and pursue "certain private objectives even if this is at the expenses of the social welfare or in contrast to social preferences". Benevolent government is obsessed with satisfaction of the (socio-economic) interest of its citizenry, and this government also consistently operates on behalf of its constituency without any regard of amassing benefits, self-interests and preferences of the elite (Beloc n.d). Political influence and interference in SOEs has been considerable in both developed and developing countries. A plethora of literature (Akoum 2012; Irwin and Yamamoto 2004; Sungkar 2008) reveal this influence in SOEs in the Middle East and North Africa (MENA) region, Mexico, Philippine, South Africa, Indonesia for example. Political influence compromises corporate governance in SOEs as corruption, bribes and other unethical tendencies are smuggled into the entities. For instance, Sungkar (2008) postulated that in Indonesia for example, SOEs would be highly influenced by increased involvement of well-connected business groups and individuals or influential military elite who would have significant influence and control in the entities. These factors are common in systems where big business (individuals and families) have enormous influence over the political elites and business executives in well orchestrated political captures of political and business objectives and systems through corruption and illegal behaviours involving irregular tenders which favour certain business entities over others, bribes, patronage, kickbacks, payment of huge salaries and "performance" bonuses to the executives and conflict between public responsibilities and private elite interests of a web of multiple role-players and stakeholders. The influence of the Gupta family in South Africa's business-political filed would best fit description. The Gupta family though a company linked to them is said to have used its influence on elite politicians and company executives to benefit through kickbacks amounting to approximately R5.3 billion in the current Transnet locomotive investment programme (Van Resnsburg and Brown 2017).

These factors reduce SOEs into political and business elite battle fields for the access of public resources through illicit business contracts, corrupt preferential procurement systems favouring certain business entities over others and open looting. The SOEs are looted until they become loss-making entities only surviving through government bail-out budgets. Resultantly, these SOEs are reduced into parasitic entities which are burdensome to public administration in general. The overall aim of the role-players is theft of public assets and goods. In his article "Nothing left to steal", Muzilikazi wa Africa (Mzilikazi WaAfrika 2014) demonstrates how these syndicates operate in plundering state resources to enrich (small) cabals of well-connected political and bureaucratic elites. Political influence in SOEs begins by increasing determination of company executives such as Chief Executive Officers (CEOs) and company board members through political elites and some powerful individuals in private business. In the South African context, these cabals exploit the ruling party's cadre deployment policy to their advantage in influencing the appointment of their own "deployees" who would do the job for them. The influence of the powerful business individuals in the appointment of company executives ensures that these individuals maximally benefit from business transactions taking place within those enterprises while the chosen "deployees" also distribute the resources to the supporters of the scheme. To entrench these cabals within the SOEs, high powered political elites and their business associates through symbiotic relationships capture, centralise and control the SOEs systems in order to eliminate lower-order, rent-seeking competitors for instance (Bhorat et al. 2017). First and foremost these cabals capture state systems, and in addition specific company executives—especially of those companies targeted by the cabals. For the purpose of this article, two scenarios are presented to illustrate how politics plays itself out in the SOEs sector in South Africa. The purpose of these two scenarios is to demonstrate how intertwined these scenarios are in serving the interests of politico-business cabals in the looting of state resources and paralysis of SOEs for example.

6   The Brian Molefe Scandal

Brian Molefe is the (former) Chief Executive Officer (CEO) of Eskom. He could be called "former" CEO because he was finally dismissed from Eskom by the Minister of Public Enterprises after the minister was pushed by the ruling party to do so after the return of Brian Molefe from parliament to Eskom. This issue had caused immeasurable public criticism of government and the ANC to an extent of the ANC to force the minister to intervene. The Brian Molefe scandal at Eskom might shed light on the role played by politics in the affairs of SOEs. Brian Molefe "resigned" as Eskom CEO after being fingered in what has become known as the State of Capture Report of the Public Protector (PP) for being part of the allegedly corrupt Gupta family, and the family's subsequent allegedly corrupt business interests at Eskom. However, when Molefe returned to Eskom after failing at parliament to be appointed Minister of Finance, the Eskom Board led by Ben Ngubane re-appointed Brian Molefe as CEO of Eskom. Ngubane and the Eskom Board released a statement that Brian Molefe instead never resigned from Eskom but had taken early retirement. Ngubane argued that after failing to reach retirement package due to Brian Molefe with Eskom, the Eskom Board felt Brian Molefe should instead be re-instated to his position. This was "spin-doctoring" the whole Brian Molefe scandal. After the intervention of the Minister of Public Enterprises after being pushed by the ANC to do so, the Eskom Board finally releases Brian Molefe from his position. However, Brian Molefe took the Eskom Board to the Labour Court for breach of contract and unfair dismissal. The court's ruling is pending.

After Brian Molefe has resigned from Eskom to save face over the State of Capture Report as it involves the Gupta family influence over the State; the presidency in particular, Brian Molefe was instead chauffeured through the back door into the South African parliament as Member of Parliament (MP) for the ANC. Molefe's elevation into parliament caused intense strain within the already faction fighting politics of the ruling party; the ANC where some had voiced their concerns of how the former Eskom boss was "deployed" there—especially with a cloud of possible corruption still hanging over his head in the contentious State Capture scandal. Those privy with Brian Molefe's "promotion" to parliament proposed that he was meant to replace the uncooperative Minister of Finance Pravin Gordhan as Minister of Finance during a President Jacob Zuma's cabinet reshuffle that had taken everyone by sur-prise—including the ANC structures. This reshuffle was followed by an open rebellion within the ruling party—especially by those opposed to the removal of the Minister of Finance Pravin Gordan. The issue was so volatile within the ruling party that it is on record that it was for the first time in the history of the post-apartheid South African government that a Deputy President criticised the president in public media in the manner in which Deputy President Matamela Ramaphosa did on President Jacob Zuma. However, after severe pressure from within the party structures at Luthuli House; the ANC's administrative palace in down-town Johannesburg, civil society and opposition parties in parliament, it has been alledged that President Zuma could not continue with his plans to appoint Brian Molefe as the new Minister of Finance to replace Pravin Gordhan but another perceived stooge of the Gupta family Malusi Gigaba was instead apointed the new minister. The appointment of a different minister instead of Brian Molefe suggested that Molefe's mission to parliament had failed—rendering him irrelevant in parliament. To the surprise of many, Brian Molefe hastily resigns from parliament forthwith to return to Eskom as its "new" CEO. Immediately after his returning to Eskom, the ANC summons Minister Lynn Brown to Luthuli House—because the minister is a deployee of the ANC to explain how possible it was for her to approve Brian Molefe's return to Eskom considering the complexities his appointment could cause to government and the parastatal. In addition, Brian Molefe still had pending issues at Eskom regarding his pending "early retirement" pension pay-out which was already approved by the Eskom Board to the tune of R30 million. Brian Molefe was the CEO of Eskom for approximately 18 months, and he amasses a pension payout which could have paid out no fewer than 22 professional nurses who might have been in public service for no fewer than 24 years for example. This illustrates how deeply unequal the post-apartheid South African economy has become. The resource gap between the poor and the rich is instead widening despite government's intended policy of closing the resource gap in society. Many commentators concede that Brian Molefe is the project of the Gupta family within Eskom where the family had huge interest worth billions of rands in direct and indirect contracts. Consensus amongst commentators and some key informants is that Brian Molefe's return to Eskom is at his "redeployment" by the powerful Gupta family who really wanted Brian Molefe there. Secondly, some opine that Brian Molefe was chauffeured to parliament by the Gupta family with the help of their connections within the politics of the ruling party who facilitated his transfer from Eskom to parliament so he could be appointed Minister of Finance after Minister Pravin Gordhan would have been fired by the president. Argument is that the Gupta family would have used their influence on President Jacob Zuma to get Brian Molefe appointed minister. The Gupta family is said to have undue influence on President Jacob Zuma and other powerful politicians within the ANC which makes the Gupta family business empire gain advantage in private-State business deals, and also power to dictate appointment of ministers for example.

7 The Gupta Brothers and Their Role in the SOES Sector in South Africa

This article details the role played by the Gupta brothers Ajay, Atul and Rajesh who have risen into undeniably business-political heavyweights in South Africa by forging unbreakable ties with influential politicians and business executives since 1993 when they arrived from Rani Bazar, Saharapur, Uttar Pradesh in India to settle in South Africa after being sent by their businessman father Shiv Kumar Gupta (Bhorat et al. 2017). It is popular opinion in South Africa that the powerful Gupta family for instance invaded the business-political space in the SOEs firstly by capturing party politics, government; the presidency and executive; that is, ministerial level in particular, national and provincial politics; parliament in particular (Bhorat et al. 2017). The influence of the Guptas on political-business environments of a country is not only unique to South Africa. Issues of state and presidential capture by influential business individuals and syndicates have been matters common in global politico-economic space for decades. Reddy (2016) corroborates this assertion in a Brazil's so-called "Car Wash" scandal involving corporate and political heavy weights and company executives where President Dilma Rouseff and former president Lula da Silva were caught in this famous scandal.

In South Africa, at party political level, the extent of the capture is evidenced by party structures such as the ANCYL, Umkhontho We Sizwe Veterans League and the ANCWL all towing the line to promote, defend, protect and sustain the Gupta onslaught in business and politics in South Africa. Each time there is a controversial issue affecting the Guptas, these structures rise to defend them. The defence mechanism varies from public attacks on the perceived Gupta enemies by branding about a distorted assertion that the Guptas were attacked by conservative imperial sinister forces in cahoot with Western and White monopoly capital to discredit the transformational Black Guptas or personal attacks directed to such individuals. Although South Africa has credible media which "has played a watchdog role in bringing instances of corruption [and political interference in SOEs practices] to light" (Thomas 2014), parallel electronic and print media instruments have also been invented in the country to undermine this credibility. Such invented media tools also disseminates misinformation to the public—especially in cases where the handlers of these media tools feel that key people in the SOEs-political elite syndicates are threatened. In the process, television channels and newspaper have emerged as competent agents of the pro-Gupta and president's campaign in clearly designed propagandistic mouthpiece fashion. Members of the public who could be influential are roped in to provide competing views against those others used by other perceived anti- or Gupta-unfriendly and president's campaign. These hired "experts" use political and economic analyses to distort and mislead the public. Whenever their services are enlisted in the controversial media mouthpieces, these "experts" have a clear mandate of positive image building of the president, and of the Guptas. This is achieved by deceptively "trumpeting" small achievements into big national and international achievements in pure propaganda. Open discussion on issues of state performance is curtailed by denying the public any space for conversation. Van Vuuren (2017) summarised this approach thus "the truth suffers when there is no room for nuanced conversation" Also, the president is portrayed as someone who is championing the transformation of South Africa into a country which has championed the development and empowerment of Black people—especially with regard mainstream formal economic inclusivity and participation. President Zuma must be portrayed as an independent transformative president leading South Africa's so-called radical socio-economic transformation agenda while all those who are perceived as fighting the president are viewed as being anti-revolutionaries hell-bent to undermine the president's efforts to "radicalise" his government's attempts to transform South Africa. Those perceived as anti-president are labelled "anti-revolutionaries" and "anti-Black people"—especially those who demonstrate resentments towards the Guptas. Despite the obvious destruction of the ANC, the pro-Zuma-Gupta footsoldiers need this factional rhetoric to entrench themselves and their agenda in the political machinery. The media instruments purporting the onslaught are portrayed as informationally transformative. They are also flavoured with the "Black" tag to portray them as being Black owned. Evidently, the strategy employed is similar to elsewhere in places such as Angola, Zimbabwe and so forth. In case of difficult court cases for example, the strategy is to exploit existing gaps in the law to scupper any attempts by detractors. The cases are either delayed by tactics that would "buy" or "delay" or "de-list" the cases from proceeding. Higher court decisions such as those of the Constitutional court are calculatively ignored and eventually sidelined. Some are referred to reviews while some are taken to parliament for decisions. The findings of Advocate Thuli Madonsela's inquiry as Public Protectors were referred to parliament, and sarcastically even to the Minister of Police for adjudication. Being a Chapter 9 institution, the findings of the Public Protector should instead have been implemented as they have been. The Security Cluster which includes the police is invaded and stuffed by complying deployees. Politicians and ministers who do not comply, and fail to tow the line are gotten rid of in unannounced cabinet reshuffles. Letsoalo (2017: 5) summarised this sentiment thus "[President] Zuma has in the past dealt harshly with anyone in the ANC who held a different view from him" Weaker and inexperienced politicians are appointed into critical portfolios to fast track project targets. In December 2015 the replacement of the industrious Minister Nhlahla Nene by the completely unknown novice David "Des" Van Rooyen sent the financial markets into a nose dive ever experienced in South Africa, costing the country approximately R500 billion over 4 days (Mathekga 2017).

Bhorat et al. (2017) details the role played by the powerful Gupta family in South African business-political space. According to Bhorat et al. (2017), President Jacob Zuma, certain members of his family and some politicians are said to have been captured by the Gupta family to influence their business interests in the SOEs in particular. The famous State of Capture Report released by the office of the Public Protector Advocate Thuli Madonsela chronicles the extent of this capture on the president and subsequently the state. This Report revealed that even the appointment of politicians—ministers in particular would have to be vetoed by the powerful Gupta family before the president would appoint such a minister. Effectively, the state is reduced into proxy for self-interest by these individuals who not only render the state powerless and useless but the whole political system of the country a mockery. The Guptas have reduced South Africa into a banana republic whose highest office; the presidency has effectively been reduced into a lackey, puppet and a conduit used for perpetual criminality.

Constitutionally, it is the prerogative of the president of the Republic to appoint ministers. The appointment of ministers by ordinary citizens such as the Gupta family undermines and violates state protocol. This in addition exposes the state to serious security risks. This practice suggests that powerful business individuals might become "shadow presidents" in a "silent coup". Allegations are that in current South Africa, the would-be ministers are summoned to the Gupta compound at Saxonwold (Bhorat et al. 2017), to be initiated and schooled on how to work in the system. The country is therefore captured and micro-managed. Saxonwold has replaced Pretoria. The Guptas become *de facto* heads of state who micro manages the country to promote and sustain their family interests (Mathekga 2017: 50). The whole machinery operates like a movie; a soapie, and in Africa where the majority of people believe in the power of invisible powers and their influence on humans, some have even suggested that what is currently happening in South Africa could be pure witchcraft. Sophistications which can't be explained by any possible means in the same way as the lootings currently taking place All the state apparatus can only watch when the state is being plundered and looted without recourse. Parliament has failed because it has also been captured by the powerful business cabal. Whatever motion and parliamentary debate would emerge seen to be against these cabals would be defeated. The ruling party; the African National Congress (ANC) which is in the majority in parliament would always and nonetheless vote against any encroaching debate and motion on the business space of the powerful cabals. Unfavourable parliamentary debates and motions sponsored by opposition parties would be thrown out and effectively reduced into some minor complaints by the huge ANC majority in parliament. Despite some cracks within the ruling party beginning to emerge of late, the number of the pro-*mafias* in parliament remains overwhelming to still effect favourable decisions. The reshuffling of cabinet by president Jacob Zuma which saw the removal of the Minister of finance Pravin Gordhan from office and his subsequent replacement by a perceived captured minister Malusi Malusi Gigaba was vehemently defended by the pro-mafia parliamentarians. Minister Gigaba has been linked on several occasions to the Gupta empire. Many commentators opine that Gigaba would be able to push the Gupta deals much faster within the SOEs band than the perceived anti-Gupta Pravin Gordhan.

Some ministers even get to know about their appointments as ministers through the Gupta family, not the president. Sometimes towards the end of 2016, Deputy Minister of Finance Mr Mcebisi Jonas made some serious allegations on the Gupta family regarding his impending appointment as minister of finance to replace the soon-to-be axed Pravin Gordhan. Powerful government systems such as the Treasury are captured to achieve the objectives of the cabals (Bhorat et al. 2017). It is unfortunate that in the process, the constitutional state is undermined, destroyed and replaced by a "shadow state" controlled by a group of *mafias* in a strategically coordinated *"silent coup"* whose primary objective is to amass personal assets and resources (Bhorat et al. 2017). What should have been pure business has degenerated into some sophisticated political power play of the pro and anti-Gupta groupings. These groups are divided by the so-called "State Capture" meted out by the Guptas on business and politics of the country. This division continues to haunt and divide the tripartite alliance; the ANC, SACP and COSATU to an extent of affecting internal party functioning and operation of the ANC, and the alliance in general. Currently, the impending ANC elective conference has campaigns characterised by the pro and anti-Gupta-Jacob Zuma sentiments. Already Jacob Zuma's former wife, Nkosazana Dlamini-Zuma who is favoured by the president and his supporters to take over the leadership of the ANC post-electoral conference of December 2017, and of government as president of the country in 2019 after president Zuma's tenure would have ended is seen by many as a would-be deployee of the Gupta dynasty to continue where her former husband would have left off. Some view Nkosazana as that "soft" candidate punted by the president to safeguard his fragile freedom after his tenure would have ended because of the many prosecutable scandals the president would carry into his end of office. In addition, Nkosazana presents the Guptas with that continuation of their hold on the state and business affairs—especially their business empire in South Africa. Although at the core of the Gupta state capture lies the subtle move to acquire business space and influence in the SOEs in particular, this desire might not be fulfilled without political control of influential individuals such as the president and some party political structures. The actions of the SOEs cabals undermine the fact that SOEs were meant to enhance socio-economic advancement and improvement of the standards of living of the masses of the millions of resource-poor populace in the country (Kuye 2016).

8 Mapping the Way Forward for the SOES in South Africa

This article takes cognisance of the fact that existing research forwards useful tools and frameworks to assist the course of SOEs in South Africa. For example, Makhado (2016) and Sadiki (2015) propose the whole lot of policy and organisational strategies, legislative and policy instruments to improve conditions in the SOEs in South Africa. It is therefore unnecessary for this article to reduplicate the suggestions lest this literature ends with another wheel. However, this article first and foremost postulated that the majority of factor complexities affecting SOEs in South Africa are political factors. This article therefore forwards a way forward inclined to political realignment of party and state politics in relation to SOEs environment in South Africa. The fact that the SOEs environment is highly politicised and unfolding at the background of a political discourse which also involves government and party politics, it emerges that to resolve these complexities would be demanding. The level of difficulty in resolving the complexities would be determined also by the strength of political will there is amongst the political elite to facilitate for such transformation of the SOEs sector. It is unfortunate that political machinery in South Africa has been disenfranchised and has in addition disintegrated by the divisive nature of the battle to access state resources by various structures of mainstream party and state politics in the country. Political factionalism propagated by those "gatekeeper" political elites deployed by criminal elements hell-bent to loot state resources who operate from party and state political machinery, SOEs and public service administration to regulate access to state resources and opportunities has split party politics in the middle; pitting anti-corruption activists of transformation and corruption *mafias* on the one hand. Effective and efficient reform under these conditions might be difficult. This assumption is based on the fact that corruption perpetrators benefit from the perpetual unstable politico-economic environment currently at play in South Africa. In the article entitled "Power, patronage, and gatekeeper politics in South Africa" Beresford (2015) demonstrates the extent of the volatility of the current battle for access to state resources by competing groups in South Africa.

The South African politico-SOEs business environment has in fact degenerated into chronic and worsening volatility where the battle for inclusion and exclusion in mainstream politico-economic space of rival elites compete for dominance in the acquisition of state resources has provoked some bitter party political factionalism to an extent of causing an obvious paralysis of government, public administration and governance in the country. People enter politics to "eat", and they enter public service such as in the SOEs as conduits for corruption and state resource access. Out there in public—in the *Tshivenda* native language of these athours, this kind of politics is known as "politics of *Vhanani*" that is politics of the "eaters". There is so much instability in mainstream (party and state) political space, government and mainstream business—especially in SOEs sector that transformation remains seriously compromised. The instability is strategically created by the *mafias* to perpetuate anarchy while they continue to loot the state. Any transformational measures which could be perceived as denial of space of the *mafias* into state resources, and also those perceived as being punitive to transgressors might be suppressed. There should be political actors who postulated transformation in the same way as China's Deng Xiaoping who emphatically argued that "stability overrides everything," (Wang 2014) in order to bring stability in the SOEs sector. Dealing with transgressors with regard SOEs corruption and involvement in illegal transactions such as kick-backs, bribes and inflated contracts for example in the sector, Xi Jinping's approach of cleaning up the system from the "tigers"; that is, the elite and thereafter the "low flying flies", that is the ordinary citizens who are roped into these activities should be promoted. Xi Jinping advocates for severe punitive measures against transgressors. Politicians found guilty in perpetrating SOEs corruption should be severely punished. In the same way as it happened in Brazil during the Petroleo Brasileo S.A. (Petrobas)—President Dilma Rouseff's scandal which got Dilma Rouff suspended, and subsequently impeached from office by the Senate (Reddy 2016), South Africa should also introduce such harsh measures. In South Africa however, it is emerging that to successfully prosecute alleged transgressors has not been easy. One example is that of President Jacob Zuma who instead of facing prosecution over alleged involvement in corrupt deals in the famous Arms Deal scandal went on to become president of the country. The Nkandla gate scandal where the president was said to have benefited illegally from the state during the building of his lavish private residence in his rural home of Nkandla never yielded anything significant despite the ruling of the PP and the Constitutional Court. President Zuma used his political power in the ruling party, parliament and government to evade any prosecution. President Zuma has proven in many occasions that there is no political will at higher political office of the country to deal with corruption anywhere and anyhow in the country both in government and the SOEs sector.

Company executives found to have contravened SOEs frameworks should also be prosecuted in the same as Brazil prosecuted their 117 company executives involved in the Petroleo Brasileo S.A. (Petrobas)—President Dilma Rouseff's scandal. For example, it took President Xi Jinping of China to deal with SOEs corruption in scandals involving Petrochina, China Southern Airlines and Sinopec amongst others where approximately 115 officials were publicly named as being corrupt and thereafter dully investigated and prosecuted (Reddy 2016). Reviewed literature (Gumede 2016; Sungkar 2008) for instance revealed that a number of economies around the world have sought improvement of SOEs through privatisation. According to Sungkar (2008), privatisation could be used as a tool to reduce government expenditure by abolishing or reducing subsidies to SOEs, thus, governments therefore reasonably expected to gain extra revenue from the economically viable and competitive SOEs which would make profits. Following this sentiment, it could be argued that privatisation therefore promotes competition, viability, efficiency and profitability while indirectly saving government resources. Looking at additional bail-out expenditure which the South African government undergoes at every economic cycle for SOEs such as the SAA, SABC, Eskom for instance, privatisation seems to be the best option a tool to sustain these entities. However, privatisation of SOEs in South Africa has had some serious implications for the state. Some of these implications have resulted in the state-workers clashes on several occasions. These tensions and resistance for privatisation are however not only common in South Africa. Sungkar (2008) revealed the same in Indonesia for instance.

9 Conclusion and Policy Recommendations

This chapter concludes that SOEs are critical instrument for economic development in South Africa. There is a need for better organisation, structuring, governance systems based on the rule of law and combating of corruption in the sector to improve on the viability, sustainability and competitiveness of SOEs in their current forms in South Africa. First, the SOEs sector has to be depoliticised. It has become increasingly evident that the reforms needed in the SOEs would require "strong political will as well as state capacity" (Sungkar 2008) to effect. Considering that the majority of complexities impacting on the operation of SOEs are corporate while those revealed in this article point to highly politicised factors, and that most of these factors could be chronic, this article recommends that the transformation of SOEs in South Africa should begin by regularising mainstream politics and its influence in SOEs environment.

Keywords Definitions

State Owned Enterprises (SOEs) The operational definition for SOEs in this article shall mean "state owned entities or companies which are legal entities that tend to carry out business activities on behalf of the state" (Chilenga 2016). The definition supplied by Chilenga (2016) is consistent with that of the Public Finance Management Act (Act of 1999) (PFMA), Section 1 (a), (b), (c) and (d) (i, ii) as amended by Act 29 of 1999 which describes the entities as "National Government Business Enterprise" which (a) "is a juristic person under the ownership control of the national executive (b) has been assigned financial and operational authority to carry on a business activity (c) as its principal business, provides goods and services in accordance with ordinary business principles (d) is financed fully or substantially from sources other than the National Revenue Fund or by way of a tax, levy or statutory money" (Chilenga 2016; Sadiki 2015).

Financial Guarantees According to Sadiki (2015), financial guarantees refer to undertakings by the state to pay, after the occurrence of certain events which might negatively impacted substantially on the creditworthiness of the particular institution requesting that guarantee the amount of which could be paid directly to the beneficiary or to its creditors.

Loan A loan is money lent which has to be returned usually with interest (Sadiki 2015).

State guarantee Sadiki (2015) defines state guarantee as a promise by a person (the guarantor) to settle a debt or fulfil the promise of someone else. The obligations of the guarantor in the guarantee are equivalent to those of the borrower.

References

Akoum, A. (2012). The political economy of SOE privatization and governance reform in the MENA region. *International Scholarly Research Network, 2012*, 1–9. https://doi.org/10.5402/2012/723536. Article ID: 723536.

Beloc, F. (n.d). Innovation in state-owned Enterprises: Reconsidering the conventional wisdom. Department of Economics, University "G. d'Annunzio", Pescara, Italy.

Beresford, A. (2009). Comrades 'back on track'? The durability of the tripartite alliance in South Africa. *African Affairs, 108*(432), 391–412. https://doi.org/10.1093/afraf/adp021.

Beresford, A. (2015). Power, patronage, and gatekeeper politics in South Africa. *African Affairs (London), 114*(455), 226–248. https://doi.org/10.1093/afraf/adu083.

Bhorat, H., Buthelezi, M., Chipkin, I., Duma, S., Mondi, L., Peter, C., Qobo, M., Swilling, M., & Friedenstein, H. (2017). *Betrayal of the promise: How the nation is being stolen*. State Capacity Research Project.

Chilenga, A. (2016). *State owned enterprises: A policy analysis of South African Airways (SAA)*. Unpublished Masters dissertation, University of KwaZulu-Natal, Pietermaritzburg.

Crowell, S. M. (2012). *The rise of Julius Malema*. Unpublished Hons Dissertation, Wesley College.

Edoun, E. I. (2015). The impact of governance on state owned enterprises (SOEs) in Africa. *Mediterranean Journal of Social Sciences, 6*(1), 352–358.

Faccio, M., Masulis, R. W., & McConnell, J. J. (2006). Political connections and corporate bailouts. *The Journal of Finance, LXI*(6), 2597–2635.

Fourie, D. (2014). The role of public sector enterprises in the South African Economy. *African Journal of Public Affairs, 7*(1), 30–40.

Frank, S. (2013). State-owned enterprises and economic reform in Vietnam. Paper for Joint Military Operations Department, Naval War College, Newport, Report No. RI 02841-1207. 01.11.2013.

Gumede, W. (2016). The political economy of state-owned enterprises restructuring in South Africa. *Journal of Governance & Public Policy, 6*(2), 69–97.

Irwin, T. & Yamamoto, C. (2004). *Some options for improving the governance of state-owned electricity utilities. Energy and Mining Sector Board Discussion Paper* (Paper No.11). Washington, DC: The World Bank.

Kanyane, M., & Sausi, K. (2015). Reviewing state-owned entities' governance landscape in South Africa. *African Journal of Business Ethics, 9*(1), 28–41. https://doi.org/10.15249/9-1-81.

Karodia, A. M., Soni, P., & Nedelea, A. (2017). A reckless shot at the central bank of South Africa by the Public Protector spells economic disaster for the country amidst a recession and ratings down grades: More kicks for the economy and South Africa in turmoil. *Ecoforum, 6*, Issue 3 (13), 1–15.

Klippenstein, C. E. (2009). *Leadership and the ANC: The Thabo Mbeki era in South Africa*. Unpublished Masters Dissertation, University of Saskatchewan, Saskatoon.

Kuye, J. O. (2016). Quangos and Chapter 9 institutions in the governance of the state Leadership issues and reforms in developing and emerging nations. *African Journal of Public Affairs, 9*(1), 86–109.

Kuye, J. O., & Cedras, J. P. (2011). Dialogue between the ANC, COSATU and the SACP: The impact on leadership, governance and public policy in South Africa. *African Journal of Public Affairs, 4*(3), 73–84.

Letsoalo, M. (2017). Zuma, wake up and smell the stench. *Mail and Guardian*, June 2 to 8, 5.

Mafukata, M. A. (2016). The consequences of China's impending economic crisis on global economy: A predictive scenario on Sub-Saharan Africa. *Journal of Finance and Banking Studies, 5*(6), 24–41.

Makhado, R. (2016). The role of PAC in enhancing oversight and accountability by the state-owned enterprises in South Africa. *African Politics and Policy: Online*, March 25.

Mathekga, R. (2017). *When Zuma goes*. Cape Town: Tafelberg.

Mbo, M., & Adjasi, C. (n.d). *Drivers of organizational performance: A state-owned enterprise perspective*. Paper for presentation at the Biennial conference of the Economic Society of South Africa, University of the Free State, Bloemfontein, South Africa, 25–27 September.

Mfuku, M. (2006). *Privatisation and deregulation policies in South Africa*. Unpublished Masters Dissertation, University of the Western Cape, Bellville, Cape Town.

Mhlanga, O., Steyn, J. N., & Spencer, J. P. (2017). Impacts of the micro environment on airline operations in southern Africa: A literature review study. *African Journal of Hospitality, Tourism and Leisure, 6*(1), 1–13.

Musacchio, A., & Lazzarini, S. G. (2012, June 4). *Leviathan in business: Varieties of state capitalism and their implications for economic performance* (Working Paper 12-108). Harvard Business School.

Muzapu, R., Havadi, T., Mandizvidza, K., & Xiongyi, N. (2016). Managing state-owned enterprises (SOEs) and parastatals in Zimbabwe: Human resource management challenges—Drawing lessons from the Chinese experience. *Management, 6*(4), 89–102. https://doi.org/10.5923/j.mm.20160604.01.

Mzilikazi WaAfrika. (2014). *Nothing left to steal*. Johannesburg: Penguin Random House.

Radygin, A., Simachev, Y., & Entov, R. (2015). The state-owned company: "State failure" or "market failure"? *Russian Journal of Economics, 1*(2015), 55–80. https://doi.org/10.1016/j.ruje.2015.05.001.

Reddy, Y. R. K. (2016). State-owned enterprises and corruption: An international perspective. *Seven Pillars Institute Moral Cents, 5*(2), 57–61.

Sadiki, M. (2015). *Financial assistance to state-owned enterprises by the state in South Africa: A case study of Eskom*. Unpublished Masters Dissertation, University of South Africa, Pretoria.

Sungkar, Y. (2008). Indonesia's State Enterprises: From State Leadership to International Consensus. *Journal of Indonesian Social Sciences and Humanities, 1*(2008), 95–120.

Thomas, A. (2012). Governance at South African state-owned enterprises: What do annual reports and the print media tell us? *Social Responsibility Journal, 8*(4), 448–470. https://doi.org/10.1108/17471111211272057.

Thomas, A. (2014). Media-reported corporate governance transgressions in broad-based black economic empowerment deals in the South African mining sector. *African Journal of Business Ethics, 8*(2), 89–107.

Van Resnsburg, D., & Brown, J. (2017). Is the PIC in too deep? *City Press Business and Tenders Newspaper*, 4 June: 1.

Van Vuuren, H. (2017). *Apartheid, guns and money: A tale of profit*. Sunnyside, Pretoria: Jacana.

Wang, J. (2014). The political logic of corporate governance in China's state-owned enterprises. *Cornell International Law Journal, 47*(3), 631–669.

Part III
Strategic and Innovative Thinking

Strategic Thinking and Dimensions of Effective Leadership

Kürşad Zorlu

Abstract The concept of strategic thinking, which becomes a necessity in today's management understanding, requires to think about every issue which is meaningful from strategic point of view. Leadership, on the other hand, appears to be the most important organizational variable providing a basis for this perspective. Strategic thinking provides the managers with the courage to make the right decision at the point they want to get opportunities, the convenience of gaining problem-solving skills and being able to see the big picture and identify threats. In this study, it is aimed to examine the relationship between strategic thinking and leadership and to reveal the areas of interaction according to the basic dimensions of both concepts. In the study, the conceptual framework for strategic thinking and leadership is first presented, and then the relational context is explained. It is understood that the sub-dimensions of strategic thinking and leadership variables are mutually complementary and that the strategic thinking capacity of the organization can be guided through the interaction of two variables in the framework of the findings and evaluations revealed in the study.

1 Introduction

While almost everything in the world tends to change, innovations in technology determine consumption habits, national economies grow rapidly, and social dynamics differ. The ruthless competition brought by the market economy and the increasing complexity of organizations increase the tendency of uncertainty and strategic understanding is gaining importance for solution of problems. Contrary to classical management thinking, it is becoming a necessity to look at organizations long term and to be able to direct the future. This obligation is crucial for many small and very small organizations to gain competitive advantage and to mobilize their resources.

K. Zorlu (✉)
Ahi Evran University, Political Science and Public Administration, Kirsehir, Turkey
e-mail: kzorlu77@gmail.com

© Springer International Publishing AG, part of Springer Nature 2018   173
H. Dincer et al. (eds.), *Strategic Design and Innovative Thinking in Business Operations*, Contributions to Management Science,
https://doi.org/10.1007/978-3-319-77622-4_9

Thus, the unpredictability of the cycle makes future-oriented thinking indispensable, and the leadership qualities and/or behaviors of the management decision which is accepted as the ultimate formation center of strategic decisions are centered on the developing strategic point of view.

For this reason, researches in the field of management give more weight to leadership matter every day. That the informal organizational structure of groups, especially for the organization and the human-based approaches present the undiscovered findings for effectiveness and efficiency highlights the leadership concept. It seems that there is diversity in the definition of leadership as well as the increase in work done. The different preferences about the leader's features, behaviors and consequential effects lie behind the differentiation.

Nevertheless, managers, whether in private or public sector, concentrate on the assumption that there is only one way and a method to follow each organization. However, the parts of every organization and the holistic systems that are constituted with these parts are different from each other. Managers must firstly tie these pieces together carefully for an effective strategy and direct them in a specific order. In addition, continuous decisions must be made in different fields of business such as sports, art, politics and economy. On the one hand, there is a conflict between the correctness of mutual decisions and action plans in many lines of business. Collis and Montgomery (1990) say that "For any company strategy, as a testing benchmark, the work that the company has done should not be more valuable for another business owner." It is expected that scientific methods should be taken as basis for determining the strategy to follow the change processes.

So one of the effective concepts that bring organizations to the future is strategy. As a military concept, the strategy shaped by the ideas of Sun Tzu as from 500 B.-C. became a sub-discipline in the field of management, especially in the 1980s, with increasing emphasis (Haycock et al. 2012: 1). Generally, the concept of a strategy that reveals the necessary ways and methods for reaching the goals of the organization and achieving success is a road map of the foreseen goal in the future or the modeling of final organization habit. In the construction of the strategic future, strategic thinking is a mental state and a synthesis process that reveals what must be done for this construction. Thus, the strategy evolves into a governance process by its nature and transforms into a field of resistance that carries it to its goals concordantly beyond building the future.

Strategic thinking, which is used in the same meaning with "strategic planning" or even "strategic management" in some of the studies, stands in a vital area where you can get the better of your competitor or your competitor can get the better of you. Managers in business life, politicians in politics, technical directors in football, parents who want to raise good behavior in their children have to think strategically (Dixit and Nalebuff 2010: 3–4). Although the strategic thinking organization is an individual orientation in terms of human resources, it gains effectiveness when the organization as a whole adapts to this process. Because in organizations, the production of goods and services takes place through a collective mechanism consisting of parts. Here, management activity is very important for the formation of strategic thinking climate, motivation of employees and preparation of all subsystems for this. Two important requirements for the management device at this point show themselves: To have a strong intention for the strategy and the ability to make it reach a conclusion. Therefore, the level of leadership and content in an organization is closely related to strategic thinking.

From this point of view, leadership and strategic thinking are becoming an inseparable whole. To be able to read the change in the environment, to be able to see organizational variables as a whole, and to be able to express a visionary perspective are the obligations to think strategically. Leaders with strategic thinking have distinctive features such as long-term thinking, predicting retrospectively, constructing an organizational system, and reinforcing creativity level.

In this study, it is aimed to examine the relationship between strategic thinking and leadership and to reveal the areas of interaction according to the basic dimensions of both concepts. In the study, the conceptual framework about strategic thinking and leadership is firstly presented, and then the relational context is explained. As a constraint, scaling and analyzing the dimensions obtained from this study, which is not based on field research and examined in the case of literature review, will contribute to future studies.

2 Conceptual Framework

2.1 The Concept of Strategy

It is stated that the strategy term is composed of the words; 'stratos' meaning army and vast community of people, and 'egy' meaning to administrate and conduct in Greek (Adair 2003: 15). The concept of strategy, origin of which is based on the military field means to gain a victory by taking advantage of existing resources effectively and efficiently in this field (Adair 2003: 42; Blackerby 1994: 23; Bracker 1980: 219).

In management literature, the concept of strategy began to gain importance and become widespread in the business world toward the end of twentieth century (Johnson et al. 2003: 10). In 1938, Chester Barnard conducted a scientific study on the individual role of the manager in the strategy of organization and this study preserves its effect in terms of the examination of the organization as a whole (Jerkins et al. 2007: 1). Herbert A. Simon in 1945, Philip Selznick in 1957, and Michel Crozier in 1963 stated that they discovered the strategy as the main tool for managers responsible for keeping the organization in balance (Hafsi and Thomas 2005: 509).

The concept of strategy is expressed as an integrated and comprehensive plan which is identified with the aim of the achievement of a defined objective (Luffman et al. 1996: 65; Katsioloudes 2006: 13–14) in organizations (Glueck 1976: 4). According to Ansoff; strategy means all of the decisions taken under conditions of partial uncertainty, in which future situations will not be predicted in the future (Ansoff 1991: 454). According to Andrews strategy means all of the purpose and tasks indicating what type of work the business is doing or wants to do, what type of business it is or wants to be and methods required to perform all of these (Andrews 1971: 28).

Traditionally, strategy has always been associated with the idea of direction for an organization. It is essential to understand an organization's past and current situation for determining new directions. This requirement has emerged as a result of Mintzberg's (1994) defining the strategic consideration as "see the forward—see the top—see the under—see the side—see the beyond" The strategy should be considered as a perspective beyond being associated with a plan. Thus, the idea of establishing a clearer direction to create strategic alignment will emerge (Davies 2004: 12).

The strategy is a comparison between the opportunities, the risks, the threats that an organization's external environment creates and the sources possessed by the organization. For this reason, the strategy can be thought of as a key line between policies that are considered as a guide on what the organization wants to do and achieve (Bowman and Asch 1992: 36; Arogyaswamy and Byles 1987: 651). In addition, the strategy is highly correlated with the vision of the managers because of an intellectual activity element and presence in the manager's mind (Fahey and Randall 1994: 8). Therefore, managers need to think strategically in terms of their organizational vision.

2.2   Strategic Thinking

In management literature, the concept of strategic thinking has begun to take place with the aim of being able to predict the future and discover new and creative strategies over 25 years (Heracleous 1998: 481). Although strategic thinking has become an increasingly common concept in current management studies, it can be said that the necessary infrastructure and identification framework for the concept protects its ambiguity. Within this scope, there are three important problem areas. The first problem is related to the fact that strategic thinking is being used in a very large area other than the self-service area. It seems that all the events and facts about strategy, strategic management are covered within its scope. However, strategic thinking is an input of them and is a process of thinking about non-linear dreams and designs. The second problem is that strategic thinking is used in the same meaning with strategic planning and strategic management. Some researchers have studies attempted to demonstrate this difference (e.g. Ansoff and McDonnell 1990; Mintzberg 1994; Heracleous 1998). The third problem is that the concept can be diverted from its basic elements by a very wide variety of definitions (Taş et al. 2017: 154–158).

The conceptual confusion about strategic thinking is also related to the fact that it is expressed in two ways, narrow and broad. In a narrow sense, strategic thinking means that the task of the strategist is to deal with mission and vision, and has more orientated, creative, synthetic, and separating qualities. However, in the broad sense these features give way to western, rational, analytical, integrative thinking processes and problem-solving thinking. In a broad sense, strategic thinking is highly concerned with problem solving at the individual and organizational level, as well as with mission and vision (O'Shannassy 2003: 54–55).

Ohmae, one of the leading researchers in the concept of strategic thinking states that there is a success method that one has developed by using analytical method which can analyze effectively independently from others, reach correct results and synthesize expressions for solving and elastic logic (Ohmae 1982: 35). Liedtka, another researcher who has done research on this field and has made significant contributions to the development of the concept of strategic thinking states that the concept of strategic thinking is only considered as only thinking about the strategy by many researchers but it is a way of thinking that includes matters such as having a certain system thinking, being goal oriented and hypothesis oriented, improving timely thinking ability and having opportunistic intelligence (Liedtka 1998: 121). According to Bonn, strategic thinking is a method which tries to depends eliminate uncertainties as well as it solves strategic problems related to system thinking, creativity and vision (Bonn 2005: 338–340). Therefore, it can be said that strategic thinking includes thinking about not only strategy but also every matter that is meaningful strategically. Mintzberg argues that strategic thinking is a form of governance which has features making a difference uniquely and transparently and at the same it occurs with a synthesis of intuition and creativity (Mintzberg 1994: 15).

The most important goal of strategic thinking is to get information about the future in lively, complex and unclear environmental conditions that affect organizations directly by taking lessons from the past. Successful organizations have to synthesize the knowledge they have acquired and the strategies they have developed to cope with future uncertainties (Liedtka 1998: 121). In this way, strategic thinking will help to make choices for managers in vital decisions, and will provide them with a vision of their future situation (Rosche 2002: 2). However, strategic thinking is a process having a good beginning and continuity (Macmillan and Tampoe 2000: 2).

2.2.1 Sub-dimensions of Strategic Thinking

When the literature on strategic management is examined, it is seen that many authors have been working on the sub-dimensions of strategic thinking by revealing both common and different dimensions. If it is noted that there are more than 4.8 billion articles in which the strategy word was used and 17,500 articles, title of which included strategy in 1-year period from 2015, it is understandable that the strategy is being studied in many different disciplines (Young 2016: 6). When clustering analysis is applied with classifications obtained from 55 different sources, it is seen that the characteristics of strategic thinking are examined in 18 different dimensions in general (Leon 2016: 9). Liedtka (1998) examines strategic thinking in five dimensions. Rahnama and Rahpeyma (2015) reduce to four dimensions. Table 1 shows the dimensions commonly used in the literature.

In this study, strategic thinking is considered in five dimensions; Visionary Thinking, System Thinking, Creativity, Synthesis, Hypothesis-driven.

Table 1 Strategic thinking dimensions used

Leon (2016)	Liedtka (1998)	Rahnama and Rahpeyma (2015)	Thomson and Strickland (1996)	Heracleous (1998)	Graetz (2002)	Rowe et al. (1986)	Nuntamanop et al. (2013)
Synthesis	Thinking in time	Systematic thinking	Analytical	Creativity	Creativity	Creativity	Creativity
Intuition	İntent-focused	Creative thinking	Conceptual	Synthetic	Synthetic	Flexibility	Analytical thinking ability
Hypothesis driven	Systems perspective	Vision-driven thinking	Visionary	Divergent	Divergent	Vision	Visionary thinking
Analytical thinking ability	Hypothesis-driven	Market-oriented thinking	Synthesizing skills		Intuitive Innovative	Entrepreneurship	Learning ability
Problem solving	İntelligently opportunistic		Knowledge				Synthesizing ability
Creativity							Objectivity
System thinking							
Visionary thinking							

Visionary Thinking

Strategic thinking is based on a perspective that can be called futurist in order that the organization can achieve its goals and desired vision. Being future-referenced requires to have a mission and vision. Having a vision and being able to develop this vision is one of the most basic tasks of strategic thinkers (Bonn 2001: 68). When managers in organizations face uncertainty and inadequacy of information and they have to understand complex projects, the thing which will supply their need for guidance to define valid strategies is the vision. The vision provides orientation and future focus for all activities in the organization and increases organizational commitment by penetrating the entire organization (Bonn 2001: 68, Rahnama and Rahpeyma 2015: 27; Mintzberg 1994: 112).

System Thinking

One of the elements of strategic thinking is to achieve to have the idea of a system. The inclusion of system thinking in strategic thinking is based on the power of holistic thinking (Leon 2016: 9). System approach in strategic thinking comes out with their having a mental model in all sense for the formation of appreciation in the organization and their understanding of the relationship between them. Peter Senge has stated that mental models have an important place in affecting behavior (Senge 1992: 4–10). In other words Senge; emphasizes that, a manager must tend towards all the structures and systems that make events happen rather than the superficial consequences of events in organizations (Liedtka 1998: 122). Also according to the system thinking; any problem must be resolved by starting from its whole and it must be known that the components are not independent of each other (Rahnama and Rahpeyma 2015: 27). Moreover, strategic thinking requires managers to think strategically about management of confluent areas, the knowledge of the position among competitors and within that ecosystem (Liedtka 1998: 122).

Creativity

Within the scope of strategic thinking, the creativity process involves the level of consciousness that creates the problem for solving a problem, a different superior level of consciousness from the approach, and the ability to exhibit a new approach (Kneller 2005: 26). Managers with strategic thinking skills must find ways to demonstrate the new approaches needed to achieve sustained competitive advantage in the best way. To provide this, creativity comes first at the core of these requirements. In particular, to be able to perceive existing concepts and phenomena in different ways and to find solutions that provide lasting competitive advantage by discovering the hidden dependencies between them discovering the hidden dependencies among them constitute the most important necessity of creative thinking (Robinson and Stern 1997: 56; Bonn 2001: 67). In this case, it is possible to say that creativity takes place in the process of innovation and invention (Leon 2016: 10). In addition, in the process of strategic thinking, the creative spirit should be supported and creativity should be promoted (Graetz 2002: 458).

Synthesis

One of the elements of strategic thinking is the ability to synthesis meaning to be able to unify the parts and to think in higher level. According to Mintzberg, strategic management should now proceed in a more synthetically oriented manner and this situation will also make a significant contribution to the development of strategic thinking (Mintzberg 1994: 108). Formal planning method businesses in large organizations which is typical practice in the US and Europe in the 1970s; deprive them of the ability to make strategic changes (Betz 2001: 233). While this practice emphasized strategic planning, it kept the strategic dimension of thinking, which has an extremely vital prescription for organizations in the background But; strategic thinking is an indispensable requirement for organizations because it is a synthesis-oriented structure (Heracleous 2003: 39).

Hypothesis-Driven

The hypothetical focus of the last dimension of strategic thinking means that a strategic thinker assumpts about the future and tests these assumptions. Hypothesis-focused thinking is a concept which many managers who don't gain the ability of strategic thinking are quite stranger to even though an organization is one of the main requirements to be able to prepare for the future and achieve its goals and objectives. However, constant changes in the environment and related factors that affect both individual and organizational performance require to be hypothesis-driven. Organizations should estimate how environmental conditions in which they operate and how they will be affected by this change and should schedule according to the evolving situation. Otherwise, it will not be possible to sustain continuity and focus on the future (Liedtka 1998: 123–124).

2.3   Strategic Thinking and Leadership

People's living together, acting in groups and needing a group that uses an initiative together, finds a solution to the problems and can lead the group around a common goal has revealed the concept of leadership (Glueck 1980: 459). Although today it is the platform of different Dynamics, the thing that reveals the leadership mechanism is this necessity. The change in the world, however, continues. The evolution of post-industrial revolutionary developments, especially in the age of information, has led to greater need for leadership, both social and organizational, than ever. That the employees in organizations need to be guided by a leader in order to have high motivation and success makes variables such as organizational culture which they share, high organizational commitment and organizational citizenship relevant.

Thus, the importance of leadership for the organization's future is increasing gradually (Luthans 2005: 546).

Many researches on the structure of society have revealed that some individuals have had superiority over others and they have made the masses trail behind them. This differentiation and domain in society has prompted the researchers in search of solutions to organizational problems to work on leadership. It is a distinctive skill to be able to move, direct and organize a particular community within the framework of pre-determined goals. For this reason, the field of work on leadership is expanding day by day (Özkalp 1982: 211, Eren 2004: 431).

Although there is a great deal of research on leadership, there is no full consensus on definition and content (Feldman and Arnold 1993: 283). The goal of many researchers is to determine which factors determine the effectiveness of leadership behavior. The researchers in this area have tried to find out what the qualities, the capabilities, the power sources, the behavioral and situational conditions that will enable the leader to influence on the group goals that they want to achieve with their followers are (Yukl 2010: 2).

In the 1960s and 1970s, it was predominant the thought that the situations and conditions businesses meet are fundamental determinants of managerial behavior and organizational outcomes, and that managers do not have much ability to make decisions that affect business performance (Ireland and Hitt 2005: 45). In addition, during the 1950s and 1980s, in the literature on leadership, there were studies on only the lower and middle level managers in organizations (Yukl 2010: 368). However, after the 1980s, innovation and change have been seen in leadership research, particularly since the second half of 1980, change has begun to be explored in terms of strategic leadership research of executive leadership researches and senior managers (Boal and Hooijberg 2000: 515–516; Yukl 2010: 368–369). As a result of living changes and innovations, the concept of strategy has become one of the focal points in leadership researches.

The strategy is the main intellectual management activity because of its providing organizations with long-term and effective leadership. In this regard, the strategy is the basic building block for effective leadership. If there is not a leader providing long-term orientation in an organization, that organization can not show improvement and adapt a change. In addition, the absence of a leader that provides long-term orientation in the organization is causing the organization to remain vulnerable in a constantly changing competitive environment. (Betz 2001: I).

At the heart of effective leaders' success is the fact that they have the ability to think strategically and act. Strategic thinking ability is considered to be a very important leadership skill for the managers because of the importance of the basic building block that the strategies have in order to ensure the continuity of the organization. (Betz 2001: 5). In addition, strategic thinking provides managers with the courage to make the right decision at the point of opportunity they want to gain and facilitates managers to be future-oriented, to see big picture, to detect threats, to become skillful at making decisions and to solving problems (Alsaaty 2007: 68–69).

New problem areas require need for new synthesis and solutions. The manager must be a good strategist then a leader. According to a research on leadership and

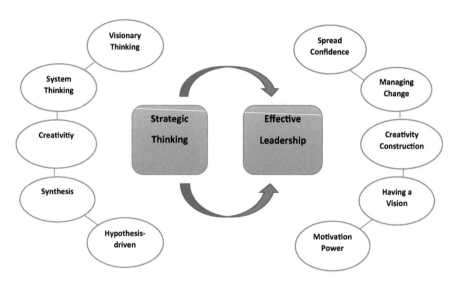

Fig. 1 Outstanding strategic leadership cycle

strategic thinking, the level of strategic thinking, which is the interface of mental perception and processes, influences the formation of leadership styles. In this respect, the strategic competencies of managers have an influence beyond the organizational life (Bajcar et al. 2015). In Fig. 1, it can be seen which sub-dimensions strategic thinking and corresponding of leadership process should possess It can be suggested that these subdimensions are complementary and catalyzer for each of the two variables.

From this point of view, strategic thinking is also a way of thinking about organizational leadership. Because the only representative of the intellectual context related to the strategy leads the management in the organization to the leadership skill. That visionary leadership gains importance with the advantage of creative ideas in competition is also used to eliminate the gaps occurring in the strategic planning. Because, strategic thinking helps downward decisions and ideas spread throughout the organization and gain efficiency although strategic planning which approaches the classical management model focuses upper, It is stated that strategic thinking indicates a skill of synthesizing based on the scientific knowledge in the perspective of organizational leadership, establishment of organizational climate which is dominated by trust, an understanding of human resources based on motivation, and an excellent understanding of management that increases the participation of employees (Bouhali et al. 2015: 75–77). In this part of the work the general framework of the leadership sub-dimensions mentioned above is presented.

2.3.1 Effective Leadership Sub-dimensions Based on Strategic Thoughts

There are a number of widely-adopted views on the characteristics providing the leaders' efficiency (Barutçugil 2004: 268). It is not enough that a person has only leadership qualities in the frame of these opinions. Some efforts must be made to comply with the rules and to make it effective in this regard. The attitudes, behaviors and strategies which the leaders adopt in society, group or organization determine their effectiveness (Güney 2012: 53, 59). It is very important to ensure the suitability of the behaviors that result in decisions to realize a characteristic. The success of the leadership mechanism in today's management understanding necessitates these attitudes and behaviors to reach a strategic position.

In this study, the necessary qualities for leaders to achieve success and to be effective on the basis of strategic thinking can be examined in five sub-dimensions. These can be organized as spreading trust, managing change, having vision, building motivation and creativity.

Spread Confidence

Much of the work of leaders in organizations is to manage employees and solve their problems, however obtaining the information they need to solve these problems is related to how employees trust on their leaders. Trust and reliability are important for leaders in reaching information and collaboration and increasing effectiveness. Trust is a tool of desire and conditioning to think strategically. Trust, therefore, expresses the willingness to make yourself vulnerable due to the presence of positive expectations about how work will be shaped. The shaking of trust can not only lead to a departure from the strategic point of view, but also to harmful effects on the performance of employee in the organizations (Robbins and Judge 2013: 387).

Managing Change

The ability to manage the change of strategic thinking leaders has begun to be seen as their most distinctive feature and strength, as in the recent years rapid changes in the business environment have occurred and the effects of these changes on organizations have become more evident (Hussey 1998: 10). One of the main tasks of the leader is to learn new things by meeting passion for change and to create an organization spirit and organizational culture by transforming new things into experiences. Leaders who manage change offer opportunities to help embrace organizational learning and new developments by acting forward rather than reacting to change (Tapscott 2014: 242). From this point of view, a leadership understanding that takes the strategic thinking of organizing the future and organizational renewal into itself and organizational learning gains importance.

Having a Vision

From an organizational point of view, the vision expresses the organizational future's being portrayed as well as the ability to design, develop, and share the imagined future (Senge 1998: 17). For a successful strategy, it must have a good leader and a good strategic vision. It is also expected that this vision can be successfully transformed into effective operational plans (Betz 2001: II). One of the key elements of leadership is to have a vision that guides them. If an individual does not know where and what he wants to reach, it is not possible to get there. Leaders have loud and clear ideas individually and professionally about what they want to do on the basis of strategic thinking in organizations. This situation shows that they have vision. The leaders having vision makes them have the power to continue, even in regressions and failures (Bennis 2009: 34). So it can be said that the leader who can not draw a vision or does not make such an effort is far away from strategic thinking.

Motivation Power

For an effective motivational force, leaders must have the ability to move organization employees in the desired direction, initiate action, activate and thrill them (Adair 2003: 167). Leaders with strategic thinking skills can achieve effective networking with their employees and motivate them towards organizational goals and vision. Because effective leaders can ensure that employees feel strong, capable, equipped and connected to their work, and can mobilize them. The motivation tool for effective leadership at this point regards a strong communication ability as a necessity. Effective leaders must share their knowledge and ideas with them in order to mobilize employees. Otherwise, the motivation power of the leaders will tend to weaken (Maxwell 2007: 29).

Creativity Construction

Creativity, which is the ability to create new ideas (Barker 2002: 23), is the key element of leadership that enhances the efficiencies of leaders and is a creative problem-solving ability and can approach the problem in many ways (Puccio et al. 2007: 13). In development of employees' creativity skills in organizations, it is also a very important issue that Followers are provided incentives, support, open and continuous communication by the leader they follow and the leaders show feedback on the basis of their work (Madjar et al. 2002: 757). For this reason, there is a need for sufficient numbers of strategically thought leaders to be able to develop creativity (Mumford et al. 2003: 411). Leaders outside of custom and tradition play a crucial role in the development of creativity in organizations, and the reinforcement of organizational climate for strategic thinking is the most important one. In such a climate, employees are directed to think creatively, organizational benefits and gains are maximized (Jaussi and Dionne 2003: 495).

3   Conclusion

It is understood that organizations should focus on problem solving in management other than production and marketing functions, based on global developments in the world, changes in consumption habits and increasing competition. This situation translates into a social expectation at a level that exceeds customer relationships.

However, whether profit-oriented or non-profit organizations, the framework for the routine service requirement expected from the managers in today's management concept is expanding and it involves predicting the future, increasing the forecasting hits and a vision-based management perspective. In this way, all organizations, small and large, meet with the concept of strategy and face the necessity of making the perspective of the organization dominant in the life of the organization.

The concept of strategy adapted from the military terminology has gradually gained a special position within the management discipline since the 1950s, and has been increasing its influence by holistic orientations such as strategic planning and strategic management. As an adaptable and dynamic concept in this process, strategic thinking is used as a strategic road map for managers. A perspective that encompasses the organization's culture and climate seems appropriate to the nature of strategic thinking beyond its goal of achieving in only a few predictions, predicting organizational variables or parameters. Strategic thinking requires to think about every issue that is meaningful from a strategic point of view.

On the other hand, strategic thinking brings together an understanding that promotes manager into a leadership position by its nature. Building the future, positioning the organization in this direction and ensuring its continuity mean moving the organizational purpose partnership to higher levels in terms of professional management. Therefore, the power and the spread of strategic thinking and the effectiveness of leadership have a certain co-ordination. The existence of managers who do not have certain leadership qualities in an organization does not seem to be sufficient in terms of the emergence of strategic thinking as a system.

In this study, it is aimed to present the interaction and coordination between strategic thinking and leadership based on literature. In the scientific literature, studies conducted in this direction were examined and it was attempted to determine in which dimensions the strategic thinking and appropriate leadership style could come together. According to this, while the strategic thinking is analyzed with the sub-dimensions of Synthesis, Visionary Thinking, System Thinking, Creativity and Hypothesis-driven, the leadership dimensions coordinating with the strategic thinking are determined as spreading trust, managing change, having vision, building motivation and creativity. It is revealed that mutual sub-dimensions are complementary in the framework of these findings and evaluations and that the strategic thinking capacity of the organization can be guided through the interaction of two variables. It can be said that supporting the general framework and literature contribution drawn in the study with field research is important in order to measure generalizability as well as obtaining empirical findings.

References

Adair, J. (2003, May). *Effective strategic leadership: An essential path to success guided*. London: Pan Books.

Alsaaty, F. M. (2007, February). Entrepreneurs: Strategic thinkers in search of opportunities. *Journal of Business & Economics Research, 5*(2), 65–71.

Andrews, R. K. (1971). *The concepts of corporate strategy* (3rd ed.). Homewood, IL: Dow Jones-Irwin.

Ansoff, H. I. (1991). Critique of Henry Mintzberg's 'The design school: Reconsidering the basic premises of strategic management'. *Strategic Management Journal, 12*, 449–461. https://doi.org/10.1002/smj.4250120605.

Ansoff, H. I., & McDonnell, E. J. (1990). *Implanting strategic management*. Englewood Cliffs, NJ: Prentice Hall.

Arogyaswamy, B., & Byles, M. C. (1987). Organizational culture: Internal and external fits. *Journal of Management, 13*(4), 647–659.

Bajcar, B., Babiak, J., & Nosal, C. (2015). When leaders become strategists. A new look at determinants of leadership styles through their relationship with strategic thinking. *Procedia Manufacturing, 3*, 3669–3676. https://doi.org/10.1016/j.promfg.2015.07.777.

Barker, A. (2002). *The alchemy of innovation: Perspectives from the leading edge*. London: Spiro Press.

Barutçugil, İ. (2004). *Stratejik İnsan Kaynakları Yönetimi*. İstanbul: Kariyer Yayınları.

Bennis, W. (2009). *On becoming a leader* (4th ed.). New York: Basic Books.

Betz, F. (2001). *Executive strategy: Strategic management and information technology*. New York: Wiley.

Blackerby, P. (1994). History of strategic planning. *Armed Forces Comptroller Magazine, 39*(1), 23–24.

Boal, K. B., & Hooijberg, R. (2000). Strategic leadership research: Moving on. *Leadership Quarterly, 11*(4), 515–549.

Bonn, I. (2001). Developing strategic thinking as a core competency. *Management Decision, 39*(1), 63–70.

Bonn, I. (2005). Improving strategic thinking: A multilevel approach. *Leadership & Organization Development Journal, 26*(5), 336–354.

Bouhali, R., Mekdad, Y., Lebsir, H., & Ferkha, L. (2015). Leader roles for innovation: Strategic thinking and planning. *Procedia—Social and Behavioral Sciences, 181*, 72–78.

Bowman, C., & Asch, D. (1992). *Strategic management*. New York: McMillan.

Bracker, J. (1980). The historical development of the strategic management concept. *Academy of Management Review, 5*(2), 219–224.

Collis, D. J., & Montgomery, C. A. (1990). Competing on resources: Strategy in the 1990s. *Harvard Business Review, 73*(4), 118–128.

Davies, B. (2004). Developing the strategically focused school. *School Leadership & Management, 24*(1), 11–27.

Dixit, A. K., & Nalebuff, B. J. (2010). *The art of strategy: A game theorist's guide to success in business and life*. New York: W.W. Norton.

Eren, E. (2004). *Örgütsel davranış ve yönetim psikolojisi (8. Baskı)*. İstanbul: Beta Yayıncılık.

Fahey, L., & Randall, R. M. (1994). *The portable MBA in strategy*. New York: Wiley.

Feldman, C. D., & Arnold, H. J. (1993). *Managing individual and group behaviour in organizations*. New York: McGraw Hill.

Glueck, W. (1976). *Business policy: Strategy formation and management action* (2nd ed.). Tokyo: McGraw-Hill.

Glueck, W. F. (1980). *Management*. Insdale, IL: Dryden Press.

Graetz, F. (2002). Strategic thinking versus strategic planning: Towards understanding the complementaries. *Management Decision, 40*(5), 456–462.

Güney, S. (2012). *Liderlik*. Ankara: Nobel Yayıncılık.

Hafsi, T., & Thomas, H. (2005). The field of strategy: In search of a walking stick. *European Management Journal, 23*(5), 507–519.

Haycock, K., Cheadle, A., & Blustone, K. S. (2012). Strategic thinking: Lessons for leadership from the literature. *Library Leadership & Management, 26*(3/4), 1–23.

Heracleous, L. (1998). Strategic thinking or strategic planning. *Long Range Planning, 31*(3), 481–487.

Heracleous, L. (2003). *Strategy and organization: Realizing strategic management.* New York: Cambridge University Press.

Hussey, D. (1998). *How to be better at managing change.* London: Kogan Page.

Ireland, R. D., & Hitt, M. A. (2005). Achieving and maintaining strategic competitiveness in the 21st. century: The role of strategic leadership. *Academy of Management Executive, 19*(4), 63–74.

Jaussi, K. S., & Dionne, S. D. (2003). Leading for creativity: The role of unconventional leadership behavior. *The Leadership Quarterly, 14,* 475–498.

Jerkins, M., Ambrosini, V., & Collier, N. (2007). *Advanced strategic management: A multi-perspective approach* (2nd ed.). Hampshire: Palgrave Macmillan.

Johnson, G., Melin, L., & Whittington, R. (2003, January). Micro strategy and strategizing: Towards an activity-based view. *Journal of Management Studies, 40*(1), 3–22. https://doi.org/10.1111/1467-6486.t01-2-00002.

Katsioloudes, M. I. (2006). *Strategic management: Global cultural perspectives for profit and non-profit organizations.* Burlington: Butterworth Heinemann.

Kneller, G. (2005). *The art of science and creativity.* New York: Holt, Rinehart & Winston of Canada.

Leon, M. Y. (2016). Developing strategic thinking. *Australian Army Journal, 8*(2), 5–22.

Liedtka, J. M. (1998, February). Strategic thinking: Can it be taught? *Long Range Planning, 31*(1), 120–129.

Luffman, G., Lea, E., Sanderson, S., & Kenny, B. (1996). *Strategic management an analytical introduction.* Oxford: Blackwell.

Luthans, F. (2005). *Organizational behaviour.* Boston: McGraw-Hill Irwin.

Macmillan, H., & Tampoe, M. (2000). *Strategic management.* New York: Oxford University Press.

Madjar, N., Oldham, G. R., & Pratt, M. G. (2002). There's no place like home?: The contributions of work and nonwork creativity support to employees' creative performance. *Academy of Management Journal, 45,* 757–767.

Maxwell, J. C. (2007, September). *The 21 irrefutable laws of leadership: Follow them and people will follow you (10th Anniversary Edition).* Nashville, TN: Thomas Nelson. Revised & Updated.

Mintzberg, H. (1994, January). The fall and rise of strategic planning. *Harvard Business Review, 72*(1), 107–114.

Mumford, M. D., Connelly, M. S., & Gaddis, B. (2003). How creative leaders think: Experimental findings and cases. *The Leadership Quarterly, 14,* 411–432.

Nuntamanop, P., Kauranen, I., & Igel, B. (2013). A new model of strategic thinking competency. *Journal of Strategy and Management, 6*(3), 242–264.

Ohmae, K. (1982). *The mind of the strategist: The art of Japanese business.* New York: McGraw-Hill.

O'Shannassy, T. (2003, January). Modern strategic management, balancing strategic thinkking and strategic planning for internal and external stakeholders. *Singapore Management Review, 25,* 53–67.

Özkalp, E. (1982). *Davranış bilimleri ve organizasyonlarda davranış.* Eskişehir: Eskişehir İktisadi ve Ticari İlimler Akademisi Yayınları.

Puccio, G. J., Murdock, M. C., & Mance, M. (2007). *Creative leadership: Skills that drive change.* Thousand Oaks, CA: SAGE.

Rahnama, S., & Rahpeyma, A. A. (2015). The influential factors of strategic thinking at the organizational level. *Journal of Marketing and Consumer Research, 12,* 26–35.

Robbins, S. P., & Judge, A. T. (2013). *Organizational behavior.* Harlow, UK: Pearson, Prentice Hall.

Robinson, A. G., & Stern, S. (1997). *Corporate creativity.* Warriewood: Business & Professional.

Rosche, A. L. H. W. (2002). *Personality correlates of strategic thinking in an organizational context.* California School of Organizational Studies, San Francisco: Alliant International University.

Rowe, A. J., Mason, R. O., & Dickel, K. E. (1986). *Strategic management – A methodological approach*. Boston, MA: Addison-Wesley Publishing Company International.

Senge, P. (1992, March/April). Mental models. *Planning Review, 44*, 4–10.

Senge, P. (1998, Summer). The practice of innovation. *Leader to Leader Journal, 9*, 16–22.

Tapscott, D. (2014). *Digital economy anniversary edition: Rethinking promise and peril in the age of networked intelligent*. New York: McGraw Hill.

Taş, A., Hızıroğlu, M., Ersoy, A. Y., & Özer, K. (2017). Kutadgu Bilig'de stratejik düşünmenin izini sürmek. *Bilig, 80*, 147–178.

Thompson, A. A., & Strickland, A. J. (1996). *Strategic management* (9th ed.). Irwin, Sydney: Times Mirror Higher Education Group.

Young, M. L. (2016). Developing strategic thinking. *Australian Army Journal, 8*(2), 5–23.

Yukl, G. (2010). *Leadership in organization* (2nd ed.). Upper Saddle River, NJ: Prentice-Hall.

How to Create a Culture of Innovation?

Mehmet Saim Aşçı

Abstract As a consequence of economic, social and political developments, the human, social and cultural structures of institutions have begun to attract the attention of those who work in the theoretical and practical fields of management. It is concluded that cooperation systems can be successful in the direction of the individual talents and in particular the desires of the participators that establish them.

Therefore, an effective and productive management depends on the knowledge of the factors determining the attitudes and behaviors of a person, either as an individual or as a member of a group, and the existence of possibilities to influence them.

Each organization creates its own culture (value system), but also it is a product of the cultural influence of the surrounding environment. International business management has led to comparative cultural research, which has made the culture to become part of management field and made the managers be more interested in the subject.

The age of transformation we live in demands new perspectives and approaches from all of us. Information changes our lives rapidly. Recently, we have been more often using concepts like "**innovation**", "**restructuring**", "**change**" or "**transformation**". All of these concepts we use about our individual, institutional or social life indicate that we are not satisfied with "our present situation". Today, the methods, ways, styles, and processes we have been applying are not as useful as they used to be. This increases uncertainty in the business world as well as in all areas of life. In this age, where we are surrounded by uncertainty, the way to overcome uncertainty is through making innovations, that is, from "**innovativeness**".

Innovation cannot always be made and in everywhere; the source of innovation is the creativity. But successful innovation requires more than that; some conditions— social, economic and political conditions—should arise. Innovativeness needs a culture to flourish. This study tries to explain what these conditions might be and if they could be recreated intentionally.

M. S. Aşçı (✉)
İstanbul Medipol University, Istanbul, Turkey
e-mail: msasci@medipol.edu.tr

© Springer International Publishing AG, part of Springer Nature 2018   189
H. Dincer et al. (eds.), *Strategic Design and Innovative Thinking in Business Operations*, Contributions to Management Science,
https://doi.org/10.1007/978-3-319-77622-4_10

1 Introduction

What is culture? Today it is difficult to answer this question in a way to satisfy everybody. Indeed, the efforts of almost all scientists, working in fields related to culture, to redefine culture proves this. In understanding the difficulty to define culture, one should, in many times, seek reasons other than lack of existing knowledge and tools. First, the terms should follow the advances of the sciences they belong to, and be redefined accordingly (Turhan 1987: 34).

Nevertheless, if all the definitions presented up to now are considered, it is easy to understand the common points in them and what is meant by "culture".

2 Literal Meaning of the Culture

Culture is considered to come from "colere" or "cultura" which are classical Latin verbs, meaning "to look" or "to grow". It is necessary to wait until the beginning of the 1750s to link this word to the lifestyle of human in the history of humanity (Lubben 1970: 86).

Before the eighteenth century, the word *cultura* was used in the meaning of *cultivating*. This word, which is used in French in the same sense, was first used by Voltaire to mean the establishment, improvement, and development of human intelligence. The word passed from here to German used as *cultur* in a German language dictionary dated 1793 and later became the *Kulture* (Güvenç 1972: 96).

2.1 The Meaning of Culture in Social Sciences

The culture is a technical term regarding social sciences. This could not prevent the culture from being used in various non-technical meanings (Erdoğan 1975: 8). Sometimes it is said that anybody who is cultured has extreme subtlety and behavior and knows the aesthetic aspects of life. In this narrow sense, culture is something that relatively few people have, who allocates leisure, wealth, competence, and interest for such elegancies (Fichter 1960: 196).

Culture is defined as a heredity in social sciences which includes knowledge, beliefs, and customs. The knowledge and skills in here are those which are useful for members of society. In this case, the culture is the limitation of the way of life of society. The culture does not cover people's random and all behaviors that they particular have. The culture includes patterns of behavior or habits that are common in society (Erdoğan 1975: 9).

According to anthropologists, the culture has a meaning that goes beyond the aesthetic pleasure of man. The culture encompasses scientific beliefs, beliefs about miracles, religious beliefs, and beliefs as authority, organization and business, that characterize society (Penfield 1969: 41–42).

3 Organizational Culture

Since the emergence of Japan as a leading industrial power, organizational theorists and managers have become more aware of the relationship between culture and management. In the 1960s, the confidence and influence created by American management and industry were at the highest level. In the 1970s, the performance of Japanese automakers, electronics, and other manufacturing industries began to change this picture, with a gradual but increasingly powerful force. Japan has become dominant in international markets and has gained a solid reputation for quality, reliability, value, and service. With a population of over 110 million clustered in four small mountainous islands, with almost no natural resources and energy, Japan has managed to achieve the lowest unemployment rate with the highest growth rate and recruited the world's best paid and healthier workers, at least in relatively bigger and successful corporations. It established a leading industrial empire out of the ashes of the Second World War.

Most of the different theorists, who discussed the reasons for this transformation, came to a consensus that the cultural and general lifestyle of this mysterious Eastern country played an important role in this issue. Thus "culture" became a hot topic in the field of management in the 1980s and early 1990s. Japan's indigenous character has led to Western management theorists to take a special interest in the culture and character of their own countries and their ties to organizational life (Morgan 1998: 139).

What is this phenomenon we call culture? The word is derived from the figurative meaning of cultivating the land. When we speak of culture, we are talking about a model of development that is usually reflected in society's knowledge, ideology, value, law and daily ritual system. The word is often used to indicate the degree of education that appears in the belief and tradition systems, as it is in the concept of being "cultured". Both uses arise from observations of "primitive" societies in the nineteenth century and express the idea that different societies reveal different levels of social development. However, at present, the concept of culture does not include this old point of view towards evaluation; rather, it is used to express that different groups of people have different lifestyles. As it is defined by the anthropologist C. Wissler, "Culture is society's way of living" (Turhan 1987: 37).

In speaking of society as a culture, we use a metaphor related to agriculture to draw attention to a very specific aspect of social development (Morgan 1998: 140). This is a metaphor having great relevance to the understanding of the organization.

The business operates in a specific society. Members of this society have peculiar beliefs, value judgments and specific attitudes towards various events. It is significant to know these cultural elements for the manager. However, the informational characteristics, laws, technological level of the society will also affect the business that continues to work within a society. Thus, the culture, for business and business manager, is all of the beliefs, values, customs and other interpersonal relationships created by specific human communities and affecting the way the organization works and the outcome of its activities. From this point of view, it is possible to draw the conclusion that the culture is the societal values surrounding the business activities and having material and spiritual characteristics (Erdoğan 1975: 13).

While the manager wants to understand better the social environment she lives in, on the one hand, she wants to base the staff's behavior to certain principles on the other. Today's manager wants to know the factors that affect the working conditions of the environment where she sustains efforts and to predict the behavior of the individuals she works with. Knowing people's behaviors in advance and recognizing the various characteristics of the community is possible by knowing the cultures of people and society.

The manager must know the behavior of both the individuals in the organization and the members of the society encircling the organization. If we are aiming at predicting people's behaviors over a long period, or if we want to be able to orientate people's behavior to specific goals, we need to be aware of the developments in beliefs and attitudes and the processes that occur during their change. Managers, reformers, minority group leaders and people in business are not content with knowing the general characteristics of the attitudes; they want to know more and even the very specific beliefs and attitudes of people. Again, these people want to know how to create beliefs and attitudes that do not exist in people, and how to change their current beliefs and attitudes (Krech and Crutchfied 1967: 204).

This information does not only give an opportunity to understand and predict the behaviors of the members of such culture but also identifies what activities are possible to make (Flippo 1966: 76).

The important thing in this context is how leaders will deal with the intellectual entity in their organizations. The knowledge, insight, and skills of the workforce in their hands will determine whether this organization will be successful. The task facing the leader is to think about how to utilize this asset as leverage to improve performance (Rosen and Brown 1996: 176–177).

4   Organizational Culture and Sub-cultures

The impact of a culture is rarely uniform. As the individuals in culture have different personalities despite many commonalities, the same is true for groups and organizations.

This is what is now considered as "corporate culture". Organizations are mini-communities that have their own distinctive culture and sub-culture models. An organization can see itself as a tightly integrated team or family that believes in working together. The idea of "We are the best in the business, and we intend to stay so" may be the judgment of other. The other may be divided into and highly fragmented among different groups who think quite differently and have different aspirations as to how the corporation should be. Such belief or common-sense models supported by different norms of functioning and rituals, fragmented or integrated, may have a decisive influence on the ability of the organization to overcome the challenges it faces.

One of the easiest ways to understand the nature of the company's culture and subculture is to observe the daily functioning of a group or organization to which a person belongs to as if looking from the outside. It is to assume the role of an anthropologist. As the interaction models of the individual, the language used, the images and the themes used in the conversations, and the various rituals of the daily routine are understood, the characteristics of the observed culture will gradually emerge. As the rationale of the culture related to such aspects is examined, one usually realizes that the way in which work is conducted has a sound historical background (Morgan 1998: 150).

Common values, common beliefs, common sense and common understanding, are all different forms of defining culture. When referring to culture, we are talking about the process of establishing a reality that allows people to see and comprehend certain events, actions, objects, words or situations in different ways. These comprehension models help us to overcome these situations and provide a basis rendering our behavior reasonable and meaningful (Morgan 1998: 159).

But how does this happen? How is culture created and sustained?

5 Creating a Common Mindset: Reorganizing the Company Culture

Usually, neither reorganization of business process nor strategic reorientation alone is enough to reverse the situation of a company. Sometimes the company mindset must be entirely transformed (De Vries 2006: 192).

The challenge faced by the inspirers of any change process is to ensure that everyone in the organization takes personal responsibility for a part of the process. Everyone in the organization should ask the following question: What are the things that keep me away from doing the task I want to do? How can I get rid of these obstacles?

As any person in the leadership position can discover in a short time, you cannot make people sensitive only by demanding to be so. In other words, the leader has to create a "common mindset". To do this, you need to ask personal questions like "what are the obstacles ahead of you?" to the people. The reactions people show to these questions push the process of institutional transformation and determine whether this process will continue and how would it be possible.

The common mindset required for successful change combines the concrete future objectives with the characteristics of an organizational culture that supports the desired future. This is a difficult task, however, because of organizational culture—the mosaic of fundamental assumptions expressed as behavioral patterns, beliefs, values, and characteristic behavioral patterns adopted by members of an organization in the struggle to cope with internal and external pressures—is largely out of the awareness of people. Organizational culture is kind of an "invisible hand" that structures activities in the organization (De Vries 2006: 194).

Organizational culture provides rules for behavior. It helps employees understand what to do and what not to do in the organizational life. At the same time, the organizational culture is "descriptive", expressing the uniqueness and identity of the organization; it includes certain symbolic elements like language, rituals, stories, metaphors, narratives, behaviors, and other structures. They have become integral parts of the experiences of everyday life. Because their roots are in the identity, the organizational culture tends to continue over time, and it is not easily changeable.

The values create the company culture values, and these are reflected in the way they work. Model persons, events, celebrated and rewarded subjects determined the company culture. The rewarding of innovation in a company determines its value. An employee's initiative towards customer satisfaction can be appreciated from mouth to mouth. An unsuccessful investment in a new market made by someone else can be seen as a negative experience. These are clear indications of the corporate culture (Zoltners et al. 1997: 111–112).

The company values determine what matters in the company. These are principles, standards, and guides of behavior. These values often contribute to the resolution of conflicts and contradictions in the company.

It is not easy to determine the values that establish the culture in our organization. However, no matter how difficult it is, determining these values is vital for any change effort. The leader should know which values are shared. Otherwise, she can't know if these values are worth pursuing. Knowing this is very valuable for leaders who want to be able to create an open, collaborative and trust-based "able-to-do" atmosphere (Hudson 2003: 119).

While the point of departure of the industrial society is freedom of the individual, the structure and institutionalization have been realized at the societal level (national level). This has limited participation at the political and social level. The class-based structure of the conventional society as aristocrats-servants has continued in the employee-employer form.

These social structures are reflected in the values, norms and behavioral patterns, i.e. the cultural system, of the individual. In the industrial society, freedom, equality, justice, security, and welfare have developed as a reaction to the existence of opposing categories in society. There is a need for policies to disseminate these basic social values against dependency, bigotry, inequality, poverty, uncertainty, and risks that exist in the society.

It has become a necessity **to protect the freedom of the individual** against values, norms, rules, and behaviors that limit the individual and make her a dependent (Erkan 1994: 209).

6 Changing the Culture

The culture of a company can only be changed by its employees. Employees, as a new visionary, can change the existing culture by insisting on spreading the desired values and working styles, adapting their movements to the desired new culture and rewarding the behaviors appropriate to the new culture.

The cultures should be continually adapted to the conditions and spread by articulation. Decisions should be given according to the desired culture, the achievements should be celebrated accordingly, values should be expressed, and appropriate working styles should be chosen. The vision that will guide the company culture should be spread continuously, insistently and persuasively. It should be included in the speeches and writings of the leaders. The managers should take it as a guide while guiding and giving ideas. All employees should carry out their daily activities and relations with each other according to that vision. Events and heroes should be celebrated by that vision. Appropriate values and patterns of work should guide the company's strength. When appropriate values and work styles are celebrated, different values should be countered and prevented.

The culture changes when people do what they say. If employees cannot live by the desired culture, culture cannot live long. What is told should be consistent with what is done in a company. When the behaviors are different from the expressions, there grows doubt and insecurity. When the two are compatible, the values are strengthened and spread throughout the organization.

A sound culture should reward sound events. Companies must reward the values and work that build the desired culture. If an open communication needed to become sound, those who say all the positive and negative information and ideas should be rewarded, never be punished. The bad news should be taken as a signal for change, not to punish and exclude the informant. Risk taking should not be punished. Errors help people learn and improve. This understanding should be a part of the culture (Zoltners et al. 1997: 246–256).

7 Creativity

There is no doubt that human being is the most important source of creativity. Without creativity, there would be no progress; we would always repeat the same pattern (de Bono 2000: 159).

The person, who develops a physical object or thought which have never been made or thought, or new for her, is called the creator. A created thing is not required to emerge for the first time on the earth. It is sufficient to be new for the creator himself and her around.

Regarding our intellectual functions, creativity can be defined as "producing new concepts or ideas from the relations between existing concepts". That is, the creative thinking is about bringing "innovation" or "difference" (Yıldırım 1998: 21).

The creativity is personal, but not private! In other words, the creation process takes place with personal characteristics, but the share of the surrounding in the creation of these characteristics is crucial. For example, if it was possible to isolate a baby before she starts to recognize her surrounding, it would be observed that over the years she would make some creative initiatives only with her innate abilities. For example, she would protect herself from cold, fall fruits from trees with sticks or make simple devices. However, if the same child is trained in a civilized environment and has a profession, she will be able to make a much higher level of creative initiatives. In addition to the effect of raising the level of creativity, the environment also has a negative effect that limits it.

The creativity is not a coincidental event. Every creative initiative and its success is based on a reason. In addition to the innate abilities of the creative person, reasons like the previous knowledge, incentive effects, belief in personal and social goals, trial, patience, determination, and endurance also plays a role in creativity. Why Beethoven emerged in a certain region of Europe and at the beginning of nineteenth century can be explained by certain reasons as well as by some coincidences.

Humanity is at the zenith of creativity in the age of infancy. But because of lack of judicial power, knowledge, and experience, the level of things she creates is much lower than adults. The first signals that limit the child's creative power come from the family environment. It is always instructed and even ordered to accept, what should and should not be done as well as what the good and the bad is. This also goes on in education from primary school to graduation from college. As the social environment is in the same attitude as well, the creativity of the person becomes very limited (Kobu 1981: 356).

Knowledge has become the most important source of individuals, institutions or societies today. Our future success will depend on our ability to produce and use knowledge and thus the thinking activity.

Our thinking activity depends on innate traits, but it is also a skill to be developed. As a matter of fact, what we have learned from education, experience or a variety of sources increase our ability to think as much as developing our "knowledge store". But we cannot achieve the intellectual capacity we need "in the information age" just "indirectly". Also, we must improve our potential and use it better.

The ever-accelerating "change" brings new challenges, new options, and perspectives. So, in addition to making what we do better in the future, we will need more of our creativity, "searching and finding innovation".

Like our other intellectual skills, we can develop our creativity with a conscious effort. It is possible to use a variety of tools from using specific methods and approaches to adopting certain attitudes and behaviors, changing our lifestyle and education. Even if conscious efforts do not assure making all of us "geniuses", they will definitely make us more creative and innovative. Apart from groundbreaking innovations, we need to bring small but constant innovations about our private, business and social life (Yıldırım 1998: 243–244).

8 The Use of Creativity in an Organization

Creativity in an organization can be used in two ways (De Bono 2000: 163–165).

1. As a part of the general idea of everyone in the organization. When the creativity is used in the production stage, it will make processes more effective, such as quality improvement, business improvement, and cost reduction. The creativity does not only provide concrete ideas, but it also creates an important driving force because it leads people to think about what they are doing.

   The creativity is a fundamental part of total quality management and all cost-reduction applications. An analysis can bring you only to a certain stage. Options and new ideas are necessary to go further. Problem solvers have a great need for creativity especially when the reasons for the problem cannot be eradicated, and there is a need for a way out. The improvement, especially with successive small steps, depends on creativity to a very large extent.

   All senior managers, including top executives, should be involved in creativity. Assigning this task to someone else is not enough. It Is extremely important that senior management understands the logic and methods of creativity. Creativity is part of thinking; putting this piece on edge and taking care of it cannot be called the work of others.

2. The creativity that focuses on specific areas such as strategy, research, product design, marketing, worker relations, finance, and production methods is also necessary. In these areas, there is a constant need for new ideas to solve problems or create opportunities. Relying merely on experience, knowledge, and analysis are no different than driving a car with only three wheels.

9 Innovation

As it is in our every skill, our creativity is meaningful to the extent that we can use it. Therefore, we need to touch briefly on what purpose, where, and when to use this skill. Theoretically, creativity is necessary for everyone and in every aspect of the life. Indeed, some of the great inventions of the past was made by established connections or unexpected connotations while doing another activity. However, some situations are more conducive to creativity by nature.

A university research lab or a company's product development department has already been established for the use of creativity. So, we can make some generalizations even if we can't draw exact boundaries about the use of our creativity.

The words of "creativity" and "innovation" often come out together. When you want one of them, it is as if you have to ask for the other as well. Indeed, when we look at the use of company language—annual reports, job advertisements, vision and mission statements, etc.—we can have the doubt that the two words express the same thing.

We need to distinguish these two terms from each other. Let's start with a simple definition: *Innovation is creating new resources for customer satisfaction.*

It not only brings new ideas to an organization but also to the environment of the organization and applies them.

This practice is something—a product or service—that customers realize. The novelty of this good or service and their value as innovation is from the customer point of view, not from the innovativeness itself. Creativity can be defined in the same way: The *creativity is the ability to create new ideas.*

Innovation is a process, and the creativity is the set of skills or natural pre-dispositions enabling such process. Creativity is an act of innovation (mainly mental) while innovation is a physical or external consequence of the creativity.

9.1 Using Innovation and Creativity

We use creativity to produce new concepts or relationships. This can arise as a new solution to a problem, as a new product or as a new form of behavior. When we ask, "why do we do this?", we can give answers such as "not satisfied with the present", "finding the present insufficient", "to think we can do better than the present", "others can do better than the present" and "getting used to and be bored of the present". In summary, we use our creativity to "develop our present situation in any matter" and thus "bring innovation at any level".

Creativity is often seen as individualistic and partly capricious: difficult to define, and even more difficult to manage. Innovation, on the other hand, is often seen as a structured group of processes that provide economic or Market advantage. The senior managers show greater interest in consultants who offer to increase their capacity to innovate, compared to projects aimed at unveiling the creativity of people. Creativity is seen as something very good; whereas what brings real rewards is innovation (Barker 2002: 23).

The concept of innovation also related to "change" and "improvement". The change means that something new emerges, and improvement means that these innovations are positive. As a matter of fact, we say that our everyday life changes continuously and with and increasing pace (Yıldırım 1998: 121–122).

10 Creating Innovation Culture

Innovation cannot always be made and in everywhere; the source of innovation is the creativity. But successful innovation requires more than that; some conditions—social, economic and political conditions—should arise. Innovation requires a culture to flourish inside; it opens the windows of mind sanctuary and necessitates a blend of expertise and experience that brings us to new ideas, new processes, and new products (Hammer and Champy 1993: 29).

We need a mix of rich expertise and experience that will open the windows of our mind cathedral, bring us new ideas, new processes, and new products.

"Culture" is a word we use for both societies and organizations. The definition is almost as difficult as "innovation" and "innovativeness"; but when we say "culture" in this context, we are referring to the complex values and attitudes that give information about what people do. These values can be difficult to distinguish: most of them are not articulated in the law or similar documents, but tacitly included (Dodgson 1993: 379).

Some cultures seem to be more inclined to innovation than other cultures. What kind of values do these cultures possess? If we can detect them, maybe we can improve those values ourselves as well. This desire has led some organizations to develop industrial complexes, science parks and exchange programs (Barker 2002: 63–64).

In this context, how the values of the cultures close to the innovation function gain importance.

10.1   Industrial Zone as a Culture of Innovativeness

Innovativeness is essentially an urban phenomenon. Historically, the creativity has emerged not in remote rural areas, but in crowded cities. Indeed, it appears that your innovation has emerged in certain cities at certain times.

A century ago, economist Alfred Marshall realized that innovation was booming in certain zones. For example, he found such zones in London's East End, Manchester, Stoke-on-Trent, Birmingham, and Glasgow. They called them "industrial zones" and explained how they flourished innovated.

> When an industry chooses a venue for itself, there is a high probability of staying there for a long time: the advantages of close neighbors with the same artisanship are huge. The secrets of that craft are no longer mystery and become things that can be found everywhere like the air, and the children learn them without even realizing it. A good job is appreciated with its worth. There is an immediate exchange of views on the virtues of innovations and improvements in machines, processes and general business organization: When someone develops a new idea, others take it and combine it with his proposals so that the idea becomes a source of further ideas.

In this striking expression in the paragraph above, which we call today "brain storm", the realization of the idea of an innovative culture is explained. This paragraph might well describe the coming together of technology companies in the Silicon Valley or the virtual networks of software houses, design companies, microelectronics manufacturers, assemblers and servers who operate in the dot.com field.

This kind of zones has some characteristics of the complexity theory. For example, "the vertical production is fragmented": A large number of companies in the individual property are producing materials or components for each other. This creates very complex production networks. To alleviate shipping and adaptation issues, companies need to be grouped in the same place. But such economic complexity also creates the social complexity of communities that enable people to meet each other, learn from each other and exchange ideas. The meeting of minds is as important as the production networks regarding the development of innovativeness.

The economists and geographers have explored the basic features of such innovative environments since Marshall. Peter Hall, for example, examines Manchester of the eighteenth century, Glasgow and Berlin of the nineteenth century, Detroit of the early twentieth century and San Francisco of the mid-twentieth century in his book, *Cities in Civilization*. Hall has seen that all of these major industrial areas have some common characteristics (Hall 1998).

- They are all **commercial centers**. Most of them are ports.
- **The rise and decline of all of them are happening around innovative activity**. Technological innovation is creating urban development. These cities are showing rapid growth—and this speed often takes the form of a boom. As the innovation passes to somewhere else, their collapses can become disastrous.
- All of these cities are **located right on the edge of economic and cultural areas**. They are located somewhere in the middle of established industrial and political power centers. They are not isolated, but they are marginal.
- They all **have a tradition of developing the connected industries**. Successful companies meet demand which is specific to the local market: Shipping in Glasgow, T-model Ford production for local farmers in Detroit, electronic manufacturing for the needs of the army in San Francisco are dominant. Innovation is often the result of the dialogue between the connected established industries.
- In all of them, there is **relative cultural freedom**—free from choking prejudices, tradition, political or social constraints. They have an egalitarian social structure that is hardly based on hereditary richness. Likewise, religious or moral atmosphere conditions often promote openness and success.
- All have an activity network that nurtures learning and idea exchanges. Academic education or—in essence—training in the form of apprenticeship is more or less free. There are channels to transfer information into new application areas.
- They all benefit from the **new wealth** in the hands of people who are willing to use it as a venture capital.

Two Swedish academics have developed more theoretical models of innovative culture (Barker 2002: 69–71). Gunnar Törnqvist argued that any innovative culture has four main elements (Törnqvist 2004: 234):

- Information that people transmit to each other;
- Information stored in real or mechanical memory;
- Competence in activities to meet the needs of an external environment;
- The creativity that creates something new from all three activities.

A similar concept was developed by another Swedish scholar, Ake Andersson. Andersson believes that some factors come together in a "dynamic synergy process" to create innovative cultures:

- A sound financial system subject to moderate regulation;
- Original basic knowledge and competence;
- An imbalance between the needs and the existing possibilities;
- A culturally diverse community;
- Good communication.

Both Törnqvist and Andersson emphasize the idea of "structural instability" in their models. This idea reminds the theory of complexity. According to these two models, culture becomes "innovative" when it is "at the edge of chaos"—its internal order is at a point of transition or a radical transformation. Stable cultures—or collapsing cultures—are often largely devoid of innovation (Those who work in well-established—or worn and disordered—organizations call well understand this). It is interesting that both Törnqvist and Andersson prefer to explain this concept of structural instability, which is alarming in a sense, with a river metaphor. This may be because of Sweden's strong rivers.

Think about a culture that flows like a river in a social and economic "land". Regulation and technology cooperate to open a well-defined river bed allowing a fast flow at the first stages of the development of this culture. Then the land is flattened. Then the culture can stagnate, or the bed may become blurry and unstable. Uncertainty about the future allows for creative change. A small group of people with a vision can intervene in the situation and bring society into a new stable state. These are "New Humans", as Schumpeter mentions; they are courageous entrepreneurs who can keep up with the conditions of uncertainty (Andersson 1985: 59).

10.2   Two Different Innovative Cultures: From Top-Down or Bottom-Up?

So far, we have dealt with innovation as a "bottom-up" phenomenon. Outsiders—visionary, destructive, marginal and often young—creates chaotic entrepreneurship networks. New ideas emerge in these networks, and innovation takes off towards a very energetic and impossible to a predictable outcome.

However, there are the two historical developments that make this outcome difficult. When looking at these developments, it appears that innovation also has a "top-down" dimension. This dimension has been systemized and institutionalized within large companies during the last century. For the majority of us, these developments have determined how we have experienced these innovations (Gardner 1993: 7).

The first key development is the emergence of research and development (R&D). The industry—and the science supporting it—was institutionalized at the end of the nineteenth century, especially in Germany and in the United States. The vertically fragmented "industrial zone" became a highly integrated global company controlling all aspects of production and distribution. The entrepreneur has left its place to the manager and innovation has no longer been a product of visionary individuals but of scientists working in laboratories that are commercially financed. The first R&D laboratory was founded in 1872 by Siemens in Germany. The Bell Laboratories, founded in the 1920s, and DuPont's development department are the next examples. The R&D became a bedrock of innovativeness for the world's biggest companies in the fields of telecommunication, medicine, and even automobile production. As a consequence of this, the innovativeness was started to be seen dominantly as something belonging only a part of the organization.

It is common for innovation to look at something that belongs to only a part of the foundation. The biggest challenge facing many large companies today is taking innovation out of the laboratory and making a product of entire organization (Barker 2002: 73).

The second major development in innovation over the past century has been the increase in state intervention. Its birthplace is Germany as well. Berlin became the power plant of Prussian war machine in the nineteenth century, while it had been nothing but the capital of the small German state. The innovation—and its supporting educational institutions—were incentivized by the state for apparent militarist purposes. Then the development of the Silicon Valley in the 1940s and 1950s was, at least in part, was realized as the product of military imperatives. This time it was the Cold War policy. The companies were heavily financed by Washington to make an investment in R&D. Therefore, the innovation has started to focus increasingly on more advanced military technology.

The difference between the two is in the way the organizations are organized. The industrial innovations in Berlin were dominated by two giant companies—Siemens and AEG; but in California, on the contrary, Stanford University set a stage for the growth of many small firms. The increase in defense procurement has led to an extraordinarily large number of small subsidiaries financed by venture capital rather than creating a local production complex that reproduces itself. In addition to hosting a research institute, Stanford became the world's first science park. The Silicon Valley has become an industrial zone no different from the Victorian period the United Kingdom. Initially, those who maintained this network were large companies, which are part of the military—industrial complex; But this network was also largely fed from local skill, knowledge and labor pool. It became a dynamic network created by small firms—competing fiercely with each other in mutual dependence, yet cooperating extensively—that transformed the aircraft manufacturing into a new aviation industry and electronics into computer technologies (Tudor 1999: 79).

The state has also had a decisive impact on Japan, another great innovative culture of the last century. The extraordinary success of Japanese companies is a complex story that is often emphasized. The main actor of this story is the MITI (Ministry of Foreign Trade and Industry). Founded in the 1920s, this ministry has roots dating back to the 1870s, the first years of Meiji restoration. Linking the government, banking, and industry together through a tight and sensitive social network system, the MITI applied an agreement planning that guided large Japanese companies throughout the period from 1950 to the mid-1970s, which was called "catching period". However, the role the government played in Japan was completely different from that of the government in the United States. It was the market mechanism that led innovation in Japan at a time when military spending was tightly constrained. The technological revolution was serving to the purchasing demands of consumers, not the satisfaction of military goals at all costs. The success of Japan's innovations emerged not because it created new basic technologies, but because it produced many perfect and flawless consumer goods, from automobiles to laptops. Moreover, the miracle that the Japanese created after the war—whether ending or not, now—was largely based on vague intervention by the state in the politics, strategy, and financing of companies (Kodama 1996: 147).

10.3   Science Park: A New Vision for the Culture of Innovativeness

A lot of imitations of the science park at Stanford have emerged all over the world. Science parks are attempts to recreate the nineteenth century "industrial zones" in a planned way. The aim here is to create a resemblance to that old chaotic innovativeness-but without paying for its terrible social and environmental costs. The science parks combine two traditions of innovation: the "bottom-up" tradition of the small entrepreneurship companies established at home garages or basements, and the "top-down" innovativeness tradition, organized in research laboratories of large companies and often benefit from state support and sponsorship (Scarborough et al. 1999: 97).

The UK Science Park Association describes the science park as "a support and a technology transfer initiative to the business life". Here's what they do:

- Encouraging and supporting the establishment, incubation, and development of innovation-driven, fast-growing and knowledge-based companies;
- Creating an environment where large international companies can engage in a special and close interaction with a specific information creation center by mutual benefit;
- Establishing formal and functional links with knowledge creation centers such as universities and research organizations.

A science park usually begins with a kind of co-operation between the government and higher education institutions. One of the first science parks in the United Kingdom was in Cambridge. This project owned all the basic features of science parks—a link between a major university (which basically has a large land) and government and industry. In the United Kingdom, the Labor Party government, taking office in 1964, forced universities to strengthen their links with the industry and increase their returns from the investment in basic research. The Discussion Committee of the University of Cambridge responded this with a report in 1969. The Committee recommended the expansion of the "science-based industry" near Cambridge to enable the university's scientific expertise, equipment and libraries to be used and the Cambridge science community to receive more feedback from industry.

These ideas attracted the attention of Trinity College in Cambridge. Trinity has had a long tradition of scientific research and innovation since Isaac Newton. It also had some land in its possession.

The general plan permission was issued in October 1971 and the first company, Laser-Scan, moved to this campus in 1973. The development of the park in the first 5 years was slowed. The branches of multinational companies in the UK started to settle here (Sweden's LKB Biochrom and US laser expert Coherent were first settlers) and the number of companies grew steadily, reaching 25 by the end of the 1970s. The concept of the science park was not yet popular; what initially attracted companies here was to establish university-based research links. The fact that Trinity agreed to slow investment return has played a major role in the success of this park. During the economic recession of the 1980s and 1990s, Trinity adhered to the vision of keeping the park as a venue specific to high-tech industries and opposed the tendency to fill the space with companies from other sectors.

The park began to make a breakthrough in the 1980s. The Cambridge science park, which has about 70 companies and 4000 employees—along with its accompanying campuses around the city—is a successful initiative to regenerate the industrial region that Marshall describes very vividly in the late nineteenth century. This park has all that is needed for the Alchemy of innovative collaboration (Barker 2002: 75–80):

- A university with large resources and a worldwide research reputation,
- A well-developed consulting in both the technical and managerial fields,
- Venture capital,
- An advanced property management conducted by a landowner who has interest in intellectual and technological innovations,
- Some different types of firms close to each other

10.4 Internalization of the Industrial Region: Creation of an Innovative Culture in Organizations

So far we have examined the possible functioning of an innovative culture within the society. We have addressed this as a wider influence, or more concretely as an engine, of the innovative activities of firm networks in the industrial zones or modern cases like science parks. But is it possible that some of these ideas can also be applied by the organizations themselves? How can we begin to transform the cultures of our organizations so that innovation can flourish more effectively?

The fact that most companies in the West are choking and far from being creative is well-known. Crossing the border of the "system" as an outsider entrepreneur seems to be the unique way of making innovation. This idea represents a broader phenomenon peculiar to western societies: the cult of the individual. We exalt the individual as the source of creativity and the organizations as the emblem of social order, but we often see these two, as things that are against each other. As a result, we think that radical changes can only happen with the efforts of heroic individuals. We say to ourselves, "If you really want something to be done, do it yourself". However, creativity and initiative are almost inevitable to disappear when we put the individual into an organizational structure (Barker 2002: 81).

However, this understanding of the tension between creative individualism and corporate inertia is not universally shared. For example, institutions in Japan have been surprisingly successful even though they have many of the organizational characteristics that would inevitably lead to failures in the West. Many of the most innovative Japanese companies of the past 50 years are the largest and oldest companies—operating in a society renowned for their inherent conservatism. Researchers have stared their eyes on Japan for years so that the Western companies can take courses. However, the post-war conditions of Japan have become much different from the US or developed European economies; besides, the adaptation of the root features of Japanese cultures to conditions outside the Japanese context is never an easy task.

First, Japanese companies had no choice but to innovate in the post-war period. In the face of some local wars erupting in the region, intense international competition, numerous economic crises and increasingly volatile markets, the only thing Japanese companies can do to survive is innovation (Barker 2002: 82). Being able to cope with uncertainty has become a matter of life and death even for the most successful Japanese companies. Most of the Western companies did not have to make such a life-and-death struggle to survive (Kodama 1996: 154).

Secondly, great importance is attached to learning-by-doing in the Japanese culture. From the time when Zen Buddhism became established, the Japanese knew the body and mind unity. That is why the Japanese managers highly value the teaching of the experience: they initiate new experiments and think a lot about them. On the other hand, learning in the West is seen mainly as an academic activity. Practical experience-based learning is systematically less valued than learning from educational institutions—or from books.

Thirdly, the Japanese society values collectiveness more than individuality. The Japanese companies are very happy when they benefit from their foreign partners— suppliers, customers, external experts and even competitors. They have long mastered in internalization of such information as well as reforming and enriching it by its adaptation to their companies' identity and strategy.

Japan is well known for the coverage of this collective sense of responsibility through the relationship between individuals with companies. Creativity in Japan is largely based on the employees' personal commitment to the company and its mission, and their identification with it. Western organizations are renowned for their inability to create a similar sense of loyalty or commitment among their own employees.

These three factors are difficult to create in the West. We have not been forced to make such an innovation; we tend to underestimate the value of practical experience systematically, we prefer to grant reputation and power to those having academic qualities; and we live in a society that values individual achievement much more than any collective loyalty. For that reason, in our own global village, the problems facing the organizations are (Barker 2002: 83):

- How can we flourish the sense of urgency that is the engine of innovation?
- How can we establish a balance between an excessively rational point of view and learning that values experience and experimentation?
- How can we develop a culture of commitment among workers that seem to be highly individualized?

10.5 Development of Innovative Environments

Most people would prescribe the improvement of the physical working environment. Managers realized that giant office buildings are not suitable places for creativity; the innovative work is a multidisciplinary effort and can leap up thanks to the exchange of ideas among people having different expertise. Some organizations purposefully abandoned the special meeting areas of departments so that people would have to leave their work areas to eat or drink. Going to a canteen or coffee machine allows the possibility of merging people from other departments or disciplines.

Some would say that the organizational culture finds an expression not only in the physical environment but also in organizational relations. What are the most favorable organizational structures for creating an innovative culture?

It can be said that there are three general organizational types: "top-down," "bottom-up" and "mid-level management" models (Barker 2002: 85).

The "top-down" organization is essentially an enterprise shaped by its founder. It is run by a charismatic person with an innovative vision. The leader is a source of inspiration with his model for the people in his organization. The freedom to innovate comes from a very personal vision that is paradoxically imposed to the organization. Many innovative companies fit this pattern. The efforts of a single inspiring leader can miraculously transform a department of a large organization. Such a model can be very successful—but usually on a limited scale. When the size of the company grows—or when the leader leaves the company—the effects of the inspiring leadership are often disappeared (Senge 1993: 49).

The "bottom-up" model envisions the company or organization as an aggregation of small initiatives. A holding can be formed by a multitude of companies, each innovating in its own way and benefiting from the parent company's support or umbrella against the risks.

In their groundbreaking book, *The Knowledge-creating Company,* Nonaka and Takeuchi point out that mid-level management in traditional companies can play a decisive role in the development of innovation. They say that the mid-level management has traditionally been seen as the most stubborn part of the organizational structure and the top managers usually try to remove this level completely to give leeway to innovation. Nonaka and Takeuchi see this discontent from the mid-level management as understandable but wrong. According to them, middle-level managers are the cornerstone of information management and development mechanism of an organization. They form the meeting point of information coming from different parts of the organization, and they are potentially the main motivators for identifying innovation opportunities and developing creative projects (Nonaka and Takeuchi 1995: 75).

Perhaps the issue is, a company's comprehension of its position, and then setting the most appropriate managerial structure and processes by it. However, innovation is not "something that hangs around in the void". It is a mental attitude that cannot be improved either by improvements in the environment or by changes in management. Innovation is a process; like all other processes, it should also be governed. The organizations need to develop systems and procedures that will provide a discipline required by all structure and organized work for innovation. Without them, there is no such thing as innovation (Barker 2002: 88).

11 Being Decisive in Innovation

Many companies want to be competitive in all areas, not just in one or two dimensions, but with a passionate desire. However, exceptionally competitive performance is not something that can be achieved easily. There are few companies that can do this; most cannot.

What distinguishes exceptional competition masters from others? There are two basic principles in this. First, they know that the key to the survival of a company is constantly innovating. Being innovative from time to time and in one or two areas is useless. Second, they know that the strongest changes are the changes that create value for existing and potential customers. For this reason, competitive companies constantly look for ways to change their business in every aspect. After finding its way, they ensure the transformation of changes into advantages which are appreciated and impressed by the customers (Henry 1991: 29).

The companies that know and implement these principles can offer better products at lower prices for many years in a sustainable way to their customers. The companies with an extraordinary performance that can achieve this success have a systematic vision on innovation. They know that their competitive success is based not on solely a single major success in sales, marketing or R & D fields, but on stable improvements in production, finance, distribution and all other businesses. For that reason, they ensure that there are players who constantly pass the balls, and they create organizations providing all the support these players need. This means (Pearson 2003: 39–40):

- The creation and maintenance of a corporate environment that values better performance more than anything;
- The structuring of the organization so that it values the innovative ideas more than the requirements of conducting company business;
- A clear definition of a strategic focus to ensure that the company directs its innovative efforts to realistic channels—to find a response in the market;

- Knowing where to look for good ideas and how to use them when found;
- Mobilizing all resources of the company and fast pursuit for good ideas.

When addressed individually, none of these activities are too complex and difficult to accomplish. But keeping a company always focused on all of them requires extraordinary discipline and persistence. It is this systemic effort to institutionalize innovation that gives market leaders the advantage they have. This is also what other companies need to learn from them.

11.1 Starting the Business with a Correct Mentally

To be able to transform a stable company into an aggressive competitor, you need to create an organization which not only values high performance, but also that sustains this commitment every year. This is not to increase the number of new ideas slightly for the next year, but to make a serious change in the values.

Even a brief closer look at the companies that make successful inventions is enough to see how insistent they are in making everything better. Not only a few people at the top, but everyone in the company thinks and acts like that.

Some factors are needed to sharpen the sensitivity of an organization to change. Most important of all is the obligation of top management to participate in this process profoundly and personally.

Innovative companies are managed by innovative leaders. The issue is so obvious. These are the leaders who set challenging targets for themselves and for others, who set new targets, enforcing innovation, in front of their organizations, so that they achieve it. These are precise and measurable targets that create relatively flawless performance—such as being the number one in some particular markets, not vague, difficult-to-achieve ones.

Innovative leaders are not required to be creative and idea-driven. But they are open to change because they believe that the competitive existence depends on novelty. This is a mentality that most managers can develop—as long as these beliefs are based on a precise understanding of a certain competitive environment, not just a cliché generalization (Pearson 2003: 40–41).

11.2 Shaking the Organization

Most large organizations are primarily designed to conduct business: to get the job done, to check performance, to identify problems and to achieve the projected results for that year. That's what it should be.

However, this structure, process, and people, which smoothly carry out the business, can prevent the creation of good ideas, or even stop the created ones from flowing through the corporation's system. For example, excessive hierarchy kills ideas without giving an opportunity of being examined by the top managers. The barriers encircling the R & D, marketing, production, and finance areas prevent the realization of functional problems—to the point where there is nothing left to do for effective solutions. The complex approval mechanisms end up promising innovations. Ideas are strictly reviewed by the seniors or blocked by some financial criteria before they become mature to be examined in detail.

The management has become extraordinarily complex today as organizations and markets have grown and differentiated from each other over time. Therefore, it became necessary to merge and integrate different parts of the organizations. This has brought problems such as excessive control of the management of the employees, restriction of the employees' chance of realizing their own potential, prevention of participation in the organization (Raelin 1999: 43–46).

Overcoming such organizational barriers depends on being able to distinguish between what is needed to run the company and what is needed for the creative activity. Most successful innovations need four key inputs (Pearson 2003: 45):

- An idealist person who believes that the new idea is critical and is determined to progress regardless of the looming obstacles;
- A supporter whose position in the organization is high enough to assemble the resources—people, money and time—required by the new idea;
- A combination of people who will bring together bright, creative minds (those who create ideas) and experienced practitioners;
- Simple and fast processes that would allow the ideas to be evaluated and approved by the top managers and met with the necessary resources.

12 Evaluation and Conclusion

We are operating in a global economy that is becoming increasingly complex and ambiguous. At this point of the history, innovation has become so important that it will not be left to the outsider entrepreneurs. Whether commercial, public or non-profit, in all business of the economy, both the organizations and networks that are becoming increasingly complex among these organizations, we need to learn how to innovate together.

The innovation is the essence of being a human: It benefits from our ability to cooperate, learn and create. We have made progress from cave paintings to digital cameras, from sculpting tools to computers—and from multi-piece hunting instruments to intercontinental rockets. Innovation is a dangerous activity; it often creates more problems than it solves. It creates an endless spiral of the problems to the solutions and each time from these solutions to even more complex problems requiring more innovative solutions. Innovation is a *social* phenomenon at least as much as a technological phenomenon; moreover, many of the most important innovations are cultural and social innovations rather than being scientific or technical.

Innovation is not something that can be made every time in everywhere. It is understood that some conditions are required for people to make innovation. Besides, the creation of the environment and "culture" of innovation—both in and between the organizations—is full of challenges as well as complexities.

Equipping people with innovative and productive potential can be possible only with the support of the organizational culture to the growth of skills and removal of elements restricting their ability to maneuver and creativeness.

Some steps need to be taken to make the organization more dynamic and more innovative. These can be listed as structuring the organization in a way to support the innovation, developing a strategic focus which orientates innovative efforts, well knowledge of where to seek for good ideas and how to benefit from the system to use them when they are found, mobilizing everything for the realization of these ideas when the good ideas are fully developed, but not establishment of an oppressive organizational environment on everybody—in a way to surpass some rivals by the innovation—and not in a way to choke the organization.

They all look simple at first glance because they are simple. They are Simple, but not easy; because every innovation is a constant challenge from beginning to end. It is a challenge that has to be faced because it is the element that forms the market leadership and competitive impetus. This also explains why it is necessary to make an extra effort to become an innovative company.

References

Andersson, R. (1985). Creativity and regional development. *Papers in Regional Science, 56*(1), 5–20.

Barker, A. (2002). *The alchemy of innovation*. London: Spiro Press.

De Bono, E. (2000). *Rekabet Üstü (Sur/Petition)*. İstanbul: Remzi Kitabevi A.Ş.

De Vries, K. M. (2006). *The leadership mystique*. London: Prentice Hall Financial Times.

Dodgson, M. (1993). Organisational learning: A review of some literatures. *Organisation Studies, 14*(3), 375–394.

Erdoğan, İ. (1975). Kültürün Yönetim Fonksiyonlarının Uygulanmasına Etkisi ve Faktör Analizi Yöntemi İle Bir Araştırma, İstanbul Üniversitesi Yayın No: 2060, Sermet Matbaası, İstanbul.

Erkan, H. (1994). Bilgi Toplumu ve Ekonomik Gelişme, Türkiye İş Bankası Kültür Yayınları, Genel Yayın No: 326, Bilim Dizisi: 8.

Fichter, J. H. (1960). La Sociologie, Tradvit Par: Giovanni Hayois Editions Universitaires, Paris.

Flippo, B. E. (1966). *A behavioral approach*. Boston: Allyn and Bacon.

Gardner, H. (1993). *Creating minds*. New York: Basic Books.

Güvenç, B. (1972). *İnsan ve Kültür*. Ankara: Ayyıldız Matbaası.

Hall, P. (1998). *Cities in civilization*. London: Weidenfeld and Nicolson.

Hammer, M., & Champy, J. (1993). *Reengineering the corporation*. London: Nicholas Brealey.

Henry, J. (Ed.). (1991). *Creative management*. London: Sage.

Hudson, M. K. (2003). Muhafazakâr Bir Şirketi Dönüştürmek—Her Seferinde Bir Kahkaha, Kültür ve Değişim, Harvard Business School Publishing Corporation, Çev. Kardam. A., BZD Yayın ve İletişim Hizmetleri, MESS Yayın No: 402, İstanbul.

Kobu, B. (1981). Üretim Yönetimi, İstanbul Üniversitesi yayın No: 2298. Fatih Yayınevi, İstanbul.

Kodama, F. (1996). *Emerging patterns of innovation: Sources of Japan's technological edge*. Cambridge, MA: Harvard Business School Press.

Krech, D., & Crutchfied, S. R.. (1967). Sosyal Psikoloji, Çev. Güçbilmez, E., Onaran, O., Sevinç Matbaası, Ankara.

Lubben, A. R. (1970). Recent research. In E. Lasswell, H. Burma, & H. Aronson (Eds.), *Life in society*. Glenview, IL: Scot Foresman.

Morgan, G. (1998). Yönetim ve Örgüt Teorilerinde Metafor, Çev. Bulut, G., BZD Yayıncılık, MESS Yayın No: 280. İstanbul.

Nonaka, I., & Takeuchi, H. (1995). *The knowledge—creating company*. New York: Oxford University Press.

Pearson, E. A. (2003). Yenilikçilikte Kararlı Olma Yolları, Yenilikçilik, Harvard Business School Publishing Corporation, Çev. Kardam, A., BZD Yayıncılık, MESS Yayın No: 412, İstanbul.

Penfield, V. R. (1969). Örgütte Beşeri Münasebetler, Çev. Taşçıoğlu, R., Ajans – Türk Matbaacılık Sanayii, Ankara.

Raelin, A. J. (1999). Kültürlerin Çatışması (Yönetenler – Yönetilenler), Türkiye İş Bankası Kültür Yayınları, Genel Yayın: 412, Felsefe Dizisi: 48, İstanbul.

Rosen, H. R., & Brown, B. P. (1996). *Leading people: Transforming business from the inside out*. New York: Viking/Penguin.

Scarborough, H., Swan, J., & Preston, J. (1999). *Knowledge management: A literatüre review*. London: Institute of Personnel and Development.

Senge, P. (1993). *The fifth discipline*. London: Random House.

Törnqvist, G. (2004). Creativity in time and space. *Geografiska Annaler: Series B. Human Geography, 86*(4), 227–243.

Tudor, R. (1999). *Creativity and the management of change*. Malden, MA: Blackwell.

Turhan, M. (1987). Kültür Değişmeleri, Marmara Üniversitesi İlahiyat Fakültesi Vakfı Yayınları, İstanbul.

Yıldırım, R. (1998). *Yaratıcılık ve Yenilikçilik*. İstanbul: Sistem Yayıncılık.

Zoltners, A. A., Sinha, K. P., & Murphy, J. S. (1997). *The fat firm: The transformation of a firm from fat to fit*. New York: McGraw-Hill.

Innovativeness in Family Firms: Effects of Positive Leadership Styles

Elif Baykal

Abstract Family business is an unique kind of business, that can be depicted by an ownership structure mostly dominated by members of a particular family, shared familial norms and values and a shared way of thinking accumulated over a long period of time. This socioemotional wealth of the family owning the family business and overlapping family and business goals make them more harmonious, ambitious, hard working and more engaged regarding both their familial and business goals. In family a firm, central decision making that is accumulated on the hands of founder owners and their desire for further growth result in an inclination to respond quickly to opportunities that have the probability to provide economic gains which will be useful for both the owner family and the business itself. Moreover, sustainability and long run performance in these kind of companies are significant both business goals and family honor. And in this paper it is claimed that like other firms, family businesses, also prefer to benefit from innovation for economic growth due to the fact that innovation is an activity that is fast in financial return. That is to say, engaging in innovation process is both difficult and time consuming, but once a company accomplished to innovate a certain product or service, financial returns of this accomplishment are highly satisfying and rapid. And in this process, as in the case with other kind of businesses, proper style of leadership is an important factor in motivating employers to engage in innovation processes, and unique characteristics of family businesses and antecedents of an innovative work atmosphere effects this proper leadership style.

Family business is a special form of business in which ownership or majority of shares are owned by a particular family. In family businesses members of a certain family work, make decisions and attain goals together. Family firms are much more than smaller version of major corporations. In these kind of firms, power is quite central and decision making right is often concentrated in the owner/manager's

E. Baykal (✉)
İstanbul Medipol University, Istanbul, Turkey
e-mail: enarcikara@medipol.edu.tr

© Springer International Publishing AG, part of Springer Nature 2018   213
H. Dincer et al. (eds.), *Strategic Design and Innovative Thinking in Business Operations*, Contributions to Management Science,
https://doi.org/10.1007/978-3-319-77622-4_11

hands. In these organizations, socioemotional wealth of the family is quite significant in ensuring sustainability and long run performance of the organization. Sustainability and economic growth are two essential goals for family businesses since these factors help them live for many generations. Similar to the case with many other firms, family businesses use several methods in attaining these goals and although not very common, engaging in innovative activities is one of these particular methods used in family firms.

Without doubt, leadership profile of the owner/manager is decisive in achieving corporate goals via innovativeness due to leaders' capacity to encourage innovativeness in organizations and their power to empower and motivate followers intrinsically (Amabile 1998). In the extant literature there are two conflicting views regarding family firms' innovativeness; first view claims that they are not different from other firms regarding their tendency in resorting to innovation and the second one claims that they are reluctant in taking risks and using innovation in achieving their goals. In family firms, less rigid bureaucracy, closer relationships with customers and closer interaction among different departments, easier and shorter communication lines, often triggers innovation. However, parochial structure, over concentrated management mentality and decision making processes, unsatisfactory institutionalization, too much conservatism and too much risk-aversion lowers the innovative capacity.

Among scholars it is widely accepted that family firms are reluctant innovators and they often prefer incremental innovations. In this study, innovativeness is regarded as an organization's openness to novel ideas as an aspect of organizational culture. Main goal of the study is examining innovative behaviours and preferences of family businesses and examining the relevance of positive leadership styles with innovativeness in these firms. Although, it is pervasively accepted that high quality leader-member relationships encourage innovativeness, in the extant literature there is a scarcity of researches regarding this relationship in family firms. Thus, in this study, a positive organizational scholarship perspective and positive leadership framework have been adopted in understanding the probable effects of leadership on innovativeness in family business context.

1 Introduction

In contemporary dynamic and challenging work environment factors such as creativity and innovation have become valuable assets for gaining competitive advantage. High technology, competitive pressures, turbulent economic environment make it necessary for organizations to become innovative structures in order to compete, survive and thrive. On the one hand, globalization, and frequently changing customer needs and demands put stress on today's organizations to make changes on the ways they make production and do business (Hall et al. 2001). That is why, successful cases in innovation related to new product/services and new business processes are often seen as the main issue in financial development and economic growth (Porter 1990). But, more importantly, this financial growth mostly come about despite the financial condition of the larger economy that the firm acts as a player (Craig and Moores 2006). Changes occurring in business life effecting astonishingly changing technology, make it necessary to adopt innovation processes for creating more productive companies (McAdam et al. 2010). According to Varis and Littunen (2010), irrespective of an organisation's size and other properties, innovation is vital for companies, since a company's success, survival and growth is highly effected by its ability to innovate.

As a word, the concept of innovation is more than the concept of invention, which are frequently confused with each other. They are different in the point that innovation can be both based on new knowledge creation or on the reconfiguration of existing knowledge, redesign of old methods and processes (Drucker 1985). As a management term, innovation can be described as a mechanism that create both new products/services and redesigned or improved products and services (Porter 1990). According to classic Schumpeterian innovation definition we can talk about five different innovation types: new products, novel production processes, methods, markets, new supply sources and new organizational forms (Schumpeter 1934). All kinds of innovation types necessitates innovativeness of the organization. The term innovation capacity or in other words innovativeness of a firm is related to the firm's innovation capacity and the tendency of the firm to introduce new products, ideas or processes successfully and conveniently (Hult et al. 2004).

Innovativeness of a company is affected by several factors and necessitates a well oiled engine. First of all, firm characteristics such as firm's age, size, nature and R&D expenditures are very important in innovativeness of the firm. Undoubtfully, firms having wider resources have a higher potential to engage in innovative activities. Innovative processes often necessitates high amounts of financial resources due to expensive R&D expenditures, high wages given to qualifies personnel and money spent during trials of a new product or new processes. Small scale and unprofitable firms often can not afford to engage in innovative activities. More over, organizational climate should also be proper for an innovative atmosphere. Mechanic organizations hindering risky trials are the most powerful enemies of innovation. And second major factor effecting innovativeness is properties of organization members (Hurley and Hult 1998). Teamwork, involvement of the employees in critic processes and high quality communication are all important factors effecting innovativeness of organization members. Namely, people that can easily communicate with each other and engage in critical activities in the organizations prefer to try novel methods and processes and can be successful in the innovation of new products and processes. In parallel to that approach, Romijn and Albaladejo (2002) suggests that knowledge and skills of the workforce is one of the most important factors enhancing innovation capacity. Moreover, Birdthistle and Fleming (2007) also insists that, the success of companies regarding innovations is closely related to the capabilities, skills and intellectual capacities of individuals in rapidly changing business environment. Similarly, research conducted by Mohnen and Röller (2005) showed that lack of capabilities and skills necessary for innovation are the most important obstacles creating new products and processes. The third important factor effecting innovativeness is, environmental factors. For example, intense competition, high levels of networking, and rapid changing environment as understood by organization members (Beck et al. 2009) make firms feel forced to try something new that will bring money. Especially, challenging business atmosphere and demanding rivalry among business actors are more prominent in forcing companies to become more innovative.

Likewise Siguaw et al. (2006) claims that top management should direct, encourage, appreciate, and enhance the tendency of employees to take place in innovative processes and spend their energy in the service of increasing overall collective innovation capacity of their organization (p. 565). Burns and Stalker (1961) also emphasizes importance of cross-functional teamwork in enhancing innovativeness due to the fact that it is one of the most impressive communication channels (Burns and Stalker 1961). Teamwork among different disciplines and high quality communication among different levels and departments of the organization are significant because they diminish resistance and ensures information flow (Beck et al. 2009). In his study regarding human related antecedents of innovation capacity, Beck et al. (2009) found that involving employees in decision making processes and the clarity of direction regarding organizational goals effect innovative capacities of the firms.

In the extant literature there are two major different streams of studies related to innovative capacity of the firms. Each focusing on various antecedents regarding innovation. The first of them focusing upon technological aspects effecting innovation (Leblanc and Nguyen 1997). The second stream focuses upon human aspects and presupposes that people and the organizational climate of the firm are main antecedents of innovativeness (Cooper and Kleinschmidt 1995). In this study, we had an approach that adopt the second perspective. And we turned our lens to leadership style in the organization in understanding innovative behaviours of the firms. We focused especially on family firms regarding their innovativeness, since it is a virgin area of study.

According to extant literature, unique work environment of family businesses inspires employee' care for the organization and their loyalty to the firm (Ward 1988). Family businesses often have a shared family language, that lets them communicate among the members more efficiently and transfer higher levels of data with higher levels of privacy (Tagiuri and Davis 1996). Moreover, family firms have the capacity to see the big Picture and give meaning to it. And they also have more patience regarding long-term results of their performance (DeVisscher et al. 1995) making them proper places for taking risks and engaging in innovative activities.

2 Family Firms

Family businesses are very important for contemporary economies. They are sources of economic development and growth. Worldwide, they create 40–60% of gross national products of countries and 35–70% of all job generation (Van Gils et al.

2008). When managed properly, they can be more active and effective player in economies and contribute to higher levels of growth rates and contribute to the economic growth of countries. However their unique nature necessitates special kinds of managerial methods and more attentive selection of proper leadership styles.

In fact, family firms are regarded as one of the most complex forms of organizational structures owing to the overlaps in the issues related to ownership structure, managerial control, and administration increases this complexity (Craig and Moores 2006). As an organization, family business is a kind of business where "a certain dominant family is effective on the whole company". They have the majority of the rights to make decision. They are represented in higher ranks of the hierarchical order and the management team, and members of the family perceive the firm as a family firm as their familial asset (Westhead et al. 1996). In important positions mostly family members take place and non family members often have little chance to promote and have a say in critic topics. Generally, family businesses have been considered as more conservative organizations compared to other kinds of companies (Sharma et al. 1997). In this kind of firms owner/managers insists on protecting their familial assets. Family business and family heritage is often intervened. So they are often introverted, inflexible, and often tightly bound to traditions (Kets de Vries 1993). They do not like outsiders to intervene in their business and familial relationships and often more aversive regarding financial and managerial risks (Naldi et al. 2007) and they do not like changes (Ward 1997).

Family business as an academic study area has been limited by its nomenclature. Namely, it is thought as theoretically related with a range of constructs, which are mostly have little link with financial performance indicators such as entrepreneurialship orientation and performance, high-performing firms, opportunistic risk taking or innovation (Craig and Moores 2006). In the extant literature family firms' successes have often not been linked to the similar performance indicators as non family firms. Generally succession, transition of ownership and success of the family business system, are used to understand attainment of performance in family firms (Habbershon and Pistrui 2002). In this chapter, it is claimed that financial wealth -generative actions such as innovation can also be meaningful tools for attaining organizational goals of family businesses.

3   Family Business and Innovation

In family firms innovativeness is an understudied and poorly understood phenomenon. The nature of family business has some major effects on the innovation process. First of all, family owned nature of these firms facilitate flexibility and add complexity to the daily innovation processes (Lorenzo and Núñez-Cacho 2013). They are not as bureaucratic as non family corporate organizations. They have less hierarchical levels in their organizational structure, job descriptions have gray areas and managerial decision making is quite central which is sometimes helpful in making quick decisions. Moreover, in these firms, families often show strong tendencies to protect long-term advantages of the firm (Miller and Le Breton-Miller 2005). Tendency to make profit make it more probable for them to support innovativeness as a way of ensuring growth and prosperity (Zahra et al. 2004) and protect their competitive advantages over time.

Family businesses are different from other kinds of businesses concerning their resources and capabilities. In these firms the interaction of the family and the organization creates "familiness" of the firm (Habbershon and Williams 1999). Familiness and family characteristic of a family firm are those skills and knowledge of the particular family firm within the business. Specific characteristic of these organizations have the capacity to incur original skills and competences necessary for innovativeness which are kept and protected in the organization for years (Uhlaner et al. 2007). In terms of employee motivation, loyalty to the organization, and trust among organization members generate unusual motivation and acts as a cement and increase organizational trust (Tagiuri and Davis 1996).

Barney's (1991) resource-based approach of firms is regarded as an important tool for understanding innovative capabilities of family businesses. When used properly family-owned nature of family businesses may contribute to competitive advantage of family businesses among other rivals (Habbershon et al. 2003). Having resources that are precious, rare and inimitable does not necessarily imply a competitive advantage. These resources should be properly managed by the management team, namely the owner family in order to make use of them. That is to say, innovation necessitates reconfiguration of firm's own capabilities and resources (Rumelt 1987). In family firms, innovation is useful in means of cost saving and larger market share. In addition, there are many indirect positive effects of innovation, such as making organizations more perceptive, more flexible and more adaptable to interior and exterior changes that helps accumulation of specific and unique knowledge over time, and family firm's family-owned nature supports these effects (Núñez-Cacho and Grande 2013). Therefore, it would be meaningful to expect that the dynamic capabilities of family firms will make it easy to increase these firms' competitive advantages through efficient management of innovation processes.

Unfortunately, family firms sometimes experience difficulties regarding innovativeness. There are several reasons underlying this suggestion. One of the most important underlying factor is the fact that they prone to experience more problems and adversities regarding personnel's skills and capabilities. First of all, it is probable that family firms employ members of the owner family that are not always competent regarding the job. And as Schulze et al. (2001) claims they are more likely to ignore outsiders that are more qualified compared to family members working for the family firm. And as Kets De Vries (1993) claims nepotism favoring family members hinders attracting professional managers from outside and causes inept family members remain in critical positions.

Craig and Moores (2006) claim that family firms attach great significance to innovation as a key component of their corporate strategy. Nonetheless there are two contrasting views regarding family firms' use of innovation. First claiming that family businesses are not necessarily timid about adopting innovation. Second claiming that family business have no difference from other kind of firms regarding their effectiveness on innovation, claiming that they are creative enough and they do not have problems in giving satisfactory importance to R&D projects (Pervin 1997), they are successful in self-analysis (Moscetello 1990).

In the extant literature researchers claiming that family firms can have high levels of innovation capacity, base their approach on the fact that these firms use corporate internal control mechanisms less often (Uhlaner et al. 2007). They are less bureaucratic and people can share information and ideas in these kind of organizations easily. Moreover, informal management and information systems that increase the capacity to innovate make them more effective regarding making regarding innovation with the help of easier communicate paths that delivers ideas and information between the different parts of the family business (Burns and Stalker 1961). Niehm et al. (2010) suggests that family businesses are not necessarily more risk aversive and less innovative compared to non-family businesses as some of the scholars claim who think that family businesses are not proper kind of organizations for making innovation. Supporting that view, according to agency theory, these firms melt ownership and managerial control in the same pot, thus lessen agency costs and align managers' and families' interests (Jensen and Meckling 1976). According to agency theory agents (hired managers) have aims different from their owners. This differences results in differences in the priorities of parts namely owners and managers (Fama and Jensen 1983). Some theorists claim that family businesses represent are ideal organizations since in these organizations ownership and the firm legal entity are aligned. This alignment of interests contributes to lower levels of hesitation regarding risky decisions including innovation-related decisions (Nieto et al. 2015). And contributes to sustainability of the firm and results in support for radical innovations (Zahra 2004). This is more likely to be observed when family has a larger percentage of the firm's shares due to the fact that ownership encourages higher levels of entrepreneurial risk taking (Zahra 2004). Furthermore, regarding innovativeness of family firms, Zahra (2005) claims that the younger generation family members working in family firm tend to involve in innovative processes more often compared to previous generations thus new generations in family firms are often regarded as the driving force behind innovation. That is to say. Rather than founder family members. Following generations are more prone to engage in innovative activities.

On the other hand, many scholars claim that family businesses do not have the suitable atmosphere for innovativeness. According to McAdam et al. (2010), family businesses are desirous of establishing long-lasting legacy, thus sometimes they may become more conservative regarding the risks an innovation project may create for the organisation. Similarly, Chen and Hsu (2009) claims that since innovation activities are highly expensive and involve high financial risks that makes them unattractive for small scale firms with limited financial resources, like most family firms. For fear of losing their authoritarian power and control in decision making, family firms often find it unmeaningful to take part in capital markets (Kets de Vries 1993). This desire to maintain control may limit their relationships with other shareholders and stakeholders (Le Breton-Miller and Miller 2009). Of course this aversiveness limits their financial power and hinders financing innovation activities. Moreover, the synergy that occurs as result of the interaction of business and family has the ability to create a barrier limiting firm's innovativeness (Webb et al. 2010). Furthermore, in family businesses, lack of discussion of ideas and homogeneity of ideas in families may limit input of different ideas and emergence of innovative proposals can be hindered. And in the long run this can be reflected in the rate of innovativeness.

In the extant literature, other topics have been listed supporting the view that family firms do not have the necessary climate for innovativeness. One of the most noteworthy claims is that, in family firms family fortune, career opportunities, and firm and family reputation in the society are all related to the success and fate of the family firm. Thus any kind of risky decisions and strategies may have negative consequences for the family's personal wealth, in both economic and socioemotional realms (Gómez-Mejía et al. 2007). This makes family firms more conservative organizations organizations and push them towards safer practices rather than risky innovations (Wright et al. 2002). Although scarce in number, there are studies focusing on family firms' tendency to innovate that found inconsiderable powerful interactions between family firms and innovativeness. For example: Wu (2008) examined the relationship between degree of family ownership rate of the firm and innovativeness in family firms. And found a positive but nonetheless insignificant relationship. Similarly Gudmundson et al.'s (2003) study could not find a significant difference in innovativeness levels between family firms and non-family firms.

In fact, innovation in family businesses is not something black or white. There are grey areas regarding innovative behaviours of these firms. Conventionally, there are two kinds of innovations that are incremental or radical which are valid for all kinds of firms (Anderson and Tushman 1990). These two kinds of innovations require different levels of risk taking and that is why they require different capabilities (Nieto et al. 2015). These kinds of innovations are innovations with lower levels of risk and they are incremental. Incremental innovations mostly do not invent something novel but redesign or reinvent former products. Since family businesses are frequently more conservative compared to nonfamily firms (Sharma et al. 1997), they react more slowly to change and they prefer incremental innovations rather than radical innovations which invent novel products, services or processes. Similarly, Nieto et al.'s study (2015) on innovativeness of family firms shows that family firms not only engage in innovative activities less often compared to nonfamily firms but also they prefer incremental innovations rather than radical innovations.

In this point the term strategic simplicity come to the scene. The term "strategic simplicity," helps us understand the processes of family firms' strategy making. According to Miller (1993), strategic simplicity means using old routines that worked well in the past again and again despite the strategic challenges of the business atmosphere (Miller 1993). Sometimes it may result in overuse of ready-made solutions thus hindering innovativeness (Miller 1993) and undermine firms' capabilities to try new ideas, and adopt the risks (Zahra 2005). Family firms that unite resources by new methods often do not know how to make money from innovation. They should experiment different alternatives in order to find the most successful recipe. Without doubt this is time consuming, risky and expensive. So it is quite common to see that these firms often prefer imitation in order to protect their competitive advantage rather than engaging in innovation (Zahra 2005).

Besides that, nepotism is another problem hindering innovativeness in family businesses. In family firms, hiring of family members are quite common and monitoring their performance is difficult (Dyer 2006). Founders mostly favor their own relatives, hindering full integration of competent employees (Zahra 2005). Recruitment and promotion of nonfamily managers are very uncommon thus they often face the risk of losing or even not finding the skills and creative knowledge needed for innovations (Nieto et al. 2015).

To sum up, although there are both proponents and opponents of the idea that family firms have proper atmosphere and management mentality necessary for a more innovative structure, in this study, it is suggested that flexible and less bureaucratic structure of family businesses contributes to innovativeness of these firms when proper kind of leadership and special characteristics of family businesses are melted in the same pot.

4 Factors Effecting Innovativeness in Family Businesses

Typology of the family business is effective in determining the degree of its innovativeness. Two important studies; Pittino and Visintin's (2009) study and McCann et al.'s (2001) study focused on the degree of innovation by using Miles and Snow's (1978) model. According to their innovation strategies four kinds of family businesses have been determined. First of these typologies are the *defenders*, those firms that give great importance to innovation in processes with the aim of strengthening their competitive position in their sectors. Second typology is the *prospectors*, oriented towards innovation in products and the exploration of new areas of business; the third typology is the *analysers*, have an intermediate balanced profile between innovation in products and processes, the last typology the *reactors*, do not have a clear orientation towards innovation, often stemming from lack of a clear innovation strategy. Families prefer to adopt one of these typologies and designate their strategies regarding innovation compatible with these typologies. For example: a defender firm may prefer to change their owner managers' business strategy and find novel methods of doing business in order to gain a wider market share. As an example; Ülker—a famous confectionary firm in Turkey changed its strategy after second generation and started to make business in different sectors such as real estate, technology and construction.

Of course, factors affecting innovativeness of the family firm are not limited with the typology of the family firm, the generation to which the family firms' owner managers belongs is also important (Beck et al. 2011), since it effects conditions that shapes company's culture of innovation. According to Beck et al. (2009) a family firm managed by the founder members, namely, the first generation often tend to employ greater number of family members who are not necessarily very qualified and competent for the job and this may hinder accumulation of necessary skills and knowledge that effects innovation capacity (Beck et al. 2009). Related to effects of generations on innovative capacities of family businesses Denison et al. (2004) claim that the impact of the founder owner in family firms on strategic decision making is mostly greater in family firms compared to their non-family counterparts. That is why, innovativeness in family firms often means innovativeness of the founder owner, and this does not always means that the whole company is innovative in general (Verhees and Meulenberg 2004).Furthermore, founder owners of family firms with long tenures are tend to invest in long lasting relationships that make risk taking more possible (Zahra 2004). And they often have the necessary resources to engage in innovative activities. Related to this point, in Zahra's (2004) study, 209 U.S. manufacturing family firms have been examined in order to highlight their risk taking behaviours. Results showed degree of family ownership and involvement promote entrepreneurship.

5 Leadership in Family Business

Leadership in family businesses is very important due to their organic structure shaped by the motives of founder owners. Leadership often overlaps with the personality of the founder owner and effects organizational culture and managerial style and shapes organizational strategy. Without doubt, some specific leadership styles are more proper for the unique nature of family firms. Sonderson's study on 59 small scale family firms showed that referent, expert, and participative leadership styles produce positive organizational outcomes in family firms contribute to high levels of satisfaction and organizational commitment.

Dyer's study published in 1986 is a classic regarding leadership in family business literature. He examined 40 family firms, and categorized them into four different cultures. Each culture type in Dyer's methodology shows a different type of managerial style. He chose two titles from these four cultures, participative and laissez-faire that are, in fact, titles frequently used to describe common leadership styles in family firms. Dyer (1986) claims that, the most frequently seen type of culture in family firms is paternalistic culture in which relationships are arranged hierarchically and authority is very important. In family businesses paternalism ensures sustainability and guardianship of family traditions, and ownership (Sorenson and Franzosa 1999). Paternalistic leaders control followers in a fatherly, but prefer to give them very little responsibility (Koiranen 2003). But this leadership style sometimes may lead to angry, upset or humiliated followers (Koiranen 2003).

The second culture type for family businesses is participative culture. It is relatively rare and often based on trust. This culture is member oriented; not very hierarchical and power distance is minimized. In this culture, individual progress and growth of all members are significant. Participative leadership is often seen in participative culture. This leadership style is proper for building successful cohesive teamwork, increases satisfaction, improves decision making and its quality and enriches work (Yukl 1998).

The third culture in Dyer's (1986) typology is *laissez-faire culture*. In this culture, leaders define aims and goals of the organization and encourages employees to be proactive in attaining them. In this culture employees experience excessive freedom, leaders trust employees, and lower level decision makers are highly active. This leadership style allows freedom of choice. Bass (1990) claims that laissez-faire leaders creates inefficient, unsatisfaction and unproductive followers.

The fourth culture type is *professional* culture. In this culture individual motivation and achievement are highly important. In this culture, the environment is highly competitive and individuals are given decision-making authority. However, because of lack of specificity related to leadership style in Dyer's approach, it is not easy to talk about a specific leadership in this culture. But expert leadership or referent leadership seems to be suitable for professional culture. Expert leadership has its roots in knowledge and technical skills of the leader about his business (Sorenson 2000). In expert leadership leader inspire his followers by their superior know-how. On the other hand, in referent leadership, leader is perceived as considerate, fair, respectful, and trustworthy and results in high levels of satisfaction and commitment.

In the light of Dyer's (1986) typology, Sorenson (2000) claimed that participative leadership styles provide a significant tool for creating adaptation and change in family businesses. Without doubt, tools making change and adaptation easy for family businesses are very important. One of the most famous family business researchers Ward (1987) notes that due to increased rivalry and shortened life cycles of products, thriving change for family businesses is very important. Similarly, Dyer (1986) claims that to become successful, family businesses have to make necessary changes in their organizational climate. Both of these researchers claim that family firms need satisfying leadership in order to make changes in their organizations, processes and products (Sorenson 2000). According to Sorenson (2000) participative leaders have important effects on the financial success of family firms since it promotes change which is a very important element that most family firms lack (Ward 1987). It allows flexibility and integration of different perspectives. Under participative leadership since family members take part in critic processes, they become more committed to their firms and families (Sorenson 2000).

However, in numerous family firms, management function is undertaken by professional outsiders, namely, nonfamily managers who are supposed to direct the firm as professionally and as managerially as possible. Professional management is different from paternalistic management style of an owner. Paternalistic management often involves directing, protecting, and restraining followers, whereas managerial management often involves setting standards, checking results, and controlling (Koiranen 2003).

In this study, it is proposed that authentic leadership who has both a professional approach and a participative approach regarding management will be proper for the unique structure of family businesses. Authentic and trustworthy perspective of authentic leaders is congruent for gaining confidence of both family and non family members which is a problematic issue in family businesses due to the favored status of family members. Authentic leaders are not self serving leaders and they are sensitive in treating their followers with justice. It is one of the most important points that makes authentic leadership necessary for family businesses. Their transparency, authenticity and morality are helpful in solving problems familial problems that often intervene to business life in family firms and lowers the quality of the relationships and outputs in the organization. And their caring leadership style is significant in solving problems that are experienced mostly by non family members which are caused by not being a member of the ingroup, namely, member of the family.

Also, their objectivity and transparency help them solve job related problems easily and encourage people to try novel and risky projects. Followers conviction regarding their leaders' authenticity and empowering leadership style will make them feel more self confidence in making challenging attempts. They will have less fear of failure and will not feel themselves humiliated incase of inefficacy. Under authentic leadership leader will transmit his hope, optimism, self efficacy and resilience to all over the organization. This powerful psychological capacities uniting with the familial power and socioemotional wealth of the family business will result in higher levels of feelings of efficacy and confidence among organization members and will contribute to more and higher quality organizational outputs including innovations.

6 Authentic Leadership and Effects on Innovation

Positive psychology, insists that "what is good about life is as genuine as what is bad about life, therefore it deserves equal attention" (Peterson 2006, p. 4). Having its roots in positive psychology, a new realm of psychology, positive organizational behaviour as defined by Luthans (2002b) is "the study of positively oriented psychological strengths and capacities of people that can be measured, managed and developed for performance improvement in workplaces" (p. 59) has appeared. Positive psychological capital is a significant premise for authentic leadership. It is a positive organizational behaviour construct that empowers positive sides and psychological strengths of individuals and enhances performance (Luthans 2002a).

We can talk about four main psychological capacity. First of them is optimism. Seligman (1998) defines optimism as an attribution that is helpful in explaining positive cases in life in terms of permanent, personal, and pervasive causes and negative cases in terms of temporary, external, and situational causes. Without doubt optimism has a significant performance impact in work atmospheres (Luthans et al. 2005). Regarding effects of optimism on entrepreneurship, Pinfold (2001) applied a study in New Zealand and found a positive correlation between optimism and entrepreneurship which can also be expected in the relationship between positivity and innovation. According to Jensen and Luthans (2006) optimism builds a threshold effect regarding innovation by creating a future oriented and goal oriented optimistic world view. Since one of the ways of acquiring optimism is modeling

(Peterson 2000), it is meaningful to claim that under authentic leadership followers of authentic leaders will model desired positive emotions and thus optimism is disseminated all over the organization.

Second important psychological capacity is resiliency. Luthans (2002a) defines resiliency as "the capacity to rebound or bounce back from adversity, conflict, and failure or even positive events, progress, and increased responsibility" (p. 702). Resiliency has its roots in clinical psychology and it is useful to be successful and to be tolerant in times of risk and ambiguity. Although there is not enough study regarding the relationship between innovation and resiliency there is indirect research regarding the suggestion that innovation and will be supported by the resiliency of the leaders and members. For example; in Block and Kremen's (1996) study it was seen that resilient individuals are more successful in risky and ambiguous atmospheres that are also the kind of business climates most innovators come across. Authentic leaders have the capacity to strengthen resilience, by giving support to their followers in recovering from adversities, and maintaining positive change (Zehir and Narcıkara 2016). The capacity for resilience promotes the recognition of potential setbacks and adversities and allows individuals the necessary energy, time and resources to recover, and turn back to an equilibrium point (Bonanno 2004; Youssef and Luthans 2007). In organizational terms organizational resilience contributes to deployment of resources and mechanisms that increase capabilities of the firms to recombine assets and resources in novel ways (Weick and Quinn 1999). Organizational resilience enhances firm product innovativeness by increasing the use of ideas and information/knowledge necessary for innovation.

The third important capacity is self efficacy. Authentic leaders build followers' self-efficacy, by expressing confidence and trust in them and by making them recognize their own capabilities (Gardner and Schermerhorn 2004). Bandura (1977) described self-efficacy as one's own judgments about his capabilities to coordinate his own actions in order to achieve designated goals. Self-efficacy measures one's focus on performance capabilities rather than one's physical or psychological characteristics (Zimmerman 2000). Bandura claims that self-efficacy have an important role in attaining goals because "outcomes people anticipate from their own behaviors largely depend largely on their own judgments regarding how successful they will be able to perform in a particular context". It is the belief about one's capability to fulfill a given task not one's feelings about themselves in general.

Hope is another important psychological capacity. According to extant literature high hope organizations tend to be more profitable (Adams et al. 2002) and high hope managers are more successful (Peterson and Luthans 2003). In workplace, high hope employers prone to be more resolute about their goals; value progress toward their goals; enjoy collaboration with others; are often less anxious, and often have high adaptation capabilities that are necessary for change and innovation change (Snyder 2000). In a related study by Peterson and Luthans (2003), results showed that leader's hope may be a healthy antecedent of high employee performance, positive retention habits, and high levels of job satisfaction. Namely, leaders with high levels of hope often have positive impacts on positive work outcomes. Hopeful, reliant, confident and optimistic followers are often more inclined to engage in novel activities, try novel ways and do not hesitate in challenging situations (Černe et al. 2013). These positive capacities triggered by authentic leadership enable flexible, innovative and creative decision making (Avolio et al. 2004). Under authentic leadership employees use experimentation with self confidence. Thus, employees do not afraid to experiment, even when their ideas are too novel and have the risk to fail. Therefore, this confidence contributes to higher creative performance (Černe et al. 2013).

Properties of authentic leadership can be summarized in three main categories; self-regulation, self-awareness, and positive modelling (Černe et al. 2013) which are all very important factors in encouraging and triggering, innovativeness, creativity and entrepreneurship. Under authentic leadership, through relational transparency, which is a part of self-regulation process of authentic leadership, the leaders' true self becomes visible to the followers (Gardner et al. 2005). This openness resulting from high levels of relational transparency makes followers better understand the degree to which their leaders support innovativeness in the organization (Černe et al. 2013). Authentic leaders gain followers' trust, which end up with higher emotional safety (Avolio et al. 2004) that creates the necessary atmosphere for sharing ideas and trying new ways of doing the business which is very important for making innovation. Extant literature related to authentic leadership shows that a positive organizational atmosphere under authentic leadership has many positive organizational outputs. To give an example; in the research conducted by Jensen and Luthans on 148 business founder owners, results showed that there is a positive relationship between entrepreneurs' self perception of being authentic leadership and their psychological capital. A proper situation for both innovation and entrepreneurs for both surviving and thriving in a challenging and competitive business environment for particularly today's smaller organizations that are composed of mostly family firms (Jensen and Luthans 2006).

As a term, authenticity means, acting consistent with one's true self, understanding and having an integrations between one's own ideas and behaviours (Harter 2002). It means being original, natural and not a copy (Shamir and Eilam 2005). Leader's authenticity is leader's capacity to evaluate situations objectively and process information effectively related to both his own values, goals, beliefs, and feelings and others'. It is an ability to integrate their behaviour with their own self, namely having a clear personal identity (Chan et al. 2005). By knowing themselves very well authentic leaders' self-confidence is also built through self-awareness process. Authentic leaders are independent leaders, which supports creative behaviour (Patterson 1999). Under authentic leadership, identification of followers with their leader is called positive modelling and it is closely related to the leader's self-awareness (Gardner et al. 2005). During positive modelling, authentic leaders contributes to development of psychological capacities in the followers (Avolio et al. 2004). By demonstrating their true self to the followers and leading by example, authentic leaders enhances followers' innovativeness and creativity (Ilies et al. 2005).

Moreover, authentic leader is a trustworthy and caring leader. He gives equal emphasize to both goal attainment and employee development (Luthans and Avolio

2003). According to Avolio et al. (2004) authentic leaders are the kind of leaders that are deeply aware of their own and others' values, knowledges, moral perspectives and strengths. They are often deeply aware of the context in which they take place; and they are highly confident, optimistic, hopeful and resilient. They have the capability to make their followers recognize their own capabilities (Gardner and Schermerhorn 2004). And this properties of authentic leaders make them proper leaders for an innovative organizational atmosphere.

To sum up, having its roots in positive organizational behaviour, authentic leadership increase the positive emotions of followers by establishing positive, supportive, ethic and transparent interactions (Peterson et al. 2012) which in turn urge followers to become more creative. Creativity literature suggests that when team leader's self-confidence is high, independency perceived by team members is also high and this results in higher levels of employee creativity (Černe et al. 2013).

Although scarce in number there are also some studies regarding the effects of authentic leadership on innovation for example in Černe et al.'s (2013) study on 23 leaders and 289 employees in a manufacturing firm in Slovenia, researchers investigated interactions between authentic leadership and innovativeness and results of the study showed that relationship between team leaders' authenticity and creativity is mediated by perception of support for innovation. As an other example, in Müceldili et al.'s (2013) study on 142 employees working in organizations operating in Turkey, results of the study showed that authentic leadership promotes creativity within the organization and contributes to organizational innovativeness.

7 Conclusion

Without doubt, being a leader is always compelling and difficult in challenging business atmospheres, but today's rapidly changing and stressful business environment necessitates a renewed focus on what makes genuine leadership (Avolio et al. 2004). Challenges of modern world is unfortunately more bothersome for small scale firms which are mostly composed of family firms. And these special kind of firms also need a specific kind of leadership that will be suitable for their and they often prefer incremental innovations. In this study, innovativeness is regarded as openness to new ideas as an aspect of a firm's culture. Main goal unique structure and management mentality. Since family firms are emotional organizations in which families and business overlap, this particular situation necessitates more authenticity, more intimacy and more openness. In family firms, strict familial relationships among organization members may result in moving away from professionalism and results in nepotism and injustice that may disturb both family members and non family members among the employees. Moreover, existence of non family members among colleagues may create problems and confidence crises among organization members and toward owners/managers.

Being inspired from extant literature we claim that authentic leaders are among the most congruent leaders with the unique climate of family firms, since they have the inner power to create the necessary atmosphere for innovativeness in these kind of organizations. With the help of their trustworthy nature and authentic leaders enhances positive psychological capabilities of employees, namely followers' own self-esteem (Luthans and Avolio 2003), trust (Clapp-Smith et al. 2009), resiliency (Gardner and Schermerhorn 2004), hope (Clapp-Smith et al. 2009), and optimism (Avolio and Gardner 2005). Being exposed to authentic leadership, more optimistic, hopeful, and confident employees become more prone to try novel things more often and not be afraid of a possible failure (Černe et al. 2013). Creative and innovative managers that are most likely to derive from authentic leaders who have high self-awareness tend to appreciate, encourage and model creativity and innovation for their followers. They have the ability and tendency to enable and motivate their followers to work towards the implementation of innovative ideas and processes (Tierney 2008).

The four dimensions of authentic leadership: (1) Self-awareness, namely leader's understanding about his or her strengths, insufficiencies, others' perceptions, and how (s)he effects others (Walumbwa et al. 2008); (2) Balanced processing, namely his capacity regarding making objective analyzes and decisions (Gardner et al. 2005) and (3) Relational transparency, namely presenting his (leader's) true self to others, expressing his true thoughts and feelings, speaking and acting frankly and, (4) Internalized moral perspective namely setting high moral standards and acting in congruent with them (Walumbwa et al. 2008); reinforce openness among followers and ensure the proper climate to try new opportunities, share their ideas and take risks which are required for innovativeness.

Not sharing the same approach with scholars claiming that family firms' conservative nature will make them resistant to change and risk aversive, in this chapter it is claimed that under proper kinds of leadership, in our case under authentic leadership, family firms do show significant differences with their nonfamily counterparts regarding innovativeness. Both family and nonfamily firms become innovative under proper kind of leadership and organizational atmosphere. Authentic leaders' positive effect on the organizational climate of family firms contribute to growth and competitiveness of these firms and may provide them with the necessary motivation to adopt a more proactive managerial style which will result in higher levels of innovativeness.

References

Adams, V. H., Snyder, C. R., Rand, K. L., King, E. A., Sigmon, D. R., & Pulvers, K. M. (2002). Hope in the workplace. In R. A. Giacalone & C. L. Jurkiewicz (Eds.), *Handbook of workplace spirituality and organizational performance* (pp. 367–377). Armonk, NY: M.E. Sharpe.

Amabile, T. M. (1998). *How to kill creativity* (Vol. 87). Boston, MA: Harvard Business School Publishing.

Anderson, P., & Tushman, M. L. (1990). Technological discontinuities and dominant designs: A cyclical model of technological change. *Administrative Science Quarterly, 35*, 604–633.

Avolio, B. J., & Gardner, W. L. (2005). Authentic leadership development: Getting to the root of positive forms of leadership. *The Leadership Quarterly, 16*(3), 315–338.

Avolio, B. J., Gardner, W. L., Walumbwa, F. O., Luthans, F., & May, D. R. (2004). Unlocking the mask: A look at the process by which authentic leaders impact follower attitudes and behaviors. *The Leadership Quarterly, 15*(6), 801–823.

Bandura, A. (1977). Self-efficacy: Toward a unifying theory of behavioral change. *Psychological Review, 84*(2), 191.

Barney, J. (1991). Firm resources and sustained competitive advantage. *Journal of Management, 17*(1), 99–120.

Bass, B. M. (1990). From transactional to transformational leadership: Learning to share the vision. *Organizational Dynamics, 18*(3), 19–31.

Beck, L., Janssens, W., Debruyne, M., & Lommelen, T. (2011). A study of the relationships between generation, market orientation, and innovation in family firms. *Family Business Review, 24*(3), 252–272.

Beck, L., Janssens, W., Lommelen, T., & Sluismans, R. (2009). *Research on innovation capacity antecedents: Distinguishing between family and non-family businesses*. Diepenbeek: KIZOK Research Centre.

Birdthistle, N., & Fleming, P. (2007). Under the microscope: A profile of the family business in Ireland. *Irish Journal of Management, 28*(2), 135.

Block, J., & Kremen, A. M. (1996). IQ and ego-resiliency: Conceptual and empirical connections and separateness. *Journal of Personality and Social Psychology, 70*(2), 349.

Bonanno, G. A. (2004). Loss, trauma, and human resilience: Have we underestimated the human capacity to thrive after extremely aversive events? *American Psychologist, 59*(1), 20.

Breton-Miller, L., & Miller, D. (2009). Agency vs. stewardship in public family firms: A social embeddedness reconciliation. *Entrepreneurship Theory and Practice, 33*(6), 1169–1191.

Burns, T., & Stalker, G. M. (1961). *The management of innovation*. London: Tavistock.

Černe, M., Jaklič, M., & Škerlavaj, M. (2013). Authentic leadership, creativity, and innovation: A multilevel perspective. *Leadership, 9*(1), 63–85.

Chan, A. W. L., Hannah, S. T., & Gardner, W. L. (2005). Veritable authentic leadership: Emergence, functioning, and impact. In W. L. Gardner, B. J. Avolio, & F. O. Walumbwa (Eds.), *Authentic leadership theory and practice: Origins, effects and development* (pp. 3–41). Oxford: Elsevier.

Chen, H. L., & Hsu, W. T. (2009). Family, ownership, board independence, and R&D investment. *Family Business Review, 22*(4), 347–362.

Clapp-Smith, R., Vogelgesang, G. R., & Avey, J. B. (2009). Authentic leadership and positive psychological capital: The mediating role of trust at the group level of analysis. *Journal of Leadership & Organizational Studies, 15*(3), 227–240.

Cooper, R. G., & Kleinschmidt, E. J. (1995). Benchmarking the firm's critical success factors in new product development. *Journal of Product Innovation Management, 12*(5), 374–391.

Craig, J. B., & Moores, K. (2006). A 10-year longitudinal investigation of strategy, systems, and environment on innovation in family firms. *Family Business Review, 19*(1), 1–10.

Denison, D., Lief, C., & Ward, J. L. (2004). Culture in family-owned enterprises: Recognizing and leveraging unique strengths. *Family Business Review, 17*(1), 61–70.

DeVisscher, F. M., Aronoff, C. F., & Ward, J. L. (1995). *Financing transitions: Managing capital and liquidity in the family business, family business leadership series*. Marietta, GA: Business Owner Resources.

Drucker, P. F. (1985). The discipline of innovation. *Harvard Business Review, 63*(3), 67–72.

Dyer, W. G. (1986). *Cultural change in family firms*. San Francisco: Jossey-Bass.

Dyer, W. G. (2006). Examining the "family effect" on firm performance. *Family Business Review, 19*(4), 253–273.

Fama, E. F., & Jensen, M. C. (1983). Agency problems and residual claims. *Journal of Law and Economics, 26*(2), 327–349.

Gardner, W. L., Avolio, B. J., Luthans, F., May, D. R., & Walumbwa, F. O. (2005). Can you see the real me? A self-based model of authentic leader and follower development. *The Leadership Quarterly, 16*, 343–372.

Gardner, W. L., & Schermerhorn, J. R., Jr. (2004). Unleashing individual potential: Performance gains through positive organizational behavior and authentic leadership. *Organizational Dynamics, 33*(3), 270–281.

Gómez-Mejía, L., Takács, K. T., Núñez-Nickel, M., Jacobson, K. J. L., & Moyano-Fuentes, J. (2007). Socioemotional wealth and business risks in family-controlled firms: Evidence from Spanish olive oil mills. *Administrative Science Quarterly, 52*, 106–137.

Gudmundson, D., Tower, B. C., & Hartman, A. E. (2003). Innovation in small businesses: Culture and ownership structure do matter. *Journal of Developmental Entrepreneurship, 8*(1), 1–17.

Habbershon, T. G., & Pistrui, J. (2002). Enterprising families domain: Family-influenced ownership groups in pursuit of transgenerational wealth. *Family Business Review, 15*(3), 223–238.

Habbershon, T. G., & Williams, M. L. (1999). A resource-based framework for assessing the strategic advantages of family firms. *Family Business Review, 12*(1), 1–26.

Habbershon, T. G., Williams, M. L., & McMillan, I. C. (2003). A unified systems perspective of family firm performance. *Journal of Business Venturing, 18*, 451–465.

Hall, A., Melin, L., & Nordqvist, M. (2001). Entrepreneurship as radical change in the family business: Exploring the role of cultural patterns. *Family Business Review, 14*(3), 193–208.

Harter, S. (2002). Authenticity. In C. R. Snyder & S. Lopez (Eds.), *Handbook of positive psychology* (p. 382). London: Oxford University Press.

Hult, G. T. M., Hurley, R. F., & Knight, G. A. (2004). Innovativeness: It's antecedents and impact on business performance. *Industrial Marketing Management, 33*, 429–438.

Hurley, R. F., & Hult, G. T. M. (1998). Innovation, market orientation, and organizational learning: An integration and empirical examination. *The Journal of Marketing, 62*, 42–54.

Ilies, R., Morgeson, F. P., & Nahrgang, J. D. (2005). Authentic leadership and eudaemonic well-being: Understanding leader-follower outcomes. *The Leadership Quarterly, 16*(3), 373–394.

Jensen, S. M., & Luthans, F. (2006). Relationship between entrepreneurs' psychological capital and their authentic leadership. *Journal of Managerial Issues, 18*, 254–273.

Jensen, M. C., & Meckling, W. H. (1976). Theory of the firm: Managerial behavior, agency costs and ownership structure. *Journal of Financial Economics, 3*(4), 305–360.

Kets de Vries, M. F. R. (1993). The dynamics of family controlled firms: The good and the bad new. *Organizational Dynamics, 21*(3), 59–71.

Koiranen, M. (2003). Understanding the contesting ideologies of family business: Challenge for leadership and professional services. *Family Business Review, 16*(4), 241–250.

Leblanc, G., & Nguyen, N. (1997). Searching for excellence in business education: An exploratory study of customer impressions of service quality. *International Journal of Educational Management, 11*(2), 72–79.

Lorenzo, D., & Núñez-Cacho, P. (2013). *Do family firms have specific barriers to innovation? A first approach.* 13th Annual International Family Enterprise Research Academy Conference, University of St. Gallen, St Gallen, Switzerland.

Luthans, F. (2002a). The need for and meaning of positive organizational behavior. *Journal of Organizational Behavior, 23*(6), 695–706.

Luthans, F. (2002b). Positive organizational behavior: Developing and managing psychological strengths. *Academy of Management Executive, 16*(1), 57–72.

Luthans, F., & Avolio, B. J. (2003). Authentic leadership: A positive developmental approach. In K. S. Cameron, J. E. Dutton, & R. E. Quinn (Eds.), *Positive organizational scholarship* (pp. 241–261). San Francisco, CA: Barrett-Koehler.

Luthans, F., Avolio, B. J., Walumbwa, F. O., & Li, W. (2005). The psychological capital of Chinese workers: Exploring the relationship with performance. *Management and Organization Review, 1*, 247–269.

McAdam, R., Reid, R., & Mitchell, N. (2010). Longitudinal development of innovation implementation in family-based SMEs: The effects of critical incidents. *International Journal of Entrepreneurial Behaviour and Research, 16*(5), 437–456.

McCann, J. E., III, Leon-Guerrero, A. Y., & Haley, J. D., Jr. (2001). Strategic goals and practices of innovative family businesses. *Journal of Small Business Management, 39*(1), 50–59.

Miles, R. E., & Snow, C. C. (1978). *Organizational strategy, structure and processes.* New York: McGraw-Hill.

Miller, D. (1993). The architecture of simplicity. *Academy of Management Review, 18*(1), 116–139.

Miller, D., & Le Breton-Miller, I. (2005). *Managing for the long run: Lessons in competitive advantage from great family businesses.* Boston: Harvard Business School Press.

Mohnen, P., & Röller, L. (2005). Complementarities in innovation policy. *European Economic Review, 49*, 1431–1450.

Moscetello, L. (1990). The Pitcairns want you. *Family Business Magazine, 19*(2), 135–145.

Müceldili, B., Turan, H., & Erdil, O. (2013). The influence of authentic leadership on creativity and innovativeness. *Procedia-Social and Behavioral Sciences, 99*, 673–681.

Naldi, L., Nordqvist, M., Sjöberg, K., & Wiklund, J. (2007). Entrepreneurial Orientation, risk taking, and performance in family firms. *Family Business Review, 20*(1), 33–47.

Niehm, L. S., Tyner, K., Shelley, M., & Fitzgerald, M. (2010). Technology adoption in small family-owned businesses: Accessibility, perceived advantage, and information technology literacy. *Journal of Family and Economic Issues, 31*(4), 498–515.

Nieto, M. J., Santamaria, L., & Fernandez, Z. (2015). Understanding the innovation behavior of family firms. *Journal of Small Business Management, 53*(2), 382–399.

Núñez-Cacho, P., & Grande, F. (2013). The importance of mentoring and coaching for family businesses. *Journal of Management and Organization, 19*(4), 386–404.

Patterson, F. (1999). *Innovation potential predictor.* Oxford: Oxford Psychologists Press.

Pervin, A. (1997). A conversation with Henry Mintzberg. *Family Business Review, 10*(2), 185–198.

Peterson, C. (2000). The future of optimism. *American Psychologist, 55*(1), 44.

Peterson, C. (2006). *A primer in positive psychology.* Oxford: Oxford University Press.

Peterson, S. J., & Luthans, F. (2003). The positive impact and development of hopeful leaders. *Leadership and Organization Development Journal, 24*(1), 26–31.

Peterson, S. J., Walumbwa, F. O., Avolio, B. J., & Hannah, S. T. (2012). The relationship between authentic leadership and follower job performance: The mediating role of follower positivity in extreme contexts. *The Leadership Quarterly, 23*, 502–516.

Pinfold, J. F. (2001). The expectations of new business founders: The New Zealand case. *Journal of Small Business Management, 39*(3), 279–285.

Pittino, D., & Visintin, F. (2009). Innovation and strategic types of family SMEs. A test and extension of miles and Snow's configurational model. *Journal of Enterprising Culture, 17*, 257–295.

Porter, M. E. (1990). The competitive advantage of nations. *Harvard Business Review, 68*(2), 73–93.

Romijn, H., & Albaladejo, M. (2002). Determinants of innovation capability in small electronics and software firms in southeast England. *Research Policy, 31*, 1053–1067.

Rumelt, R. P. (1987). Theory, strategy, and entrepreneurship. In D. J. Teece (Ed.), *The competitive challenge* (pp. 137–158). Cambridge, MA: Ballinger.

Schulze, W. S., Lubatkin, M. H., Dino, R. N., & Buchholtz, A. K. (2001). Agency relationships in family firms: Theory and evidence. *Organization Science, 12*(2), 99–116.

Schumpeter, J. (1934). *The theory of economic development.* New York: Irwin University Books.

Seligman, M. (1998). *Learned optimism.* New York: Pocket.

Shamir, B., & Eilam, G. (2005). 'What's your story?' A life-stories approach to authentic leadership development. *The Leadership Quarterly, 16*(3), 395–417.

Sharma, P., Chrisman, J. J., & Chua, J. H. (1997). Strategic management of the family business: Past research and future challenges. *Family Business Review, 10*, 1–36.

Siguaw, J. A., Simpson, P. M., & Enz, C. A. (2006). Conceptualizing innovation orientation: A framework for study and integration of innovation research. *Journal of Product Innovation Management, 23*, 556–574.

Snyder, C. R. (2000). *Handbook of hope.* San Diego, CA: Academic Press.

Sorenson, R. L. (2000). Planning for family and financial success in family businesses. *Family Business Review, 13*(2), 133–142.

Sorenson, M. D., & Franzosa, E. A. (1999). *TreeRot, version 2*. Boston, MA: Boston University.

Tagiuri, R., & Davis, J. (1996). Bivalent attributes of the family firm. *Family Business Review, 9*(2), 199–202.

Tierney, P. (2008). Leadership and employee creativity. In J. Zhou & C. E. Shalley (Eds.), *Handbook of organizational creativity* (pp. 95–123). New York: Lawrence Erlbaum.

Uhlaner, L., van Stel, A., Meijaard, J., & Folkeringa, M. (2007). *The relationship between knowledge management, innovation and firm performance: Evidence from Dutch SMEs* (pp. 1–26). Zoetermeer: Scientific analysis of entrepreneurship and SMEs.

Van Gils, A., Voordeckers, W., & Hagedoorn, J. (2008, July 2–5). *Nurturing innovation in family firms: The influence of managerial and family characteristics*. Paper presented at conference "the entrepreneuring family", Neyenrode.

Varis, M., & Littunen, H. (2010). Types of innovation, sources of information and performance in entrepreneurial SMEs. *European Journal of Innovation Management, 13*(2), 128–154.

Verhees, F. J. H. M., & Meulenberg, M. T. G. (2004). Market orientation, innovativeness, product innovation, and performance in small firms. *Journal of Small Business Management, 42*(2), 134–154.

Walumbwa, F., Avolio, B., Gardner, W., Wernsing, T., & Peterson, S. (2008). Authentic leadership: Development and validation of a theory-based measure. *Journal of Management, 34*(1), 89–126.

Ward, J. L. (1987). *Keeping the family business healthy: How to plan for continuing growth, profitability, and family leadership*. San Francisco: Business Owners Resources.

Ward, J. L. (1988). The special role of strategic planning for family businesses. *Family Business Review, 1*(2), 105–117.

Ward, J. L. (1997). Growing the family business: Special challenges and best practices. *Family Business Review, 10*(4), 323–337.

Webb, J., Ketchen, D., & Ireland, R. D. (2010). Strategic entrepreneurship within family-controlled firms: Opportunities and challenges. *Journal of Family Business Strategy, 1*(2), 67–77.

Weick, K. E., & Quinn, R. E. (1999). Organizational change and development. *Annual Review of Psychology, 50*(1), 361–386.

Westhead, P., Cowling, M., & Storey, D. (1996). *The management and performance of unquoted family companies in the United Kingdom* (Working paper 42). Coventry: The University of Warwick, Coventry, Center for Small and Medium Size Enterprises.

Wright, P., Kroll, M., Lado, A., & Van Ness, B. (2002). The structure of ownership and corporate acquisition strategies. *Strategic Management Journal, 23*(1), 41–53.

Wu, H. (2008). When does internal governance make firms innovative? *Journal of Business Research, 61*, 141–153.

Youssef, C. M., & Luthans, F. (2007). Positive organizational behavior in the workplace: The impact of hope, optimism, and resilience. *Journal of Management, 33*(5), 774–800.

Yukl, G. A. (1998). *Leadership in organizations* (4th ed.). Englewood Cliffs, NJ: Prentice Hall. 1989 - 2nd ed.

Zahra, S. A. (2004). Negative relationship it CEO- tenure. No relationship with CEO–owner duality, positive relationship with high family ownership, higher the number of generations from the same owner family that are active in the company, the higher the firm's focus on innovation.

Zahra, S. A. (2005). Entrepreneurial risk taking in family firms. *Family Business Review, 18*(1), 23–40.

Zahra, S. A., Hayton, J. C., & Salvato, C. (2004). Entrepreneurship in family vs. non-family firms: A resource-based analysis of the effect of organizational culture. *Entrepreneurship Theory and Practice, 28*, 363–381.

Zehir, C., & Narcıkara, E. (2016). Effects of resilience on productivity under authentic leadership. *Procedia-Social and Behavioral Sciences, 235*, 250–258.

Zimmerman, B. J. (2000). Self-efficacy: An essential motive to learn. *Contemporary Educational Psychology, 25*(1), 82–91.

Innovation Strategies in European Developing Countries

Ljiljana Kontic

Abstract The main aim of this study was to determinate key factors of innovation strategies choice for global competitiveness. The starting hypothesis was that innovation performance correlating with national competitiveness of European developing countries. Meta data from European Innovation Scoreboard in period 2011–2016 and Global Competitiveness Report have been used in this study. Research methodology consisted of comparative method and relevant statistical methods. The findings revealed the main factors of better innovation performances that caused higher ranking according to Global Competitiveness Index. The limitations and future research avenues are presented too.

1 Introduction

One of three main areas in the Lisbon Strategy is knowledge and innovation for growth. The need for organizations to innovate and to gain the benefits of innovation comes from increasing competition and customer demands. *"Innovations involve new working methods, new ideas, new products, new processes, new form of organization, and new management. The most common criterion in any definition of innovation is newness"* (Kontic 2008).

Along with innovation, competitiveness has become a dominant economic theme. In addition to the traditional need to be more competitive, is better than others, its global importance has contributed to the global economic crisis through which all economies pass through. In the world economy, the decline is now stopped, but it is still uncertain what will happen next, whether and when growth will be restored, and when the level of GDP that existed before the crisis will reach. It is certain that Serbia will have to change its model of growth and prosperity, which it has pursued so far, by abandoning the expansion of domestic demand as a key generator of growth.

L. Kontic (✉)
University of Belgrade, Belgrade, Serbia

© Springer International Publishing AG, part of Springer Nature 2018
H. Dincer et al. (eds.), *Strategic Design and Innovative Thinking in Business Operations*, Contributions to Management Science,
https://doi.org/10.1007/978-3-319-77622-4_12

Increasing competitiveness is the process of improving the business environment that should enable the increase of domestic investments, inflows of foreign and domestic investments, exports, imports, etc. Each of these factors depends on the level of competitiveness of the national economy. Investors, domestic and foreign, will not invest capital until the country provides an attractive value proposition, and exports will only start to grow when products reach the required quality with efficient production.

Eleven countries are in a group of European developing countries e.g. Albania, Belarus, Croatia, Moldova, Montenegro, Serbia, Bosnia and Herzegovina, Macedonia, Russia, Turkey, and Ukraine.

2 Systems of Innovation

The systems of innovation (SI) approach has been used in theoretical discussions as well as practically in introducing innovation policy and implement by Governments. Organizations and institutions are the main components of SI.

The system of innovation can be regarding as a network that includes individual and collective processes of research, study and selection of various innovative features, mainly including technological and economic dimension. Innovative activities create a system of innovation. In this context, innovations have two dimensions: technological and market selection. Innovative activities are activities of "seeking knowledge" in order to develop the economic value. System innovation is important for the expansion link enterprises and institutions whose impact can be positive-help identify new innovative capacities, but also a negative-giving information that does not reflect wider trends at the market or in technology.

In creating "new knowledge" and to determinate goal of future research this approach can be useful. Another role of SI is to concentrate various resources and to exchange information with wider environment.

The contributions of national innovation system for development economics can be summarized in following (Lundvall et al. 2011):

- Political institutions affect economic processes.
- Raising important of behavioural models that replaced rationality presumption.
- Different approach to public policy
- Deeper connection with institution theory and community characteristics.
- Pluralism in methodological approaches.
- Problem solving in interaction with others
- Firm heterogeneity.

Some authors stated that establishment of regional innovation systems might overcome the national deficits (Lundvall et al. 2011; Doloreux 2002).

ERA Initiative, EU policy in the field of science and technology, uses regional competencies. This does not mean that states completely lose their power, but their significance and management function is changed.

The excellent performances of individual actors are not enough for the success of regional innovation. The sustainable success of innovation suggests that a complete regional innovation system functions.

The European regions differ in their ability to develop regional innovation systems. Factors that determine the development and different performance of regional innovation systems are (Kontic 2007:67–68):

- Regional companies differ in their innovative capabilities due to their specialization within the industry, as well as functional and organizational characteristics.
- Regional enterprises differ in their interactions with clusters, behaviour of actors within the cooperation.
- Regions vary according to capacity to build relevant institutions (research, education, technology transfer), governance model, decision-making power, financial resources and orientation of innovation policy.

3 Types of Innovation Strategies

The innovation strategy enables firm to adopt, learn from experience, and to react to new challenges and chances. They are different classifications of innovative strategies. According to Freeman (1982), there is offensive, defensive, imitative, traditional, and opportunistic innovative strategy. Strategic choice depends on scientific and technological capacities of firm. Basic scientific research implicates the choice of offensive innovation strategy. If firm has capacity for experimental development managers will choose offensive or defensive strategy. High level of product engineering function determinates imitative, opportunistic or traditional innovation strategy. In order to legally protect innovation managers will choose offensive strategy. Long term prediction and planning new products implicates strategic choice between offensive and opportunistic innovation strategies.

According to level of R&D expenditures and different patterns of organizational behavior, three main innovative strategies can be distinguished: conservative, imitative, and absorptive strategy. First strategy called conservative focused innovation activities exclusively on internal research. Conservative behavior neglects changes in innovation process. Innovation attempts are directed to exploitation of current technology—process improvements and to exploration of new technology—product innovations.

Imitation strategy is based on external knowledge and possibilities. Main intension of managers is to avoid risk and to learn on competitors mistakes. This strategy enables firms to implement technological change which is introduced by other firms. Because of specific characteristic of technological knowledge in some cases technological transfer is expensive as internal R&D. Absorptive strategy is based on combination of internal and external knowledge. Internal R&D have two goals: process improvement, and product innovation (same as conservative strategy). Firms also use external knowledge, but not to imitate competitors, in order to realize effects of cross sector fertilization. Managers expect synergetic effects of both strategies.

Precondition for implement conservative and imitative strategy is managers' abilities for use knowledge in similar technologies. Absorptive strategies is less efficient when there is need for complete knowledge. There is clear distinction between aforementioned innovation strategies.

4 Determinants of Innovation Strategies

The analysis of relevant literature showed that there is voluminous literature on determinants of innovation strategy choice. Some authors pointed to following determinants of innovation process (Ortt and van der Duin 2008:528): product or process innovation, organization structure, industry sector (e.g. technological progress in certain industry), and national culture. Majority of studies analyzed firm's size and effects of perfect and monopolistic competition (Saviotti and Nooteboom 2000).

There is many innovation in monopolistic industries because monopolistic firm can prevent imitation and gain large profit from innovation.

Large firms are more innovative than small because they are able to finance a number of R&D staff, are better to exploit unforeseen innovations, and the indivisibility of reducing costs makes them profitable.

Large firms have a wide front and technological activities. The main technological strength is based on R&D (usually chemical and electronic products) or design a complex production processes. Small firms are usually specialized in product innovations such as tools, scientific instruments, certain chemicals and software. Their main strength is the ability to adapt technologies to specific customer requirements. Strategic management requirements are found and maintain a stable niche for products and benefit from users' experience.

In addition to the firm size, there are other factors that result in innovation. The main factor in deciding on the selection of innovative projects is the expected income from investments. This test is always applied before implementation of innovation strategy. However, it cannot be applied outside the context of the firms and their environment. According to Webb (1996:27), following factor can be used in order to choose adequate innovation strategy: firms' goals, position in market, product life cycle, current and potential competition, technology, capacity of factory, level of development, market forecasting, technological forecasting.

With this range of factors, there is no single strategy that will be the best in all conditions. The following question arises: Which factors determinate innovation strategy choice? First important factor is influence of **size** on strategic choice according to the most used classification of innovation strategy (i.e. conservative, imitative, and absorptive innovation strategy). Second factor is **industry sector**. It is important to examine the influence of industry on innovation strategy. Third examined factor is **knowledge source**. This opens up the possibility of firms embodying new knowledge and innovation within the organizational culture from a wide range of new sources. If managers want to introduce many innovation in relative short time, they combined external knowledge and internal research and development.

Environmental conditions such as **crisis** have significant influence on innovation strategies. For the majority firms crisis will be innovation obstacle, and therefore some options could be limited.

The alternative is that there is no strategy (*laissez-faire* approach). This can sometimes be successful if there are facilities for rapid development of new ideas into products. However, the approach can lead to waste of resources, missed opportunities due to the concentration of efforts in a particular direction in the critical time, and for this reason is not recommended.

Main characteristics of innovation process are complexity and stochastically. In this process there are numerous barriers, that might came from environment, suppliers, buyers, as well as from inside factors. One piece of empirical research has tried to reveal the relationship between export activity and innovation in manufacturing sector that is crucial for economic development (Mahagaonkar et al. 2009: 14). The results showed the strong correlation between innovation and export activities. The more intensive export the higher number of innovation in manufacturing industry. In detailed analysis, the exchange rate volatility has been introduced in aforementioned study. To intensive export and innovation the real rate needs to be the lowest as possible. Regarding the European developing countries, the world economic crisis caused decline of expert performance of their economies and therefore low level of innovation activities in manufacturing firms. This was significant obstacle for majority firms.

Internal obstacles are situational factors such as size, technology, age, human resources etc (Piater 1984). In this study, the most important internal determinants can be lack of finance, lack of human capital, lack of information, and lack of sharing knowledge. Aforementioned internal obstacles have significant influence on innovation management.

5 Model Competitive Advantages

The term competitive advantages in economic theory was introduced by American economist Michael Porter. Analyzing more than 100 economies in ten of the most developed countries, Porter (2008) concluded that some countries are more competitive than others in different economic sectors and that no country can be competitive in all economic sectors and activities. It is therefore very difficult to compare the competitiveness of different national economies if they are based on different economic branches. Porter (2008) created a model of competitive advantages based on four factors and called it a "diamond". National competitiveness, specific for each country, is created by the interaction of four groups of factors and two external variables.

Two external variables are government and opportunity (chances), while the factors are:Factor conditions, related and supportive industries, conditions of demand—quality of domestic demand, company strategy and structure, and level of competition.

By its policy and action, the Government has an impact on all four factors. The brief explanation of the framework, known as the Porter Diamond is following.

FACTOR CONDITIONS are the conditions of the country's competitiveness, but if they are not available effectively, they are not sufficient. These include:

- Human resources, which are today with the technology of basic resources, influence the knowledge and therefore the creation of technology, with a special importance of highly educated workforce
- Physical resources include natural factors such as quality, abundance and accessibility of national land, geographical location and distance from the market.
- Knowledge resources, that is, technology is important after human resources. Measures are taken by the scope of scientific, technical and market knowledge necessary for the production and placement of goods and services.
- Capital resources—capital is generated from gross domestic product, elasticity of savings and the structure of the national capital market. This is a particularly mobile resource. The globalization of the capital market leads to the equalization of the conditions on the national capital markets. Increase of capital is realized through investments and they are also a significant factor in adjusting the economic structure of a country to the world market.
- Infrastructure includes transport system, communication system, business services and business infrastructure.

CONDITIONS OF REQUIREMENTS include the following components: advanced customer demand, size of domestic market, number of independent customers, growth and domestic demand. Satisfying the needs of a domestic customer is especially important for the company that builds its competitive advantage, as it prepares in advance for the future requirements of foreign customers. The number of potential customers, as demographic characteristic, is particularly important for developing countries. Due to high domestic demand, big countries are at a disadvantage, while small countries forced earlier exported to foreign markets, which are more demanding than the domestic. The structure of demand and the demands of local consumers are important for performance on foreign markets, because it depends on the quality of the products.

RELATED and SUPPORTIVE INDUSTRIES are for specialized local suppliers and subcontractors and complementary production and manufacturing that share certain common components, which together make up the competitiveness of an entire sector. Abandoned the concept factory at the entrance has a raw and production materials, and on the way out the finished product, because within these production units cannot be on remunerative way to install all the necessary technology and specialist knowledge required for global competitive product. Therefore, it is used to access, still in phase of development and research to create products, in the process include companies that are in the vicinity, whereas subcontractors and suppliers. Their proximity is important for purposes of direct contacts, exchange of information and ease of construction, feeling that it creates a common product.

STRATEGY AND STRUCTURE OF ENTERPRISES AND COMPETITION LEVEL involves the conditions under which enterprises are established, organized and managed and the nature of domestic competition. The strategy is a set of activities that will achieve a certain vision. The strategy relates to the positioning of a company on the market and it represents the realization of activities that are different in relation to those achieved by competitors or the realization of similar activities that are performed by competitors in different ways. The actions that make up the strategy must be mutually consistent with strong positive interactions so that they act as a system, and the hierarchy of responsibility should be as divided as possible. Strong competition on the domestic market is significant especially in the initial steps of preparing the company for participation in the international market. The domestic market, as an initial step, is necessary because some of the operations are too expensive and prerequisite to be realized abroad, before gaining security in the domestic market. It is difficult to assume that a foreign company can gain competitive advantage without having succeeded in the domestic market.

The interaction between these four determinants determines the competitive advantage. The links between the factors are interactive, and the good position of one factor positively reflects on the other. Similarly, weakness in any factor limits the potential of all others.

ROLE OF CHANCE is one of Porter's external variables. Technical progress brings new materials, processes and applications, creating the possibilities of substitutes that form the basis for gaining a competitive edge. Timely understanding of the potential and scope of new phenomena represents a new competitive advantage.

THE ROLE OF GOVERNMENT is of paramount importance for the country's competitive ability. Opinions are divided between two extremes, one is that the state should not be confused with problems, and the second is that the state should manage all segments of that process. Porter's proposal to economic policymakers is to reduce the government's industrial and strategic trade policy, and instead open the domestic market and create tempting conditions for foreign direct investment.

6 Other Relevant Study

The Enterprise Surveys contain information about the external national and industry specific factors. They used mixed method for collecting relevant data. The quantitative data were meta data from relevant statistical sources. The interview method has been realized directly with company managers and/or owners.

The qualitative and quantitative data collected through face to face interviews with firm managers and owners.

The information about each country have been standardized into ten sections.

The first indicators measure quality of product (firm investing in Internationally Recognized Quality Certification) and transparency of financial statements. The further indicators provide information about the use of ICT, especially possess of own web site and email communications with business partners. The third set of indicators includes three ratios: percentage of temporary workers, percentage of permanent workers and the percentage of female workers.

Due to sampling method used in the World Bank Enterprise Survey i.e. random sample of firms as well as limited usefulness of ratio analysis, this comparative analysis has rudimentary character.

7 Objective of the Chapter

The objective of the present chapter is to analyze whether the poor countries' innovation performance was correlating to the national competitiveness for the period 2011–2016 in a case of European developing countries.

8 Data and Methodology

In this study two relevant methodology have been used: Innovation Union Scoreboard and Global Competitiveness Index. To assess the relative innovation performance in EU countries and selected other countries, European Commission calculated Innovation Scoreboard.

> Methodology consisted of seven dimensions grouped into three main blocks namely, enablers, firm activities and outputs. The main drivers of innovation—enablers were: human resources and finance and support. Indicators in the domain of human resources were followed five: S&E and SSH graduates per 1000 populations aged 20–29 (first stage of tertiary education), S&E and SSH doctorate graduates per 1000 populations aged 25–34 (second stage of tertiary education), a population with tertiary education per 100 populations aged 25–64, participation in lifelong learning per 100 populations aged 25–64, youth education attainment level. Indicators of finance and support were: Public R&D expenditures (% of GDP), venture capital (% of GDP), private credit (relative to GDP) and broadband access by firms (% of firms).
>
> Firm activities have been consisted of firm investment (3 indicators), linkages and entrepreneurship (4 indicators), throughputs (4 indicators).
>
> Outputs were innovators (3 indicators) and economic effects (6 indicators). Based on their average innovation performance, the countries classified into one of four groups: Innovation leaders, Innovation followers, Modest innovators and Moderate innovators. (Innovation Union Scoreboard (IUS) 2011:6).

This is a huge research with relevant statistical data. Data sources were: Eurostat, Science Metrix/Scopus, CWTS/Thomson Reuters, OECD, OHIM, and United Nation. To improve comparability between countries, the international data sources have been used. Time line is a period from 2011 to 2016.

From the group of European developing countries, the following countries participated in IUS: Russia, Serbia, Croatia, Turkey, and Former Yugoslav Republic of Macedonia. It is evident that observed countries have not participated in this survey in overall period. Therefore, data for some years were missing. The conclusion will be reliable because of numerous and relevant statistical data.

Changes in the past report (Hollanders et al. 2016) caused that data from this survey cannot compared to previous reports. First, the report got new name European Innovation Scoreboard. Second, the following changes have implemented (Hollanders et al. 2016: 9–10):

1. Data source for international scientific co-publication, and Most-cited scientific publications have changed.
2. Definition and formula for Venture capital investments have change.
3. Data revision for Public-private co-publications.

4. New definition of PCT patent applications in societal challenges.
5. Data source for Community trademarks.
6. Definition and data source for Community designs.
7. Methodology for calculating Balance of Payments statistics for Exports of knowledge-intensive services.
8. Methodology for calculating Balance of Payments statistics for License and patent revenues from abroad has change as well.

Today, with the World Bank, the World Economic Forum is the most important institution dealing with analysis and measurement The Global Competitiveness Index (GCI). To measure and compare the competitiveness of national economies, the relevant factors assess and then combine into composite index.

All factors are grouped into twelve pillars:

1. Institutions. Institutional ambience is framed by national legislative. The arrangement of the institutional environment is an extremely complex job. First, it means ensuring the protection of all forms of ownership, as this is a basic precondition for attracting foreign investments. Also, institutional support for the development of market freedoms, finding an optimal level of regulation, preventing corruption, freeing the judiciary from political dependence, protecting the environment, etc. is very important. Although these activities create significant economic costs and slow down economic growth, it is necessary to strive for the creation of an institutional environment that enables fair and fair business.

2. Infrastructure. Developed infrastructure is important for the efficiency of the functioning of the economy because it determines an industry profile that can be developed. Developed transport and communication infrastructure is a prerequisite for linking to less developed regions. It is important to build the roads, railways, ports and air transport enable the transport and timely placement of products and services, as well as efficient transport of workers to their jobs. Modern economies require a developed energy infrastructure that will prevent shortages and disruptions in distribution. Also, the development of telecommunication infrastructure is extremely important, because the quality telecommunication network contributes to the quick and free flow of information that allows making better decisions and increases the overall economic efficiency.

3. Macroeconomic environment. For the development of competitiveness, the stability of the macroeconomic environment is extremely important. In other words, it is necessary to ensure that higher economic growth, reduce unemployment, ensure price stability (low inflation) and avoid balance of payments deficits. These macroeconomic policy objectives are in mutual relations that depend on aggregate demand and changes in the economic cycle. For example, in the expansive phase of the business cycle, it is rapid reducing unemployment, and increasing aggregate demand, fueling inflation and stimulating imports (due to the narrowing of gaps between real and potential outputs). Inflation diminishes the competitiveness of domestic products, which reduces exports, while at the same time, due to the increase in demand, imports increase, which ultimately leads to a deficit in the balance of payments. There are also many other mechanisms that confirm the dependence of macroeconomic variables, whose quantification, importance, and validity are the subject of vigorous economic

discussions. The general conclusion is that macroeconomic stability helps to raise competitiveness, and that every government should work on its maintenance, trying at the same time to reduce its costs to a minimum.

4. Health and primary education. The poor health picture of the workforce increases the costs of doing business, due to the frequent absence of sick workers and the low level of efficiency of their work. Therefore, investments in raising the level of health care are important, both economically and morally. On the other hand, education is important for raising the quality of people's lives and ensuring social and economic progress. Insufficiently educated workforce can only perform basic manual tasks and there are often serious difficulties in adapting advanced production processes and technologies. The levels of health and education are much higher in economically developed countries, due to higher investment opportunities in education and health.

5. Higher education and training. All countries that strive to increase prosperity must increase the quality of education. The global economy implies that employees are educated and able to adapt to an environment that is rapidly changing. The importance of continuous professional training, which is neglected in many economies, is important if it ensures continuous upgrading of skills and knowledge of employees, in accordance with the needs of production systems.

6. Efficiency of the commodity market. The effectiveness of the commodity market implies the ability and ability to produce a wide range of products and services in given supply and demand relationships. The efficiency of this market segment depends on demand conditions, which are determined by consumer orientations and their sophistication that corresponds to purchasing power. Globalized markets are characterized by excess supply in demand, which favors the position of consumers. That's why manufacturers should focus on them, in terms of increasing the degree of consumerization of the offer. On the other hand, large tax rates or restrictive and discriminatory rules related to the ownership of foreigners or foreign direct investment can greatly affect the reduction of the efficiency of the commodity market, and hence competitiveness.

7. The efficiency of the labor market. The mobility of labor market is very important for the development of the competitiveness of each economy. In advanced economies, the employees are assigned appropriately, in accordance with their knowledge, skills and abilities, which gives full contribution to their places of employment. Also, efficient labor market must provide the ability for the reallocation of workers from one of economic activity to another, without causing major social disorders. Efficient labor markets must provide talents come to the fore, as well as equality between men and women.

8. Sophistication of financial markets. Sophisticated financial market provides efficient routing of financial resources to the best entrepreneurs and investment projects. Mentioned resources include savings of citizens, as well as domestic and foreign investment. In addition to a stable banking sector, an efficient financial market requires developed and alternative ways of funding. This means that the market should be a deep secondary market for a wide range of financial instruments and derivatives.

9. Technological equipment. In a globalized world, technologies are becoming one of the key elements for creating and maintaining competitive advantage. America must be ready for adoption of new technologies and to provide the necessary conditions for their effective use. Special emphasis should be placed on the ability to use information and communication technology (ICT) and to their implementation in all daily activities production processes. ICT can be called a "technology of general purpose which is to build the infrastructure of this type is inevitable for the maintenance and enhancement of economic competitiveness. Also, it is very important to provide access to sources of modern technology. When it comes to less developed countries, it is primarily achieved through foreign direct investment. On the other hand, developed countries that set technological standards, must rely on innovation and investing in our own research and development".

10. Market size. The size of the market is extremely important to raise competitiveness. Countries with large markets can use the effects of economies of scale or to its businesses provide increase of production capability by lowering the cost per unit of product. In an era of globalization, international markets are increasingly replacing national markets, which is particularly characteristic for small countries. There are several empirical evidences that openness to trade positively correlated with economic growth, especially when it comes to countries with small national markets.

11. Business sophistication. The productivity of a country depends on the productivity of companies who operate in it. The sophistication of the country's business involves the quality of relationships. Therefore, it is necessary that each company continuously improves operational efficiency, based on the best global practices. As for the strategic approach, it is desirable to implement a strategy of differentiation, including the development of innovation. Using alternative strategies that focus on leadership in costs, leads the actors in the so-called "price war", which often results in a reduction in the quality of products, and therefore competitiveness. Also, networking companies (clusters, incubators, Strategic Alliance) represents an important link in the development of competitiveness, due to synergetic effects that can be achieved in many segments of business (growing negotiating power, conquest new markets, acquiring new knowledge, etc.).

12. Innovation. Developing countries have the privilege of your productivity can improve with the adoption of existing technologies, which developed countries does not apply. Companies in developed countries should devise and develop new products and processes, to maintain a competitive advantage. It requires an environment that supports the development of innovation, i.e. investment in research and development. Businesses must leave the concept of traditional hierarchical organizational structure and improve shallower structures that provide more decentralization of power, informal communication that provides a faster flow of information and flexibility, as well as anything else that encourages creativity of employees and leads to the desired innovation.

The 12 pillars of competitiveness are grouped into three separate units, that represent a key for the different ways of running the economy, namely: basic factors driven by economics, efficiency driven by economics and innovation driven economy.

9 Results and Discussion

9.1 Graphical Analysis

To have a quick view on the innovation performances among the countries a graphical analysis has produced (see Fig. 1).

Primary, the intention was to include all eleven countries, but majority of them have not included in large study conducted by European Commission. Therefore, the sample consisted of following countries: Croatia, Russia, Serbia, Turkey, and Former Yugoslav Republic of Macedonia.

Then, analysis of relative straights and weakness in period 2011–2015 had performed. The Table 1 presents the results.

In 2011, Croatia was the moderate innovator (Innovation Union Scoreboard 2011: 52). It can be noticed a high growth, compare to EU27, for transfer of external knowledge and registration cost for Croatia's trademarks in European Union, for one side. For the other side, a trend of diminishing is observed for buying and licensing new ideas as well as foreign payments from previous registered patents.

In 2011, Serbia was the moderate innovator (Innovation Union Scoreboard 2011: 57). It can be noticed a high growth, compare to EU27, investing in research and development in public sector, joint publications between scientific society and private partners, and registration cost for Serbia's trademarks in European Union,

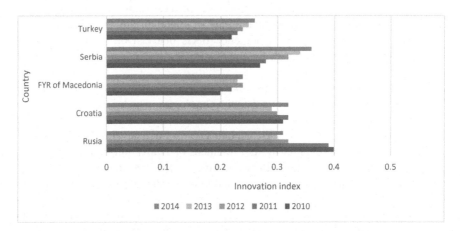

Fig. 1 Innovation performances in selected countries

Table 1 Relative straights and weaknesses in selected countries

Country	Year							
	2011		2013		2014		2015	
	Straights	Weaknesses	Straights	Weaknesses	Straights	Weaknesses	Straights	Weaknesses
Russia	Tertiary education	International co-publications, PCT patents	Tertiary education	International co-publications, PCT patents	Tertiary education	License and patent revenues from abroad	Tertiary education	License and patent revenues from abroad
Serbia	Human resources, Open, excellent and attractive research systems finance and support and economic effects	Firm investments, linkages & entrepreneurship, intellectual assets and innovators	Finance and support and innovators	Intellectual assets	Finance and support and innovators	Community designs	Firm investments, linkages & entrepreneurship	Intellectual assets
Croatia	Human resources, finance and support, innovators and economic effects	Infrastructure for developing innovation	Human resources, and economic effects	Infrastructure for developing innovation	Human resources	Intellectual assets	Human capital	Infrastructure for developing innovation
Turkey	Open, excellent and attractive research	Human resources, firm investments, intellectual assets	Innovators and economic effects	Human resources, and firm investments	SMEs with Marketing	Community trademarks	Firm investments	Linkages entrepreneurship

(continued)

Table 1 (continued)

Country	Year							
	2011		2013		2014		2015	
	Straights	Weaknesses	Straights	Weaknesses	Straights	Weaknesses	Straights	Weaknesses
	systems, finance and support, innovators and economic effects							
FYR of Macedonia	Human resources, finance and support, and economic effects	Infrastructure for developing innovation entrepreneurship, intellectual assets Financial support	Innovation and economic effects	Linkages & entrepreneurship, intellectual assets Finance and support	Human resources, finance and support	Linkages & entrepreneurship, intellectual assets Finance and support	Human resources	Intellectual assets

for one side. For the other side, a significant small number of PhD students from countries outside European Union has evidenced.

In 2011, Turkey was the modest innovator (Innovation Union Scoreboard 2011: 53). It can be noticed a high growth, compare to EU27, for visibility of national results in high ranking journals in the world, investing in private research and development activities, and registration costs of Turkey's trademarks in European Union. In same period, it can be noticed diminishing number of registered national designs in European Union.

In 2011, FYR of Macedonia was the modest innovator (Innovation Union Scoreboard 2011: 58). It can be noticed a high growth, compare to EU27, for people with university or college degree, joint publications with foreign participations, and registration costs of Macedonia's trademarks in European Union, for one side. For the other side, the decrease number of PhD students from countries outside European Union is noticed as well as less investing in Government research and development system.

It was expected that the effects of economic crisis on innovation would be evidenced in Innovation Union Scoreboard 2013. Although there were not radical changes regarding innovation performance of observed countries.

In 2013, the trend of growth in for transfer of external knowledge and registration cost for Croatia's trademarks in European Union continued in Croatia (Innovation Union Scoreboard 2013: 55). Croatia's gap has increased in PCT patents applications and national designs tried to be registered in European Union.

In 2013, it can be noticed Serbia has significantly invested in small and medium enterprises. In same period, private investing in research and development, and export of the intellectual assets have decreased (Innovation Union Scoreboard 2013: 60).

In 2013, Turkey was still the modest innovator (Innovation Union Scoreboard 2013: 56). It can be noticed increased number of PhD students and Community trademarks. Turkey's gap has increased in national designs trying to register in European Union.

In 2013, many people with tertiary education, especial group aged 30–34 years has increased in FYR of Macedonia (Innovation Union Scoreboard 2013: 61). Public-private scientific co-publications has well below EU27 average.

The main conclusion of the Innovation Union Scoreboard 2014 was that negative effects of financial crisis on innovation performances had not as severe as researchers expected.

In 2014, same trends were in Croatia, and its innovation performance were 55% of EU27 average (Innovation Union Scoreboard 2014: 53).

Most indicators of innovation performance have been positive in Serbia regardless the economic crisis (Innovation Union Scoreboard 2014: 75). One question arises: If the country performing below the average, the effect of crisis will be lower than in developed countries?

The same situation was with Turkey's innovation performance in same study (Innovation Union Scoreboard 2014: 76). Relative performance was 40% of EU27 average.

The following indicators have increased in FYR of Macedonia: New doctorate graduates, Community trademarks, and Most cited scientific publication (Innovation Union Scoreboard 2014: 74). The Macedonia's gap has increased in private investing in research and development, PCT patent applications, and joint university business publications. Relative innovation performance was 44% of EU27 average.

During the period, in majority of observed countries innovation performance raised with minor differences in national straights and weaknesses.

Although changes introduced in past report with new name European Innovation Scoreboard (Hollanders et al. 2016), major results will be presented for observed countries.

Russia's innovation performance was worst the EU27. It is important to note that 69% of population has completed tertiary education. The largest gap has evidenced in number of people with PhDs, investments in research and development, and PCT patents (see Table 2).

According to the latest Report, Croatia was still in same group with innovation activities lower than other countries from European Union (Hollanders et al. 2016). The better performance was only in Human resources. The largest gap has evidenced in Finance and support, and investing in infrastructure for innovation.

The FYR of Macedonia's innovation performance was well below European average.

Serbia was a Moderate innovator with relative straights in acquiring external knowledge. Innovation activities significantly intensified in period 2008–2015.

Same situation was with Turkey. In nearly all indicators Turkey's performance has improved.

In this report, the data for Ukraine presented. Ukraine was a Modest innovator and performed well below EU27 average on almost all dimensions Global Competitive Index by main pillars is presented in Table 3.

Regarding the stage of development, Croatia, Russia, and Turkey were in transition stage from efficiency driven to innovation driven economies. Although, Serbia and FYR of Macedonia had efficiency driven economies.

It is worth to note that main problematic areas in doing business have identified too (Schwab et al. 2015).

The following factors have identified in Croatia, Macedonia, Russia, and Serbia: inadequate business behavior, crime and theft, Government instability/coups, low innovation activities, foreign currency regulations, high inflation, and bad social systems. All these countries had insufficient capacity to innovation, expect Turkey.

Analysis of top and middle-level Serbian managers attitudes towards desirable characteristics of their employees gave the following results (Kontic and Cabrilo 2009): competencies, collaboration, initiating new ideas, effectiveness, and innovative spirit. According to this research, the key characteristics of employees in Serbian industry are: expertise, cooperativeness, commitment, efficiency. To obtain and sustain competitive advantage, it is necessary to innovate. In this process, abilities to increase competence of employees and managers along with promotion of innovative spirit are essential. The results revealed the fact that managers in Serbia are not aware of this. Furthermore, small number of product and/or process innovation have resulted from managers unawareness.

Table 2 Russia relative performance in 2016

Indicator	Relative performance	Difference in performance growth (in %)
PhD education	78.3	–3.8
Tertiary education	168.8	–3.1
Joint publications with foreign partners	49.9	–1.2
International transparency of national journals	31.3	–0.4
Investments in research and development	66.4	0.8
Joint publications	57.8	–2.1
PCT patents	4.9	–2.2
PCT pat. social changes	34.4	–0.1
Exports med. & high-tech prod.	11.5	–3.7
Exports of sophisticated services	16.9	0.0
License and patent revision	75.0	–0.5
	6.1	–0.4

Source: Hollanders et al. (2016):35

Table 3 GCI by main pillars in selected countries

Pillar	Croatia	FYR of Macedonia	Russia	Serbia	Turkey
Institutions	3.63	4.14	3.46	3.24	3.84
Infrastructure	4.59	3.77	4.81	3.87	4.43
Macroeconomic environment	4.19	5.09	5.29	3.60	4.75
Health and primary education	5.85	5.61	5.94	5.87	5.69
Higher education and training	4.62	4.79	4.96	4.27	4.58
Goods market efficiency	4.05	4.65	4.16	3.74	4.53
Labor market efficiency	3.83	4.07	4.40	3.72	3.46
Financial market development	3.59	4.09	3.53	3.23	3.93
Technological readiness	4.65	4.15	4.22	4.47	4.08
Market size	3.59	2.94	5.93	3.7	5.41
Business sophistication	3.74	3.87	3.79	3.14	4.07
Innovation	3.13	3.38	3.29	2.90	3.35

Source: Schwab et al. (2015)

Processes of knowledge sharing are not sufficiently represented in the observed companies. The reasons for insufficient knowledge sharing could be partly in organizational culture, which is characterized by an atmosphere of mistrust, fear and insecurity of employees. Such atmosphere adversely affects employee motivation and commitment as well as knowledge sharing. The absence of employee satisfaction and encouraging organizational culture, dominated by the trust and openness, are the essential reasons for insufficient employee motivation, which further cause the lack of employee incentive and 'entrepreneurial approach' to work.

It is evident a correlation capacity to innovate and national competitiveness in observed countries according to meta data in these two relevant studies.

10 Conclusion and Policy Suggestions

In this study, the relationship between innovation and competitiveness has been exposed. It is worth to mentioned that effects of global crisis on innovation performance in observed European developing countries were minor. Although, the presented meta data were relevant and accurate the full picture should be with all eleven countries.

Most indicators of innovation performance have been positive in observed countries regardless the economic crisis.

For some of those countries, the accession to the EU will lead to intense learning about how to enhance innovation capacities. As a policy suggestion, following activities can be useful in European developing countries:

1. Promotion innovation culture,
2. Place innovation at the core of legal and regulatory reforms,
3. Increase the number of small and medium innovative firms,
4. Strengthen transfer of knowledge in national economies,
5. Establish proactive innovation policy.

There is still a wide variation among the developing countries that should be chronologically reduced by structural developments.

Key Words Definitions

Innovation In this survey, CIS definition of innovation has been used. CIS methodology defining innovation as new or significantly improved goods and/or the processes used to produce or supply all goods or services that the business has introduced, regardless of their origin.

Strategy The main aim of the strategy of innovation is to maximize organization's innovative potential. To obtain and sustain competitive advantage, strategic managers should elaborate current and future innovation strategy.

Competitiveness "Ability of a firm or a nation to offer products and services that meet the quality standards of the local and world markets at prices that are competitive and provide adequate returns on the resources employed or consumed in producing them."

Innovation performance The outcomes and the benefits generate by the process of innovation.

European developing countries A developing countries, measuring by GDP per capita in Europe are Albania, Belarus, Croatia, Moldova, Montenegro, Serbia, Bosnia and Herzegovina, Macedonia, Russia, Turkey, and Ukraine.

References

Doloreux, D. (2002). What we should know about regional innovation systems. *Technology in Society, 24*(3), 243–263.

Freeman, C. (1982). *The economics of industrial innovation*. London: Frances Pinter.

Hollanders, H., Es-Sadki, N., & Kanerva, M. (2016). *European Innovation Scoreboard 2016*. European Commission.

Innovation Union Scoreboard. (2011). Available at: http://ec.europa.eu/enterprise/policies/innova tion/files/ius-2011_en.pdf. Accessed 2 August 2017.

Innovation Union Scoreboard. (2013). Available at: http://ec.europa.eu/enterprise/policies/innova tion/files/ius-2011_en.pdf. Accessed 2 August 2017.

Innovation Union Scoreboard. (2014). Available at: http://ec.europa.eu/enterprise/policies/innova tion/files/ius-2011_en.pdf. Accessed 2 August 2017.

Kontic, L. (2007). Regional innovation systems. *Annals of Faculty of Economics Subotica, 17*, 63–73.

Kontic, L. (2008). *Innovations—challenges for future*. Belgrade: Zaduzbina Andrejevic.

Kontic, L., & Cabrilo, S. (2009). A strategic model for measuring intellectual capital in Serbian industrial enterprises. *Economic Annals, 54*(183), 89–117.

Lundvall, B. Å., Joseph, K. J., Chaminade, C., & Vang, J. (2011). *Handbook of innovation systems and developing countries: building domestic capabilities in a global setting*. Northampton, MA: Edward Elgar.

Mahagaonkar, P., Schweickert, R., & Chavali, A. S. (2009). *Sectoral R&D intensity and exchange rate volatility: A panel study for OECD-countries* (Kiel Working Paper 1531). Kiel: Kiel Institute for the World Economy.

Ortt, J. R., & van der Duin, P. A. (2008). The evolution of innovation management towards contextual innovation. *European Journal of Innovation Management, 11*(4), 522–538.

Piater, A. (1984). *Barriers to innovation*. London: Frances Pinter.

Porter, M. E. (2008). *Competitive advantage: Creating and sustaining superior performance*. New York: Simon and Schuster.

Saviotti, P., & Nooteboom, B. (Eds.). (2000). *Technology and knowledge*. London: Edward Elgar.

Schwab, K., Sala-i-Martin, X., & Brende, B. (2015). *The Global Competitiveness Report 2015-2016* (Vol. 5).

Webb, A. (1996). *Managing innovative projects*. London: International Thomson Press.

Strategic Thinking and Risk Attitude

Yunus Emre Taşgit, İstemi Çömlekçi, and Kübranur Çakır

Abstract In recent years, strategic thinking and risk attitude are demonstrated among the most interesting topics in strategic management literature. However, when the literature on the subject is examined, it is seen that there is not enough comprehensive correlational studies, although it is understood that there is significant logical linking between the two subjects. The purpose of this study is to explore the relationships between strategic thinking and risk attitude, to carry out a pioneering step towards filling this gap in the literature and to encourage further work. Qualitative research method will be used in the study and conceptual association will be done by analyzing the secondary sources with the document review technique.

1 Introduction

It seems to be widely used strategic thinking in the literature at the field of problem solving, decision making and scenario preparation for anticipating the future of the organization and is evaluated as a synthesis activity that can be developed in individuals at every stage of an organization (Haycock et al. 2012: 3). On the other side strategic thinking contributes to comprehensive concepts that determine the future direction of an organization based on expected environmental conditions (Goldman et al. 2009: 6).

Heracleous (1998) defines the purpose of strategic thinking as "discovering new and innovative strategies that rewrite competitive game rules and foresee significant different potential futures from now." Goldman et al. (2009: 6) explains the purpose

Y. E. Taşgit (✉) · İ. Çömlekçi
Faculty of Business, Düzce University, Düzce, Turkey
e-mail: yunusemretasgit@duzce.edu.tr

K. Çakır
Düzce University, Düzce, Turkey

© Springer International Publishing AG, part of Springer Nature 2018 253
H. Dincer et al. (eds.), *Strategic Design and Innovative Thinking in Business Operations*, Contributions to Management Science,
https://doi.org/10.1007/978-3-319-77622-4_13

of strategic thinking as exploring competitive strategies to bring the organization at a significant different position from the current situation.

2 Strategic Thinking and Risk Attıtude

2.1 What Is Strategic Thinking?

Although the term "strategic thinking" frequently and commonly used in the field of strategy today, there is a clear lack of understanding of what is meant by strategic thinking in the literature (Liedtka 1998: 121). Strategic thinking is often used to describe concepts such as strategy, strategic planning, or strategic management rather than a specific form of thinking with specific characteristics. For example, Wilson (1994: 14) argues that strategic thinking causes the evolution in strategic planning processes and changes the character of strategic planning. According to Nasi (1991: 29), strategic thinking extends both to the creation and implementation of strategies by business leaders, and to the strategic performance of the total enterprise. In addition strategic analysis, strategic planning, organization and control, and even strategic leadership are considered in this context. For this reason, strategic thinking is basically associated with all these concepts that can be labeled as "strategic".

On the other hand, the first advocates of the concept of strategic thinking are expressing it as a form of thinking that has certain characteristics. For instance, according to Mintzberg (1994), considered as one of the leading advocates of strategic thinking, strategic thinking is a synthesis process that uses intuition and innovation which results in an "integrated perspective of the enterprise" (Liedtka 1998: 121). Goldman et al. (2009: 6) who argue that effective strategic thinking leads to competitive advantage, evaluated strategic thinking as an individual thought activity. Ohmae (1982) defines strategic thinking as "the ultimate non-linear thinking tool", as opposed to traditional, system-based thinking approaches. Maxwell (2003) describes the concept as planning and managing the most advantageous position of aside from tactics and before engaging with a competitor actually. Game theorists define strategic thinking as the art of accomplishing with the rival and emphasize that "the opponent is trying to do the same with you". According to Stacey (1992), strategic thinking is not an intellectual work to discover the possible, but rather to use analogy and qualitative similarities to develop innovative new ideas. Raimond (1996: 210–212) divides strategic thinking into two; "strategy as intelligent machine" (data-oriented, information processing approach) and "strategy as innovative imagination". The essence of the strategy method as an intelligent machine is: to define the goal, to determine a course to achieve the goal, taking into account the inactivity conditions and internal capabilities; and like a route tracker, to keep on going in the right direction, constantly making progress to reach the goal. Strategy as innovative imagination works differently. The first stage is ideally starting to imagine where you want to be. Innovative imagination creates a complete picture of how an ideal company and its situation will be in all its aspects. The second step is how to plan the ideal design. Kaufman et al. (2003) sees strategic thinking as a "practical dream" in which people within an organization evaluate and display the future for themselves and their associates through the identification and prediction of value-adding results. Haycock et al. (2012: 4) defines strategic thinking as a focus on finding and developing unique opportunities to create value by building a provocative and innovative dialogue among those who can influence a company's vision.

2.2 How to Think Strategically?

According to Perkins (2012) in order to think strategically, it is necessary to criticize the company, to design an executive strategy and to allocate resources. For example; having alternative sources of information to reach new and accurate information about companies, competitors and industry. Taking the time to think in detail about learned new information. To be able to create road maps but not always to be obsessed with "a strategy needs to be", sometimes let it go and be flexible. Sharing the roadmap with the team to be proactive. When deciding, not only information but also using ideas and setting the priorities and effectively allocate the necessary resources. Avoiding saying "yes" to everything and being overly concerned with "thin things".

Watkins (2007) focuses on six key applications to improve strategic thinking ability. These; immersion (dip), apprenticeship, simulations, game theory training, case-based training and cognitive reshaping. *Immersion*; to understand the core dynamics of each new situation, and to ensure that people spend time in related environments (complex business environments) to create powerful mental models. *Apprenticeship*; to provide low-risk environments to the beginner (novice) where they can observe, learn and think through their masters' work (how they act against competitors, how they behave under certain circumstances). *Simulations*; to create a "manageable complex" environment (e.g., Executive Challenge Simulation) to enable administrators to experiment safely on cause-and-effect relationships and apply various alternatives according to changing circumstances to understand all aspects of the event. *Game theory education* is related to direct the work schedule in which there are movements that lead managers to certain potential gains with conflicting interests, and the "games" where smart actors take part to play the game. *Case-based education*; exposing managers to a variety of "real cases" to reveal an experience process involving comparison of cases. *Cognitive reshaping* is about creating new mind habits by doing mental exercises with the "act on abstraction levels" method on management's ways of evaluating the events or making decisions.

2.3 Why Is Strategic Thinking Important for Business Success?

Strategic thinking requires a number of decisions about what actions the company wants to accomplish in order to achieve its goals quickly and more successfully. Companies should try to do strategic thinking throughout the year rather than in the interim. At the heart of strategic thinking is the ability to identify and use the opportunities that arise from predicting key gaps in the competitive marketplace.

According to Hill (2017), strategic thinking primarily allows an executive to determine how to use the finite resources available most effectively and advance the company towards its goals. At the same time, it enables the company to be prepared for emerging competitive threats and various situations that may arise as a result of changes in the national and local economy. Companies with strategic thinking ability are strengthening their managers' hand on the right time and the best tools to attack rivalries as they continuously assess the strengths and weaknesses of their businesses and the strengths and weaknesses of major competitors. On the other hand, strategic thinking encourages surviving and growing by contributing to business is innovative in every way. Finally, it provides managers with the ability to use improved decision-making methods, so they become strategic thinkers over time.

According to Bianca (2014) strategic thinking can be a critical factor in the success of companies as it allows managers to identify and assess loss opportunities while helping managers to identify and benefit from lucky opportunities. It also offers different suggestions to focus on problem solving about the company's business model and operations, as it directs the business manager and employees to think critically about the root causes of the problems. Likewise, it enables the formation of a set of in-house strategic mindset that makes the company active in creating a clearer strategy. Finally, strategic thinking takes the company forward in being proactive because it requires working on the early sign indicating-oriented programs about how to succeed in current business conditions and more difficult times.

2.4 Strategic Thinking Process

According to Zand (2010), Peter Drucker's observations have influenced the strategic considerations of managers for years. Drucker's thinking model gives valuable information to managers, especially to improve the strategic analysis process. There are three stages in the thinking model many of critical subject are taken into consideration: Phase one: asking influential questions to produce innovative options, Phase two: redirecting to activate the arrangement, Phase three: thinking about alternative assumptions and research results. The first phase of the strategic thinking process; is beginning to question the current situation (status quo) within the framework of analytical thinking and to ask intrusive questions to produce innovative options. Influential questions to form better strategies are a very important resource. In this context, two questions are addressed, focusing on the essence of the subject and evaluating it quickly and logically, and liberating management's thinking: (1) Which work should we not be? (2) What are our notifications? Can we get into this now? According to Drucker, these two questions help us to catch the strategic essence of the subject. With the first question, regarding the current situation of the company; outcomes, targets, resources, abilities, etc. are critically evaluated in order to understand current and future facts, bad/well-made decisions and incorrect/correct assumptions are determined. With the second question, it is possible to evaluate the development of innovative alternatives using critical information that the company is aware of about the activities that has some experiences. For example, we know that this business is highly competitive, requires constant investment, as far as we can see, it offers low returns and can not achieve a sustainable competitive advantage. Then why do we have to go into this business and invest now? These questions encourage executives to confront tough facts and encourage them to deal with strategic choices and to be as dissatisfied as possible. The second phase involves redirecting companies in order to look for competitive advantage, in order to conduct an in-depth review and re-enact necessary regulations to ensure that the essence of the subject is rescheduled. Working with the right information (acquisition and use) is of great importance for in-depth analysis. It seems impossible for companies lacking the source (technical-human) to direct the strategic thinking process. At this stage, managers try to obtain information on what critical information will enable them to achieve competitive advantage and how they will contribute to the company's competitive edge, synthesizing information using concepts to organize ideas and data, to redirect and decide what to do and how to do it for the current and future direction of the firm. In the third phase, alternative hypotheses are developed to think strategically about the future of the firm and the possible consequences of decisions are considered extensively. In this context, it is generally suggested that develop in-house opposition and should be directed discussions constructively within the institution. It is also suggested to use different problem-solving techniques that are accepted in the field.

2.5   Five Factors of Strategic Thinking

Liedtka (1998) has developed a model that defines strategic thinking as a form of thinking that has very specific and clearly identifiable characteristics. Figure 1 shows the five elements of strategic thinking.

2.5.1   System Perspective

The first element is the system perspective. The system thinking, Senge (1990) regards as it the most critical issue for organizational learning, presents an important

Fig. 1 The elements of
strategic thinking

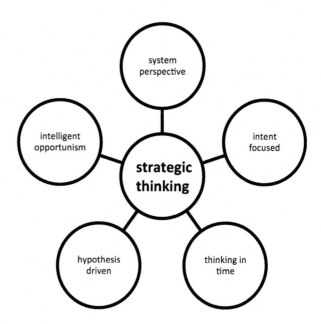

point of view in strategic thinking. System thinking is able to think together the whole, the parts that make up the whole, the relationships between the parts and the parts, and between the whole and the parts. In today's business world one of the most fundamental problems that companies face is their failure to identify problems and make decisions (Lawrence 1999: 5). The underlying reason for this problem is not thinking holistically, but focusing on just one part of the whole. According to Liedtka (1998), without systemic thought, it is impossible to identify the problem in all its aspects and to optimize the results of the decisions taken.

In strategically thinking, there is a mental model of the value creation system from start to finish and understanding of interdependence in the chain. This mental model of "how the world continuious" includes both external and internal context of the establishment. While the internal context dimension of the mental model is based on organizational dynamics such as organizational resources, abilities, structure, culture, and their interrelationships; the external context dimension is based on competitive environment and industry environment. According to Moore (1993) the external dimension needs to be perceived in a broader context from the industry. Because for strategic thinking, the company should be seen not as a member of a single industry but as part of a business ecosystem that transcends various industries. In this context, companies need to pay close attention to their position (present-future), competition and cooperation in the business ecosystem, innovative tendencies, talents and investments (Lawrence 1999: 5).

Strategic thinkers not only understand the external business ecosystem that the company is involved in, but also try to understand the interrelationships between all the parts covered together. Such a point of view identifies the role of each part in the larger system and clarifies the effects and consequences of its behavior on other parts of the system. Sometimes from the perspective of vertical connections; by associating an in-house application with a development in the external environment; sometimes solving the linkages between in-house developments from the perspective of horizontal links (Liedtka 1998: 122).

2.5.2 Intent Focused

The second element of strategic thinking concerns the intention to focus and be willing. According to Hamel and Prahalad (1994), the strategic objective should show a direction and imply a certain point of view on the long-term competitive position. Strategic intent is to provide a unique perspective on the future. It promises to discover new areas of competition for employees. For this reason, there is a sense of discovery. At the same time, strategic intent has an emotional appeal; it is a goal that employees perceive as valuable. Strategic thinking and intention must be internalized within the institution in order for the strategic thinking to take place in a healthy way. In this scope; it is necessary to collect the employees' energy on the attention around purpose and intention, to intensify attention during the time required to reach the target, and to remove the distracting forces becoming the leverage effect (Liedtka 1998). In the swirling vortices of the variable, such a psychic energy can be the most limited source of having an organization, but only those who use it will be successful (Lawrence 1999: 6).

2.5.3 Intelligent Opportunism

The third element of strategic thinking is intelligent opportunism. The essence of this thinking is based on the idea of openness to new life and the possibility to take advantage of alternative strategies that can be related to the rapidly changing business environment. For this, it is necessary to recognize the difference between the strategies, conceptualized by Mintzberg and Waters (1985), the emergent strategy and the deliberate strategy. In order to be successful in implementing smart opportunism, it is necessary to input the innovative work of employees at all levels of the organization as input and to embrace alternative strategy recommendations (Lawrence 1999). According to Hamel (1996) this situation is not as easy as it seems and even though it means giving a disproportionate share of promise to people who have been abandoned in strategy formulation process until now, if requested to create a sense of the future, a meaningful strategy, and a hierarchy of dreams in the company this is a necessity. Such an approach can create a tremendous amount of communication and interaction points that can lead to opportunistic possibilities by providing the flow of ideas and probabilities between the management levels -top management-middle management-bottom management-employees.

2.5.4 Thinking in Time

The fourth element of strategic thinking is to think in time. According to Hamel and Prahalad (1994) it is a misleading view to think only of the future or only today. It is necessary to establish an effective link between the present reality and the intention towards the future. From a wider perspective, the strategic thinking leads to connect the past to the present and the present to the future. While traditional view focuses on aligning with existing resources and opportunities (Lawrence 1999: 7), strategic thinking goes beyond this and emphasizes to anticipate the potential sources and opportunities. Thus, it argues that "timely thinking" will take place by exhibiting a tendency of thinking the past, the present and the future at the same time and both will be provided learning from the past and will be prevented missing future opportunities. Thinking in Time consists of three components. First, it is to accept that the past is a predictive value of the future. Secondly, it is to recognize the things that are important for the present and toward the future (actual router changes). The third component is the continuous comparison. It is related the critical points about the possible changes that will take place to associate with the past and make presentations for the present and for the future (Neustadt and May 1986: 251). On the other side, Thinking in Time uses both the memory of the institution and the vast historical content of creating the future. It requires the ability to select, define and use appropriate analogies both its' own and others' histories. Therefore, the strategic question is not only "what is the future we want to create" but "how we will use the past to create the future" (Liedtka 1998: 123).

2.5.5 Hypothesis Driven

The fifth element of strategic thinking is to follow up a hypothesis-based process. This method, which is somewhat foreign to most managers, needs critical skills to develop good hypotheses and test them efficiently in today's conditions, where information availability increases and time for thinking decreases (Liedtka 1998; Lawrence 1999). Therefore, companies have to increase their capacity to create and test hypotheses by incorporating them into innovative and critical thinking processes. Strategic thinking uses analytical and intuitive thinking together in hypothesis-based focus. Hypothesis generation and testing continues in the form of repeated cycles. Hypothesis production begins with a critical and well-defined question. The inquiry continues in the form of "if ... so ...". For the evaluation of the developed hypothesis, various data on related topics is collected and analysis is carried out together with assumptions open to commentary. This repeated sequence ensures that hypotheses developing every time without losing the ability to discover new ideas. Such an application, while supporting the continuous learning of an organization, causes it to go beyond simple cause and effect associations.

2.6   Strategic Thinking and Business Planning

There are close relations between strategic thinking and planning in the literature, but it is noteworthy that there is scope and understanding difference in some points. While planning is an embedded function of general decision making in the organization, strategic thinking requires more synthesis of innovative games as it tries to create a different vision. Actions that motivate strategic thinking are based on open-ended, emerging proposals, different perspectives, and convergence-focused freeforms (Sloan 2006: 106). Amitabh and Sahay (2008) argue that strategic thinking has completed strategic planning and strategic management, but allows for a faster and more innovative response; because strategic planning is based on rational, linear thinking, which is used to facilitate progress in an accepted strategic position. Strategic thinking enables traditional organizational planning processes to transform from consecutive and systematic activities into highly interactive processes. On the other hand, the mental model defended by strategic thinking may not be a measurable result during the strategic thinking process; sometimes it may engender a concern that it may cause time loss. But according to Hamel and Prahalad (2005), innovative strategies rarely emerge from the annual planning ritual. In it the starting point of next year's strategy is almost always the strategy of this year. Improvements are gradual. The company has binding elements. As it is known that real opportunities are elsewhere, it is necessary to go beyond traditional planning rituals. Therefore, strategic thinking can be regarded as an important tool in this context that can change the functioning of planning.

2.7   Strategic Thinking and Managerial Competencies

High-performance managers integrate strategic thinking into the organization as a critical element for achieving and sustaining organizational success. In this context, four areas of competence that managers can use are discussed. These; organizational analysis, vision shaping, strategy formulation and organizational design (Collins et al. 2000: 18).

Organizational Analysis is a competency that includes a systematic information gathering process to recognize the purpose of the organization, to assess environmental forces, and to identify strategic issues that lead to the development of an effective strategy. Managers for the activity of this competency provide the acceptance of the strategic planning process as a method. In this framework, they carefully consider the aim of the effort, process steps, strategic action methods, individual roles and group roles, and resource commitment (Bryson 1995). However, critical issues, including core beliefs, values, priorities, and corporate image, are clarified with the strategic planning team. On the other hand, they analyze power sources in the external and internal environment to determine strategic issues, and undertake evaluations consistent with the organization's mission and objectives (Porter 1980;

Wright et al. 1992). In external evaluation; it is synthesized the effects of political, economic, social and technological forces on competitors, customers and suppliers; In internal evaluation; by analyzing the effects of changes on the dynamics such as resources, business processes, information technology, competencies, culture and performance it is determined that what the strengths and weaknesses, opportunities and threats of the firm are.

Vision shaping is a competency that provides the context for everything that happens in the organization and guides and coordinates everyone's decisions and actions because it draws a picture of how it should look after successfully implementing the strategies (Albrecht 1994). For the activity of this competency, managers develop a picture of what function is required to achieve the outputs expected from the foundation processes of the organization. Later, they identify stakeholders who can contribute to shaping the vision, and work with these stake-holders by using a variety of communication and collaboration methods to design a vision that is more attractive than the vision of the existing organization and to create a shared vision. At the same time, they tries to analyze how the business units have a structure, how the units work, and how the units affect each other (Nanus 1996), and they link mechanisms to achieve vision-driven output by emphasizing structural change.

The Strategy Formulation is a competency in efforts to develop effective perfor-mance strategies for competing in a continuously changing environment. It requires to formulate action plans through collaborative efforts and to determine the appro-priate culture to carry out the organization's mission. Managers, for the activity of this competency, gather information through gap analysis by comparing environ-mental analysis, current situation and future vision for the development of a new strategic direction. The strategic issues that need to be resolved in the direction of the findings are highlighted and the problems are framed to formulate the needed strategy. Then it is evaluated that how each alternative can affect the critical organizational system to determine the criteria for solving strategic issues. When evaluating alternative forms of action, managers consider factors such as human resources, financial resources, core processes and strategic partnerships. In addition for an effective measurement strategy, along with targets and action paths, perfor-mance indicators and potential hurdles (for early identification) are included in strategic plan. High-performance managers become visible role models to define an organizational culture that supports the developed strategy, and send clear signs related to the organizational form, key values and expected behaviors that they want, and provide direction and energy for their subordinates (Nadler and Tushman 1988). They focus on explicit values and beliefs that are determined by their core values. They communicate their priorities, values and concerns openly and honestly, for-mulate measures that promote ethical behavior, and reward ethical behavior formally and informally (Nadler et al. 1995).

Organizational design is a competency that enables to be designed the changes related to organizational structure in the way of contributing to the solution of strategic issues. In order for strategic thinking to result in performance, the different components of the organization need to be organized properly (Rummler and Brache

1995). Strategic leaders formulate a design intent in accordance with identified problems, develop a concrete list of design criteria, and configure grouping and linking the options (alternatives) (Nadler and Tushman 1997). For successfully implementing the strategy, they develop designs to create meaningful and motivating work for individuals. For the activity of this competence, managers try to predict the new structure before designing the organization, balancing the design process with informal organizational elements and individual concerns, taking into account the basic structure of the organization. Then they evaluate the design alternatives and determine the appropriate links to the new strategic design in the formal organizational structure. Also they assess the harmony of organizational strategy, operating systems, management processes and organizational culture and climate to optimally respond to customer needs and environmental demands (Semler 1999). Though the line between design and application is blurred, the thought process before application is taken attention as the most important factor in developing a design (Nadler and Tushman 1997).

2.8 Strategic Thinkers' Features

According to Keelin and Arnold (2002) there are five basic features / habits that strategic thinker has. These are: entering game, accepting confusion and contradictory thoughts, assuring mental calm, managing thoughts, developing expression clarity.

Entering the game Strategic thinkers generally argue that they must engage in struggle rather than looking from the edge to win. For them, the strategic point of view is developing in intensive learning environments and disappearing in passivity and routine. Walking in structured patterns they see as a barrier to strong and timely thinking. Also they think that many talented people can not reach the running potentials because they do not enter the game. They are hampering their progress with restrictive assumptions. For example, they mostly say "My task is to manage numbers; the CEO's job is to interpret them". Strategic thinkers are very well aware of where they should stop at the best time to manage the game during crisis times and are engaged in a series of interrogations and discussions on game rules and conclusions: such as "Are these alternatives tactical or strategic?" , "What do these results mean, why are they important, or are they not?" "Can we explore other ways?", "What different points of view do we need to address, what more do we need to address them?" On the other hand, they prefer to have active participation in difficult issues to develop a strategic perspective. For this reason, they try to identify a difficult problem that is really important for your organization, then concentrate on looking at where their minds lead them.

Accepting confusion and contradictory thoughts According to strategic thinkers, the side-by-side placement of apparently contradictory ideas is the root of innovation. Managers should learn to live regularly with contradictory ideas. Such as seesawing innovative products/services requirements and financial situation; balancing customer anticipations and shareholder expectations; staying between the reflections of the past and the imagination of the future. Such situations are a failure pretext for some managers, but not for strategic thinkers. They argue that such situations lead people to find a mental framework, to interpret everything according to their conditions and to learn more. Therefore, beyond abstaining or acting wildly, they prefer to consider the issue from different angles, to work at a level that everybody can appreciate, to see through the eyes of others, and to consider the consequences for all stakeholders. They know that avoiding from confusion and contradictory thought limit the rate of learning, adopting them helps to learn quickly and make better decisions.

Assuring mental calm Strategic thinkers are able to remain calm even in critical conditions and stressful environments. Their calm is perceived as a powerful "asset" and is regarded as a quality indicator that distinguishes them from others. Calmness of mind allows for incubation and development of strong opinions. In general it is said that an executive's day is full of interruptions and crises, and it is almost no time to think quietly. But strategic thinkers, despite the complexity of everyday tasks, are creating filters that will allow the mind to calm down and for the emergence of strong thoughts. They can successfully evacuate their mental space by easily extracting insignificant topics and distracting thoughts; easily catch warriors who can open doors to good ideas. Despite the intensity, this feature contributes to the formation and development of mental calmness, and it is also reflected in the surrounding people.

Managing thoughts The thoughts are sometimes like explosions of corn, they are not there for a moment and you are looking at a new idea emerges. It does not matter how ideas come out, strategic thinkers usually ask the question: "Is this a good idea? If so, what do I do with it?" Such an approach can provide a good framework for managing thoughts. On the other hand managing thought requires a discipline for throwing offensive or irrelevant thoughts, spending time, and intensifying thoughts that will help reach the goal. When strategic thinkers meet a good idea or when a good idea arises, they show a great deal of effort to keep it and not to allow it to slide off their fingers. They label consciously the irrelevant thoughts that are not purposive as trivial, and only consciously focus on remarkable thoughts. So they empty their heads to catch remarkable things.

Developing expression clarity There is not even one area where good communication skills are not necessary for progress. You may have developed a strong strategic perspective, but if you misrepresent it, others will not benefit from it and you can not do what you want. Strategic thinkers often view their words as ammunition, choose words that make the message clear, and strongly avoid every unnecessary word because it reduces the value of the expression. They always keep in mind the target masses and take into account who they are, what their interests are, and their opinions on the subject. They do not derive from the fact that different people learn in different ways. Also they improve the internal logic of expressions by using stronger or reminders in their direction; they convey their messages by emphasizing the connection between the ideas and the interests of the spectators.

Those with these characteristics are more successful in developing strategic perspectives whether they are business managers, management consultants, or other professionals. They are also able to see the main source of more complex problems and to express solutions that others will adopt, and know better how to set up research and direction.

2.9 Risk and Uncertainty

Risk is defined as the probability of encountering unexpected outcomes in the future and refers to deviation from expected situations (Schroeck 2002: 24). Although theoretically, risk includes both positive and negative deviations between the expected value and the actual value, the concept of risk is generally perceived as negative deviations (Sayılgan 1995: 324). On the financial side, the positive difference between the expected result and the actual result is expressed as profit, income, return, etc.; the negative difference is explicated as losses, losses, expenses, etc. When the definitions of risk are examined, the point of common consensus is that risk is considered as a possible deviation from the outcome. The source of this possibility is the uncertainty of the future. Uncertainty covers the risk and consists of two dimensions: the ignorance and the surprise shock. Therefore, the concept of uncertainty has unpredictability and no precautions can be taken. However, because the danger and possibility is in risk concept, predictability and preventability are mentioned (Yalçınkaya 2004: 9–10). On the other hand the risk that arised form the uncertainty is an inevitable element of the economy (McDonald 2006: 5). With the help of the risk-protection tools, businesses are trying to reduce or eliminate these risks (Lin and Chen 2009). In addition, different types of risk-protection strategies are followed by firms where the level of uncertainty is different (Frey and Runggaldier 1999).

2.10 Risk Management

Risk management is defined as the planning, organization, management and control of the necessary resources and activities for controlling with the least cost the negativity and damages that may arise in the enterprises (Emhan 2009). Risk management involves a dynamic process in which many indicators are associated with specific situations of the business, continuous monitoring of decisions is made and taking new precautions if necessary. For risk management to be successful, it is necessary to determine the sources of risk, to measure risk, to determine the possible effects on the operation, to decide whether this risk is feasible, and to include the steps of selecting and implementing the risk protection technique (Sayılgan 1995).

Risk management is an important part of the general strategy of businesses (Guay and Kothari 2003). Businesses strive to reduce existing risks through risk management or to provide an optimal balance between risk and return. Risk management consists of some stages such as the foreseeing of the future, the creation of a strategic plan in this predictive light, making a decision to protect or not to protect from the risk, the selection of a preventive tool and the application of a risk protection program (Moosa 2003).

2.11 Risk Attitudes

In microeconomics and finance theory, it is generally accepted that individuals have a style of behavior that avoids from the risk (Bolgün and Akçay 2003: 111). However, there are individuals who love to take risks and who think that the difference between the expected value and the realized value will result in a positive result. It is also expected that individuals and businesses will be exposed to different risk attitudes in different conditions against risk. However, factors such as the level of knowledge about the markets, past work experience, potential future business opportunities, age, gender and educational status are thought to be influential on individual risk perceptions (Sepúlveda and Bonilla 2014), it is argued that the risk perception of the enterprises can be affected by factors such as the size of the value that exposures to risk, the effectiveness of the risk protection method to be used, having information about the risk protection methods and the cost of risk protection procedures.

Hillson and Murray-Webster (2007: 47) put forward four different categories based on two basic components: comfortable response and discomfortable response to uncertainty that can explained the individuals' risk attitudes. As came near to the extreme limits of each category, the risk sensitivity increases and because of the risk averse behavior increases, risk paranoid is formed.

The first category is risk-averse group It is the group of people with low uncertainty tolerance and has discomfort response to uncertainty. They are always in search of a solution to the risk. This group, which is responsive to risk, can overreact to threats. On the other hand, the ability of the individuals in this group to foresee opportunities is limited. In general, these groups tend to overreact to the threats, but remain insensitive to the opportunities.

The second category is risk-tolerance group It is the group of people who accept uncertainty as a part of everyday life and business world and who are inclined to live with uncertainties. This can lead to negative consequences for opportunities and threats. Because they think that the risk can not be managed, they cause threats to grow and opportunities can not be assessed in time. Therefore, this group is the most problematic group in the risk attitude groups. The risk tolerance may seem balanced, but progress can not be made when it is perfectly balanced.

The third category is risk-neutral group Individuals in the neutral (risk-neutral) group seek neither a risk aversion nor a risk-seeking. They are looking for strategies and tactics that will generate high profits in the future. A neutral approach to risk, in terms of both threats and opportunities, moves long-term and takes action when thinks it will only provide long-term benefits.

The fourth category is risk-seeking group It is the group of people who tend not to be afraid of taking action. The excitement of chasing opportunities of them is superior to their potential to see negativity and can cause making non-rational decisions. They see the risk as part of the normal workflow, but the risk they perceive is usually lower than the current risk. For this group, the emerging threats are either ignorable or acceptable in terms of their possible consequences. Risk seekers are more sensitive to opportunities and are more eager to evaluate those opportunities. Finally, outside of these groups there are risk-addicted and risk-paranoid groups. The first is on the extreme end of comfort response to uncertainty, the other is on the extreme end of discomfort response to uncertainty.

On the other hand, the attitudes of the firms to risk are realized in three different ways as full protection from risk, partly protection from risk or no protection from risk (Heaney and Winata 2005). There are two basic reasons why businesses confront with the unprotected risk status. The first is that business is not aware of the risks involved or is not aware of the methods of risk protection; and the second is that business has an opinion that prices, interest rates or exchange rates will change in their favor or will be at the current level. Also some businesses leave open positions in order to benefit from the risks, this is explained as a partly risk protection. If businesses try to close all positions in order to be protected from risk, it is defined as total protection from the risk. In addition, it can be said that some businesses are unresponsive to risk.

While firms develop different attitudes towards risk, they are affected by two fundamental conditions: the financial value and of the uncertainty of the entity that exposure to risk. As the value of the entity varies depending on the size and the smallness, the level of uncertainty varies between high and low. If the value is great and the level of uncertainty is high, the risk perception of the enterprises increases and an attitude which does not accept the risk is displayed and for all risk issues, internal and external, risk protection methods are applied. If the value is great and the level of uncertainty is low, the risk perception of the enterprises is decreasing and a positive attitude towards the risk is displayed and trying to increase the risk issue by considering that the risk is likely to result in profit. On the other hand, if the value of the entity that exposure to risk is small and the level of uncertainty is high, the risk perception of the business is changing positively and the risk seems to be insignificant and no risk protection methods are applied. Likewise, when the value and the level of uncertainty are low, the risk perception of the business is reduced and the risk is considered as unimportant, so no need for protection methods (Parlakkaya 2005: 95).

3 Associations and Conclusion

Based on the literature, in the light of the above explanations some logical relationships can be established between strategic thinking and some characteristics of strategic thinkers and the motives of thought and behavior that reveal the risk attitude. In this context, the most basic features of strategic thinking are summarized; using different problem-solving and decision-making methods, preparing scenarios for anticipating the future of the company, identifying and using important opportunities in the competitive market, working on early-indicator demonstration programs, being proactive, developing alternative hypotheses about the future and creating internal opposition for comprehensive evaluations.

Because risk is evaluated as both positive and negative deviation between expected value and actual value, risk attitude can be evaluated from two perspectives as positive and negative. Moreover, since it is possible to predict and take precautions in the concept of risk, it can be argued that any situation that reduces uncertainty will positively affect risk attitude, and that any situation that increases uncertainty will be negatively reflected in risk attitude. On the other hand, although it is generally accepted that individuals have a behavior style of avoiding risk, it is a fact that can be readily accepted in individuals who love to seek and take risks. Strategic thinkers are the individuals most likely to be assessed within the scope because of the features they have.

The main elements that shape the risk perception and the risk perception of the enterprises and individuals are the financial value of the risk subject, the level of uncertainty about the risk subject, and the reactions of the individuals to the uncertainty. As sensitivity to uncertainty increases in the negative direction, the attitude of risk avoidance arises and the risk goes to paranoid. When it increases positively, risk lovers are emerging.

Strategic thinking leads managers and managers to develop positive attitudes towards risk taking because of its basic features. Namely; to work on scenarios to anticipate the future of the organization using various problem-solving techniques can ensure the more clear photographs of the results. This is reducing uncertainty about risk and making reasonable the risk-taking behavior. In the same way, working on early-indicator-oriented programs and developing alternative hypotheses about the future reduces the uncertainty about the risk subject, making the risk for firms and individuals volatile, and positively affects the risk attitude. On the other side, creating an internal opposition to evaluate the issue in a comprehensive way raises concerns that it may lead to unnecessary worries and anxieties in some situations while creating an environment for examining the issue from different angles, causing uncertainty about the risk. This indecisive environment prevents proactive and risk attitude is on the negative side.

Due to some distinguishing features strategic thinkers will be able to understand all the relationships and influences in the business ecosystem, to create a specific point of view and direction about the long-running competitive position, to internalize strategic purpose and intention within the institution, to gather the employees' energies around the aims and intentions, to remove the resistance to reach the goal, to take into consideration the innovative work of employees at all levels of the institution with intelligent opportunism, to compare the critical points of possible changes that are likely to occur with past experiences and make present and future extractions.

Today, managers are struggling in a business world where the amount of information is so much increased and facilitated accessing to information and with this the time of thinking decreases. While the increase in the amount of information makes it more difficult to reach the right information, the ease of accessing information cause to an increase in the violence and intensity of competition. Because these conditions trigger the increase of uncertainty, the attitudes towards risk and risk perception affected negatively. But strategic thinkers are able to reduce ambiguity by generating hypothesis-based critical ideas and testing them efficiently, they can change the attitudes towards risk and risk perception positively.

As strategic thinkers integrate organizational changes into organizational processes, because they address the basic structure of the organization from a strategic standpoint and balance organizational and individual concerns, the new organizational design can be bring about a more concrete. Despite the fact that the line between design and application is blurred, these concrete indications provide less uncertainty. Decrease in uncertainty affects the risk perceptions and positively reflects the risk attitudes.

Because strategic thinkers defend the necessity to enter the game to win, they generally prefer to active participation in difficult situations in order to avoid passivity and routine. The motivation to intervene in the game without looking from the edge creates a tendency that will make easier to take risk, and it can ensure that the risk attitude develops positively.

According to strategic thinkers, learning to live regularly with contradictory and conflicting ideas can be regarded as the root of innovation and help to learn more quickly. Therefore the situations with threats in terms of possible outcomes are considered by them to be ignorable or admissible, and the behavior of risk avoidance is generally not preferred. Likewise, because strategic thinkers are able to remain calm even in critical conditions and stressful environments, their mental calmness is able to incubate innovative strengths ideas and gives opportunity them for development. Also, when a good idea emerges, they make a serious effort and empty their heads to catch up it. This approach makes strong them about reducing uncertainty, changes positively the risk perceptions and reflects positively the risk attitudes. Knowing very well the most critical features of the target masses and conveying their messages by emphasizing strong expressions the connection between ideas and the interests of the audience in direction, cause positive attitudes towards the risk to emerge at the other individuals around them.

On the other hand, the mental model defended by strategic thinking does not predict a measurable consequence because it deals with more innovative game syntheses, open-ended proposals, convergence-focused freeforms throughout the strategic thinking process. This situation leads to worries that the process may sometimes be inconclusive or cause time loss. In such an environment, because the uncertainty is increasing, it is inevitable that negative attitude towards risk will develop negatively.

These shared features related to the strategic thinkers extract from them; *the risk-averse group* with low uncertainty tolerance and discomfort from uncertainty, overresponsible to threats, limited ability to predict opportunities, and insensitivity to opportunities; *the risk-tolerant group* that does not care about uncertainty, thinks that risk can not be managed, for being unconcerned causing the threats to grow and can not be timely assessed the opportunities; *the risk-neutral group* that not avoiding from the risk and not seeking risk, only when try to do something it finds strategies and tactics that will generate very high earnings in long-term; and enter in them *the risk-seeking group* that is not afraid to act, sees the risk as part of the normal workflow, perceives the risk generally lower than the existing risk, is more sensitive to opportunities and more willing to consider opportunities.

Key Words Definitions

Strategic thinking It is a synthesis process that basically associated with all these concepts that can be labeled as "strategic" and focused on findings and developing unique opportunities to create value by building a provocative and innovative dialogue among those who can influence a company's vision.

Strategic thinking process The process is consisting of three stages in it many of critical subject are taken into consideration: Firstly, asking influential questions to produce innovative options, Secondly, redirecting to activate the arrangement, Thirdly, thinking about alternative assumptions and research results.

The Elements of Strategic Thinking There are five elements; system perspective, intent focused, intelligent opportunism, hypothesis-driven, thinking in time.

Strategic thinker He is a person who has five basic features / habits such as entering game, accepting confusion and contradictory thoughts, assuring mental calm, managing thoughts, developing expression clarity.

Strategic Thinking and Managerial Competencies In order to integrate strategic thinking into the organization as a critical element for achieving and sustaining organizational success, there are four areas of competence; organizational analysis, vision shaping, strategy formulation and organizational design can be used by high-performance managers.

Risk It is defined as the probability of encountering unexpected outcomes in the future and includes both positive and negative deviations between the expected value and the actual value.

Risk management It is defined as the planning, organization, management and control of the necessary resources and activities for controlling with the least cost the negativity and damages that may arise in the enterprises.

Risk Attitudes The attitudes that a pattern of behaviors and repetitive behaviors that individuals possess to avoid from the risk or to take risk. They are influenced by factors such as the level of knowledge about the markets, past work experience, potential future business opportunities, age, gender, educational status and etc.

References

Albrecht, K. (1994). The northbound train. In *Finding the purpose, setting the direction, shaping the destiny of your organization*. New York: American Management Association.

Amitabh, M., & Sahay, A. (2008, May). *Strategic thinking: Is leadership the missing link: An exploratory study*. In 11th Annual Conversation of the Strategic Management Forum, Kanpur, India.

Bianca, A. (2014). Why is strategic thinking important to the success of Business?, accessed July 9, 2014, from http://yourbusiness.azcentral.com/strategic-thinking-important-success-business-9612.html

Bolgün, E., & Akçay, B. (2003). *Risk Yönetimi*. İstanbul: Scala Yayıncılık.

Bryson, J. (1995). *Strategic planning for public and nonprofit organizations: A guide to strengthening and sustaining organizational achievement*. San Francisco: Jossey-Bass.

Collins, D. B., Lowe, J. S., & Arnett, C. R. (2000). High-performance leadership at the organization level. *Advances in Developing Human Resources, 2*(1), 18–46.

Emhan, A. (2009). Risk Yönetim Süreci ve Risk Yönetmekte Kullanılan Teknikler. *Atatürk Üniversitesi İktisadi ve İdari Bilimler Dergisi, 23*(3), 209–220.

Frey, R., & Runggaldier, J. W. (1999). Risk minimizing hedging strategies under restricted information: The case of stochastic volatility models observable only at discrete random times. *Mathematical Methods for Operations Research, 50*, 339–350.

Goldman, E., Cahill, T., Filho, R., & Merlis, L. (2009). Experiences that develop the ability to think strategically. *Journal of Healthcare Management, 54*(6), 7–416.

Guay, W., & Kothari, S. P. (2003). How much do firms hedge with derivatives? *Journal of Financial Economics, 70*, 423–461.

Hamel, G. (1996, July–August). Strategy as revolution. *Harvard Business Review*, 69–82.

Hamel, G., & Prahalad, C. K. (1994). *Competing for the future*. Boston: Harvard School Press.

Hamel, G., & Prahalad, C. K. (2005, July-August). Strategic intent, the high-performance organization—the best of HBR. *Harvard Business Review*, accessed September 7, 2017, from https://www.europeanleadershipplatform.com/assets/downloads/infoItems/148.pdf

Haycock, K., Cheadle, A., & Bluestone, K. S. (2012). Strategic thinking lessons for leadership from the literature. *Library Leadership & Management, 26*(3/4), 1–23.

Heaney, R., & Winata, H. (2005). Use of derivatives by Australian companies. *Pacific Basin Finance Journal, 13*, 411–430.

Heracleous, L. (1998). Strategic thinking or strategic planning? *Long Range Planning, 31*(3), 481–487.

Hill, B. (2017). Why is strategic thinking important to the success of business?, accessed 9 July, 2017, from http://smallbusiness.chron.com/strategic-thinking-important-success-business-4661.html

Hillson, D., & Murray-Webster, R. (2007). *Understanding and managing risk attitude* (2nd ed.). Aldershot: Gower.

Kaufman, R., Oakley-Brown, H., Watkins, R., & Leigh, D. (2003). *Strategic planning for success: Aligning people, performance, and payoffs*. San Francisco: Jossey-Bass.

Keelin, T., & Arnold, R. (2002). Five habits of highly strategic thinkers. *Journal of Business Strategy, 23*(5), 38–42.

Lawrence, E. (1999). Strategic thinking—A discussion paper, Research Directorate, April 27, Public Service Commission of Canada.

Liedtka, J. (1998). Strategic thinking; can it be taught? *Long Range Planning, 31*(1), 120–129.

Lin, C. T., & Chen, M. Y. (2009). Hedging strategic flexibility in the distribution optimization problem. *Omega, 37*(1), 826–837.

Maxwell, J. (2003). *Thinking for a change: 11 ways highly successful people approach life and work*. New York: Warner.

McDonald, R. L. (2006). *Derivatives market*. Boston: Addison Wesley, Pearson.

Mintzberg, H. (1994). The fall and rise of strategic planning. *Harvard Business Review, 72*(1), 107–114.

Mintzberg, H., & Waters, J. (1985). Of strategies, deliberate and emergent. *Strategic Management Journal, 6*, 257–272.

Moore, J. (1993). Predators and prey: A new ecology of competition. *Harvard Business Review, 7* (13), 75–86.

Moosa, A. I. (2003). *International financial operations.* New York: Palgrave Macmillan.

Nadler, D. A., & Tushman, M. L. (1988). *Strategic organization design. Concepts, tools and processes.* Glenview, IL: Scott, Foresman.

Nadler, D. A., & Tushman, M. L. (1997). *Competing by design. The power of organizational architecture.* New York: Oxford University Press.

Nadler, D. A., Shaw, R. B., & Walton, A. E. (1995). *Discontinuous change: Leading organizational transformation.* San Francisco: Jossey-Bass.

Nanus, B. (1996). *Leading the way to organizational renewal.* Portland, OR: Productivity.

Nasi, J. (1991). *Arenas of strategic thinking.* Helsinki: Foundation for Economic Education.

Neustadt, R., & May, E. (1986). *Thinking in time: The uses of history for decision-makers.* New York: Free Press.

Ohmae, K. (1982). *The mind of the strategist.* New York: McGraw-Hill.

Parlakkaya, R. (2005). *Finansal Türev Ürünler ile Mali Risk Yönetimi ve Muhasebe Uygulamaları (2 Baskı).* Ankara: Nobel Yayın Dağıtım.

Perkins, L. (2012). 3 Essential steps to thinking strategically. Accessed July 7, 2017, from https://www.inc.com/lauren-perkins/three-essential-steps-to-thinking-strategically.html

Porter, M. (1980). *Competitive strategy: Techniques for analyzing industries and competitors.* New York: Macmillan.

Raimond, P. (1996). Two styles of foresight. *Long Range Planning, 29*(2), 208–214.

Rummler, G., & Brache, A. (1995). *Improving performance: How to manage the white space on the organizational chart.* San Francisco: Jossey-Bass.

Sayılgan, G. (1995). Finansal Risk Yönetimi. *Ankara Üniversitesi Siyasal Bilgiler Fakültesi Dergisi, 50*(1–2), 323–334.

Schroeck, G. (2002). *Risk management and value creation* (1st ed.). New Jersey: Wiley.

Semler, S. (1999). Operationalizing alignment testing alignment theory. In P. Kuchinke (Ed.), *Proceedings of the Academy of Human Resource Development.* Baton Rouge, LA: Academy of Human Resource Development.

Senge, P. (1990). *The fifth discipline: The art and practice of the learning organization.* London: Century Business.

Sepúlveda, J. P., & Bonilla, C. A. (2014). The factors affecting the risk attitude in entrepreneurship: Evidence from Latin America. *Journal of Applied Economics Letters, 21*(8), 573–581.

Sloan, J. (2006). *Learning to think strategically.* Oxford: Butterworth-Heinemann.

Stacey, R. (1992). *Managing the unknowable.* San Francisco: Jossey-Bass.

Watkins, M. D. (2007). How to think strategically. *Harvard Business Review.*

Wilson, L. (1994). Strategic planning isn't dead-it changed. *Long Range Planning, 27*(4), 12–24.

Wright, P., Pringle, C., & Kroll, M. (1992). *Strategic management text and cases.* Needham Heights, MA: Allyn and Bacon.

Yalçınkaya, T. (2004). Risk ve Belirsizlik Algılamasının İktisadi Davranışlara Yansımaları. *Muğla Üniversitesi İİBF Tartışma Tebliğleri*, Muğla, No: 2004-05.

Zand, D. E. (2010). Drucker's strategic thinking process: Three key techniques. *Strategy & Leadership, 38*(3), 23–28.

Industry 4.0 and Turkey: A Financial Perspective

Sibel Yılmaz Türkmen

Abstract All sectors globally are going through a new industrial revolution which is called "Industry 4.0". It is said to have a huge impact on manufacturing, lifestyle and future of people. Industry 4.0 demands a significant amount of investment in new technology. Major changes will have to take place in the global economy, because of migrating to Industry 4.0. The study aims to discuss Industry 4.0 and its influences on people, in an economic and financial perspective, in the world, particularly in Turkey.

1 Introduction

The term Industry 4.0 was first heard in the Hanover fair (Hannover Messe) in 2011 (Pfeiffer 2017, p. 107). The German federal government presented "Industrie 4.0" as its future cutting-edge industrial development strategy (Huang et al. 2017, p. 711). The workgroups proposed recommended Industry 4.0 implementations to the German government in 2012.

The fourth industrial revolution, which is named as the Industry 4.0, refers to the current trend of automation and data exchange in the management and the organization of the whole value chain process in manufacturing technologies. The Industry 4.0 concept is commonly used across Europe, particularly in Germany. In the English-speaking world, especially in the United States, it is generally called the "Internet of Things" or the "Internet of Everything" (Deloitte 2015, p. 3).

With the introduction of mechanical production equipment at the end of the eighteenth century, industrialization began, thus the industrial revolution. The first equipment involved water or steam powered machinery such as the mechanical loom for goods manufacturing. With the advent of electrical machinery, the second industrial revolution introduced mass production and the assembly line at the end

S. Y. Türkmen (✉)
Marmara University, Istanbul, Turkey
e-mail: sibelyilmaz@marmara.edu.tr

© Springer International Publishing AG, part of Springer Nature 2018   273
H. Dincer et al. (eds.), *Strategic Design and Innovative Thinking in Business Operations*, Contributions to Management Science,
https://doi.org/10.1007/978-3-319-77622-4_14

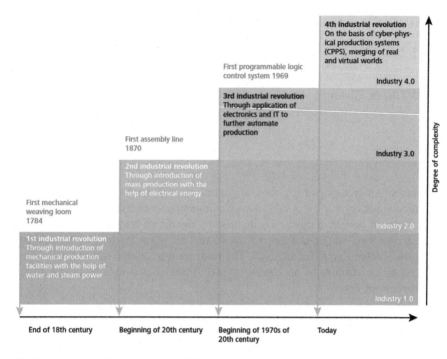

Fig. 1 Industry 4.0. Source: Deloitte (2015, p. 3)

of the nineteenth century. The third industrial revolution was based on automating the production process with the use of information technologies and electronics, starting in the early 1970s. Computing became widespread with the unstoppable progress of the Internet, along with steady miniaturization. Linking of computers to each other results in a constantly growing network. With all the sensors and the computing power of the devices and machinery, Internet of Things, enables real-time communication and cooperation of cyber-physical systems, with each other and with humans; which is the enabler of the fourth industrial revolution. The major idea of Industry 4.0 is the introduction of internet technologies into industry (Gabriel and Pessl 2016, p. 132; Fig. 1).

Mechanization characterizes the first three industrial revolutions. High electric energy usage, automation and electronics, also respectively define the preceding industrial revolutions.

The first industrial revolution introduced automation. High manufacturing costs encouraged producers to invent mass production tools and build factories in the eighteenth century. Decades later, large cities inhabited by industrialists, encouraged them to build assembly lines to support major supply-chains.

The second came with the mass production. The third industrial revolution came with the utilization of robots. Over the past 50 years, global competition has spurred the rise of systems that allow managers to reconfigure factories quickly and cheaply to produce different items (Grier 2017, p. 120).

Industry 4.0 brings smart production robots that can decide according to the data flowing from the sensors and the market. The purpose of the origination is to make adaptive, custom production economical, and to use assets productively. A central production control system executes the organization of information flow (Gubán and Kovács 2017, p. 112) requiring each device in the production to communicate with each other. Every industrial revolution took place in a shorter period than before. Also unlike other industry revolutions, Industry 4.0 was foreseen before it was realized.

The fourth industrial revolution, which is defined by the use of smart factories, service innovations and cyber-physical systems, is the target of today's economy. The German federal government conceptualized the idea of Industry 4.0. The main goal is promoting computerization or digitalization. That is why Germany is leading the change, and expecting an increase in the German economy for 267 billion euros (Shamim et al. 2017, p. 1).

The third industrial revolution was concentrated on individual processes and machinery. Whereas Industry 4.0 concentrates on the digital transformation of physical systems and integrating them into a digitally interconnected infrastructure. Network of devices with the newest technologies all communicate data that plays a huge role and producing, transferring and analyzing it establishes the real benefits assured by Industry 4.0.

Capital has to introduce new technologies to both resist the over-production crisis and compete in market conditions. According to this law, as the firms grow, the machines that make up the unchanging part of the capital tends to increase in proportion to the changing power of the labor force, which is an explanation of the change we are in now (Aksoy 2017, p. 42). Industry 4.0 is not a one-fits all solution for implementing directly, but a concept of improving the manufacturing process by best practices and new technology (KPMG 2016, p. 16).

Increasing public acceptance of Interconnected Things (IT) encourages the increasing interest in Industry 4.0, leading to an augmented interest on investment and development (Batista et al. 2017, p. 16).

The organization of the manufacturing processes is described by Industry 4.0 with a "smart" factory which is a virtual environment constructed by data provided by physical systems. Smart factory is simply a virtual copy of the real production environment being monitored by computer-driven systems, which drives decisions and maintain organization based on the calculations all of which depend on devices communicating with each other (Smit et al. 2016, p. 20).

Technological advances reversed the logic of the manufacturing process from conventional methodologies to a way that the product is no longer "processed", but it communicates with the manufacturing facility to tell them what to do exactly. This paradigm shift represented by Industry 4.0 is a movement from centralized production to decentralized (GTAI 2014, p. 6).

The shift from Industry 3.0 to Industry 4.0 is more than one number for manufacturers. It is a different approach, which means a comprehensive transition (KPMG 2016, p. 18). Industry 4.0 seeks to alter the fundamental interaction between worker and machine (Young and Solberg 2017, p. 22). Integration of business partners and customers, productivity, versatility and functionality characterizes this process (Srivastava 2015, p. 23).

Many of the technologies that are dramatically changing the manufacturing processes are not new. The technologies like artificial intelligence, sensors, 3D printing, drones, robotics and nanotechnology were, in fact invented nearly 30 years ago. What makes them more adaptive and accelerate the industrial process is the massive increase in computing power and cost reductions (Deloitte 2015, p. 5).

The main features of Industry 4.0 are (Smit et al. 2016, p. 21):

- Interoperability: The ability of all devices and humans to connect and communicate with each other and exchange data to maintain and even further improve the processes. Any machinery or device can be a source by collecting the information from sensors.
- Virtualization: The ability of information systems to create a virtual manufacturing plant model of the real environment by gathering information from the sensors and aggregating the raw data to the context information for simulating the production.
- Decentralization: The ability of cyber-physical systems to make their own decisions unless there are interferences or conflicts. The gain increases as systems perform their processes more autonomously.
- Real-Time Capability: The ability to enrich and analyze data that is flowing from the sensors or any source and present insights instantly.
- Service Orientation: A design approach in the form of services for computer software. Service-oriented design principles emphasize the separation of software concerns.
- Modularity: The ability of smart factories to be flexible and adaptive to the changing requirements and be able to expand or replace any part of the infrastructure or system.

The Industry 4.0 has been proposed for a period. Industrialization and information technology integration faces new opportunities (Pei et al. 2017, p. 151). The expectations from Industry 4.0 are supposed to occur within 10–20 years.

The introduction describes Industry 4.0 and other industry revolutions, features of Industry 4.0. Then, some of the studies on the subject related to the literature have been mentioned. In the following section, we tried to explain the location of the Industry 4.0 in the World, and finally the Industry 4.0 in Turkey was mentioned and the work is completed.

2 Review of Related Literature

Industry 4.0 has begun to be examined in many dimensions in the world in recent years. A few of these studies are listed below.

Prause (2015), searched how new and sustainable structures and business models for Industry 4.0 might look like and in which direction existing traditional business concepts have to be developed to deploy a strong business impact of Industry 4.0 and also discussed why e-residency might be the appropriate concept in the context of Industry 4.0.

Sommer (2015), examined the capability, readiness and awareness of companies, considering the role of the SMEs, to face Industry 4.0 challenge.

Wahl (2015), analyzes in which degree Estonia is prepared for Industry 4.0 by employing strategic factor analysis, adding the refinement of a strategic knowledge vision is necessary in order to be ready for the new technological advancement.

Wang et al. (2016), implemented a reconfigurable and adaptive smart factory that is vertically integrated, proposing a framework which involves industrial wireless networks, smart terminals and machinery, conveyors, products and the use of cloud.

Kroh (2016), criticized the technocratic ways documented in strategic governmental guidelines and dealt with the socio-economic outcomes of Industry 4.0 by pointing on the key problem being the social dimension of the fourth industrial revolution.

Dai and Vasarhelyi (2016), aimed to imagineer the effects and usage of the technologies that encompass Industry 4.0 upon the audit process, prior to their widespread implementation in business.

Ganzarin and Errasti (2016), proposed a procedure as a directing infrastructure for Industry 4.0 collective enhancement vision, methodology and process building. They recommended a phase procedure model to guide and prepare organizations to recognize new possibilities for broadening the use of Industry 4.0.

Gabriel and Pessl (2016), discussed potential social and environmental impacts of Industry 4.0 with a focus on small and medium-sized enterprises and referenced to an empirical study in Austria.

Stock and Seliger (2016), presented a state of the art review of Industry 4.0 based on recent developments in research and practice and different opportunities for sustainable manufacturing in Industry 4.0.

Zhang et al. (2016), analyzed the main problems existing in the development of the Chinese manufacturing industry and the enlightenment of German "industry 4.0" to the Chinese manufacturing industry.

Shamim et al. (2017), proposed a framework of management practices which can promote the environment of innovation and learning in an organization, and hence facilitate business to match the pace of Industry 4.0 by facilitating technology acceptance e.g., digital enhancements and implementation of cyber physical systems (CPS).

Pfeiffer (2017), aimed to debunk the myth about the origin of this powerful vision and to trace the narrative back to the global economic crisis in 2009 and thus to the real actors, central discourse patterns, and hidden intentions of this vision of a new Industrial Revolution.

Stancioiu (2017), in particular, assessed the state of Romania against industry 4.0, examining the benefits and needs to do.

Alçın (2016) studied the trivial characteristics and conceivable impacts of the Industry 4.0 concepts. Macit (2017), proposed a structural framework system for the Industry 4.0 process. Aksoy (2017) reviewed and explained Industry 4.0 with the title evolution or revolution.

3 Industry 4.0 and World

Industry 4.0 started in Germany. The momentum is gradually picking up in the United States, Japan, China, the Scandinavian countries and the United Kingdom to bring this approach into the system. Companies all over the world are expecting to increase digitization over the next 5 years dramatically. By 2020, the US aims to achieve 74% digitization from the current levels of 32%, Asia Pacific to 67% from current 36% and the Europe, the Middle East and the Africa to 71% from current 30% (Grant Thornton 2017, p. 15). According to PWC, costs are expected to reduce by $ 421 billion p.a., revenue to rise by $ 493 billion p.a. and investments to increase up to $ 907 billion p.a. (www.pwc.com, 03.07.2017).

There are divided opinions on using the terms revolution or evolution. The concept was launched in Europe, and German government supports programs and leading companies like Siemens and Bosch (Stancioiu 2017, p. 76).

Inspired by Industry 4.0, China has launched China Manufacturing 2025 (CM2025), which is on the track of Industry 4.0 and moved further. Industry 4.0 is about technological advancement, whereas CM2025 is about restructuring the entire industry and making it more competitive, using advancement in production technology as just one of the instruments (Lu 2017, p. 27).

The US and Germany being the lead for traditional industrial economies, plan to relocate production from low-wage countries to local manufacturing facilities in North America and Europe, and improve the global competitiveness by using some of the advantages of Industry 4.0, like productivity and digitalization (Deloitte 2015, p. 4).

Japan and Germany are implementing digitization primarily to increase their efficiency and product quality. In the US, the trend is to develop new business models using digital offers and services and to provide these products and services digitally as quickly as possible. China's manufacturing companies focus on ways to cope with international competitors by cutting costs (Stancioiu 2017, p. 77).

China's R&D investment rose from the year 2008 to 2012. However, compared with the United States, Germany, Japan and other manufacturing powers, China's R&D funding input intensity (the ratio of R&D expenditure and gross domestic product) is significantly lower. This shows the percentage of R&D funds for of the world's major six countries. In 2014, China's R&D expenditure reached 1331.2 billion Yuan, an increase of 12.4% over the previous year. The intensity of R&D funds increased to 2.09%, while Germany's R&D had reached 2.69% in 2008 (Zhang et al. 2016, p. 100).

New business processes and manufacturing technologies are needed as the competition and customer demands increases because of the changing economic environment and globalization (Gubán and Kovács 2017, p. 114). Industry 4.0 influences the global business of all companies: value chains will be more flexible and agile and organized in a more fragmented manner. Real-time data will be of the utmost importance and data analytics skills a key requirement (S-GE 2016, p. 2).

Germany, an industrial location, could benefit potential changes by implementing Industry 4.0 like increased production flexibility, increased global competitiveness,

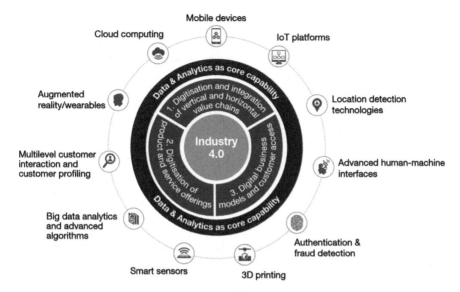

Fig. 2 Technologies of Industry 4.0. Source: PWC (2016, p. 6)

improved adaptation the ongoing change in customer needs, new business processes and the consideration of demographic change (Sommer 2015, p. 1513; Fig. 2).

Nine technologies are giving momentum to the industrial production of the future:

Big Data Nowadays, through the rapid development of Internet, such a huge amount of information is produced and collected on a daily basis that, their processing and analysis is beyond the capabilities of traditional tools. However, there is a technology by which we can conduct analysis, and that is Big Data. Big Data allows quickly and efficiently managing and using a continually growing database. With this technology, even data that has been collected in various mutually incompatible systems, databases and websites is processed and combined to give a clear picture of the situation in which there is a specific company or person (Witkowski 2017, p. 767). Big Data is recognized as an area where skills need to be developed, especially when more data will become available and people need to turn data into value-added insights (PWC 2017, p. 9).

Autonomous Robots Producers used robots for a long time to deal with complex tasks. As the technology and the computing power advances, robots are evolving to become more cooperative, autonomous and adaptive. They will, eventually learn from humans that are working safely near them and communicate with each other. The evolved robots will play a more versatile role in production and cost less than the ones that are used today (Rüßmann et al. 2015, p. 3).

Simulation The simulations of systems allow assessment of various scenarios. Once the scenarios are assessed, cost-effective solutions can be developed, tested and implemented much quicker leading to reduced cost and time to market (Grant Thornton 2017, p. 8).

Horizontal and Vertical System Integration Most of the information technology used today are not integrated fully. Companies, suppliers, and customers are rarely linked closely. What Industry 4.0 proposes is, the capability to become more cohesive and integrated between companies and departments, as networks evolve, increase the amount of data integration and enable truly automated value chains (Rüßmann et al. 2015, p. 3).

Internet of Things Network of devices, sensors, assets, people and any machinery with embedded software or electronics interoperating with the existing Internet infrastructure like wireless networks, wide-area networks or wired high-capacity networks (CGI 2017, p. 4).

Cybersecurity Traditional information technology security is not enough to protect the business and sustain a digitally connected value chain. As more companies implement innovations, the "attach surface area", the area that is vulnerable increases. Cybersecurity risks must be minimized as, a single manufacturing facility closing down means a loss of productions that can cost millions of dollars for each day. To disregard this possibility is to jeopardize the security and the stability of the company (CGI 2017, p. 14).

The Cloud Computing The cloud is being used for applications such as remote services, color management, and performance benchmarking and its role in other business areas will continue to expand. With continuous advancements in technology, machine data and functionality will only continue to shift towards cloud solutions. The cloud allows for a much faster roll out of updates, performance models, and delivery options than standalone systems (Grant Thornton 2017, p. 8).

Additive Manufacturing 3D printing makes it possible to produce complex parts without the need for assembly or any individual parts. As productions shift to selective laser sintering and 3D printing, new jobs in R&D and engineering are needed in 3D modeling and 3D computer-aided design. This causes a loss of jobs in parts assembly (Lorenz et al. 2015, p. 6).

Augmented Reality The process efficiency increases significantly by the use of augmented reality. To support service technicians who Companies are required to build new large scaled capabilities in digital assistance systems, IT and R&D (Lorenz et al. 2015, p. 6; Fig. 3).

Across the world, companies are expecting a significant impact on digitization and integration. The investors will start seeing the advanced implementation of Industry 4.0 as a qualifier for funding and it will become a qualifier to compete (S-GE 2016, p. 6).

Digital transformation is having in Europe and the United States, where highly automated and flexible factories can now compete against low-cost factories in Asia (BDC 2017, p. 1).

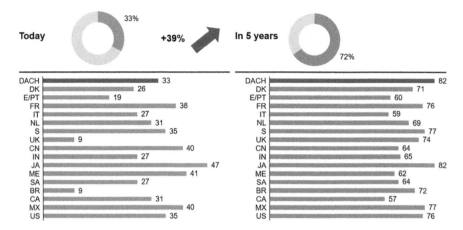

Fig. 3 Digitization levels across the world. Source: Switzerland Global Enterprise (2016, p. 2)

As seen in the Table 1, there is huge gap between developed nations and developing ones. Singapore topped the rankings. Turkey's rank was 48. Network readiness index is a key indicator of how countries are doing in the digital world. This depends on whether an individual country has the necessary infrastructure to meet the potentials of digital technology and whether these technologies are effective on the economy and society. The digital revolution may change the nature of innovation. This is increasingly based on the new business models and the digital technologies it allows (Grant Thornton 2017, p. 11; WEF 2016).

The benefits of Industry 4.0 are as follows (Stancioiu 2017, p. 76):

Time Engineers spend 31% of their time, which could be used for more valuable activities, searching for information. Optimization of the process makes every employee more efficient.

Cost Taking the right decisions require accurate data in the right context and format needed. Inaccurate decisions taking by the consideration of incorrect information can cost 25% of the company's income.

Flexibility They create flexible systems ready for change and ready for new opportunities. Only 36% of companies are ready to optimize processes based on data analysis.

Integration The digital manufacturing involves the simultaneous development of the product and the production process. The companies reduce 80% time with production interruptions if they use digital validation.

Industry 4.0 presents a possibility to save crucial resources besides decreasing costs and improving efficiency (S-GE 2016, p. 42).

At a relatively low cost, Industry 4.0, driven by the Internet of Everything, offers high potential effects. Each company and each industry can become a digital company, implementing a suitable technology stack to enable agile processes and

Table 1 Network readiness index

Networked readiness index 2016	Global rank
Singapore	1
Finland	2
Sweden	3
Norway	4
United States	5
Netherlands	6
Switzerland	7
United Kingdom	8
Luxembourg	9
Japan	10
Denmark	11
Hong Kong SAR	12
Korea, Rep.	13
Canada	14
Germany	15
Malaysia	31
Turkey	**48**
China	59
Thailand	62
India	91
Pakistan	110

Source: World Economic Forum (WEF)

new revenue streams as data from the interconnected devices that depend on software applications are transformed into real business results. Investment should be made for the most suitable technologies and platforms. The technical infrastructure must be highly scalable to be able to work with self-learning distributed devices in real-time (McKinsey Digital 2015, p. 13).

Manufacturers can develop the growth of their revenues by taking one or more actions (Lorenz et al. 2015, p. 7):

- Making manufacturing more flexible by the use of robotics and 3D printing, the latter offering high level customization to the product
- Utilizing new markets by implementing innovative business models, like machines as a service
- Making use of augmented reality by service professionals to develop new services and to improve post-sales service
- Increasing the effort to cope up with the high demand for Industry 4.0 technologies, such as autonomous robots

The Internet and networking drives and enables Industry 4.0. The Industry 4.0 vision encompass all segments, areas and functions of the manufacturing industry including economic action. To begin with, companies must create the general conditions. However, they must invest in network infrastructure, processing and the digitalization of their processes (KPMG 2016, pp. 9–10).

A significant amount of investment is required for the development and implementation of Industry 4.0 technologies. In this manner, the question of what financing is accessible for enterprises emerges. Users are mostly technology-driven manufacturers who have high capital operations. These types of companies have good financing conditions. Whereas, information and communication technology companies who are young and innovative have more difficult the conditions for financing the development of their applications for Industry 4.0. These companies depend on external capital and lack a positive cash flow initially. Credit allocation is risky for banks, as they do not receive enough collateral; however, they often do not understand the usually completely new business models or products of young ICT companies. Venture capitalists can close the financing gap, however, they supply equity capital to a few number of companies and mostly specialize in a specific sector. Their specialization gives them expertise and networks for particular sectors and thus they are able to increase the probability that innovative young companies will survive. In contrast to banks, venture capitalists take an equity position in the relevant company, rather than receiving interest (Schröder 2016, p. 16).

The investment of global industrial manufacturing companies that sums up to $907 billion per year through to 2020 reveals that the investments for Industry 4.0 are already significant. Sensors and connectivity devices are the major focus of this investment, which are followed by software and applications like manufacturing execution systems. As the need for trained employees increase, companies, in addition, also invest in driving organizational change and training. More than half of respondents expect their Industry 4.0 investments to yield a return within 2 years or less, given the investment of around 5% p.a. of their annual revenue (PWC 2016, p. 9).

Investment and innovation projects allow using new advances to get high profit. Investments can give the investor net present value or great profit while, using innovations allows applying the company's new technical equipment, technologies, materials and other facilities. Most funded projects ensure the production of high quality, competitive goods. For the success of the project also important is the form of fundraising and the methods of financial support. The system of the financing of innovation and investment projects is a combination of direct and indirect ways of financing as shown in the Fig. 4 (Chirkunova et al. 2016, p. 2).

The Internet of Things and Industry 4.0 will certainly introduce a reduced consumption of resources in the near feature and proves that they are feasible technologies (Pfeiffer 2017, p. 115). The success of Industry 4.0 will be because of a demand by the global economy (Grier 2017, p. 120).

Technological change can have both a positive and a negative impact on employment, although the value creation effects from gains in efficiency and new business models is one positive aspect of Industry 4.0. The restructuring of jobs will be the challenge because some of the less-demanding occupations will quickly disappear (Roblek et al. 2016, p. 3). To meet new requirements on their own initiative, financial incentives could help encouraging employees to improve their qualifications (Schröder 2016, p. 19).

While having a negative impact on medium to low-skilled workers, innovation is increasing the pay for high-skilled employees is a phenomenon that economists

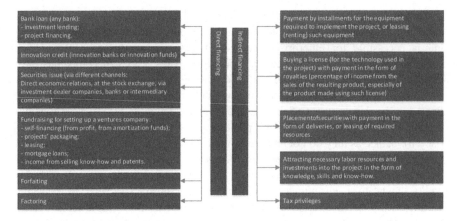

Fig. 4 Financing of innovation and investment projects. Source: Chirkunova et al. (2016, p. 2)

agree, who even debate on the extent and duration of it. The problem is posed by technology transitions, as it seems that "technological unemployment" is increasing in the world. In fact, some credible academic studies predict that computerization could make up to half of current jobs redundant within the next two decades (Ashby 2017, p. 18). Employees will have to be open to change, possess greater flexibility to adapt to new roles and environments, and get accustomed to continual interdisciplinary learning (Lorenz et al. 2015, p. 10). Industry 4.0 will create digital networks and ecosystems that in many cases will span the globe but retain distinct regional footprints (PWC 2016, p. 9).

4   Industry 4.0 and Turkey

Each country will adhere to Industry 4.0, which will provide revenue, cost and efficiency advantages with different speeds and applications. The awareness of Industry 4.0 and its competitive advantage is quite high in Turkey. In the future, those who deliver a good with the best quality, at the lowest cost, and in the fastest manner will be successful. This is why the steps taken by Turkey in Industry 4.0 are very important. In fact, Turkey's industrial enterprises are between Industry 2.0 and Industry 3.0.

However, Turkey faces some structural challenges to keep up and grow its participation in the global value chain (TÜSİAD and BCG 2016, p. 36; Fig. 5):

- High import dependency for exports: Proportion of imports covered by exports has been consistently high for decades.
- Low share of value-add products: Despite rising global demand for value-added products, the share of high-technology products in Turkish manufactured exports is approximately 4%.

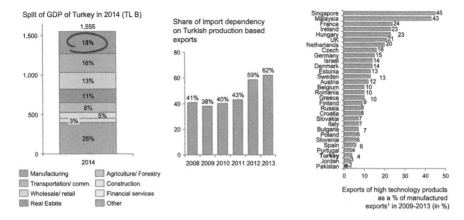

Fig. 5 The position of Turkish manufacturing sector. Source: TÜSİAD and BCG (2016, p. 36)

- Limited workforce skills/capabilities: Limited skilled workforce and ecosystems hinder the adaptation to new technologies.
- High employee turnover: The shift of workforce from industrial to service sectors leads to high turnover rates in manufacturing sectors.

Within this framework, conversion to Industry 4.0 is expected to result in development in four important categories (TÜSİAD and BCG 2016, p. 13):

Productivity In the current economic conditions, production sector can earn up to 50 billion TL, if the manufacturers implement Industry 4.0 successfully. This estimation is based on the increase in productivity of 4–7% considering the total production costs. The projected productivity further increases up to 15% taking into account the cost of conversion alone.

Growth The integration with the global value chain and the competitive advantage gained through the economy that thrives within the framework of Industry 4.0, is expected to boost the industrial production 3% a year, which achieves 1% or more growth to Turkey's GDP, which results to an extra revenue of 150–200 billion TL.

Investment For integrating Industry 4.0 manufacturing process, 15 billion TL must be invested per year over the next decade, based on the current size of the economy and the prices.

Employment It is assumed that while the need for high-skilled workers increase, as a whole the need for employed labor will grow, based on the realization of the growth targets. The high-skilled work force will need to be better educated and thus, will earn higher wages. The expectation is that the medium to low-skilled jobs will decline, but the increase in industrial production will expand the absolute overall employment. The development of a skilled workforce will improve Turkey's knowledge infrastructure and the income pyramid.

The following figure shows Turkey's Employment Projection. The need for skilled workmanship will gradually increase while the need for unskilled

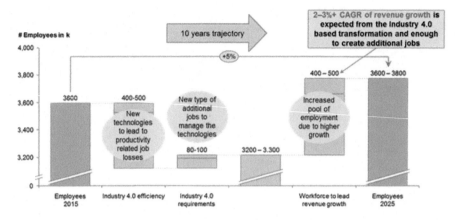

Fig. 6 Employment projection for Turkey. Source: TÜSİAD and BCG (2016, p. 49)

workmanship will decline over the next 10 years. With an increase of 2–3% due to Industry 4.0 is considered enough to compensate for the loss of employment (Fig. 6).

The relatively low cost of labor in Turkey reduces the potential impact of new technologies on productivity. This is mainly due to the smaller share of labor costs among the total cost of production. Essentially, the same rate of productivity improvement yields less cost improvement in Turkey compared to countries with higher labor costs. Structurally cheap labor costs lengthen the break-even period of return on investments, yielding less incentive to invest in advanced capex intensive systems (TÜSİAD and BCG 2016, pp. 50–61).

According to the research conducted by TÜBİTAK (2016, p. 4), only about 22% of Turkish firms have extensive knowledge about Industry 4.0. The sectors with the highest awareness are electronics, software and materials.

Finance, logistics, and software and system integration, which are production solution partners, are also important areas. Strengthening the logistic sectors' integration in value chains with regard to Industry 4.0. Keeping manufacturing sectors' solution partners up-to-date in terms of innovation needs and competencies required. Adapting financial institutions to new risk assessment needs due to changing balance sheet structures (TÜSİAD and BCG 2016, p. 63).

Companies will lose their competitive advantage if they fail to invest in pilot projects and to educate themselves on these new technologies, thus miss the opportunity to lead the transformation that is currently sweeping across the industry (CGI 2017, p. 22). Companies that have completed their digital infrastructure and have been able to dig into the corporation have taken one of the most important steps in capturing Industry 4.0. Firms in certain sectors in Turkey have begun to implement Industry 4.0, albeit at various levels. Businesses should allocate a certain share of their R&D budget.

It is understood that the telecommunication sector separates 70% of the investments that make the most investments into the digital structure. Apart from this, the two sectors that make the greatest contribution to digitalization are insurance and

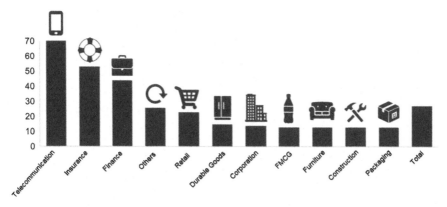

Fig. 7 Investments made on digital transformation. Source: TÜSİAD et al. (2016, p. 16)

banking. As an important part of their investments can be seen in this area, the financial sector is paying great attention to digitalization (Fig. 7).

In order for Turkey to be among the world's top ten economies in 2023, it has to grow at an average annual rate of 8.5%. This growth can be possible through the effective and efficient use of technologies. With Industry 4.0, new products can reduce the time to market from 25% to 50%, engineering fees can be reduced by up to 30% having up to 70% energy savings. First, the business processes in which the Internet of Things is used must be managed correctly. Giving a higher emphasis to computer education in Turkey, educating developers and programmers and accelerating the research of the Internet of Things can provide us the side of developing innovations (Ersoy 2017).

Turkey has not yet completed the process of transition to the automation and information systems which are required by the third industrial revolution. Generally speaking, the industrial value added of high and medium level technological structure is only 25% of total added value. This weakens Turkey's chances. Turkey should be structured to give priority to high-tech production. What appears to be now is that trade is in front of production, and this situation is unsustainable. Industry 4.0 is a golden opportunity for trained manpower. It is obvious that more technical staff will be needed. Generally speaking, Industry 4.0 is an industrial revolution that uses and promotes trained manpower. It is essential to train qualified human power as sectors and the days are gradually decreasing in which unqualified human power will work (Şişbot 2016, p. 25).

It is crucial to take place within the leading economies implementing Industry 4.0 for Turkey. Lower labor costs and logistical advantages should increase the competitiveness and provide Turkey a significant gain on the construction of a framework. Turkey should focus on creating an industry that will obtain a larger share of the global production value chain, and develop and maintain a sustainable and competitive advantage with Industry 4.0. Turkey's goal of shifting from an emerging market to the next level can be achieved at such a time when the indicators of competitive strengths are so diverse and rapidly changing (TÜSİAD and BCG 2016, p. 13).

The simulation of the new business model may be decisive in the need for financing. Inadequate or underdeveloped features arise as a result of a data analysis on the targets. It can provide a solution to the company's own product and service portfolio in a radical way and to develop new products and services. For this reason, companies' tax and legal departments should be involved to avoid foreseeable risks and utilize the potential for tax breaks (KPMG 2016, p. 18).

For Turkey, the Industrial 4.0 approach means to produce products and services with high added value, competitive power and sustainability in the production economy. The productivity increase in Turkey's production sectors is estimated to be 4–7%. The competitive advantage to be gained through the economy around the industry 4.0 is expected to provide an increase in industrial production of up to around 3% per year. In order to include the industry 4.0 technologies in the production process, it is estimated that about 10–15 billion TL investment should be invested in the next 10 years, corresponding to about 1–1.5% of the producers' revenues per year (Şuman 2017). If these steps can not be taken, if Turkey can not keep up with Industry 4.0, Turkey's market share in the world will shrink and competition power will weaken.

5 Conclusion

Turkey is faced with the opportunity to have an important place in the world economy with Industry 4.0. To reach the level of leading countries, and increase and develop competition level, it is vitally important to internalize developing technology and even be a part of the technology development. It is imperative to put forward the steps interactively with all stakeholders that will capture this opportunity at all levels, and work on this path.

In this long-term process, education, in particular, must be elaborated to prevent the potential difficulties that may arise in introducing qualified workforce. Vocational schools for Industry 4.0 are opened in Turkey, and some universities teach about industry 4.0.

It is necessary for all interested parties to follow up the technology related to Industry 4.0 by taking strategic steps, to devote themselves to innovation and roadmaps. In order to be able to approach the level of advanced countries in this area, in accordance with the needs of Industry 4.0 in the country, the state should support research and development activities in universities and various institutions and technological innovation. For developing Industry 4.0, the state has to prepare the investment and incentive environment and tax deduction if necessary.

Turkey should not only be a consumer in the field of computing and technology, but also a manufacturer. In Turkey, Industry 4.0 should be applied not only by certain companies, but also by all industrial organizations, and should be spread broadly. Providing the necessary resources for Industry 4.0 in a financial sense is not a big problem and the financial environment is prepared. It is important to start taking the steps for applying Industry 4.0. Industry 4.0 will allow those with a positive contribution to gain momentum, rather than sectors with a slow economic contribution. In the world, those who shape both education and industry programs into Industry 4.0 will win. Those who can not take the necessary steps will miss a great opportunity.

Keywords Definitions

Industry 4.0 Fourth industrial revolution, most commonly called "Industry 4.0", which is a reminiscence of software versioning, refers to the current trend of automation and data exchange in the management and the organization of the whole value chain process in manufacturing technologies.

Internet of Things Internet of Things enables real-time communication and cooperation of cyber-physical systems, with each other and with humans, being the major idea behind Industry 4.0.

Smart Factories (Smart factory is a virtual copy of the real production environment being monitored by computer-driven systems, which drives decisions, maintain organization based on the calculations all of which depend on devices communicating with each other, and is defined as a context-aware factory.

References

Aksoy, S. (2017). Değişen Teknolojiler ve Endüstri 4.0: Endüstri 4.0'ı Anlamaya Dair Bir Giriş. *Katkı Teknoloji, 4*, 34–44.

Alçın, S. (2016). Üretim için Yeni Bir İzlek. *Journal of Life Economics, 8*, 19–30.

Ashby, B. (2017, February). How industry 4.0 will impact industry. *Industrial Heating – Federal Triangle*, 18.

Batista, N. C., Melício, R., & Mendes, V. M. F. (2017). Services enabler architecture for smart grid and smart living services providers under industry 4.0. *Energy and Buildings, 141*, 16–27.

BDC. (2017). *Industry 4.0: The new industrial revolution – Are Canadian manufacturers ready?*. Business Development Bank in Canada.

Chirkunova, E. K., Kireeva, E. E., Kornilova, A. D., & Pschenichnikova, J. S. (2016). Research of instruments for financing of innovation and investment construction projects. *Procedia Engineering, 153*, 112–117.

CGI. (2017). *Industry 4.0 – Making your business more competitive.*

Dai, J., & Vasarhelyi, M. A. (2016). Imagineering audit 4.0. *Journal of Emerging Technologies in Accounting, American Accounting Association, 13*(1), 1–15.

Deloitte. (2015). *Industry 4.0: Challenges and solutions for the digital transformation and use of exponential technologies.* Switzerland.

Ersoy, A. R. (2017). *Endüstri 4.0 Sürecinde Neredeyiz?* Retrieved August 28, 2017, from www.endustri40.com/endustri-4-0-surecinde-neredeyiz/.

Gabriel, M., & Pessl, E. (2016). Industry 4.0 and sustainability impacts: Critical discussion of sustainability aspects with a special focus on future of work and ecological consequences. *International Journal of Engineering, 14*(2), 131–136.

Ganzarin, J., & Errasti, N. (2016). Three stage maturity model in SME's towards industry 4.0. *Journal of Industrial Management and Engineering, 9*(5), 1119–1128.

Grant Thornton. (2017). *India's readiness for industry 4.0 – A focus on automotive sector*. Grand Thornton and Confederation of Indian Industry.

Grier, D. A. (2017). The radical technology of Industrie 4.0. *Computer – Global Code.*, IEE Computer Society, *50*(4), 120–120.

GTAI. (2014, July). *Industrie 4.0 – Smart manufacturing for the future*. Germany Trade and Invest.

Gubán, M., & Kovács, G. (2017). Industry 4.0 conception. *Acta Technica Corviniensis – Bulletin of Engineering, Fascicule 1*(January–March), 111–114.

Huang, Z., Yu, H., Peng, Z., & Feng, Y. (2017). Planning community energy system in the industry 4.0 era: Achievements, challenges and a potential solution. *Renewable and Sustainable Energy Reviews, 78*, 710–721.

Kroh, M. (2016). A socio economic context of the "fourth industrial revolution". *Education and Science without Borders, 14*(7), 10–13.

KPMG. (2016). *The factory of the future: Industry 4.0 – The challenges of tomorrow*, KPMG Guide Part 1.

Lorenz, M, Rüßmann, M., Strack, R., Lueth, K. L., Bolle, M. (2015, September). *Man and machine in industry 4.0 – How will technology transform the industrial workforce through 2025?*. The Boston Consulting Group.

Lu, Y. (2017). Industry 4.0: A survey on technologies, applications and open research issues. *Journal of Industrial Information Integration, 6*, 1–41. Accepted Manuscript. Accepted April 15, 2017. https://doi.org/10.1016/j.jii.2017.04.005.

Macit, İ. (2017). Kurumsal Kaynak Planlamasının Endüstri 4.0 Kazanımları: Bir Yapısal Çatı Modeli Önerisi. *Yönetim Bilişim Sistemleri Dergisi, 2*(1), 50–60.

McKinsey Digital. (2015). *Industry 4.0: How to navigate digitization of the manufacturing sector*. McKinsey & Company.

Pei, F., Tong, Y., He, F., & Li, D. (2017). Research on design of the smart factory for forging enterprise in the industry 4.0 environment. *Mechanika, 23*(1), 146–152.

Pfeiffer, S. (2017). The vision of "Industrie 4.0" in the making – A case of future told, tamed, and traded. *Nanoethics, 11*, 107–121.

Prause, G. (2015). Sustainable business models and structures for industry 4.0. *Journal of Security and Sustainability Issues, 5*(2), 159–169.

PWC (Price Waterhouse Coopers). Retrieved July 3, 2017., from www.pwc.com.

PWC. (2016). *Industry 4.0: Building the digital enterprise*. Price Waterhouse Coopers 2016 Global Industry 4.0 Survey.

PWC. (2017). *Industry 4.0: Hype or reality? The current state of play in Flemish manufacturing*. Price Waterhouse Coopers 2017 Industry 4.0 Survey.

Roblek, V., Mesko, M., & Krapez, A. (2016, April–June). A complex view of industry 4.0. *SAGE Open, 1*, 1–11.

Rüßmann, M., Lorenz, M., Gerbert, P., Waldner, M., Justus, J., Engel, P., & Harnisch, M. (2015). *Industry 4.0 – The future of productivity and growth in manufacturing industries*. Boston, MA: BCG – The Boston Consulting Group.

Schröder, C. (2016). *The challenges of industry 4.0 for small and medium-sized enterprises*. Friedrich Ebert Stiftung.

S-GE. (2016, April). *Industry 4.0: Whitepaper – Opportunities for the Swiss export industry*. Switzerland Global Enterprise.

Shamim, S., Cang, S., Yu, H., & Li, Y. (2017). Examining the feasibilities of industry 4.0 for the hospitality sector with the lens of management practice. *Energies, 10*(499), 1–19.

Smit, J., Kreutzer, S., Moeller, C. & Carlberg, M. (2016). *Policy department A: Economic and scientific policy, industry 4.0, European parliament*. Study for the ITRE Committee, European Union.

Sommer, L. (2015). Industrial revolution – Industry 4.0: Are German manufacturing SMEs the first victims of this revolution? *Journal of Industrial Engineering and Management, 8*(5), 1512–1532.

Srivastava, S. K. (2015, November 15). *Industry 4.0* (pp. 23–24). Lucknow: BHU Engineer's Alumni.

Stancioiu, A. (2017). The fourth industrial revolution "Industry 4.0". *Academica Brâncuşi Fiabilitate si Durabilitate – Fiability & Durability, 1*, 74–78.

Stock, T., & Seliger, G. (2016). Opportunities of sustainable manufacturing in industry 4.0, 13th global conference on sustainable manufacturing. *Procedia CIRP, 40*, 536–541.

Şişbot, S. (2016). *Sanayi Devrimi ile Teknik Elemana İhtiyaç Duyulacak.* TOBB Ekonomik Forum (p. 25).

Şuman, N. (2017). Akıllı Üretim Çağı: Endüstri 4.0, *Fortune*. Retrieved August 19, 2017, from www.fortuneturkey.com/akilli-uretim-cagi-endustri-40-42841.

TÜBİTAK. (2016). Yeni Sanayi Devrimi akıllı Üretim Sistemleri Teknoloji Yol Haritası, TÜBİTAK Bilim Teknoloji ve Yenilik Politikaları Daire Başkanlığı, V.27.12.2016.

TÜSİAD & BCG. (2016). *Industry 4.0 in Turkey as an imperative for global competitiveness: An emerging market perspective.* Turkish Industry and Business Association, Boston Consulting Group, Publication Number: TÜSİAD-T/2016-03/576, İstanbul.

TÜSİAD, Samsung Electronics Türkiye, Deloitte Türkiye, & GfK Türkiye. (2016). Türkiye'deki Dijital Değişime CEO Bakışı, İstanbul.

WEF (World Economic Forum). Retrieved August 10, 2017., from http://reports.weforum.org/global-information-technology-report-2016/networked-readiness-index/.

Wahl, M. (2015). Strategic factor analysis for industry 4.0. *Journal of Security and Sustainability Issues, 5*(2), 241–247.

Wang, S., Wan, J., Li, D., & Zhang, C. (2016). Implementing smart factory of Industrie 4.0: An outlook. *International Journal of Distributed Sensor Networks, 12*(1), 1–10.

Witkowski, K. (2017). Internet of things, big data, industry 4.0 – Innovative solutions in logistics and supply chains management. *Procedia Engineering, 182*, 763–769.

Young, S., & Solberg, D. (2017, March). Industry 4.0 through the "eyes" of metrology. *Foundry Management & Technology, 145*, 22–23.

Zhang, X., Peek, W., Pikas, B., & Lee, T. (2016). The transformation and upgrading of the Chinese manufacturing industry: Based on "German Industry 4.0". *Journal of Applied Business and Economics, 18*(5), 97–105.

A Heterogeneous Panel Causality Test: Research and Development Expenditures and Economic Growth in OECD Countries

Asuman Koc Yurtkur and Tezcan Abasız

Abstract The rapid spread of technology since the 1990s brought with it various advantages such as high efficiency and low cost in terms of production processes. These advantages have led countries to pay more attention to different variables for this processes. Research and development activities are also among these variables. Theoretically, research development is given an important place in endogenous growth models. Many studies have been made by economists that technological innovation is an endogenous variable and technological innovations with research investments are an important source of economic growth. This study examines the interaction between this variables by heterogeneous panel causality test. According to the empirical findings of the study, the existence of a heterogeneous causal relationship between these two variables is implied for all countries. In this context, today's system where economic and technological ties are increasing, it can be said that R&D is an important dynamic in terms of economic growth from the point of view of working country sample.

1 Introduction

With the use of every field of information technology and the intensive use of technology in almost every field, a period called the New Economy has begun in the literature. (DeLong and Summer 2001). This definition includes innovations and technological developments that contribute to production and economic growth using new technologies. Rapidly developing technology has made the relationship between R&D activities and economic growth is among the most important topics in the literature. Thus, R&D began to be shown as one of the most important dynamics of economic growth. Significant development differences between countries today

A. K. Yurtkur (✉) · T. Abasız
Faculty of Economic and Administrative Sciences, Department of Economics, Bülent Ecevit University, Zonguldak, Turkey
e-mail: asuman.ky@beun.edu.tr; tezcan_abasiz@beun.edu.tr

© Springer International Publishing AG, part of Springer Nature 2018   293
H. Dincer et al. (eds.), *Strategic Design and Innovative Thinking in Business Operations*, Contributions to Management Science,
https://doi.org/10.1007/978-3-319-77622-4_15

depend on the level of technological development and therefore the level of R&D activities.

Economic theory shows that knowledge development (Schumpeter 1949) and technical changes (Solow 1957) are among the main sources of long-term productivity growth. R&D is seen as the most important source of technological change (Romer 1990) it is also regarded as the main component for knowledge-based growth of economic competitiveness, growth and productivity (Mowery and Rosenberg 1989; Coccia 2008). Guellec and Potterie (2001) studies, likewise, emphasizes the importance of technology for growth. The technological developments are emerging as inventions and innovations (innovation), made by companies (OECD 2003: 11). Technological developments and innovations are growing economically from the macro point of view, and from the micro point of view, the R&D activities which are realized in order to increase the profitability and market share of the companies, represent the innovations and inventions that have emerged.

In R&D-based growth models, firms include expenditures, research and development expenditures determined by their price-determining role in monopolistic competition market conditions. As a result, the innovative firm that has the final market power of R&D activity will continue to spend on R&D with the demand for new inventions and innovations due to the limited market power, as it can make mark-up pricing (Tuluce and Yurtkur 2015). The continuation of the profit potential will lead to the emergence of new profit opportunities as an incentive for R&D expenditure (Aghion and Howitt 1998: 79–80). With Schumpeter's point of view, Schumpeter has argued that entrepreneurs contribute to economic growth by creating innovations in the face of competition (Schumpeter 1934, 1942).

In fact, many of the arguments favoring policies to increase the level and efficiency of R&D are based on assumptions that there is a close link between R&D investment and microeconomic and macroeconomic performance (Mitchell 1999; Kafouros 2008). Technological improvements and innovations result in exogenously that cause economic growth in the long run, leading to an increase in the overall economy (Jones, 1998: 73–78). Promoting institutional R&D activities, not only in terms of productivity growth but also in terms of profitability, sales, employment growth, competition and socio-economic well-being, brings with it micro and macro convergence (Griliches 1994; Hall et al. 2010; Moncada-Patern-ò-Castello 2016).

In this context, it can be said that R&D expenditure is an important innovation input. Research and development intensity is expressed as an indicator of the proportion of R&D expenditure in GDP and the relative investment level that an economy uses to generate new information. R&D intensity can also be considered as one of the indicators adopted as a goal in terms of political decision-making processes and public financing. In addition, since R&D intensity indicates the concentration ratio of countries to R&D expenditures, R&D expenditures of countries can allow for evaluated more healthily. R&D intensity in OECD countries average is 2.3% (OECD 2011).

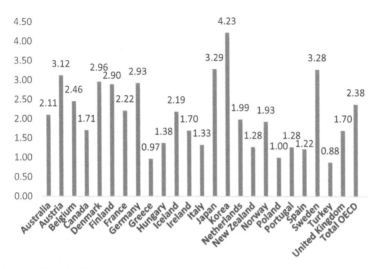

Fig. 1 R&D Share in GDP. Source: www.oecd.org, 22.09.2017

Figure 1 shows the ratio of R&D expenditures to GDP in 2015 by the 24 OECD countries making up the sample of the study. As of 2015, Korea has become the country that has the largest share of GDP in R&D. Korea has been promoted to a high-income country class by getting rid of the middle-income trap with the acceleration that it has caught with R&D. In turn, Korea is followed by Japan, Sweden, and Austria. Greece, Turkey and Poland are the countries with the least share.

In the continuation of the work, theoretical explanations and macroeconomic modeling of the subject are being made. Then, the literature, which is composed of studies that examine this relationship, is mentioned in detail, especially the work done for OECD countries. Then the study continues with the empirical part and is concluded with the result part.

2   Ar-GE Based Endogenous Growth Models

Neoclassical growth theories have shown that technology has a significant share in the economy, but they cannot explain the technology within the model and have accepted it as exogenous. The technological factor, which cannot be explained by the growth theory of Solow (1956), is explained by the development of endogenous growth theories within the framework of Romer (1994). Lucas (1988) will in the manner contributing to the development of endogenous growth theories than evaluates the difference between endogenous growth theories and neoclassical growth theories in two point. The first point that is emphasizing is that growth is not a result of the forces that affect the system from the outside, but a product of the in-model elements. The second point is that technological development is not exogenous, and it is in the economic system.

Within the economic growth activities, the importance given to these activities has begun to develop since the 1980s. It is theories that argue that endogenously growth theories, technological developments, and human capital are the main determinants of growth. In the endogenously growth models emerging by determining the variables such as knowledge, human capital, R&D and technological development in the system itself, both new products and efficient production methods are emerging. This process contributes to the R&D activities, which are made possible by the human capital created by the expenditures made in education, health and technology, and some features in the economy (Palley 1996: 124–125). In this context, R&D activities among the working models are the work of the Romer (1990) which develops the growth model based on R&D, emphasizing the importance of growth. Earlier, in studies dealing with the relationship between R&D activities and economic efficiency, from a Cobb-Douglas production function was acted upon (Griliches 1979; Griliches and Lichtenberg 1984).

R&D-driven growth models have become important together with insufficient capital accumulation in the explanation of long-term growth and endogenous technological knowledge in explaining technological developments. In these models, technological developments are dealt with as a result of individuals seeking new knowledge, with the thought of getting a share of the profit generated by the creation of new creative ideas (Aghion and Howitt 2009: 226–233). In the R&D-based endogenous growth models, the R&D sector contributes to growth through increased returns created by creating externalities. The basis of Romer (1990) model is R&D activities, human capital and new ideas and methods produced in the sector. In the Solow model, technological developments considered exogenously are endogenous. This endogenous situation is making researchers who are interested in profit making and are in search of new ideas. Jones (2002), for example, considers variables such as health expenditure and lifetime as endogenous variables driven by technological advances (Jones 2002: 32). Technological development is driven by advanced R&D activities in the world (Jones and Vollrath 2013: 99).

In the Romer model, technological change has two basic elements. The total production function in the model is as in Eq. (1):

$$Y = K^{\alpha} (AL_Y)^{1-\alpha} \qquad (1)$$

K, capital stock; L_Y, the amount of labor used to produce the output; Y, the amount of output produced A shows the creative idea stock used. α is a parameter changing between 0 and 1. For the given technology level (A), the production function exhibits constant return characteristics on a scale relative to the K and L_Y variables (Jones and Vollrath 2013: 99–107). However, the creative idea is that when A is accepted as an input in production, there are increasing returns to the scale. The doubling of labor, capital and creative idea stock in the new production function will lead to an increase in production of two quarters (Jones 2001: 92).

The capital will be abandoned by the people in the society to cautious from consumption at the rate of s_k and will be extinguished by the accumulation to the exogenous δ ratio. The labor equivalent to the population grows exponentially in an exogenous and constant manner, such as n (Jones 2001: 93). Definitions of capital and labor are defined in the model as the same as the Solow growth model and as shown in Eqs. (2 and 3) (Jones and Vollrath 2013: 100–104).

$$K = s_k Y - \delta K. \tag{2}$$
$$L/L = n \tag{3}$$
$$\dot{A} = \theta L_A \tag{4}$$

In the Romer model, the growth in A is endogenous. $\dot{A}$ represents the number of new creative ideas generated by time, θ represents the rate of R&D to create new ideas, and L_A represents the amount of labor used to search for new ideas. A in Eq. (4); equal to the number of people who are trying to produce new creative ideas (L_A) multiplied by the new creative idea generation rate (θ). If $\theta > 0$, then A is the increasing function. The efficiency of research with newly discovered ideas increases, that is, past ideas increase the efficiency of current research. $\theta < 0$, it represents a difficult rising situation. $\theta = 0$ means that the efficiency of the research is independent of the information stock.

If the number of people seeking new ideas is a factor that affects the average productivity of the research, the overall production function is as follows:

$$\dot{A} = \theta L_A{}^\lambda A^\phi \tag{5}$$

L_A, represents new ideas that enter the production function. In other words, LA is used instead of L to represent new creative ideas. It is a parameter between λ, 0 and 1. A^ϕ, indicates that the individual agent is taken as exogenously. It is possible to see how the resource allocation of the resources is done, namely the resource constraint, from the following Eq. (6). Equality means that it is necessary to decide how much of labor is to be used to produce output and how much to use to produce ideas.

$$L_Y + L_A = L. \tag{6}$$

Romer (1990) says that the growth model will be a continuous growth in the presence of the continuous research effort with the assumption of $\lambda = 1$ and $\varphi = 1$. This can be illustrated in Eq. (7):

$$\dot{A}/A = \theta L_A \tag{7}$$

Acting on the assumption that it is a fixed fraction, it can be expressed by $L_A/L = S_R$. S_R is the part of the labor that is separated from R&D to produce new ideas, and $1 - S_R$ is the part of the work that is devoted to output.

In the Fig. 2, if the technological development is taking place while the economy is in the beginning balance, the change that is happening is shown. An increase in S_R, which is part of the R&D part of labor, will increase L_A/A and a higher growth rate will be achieved by researchers producing new ideas. A growing number of additional researchers are generating new ideas and the growth rate of technology is higher at this point. This point corresponds to point x. At point X, the technological

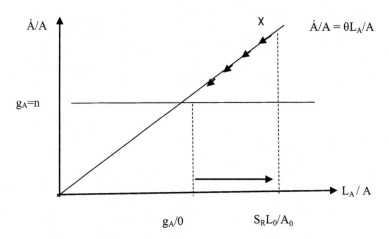

Fig. 2 Technological progress: an increase in R&D share

progress ($\dot{A}/A$) exceeds population growth (n), therefore the L_A/A ratio will decrease over time as shown by arrows. This decline will continue gradually until the economy returns to its former stable growth point ($g_A = n$). As a result, the share of population growth in R&D temporarily increases technological progress and this effect does not occur in the long run (Jones and Volrath 2013: 109). This is explained by Jones (1998): The continuous increase of the growth process takes place with the continuous increase of the population. More researchers will mean constant growth in the model. However, even in the models in which technological progress has been dealt with endogenously, the long-term growth is not affected by the increase in the labor force employed in R&D. Because everyone who is in the economy benefits from these ideas because new ideas of technological progress are not competitive. In the early periods, the rate of increase in stock rate with new ideas starts to fall over time. In fact, technology does not stop at all, but every new 100 creative idea stock becomes less visible in stock than it accumulates and be reduced.

Technology quality is constantly increasing because there is a steady increase in R&D. In the Romer (1990) model this stable increase is defined as a permanent increase in the rate of S_R, that is, the fraction of labor devoted to R&D to generate new ideas. The continuous increase in technology level can be shown as follows Fig. 3 (Jones and Volrath 2013: 110).

In the model of Grossman and Helpman (1991), while the sources of growth are examined are moving from two sources. The first of these sources is expressed as the increase in the diversity and quality of new products, which are the result of technological improvements. The second is specified as information, which is a feature of the public goods. In the model which focuses on product innovations, it is aimed to increase the qualifications of existing products or to increase the product variety by means of consuming these products and to help them to benefit from economic growth. The fact that the information is in the nature of public property

Fig. 3 The level of
technology over time

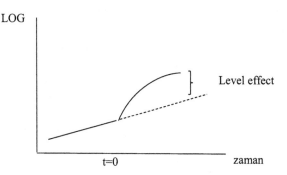

gives the properties of being non-crowding out and non-competitive. Thus, technological innovations contribute to the economic growth process, spreading through
information flows between sectors and producers. (Grossman and Helpman 1994:
31). The social return ratios of R&D expenditures considerably exceed special return
ratios. Mansfield et al. (1977) support that resources expenditure on commercial
research can be productive, especially when producing new output. Studies by
Bresnahan (1986) and Trajtenberg (1990) are among the studies supporting this
situation. Aghion and Howitt (1992) developed a model that explains effects of
technological innovations on economic growth based on the creative destruction
process, starting from Schumpeter's view of creative destruction. Each innovation
has its vision of being able to produce the final output more efficiently than before.
The endogenous growth literature involves industrial innovations that increase
product quality, which is not considered much. In the model, the process of contributing to growth by accumulating R&D expenditures, or physical or human
capital, affecting the ratio of innovations on output will work.

3 Review of Related Literature

Economic growth process is explained in the framework of Neoclassical growth
model developed by Solow and Swan in 1956. In the process up to the 1980s,
economic growth has been assessed in this context. Romer (1986) and Lucas (1988)
considered technology as an important variable that has an impact on economic
growth. Thus, endogenous growth models have become known as models in which
technological innovations realized through R&D investments are regarded as a
source of economic growth (Jones 1995: 759). Trajtenberg (1990) expresses that
research and development investments are one of the key strategies to protect the
potential of technology. The discovery of R&D activities in terms of economic
growth has led to the creation of various policies to support these activities and the
promotion of R&D investments (Goel and Ram 1994).

The contribution or effect of R&D to economic growth is revealed in two different studies in the literature. These studies can be evaluated in both the case studies on the historical dimension and the econometric methods of researching the production functions that are included in the R&D variable. A number of detailed case studies of specific innovations have been carried out that trace the outcomes that will emerge later on. Griliches (1958), Mansfield et al. (1977), and Griliches (1973) are examples of case studies. Because case studies are costly in terms of time and tend to focus on specific areas of success, it is difficult to achieve a clear conclusion on the basis of these studies in general. The econometric production function approach focuses on total output or total factor productivity as a function of R&D investments in the past, rather than the interesting details of case studies. The overall productivity increase in this area is due to expenditures on R&D (Griliches 1979: 92–93).

The literature is highly enriched in terms of studies investigating the relationship between these two important variables. These studies differ in terms of selected econometric methods, the selected country or group of countries and the findings obtained. OECD organization represents an association formed in order to obtain a certain level of economic and social prosperity in terms of the member countries. Member States serve to assist and guide each other when they face any problem and to contribute to the development process of the countries in the development path, as an accelerator. Researches that are important for OECD countries are important in the literature, as regards R&D investments and growth, which are considered important for countries in the development path.

It has become possible to identify the effects of R&D investments on a country, with the theoretical demonstration that the trade partners of R&D investments in a country affect the total factor productivity. The Coe and Helpman (1993) study, suggests that R&D expenditures for 22 OECD countries help explain the growth in total factor productivity. In the survey, it was found that one fourth of the R&D investments were made by commercial partners. Porter and Stern (2000) investigated the ideal parameters for economic growth models for 17 OECD countries during 1973–1993. The number of patents in the study was identified as the technological variable used as an R&D input and affecting economic growth, and this study has been among the pioneering studies in this area.

In the literature from the beginning of the 2000s, the number of studies investigating this relationship for the OECD countries has started to increase rapidly. Freire-Seren (2001) investigated how R&D expenditures affect productivity growth. In the study, it was determined that the increase in total R&D expenditures increased the gross domestic product. It also emphasized the importance of encouraging research and development investments and said that these investments will have more impact on growth through capital increase. Guellec and Potterie (2001) investigated the long-term spillover effect of R&D expenditures during 1980–1998 using panel regression. Sylwester (2001) investigated the same relationship using data from 1989 to 1996 for 20 OECD countries, but could not identify any relationship. However, when researching for the same G7 countries during the 1989–1999 period, research results showed a positive effect between these two variables. Keller

(2002) is among the studies linking R&D and production efficiency. In the study conducted for the period of 1970–1991 for 8 OECD countries, 20% of the R&D efficiency levels are due to international R & D spillovers and 80% are due to domestic R&D.

Zachariadis (2004) investigated the effect of R&D expenditure growth in 10 OECD countries on economic growth and found that the increase in R&D expenditures positively affected the increase in productivity growth and output in the OECD country in its study covering the period 1971–1995. Ulku (2004) studied the same relationship for OECD countries, covering the period 1981–1997 with GMM model. The results are a support provider for endogenous growth models. Falk (2007) the dynamic panel data model explored the relationship between R&D investments and economic growth during the 1970–2004 period for 15 OECD countries. Findings show that R&D investments in GDP increases, per capita GDP is increases and supports the focus on R&D investments. Wang (2007) countries using 30 countries' data (23 of which are OECD members; 7 are non-OECD countries) indicate that countries using R&D expenditures effectively will achieve better economic growth performance. Studies conducted by Özer and Çiftçi (2008), Saraç (2009), Eid (2012), Gülmez and Yardımcıoglu (2012), Güloğlu and Tekin (2012) and Özcan and Arı (2014) constitute other studies of similar analyzes for OECD countries. All of these studies have been supporting this significant relationship.

In addition, studies on the same relationship for different countries or groups of countries are found in the literature. There are also studies in which studies have not established any relationship as there is a large number of studies showing that there is a long-run causality relationship between R&D and growth and that R&D expenditures are the cause of growth. Lichtenberg (1992), Goel and Ram (1994), Coe and Helpman (1995), Griliches (1998), Bilbao-Osorio and Rodriguez-Peso (2004), Goel et al. (2008), Sadraoui and Zina (2009), Samimi and Alerasoul (2009), Altın and Kaya (2009), Yaylalı et al. (2010), Korkmaz (2010), Alene (2010), Genç and Atasoy (2010), Horvath (2011), Kirankabeş and Erçakar (2012), Gülmez and Akpolat (2014) and Dam and Yıldız (2016) studies are among these studies.

4   Empirical Analysis

Today, in the economic sense, countries are getting closer and interacting with each other. This causes the classical approaches that claim shocks affect groups of countries of the same size to lose significance. Classical approaches are replaced by new statistical methods that will overcome the shortcomings of the more innovative and classical approach. Particularly in the stacked data set in which the feedback case was searched, the causality relation was based on the assumption that the null hypothesis was not causally tested and that autoregressive parameters did not change over the entire cross section. So the fact that a variable in a stacked data set is the basis for the other variable and that the causality can be located in any section of the stacked data (Granger 2003), may be stronger than the null hypothesis testing.

In the study with this thought, the causality relation is taken into account in the context of heterogeneity. Moreover, the fact that heterogeneity is not taken into consideration with the assumption that the coefficients are constant along the cross section in the causality relation leads to the heterogeneity deviation as expressed by Peseran and Smith (1995). This means that the estimators obtained are inconsistent. Therefore, the fact that this effect is not taken into account causes different findings to appear in the literature. Similar structure studies Holtz-Eakin et al. (1988) study, in which the constant term is inter-sectional, Hurlin (2005, 2008) studies, which allow heterogeneity of autoregressive parameters, Hurlin and Venet (2003, 2008) causality tests can be shown as a pioneer. In this study, the causality test without the mean group estimator cointegration vector mentioned in the Pedroni (2001, 2007) studies with the assumption that both the constant term and the coefficient parameter change along the section is estimated in the standard Granger format as in Eq. (8).[1]

$$
\begin{aligned}
\Delta R\&D_{jt} &= \alpha_j + \sum_{i=1}^{n}\sum_{j=1}^{m} \gamma_{ji} \Delta R\&D_{jt-i} + \sum_{i=1}^{n}\sum_{j=1}^{m} \delta_{ji} Growth_{jt-i} + \varepsilon_{jt} \\
\Delta Growth_{jt} &= \beta_j + \sum_{i=1}^{n}\sum_{j=1}^{m} \phi_{ji} \Delta R\&D_{jt-i} + \sum_{i=1}^{n}\sum_{j=1}^{m} \varphi_{ji} Growth_{jt-i} + \varepsilon_{jt}
\end{aligned} \tag{8}
$$

Growth and research and development variables in Eq. (8) are in a static structure, and for countries γ_{ji} and φ_{ji} degree from i autoregression parameters, the parameters δ_{ji} and ϕ_{ji} indicate the coefficient parameters. In the case of an assumption of $\gamma_{ab,ij} \sim N(\overline{\gamma}_{ab,j}, v_{ab,j}); a, b = 1, 2, \ldots, n)$ for the coefficient parameters, the principal diagonal element values in the variance covariance matrix are not constant across the cross-section, but are heterogeneous. In the estimation of $\overline{\gamma}_{ab,j}$ parameter Pesaran and Smith (1995) used the mean group estimator (MGE) which allowed heterogeneity.[2] The average group estimator for the coefficient parameters is obtained as $\hat{\overline{\gamma}}_{ab,j}^{MG} = N^{-1} \sum_{i=1}^{N} \hat{\gamma}_{ab,ij}$. MGE is a estimator of consistent and asymptotic distribution predicted by least square (LS) for each section (Hsiao et al. 1989). The mean group estimator for the variance values of the coefficient parameters is estimated as $\hat{v}_{ab,j}^{MG} = (N-1)^{-1} \sum_{i=1}^{N} \left(\hat{\gamma}_{ab,ij} - \hat{\overline{\gamma}}_{ab,j}^{MG} \right)^2$. The heterogeneity causality test is obtained by comparing the Wald statistic value obtained from the test of the null hypothesis involving $\overline{\gamma}_{ab,j} = 0$ hypothesis for each section with the critical value in the chronological degree of freedom at the lag length n. For the whole cross section, causality results are obtained by limiting the coefficient parameters to

---

[1] The WinRATS 9.1 SWEEP referral was used for the test procedure related to the assumption that parameters and variances were cross-specific.

[2] For the corresponding estimator, Swamy (1970) and Hsiao et al. (1989), the GLS method is the preferred alternative method.

the lag length of n and by comparing the values of the N*n degrees of freedom with the value of the square table. The covariance in Eq. (8) needs to be checked to see if the variables used in the estimation of a stationary PVAR model return to their post-shock averages. Also Breusch and Pagan (1980), Pesaran (2004), and Pesaran et al. (2008) proposes to check whether the covariance between error terms has changed. Relevant tests vary by time and cross-sectional size. Therefore, considering cross-sectional dependency will affect unit root test results and heterogeneous panel causality test results (O'Connel 1998). The null hypothesis that there is no horizontal section dependency $Cov(u_{ij}, u_{jt}) = 0$ is being tested against the alternative hypothesis, by comparison with $LM = T \sum\limits_{t=1}^{N-1} \sum\limits_{j=i+1}^{N} \rho_{ij}^2$ statistic and the critical value at the $\chi_{(n^2-n)/2}^2$ degree of freedom. The corresponding test statistic is valid if the time dimension is greater than the cross-sectional dimension. Other horizontal section dependency tests are CDLM and adjusted CD tests recommended by Peseran. The relevant test statistics are given as

$$CD_{lm} = \sqrt{T/N(N-1)} \sum_{t=1}^{N-1} \sum_{j=i+1}^{N} \rho_{ij}^2, \quad CD_{adj} = \sqrt{2T/N(N-1)} \sum_{t=1}^{N-1} \sum_{j=i+1}^{N} \left(T\rho_{ij}^2 - 1 \right)$$

and $\quad LM_{adj} = \sqrt{2/N(N-1)} \sum\limits_{t=1}^{N-1} \sum\limits_{j=i+1}^{N} (\rho_{ij}) \dfrac{(T-k-1)\rho_{ij}^2 - \mu_{Tij}}{V_{Tij}} \quad$ respectively.

Adjusted LM statistical normal distribution is an appropriate statistical value. Levin, Lin and Chu (LLC) and Im, Peseran, Shin (IPS) panel unit root tests were used for stationarity of all variables in Eq. (8). LLC (2002) Panel Unit Root Test assumes that all individuals in the panel are partially autocorrelated from the first order, but that the horizontal dimension of all other deterministic components of the model allows variation between cross-sections (Herwartz and Siedenburg 2008: 143). LLC (2002) panel unit root test is based on the assumption that horizontal section independence, stationary effects change horizontal section from horizontal section and δ_i coefficient is homogenous for all horizontal sections in the panel data set.

$$\Delta Y_{i,t} = \alpha_i + \rho Y_{i,t-1} + \sum_{k=1}^{n} \phi_k \Delta Y_{i,t-k} + \lambda_i t + \delta_t + \varepsilon_{it} \qquad (9)$$

Shown here as i = 1, . . ., N and t = 1, . . ., T.

In Eq. (9), each individual has observed the year t stochastic process i = 1, 2, . . ., N for individual panel $Y_{i,t}$ stochastic process observed to include the time series t = 1, 2, . . ., T. When it is desired to determine whether there is a unit root at $Y_{i,t}$; for each individual in the panel it is assumed that all individuals in the panel have first-degree partial autocorrelation, but that other parameters in the error process are allowed to vary throughout the individual (Levin et al. 2002: 4). In the LLC test, there is a common unit root and the null hypothesis is tested. This method requires the determination of the kernel density and the lag numbers used in each horizontal section ADF regression.

The IPS assumes that the δi coefficient in the LLC test is homogeneous for all horizontal sections in the panel data set as the weakness of the LLC test. In the IPS test, the LLC test was extended to ensure that the δi coefficient is heterogeneous for all horizontal sections in the panel data set. In the IPS test is it being tested that, the null hypothesis tests that each horizontal section contains a unit root (H0: δi = 0) and the alternative hypothesis tests that at least one horizontal section does not contain a unit root (H1: δi < 0) 225). The IPS test is an expanded form of the LLC test and provides heterogeneity in short-term dynamics (Osbat 2004: 35). The most important feature of the IPS test is to apply a separate unit root test to the time series for all units instead of combining the data and IPS Panel Unit Root Test Statistic is a mean of all individual ADF test statistics (Tatoğlu 2012: 212).

5   Data Set Identification and Evaluation of Test Results

In this study, heterogeneous causality test between Ar-GE and Growth is being investigated. The dataset used is annual frequency and covers 24 OECD countries for 1990–2015. Logarithmic transformation is applied to the variables in the model and the related variables are expressed in terms of purchasing power. Horizontal cross-section dependence and panel unit root tests must be performed before the heterogeneity causality test can be performed (Table 1).

Due to the presence of deterministic trends in the variables, test results are taken into account according to the fixed and trending models. Accordingly, all variables used in Eq. (8) are stationary in the first difference and also have cross sectional dependency.

Following the unit root test and cross sectional dependency test, causality test results are discussed. The PVAR model in Eq. (8) is estimated for 5 lags, and five degrees of freedom for each cross section will be considered. For all of the panel chi-square degree of freedom is 120 and the test results are listed in Table 2.

Table 1 Panel unit root test results and cross-section dependency

	LLC panel unit root test results				IPS panel unit root test results			
	Constant	Prob	Constant + Trend	Prob	Constant	Prob	Constant + Trend	Prob
R&D	−4.00968	0.0000	1.50216	0.9335	2.17375	0.9851	−0.95353	0.1702
ΔR&D	−6.88661	0.0000	−8.02713	0.0000	−9.07204	0.0000	−9.73443	0.0000
Growth	−5.57545	0.0000	0.12264	0.5488	−0.16991	0.4325	2.53392	0.9944
ΔGrowth	−11.2505	0.0000	−7.54369	0.0000	−11.1472	0.0000	−8.11035	0.0000
Cross-section dependency								
LM	2175.805	0.0000						
CDLM	79.83955	0.0000						
CDLM1	73.17806	0.0000						
LMadj	8.061199	0.0000						

Table 2 Heterogeneous non-causality test results in heterogeneous panel

Countries	$H_0 : R\&D \neq Growth$		$H_0 : Growth \neq R\&D$	
	χ_5^2 statistics	Prob.	χ_5^2 statistics	Prob.
_AUS	10.4460	0.0635	3.1420	0.6781
_AUST	10.8950	0.0535	11.6480	0.0399
_BEL	12.0890	0.0336	6.9870	0.2216
_CAN	23.4380	0.0003	24.0790	0.0002
_DEN	7.4300	0.1906	31.1380	0.0000
_FIN	16.6320	0.0053	5.5650	0.3509
_FRA	4.4280	0.4896	6.1870	0.2885
_GERM	10.2140	0.0694	16.4900	0.0056
_GREEC	9.8020	0.0810	19.1350	0.0018
_HUNG	13.9250	0.0161	2.0830	0.8375
_ICELAND	3.1600	0.6754	22.6190	0.0004
_IRELAND	13.8820	0.0164	23.6800	0.0003
_ITA	10.8820	0.0538	16.6120	0.0053
_JAP	29.3270	0.0000	1.5540	0.9068
_KOR	12.4000	0.0296	21.0410	0.0008
_NETH	1.5280	0.9098	11.8500	0.0369
_NEW	20.9640	0.0008	16.3750	0.0059
_NORW	35.6880	0.0000	12.6350	0.0271
_POL	9.1770	0.1022	16.5570	0.0054
_POR	13.6510	0.0180	8.9530	0.1110
_SPAIN	16.6160	0.0053	14.3700	0.0134
_SWEE	11.4520	0.0431	12.2940	0.0310
_TUR	18.2130	0.0027	2.6470	0.7542
_UK	9.6160	0.0869	20.2360	0.0011
ALL	389.5808	0.0000	460.4832	0.0000

According to the test results, there is a two-way causality relation in the entire panel, also there exists at least one individual causality relationships in overall panel. If the results of the causality test will be evaluated in a cross-specific manner, it is observed that there is a causality relation between R&D and growth in all country groups except Denmark, France, Iceland, Netherlands, Poland. For all countries, growth is the cause of R&D expenditures result is reached except for Australia, Belgium, Finland, France, Hungary, Japan, Portugal and Turkey.

6 Conclusion

In the present economic system it experienced rapid technological developments, as well variables such as human capital or physical capital, as well as R&D seems to be participant in economic development. The discovery of the different elements that will contribute to economic growth has led countries to contribute to economic growth. In this study, R&D expenditures and economic growth relationship is examined by heterogeneous causality test using panel data model for 24 OECD countries. According to empirical results, research development and economic growth are in causality relation in the sample of the studied countries. Denmark, France, Iceland, the Netherlands, Poland are out of this. Also the result is reached the growth is the cause of R&D expenditures in all countries. Australia, Belgium, Finland, France, Hungary, Japan, Portugal and Turkey are out of this. Although causality relationship differs from country to country, findings in the study reveal the existence of an important relationship. In terms of countries with no causality relationship, it can be concluded that research and development expenditure alone is not a source of economic growth.

Key Words Definitions

Research and Development (R&D) It is a creative effort based on a systematic basis in order to increase research and development scientific and technical know-how and the use of this knowledge in new applications

Economic Growth A country, increasing the amount of scarce resources owned or limit the expansion of the production facilities by improving their quality. Or a country has to change its production technology to reach higher production levels.

Heterogeneous Panel Causality The assumption that both the constant term and the coefficient parameter change throughout the panel section.

OECD Countries Austria, Australia, Belgium, Canada, Denmark, Finland, France, Germany, Greece, Hungary, İceland, İreland, Italy, Japan, Korea, Netherlands, New Zeland, Norway, Poland, Portugal, Spain, Sweden, Turkey, England.

References

Aghio, P., & Howitt, P. (1992). A model of growth through creative destruction. *Econometrica, 60*, 323–331.
Aghio, P., & Howitt, P. (1998). *Endogenous Growth Theory*. Cambridge, MA: MIT Press.
Aghio, P., & Howitt, P. (2009). *The economics of growth*. London: Massachusetts Institute of Technology.
Alene, A. D. (2010). Productivity growth and the effects of R&D in African agriculture. *Agricultural Economics, 41*, 223–238.
Altın, O., & Kaya, A. (2009). Türkiye'de Ar-Ge harcamaları ve ekonomik büyüme arasındaki nedensel ilişkinin analizi. *Ege Akademik Bakış, 9*, 251–259.
Bilbao-Osorio, B., & Rodriguez-Peso, A. (2004). From R&D to innovation and economic growth in the EU. *Growth and Change, 35*, 434–455.
Bresnahan, T. (1986). Measuring the spillovers from technical advance: mainframe computers in financial services. *American Economic Review, 76*, 742–755.

Breusch, T., & Pagan, A. (1980). The lagrange multiplier test and its application to model specifications in econometrics. *Reviews of Economics Studies, 47,* 239–253.

Coccia, M. (2008). Science, funding and economic growth: analysis and science policy implications. *World Review of Science, Technology and Sustainable Development, 5,* 1–27.

Coe, D., & Helpman, E. (1993). *International R&D spillovers.* The Foerder Institute for Economic Research, Working Paper No. 5-93.

Coe, D. T., & Helpman, E. (1995). International R&D spillovers. *European Economic Review, 39,* 859–887.

Dam, M. M., & Yıldız, B. (2016). Impact of R&D and innovation on economic growth at BRICS-TM countries: An econometric analysis. *Journal of Akdeniz İİBF, 33,* 220–236.

DeLong, S. B., & Summers, L. H. (2001). *The new economy: background, questions and speculations.* Federal Reserve Bank of Kansas City: *Economic Policies for the Information Age.*

Eid, A. (2012). Higher education R&D and productivity growth: An empirical study on high-income OECD countries. *Education Economics, 20*(1), 53–68.

Falk, M. (2007). R&D spending in the high-tech sector and economic growth. *Research in Economics, 61,* 140–147.

Freire-Seren, M. J. (2001). R&D expenditure in an endogenous economic growth. *Journal of Economics, 74*(1), 39–62.

Genç, A. C., & Atasoy, Y. (2010). The relationship between R&D expenditures and economic growth: Panel data analysis. *The Journal of Knowledge Economy and Knowledge Management, 5,* 27–34.

Goel, R. K., & Ram, R. (1994). Research and development expenditures and economic growth: A cross country study. *Economic Development and Cultural Change, 42,* 403–411.

Goel, R. K., Payne, J. E., & Ram, R. (2008). R&D expenditures and US economic growth: A disaggregated approach. *Journal of Policy Modeling, 30,* 237–250.

Granger, C. W. J. (2003). Some aspects of causal relationships. *Journal of Econometrics, 112,* 69–71.

Griliches, Z. (1958). Research costs and social returns: Hybrid corn and related innovations. *Journal of Political Economy, 66,* 419–437.

Griliches, Z. (1973). Research expenditures and growth accounting. In B. R. Williams (Ed.), *Science and technology in economic growth* (pp. 59–95). London: Palgrave Macmillan.

Griliches, Z. (1979). Issues in assessing the contribution of research and development to productivity growth. *The Bell Journal of Economics,* 92–116.

Griliches, Z. (1994). Productivity, R&D, and the data constraint. *The American Economic Review, 84*(1), 1–23.

Griliches, Z. (1998). Productivity, R&D, and the data constraint. In Z. Griliches (Ed.), *R&D and productivity: The econometric evidence* (pp. 347–374). Chicago: University of Chicago Press.

Griliches, Z., & Lichtenberg, F. (1984). Interindustry technology flows and productivity growth: A reexamination. *The Review of Economics and Statistics, 66,* 324–329.

Grossman, G. M., & Helpman, E. (1991). *Innovation and growth in the global economy.* Cambridge, MA: MIT Press.

Grossman, G. M., & Helpman, E. (1994). Endogenous innovation in the theory of growth. *The Journal of Economic Perspectives, 8*(1), 23–44.

Guellec, D. & Potterie, B.P. (2001). R&D and productivity growth: Panel data analysis of 16 OECD countries. *OECD Economic Studies,* No. 33, 2001/II, 103–126.

Gülmez, A., & Akpolat, A. G. (2014). Research & development, innovation and economic growth: A dynamic panel analysis for Turkey and European Union. *The Journal of AİBU Social Science Institute, 14*(2), 1–17.

Gülmez, A., & Yardımcıoğlu, F. (2012). R&D expenditure and economic growth in OECD countries: Panel cointegration and panel causality analysis (1990-2010). *Finance Magazine, 163.*

Güloğlu, B., & Tekin, B. R. (2012). A panel causality of the relationship among research and development, innovation and economic growth in high income OECD countries. *Euroasian Economic Review, 2*(1), 32–47.

Hall, B. H., Mairesse, J., & Mohnen, P. (2010). Measuring the returns to R&D. In B. H. Hall & N. Rosenberg (Eds.), *Handbook of the economics of innovation* (Vol. 2, pp. 1033–1082). Amsterdam: North-Holland.

Herwartz, H., & Siedenburg, F. (2008). Homogeneous panel unit root tests under cross sectional dependence: Finite sample modifications and the wild bootstrap. *Computational Statistics & Data Analysis, 53*(1), 137–150.

Holtz-Eakin, D., Newey, W., & Rosen, H. S. (1988). Estimating vector autoregressions with panel data. *Econometrica: Journal of the Econometric Society*, 1371–1395.

Horvath, R. (2011). Research & development and growth: A bayesian model averaging analysis. *Economic Modelling, 28*, 2669–2673.

Hsiao, C., Mountain, D. C., Chan, M. L., & Tsui, K. Y. (1989). Modeling Ontario regional electricity system demand using a mixed fixed and random coefficients approach. *Regional Science and Urban Economics, 19*(4), 565–587.

Hurlin, C. (2005). Granger causality tests in panel data models with fixed coefficients. *Revue Economique, 56*, 1–11.

Hurlin, C. (2008). *Testing for Granger non-causality in heterogeneous panels*. Working Paper, Laboratoire d'Economie d'Orléans, University of Orleans.

Hurlin, C., & Venet, B. (2003). *Granger causality tests in panel data models with fixed coefficients*. Paris, France: Mimeograph, Universitie Paris I.

Hurlin, C., & Venet, B. (2008). *Financial development and growth: A re-examination using a panel Granger causality test*. Working Paper, Laboratoire d'Economie d'Orléans, University of Orleans.

Jones, C. I. (1995). R&D-based models of economic growth. *Journal of Political Economy, 103*(4), 759–784.

Jones, C. I. (1998). *Introduction economic growth*. New York: W. W. Norton & Company Inc..

Jones, C. I. (2001). *Introduction to economic growth* (Ş. Ateş & İ. Tuncer, Trans.). Istanbul: Literature Publications.

Jones, C.I., (2002). *Why health expenditures as a share of GDP risen so much?* NBER Working Papers, 9325.

Jones, C. I., & Vollrath, D. (2013). *Introduction to economic growth* (3rd ed.). New York, London: W. W. Norton & Company.

Kafouros, M. I. (2008). Economic returns to industrial research. *Journal of Business Research, 61* (8), 868–876.

Keller, W. (2002). Trade and the transmission of technology. *Journal of Economic Growth, 7*(1), 5–24.

Kirankabeş, M. C., & Erçakar, M. E. (2012). Importance of relationship between R&D personnel and patent applications on economics growth: A panel data analysis. *International Research Journal of Finance and Economics*, (92), 72–81.

Korkmaz, S. (2010). Analysis of relations between R&D investments and economic growth in Turkey with VAR model. *Journal of Yaşar University, 20*(5), 3320–3330.

Levin, A., Lin, C. F., & Chu, C. S. J. (2002). Unit root tests in panel data: Asymptotic and finite-sample properties. *Journal of Econometrics, 108*(1), 1–24.

Lichtenberg, F. R. (1992). *R&D investment and international productivity differences*. National Bureau of Economic Research, Working Paper No. 4161.

Lucas, R. E. (1988). On mechanism of economic development. *Journal of Monetary Economics, 22* (1), 3–42.

Mansfield, E., Rapoport, J., Romeo, A., Wagner, S., & Beardsley, G. (1977). Social and private rates of return from industrial innovations. *The Quarterly Journal of Economics, 91*(2), 221–240.

Mitchell, G. R. (1999). Global technology policies for economic growth. *Technological Forecasting and Social Change, 60*(3), 205–214.

Moncada-Paternò-Castello, P. (2016). *Corporate R&D intensity decomposition: Theoretical, empirical and policy issues* (No. 2016-02). Institute for Prospective Technological Studies, Joint Research Centre.

Mowery, D. C., & Rosenberg, N. (1989). New developments in US technology policy: Implications for competitiveness and international trade policy. *California Management Review, 32*(1), 107–124.

O'Connel, P. G. J. (1998). The overvaluation of purchasing power parity. *Journal of International Economics, 44*, 1–19.

OECD (2003). ICT and Economic Growth Evidence from OECD Countries, Industries and Firms. http://www.cla.org.pt/docs/OCDE_TIC.PDF

OECD. (2011). Innovation and growth in knowledge economies, science, technology and industry scoreboard. OECD Publishing. doi:https://doi.org/10.1787/sti_scoreboard-2011-en.

Osbat, C. (2004). Panel unit root and panel cointegration methods. *European Central Bank*, 1–84.

Özcan, B., & Arı, A. (2014). The relationship between research & development expenditures and economic growth: Panel data analysis. *Finance Magazine, 166*, 39–55.

Özer, M., & Çiftçi, N. (2008). R&D-based internal growth models and the impact of R&D expenditure on economic growth: OECD countries panel data analysis. *SÜ İİBF Journal of Social and Economic Research, 9*(16), 219–240.

Palley, I. T. (1996). Growth theory in a Keynesian model: Some Keynesian foundations for new endogenous growth theory. *Journal of Post Keynesian Economics, 19*(1), 113–135.

Pedroni, P. (2001). Purchasing power parity tests in cointegrated panels. *The Review of Economics and Statistics, 83*(4), 727–731.

Pedroni, P. (2007). Social capital, barriers to production and capital shares: Implications for the importance of parameter heterogeneity from a nonstationary panel approach. *Journal of Applied Econometrics, 22*(2), 429–451.

Pesaran, M. H. (2004). *General diagnostic tests for cross section dependence in panels*. Cambridge Working Papers in Economics, no. 0435. University of Cambridge.

Pesaran, M. H., & Smith, R. (1995). Estimating long-run relationships from dynamic heterogeneous panels. *Journal of econometrics, 68*(1), 79–113.

Pesaran, M. H., Ullah, A., & Yamagata, T. (2008). A bias-adjusted LM test of error cross-section independence. *The Econometrics Journal, 11*(1), 105–127.

Porter, M. E. & Stern S. (2000). *Measuring the "ideas" production function: evidence from international patent output*. NBER Working Paper, 7891. http://www.nber.org/papers/w7891

Romer, P. M. (1986). Increasing returns and long-run growth. *Journal of Political Economy, 94*(5), 1002–1037.

Romer, P. M. (1990). Endogenous technonogical change. *Journal of Political Economy, 98*(5), 71–102.

Romer, P. M. (1994). The origins of endogenous growth. *Journal of Economic Perspectives, 8*, 3–22.

Sadraoui, T., & Zina, N. B. (2009). Dynamic panel data analysis for R&D cooperation and growth. *International Journal of Foresight and Innovation Policy, 5*(4), 218–233.

Samimi, A. J., & Alerasoul, S. M. (2009). R&D and economic growth: New evidence from some developing countries. *Australian Journal of Basic and Applied Sciences, 3*(4), 3464–3469.

Saraç, B.T. (2009). The impact of research and development expenditures on economic growth: Panel data analysis. *Anadolu international conference in economics*, June 17–19, Eskişehir, Turkey.

Schumpeter, J. A. (1934). *The theory of economic development*. Cambridge, MA: Harvard University Press.

Schumpeter, J. A. (1942). *Capitalism, socialism and democracy*. Cambridge, MA: Harvard University Press.

Schumpeter, J. A. (1949). *The theory of economic development*. Cambridge, MA: Harvard University Press. (German Original 1912)

Solow, R. M. (1956). A contribution to the theory of economic growth. *Quarterly Journal of Economics, 70*, 65–79.

Solow, R. M. (1957). Technical change and the aggregate production function. *Review of Economics and Statistics, 39*, 312–320.

Swamy, P. A. V. B. (1970). Efficient inference in a random coefficient regression model. *Econometrica, 38*, 311–323.

Sylwester, K. (2001). R&D and economic growth. *Knowledge, Technology & Policy, 13*(4), 71–84.

Tatoğlu, F. Y. (2012). *Advanced panel data analysis (stata applied)* (1st ed.). Istanbul: Beta Publication.

Trajtenberg, M. (1990). A penny for your quotes: Patent citations and value of innovations. *The RAND Journal of Economics, 21*(1), 172–187. http://www.jstor.org/stable/2555502.

Tuluce, N. S., & Yurtkur, A. K. (2015). Term of strategic entrepreneurship and Schumpeter's creative destruction theory. *Procedia-Social and Behavioral Sciences, 207*, 720–728.

Ulku, H. (2004). *R&D, innovation, and economic growth: An empirical analysis*. IMF Working Paper, WP/04/185.

Wang, E. C. (2007). R&D efficiency and economic performance: A cross-country analysis using the stochastic frontier approach. *Journal of Policy Modeling, 29*(2), 345–360.

Yaylalı, M., Akan, Y., & Işık, C. (2010). Coentegration and causality between R&D investment expenditures and economic growth in Turkey: 1990-2009. *The Journal of Knowledge Economy & Knowledge Management, V*(II), 13–26.

Zachariadis, M. (2004). R&D-induced growth in the OECD? *Review of Development Economics, 8*(3), 423–439.

Re-define Product and Services Development: A Customer-Centric Perspective in Financial Services

Sinemis Zengin

Abstract Product and services development is the process of designing steps to create or recreate goods or services, and, in today's financial service sector, a customer-centric perspective is the key differentiator for finance providers. Financial services, as a result, have become much more complicated with multiple channels, products, tailor-made solutions, and IT systems; all of which require customer-centric methodologies to further develop these products or services and provide a better understanding of individual customer insights and needs. In this article, design methodologies are introduced.

1 Introduction

The effective development of products or services has become more critical as market competition has increased (Pitta and Pitta 2012). Furthermore, the increasing failure rates of new products have pushed companies to change their product or service development process as less than 50% of new products are successful in financial markets (Cooper and Edgett 1996). These results are caused by market-oriented traditional product and service development rather than customer experience (Kumar 2012). In fact, customer-centric approaches increase the efficiency of the product (Flieb and Kleinaltenkamp 2004). Furthermore, beyond efficiency, well-practiced service is the key element of service quality (Kingman-Brundage 1991).

In today's fast-changing world, customers are the major stakeholders of the firms, and their needs are the essentials of successful service and product design. Clearly, companies must understand the customer's needs (Aho and Uden 2013), and currently there are many methodologies being used: focus groups, surveys, and interviews. However, these techniques are not enough to understand customer insights because they don't give sufficient feedback about products or services not

S. Zengin, Ph.D (✉)
Turkish Economy Bank, Istanbul, Turkey

© Springer International Publishing AG, part of Springer Nature 2018   311
H. Dincer et al. (eds.), *Strategic Design and Innovative Thinking in Business Operations*, Contributions to Management Science,
https://doi.org/10.1007/978-3-319-77622-4_16

yet experienced (Kim et al. 2013). Hence new methodologies are required to understand the customer experience and develop a better product or service.

Current methodologies developed to understand the interaction between product, service, and customer range from drama scenarios, service interface analysis, storyboards, flowcharts, story telling, scripts, personas, and role-plays to experienced prototypes (Meroni and Sangiorgi 2011). Additionally, there are methodologies to measure customer satisfaction: to understand what customers say, how they feel, and the problems they are facing (Reichheld 2011). Yet, there are still difficulties in fully understanding the customer experience and putting it into an explainable scheme.

Design methodologies in business help designers visualize a customer's experience and provide feedback to product or service managers (Voss et al. 2008). Additionally, a customer-centric approach in design methodology helps organizations to identify issues not seen in analytics research (Reason et al. 2016), while remaining simple to apply and understand.

The aim of this paper is to provide new a customer-centric perspective product or service design methodology based on customer experience. The first part of the paper highlights the importance of a customer-centric perspective, while additional traditional product and service development methodologies are introduced to present the differences between two approaches. The second part of the paper—design methodologies—provides research into literature to identify methodologies applied and usage reasoning. The third part of the paper will focus on design methodologies that help organizations to identify customer needs, behaviors, actions, touch points and pain points using the customer experience.

2 Service and Product Development

2.1 The Importance of a Customer-Centric Perspective

Nowadays, the satisfaction of a customer or end user plays a vital role in business and organizational success. Today, product and services should be designed based on a customer's needs rather than the internal needs of the business. Innovation requires more than developing new ideas but comes with creative and well-established customer-centric perspective approaches. Hence, innovative product and service development requires a broader scope of analysis than traditional developmental steps. As stated by Kumar (2012), most innovative companies apply four common principles for innovation:

1. Building innovation on experiences: the first step in innovation is to understand the customer. Firms need to build their product or services understanding of customer usage, activities, needs, and motivations—beyond just organizational needs.
2. Thinking of innovation as a system: A new product or service is one part of the financial firm, so a new product or service should be compatible with a financial firm' offerings, organizations, and markets.

3. Cultivating an innovative culture: Innovative products and services are a result of an organizational culture. Every level in an organization requires injecting a customer-centric perspective into their daily activities.
4. Adopting a disciplined innovation process: Innovative product or service design needs to use well-developed processes, repeatable methods, and well-developed management.

Successful customer-centric methodologies involve listening to customers with a systematic approach since customer feedback supplies information about a customer's experience with an organization. Watkinson (2013) defines customer experiences as a qualitative aspect of all interactions that individuals have with firms and its product or services. Additionally, (Tseng et al. 1999) described customer experience as a service experience of a customer with their contacts (touch points) between a customer and an organization. Better customer experiences increase customer satisfaction and sales; moreover, customers who have high satisfaction scores are willing to pay higher prices—hence, customer profitability increases (Reichheld 2011). Additionally, higher customer satisfaction affects the decision-making process since the decision-making process, specifically at the point of the purchase, *is* the moment of truth (Löfgren et al. 2008).

Still, the customer experience and the moment of truth are subjective and depend on the customer. Organizations need to define their target customer or persona, a composite sketch of a key segment of your audience, in order to visualize a group of customers that share the same ideas, behaviors, needs and lifestyle (Luchs et al. 2016).

2.2   Product and Service Development

Product or service development, critical business activity, and long-term organizational success depend on successful products or services. Efficient product or service development provides a competitive advantage and increases market share. Nevertheless, in a competitive market, the new product failure rate is high (Hanna et al. 1995) due to traditional product and service development, which limits understanding of customer insights. So, even though the main purpose of product or service creation is to offer new or additional benefits to the customer, organizations also use new product development to decrease risk (Pitta and Pitta 2012). A main difference between traditional product or service development and a customer-centric approach is that idea generation starts with product managers, market insight, or organizational needs; whereas, in the customer-centric approach, ideas start with customer insight or needs.

Table 1 Summarize some of the product and service development approaches—in most of the models, the first step of the traditional product or service development is idea generation.

Table 1 Product or service development approaches

Handfield and Lawson (2007) defines the new product development process in five phases	1. Idea generation: the voice of the customer 2. Business or technical assessment 3. Product or process service concept development 4. Product or process service engineering and design 5. Prototype build, test, and pilot/ramp-up for operations
Cooper and Edgett (1996) define the stage gate approach, which help organizations to manage product development as a process by mapping key activities from initial to end. Cooper and Edgett (1996) introduced stage gate approach in 5 stage for action and 5 gates for control	• Stage1: Idea generation • Gate 1: Initial screen • Stage 2: Preliminary investigation • Gate 2: Second screen • Stage 2: Business case preparation • Gate 3: Decision on business case • Stage 3: Development • Gate 4: Post-development review • Stage 4: Testing • Gate 5: Decision to launch • Stage 5: Launch • Post implementation review
Chandra and Neelankavil (2008) suggested seven steps	1. Product idea 2. Screen and evaluate 3. Concept development 4. Prototype 5. Testing 6. Market ready product 7. Product launch
According to Kotler and Armstrong (1991), product development should include objectives that align with strategic management	1. Idea generation 2. Idea screening 3. Concept development and testing 4. Marketing strategy development 5. Business analysis 6. Product development 7. Test marketing 8. Commercialization
Pitta and Pitta (2012)	1. Scoping 2. Building of business case 3. Development 4. Testing and validation 5. Launch
Urban and Hauser (1993) suggested five steps for product development, defining opportunity identification as the identification of a company's strengths, capabilities, and growing markets.	1. Opportunity identification 2. Design 3. Testing 4. Introduction 5. Life-cycle management

3 Review of Related Literature

Design methodologies, which are researched in literature to identify methodology and scope, are used to identify customer needs. Additionally, design methodologies are not limited to develop product or service, but papers based on design methodologies are also useful for any problem and in any sector.

Ekdahl et al. (1999) used customer the satisfaction model to understand a customer's true needs. By putting customer activities in a travel process, which included the counter, lounge, gate, in flight and baggage claim. And, passenger activities were classified in three parts: as procedural activities, personal activities and planning/preparing. After identification of passenger activities, the model produced customers' needs and expectations by defining underlying patterns (Ekdahl et al. 1999). In addition, Kim et al. (2013) found out new service opportunities in Apple's App Store using user-centric service map methodology. The first step of research is to generate customer potential needs, which are arranged in a hierarchy. In the second step, a service map is designed based on the data collected on each dimension defined in the first step. The third step is the identification of a new service model using a two-dimensional grid that shows the frequency of the needs and those needs that are covered by existing services.

Cooper and Edgett (1996) state that the key drivers of the most successful new financial products are marketing synergy, building in the voice of the customer, strong marketing communication, service expertise, managerial synergy, and quality of the launch. Garg et al. (2014) define a customer experience as a set of interactions that occur between a customer and an organization. The 14 experience factors within the finance sector are diverse: convenience, service-scape, employees, online functional elements, presence of other customers, online aesthetics, customization, value addition, speed, core service, marketing-mix, service process, online hedonic elements, customer interaction. As stated by Cooper and Edgett (1996), experience factors are used to understand the customer decision journey. And, Haeckel et al. (2003) define three principles for value added experiences: dissolve experiential breadth and depth and the use of mechanics and humans to improve function and communicate emotionally three principles?. Clearly, the customer experience depends on diverse factors such as demographics; a customer's personal background; and their social, cultural, and economic foundations-changing factors definitively affect a customer's decision process (Jain et al. 2017).

Halvorsrud et al. (2016) applied customer journey methodology to define new customers onboarding process on broadband services by following five principles to identify individual service experiences over time in a multichannel environment: being customer-centric, being precise, distinguishing planned and actual customer journeys, distinguishing objective and subjective factors, and providing visual representation. Also, Löfgren et al. (2008) analyzed a customer's experience effects in the first and second moment of truth, customer satisfaction, and loyalty. According to Löfgren et al. (2008), technical quality is a key element for purchase and usage and notwithstanding these effects, information about contents and usage doesn't effect a customer's satisfaction because providing information is a basic requirement. Tseng et al. (1999) applied customer journey mapping methodology to improve operations and Tseng et al. (1999) used four steps for improvement:

1. Recognize and map customer's service experience
2. Discovery of potential problems and opportunities by examining the customer's experience
3. Re-map a customer's service experience in case changes
4. Improve a customer's perception of value

Moon et al. (2016) applied customer journey mapping methodology on mobile services. Additionally, scope of the research, daily customer activities, and difficulties faced by customers were collected to generate new service ideas, while Moon et al. (2016) suggested four stages and ten principles for customer journey mapping.

1. Preparation

   (a) Making a list to control the development process
   (b) Defining the goals and selection of the main target

2. Component development

   (a) Defining the phase
   (b) Defining the main goal
   (c) Defining the tasks to reach the main goal
   (d) Creating new ideas by brainstorming

3. Relation definition

   (a) Defining the relationships between the goals and tasks
   (b) Identification of the starting and ending point of each intention
   (c) Drawing the dividing line between the phases

4. Opportunity discovery

   (a) Assigning pain points to each goal

Geum and Park (2011) applied a service blueprints approach to identify the relationship between factors in a product service system for car sharing and the water purifier service. Furthermore, Ceric et al. (2016) applied the service blueprints and benchmark approach to define the process of resources identification that creates customer value. As well, Flieb and Kleinaltenkamp (2004) used the service blueprints approach to identify sources of efficiency problems by differentiating between customer-based and customer-free activities.

Bitran and Hoech (1990) suggested four key elements for effective service: communication between organization and customer, controlling of service delivery process, the power of control, and employees who offer respect to a customer. Morelli (2009) applied service design process for industrial companies and Morelli (2009) collected data from users to understand customer behavior. After collecting data, Morelli (2009) designed the service according to a customer's moment of truth, their interactions, and their participation. Alternatively, Teixeira et al. (2012) used service design methodology in multimedia service where 17 customers were interviewed to understand their experiences. Teixeira et al. (2012) diminished entertainment activities and then detailed contextual elements to understand the customers' experiences.

Voss et al. (2008) classified experiment-based strategies in two dimensions: the intensity of use experience and the degree of integration of experience. In addition, Voss et al. (2008) researched 49 organizations to identify customer experience usage for organization's strategy; similarly, Voss et al. (2008) concluded that customer experience centric service is rising, not only for product or service improvement, but also strategy.

Orthel (2015) implemented a design thinking methodology for teaching, learning, and the inquiry process; as well, Furue and Washida (2017) compared a scanning and a design thinking methodology for idea generation workshops. And, Shapira et al. (2017) applied a design thinking methodology to create prototypes for strategic sustainable development.

Manton et al. (2016) applied a mental mapping visualize methodology to understand cycling activities to decrease risk, and Sedlacko et al. (2014) used mental models to identify the effect of interactions on different insights regarding consumption (Table 2).

4 Design Methodologies

Innovation is more about imagining, organizing and competing in new ways than planning new products, services, brands, and technological inventions (Mootee 2013). Even still, it is hard to imagine a customer's needs, insight, pain points, and organization limits in order to develop or re-develop a product or service. Design methodologies provide organizations with ways to build new products, services, or strategies in creatively using simple images of the process (Brown 2009).

Also, design methodologies push teams towards more creative thinking and guide the team towards greater action and less planning. Design methodologies are dynamic, reflecting customer insight, behaviors, and experience and providing substantial images to organizations. Yet, there are differences between the traditional business models and designs methodologies (Table 3).

In design methodologies, the right definition of the product or service is one of the most important steps and needs to be defined by customer needs. Luchs et al. (2016) summarized three groups and nine criteria needed for an innovative product design:

1. Strategy:

    (a) Philosophy: What is the value, vision, or mission of the business?
    (b) Structure: What is the business model of the company?
    (c) Innovative: What differentiates them from others?

Table 2 Summary of literature

Author	Methodology	Scope
Ekdahl et al. (1999)	Service design	Flight journey
Kim et al. (2013)	Service design	Apple store
Cooper and Edgett (1996)	Customer journey	Customer decision process
Halvorsrud et al. (2016)	Customer journey	Broadband service
Haeckel et al. (2003)	Customer experience mapping	Principles effect customers' experience
Jain et al. (2017)	Customer experience mapping	Changing factors effect customer decision
Löfgren et al. (2008)	Customer experience mapping	Customer experience effect on first and second moment of truth
Garg et al. (2014)	Customer experience mapping	Sets of interaction between customers and organizations
Tseng et al. (1999)	Customer journey	Optimization of operation
Moon et al. (2016)	Customer journey	Mobile service
Geum and Park (2011)	Service blueprints	Car sharing and the water purifier service
Flieb and Kleinaltenkamp (2004)	Service blueprints	Source of efficiency problem
Ceric et al. (2016)	Service blueprints	Resources identification
Bitran and Hoech (1990)	Service design	Key elements for the effective service
Morelli (2009)	Service design	Industrial companies
Teixeira et al. (2012)	Service design	Entertainment activities
Voss et al. (2008)	Customer experience	Strategy management
Orthel (2015)	Design thinking	Learning and teaching process
Furue and Washida (2017)	Design thinking	Idea generation
Shapira et al. (2017)	Design thinking	Strategic development
Manton et al. (2016)	Mental mapping	Cycling activity
Sedlacko et al. (2014)	Mental mapping	Systemic insights on consumer

Table 3 Differences between traditional business models and designs methodologies

	Traditional business models	Design methodologies
Underlying Assumptions	Rational, objective: Static	Subjective, based on experience: Dynamic
Method	Aim to find only one best solution	Aim to find better alternatives
Process	Planning	Action
Decision Drivers	Quantitative, numeric information	Customer insight, behaviors, and experience models
Values	Control and stability	Novelty
Levels of Focus	Abstract or particular	Iterative movement between abstract and particular

Reference: Liedtka and Ogilvie (2011)

2. Context

    (a) Social/Human: What is the customer's needs and behavior? How will the design affect customers?

    (b) Environment: What does a design contribute to the environment? Is the design eco-friendly?

    (c) Viability: What are design targets—percentage of sales, market share, and earnings?

3. Performance

    (a) Process: Is the process of the design easy and does it cover the customers' needs?

    (b) Function: Is the design functional? Will the design provide open research for the future?

    (c) Expression: Does the design express the values of the internal and external community?

Experience design is the key element of designing a new product or service. Experience design provides information about customers and their current activities between organizations. Yet, there is not just one methodology for experienced design approaches. In 1994, Carbone and Haeckel (1994) divided experience design into four steps:

- Gain of experience design skills
- Data collection and analysis
- Service design
- Implementation and monitoring

In 2007, Berry and Carbone (2007) suggested a five-step approach for experience design:

- Identification of a customers' emotions
- Establish an experienced motif
- Gather and evaluate experience indicators
- Determine the experience gap
- Close the experience gap and monitor

4.1 Service Blueprints

Service blueprinting is a methodology that shows service delivery process in a flow diagram (Kalbach 2016). In other words, service blueprints mapping is used to tell a story about activities, capacities and connections (Ceric et al. 2016). Specifically, service blueprints introduced by Shostack (1984) aim to identify a process, isolate fail points, establish time frames, and analyze profitability. After using service blueprints, a new model was developed because of its easy application.

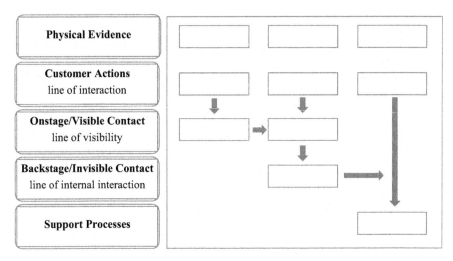

Fig. 1 Structure of service blueprint. Reference: Geum and Park (2011)

Kingman-Brundage (1991) developed service mapping techniques using the service blueprints methodology to illustrate service processes. Service mapping includes many facets: a line of interaction between customer and front-line personnel interactions, a line of visibility, a line of interaction between support team and front-line personnel, and a line of implementation. Flieb and Kleinaltenkamp (2004) developed service blueprints as a line of interaction, a line of visibility, a line of internal interaction, a line of order penetration, and a line of implementation.

Present usage of service blueprints methodology is to help organizations map internal processes of organizations including customer activity (Ceric et al. 2016). Service blueprints schemes include a product or service's physical evidence, customer actions, onstage/visible contact, backstage/invisible contact, backstage/invisible contact, support processes and their interactions. Figure 1 shows the structure of service blueprints where physical evidence refers to the touch points; whereas, customer actions are the path of the customer and how they behave. Additionally, the line of interaction is all direct interactions between customers and organizations; in comparison to the line of visibility, which is a border that distinguishes visible and non-visible issues for customer. And finally, the internal line is a border that distinguishes front line personal activities from other activities.

4.2 Service Design

First, service design models were used for industrial and product designs in mass manufacturing to manage the stage of product innovation, production optimization, and production planning (Reason et al. 2016). Later, service design methodology

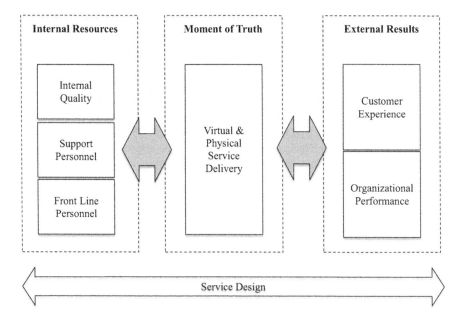

Fig. 2 Service design model. Reference: Andreassen et al. (2016)

was used to create value for a customer. Andreassen et al. (2016) defines service design as a planning activity of interaction between organizations, infrastructures, communication, and materials in order to create a value shaping customer experience (Andreassen et al. 2016).

In particular, service design provides a big picture for organizations, thereby allowing them to understand differing segments in organizations. Successful service design requires collectively embracing the customer experience components and touch points. Furthermore, new design should cover a customers' needs rather than an organizations' needs (Teixeira et al. 2012). Figure 2 states suggested a service design model for organizations wherein the first step is to identify internal recourse, the moment of truth, and targeted results. Internal recourses include quality levels of service. Support, and front line personnel. The moment of truth is the customer experience map effecting customer decisions at the point of sale, and the external results target customer experiences that are more usable and desirable for customers.

4.3 Customer Journey Mapping

Many organizations started using customer journey mapping to develop or redesign products or services, providing organizations with an emotional contact to understand customer needs, insight, and pain points. Customer journey mapping was originally obtained from service blueprint methodology; however, customer journey mapping is more useful for the identification of a customer' expectations, needs, and pain points. Also, storytelling and visualization are other key elements of customer journey mapping (Kalbach 2016).

The Customer journey is defined as a methodology that identifies key moments from end to end across the customer experience (Norton and Pine 2013) or customer's interactions with one or more service providers that achieve a specific goal (Halvorsrud et al. 2016). The aim of the customer journey is to put a costumer's desires, needs, and paint points into a map to understand how the process affects customers (McColl-Kennedy et al. 2015); moreover, the customer journey mapping visualizes a process that includes steps on how customers engage, buy, or use service or products (Peppers et al. 2016) (Table 4).

The purpose of the customer journey is to visualize a customer's interactions with an organization (Rosenbaum et al. 2017), with many models for the customer journey mapping methodology and a flexibility dependent on its sector and organization. Generally, customer journey mapping is held in workshops including different abilities of people of organizations rather than one product or service department (Moon et al. 2016). Defining this journey is an extensive process that requires top-down, judgment-driven evaluations and bottom-up, data-driven analysis- to varying degrees (Rawson et al. 2013). Kalbach (2016) defined elements of customer journey mapping as multiple elements:

1. Point of view: Customer insights
2. Structure: Chronological
3. Scope: End-to-end experience of the customer
4. Focus: This part is the customer experience and only main backstage processes effect the customer
5. Uses: Touch point analysis, optimization projects, customer experience management, marketing and branding
6. Strengths: Simple to understand, easy to apply, and suitable for team work
7. Weaknesses: Individual feedback- forget organization limits and barriers.

In regards to the customer journey mapping methodologies stated above, the main steps of the customer journey-mapping are summarized below:

1. Explore: In the explore stage, service or product definitions, internal insights, customer feedback and reasons for call center complaints are collected.
2. Define: In the define stage, personas need to define to identify who is your customer, and also organizational goals need to be clarified.
3. Map: In the mapping first stage, personas' activities such as engaging, buying, and usage need to be identified. In the second stage, activities need to visualize the end result, including end to end processing and front stage and backstage components.

   (a) Defining of user goals and expectations,
   (b) Actions between touch points and pain points are described in a timeline frame,

Table 4 Customer journey mapping methodologies

Author	Scope	Method
Rosenbaum et al. (2017)	Retail Shopping Mall	1. Developing the horizontal axis with customer research: Touchpoints were defined, and categorized before, during, and after service 2. Developing the vertical axis for service innovation: A vertical axis was created to define the interaction of department responsibility and customer touchpoints: The departments are mall shopper requirements, employee actions, employee support, mall design, and service innovation 3. Recommendation: The customer journey map was recommended to managers for better service to improve the customer experience
Voorhees et al. (2017)	Tomorrowland—a festival of dance music in Belgium	1. Three main periods were used to define the journey: Pre-core activities, core activities, and post-core activities (a) Pre-core activities are communication, information search, initial contact, and onboarding activities (b) Core service activities are core interactions: employees, technology, and environment (c) And, post-core service activities are service recovery efforts, customer feedback, reviews, crowdsourcing for new service development, and recommendations 2. Research to investigate factors was held by interviewing customers
Ament (2017)	Customer engagement	1. Description of target customers 2. Diagnosing customer engagement reasons 3. Prediction of their needs 4. Prescription: the best engagement path for organizations to work with customers 5. Cognition of a customer's emotion and their likely wants
Lee et al. (2015)	Information and Communications Technology Service	1. User research: user survey was held to collect data 2. User Experience Design and Customer Journey Map: Touch points are defined and an ideal customer journey map was designed
Canfield and Basso (2017)	Steakhouse	1. Data collection and Analysis: Qualitative and quantitative research was used to identify their cultural background, as well, semi-structured interview and internet-mediated questionnaires were held 2. Defining of target customer: personas were created 3. A cross-sectional time horizon was used to create a customer journey with application of the observation technique, in order to understand the customer journey with touch points

    (c) User thoughts, emotions and opportunities are defined to create connection with a customer with story telling.

4. Innovate: Brainstorming for redesigning a customer journey using current customer journey mapping and defining of changes.

5. Plan: Finding prior solutions and planning.
6. Apply & Monitor: Applying the new customer journey and collecting information regularly to identify customer satisfaction.

4.4 Design Thinking

A Design thinking methodology helps an organization to innovate, solve a problem, develop, and re-develop products or services in a creative way. Design thinking methodology, linked to the design method movement of the 1960s, was introduced as a scientific approach for design (Connell and Tenkasi 2015).

Luchs et al. (2016) define design thinking as a systematic and collaborative approach for identifying a problem and finding creative solutions. Mootee (2013) defines design-thinking methodology as a human-centric and holistic approach that helps to create solutions. Another key advantage of design thinking methodology is helping organizations close gaps between analytical thinking and intuitive thinking (Martin 2009) (Table 5).

4.5 Mental Model Diagram

One of the methods used for identification of customer experience is a mental model diagram- a diagram used to understand a customer's deeper needs and find solutions for those needs (Reena 2006).

The Mental Model Diagram methodology is based on concepts of cognitive mapping that emerged in the twentieth century (Seel 2003), and the diagram was first described in Craik's book, The Nature of Explanation, which was published in 1943. Johnson-Laird developed the idea as a simple, small-scale model of reality (Spicer 1998), with diagrams that include blocks showing customer insights—there are three basic information blocks (Kalbach 2016) (Fig. 3).

1. Boxes: the boxes include customers' thoughts, reactions, and principles.
2. Towers: Towers are boxed groups based on affinity.
3. Mental spaces: Mental spaces are the tower's groups based on affinity.

Young (2008) defined a process of designing mental diagrams in ten steps stated as below:

1. Defining the segment: Defining the segment stage involves listing actions practiced by groups of customers.
2. Defining targets: Defining a target that needs to be explored by an organization.
3. Setting scope for interviews: Defining a number of targeted customers and demographics and then designing questions.
4. Interviewing participants: Interviewing of customers by telephone or face-to-face and reviewing the information.

Table 5 Design thinking methodologies

Author	Method
Luchs et al. (2016)	1. Discover: Data collection and exploration of customers' needs 2. Define: Understanding of a customer's thoughts, feelings, experiences, and needs 3. Create: To develop an idea or ideas that can be shared with feedback 4. Evaluate: Evaluative steps can define the last and first steps of the process. The purpose of the evaluation stage is to get feedback from customers on prototypes
Platter (2017)	1. Empathize: Understanding of a customer 2. Define: Defining of the problem 3. Ideate: Designing with imagination to create solutions 4. Prototype: In the prototype, ideas are created for testing before the final stage 5. Test: Testing is a prototype testing stage by customers. A Customer's feedback needs to be collected

Ambrose and Harris (2010)	1. Define: Defining of the problem
	  (a) Who is the customer?
	  (b) When will the solution be needed?
	  (c) Where will the solution be used?
	  (d) Why is a solution required?
	  (e) How will the solution be implemented?
	2. Research: Collecting information about a customer's, behavior, life-style, and then receiving feedback from targeted groups
	3. Ideate: Creating of potential solutions brainstorming, sketching ideas, adapting a tried and tested design, a top-down analytical approach and a bottom-up approach
	4. Prototype: Generating prototypes to test the idea as a physical object.
	5. Select: Selecting a single idea to fit the purpose.
	6. Implement: Delivering the solution
	7. Learn: Obtaining feedback from customers

Pavie and Carthy (2015)	1. Research: Ethnological research on customers 2. Workshop 1: Identification of a problem and draft methods 3. Workshop 2: New solutions are designed by team members 4. Workshop 3: Solutions are reviewed by industry professionals 5. Workshop 4: Implementation of the final solution
Liedtka et al. (2013)	1. Visualization: Using imagery to envision possibilities 2. Journey mapping: Mapping of current experience and thoughts through the customers' eyes 3. Value chain analysis: Do current values support the current customer journey? 4. Mind mapping: Generating insight from the customer journey 5. Brainstorming: Generating creative solutions 6. Concept development: Creating an ideal customer journey 7. Assumption testing: Testing key solutions 8. Rapid prototyping: Customer testing of key solutions and later refinement 9. Customer co-creation: Creating the best solution to best fit the customer 10. Learning launch: Launching the final design and testing with market data

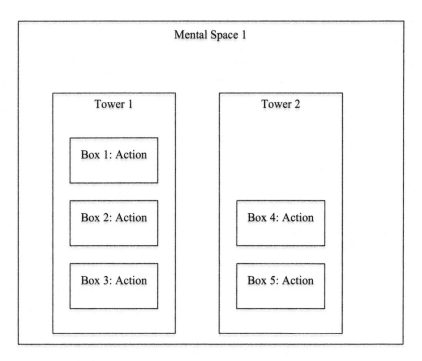

Fig. 3 Structure of a mental model diagram. Reference: Kalbach (2016)

5. Analyzing the transcripts: In the analyzing part, developers should consider details like a customer's tone of voice, their culture, their beliefs—in order to deeply understand the customer.
6. Identification of patterns: Grouping of thoughts or reactions.
7. Creating mental models: Building diagrams based on grouping and decorating.
8. Adjusting the segment: Comparing diagrams to a customer's interview.
9. Alignment and gap analysis: Drawing a proposed solution.
10. Creating a structure: Building the product or service's architecture.

4.6   Experience Maps

An experience map is a visual methodology to understand what customers are seeing, thinking, feeling, and doing when interacting with organizations (Korhan 2016). The Customer journey map and experience map are two similar approaches; whereas, the experience map focuses on general customer activity rather than specific services (Kalbach 2016).

The first stage of designing an experience map is collecting data from customers by interview or focus groups. After feedback is collected, organizations start to understand customer experiences and draw this experience as a map (Smilansky 2015). Elements of experience map (Kalbach 2016):

- Phases of behavior: Definition of a customer's activity
- Actions and steps: What is the activity of the customer?
- Jobs, goals, or needs to be done: What are the customers' needs? What are organizational targets?
- Thoughts and questions: What are a customer's thoughts about branding and process?
- Emotions and state of mind: What do customers feel about branding and process?
- Pain points: What are the problems that the customer faced?
- Physical artifacts and devices: What are the touch points?
- Opportunities: What is the value creation of an organization?

5 Conclusion

Successful product and service is based on a better customer experience, yet identifying the customer experience is complex for organizations with traditional product and service development methodologies. Design methodologies; service design, service blueprint, customer journey, design thinking, and experience mapping are introduced as new methodologies. Indeed, design methodologies provide information about the customer experience to organizations, and they can be applied easily for various reasons as problem solving, optimization, new service, or product development and redesign of service and products.

Clearly, banking is a rapidly changing industry, and the business as usual approach will not be able to keep up with these changes. The pressure is on banks to push banks to transform their approach to increase a bank's value chain. So, in order to meet a client's expectations, banks need to find new approaches to understand customers. Future banking is digitalizing, and customer centric approaches help banks to accelerate digital transformation.

References

Aho, A. M., & Uden, K. (2013). Strategic management for product development. *Business Process Management Journal, 19*(4), 680–697.

Ambrose, G., & Harris, P. (2010). *Design thinking*. Lausanne: AVA.

Ament L. (2017). Omnichannel journey design: Is your business ready? *Customer Relationship Management,* August, 38–39.

Andreassen, T. W., Kristensson, P., Lervik-Olsen, L., Parasuraman, A., McColl-Kennedy, J. R., Edvardsson, B., & Colurcio, M. (2016). Linking service design to value creation and service research. *Journal of Service Management, 27*(1), 21–29.

Berry, L. L., & Carbone, L. P. (2007). Build loyalty through experience management. *Quality Progress, 40*(9), 26–32.

Bitran, G. R., & Hoech, J. (1990). The humanization of service: Respect at the moment of truth. *Sloan Management Review, 31*(2), 89–96.

Brown, T. (2009). *Change by design*. New York: HarperCollins Books.

Canfield, D. S., & Basso, K. (2017). Integrating satisfaction and cultural background in the customer journey: A method development and test. *Journal of International Consumer Marketing, 29*(2), 104–117.

Carbone, L. P., & Haeckel, S. H. (1994). Engineering customer experience. *Marketing Management, 3*(3), 8–19.

Ceric, A., D'Alessandro, S., Soutar, G., & Johnson, L. (2016). Using blueprinting and benchmarking to identify marketing resources that help co-create customer value. *Journal of Business Research, 69*, 5653–5661.

Chandra, M., & Neelankavil, J. P. (2008). Product development and innovation for developing countries: Potential and challenges. *Journal of Management Development, 27*(10), 1017–1025.

Connell, S. E. F., & Tenkasi, R. V. (2015). Operational practices and archetypes of design thinking. In A. B. (Rami) Shani & D. A. Noumair (Eds.), *Research in organizational change and development* (pp. 195–252). Bingley: Emerald.

Cooper, R. G., & Edgett, S. J. (1996). Critical success factors for new financial services. *Marketing Management, 5*(3), 26–37.

Ekdahl, F., Gustafsson, A., & Edvardsson, B. (1999). Customer-oriented service development at SAS. *Managing Service Quality: An International Journal, 9*(6), 403–410.

Flieb, S., & Kleinaltenkamp, M. (2004). Blueprinting the service company: Managing service processes efficiently. *Journal of Business Research, 57*, 392–404.

Furue, N., & Washida, Y. (2017). Scanning and design thinking: Organizational roles for innovation. *foresight, 19*(4), 337–353.

Garg, R., Rahman, Z., & Qureshi, M. N. (2014). Measuring customer experience in banks: Scale development and validation. *Journal of Modelling in Management, 9*(1), 87–117.

Geum, Y., & Park, Y. (2011). Designing the sustainable product-service integration: A product-service blueprint approach. *Journal of Cleaner Production, 19*, 1601–1614.

Haeckel, S. H., Carbone, L. P., & Berry, L. L. (2003). How to lead the customer experience. *Marketing Management, 12*(1), 18–23.

Halvorsrud, R., Kvale, K., & Følstad, A. (2016). Improving service quality through customer journey analysis. *Journal of Service Theory and Practice, 26*(6), 840–867.

Handfield, R. B., & Lawson, B. (2007). Integrating suppliers into new product development. *Research Technology Management, 50*(5), 44–51.

Hanna, N., Ayers, D. J., Ridnour, R. E., & Gordon, G. L. (1995). New product development practices in consumer versus business products organizations. *Journal of Product & Brand Management, 4*(1), 33–55.

Jain, R., Aagja, J., & Bagdare, S. (2017). Customer experience: A review and research agenda. *Journal of Service Theory and Practice, 27*(3), 642–662.

Kalbach, J. (2016). *Mapping experiences*. Sebastopol, CA: O'Reilly.

Kim, J., Lee, S., & Park, Y. (2013). User-centric service map for identifying new service opportunities from potential needs: A case of app store applications. *Creativity and Innovation Management, 22*(3), 241–264.

Kingman-Brundage, J. (1991). Technology, design and service quality. *International Journal of Service Industry Management, 2*(3), 47–59.

Korhan, J. (2016). Map the customer experience. *Landscape Management, 54*(10), 84–86.

Kotler, P., & Armstrong, G. (1991). *Principles of marketing*. Englewood, NJ: Prentice-Hall.

Kumar, V. (2012). *101 design methods: A structured approach for driving innovation in your organization*. Hoboken, NJ: Wiley.

Lee, J. H., Kim, M. J., & Kim, S. W. (2015). *A study customer journey map for user experience analysis of information and communications technology service* (pp. 66–74). Cham: Springer.

Liedtka, J., & Ogilvie, T. (2011). *Design for growth*. New York: Columbia Business School.

Liedtka, J., King, A., & Bennett, K. (2013). *Solving problems with design thinking*. New York: Columbia University Press.

Löfgren, M., Witell, L., & Gustafsson, A. (2008). Customer satisfaction in the first and second moments of truth. *Journal of Product & Brand Management, 17*(7), 463–474.

Luchs, M. G., Swan, K. S., & Griffin, A. (2016). *Design thinking: New product development essentials from the PDMA*. Hoboken, NJ: Wiley.

Manton, R., Rau, H., Fahy, F., & Sheahan, J. (2016). Using mental mapping to unpack perceived cycling risk. *Accident Analysis & Prevention, 88*, 138–149.

Martin, R. L. (2009). *The design of business: Why design thinking is the next competitive advantage*. Boston, MA: Harvard Business Press.

McColl-Kennedy, J. R., Gustafsson, A., Jaakkola, E., Klaus, P., Radnor, Z. J., Perks, H., & Friman, M. (2015). Fresh perspectives on customer experience. *Journal of Services Marketing, 29*(6/7), 430–435.

Meroni, A., & Sangiorgi, D. (2011). *Design for Service*. Surrey, UK: Gower.

Moon, H., Han, S. H., Chun, J., & Hong, S. W. (2016). A design process for a customer journey map: A case study on mobile services. *Human Factors and Ergonomics in Manufacturing & Service Industries, 26*(4), 501–514.

Mootee, I. (2013). *Design thinking for strategic innovation*. Hoboken, NJ: Wiley.

Morelli, N. (2009). Service as value co-production: Reframing the service design process. *Journal of Manufacturing Technology Management, 20*(5), 568–590.

Norton, D. W., & Pine, B. J. (2013). Using the customer journey to road test and refine the business model. *Strategy & Leadership, 41*(2), 12–17.

Orthel, B. D. (2015). Implications of design thinking for teaching, learning, and inquiry. *Journal of Interior Design, 40*(3), 1–20.

Pavie, X., & Carthy, D. (2015). Leveraging uncertainty: A practical approach to the integration of responsible innovation through design thinking. *Social and Behavioral Sciences, 213*, 1040–1049.

Peppers, D., Rogers, M., & Kotler, P. (2016). *Managing customer experience and relationships*. Hoboken, NJ: Wiley.

Pitta, D., & Pitta, E. (2012). Transforming the nature and scope of new product development. *Journal of Product & Brand Management, 21*(1), 365–346.

Platter, H. (2017). An introduction to design thinking. Institute of Design at Stanford, https://dschool-old.stanford.edu/sandbox/groups/designresources/wiki/36873/attachments/74b3d/ModeGuideBOOTCAMP2010L.pdf (16.09.2017).

Rawson, A., Duncan E., & Jones, C. (2013). The truth about customer experience. *Harvard Business Review*, September.

Reason, B., Lavrans, L., & Flu, M. B. (2016). *Service design for business*. Hoboken, NJ: Wiley.

Reena, J. (2006). Tool: Mental models. *BusinessWeek*, Issue 4011, 5–5

Reichheld, F. (2011). *The ultimate question 2.0: How net promoter companies thrive in a customer-driven world*. Boston, MA: Bain.

Rosenbaum, M. S., Otalora, M. L., & Ramirez, G. C. (2017). How to create a realistic customer journey map. *Business Horizons, 60*, 143–150.

Sedlacko, M., Martinuzzi, A., Ropkei, I., Videira, N., & Antunes, P. (2014). Participatory systems mapping for sustainable consumption: Discussion of a method promoting systemic insights. *Ecological Economics, 106*, 33–43.

Seel, N. M. (2003). Model-centered learning and instruction, technology, instruction. *Cognition and Learning, 1*, 59–85.

Shapira, H., Ketchie, A. N. D., & Nehe, M. (2017). The integration of design thinking and strategic sustainable development. *Journal of Cleaner Production, 140*, 277–287.

Shostack, G. L. (1984). Designing services that deliver. *Harvard Business Review*, January-February, 132–139

Smilansky, O. (2015). What you need to know about customer experience maps. *Customer Relationship Management*, June, 26–29.

Spicer, D. P. (1998). Linking mental models and cognitive maps as an aid to organizational learning. *Career Development International, 3*(3), 125–132.

Teixeira, J., Patrício, L., Nunes, N. J., Nóbrega, L., Fisk, R. P., & Constantine, L. (2012). Customer experience modeling: From customer experience to service design. *Journal of Service Management, 23*(3), 362–376.

Tseng, M. M., Qinhai, M., & Su, C. J. (1999). Mapping customers' service experience for operations improvement. *Business Process Management Journal, 5*(1), 50–64.

Urban, G., & Hauser, J. (1993). *Design and marketing of new products*. Englewood Cliffs, NJ: Prentice-Hall.

Voorhees, C. M., Fombelleb, P. W., Gregoirec, Y., Boned, S., Gustafssone, A., Sousaf, R., & Walkowiakg, T. (2017). Service encounters, experiences and the customer journey: Defining the field and a call to expand our lens. *Journal of Business Research, 79*, 269–280.

Voss, C., Roth, A. V., & Chase, R. B. (2008). Experience, service operations strategy, and services as destinations: Foundations and exploratory investigation. *Production and Operations Management Society, 17*(3), 247–266.

Watkinson, M. (2013). *The ten principles behind great customer experiences* (pp. 3–23). Harlow, UK: Pearson.

Young, I. (2008). *Mental models: Aligning design strategy with human behavior*. New York: Rosenfeld.

Part IV
Risk Management Activities
in Business Operations

Trading Volume, Volatility and GARCH Effects in Borsa Istanbul

Ayhan Kapusuzoglu and Nildag Basak Ceylan

Abstract The purpose of this study is to analyze the relationship between sector indices of Borsa Istanbul in Turkey and trading volume in the framework of Mixture of Distribution Hypothesis (MDH) by using daily data covering period 23.10.1987–26.01.2017. As a model, GARCH model is used. The results of the GARCH (1,1) suggests that Borsa Istanbul sector indices show strong persistence. The findings are consistent with MDH suggesting the existence of positive volume–volatility relationships. When trading volume is added to the variance equation, the model shows the existence of a positive and statistically significant relationships between trading volume and the volatility of the sector indices suggesting that the number of information events makes the variability of the sector indices to increase. The volatility persistence also decreases in the case that the variance equation covers the volume data.

1 Introduction

In weak form market efficiency, the current market prices reflect the past stock prices which is suggested by Fama (1970, 1991). This states that in predicting the future prices of the stocks, past stock prices data cannot be used which opposes the view of the technical analysts who predicts the future prices of the stocks by using the past data of the stocks. According to technical analysts, Karpoff (1987) states that this shows the structure of financial markets. Moreover it has a great implication in the application of recent studies. One of the major issues that is under the concern in financial economics is the relationship between trading volume and stock market index.

In the related literature on the financial economics, the relationship between stock trading volume and the volatility of stock return has been an important research

A. Kapusuzoglu (✉) · N. B. Ceylan
Ankara Yildirim Beyazit University, Ankara, Turkey
e-mail: akapusuzoglu@ybu.edu.tr; nbceylan@ybu.edu.tr

© Springer International Publishing AG, part of Springer Nature 2018   333
H. Dincer et al. (eds.), *Strategic Design and Innovative Thinking in Business Operations*, Contributions to Management Science,
https://doi.org/10.1007/978-3-319-77622-4_17

topic. Karpoff (1987) has determined four major reasons why this is important. Firstly, it is important in understanding the structures of financial markets. Secondly, it is important in the case of event studies that analyze trading volume and stock price data together. Thirdly, it is important in discussing that is obtained from empirical researches carried out on the speculative stock prices. Finally, it has significant implications for the researches that are to be conducted in relation to the volume of transactions versus the price of transactions, because the market value affects the volume that is related to transactions in the futures trading market. It has significant implications for the researches that carry their research on trading volume and stock price on futures markets because price volatility affects the volume that is related to transactions in the futures market.

The Microstructure Theory, which examines the relationship, emerges as a theory that models the pass through process of private information to the stock price. This process is called information disambiguation or information assimilation. The standard microstructure model assumes a riskier asset and a market participant insensitive to the three types of risk. The first is the investor who has information about the risky assets, the second is a liquidity processor that operates entirely with liquidity gusts and the third is the market makers who forms the prices by equalizing the expected value of the final asset. The traders are in the market in a random and unsigned form and the information processors will make profits from transactions they do when the prices reach the level of information. Consecutive transactions in the market reveal that informed traders allow market makers to correct prices. This process continues until the specific information is completely reflected within the stock price and when the specific information is fully reflected in the price, all market traders or participants are in the same idea on the price of the asset. Through this process, a dynamic learning process emerges, which leads to a complete reflection of the prices of the private information through subsequent transactions and price corrections (Li and Wu 2006).

The financial markets are mainly based on two basic motives. These are information and liquidity motives. The traders who have Information perform operations on information that other traders do not know and that only they possess. The traders that trade with the motive of liquidity do not trade for the future returns of the assets and the financial institutions' that are large scale investors that operate to meet the liquidity needs of their customers or to balance their portfolios, etc. are also included (Admati and Pfleiderer 1988).

The traders who are informed assume that the profits they expect to achieve in the future will reach the maximum level and they behave as monopolists by intertemporal selection on the market. They consider the effect of the transaction they did in an auction and possible future transaction opportunities. It is assumed that the prices determined by the market makers are equal to the liquidity value of the asset and the prices depend on the information that the market maker has at the time of setting the price. For this reason, market makers make a net profit of zero on average. Market makers are unable to distinguish the trading of insiders from the noise traders and this also causes the noisy traders to camouflage the insider traders that profit (Kyle 1985).

One of the basic hypotheses that deals with the trading volume and price changes is the Sequential Arrival of Information (SAI) hypothesis revealed by Copeland (1976, 1977). According to this model, the processors get new information at a certain time, and then the processors get new information at a certain time, and then each of them changes the demand curves immediately. This period ends when the processors update the demand curves in accordance with this new information. There are N number of traders in the market and technical operation is not allowed. The trader that follows the value of a property either sells on a passive basis in the absence of new information or hides all assets. However, when new information arrives, the operator immediately changes the demand curve upwards or downwards and processes it in the active position from the passive position in the market. In addition, the traders are prohibited to make short sales in the market. As mentioned, there are N number of traders and therefore N number of demand curves, but the behavior types of the traders are taken into account based on different assumptions. The model depends on three-core assumptions. In the first assumption, it is assumed that all new information takers are optimistic. According to the first assumption, when new information comes into the market, the optimists immediately change the demand curves upwards and this process continues until all traders change their demand positions. After this process, the change in asset prices and volume levels of the assets are formed from the demand updates after the new information arrival. If there is no position update in the market where there is no initial balance in the market, the last balance is the result of the updates made in the direction of the new information. In this assumption, that is, if all traders are in the same behavioral structure as optimist, there is not much left of the original new information and only a single correction is made between the initial and final equilibrium. If there is no position update in the market where there is no initial balance information in the market, the last balance is the result of the updates made in the direction of new information. In this assumption, that is, if all processors are in the same behavioral structure as the optimist, there is not much left of the original new information and only a single correction is made between the initial and final equilibrium. In the second assumption of the model, the buyers are accepted to be all pessimist. When the first trader receives a bad news, he will immediately change the demand position and update the demand curve downwardly. If the new incoming information is bad enough, the trader may start to sell a part of his assets or continue to hold all of them and may not perform any transaction or sale. In the last assumption of the model, the traders are not only optimistic nor pessimistic. In this assumption, there are both optimistic and pessimistic traders in the market at a significant level. Unexpectedly, in the market there may be a common view on the newcoming information, but some of the traders may not agree in the same way. As a result, there will be an intermediate step between the start and end balance in the market, and there will be N number of total traders, J number of optimistic traders and Q number of pessimistic traders. Under this assumption, there will be an investor with knowledge of M (N-J-Q) quantity. When all these assumptions are considered, it is possible to summarize the model as follows: when the view of the traders are the same on the newcoming information to the market, there is a positive correlation between the price changes and the expected value of the trading volume; the trading volume increases logarithmically as a function of the number of traders in the market and the effect of newcoming information; When short sell is prohibited, the trading volume is expected to have positive skewness, related to the impact level of this information, this skewness will increase. When the investors in the market are optimistic or pessimistic, the trading volume will be indifferent.

Karpoff (1987) states that this model is open to criticism for at least two points. The first assumption is that, while some of the traders have information on the market price, the others are prohibited to do so. The second assumption is the assumption that the transaction volume will reach the highest level when both investors in the overall market agree on the meaning of the newcoming information. This assumption is in contrast to the case of making profits from the high volume of transactions (Clark 1973; Beaver 1968; Kiger 1972; Foster 1973) and do not fit the findings of Bamber (1986), Comiskey et al. (1987), Karpoff (1987).

This model, which was introduced by Copeland, was first developed by Morse (1980). In Copeland's model, the prices that are anticipated for the different traders in the market are analyzed and when each trader receives new information, he revises this information in accordance with his own beliefs and then performs transactions. These transactions cause the demand curves to change upward or downward, and the asset prices increase or decrease monotonously. By improving this existing model, Morse (1980) put forth two basic characteristics related to the usage of asymmetric information, namely trading and monotonic price movement and has reported that during the periods of high trading volume, the excess returns have serial correlation. In other words, the successful operations performed on the basis of a specific knowledge can only last for a limited period of time.

The model developed by Copeland was later replaced by Jennings et al. (1981) by using Mossin (1973)'s equilibrium analysis. Their model differs from Copeland's model and reforms the market price-fixing process by means of equilibrium analysis in a market where conditions of uncertainty and availability exist to maximize the benefits of investors. The model extends Copeland's model by associating the marginal requirement with short selling such as transaction cost and this marginal requirement causes an uneven flow trace of the demand curve of the investor. This means that the costs will vary depending on whether the investor is in a long or short position, and the demand curve following the investor's position will affect the trend of the demand curve relatively. According to the model, the demand curves of the investors (optimistic, contemporaneous and uninformed) are parallel and equal to each other. For this reason, the volume created by the optimistic investor is the same as the volume created by pessimistic investors. In other words, the total amount of volume is related to the quantity of traders in the market, not the kind of position they take in the market. Another important point that, in the traditional view, there is a positive linear link between the trading volume and the price changes, and the trading volume is higher in the bull market than the bear market and this view is also supported by some studies in the related literature (Crouch 1970; Epps 1975; Rogalski 1978). In the extended study of Jennings et al., there is a non-perfect correlation and it is generally estimated that the volume is higher compared to the bear market when the market is bull. In addition, another important point presented in the study is that an informed investor would not make speculations and would want to reach the consumptive optimum directly, but that the investor perceives that the information is at top level, he won't be satisfied with consumptive optimum in this world which can be borrowed unconditionally.

Related to the development of the relation, in the model suggested by Wang (1994), trading volume covers and reflects important information on how an asset is priced in the market. Within the model, a simple economic structure has been dealt with, and stocks and risk-free bonds and special investment opportunities have been assessed. The model assumes that the market is a competitive market, predicting a completely dynamic model of investors' dynamic transaction strategies, and models the process of optimizing investor behavior as ignorant and informative transactions. According to the process here, investors have different information on different investment alternatives and future dividends of stocks. Although informed investors have private information, non-informed investors try to find out the profit share, price signal reflected in the market etc. In other words, an informed investor performs a transaction based on specific information, whereas a non-informed investor will perform a transaction based on the factors which do not depend on information. Because of this information asymmetry, investors who are non-informed demand more discounts when they buy stocks, because they take more risk compared to the informed investors.

Smirlock and Starks (1988), who deal with the SAI hypothesis with a different view, considered the topic as process and two extreme points. According to the first extreme, all investors take the information that comes to the market at the same time and revise this information according to their expectations and perform the process. When all investors obtain information, equilibrium situation arises. There is no intermediate balance point in this process. When the other extreme part is considered, the investors get the information at a certain time and the transaction takes place after each information is received. In this case, a series of temporary equilibrium states will emerge. The point that Smirlock and Starks (1988) want to emphasize by taking these two extreme points is that the information is not only in sequential order as in Copeland (1976, 1977)'s hypothesis, but also an alternative model it can come at the same time and the result they reach is that the SAI hypothesis can provide more precise findings in describing dominant market behavior with respect to the SIM (Simultaneous Information Arrival) model.

Another hypothesis except for the Copeland (1976, 1977)'s SAI hypothesis is the Mixture of Distribution Hypothesis (MDH) hypothesis, which is introduced by Clark (1973) which deals with the relationship, out of the SAI hypothesis. Clark has introduced a stochastic process based model in relation to the speculative price series and deals with the time series related to the prices that occur in a speculative market (stock market, futures market, etc.) with short periods of time. When the new information in the market is missing, both transactions and price changes slow down. When new information is available, transactions are revived and price change process accelerates. This reveals the correlation is positive. This model, which is introduced by Clark (1973), is developed by Epps and Epps (1976). In the model, it is assumed that there is no transaction cost associated with financial assets and that investors are not subject to any limitations on short selling and borrowing. All investors are risk averse at the same level and every new information affects the distribution mean related to the end of period value of the asset. The value that the investor expects today related to the value of the asset is different from its value with respect to the previous day. The change in the market price of each day is the average of the change in the reservation prices of all the traders. They found a positive relationship. Epps (1977), as an interesting finding related to the subject, refers to the fact that positive price changes are more significant than negative price changes when trading volume and price changes occur during trading days.

According to Tauchen and Pitts (1983), these two models (Clark 1973; Epps and Epps 1976) are not sufficient and they need to be developed in two ways. Firstly, both models operate on the conditional distributions of price changes. These models need to be examined in more detailed with nonlinear regression models. Secondly, the model does not take into account the growth of the speculative markets, such as many new futures markets. At the beginning, in the new markets, the transaction volume is low, but as the market gains efficiency, the traders will recognize the opportunities of this new market and trading volume will begin to increase.

Harris (1986) reconsidered the hypothesis by stating that MDH is analyzed by considering only one stock and lacks the studies that examined inter-stock interactions. In the tests carried out on the model of Harris, the information flow ratio based on the price of the stock is different for each of the stock. Thus, the daily flow rate of information for each stock is different. As a result of the study, their findings supports MDH.

Andersen (1996) shows the relation between daily return and trading volume by combining the market microstructure approach of Glosten and Milgrom (1985) with the MDB framework with stochastic volatility. By modifying the MDH, a fully dynamic model estimation has been performed and they put forth that within the day trading volume and the volatility of returns can be predicted. Mahieu and Bauer (1998), also used the modified mixture model, which is revealed by Anderson, but unlike Andersen (1996), they used Markov Chain and Monte Carlo simulation. As a result of the modeling, it is determined that MMM is a useful model in understanding the process of trading volume and volatility.

Similarly, Lamoureux and Lastrapes (1990) use the ARCH model to make estimates on daily returns and they model the daily information flow for each of the stock and how it is reflected in the related stock returns. They model the reflection of the daily information flow to the market for each stock to the income of the relevant stocks. In this modeling process, the daily volume is taken related to the arrival time. Modelling has revealed the relevance of the ARCH model in determining the behavioral patterns of asset prices.

Bollerslev and Jubinski (1999) attempt to put a long run structure, for the relationship between trading volume and volatility addressing the MDH-modified version. The empirical findings reported are consistent with MDH, and the model provides long-term, moderate volatility estimates and a more precise pricing for long-term financial contracts. Contrary to these studies, the study of Darrat et al.

(2003), do not support the MDH hypothesis. Using EGARCH-M model, they report no strong findings to support MDH.

The main motivation for analyzing the effect of trading volume on volatility is to contribute to this growing body of the field of the literature on financial economies. To this end, an empirical work is done for the case of Borsa Istanbul, Turkey. The rest of this study is organized as follows: Second part presents the relevant literature for empirical analysis, third part introduces the data set and methodology while the results of the study is in final part.

2 Literature Review

In finance literature, there are many studies which examine the relationships in stock prices. Especially, the findings, which reports the existence of positive interactions supporting the main hypothesis of this study which is put forth in the first part of this study, have a majority in number. Richardson and Smith (1994) analyzed MDH using stock prices. As a result of the research conducted within the period of 1982–1986 and using the Dow Jones 30 index, their findings support MDH. The findings of Brock and Lebaron (1996) points out that, in the case that the demand diversity is higher than the returns volatility persistence may come from the beliefs not from the fundamentals. So that, diverse expectations related to the future return will make more investors to trade. This finding suggest that trading volume which is serially correlated with the returns show GARCH behaviour. Hutson and Kearney (2001) analyzed the effect of information presented to the market on the volatility in the prices of assets for the 1985–1993 period and using 112 daily price and transaction volume data for the case of Australia. As a result of the research, it is found out that the volatility stars to decline after an information related to an asset has arrived to the market. Lee and Rui (2002) explored the dynamic relationship as well as volatility both for the domestic country and the cross country by using the daily data of New York, Tokyo and London stock exchanges by using Granger Causality. Their findings suggest that in none of the stock markets trading volume doesn't Granger cause stock market returns. Moreover, they report positive trading volume and volatility of the stock returns in all three of the markets. In the study of Ane and Ureche-Rangau (2008), the long term relationship is analyzed based on MDF for the period 1990–2001. In the study, where daily price and volume data covering 2874 observations of London Stock Exchange show that volatility and transaction volume can move in the same way in short run, but move in different ways in the long run. Mahajan and Singh (2009) analyze the relationship between return, volume and volatility of Sensitive Index for daily data and for the October 1996–March 2006 period. Their findings suggest that there exists both statistically significant and positive relationship. Dey and Wang (2010) report that, in the analysis of the validity of the MDH and SIAH, the results obtained from 14 firms operating in the New York Stock Exchange show that these two hypotheses have very weak findings relative to their validity. Canerella and Pollard (2011) investigate the validity of the MDH hypothesis for the Russian Stock Exchange. Using GARCH model, their findings support the MDH hypothesis. In the study of Damette (2016), the effect of Tobin's tax on exchange rate is investigated with MDH, and found that in the periods where the relationship is high, there is a tendency that the relationship among these variables will develop. Takaishi and Chen (2016), using the GARCH model of daily data of trading volume, number of transactions and stock volatility for the Tokyo Stock Exchange and for the 2006–2009 period. Their findings are unable to arrive at any evidence supporting MDH. Pati (2017) analyze the relationship among the variables for Indian futures market. The period they consider is 2007–2016. Using the EGARCH model, strong findings were obtained showing that MDH is valid.

Although, there are many empirical studies supporting MDH in terms of volume and volatility in the stock returns' there are also studies showing that the hypothesis related to this relationship is not valid. In the study of Celik (2013), the relationship is examined for Istanbul Stock Exchange through MDH and SIAH hypotheses for the 2005–2010 periods and found that for the pre-crises period MDH is valid whereas it is not valid during the crises period and indicate that SIAH is completely invalid. Carroll and Kearney (2015) examine the relationship between the daily volume of 190 stocks and the price volatility of the stocks for US for the 2000–2008 period based on MDH hypothesis. They report a negative correlation, contrary to the related hypothesis.

3   Data Set and Methodology

In finance, the expectations related to the future stock market returns carry importance. The financial assets show time varying volatility characteristic which is shown by Bollerslev (1986). In the traditional ARCH type models, such as GARCH, EGARCH etc., using the lagged of the returns the future return volatility is forecasted. In an ARCH model, not only the volatility clustering identification in an autoregressive structure is allowed, but also a mixture of distributions are also allowed. The rate of information flow may also be considered as the primary mixing variable. MDH is a stochastic mixing variable which shows the rate of arrival of information flow to the market. According to MDH, the volatility of the return is proportional to the rate of information arrival and explains heteroscedasticity in returns.

In the model, when a proxy of information flow is added to the conditional variance equation of GARCH (1,1), it reduces the persistence of the volatility significantly. Lamoureux and Lastrapes (1990) reported that as a proxy of information arrival, it is good to use daily trading volume. When it is added to the conditional variance equation of GARCH (1,1), it lessens the persistency of the volatility.

In Table 1, the abbreviations used in the study are shown. Table 2 exhibits the descriptive statistics of the returns for the sector indices in Borsa Istanbul. Kurtosis

Table 1 The abbreviations used in the study

BIST 100 Price Index	BISTP
BIST Services Price Index	SERVP
BIST Financial Price Index	FINP
BIST Industrials Price Index	INDP
BIST Technology Price Index	TECHP
BIST 100 Return Index	BISTR
BIST Services Return Index	SERVR
BIST Financial Return Index	FINR
BIST Industrials Return Index	INDR
BIST Technology Return Index	TECHR

Table 2 Descriptive statistics

	Mean	Standard deviation	Skewness	Kurtosis	Jarque-Bera
BISTP	0.126265	2.604816	0.032974	7.680371	6672.576
TECHP	0.037808	2.320466	−0.210433	12.96665	17,223.75
FINP	0.125544	2.827052	−0.007558	7.021282	4382.999
INDP	0.122668	2.323805	−0.147013	8.736844	8943.788
SERVP	0.078906	2.306535	0.004977	11.33299	14,495.36
BISTR	0.096995	2.426052	−0.097148	9.100990	7777.990
TECHR	0.046575	2.322306	−0.333621	12.49327	15,675.70
FINR	0.101426	2.720764	−0.024627	8.155873	5549.712
INDR	0.101449	2.143557	−0.320626	11.81839	16,319.09
SERVR	0.087102	2.254485	−0.038558	10.58771	12,019.68
VOLUME	0.224794	31.08433	0.112783	5.816443	2431.227

shows the degree of a distribution which is denoted as fat tails or in another definition kurtosis is the shape of the tails of the distribution. As Damodaran (2006) states, fat tails causes the Kurtosis to be higher. Generally, the investors prefer the distribution to have low kurtosis, the returns that are close to the mean, as they are mostly risk averse. In the normal distribution, excess kurtosis should be equal to zero. Kurtosis is given importance by investors as it shows the possibility of change in the prices of stocks below or above the current levels (Ivanovski et al. 2015).

Jarque-Bera is a test statistic that tests whether the series are normally distributed. It reveals how the skewness and kurtosis of the series differs from the normal distribution. It is possible to compute the test statistic as follows:

$$JB = \frac{N - k}{6} \left(S^2 + \frac{1}{4} + (K - 3)^2 \right)$$

where skewness is denoted as S, kurtosis is denoted as K, and the number of estimated coefficients used to create the series is denoted as k (Lawford 2005). In normal distribution, the null hypothesis suggests that the Jarque-Bera statistic is

342 A. Kapusuzoglu and N. B. Ceylan

distributed with a degrees of freedom of two. Chen and Kuan (2003) suggests that Jarque-Bera test, can be applied to some of the GARCH-M models.

When Table 2 is observed, the descriptive statistics show that returns are mostly negatively skewed (8 out of 10) for the returns of sector indices and volume series. Negative skewness means that the likelihood of obtaining a negative return on the stock indexes and return distribution of the volume is high. If the kurtosis value is greater than 3, it indicates that there isn't available any normal distribution.

The bias on the returns being negative or positive is being shown by the skewness of the distribution. In positively skewed distributions, there exist higher probability of higher positive returns than that of negative returns. As suggested by Ivanovski et al. (2015), the positive skewness condition may cause to have excess kurtosis and for the future not to have extreme negative returns and this means the extreme returns to be positive only. This case is true in the case that the skewness is positive. In the case that there is negative skewness, because of high excess kurtosis, it is possible for the investors to come across with extreme negative returns. When skewness is smaller than −1 and the excess kurtosis is greater than one, for the return distributions, the probability of facing immediate high negative returns increases.

In the normal distributions, there is no skewness and in addition they have a kurtosis of zero. In the case of normal distribution, it is possible to measure investment by expected return and standard deviation. Expected return shows the opportunity within the investment and standard deviation shows the degree of danger as suggested by Damodaran (2006). The risk averse investors prefer positively skewed distributions to negatively skewed distributions and the distributions of returns having lower possibility to change the prices to the ones having higher possibility of higher kurtosis. Skrinjaric (2014) states that the distribution of the returns of each stock is shown by the coefficient of skewness. In the case that the distribution is positively skewed, then it means returns are greater than the expected. In most of the models, the investors are assumed to prefer the stocks which have positive skewness in the return distribution.

In the study, the data of BIST 100 Price Index, BIST Services Price Index, BIST Financial Price Index, BIST Industrials Price Index, BIST Technology Price Index, BIST 100 Return Index, BIST Services Return Index, BIST Financial Return Index, BIST Industrials Return Index, BIST Technology Return Index and total volume are obtained from EVDS-Central Bank of the Republic of Turkey. The study covers the period 23.10.1987–26.01.2017 and the frequency of the data are daily.

In Eq. (1), the logarithmic first difference of the P_t, where P_t denotes BIST 100 index, BIST 100 return index, BIST Technology index, BIST Technology return index, BIST Financial Index, BIST Financial return index, BIST Industrial Index, BIST Industrial return index, BIST Service Index and BIST Service return index are denoted as R_t:

$$R_t = [\log(P_t) - \log(P_{t-1})] * 100 \qquad (1)$$

The GARCH model, which is used by Bollerslev (1986), is considered as a model. In the model, the conditional variance of residual at time t depends on both the squared error term of the previous period and the lagged conditional variance. The GARCH (p,q) process suggested by Bollerslev (1986) can be denoted as:

$$h_t^2 = w + \sum_{j=1}^{p} \beta_j h_{t-j}^2 + \sum_{i=1}^{q} \alpha_i u_{t-i}^2 \tag{2}$$

Here in the model, the conditional variance, denoted as u_t^2 is a linear function of the q lags of the error terms or the ARCH terms (which are considered as the "news" from the past), GARCH terms, denoted as the h_t^2 which shows the lags of the past values of the conditional variances and ω denotes the constant term. The relationship between stock returns and volatility is estimated, after a set of estimations, by the GARCH (1,1) specification as shown below:

$$R_t = c + \gamma R_{t-1} + \varepsilon_t \tag{3}$$
$$\varepsilon_t \sim \left(0, h_t^2\right)$$
$$h_t^2 = w + \alpha \varepsilon_{t-1}^2 + \beta h_{t-1}^2 + \Gamma V_t \tag{4}$$

where ε's are the error term, h_t^2 is for the conditional variance and V_t is the trading volume for the day t. The trading volume is added to analyze how trading volume affects the volatility of the return. Here, the significance of Γ is tested. If it is an appropriate proxy to test information flow, it is expected that $\Gamma > 0$ holds, and that the coefficients $\alpha + \beta > 0$ when V_t is not incorporated (Lamoureux and Lastrapes 1990). V_t is expected to be positive and statistically significant.

In Table 3 we test whether the daily returns of stock market indices and volume series are stationary or not. In order to test whether the series contain unit root, Augmented Dickey Fuller (ADF 1981) test is considered. The findings shows that all the series are stationary at order 1, $I(1)$.

Table 3 Unit root test

Index	Test statistics		Critical values (CV)		
	ADF	ADF (first difference)	1%	5%	10%
BISTP	−0.074475	−77.22596**	−3.431069	−2.861742	−2.566920
TECHP	2.499797	−63.22261**	−3.431069	−2.861742	−2.566920
FINP	−0.695696	−76.05698**	−3.431069	−2.861742	−2.566920
INDP	1.016310	−74.63130**	−3.431069	−2.861742	−2.566920
SERVP	−0.655729	−70.49786**	−3.431069	−2.861742	−2.566920
BISTR	−0.351521	−47.64814**	−3.431069	−2.861742	−2.566920
TECHR	2.874151*	−43.16514**	−3.431069	−2.861742	−2.566920
FINR	−0.896771	−69.69756**	−3.431069	−2.861742	−2.566920
INDR	1.223975	−47.76981**	−3.431069	−2.861742	−2.566920
SERVR	−0.246558	−69.68029**	−3.431069	−2.861742	−2.566920
VOLUME	−2.080789	−27.98863**	−3.431069	−2.861742	−2.566920

Note: * and ** denote the significance level at 5% and 10% respectively. CV tabulated by MacKinnon (1991)

Table 4 GARCH (1,1) estimation results for the main BIST indices

INDEX	Without V_t			With V_t			
	α	β	α+β	α	β	α+β	Γ
D(BISTP)	0.1242	0.8693	0.9935	0.0669	0.5641	0.6310	0.0763 (0.0000)
D(BISTR)	0.0886	0.9049	0.9935	0.1363	0.5964	0.7327	0.0982 (0.0000)
D(MALIP)	0.0857	0.9051	0.9909	0.1108	0.5997	0.7105	0.1361 (0.0000)
D(MALIR)	0.0912	0.8992	0.9904	0.0870	0.5890	0.6759	0.1144 (0.0000)
D(SINAIP	0.1411	0.8552	0.9963	0.0760	0.5685	0.6445	0.0679 (0.0000)
D(SINAIR)	0.1728	0.8203	0.9930	0.1024	0.5710	0.6735	0.0609 (0.0000)
D(TEKNOLOJIP)	0.1537	0.8117	0.9655	0.1422	0.8170	0.9592	0.0137 (0.0000)
D(TEKNOLOJIR)	0.1572	0.8131	0.9703	0.1481	0.8149	0.9630	0.0131 (0.0000)

The estimates of the GARCH (1,1) for all the main indices which are reported in Table 4 shows that $\alpha > 0$, $\beta > 0$, and $\alpha + \beta < 1$. When incorporated the trading volume to the variance equation, the coefficient, Γ, is reported to be positive and statistically significant at a significance level of 1%. The sum of the coefficients of $\alpha + \beta$ exhibits a high degree of volatility persistence and demonstrates that when the proxy variable is omitted from the model, there exists apparent changes when compared to the model without the proxy variable. The sum of $\alpha + \beta$ with trading volume is smaller than it is without the trading volume. Overall, it shows that persistence lessens when included the trading volume in the conditional variance equation.

The findings of the GARCH (1,1) model used in the study show that Borsa Istanbul has a strong volatility persistence and past volatility can be used to give an explanation to the current volatility. When trading volume is encompassed as a proxy of new information entering into the market, trading volume appears to decrease the persistency of the volatility. The results from the GARCH (1,1) specification presents the existence of positive and statistically significant relationship between trading volume and stock volatility. This exhibits that the variability of stock returns gets larger as the number of events related to information increases. It should also be noted that the persistency of the volatility decreases when the conditional variance equations involve the trading volume.

4 Conclusion

The timing of the arrival and/or acquisition of information of investors in an active market do not have a very significant effect in terms of their investment behavior. Because the expected potential information is already priced and has already been reflected in the asset's price. That is to say, the impact of this information on the investor asset demand curves will not be so great. However, in the inefficient markets, there is no noteworthy difference depending on the level of efficiency within the market, the effect of the anticipated information on the asset is greater than that of the active market in terms of the investor's behavior. Here, the acquisition of the incoming information by the investor and the timing of this acquisition is important. The main hypothesis in this study as MDH put forth, is the investors completing the process after the post new information process and at the same time causes an increase in the number of transaction related to that asset. In the opposite case, in the case that there is lack of information, they usually take positions in terms of preserving their current situation, not doing transactions or doing very little. The key point here is that the information asymmetry existing among the investors affects the price changes that are related to the asset, not monotonously, but rather changing and volatile.

In this study, the relationship between stock returns volatility and trading volume is analyzed by using daily stock market returns and daily trading volume data of Borsa Istanbul for the period between 23.10.1987 and 26.01.2017. In the study, all sector indices of Borsa Istanbul are included. When the trading volume is incorporated in the variance equation, the results indicate that there is positive volume-volatility relationships and the findings are consistent with the MDH hypothesis. The model shows that there is a positive and statistically significant relationship between trading volume and stock market indices volatility suggesting that the variability of the stock market indices increases with the number of information events. The empirical findings reported in this study may be a guide for the policy makers and market participants. Further studies should confirm or contradict the results by using more extensive data series and specific tests.

Key Concepts and Words

Stock Market The stock market refers to the collection of markets and exchanges where equities and other sorts of securities are issued and traded.
Trading Volume The number of shares that are transacted every day.
GARCH The generalized autoregressive conditional heteroskedasticity (GARCH) process which is used to estimate volatility in financial markets

References

Admati, A. R., & Pfleiderer, P. (1988). A theory of intraday patterns: Volume and price variability. *The Review of Financial Studies, 1*(1), 3–40.
Andersen, T. G. (1996). Return volatility and trading volume: An information flow interpretation of stochastic volatility. *The Journal of Finance, 51*(1), 169–204.
Ane, T., & Ureche-Rangau, L. (2008). Does trading volume really explain stock returns volatility? *International Financial Markets, Institutions and Money, 18*, 216–235.

Bamber, L. S. (1986). The information content of annual earnings releases: A trading volume approach. *Journal of Accounting Research, 24*, 40–56.

Beaver, W. H. (1968). The information content of annual earnings announcements. *Journal of Accounting Research (Empirical Research in Accounting: Selected Studies), 6*, 67–92.

Bollerslev, T. (1986). Generalized autoregressive conditional heteroscedasticity. *Journal of Econometrics, 31*, 307–327.

Bollerslev, T., & Jubinski, D. (1999). Equity trading volume and volatility: Latent information arrivals and common long-run dependencies. *American Statistical Association Journal of Business & Economic Statistics, 17*(1), 9–21.

Brock, W. A., & Lebaron, B. D. (1996). A dynamic structural model for stock return volatility and trading volume. *Review of Economics and Statistics, 78*, 94–110.

Canerella, G., & Pollard, S. K. (2011). The mixture of distribution hypothesis and the Russian stock market. *Journal of Business & Economics Research, 1*(11), 43–58.

Carroll, R., & Kearney, C. (2015). Testing the mixture of distributions hypothesis on target stocks. *Journal of International Financial Markets, Institutions & Money, 39*, 1–14.

Celik, S. (2013). New evidence on the relation between trading volume and volatility. *Business and Economic Research, 3*(1), 176–186.

Chen, Y-T & Kuan, C-M (2003). *A generalized Jarque-Bera test of conditional normality* (IEAS Working Paper, Academic Research, No: 03-A003). Taipei, Taiwan: Institute of Economics, Academia Sinica.

Clark, P. K. (1973). A subordinated stochastic process model with finite variance for speculative prices. *Econometrica, 41*, 135–155.

Comiskey, E. E., Walkling, R. A., & Weeks, M. A. (1987). Dispersion of expectations and trading volume. *Journal of Business Finance and Accounting, 14*(2), 229–239.

Copeland, T. E. (1976). Asset trading under the assumption of sequential information arrival. *The Journal of Finance, 31*(4), 1149–1168.

Copeland, T. E. (1977). A probability model of asset trading. *The Journal of Financial and Quantitative Analysis, 12*(4), 563–578.

Crouch, R. L. (1970). The volume of transactions and price changes on the New York Stock Exchange. *The Financial Analysts Journal,* July–August, 104–109.

Damette, O. (2016). Mixture distribution hypothesis and the impact of a Tobin tax on exchange rate volatility: A reassessment. *Macroeconomic Dynamics, 20*, 1600–1622.

Damodaran, A. (2006). *Investment valuation.* New York: Wiley.

Darrat, A. F., Rahman, S., & Zhong, M. (2003). Intraday trading volume and return volatility of the DJIA stocks: A note. *Journal of Banking and Finance, 27*, 2035–2043.

Dey M. K., & Wang, C. (2010). Volume volatility in dual markets: Lessons from Chinese ADRs. Retrieved January 12, 2013, from http://ifrogs.org/PDF/EMF2010/DeyWang2010.pdf

Dickey, D. A., & Fuller, W. A. (1981). Likelihood ratio statistics for autoregressive time series with a unit root. *Econometrica, 49*, 1057–1072.

Epps, T. W. (1975). Security price changes and transactions volume: Theory and evidence. *American Economic Review, 65*, 586–597.

Epps, T. W. (1977). Security price changes and transaction volumes: Some additional evidence. *The Journal of Financial and Quantitative Analysis, 12*(1), 141–146.

Epps, T. W., & Epps, M. L. (1976). The stochastic dependence of security price changes and transaction volumes: Implications for the mixture-of-distributions hypothesis. *Econometrica, 44*(2), 305–321.

Fama, E. (1970). Efficient capital markets: A review of theory and empirical work. *The Journal of Finance, 25*(2), 387–417.

Fama, E. (1991). Efficient capital markets: II. *The Journal of Finance, 46*(5), 1575–1617.

Foster, G. (1973). Stock market reaction to estimates of earnings per share by company officials. *Journal of Accounting Research, 11*(1), 25–37.

Glosten, L. R., & Milgrom, P. R. (1985). Bid, ask, and transaction prices in a specialist market with heterogeneously informed traders. *Journal of Financial Economics, 14*, 71–100.

Harris, L. (1986). Cross-security tests of the mixture of distributions hypothesis. *The Journal of Financial and Quantitative Analysis, 21*(1), 39–46.

Hutson, E., & Kearney, C. (2001). Volatility in stocks subject to takeover bids: Australian evidence using daily data. *Journal of Empirical Finance, 8*, 273–296.

Ivanovski, Z., Narasanov, Z., & Ivanovska, N. (2015). Volatility and kurtosis at emerging markets: Comparative analysis of Macedonian Stock Exchange and six stock markets from Central and Eastern Europe. *Journal of International Scientific Publication, Economy & Business, 9*(1), 84–93.

Jennings, R. H., Starks, L. T., & Fellingham, J. C. (1981). An equilibrium model of asset trading with sequential information arrival. *The Journal of Finance, 36*(1), 143–161.

Karpoff, J. M. (1987). The relation between price change and trading volume: A survey. *The Journal of Financial and Quantitative Analysis, 22*(1), 109–126.

Kiger, J. E. (1972). An empirical investigation of NYSE volume and price reactions to the announcement of quarterly earnings. *Journal of Accounting Research, 10*, 113–128.

Kyle, A. S. (1985). Continuous auctions and insider trading. *Econometrica, 53*(6), 1315–1335.

Lamoureux, C. G., & Lastrapes, W. D. (1990). Heteroskedasticity in stock return data: Volume versus GARCH effects. *The Journal of Finance, 45*(1), 221–229.

Lawford, S. (2005). Finite-sample quantiles of the Jarque-Bera test. *Applied Economics Letter, 12*(6), 351–354.

Lee, B. S., & Rui, O. (2002). The dynamic relationship between stock returns and trading volume: Domestic and cross-country evidence. *Journal of Banking & Finance, 26*(1), 51–78.

Li, J., & Wu, C. (2006). Daily return volatility, bid-ask spreads, and information flow: Analyzing the information content of volume. *The Journal of Business, 79*(5), 2697–2739.

MacKinnon, J. G. (1991). Critical Values for cointegration tests. In R. F. Engle & C. W. J. Granger (Eds.), *Long-run economic relationships*. Oxford, UK: Oxford University Press.

Mahajan, S., & Singh, B. H. (2009). The empirical investigation of relationship between return, volume and volatility dynamics in Indian stock market. *Eurasian Journal of Business and Economics, 2*(4), 113–137.

Mahieu, R., & Bauer, R. (1998). A Bayesian analysis of stock return volatility and trading volume. *Applied Financial Economics, 8*, 671–687.

Morse, D. (1980). Asymmetrical information in securities markets and trading volume. *The Journal of Financial and Quantitative Analysis, 15*(5), 1129–1148.

Mossin, J. (1973). *Theory of financial markets*. Englewood Cliffs, NJ: Prentice-Hall.

Pati, P. C. (2017). Volatility, maturity and volume in the Indian metals futures. *Applied Economics Letters*. https://doi.org/10.1080/13504851.2017.1355536

Richardson, M., & Smith, T. (1994). A direct test of the mixture of distributions hypothesis: Measuring the daily flow of information. *The Journal of Financial and Quantitative Analysis, 29*(1), 101–116.

Rogalski, R. J. (1978). The dependence of prices and volume. *The Review of Economics and Statistics, 36*, 268–274.

Skrinjaric, T. (2014). Investment strategy on the Zagreb stock exchange based on dynamic DEA. *Croatian Economic Survey, 16*(1), 129–160.

Smirlock, M., & Starks, L. (1988). An empirical analysis of the stock price-volume relationship. *Journal of Banking and Finance, 12*, 31–41.

Takaishi, T., & Chen, T. T. (2016). The relationship between trading volumes, number of transactions, and stock volatility in GARCH models. *Journal of Physics: Conference Series, 738*, 1–4.

Tauchen, G. E., & Pitts, M. (1983). The price variability-volume relationship on speculative markets. *Econometrica, 51*(2), 485–505.

Wang, J. (1994). A model of competitive stock trading volume. *Journal of Political Economy, 102*(1), 127–168.

Assessment of the Globalization and Local Development Relationship in Terms of Political Risk Factors

Özcan Sezer and Hüseyin Çavuşoğlu

Abstract Today, globalization is an important factor affecting every aspect of life. Local development, on the other hand, is a concept aimed at progressing in the political, socio-economic and cultural field at the local level, which is the process of decision-making from the bottom up. It can be said that the effects of globalization on local development have changed both from country to country and from region to region. Globalization process develops mutual cooperation between countries in economic, cultural and social fields. This cooperation provides positive contributions to the local development process. Local development requires cooperation with both global actors and local actors. Local development is a concept that aims to promote the development of local communities in accordance with the principles of sustainable development in economic, social, cultural, physical and political contexts by activating local dynamics. Local development is motivated by local actors, although it is expressed as using countries' own local potentials to mobilize local dynamics and are exposed to global effects. Developing countries are evaluating their local potential to ensure their development. Due to the globalization, it is seen that local development has become the foreground with the participation of local, regional, national and international powers. The emergence of local development has brought about changes in the identification and implementation of local development policies. Now, states place more emphasis on local development and are increasing the authority of local governments in this direction. Today, it can be said that the concept of development is multifaceted as self-sustainable growth, structural change in the form of production, technological innovation, social political and institutional innovation and improvement in people's living standards. Local development can not be handled independently from globalization, it can not be achieved with only local dynamics. Local development has political risk factors based on international, national and local actors. Political risks are not homogeneous in all countries. The World Political Risk Report is a comprehensive review of the political risk, political

Ö. Sezer (✉) · H. Çavuşoğlu
Department of Political Science and Public Administration, Faculty of Economics and Administrative Sciences, Bülent Ecevit University, Zonguldak, Turkey
e-mail: ozcan.sezer@beun.edu.tr; huseyin.cavusoglu@beun.edu.tr

© Springer International Publishing AG, part of Springer Nature 2018   349
H. Dincer et al. (eds.), *Strategic Design and Innovative Thinking in Business Operations*, Contributions to Management Science,
https://doi.org/10.1007/978-3-319-77622-4_18

risks, transfer and convertibility, expropriation, breach of contract, abuse of sovereignty rights and financial risks, terrorism, war, civil disturbance, governmental power, government and opposition power balance, law system, local instability, economic climate, and other negative regulatory changes. The political risk factors mentioned in this study will be evaluated in terms of the relationship between globalization and local development.

1 Introduction

In the period that continued until the Second World War, there was a stable economic growth due to the large investments made by the state. Especially with the 1950s, global competitive economies have made certain formations that require cooperation at the regional scale. From the beginning of 1970s, it seems that the importance of regional policies decreased. Towards the end of the 1980s, it was observed that politics were central to the locality. Today, economic development has gained a local dimension, such as creating employment by creating local employment opportunities (Taş 2011: 7–8). After the 1970s, political powers abandoned active regional development policies and this brought about the change of the traditional, regional and economic development concept. As a result, the concept of locality has become increasingly important in the globalization process. Now, the role of the local authority in development is increasing (Aktakas 2006: 165–166). Localization together with globalization turned out for the forefront and the role of local development has increased (Genç and Erdoğan 2013: 249). The globalization phenomenon that emerged after the 1970s has led to significant changes in local development. The identification and mobilization of local dynamics in the new local development approach has gained great importance.

For an investor, the political stability of a country and the stability of the country are important factors in investing (De Moura et al. 2011: 43). Today, with globalization, the importance of political risk factors in investors' decisions is increasing. Every investor estimates what political risk factors might be. But what is important for investors is how much the inherent dynamics of each country will affect the investment risk (Robock 1971: 3). Whether it is international or local companies, will not act without considering the political atmosphere in the country to invest. There are many factors that affect the decision of the companies to settle down. Political risk is one of these factors. Among the elements affecting political risk factors are the social structure of the country, relations with foreign countries, history of the country, current political environment, practices of political parties, and social developments in the country.

In this study, emphasis is placed on the importance of local economic development with an understanding of localization that coincides with globalization and an assessment is made in terms of political risk factors. While local dynamics emphasize the importance of local development, it is stated that international investors have contributed to the local development process by preserving local values. At this point, both internal investors and the political risks affecting foreign investors are revealed, and theoretical assessments are made on what measures should be taken against political risks. The study examined the concepts of globalization and localization, the relationship between globalization and local economic development, the actors of local economic development and the political risk factors and political risk factors in local economic development.

2 Concepts of Globalization and Decentralization

Globalization is an ongoing process, with debates about the beginning. Globalization is a broad concept that can be addressed in economic, social, political, administrative, cultural, ideological and ecological dimensions, which have many field effects. Globalization implicitly means that the world shrinks and the planet becomes a globe as a whole. The most important factor is the qualitative developments in communication technologies and the transformations in the world economy (Van der Wusten 1998: 1; Robertson 1999: 21–22; Bozkurt 2000: 18; Atasoy 2005: 128). This transformation process is a process that evolves in a way that is changing in a way that is unequal and unequal, rather than describing a particular situation (James 2005: 195; Harvey 2000: 19).

In many people, globalization is simply a matter of taking power or influence from the hands of local communities and transferring them to the global arena. According to Giddens, this is one of the consequences of globalization. Because nations have begun to lose some of the economic power they had in the past. But globalization is not only an upward process; it is also a downward trend, creating new pressures in the direction of local autonomy. From this point of view it is noted that the nation state has become a unit that is now too small to solve major problems, but too large to solve small problems (Giddens 2000: 25).

Globalization is considered by some researchers as the world economy, the role of international companies, and the increase in the deregulation of finance capital, the growth of foreign direct investment, and the concentration of developments in information technology. Some researchers; new forms in the form of collective identities, emphasizing political consciousness, new forms of technology that affect the socio-cultural interactions, the daily social relations are transformed into the space of the nation state, make the national-some other authors; they perceive globalization as more abstract and perceive it as a deepening and concentration of interdependence between geographically distant places and regions very rapidly (Brenner 1999: 42).

McGrew (2005: 209) emphasizes the economic dimension of globalization by describing as the process of widespread economic relations in the world age. In parallel to this definition, Garrett (2000: 942), describes globalization as the integration of capital, service and product markets, while Das (2004: 6) defines globalization as the integration, homogenization or harmonization of countries and economies. Brenner (1999: 42–43) defines globalization as the spatial organization of world capitalism and perceives globalization as a bi-directional dialectical process. The first is the continual expansion and acceleration of the movement of money, goods, people, images and knowledge at a geographical level and the second is the transformation, re-differentiation, reconstruction and production of the transformation of the social-spatial infrastructure through rapid development.

The explanatory elements of globalization can be expressed as follows (Bonefeld 2001: 49–50):

- Increasing significance and importance in the global dimension of economic and financial structure.
- An important item in the production of knowledge.
- Increase in the speed of differentiation in specific technologies and the emergence of transnational qualities of technology.
- Global rise of multinational corporations; companies and the absence of electoral gifts outside of becoming global. Transnational banks, national governments and their national economies are becoming the most influential forces.
- Globalization of production, information and finance. This development has led to the national authority being stretched as a regulatory force and the globalization of the political authority in the form of pluralistic authority use jointly with the constitutions like the UN, G-8.

The beginning of contemporary globalization is generally accepted after 1980. In the process, a group of emerging economies have ceased to be spectators in the global economy and have begun to integrate with it. Developing countries have been able to provide comparative advantage by exporting from developed countries with abundant human resources, business-intensive manufacturing products and services. Some of them have done a pragmatic export of work-intensive products and have managed to place them on the market in certain product lines (Das 2004: 54).

Globalization is a process that comes to the forefront with more economical dimension. Globalization shows that we are witnessing the formation of a totally global economy and society in which the interconnected and nationalized national economy and the idea of a closed society is no longer valid that everyday life is linked to global forces (Bonefeld 2001: 49). In this context, economic globalization refers to the intensification and expansion of mutual economic interactions on a global scale. Large-scale capital and technology flows have encouraged trade in goods and services and new connections have emerged between national economies with the expansion of markets worldwide. The cornerstones of economic globalization are multinational corporations, economic institutions and major regional trading systems (Steger 2006: 61; Perraton 2006: 22). Economic globalization also includes the globalization of production and investment processes and financial markets. Thus, mutual dependence between national economies increases, capital, finance, labor, goods and business techniques become fluid (Karabağ 2002: 146; Das 2004: 3–5).

The notion of decentralization, which emerges from globalization, is often regarded as an anti-globalization, but it is a process that is complemented by two "global" and "local" intertwined words. In general, decentralization is understood as the process of turnover to operational units from the center of decision-making power (De Montricher 1995: 406). Decentralization is among the most controversial issues with globalization. Today, while the world is shaken by globalization tendencies, decentralization trends are strengthening at the same time, and the importance of decentralization in the globalization process is increasing steadily. In recent years, the politics of decentralization have come to be known along with the globalization of the whole world and it has started to be implemented in various countries in various forms, in which most local governments at the sub-national level have come to the forefront. The decentralization policies that the globalization process is forced to encourage governments to organize according to decentralization policies. The World Bank argues in its 1999–2000 report that both globalization and decentralization are inevitable and that a state success in the twenty-first century depends on how well these twin forces will govern. It has been stated that some powers of the nation state have to abandon the global world economy in the process of integrated world economy and the other powers to the local level.

Decision-making with the globalization process emphasizes the importance of decentralization for the development of democratic governance from the other side, along with the transfer to national and supranational institutions. In particular, it is emphasized that local people have a say in obtaining economic decisions at local level. In this direction, local autonomy, supported by the growing decentralization process in many nation-states, results in the establishment of some co-operation, networks and agreements and is pioneering a new process in the twenty-first century. One aspect of autonomy is through devolution or transfer of power to lower-level institutions. The most important steps to achieve autonomy should be continuation of the transformation process of the state, the day-to-day functioning of the administration mechanism, the arrangement of relations between administrations, and the ability to determine its own rules (Agranoff 2004: 27).

In the process of local economic development, it can be said that countries attach more importance to decentralization. In this context, more local administrations stand out as the actors of local development. When we look at the world scale, it appears that decision-making powers have been transferred to lower-level administrations. Large countries such as Australia, Canada and the United States have developed a system of decision-making responsibilities over the last few decades, with specific powers provided by different levels of government. European countries have signed the European Charter of Local Self-Government, which on their own basis forms the basis of the subsidiarity principle, and have adopted local governments as the public authorities closest to the citizen. In recent years there has been a wave of decentralization in developing countries all over the world. Latin America has entered a rapid decentralization process after the collapse of many authoritarian regimes, and China has undertaken a series of reforms in the intergovernmental finance system in the mid-1990s.

There are three key factors that accelerate the decentralization process, especially in developing countries (World Bank 2001: 4–5):

(a) **Political necessity**: Decentralization around the world is driven by a very political process rather than economic. The reaction to the domination and control of the central government for many years has revealed a strong impulse to local government autonomy in many countries.

(b) **Economic necessity**: Especially the economies of countries in transition economies have been regarded as state-controlled economies for many years, no factors that reduce the role of the state in the economy, and the provision of private goods.

(c) **Obligation of service delivery**: In the old system, central governments used central and local governments for service delivery, but enlargement of the centralization has grown and in many countries the use of all mandatory services has become financially unsustainable. In the new system, under increasing financial constraints, most countries have referred the responsibility for the provision of basic services to lower-level administrations. In many cases, local governments have had decision-making authority for preferential expenditure and have achieved their preferences so that they have met the demands and expectations of their citizens and have the capacity to implement them.

Globalization can create a favorable environment for world integration and the rise of economic borders, the support and strengthening of local development projects (Casanova 2004: 26). The necessity of implementing decentralization policies for local economic development is voiced by UNDP. There is a growing consensus that effective and good governance among the international community has a critical impetus for human development. Estimatedly, UNDP is committed to activities that promote good governance, with half of its current resources. UNDP supports local actors to ensure local economic development and tries to mobilize basic infrastructure and governance elements (Work 2001: 25–26).

3 The Relation Between Globalization and Local Economic Development

The effects of globalization have been discussed for the past 40 years. The phenomenon of globalization since the 1980s has caused significant changes in the social structure by affecting the economic, socio-cultural and political spheres of social life (Aktaş 2013: 185). With the economic dimension the phenomenon of globalization are the free circulation of trade and capital and the removal of obstacles in front. The phenomenon of globalization has turned into a valid economic policy in the world, with technological innovations emerging in the form of information processing, the widespread use of communication technologies and the minimization of transaction costs. The development of technology, the revolutionary advances in transportation, communication and information sectors, facilitated and accelerated the movement of goods, capital and people around the world (Darıcı 2007: 215–221).

In the process of decentralization that emerged along with globalization trends in the world, local economic development is regarded as one of the highest priority targets in the 1980s. In order for local economic development to be achieved successfully, it is stated that structural policies and liberalization policies should be prioritized in development policies and financial assistance should be provided to increase alternative investments (Helmsing 2001: 50–78). In the globalization process, local economic development is to mobilize local dynamics to ensure that local communities develop in accordance with sustainable development principles in economic, social, cultural and political contexts (Kaya 2007: 28). In short, local economic development is the capacity of the local economy to create prosperity for local residents (Dulupçu and Özgür 2006: 175). The local economic development approach is based on the political, socio-cultural and economic spheres built on the basis of the locale's unique qualities (Darıcı 2007: 218). Local development can be defined as a concept based on the political, socio-cultural development of the local forces, especially the economy (Darıcı 2007: 215).

As a result of globalization, there has been a change in the content of local economic development and thus the emergence of local initiatives and the emergence of a new understanding of local economic development that places great emphasis on their functioning (Tekeoğlu and Ildırar 2012: 1). The basic characteristics of local economic development, the realization of the development with the decisions taken from the local (from below), the cooperation of all actors in local economic development plans, the consideration of economic potential of each region, the improvement of basic conditions (Çetin 2007: 157).

Today, economic development has gained a local dimension, such as creating employment by creating local employment opportunities, directing local people to produce, and increasing national income per capita on a local basis (Tutar and Demiral 2007: 67). Local economic development according to the ILO; is a participatory development process with important objectives, such as the creation of a suitable business environment and the support of economic activities, which promotes partnership and cooperation between public and private sector actors in a particular region using local resources and competitive advantage, allowing for the common formation and implementation of a general development strategy (Boekel and Logtestijn 2002: 5).

Local economic development; activates actors, organizations and resources, develops new institutions and local systems with the help of dialogue and strategic activities, and reflects the idea of "think globally, act locally" (Çetin 2007: 156). Local economic development involves identifying and implementing the most effective policies to revitalize the urban or regional economy, create new business areas, and meet the economic, social and cultural needs of the local community. The phenomenon of globalization activates and influences the dynamics of local economic development. National governments and local administrations need to take the necessary precautions in any kind of risk environment in order to ensure economic development.

Global development emerges as a global development increase with the macro dimension of the countries together with the development elements. Global development elements can be listed as abolishing income inequality, eliminating the problem of unemployment, minimizing costs and ensuring competitiveness, ensuring legal regulations, ensuring inter-sectoral harmonization, and bringing R & D investments to appropriate levels (Darıcı 2007: 217–218). These elements are the basic principles of globalization and development and are also necessary elements in local development.

Especially the developments in mass media and international capital owners' decisions and movements much faster than in the past have significantly affected the local economic development. With globalization, local political participation has increased and citizens are more likely to participate in the political system because of the increased authority of local governments (Aktaş 2013: 196). Local governments have been more successful than central governments in solving political, social-cultural and economic problems because of their location (Aktaş 2013: 197). The impact of globalization on local economic development can vary from country to country and from region to region. When the literature is examined it is seen that the relationship between globalization and local development is viewed from three different perspectives: globalization is perceived as a threat to local development, globalization supports local development and local conditions, an alternative to the threat of globalization (Çetin 2007: 154).

Globalization causes free circulation of the capital on the world scale. Governments at national and local levels are required to make efforts to attract moving capital. Central government and local authorities are trying to do this by establishing financial tax incentives, direct aid, subsidized development and local economic development offices. With increasing mass unemployment and the decline of central government assistance from the other side, economic restructuring on local governments emerges as a pressure element (Mayer 1995: 319–320).

Cities, which are an important element of local units, have come to the forefront in terms of globalization and racing and competition between cities have increased. Today, when globalization is intense, local units and cities have gained economic importance. Globalization provides local governments with access to key resources such as capital and technology. Cities became one of the most important elements of local economic development, and the cities have given priority to local qualities have overcome infrastructure shortfalls in order for global capital to penetrate more into the country (Tekeoğlu and Ildırar 2012: 2–4).

Local governments are an important actor in accelerating the local economic development process in the organization, and in some cases in managing the conditions that enable economic development activities to be successful. The pressure of economic change, which is directly affecting local economies, prevents local governments from coming to ignore the problem of local economic development (Bennett 1990: 221).

The benefits of focusing on local economic development in the globalization process in terms of local governments are expressed as follows (Gibbs 2002: 86):

- Local economic development provides opportunities for those excluded from the global market.
- Local economic development can protect the social cohesion and local economic networks that are increasingly lost in the global economy.

Table 1 Key differences between traditional up-down development and local up-and-down economic development approaches

Traditional development	Local economic development
1. Regional and regional decisions are taken at the center	1. Development is carried out at the level of all territorial initiatives taken from below (local)
2. Managed by central government	2. Not managed from a single center, vertical co-operation between management layers, horizontal co-operation between public and private sectors
3. Sectoral approach applies in development	3. The developmental approach (localization, environment, etc.) is valid
4. Large industrial projects are developed to support other economic activities	4. In order to ensure alignment with the changing economic environment of the local economic system, maximum benefit from the development potential of each sector is provided
5. Financial incentives are applied to attract economic activities	5. Some basic conditions for the development of economic activities are tried to be realized

Source: Rodriguez-Pose, A. (2001), "The Role of the ILO in Implementing Local Economic Development Strategies in a Globalized World", Working Papers, London

- Local economic development can improve local differences in the face of cultural homogenization created by globalization.
- A strong local economic structure provides both a determination in the restructuring process and a new form of comparative dominance against the economic weakness brought about by globalization.

The growing importance of the local economic development approach has played an important role in shaking confidence in traditional development policies. Traditional up-and-down development approaches that adopt some standard policies and strategies to achieve economic development have failed in the globalizing world. Significant differences between local economic development and up-to-down development approaches are shown in Table 1 (Çetin 2007: 156–157).

The European Union plays an important role in support of development agencies in the regional development process. Over the last two decades, a number of territorial European Union policies (e.g. Structural Funds, Leader, Interreg or Urban programmes) have developed similar norms of action at the local level: vertical partnerships between levels of administration, horizontal partnerships between the public sector and the civil society, networking of 'best practices' (Pasquier 2005: 295).

4   Actors of Local Economic Development

The phenomenon of decentralization and local development that emerged with the phenomenon of globalization has led to a change in the actors of the development process. During periods when globalization is not heavily influenced, the central state has taken the role as the most important actor in development. However, the diversity of the dynamics of globalization process development has resulted in significant changes in the number and role of actors in this process. While the number and variety of actors in local economic development are different, their roles can be summarized in five general terms (Hazman 2011: 47–48):

- To contribute to the formation of local and regional information sharing network,
- Strengthening infrastructure capabilities for entrepreneurs and making them suitable,
- To develop sustainable development models for social capital,
- To ensure the participation of social groups in the local development process,
- Engage in basic government programs related to investment and production.

(a) **State (central administration)**: While globalization and the tendency of decentralization to evolve together enable the emergence of non-state actors in local economic development. Local economic development alone is a goal that can not be left as a private sector. The role of the state here is regulatory and incentive. The role of the state in the local development process can generally be grouped under five headings (Hazman 2011: 48):

- The state is in charge of the economy's financial and monetary policies.
- The state is a supporter of economic growth by developing and implementing growth policies.
- The state affects the distribution of income among various social groups and regions.
- The State is the regulator in nature that will take away the problems of the industry and the market.
- The state is protecting the rights of its citizens and investors.

(b) **International Actors**: International organizations such as the European Union (EU), the International Labor Organization (ILO), the Organization for Economic Cooperation and Development (OECD), the United Nations Development Program (UNDP) and the United Nations Project Services Office (UNOPS) (Rodriguez-Pose 2001: 1–19; Ecotec 2002). Some of the international organizations have implemented comprehensive programs that support the economic development process at the local level. Local development strategies and organizations are drawing attention in almost all developed economies, adapting to emerging economies (Çetin 2006: 127). Structural funds of the EU in general and methods recommended by the European Regional Development Fund in particular are used to reduce inequalities in development by improving the conditions of local development (Bennet and Payne 2000).

(c) **Local Entrepreneurs and Investors**: The various associations and organizations that local entrepreneurs have come together to contribute to local economic development. However, problems arising from inadequacy of resources for rural development entrepreneurs are a major obstacle to local development. It is important that local economic development programs are run together with central administration, local governments, entrepreneurs, development agencies.

In the field of local development, especially small and medium-sized enterprises, as one of the cornerstones of the economy, are qualitative enterprises that create employment area and accelerate regional development by contributing to economic development (Hazman 2011: 52–53).

(d) **Local Government**: It is seen that local economic development has started to transfer the authorities of the central administrations to the local governments when the development progress in the world is observed. Significant steps have been taken with the establishment of community-based local organizations. Local governments' responsibility for ensuring local economic development is particularly focused on providing public funding. Along with ensuring local development; positive developments such as out-of-country products of production oriented companies, sales made everywhere in the country, productivity increases, appraisal of idle resources, creation of good working conditions can be experienced (Hazman 2011: 47).

(e) **Non-Governmental Organizations**: One of the actors of local development in the globalizing world has been civil society organizations (NGO's). NGO's are seeking to improve job capacity at the local level, to support innovative activities, to achieve these goals by using internal resources within an integrated approach, and to take into account the social justice dimension of development. NGO's, an important actor in the decision-making process within the framework of governance, are increasingly important in the decision-making process on the world scale. Local economic development is viewed as a process in which a well-defined area of boundaries is created through the partnership of different actors, such as local governments, social groups, NGO's, and the private sector, to manage existing resources, create new business opportunities, revitalize the economy and increase competitiveness. In the civil society-state relationship, as an actor of development, civil society becomes stronger and decisive, contributing to the widespread adoption of the governance principle (Zengin and Öztaş 2008: 86).

(f) **Local (Regional) Development Agencies**: Countries have begun to make structural transformation in regional development policies in order to cope with the pressures and threats that emerged from rapid economic change in the globalization and increasing economic competition environment and to take advantage of the opportunities that arise in this process. The most important actor of this new approach is seen as Regional Development Agencies (RDA's) (Akiş 2011: 238). The RDA's are organizations created to revitalize, organize and improve the economy at the regional level. The main function of the RDA is to identify the sectoral and general development problems, to identify the solutions for these problems and to develop the solutions to these problems. The basic function of the RDA is to attract the foreign investment to the region and to develop the economic and social aspects of the region by developing and developing the internal potential. The objectives of the RDA should be broad and include elements such as the development of regional competitiveness, increasing the competitiveness of local small and medium-sized enterprises (SMEs), creating an attractive zone for foreign investment (Aslan 2005: 286).

RDA provides information to regional and local governments on a variety of topics ranging from investment areas to labor force and transport infrastructure; contributes to the marketing of the region and the renewal of its image and pioneers in bringing new investments to the region. It is also the duty of the RDA to establish close ties with universities and other educational institutions in the region and to develop joint project (Akiş 2011: 247). The structural adjustment policies brought about by the globalization process necessitated the development of original processes and tools in many areas. It has been stated that in the negotiations for full membership to the EU, regional planning in Turkey should be dealt with a new understanding, and that the most effective tool is the RDA (Akiş 2011: 249).

5 Political Risk and Political Risk Factors in Local Economic Development

Another dimension of the change in globalization's perception of time and space is also the cities. In one view, globalization has led to the loss of the significance of the nation-state concept. It is argued that the state, which played an active role in the development of the previous period, is now no longer a decision maker in some economic decisions and that the current regulations on the world economy, including nation states, are also limited. For this reason, while the constitutionality of the nation-state has been questioned, local units, cities and regions have begun to come to the forefront in terms of economy (Eraydın 2001: 368–370). There are also some risk factors for local development to be indexed to localization. Some of these risk factors will be addressed below.

5.1 Definition of Political Risk

Decentralization and the development of local development, which have coincided with the globalization process, have spread all over the world as a new development model, which has opened new opportunities for commercial opportunities and markets. While the globalization process has revealed these important opportunities and expansions, it has also brought the concept of "risk" to the agenda at the same time. Although the term "politic risk" occurs frequently in the international business literature, agreement about is meaning is limited to an implication of unwanted consequences of political activity (Kobrin 1979). Identification and measurement of risk is, in particular, the most fundamental problem of international investment decision makers. In this context, rule changes or dysfunctions of the rules of the national state and the international rule-making institutions, which set the rules of the game, can cause important developments in the fate of investors' investments.

Political risk can be defined as economic and social events, situations and developments that can lead to country risk (Nagy 1984).

Kennedy (1987) explains the political risk separately from the concept of the country's risk. The country's risk is defined as "events and developments stemming from the political-economic-social structure of the country in which an enterprise does business"; political risk is defined as "the political event or developments that can lead to the financial loss of the company, the strategy change and the problem of the employee" (Kennedy 1987).

5.2   Political Risk Factors

Risk factors are the most important obstacles to globalizing capital in the globalizing world. The political risks, which vary from country to country and are very diverse, are restricted by the policies of the host country of foreign investments of multinational corporations. Political risk is usually defined as developments such as elections, government changes, tax changes, strikes, legal regulations, public figures, structural collapses. Violent political activities, such as terrorism, kidnappings, military coups, ethnic and racial wars, civil war, are some of the political risks.

When multinational corporations invest in a country they have to examine the circumstances of that country. This is because; to make correct predictions and decisions on issues such as political situation, competition, level of technological development, socio-cultural changes, and to provide correct approaches to issues, including long-term plans based on this information. In this study, political risk factors will be tried to be divided into internal and external factors (Table 2).

5.2.1   Internal Factors

Political risk factors within the country need to be taken into account when making investment decisions in terms of international businesses. The globalization of business life brings with it the growing tensions, conflicts and different political,

Table 2 Politic risk factors

Internal factors	External factors
1. Country's management style	1. Migration, conflict and terrorism
2. The legal arrangement of the country	2. Foreign direct investment
3. Government-opposition power balance	3. Participation in international organizations
4. Political stability	
5. The impact of NGOs and pressure groups	
6. The nature of the bureaucracy	

Source: Table 2 is organized by the authors of the study

economic and social goals between investors and host countries, with increasing political, economic and social vulnerabilities at the national and local level as well as the increasing importance of local economic development. Developments related to this relationship between investors and political power around the world are causing political rage (Keleş 2007: 1).

Legal Arrangement of the Country

The development of the established legal system of the countries and their harmony with the world is one of the important factors in investors' investment decision in that country. The fact that the legal system applied in the country is fair and reliable in and out of the country has an effect in applying the policies of economic decision makers at the local level. The geographical structure, culture, competitiveness, human capital, institutions and institutional infrastructure of the countries are the main determinants of the economic growth of an country (Ünsal 2007: 286–291). Therefore, the legal order the country has one of the main institutions in the development of that country. The risk of financial damage or reputation of operators and investors is the risk of the country due to legal or regulatory means, due to difficulties in complying with the laws, regulations or other regulatory procedures of the host country. Risk; government activity measures, rule of law, property rights and legal nature (Aon Risk Solutions 2016: 19).

In countries such as Turkey, which accepts the Land Europe legal system, execution comes from within the legislature, and against these two powers the judiciary remains alone. As a result, some arbitrary implementations of the executive are corrected by the judiciary. But the executive body, which is so intertwined with the legislature, is trying to save itself from under the jurisdiction of the judiciary by making the necessary legal arrangements. In Turkey, for example, this practice is quite common. A law stipulating that any transaction should be made in accordance with the government's discretion is being tried by law to prevent all judicial obstacles. In this context, in order to ensure that the executive is single, the Constitution referendum was introduced in Turkey in April 2016 and the system of the Presidency was adopted. However, it is necessary to state that the political risks in Turkey arise from judicial decisions from time to time.

In terms of investors and businesses, the most important problems in terms of legal order are mostly between the government, which is the main center of international companies, and the host country. Such diplomatic problems and the willingness of international businesses to attract attention sometimes oblige governments to make constructive legal amendments. These are often confronted as laws against international arbitration. Arbitration is perhaps the antithesis of a kind of risk insurance that governments have found to unravel themselves. Apart from this, the widespread international trade and the development of technology are the result of legally protecting the rights of intellectual property. Governments need to protect their intellectual property by enacting laws. If it is not protected, it will be a very bad situation for companies that develop new technologies. In the process of local economic development, political risks originating from the legal order must be analyzed and evaluated before investment decisions are made.

Country's Management Style

The point that we need to understand from the way of the government of the country is whether or not it is a democratic administration. Oppressive governments, systems dominated by one person, or where the weight of the soldier's politics is high, are not preferred by investors. Because they are all negative factors for investors (Aktepe 1998: 46).

Government-Opposition Power Balance

The government-opposition power balance is an important point to consider, which is taken into account before investment by foreign investors. Depending on the power of the government, political and bureaucratic environment in the countries, government-business world relations are shaped. Governments that are strong in the political system can apply stronger policies. It can be said that the continuity of the governments depends on the success of the policies that they apply. Another point that investors take into consideration is the power ratios of the opposition parties in the system. Investors closely monitor the programs and actions of the opposition parties (Aktepe 1998: 47).

Political Stability

Political power comes to work in order to improve the country in every aspect, and political power is among the most prominent players in the international system. From the perspective of political stability, investors want political parties to have a long period of power. This continuity is very important for investors. Particularly the implementation of economic policies requires a long time. The investors also want a long-term political power to realize these policies. The stay of the same party in political power for a long time means that radical changes will not take place in the bureaucracy. This is a development in favor of investors. Political instability is increasing in situations like civil war, rebellion, confusion, assassination in a country (Aktepe 1998: 47).

Impact of NGO and Pressure Groups

Apart from the political parties, non-governmental organizations and pressure groups play an important role in the political system. Non-governmental organizations and pressure groups work in order to make decisions in their favor by making pressure on the political system. Methods used by these groups include direct interviews, strikes, rallies, dissemination, signature collection, use of mass media. The main factors determining the power of NGOs and pressure groups are the number of members, financial power, social status, level of organization, leadership. Non-governmental organizations and pressure groups are seen as an important force that investors consider in the political environment before investing (Aktepe 1998: 47).

The Nature of the Bureaucracy

The bureaucracy is an advanced structure that emerges with modern states. Bureaucracy has emerged as a means of determining the field of action of political power with the modern state. Thanks to the bureaucracy, the privileges of political power continue and political commitment continues. At the core of the bureaucracy is the absolute loyalty of political power. The bureaucracy can be described as a civil servant who can unquestioningly make the decisions of political power. Political power can organize the society and this is done thanks to the bureaucracy. Bureaucracy provides easy management. By Weber's statement; *"Through political power, bureaucracy, has the possibility to shape all patterns of everyday life to fit their own legitimate patterns."* The importance of bureaucracy at the political risk is understood when political power changes. The power of the bureaucracy means that it can bring down the dangers that might emerge when governments change (Demirci and Önder 2015: 559–574).

5.2.2 External Factors

Foreign Direct Investments (FDI)

Another of the political risk factors is the amount, volume, diversity and level of foreign direct investment (FDI). The amount of foreign capital investments that came with the globalization process has increased all over the world. The determinants of direct foreign capital movements can be considered as driving and attractive factors. Pushing factors are global factors that have direct or indirect influence on FDI among countries and that are created by investor countries and international conditions. These are the direction of the supply of investment. Attractive factors are local factors specific to the invested countries and indicate the demand direction of FDI (Albuquerque et al. 2005: 269, 272; Candemir 2009: 660). Attractive factors affecting foreign direct capital flows refer to country-specific characteristics, opportunities and risks to be invested. Factors such as macroeconomic stability, access to finance, access to education, market opportunities, infrastructure capacity, the existence of corruption, and political risks are important determinants that can provide prior information on how much an individual can be host direct foreign investment flows (Bayraktutan and Özgür 2016: 90–91).

Political risks arising in terms of FDI in the local economic development process refer to other risks other than commercial risks. These risks may be from the host country or the international environment. Political risks that have not been fully predicted in the past can cause the investment climate to deteriorate by causing weakening of the rights of the investors on their assets through sudden changes in the political environment of the host country. The prominence of political risks is set out in the WIPR 2013 Report, where the World Bank Group's policy risk insurance and credit rating augmentation MIGA assesses the challenges that foreign investors may face in developing countries (Bayraktutan and Özgür 2016: 92).

The volume of foreign capital investments, which generate annually globally, has increased about 16 times between the years 2010–2013 compared to the 1980s. Developing countries, beginning to see FDI as a means to get rid of the middle income, have hosted more than half of this volume for the first time in 2012 (Bayraktutan and Özgür 2016: 87–88). Decreasing international direct investments, such as macroeconomic fragilities in the world in 2014, economic policy uncertainties, escalating geopolitical risks and the localization of some international direct investments, amounted to $1.76 trillion with a significant increase of 38% in 2015 and the effects of the global crisis it has reached the highest level since 2008 (T.C. Ekonomi Bakanlığı 2016: 1).

With the impact of globalization, the share of FDI in emerging countries, which have a relatively high political and economic vulnerability after 2000, is increasing. This situation worries investors. The multilateral investment institutions (MIGA) 2013 World Investment and Political Risk Report (WIPR) show that political risks are in the second place after macroeconomic stability (World Bank 2014). Political uncertainties and geopolitical risks are highlighted as the most important risks for FDI in 2017. Global investment is seeing a modest recovery, with projections for 2017 cautiously optimistic. Higher economic growth expectations across major regions, a resumption of growth in trade and a recovery in corporate profits could support a small increase in FDI. Global flows are forecast to increase to almost $1.8 trillion in 2017, continuing to $1.85 trillion in 2018—still below the 2007 peak (UNCTAD 2017: x) . Political and geopolitical risks are pushing foreign capital investors in the decision-making process. According to UNCTAD's 2017 World Investment Report; "Investment policymaking is getting more complex, more divergent and more uncertain. Sustainable development considerations make investment policies more challenging and multifaceted. Policymaking is also becoming more divergent, reflecting the variety of approaches with which societies and governments respond to the effects of globalization. This, together with more government interventions, has also reduced the predictability of investment policies for investors. A rules based investment regime that is credible, has broad international support and aims at sustainability and inclusiveness can help reduce uncertainty and improve the stability of investment relations" (UNCTAD 2017).

FDI in Turkey were announced as USD 16.5 billion in 2015. In 2015, there was a 36% increase compared to 2014. In this respect, Turkey is among the countries that attract the highest international direct investment in the world in 2015. Thus, it rose

Table 3 Top FDI countries and Turkey (billion USD, year 2015)

Number	Country	FDI
1	USA	379.9
2	Hong Kong	174.9
3	China	135.6
4	Ireland	100.5
5	Netherlands	72.6
6	Switzerland	68.8
7	Singapore	65.3
8	Brazil	64.6
9	Canada	48.6
10	India	44.2
20	Turkey	16.5
	World Total	1762.2

Source: UNCTAD (2016). World Investment Report (WIR)

to second in 2014 and rose to third place in the eighth place among the developing countries (Table 3).

In the UNCTAD World Investment Report 2017, the importance of the incentive packages that Turkey gave for the development of local economies was emphasized. In particular, reforms such as incentives from the R & D field and foreign citizenship in 2017 have been highlighted. Likewise, the UNCTAD report noted that Turkey is the most active country in signing seven agreements in 2017 in the area of mutual encouragement and protection of investments. According to the UNCTAD 2017 World Investment Report, FDI in developed countries grew by 5% in 2016, while FDI in developing countries declined by 14%. However, in many developed and developing countries, FDI inflows registered a sharp decline. In 2016, FDI inflows are 88% in Ireland, 84% in Indonesia, 73% in Thailand, 71% in Germany, 40% in France, 19% in Mexico, 16% (UNCTAD 2017).

The achievement of political stability in Turkey has shown that the greatest reduction in political risks is the result of the increase in global direct foreign capital. FDI inflows in Turkey decreased by 30% in 2016. In 2016, despite all the adversities and political risks, Turkey has attracted $12.3 billion in FDI. According to the results of the FDI intelligence report on the results of the year 2016, there has been a 55% increase in direct investments from the scrutiny, which provided significant contributions to economic development, employment and industry. Direct investments from scratch will transform the Turkish economy in the long run to provide more integration into the global value chain (http://www.ntv.com.tr/ekonomi/unctad-2017-dunya-yatirim-raporu aciklandi,3iad7qUILkq7K-47r08_fw).

Participation in International Organizations

Political risks can lead to huge declines in the profit rate of foreign companies invested in this country due to sudden chaotic processes in the political environment of a country. In such a case, investors are also likely to lose all their assets. The fact that international arbitration is recognized in agreements between countries as a legal means to resolve such cases is a factor that relaxes foreign investors (Bayraktutan and Özgür 2016: 93). Participation in international organizations such as the World Bank, the IMF, WTO, the European Monetary Fund (EMF), OECD, and the other international organizations established at regional scales is a situation that reduces political risk in terms of businesses that will invest in that country.

There was a significant contribution to the formation of economic policies of the international economic institutions, especially the IMF, around the world. This tendency started to disappear from the second half of the 1980s. As the developed countries tend to discuss their problems at the G7 meetings, the impact of the IMF has begun to shift to more developed countries, just as it is in the World Bank. The WTO is actively involved in the development of these three international economic institutions and is influenced by their decisions. All of the countries that are members of the WTO are therefore influenced by their decisions and direction as they shape the foreign trade policies in the context of the WTO's decisions. The membership of the invested country to such international organizations is an assurance element in case of any risk in terms of investment decision-making enterprises. International organizations such as the EU, ILO, OECD, UNDP, and UNOPS support local development practices in many developed and developing countries (Çetin 2007: 153). Local development is affected by globalization and coincidental decentralization processes. One of the main trends that emerged with globalization is the gradual increase in homogeneity. As a result, similar products, similar preferences and similar cultures are formed almost everywhere in the world. The decentralization emphasizes the differences among the phenomenal places, which brings together various opportunities and risks (Casanova 2004: 14–15).

Migration, Conflict and Terrorism

Political instability is increasing in situations such as civil war, rebellions, confusion, assassinations in a country. The wars can be divided into two, hot and cold war. Investors are afraid of negative situations such as not being able to make payments in the battlefield, hesitating investments, and reducing income considerably. The war is a factor that affects neighboring countries as well as countries that have experienced this conflict. Political risks are also seen in the neighboring countries in the region where there is war. In order for a group of people to have a say in the management of a country, holding silos, bombed actions, assassinations can be considered as terrorist activities. Investors do not prefer to invest in the region where terrorist acts are present, and it can be said that the negative effects of terrorism are more prevalent in underdeveloped countries. Political power is the supreme power in a country and it can provide countries with more investment opportunities with their decisions. In Turkey, especially in the Eastern and Southeastern Anatolia, political power seems to attract a variety of incentives to attract investors (Tunalı 2012: 52–57).

6 Conclusion

The phenomenon of decentralization that coincides with the globalization process aims to integrate local economies with the global economy while trying to maintain development by protecting local values and cultures from one side. Today, the only actor in the concept of economic development is not the state. Local, national and international investors, NGOs and local governments play an important role in the process of local economic development. The most important goal of a country is the development of the country from the beginning to the whole country. For this, central government and local governments support the development process by giving incentives by making many legal arrangements in order to invest in domestic and foreign businesses. Multinational corporations are also evaluating the country they invest in. In these evaluations, political risk factors are prominent in the investment process. A high level of political risk in a country will prevent investors from investing in any amount of investment capital in the country concerned.

In a globalizing world, political risks can arise in many different ways. When investors evaluate the political risks associated with a country, they do not simply rely on financial indicators. In addition, it is necessary to evaluate the political and investment environment of a country by using socio-economic, social and environmental indicators. Political risk analysis includes both macro and micro risk content. Companies that will invest at the local level have a high degree of inequality in the distribution of their assets in rural areas and cities; an economic development near developed zero with a high debt weight; the potential for unemployed adult labor force; a serious population growth problem, a large number of politically conscious young people entering a job market that is carrying more work than they can carry; a past land rent system; rapid urbanization and the resulting population in cities as a result. These factors may also include serious economic strains from global conditions.

The development of local economies and the promotion of the welfare of the people at the local level are the most important policies of the states. For this, the most important task of national governments is to reduce the most political risk factors that investors will give up investment decisions. When we look at the causes of the political risk, it can be said that local instability arising from actual political or social disorder, the war or terrorist events in the country considered to be invested, the political or economic climate of the government, the actions of opposing groups that do not like management within the country, the expropriation movements of the immovables to the property of the state and the government's attitudes towards foreign investors.

It is necessary to implement measures to reduce political risks in order to ensure the local economic development of a country. Political stability, institutionalization and an established legal system are the most important elements in this direction. In today's geopolitical and economic environment, investors need to have a comprehensive view of the political dimension of risk that they will be exposed to in the market they will invest in. It is important to plan ahead and formulate strategies according to the types and ranks of the country in terms of the investing businesses. In the world, investors measure the political risk factors of countries through various institutions. Political risk factors will become one of the main elements in future investment decisions in a country. This study concludes that political risk factors need to be taken into account by central and local authorities, and that new work and regulation are needed at the legal, economic and socio-cultural scales in the light of global development in order to ensure local development.

References

Agranoff, S. (2004). Autonomy, devolution and intergovernmental relations. *Regional and Federal Studies, 14*(1), 26–65.

Akiş, E. (2011). Küreselleşme sürecinde bölgesel kalkınma yaklaşımındaki gelişmeler ve bölgesel kalkınma ajansları. *İstanbul Üniversitesi Sosyoloji Konferansları, 44*, 236–256.

Aktakas, B. G. (2006). *Bölgesel yerel kalkınma bölgesel gelişme için bir model* (Yayımlanmamış Yüksek Lisans tezi). Adana: Çukurova Üniversitesi SBE.

Aktaş, M. (2013). Küreselleşme sürecinde yerel kalkınma devlet ve demokrasi. In B. Özer & G. Şeker (Eds.), *Yerel ve Bölgesel Kalkınma: Küresel ve Yerel Bakış Açıları* (pp. 185–200). Manisa: Celal Bayar Üniversitesi.

Aktepe, C. (1998). *Türkiye'de yabancı sermaye yatırımlarını etkileyen bir faktör: poliitik risk* (Yayımlanmamış Yüksek Lisans tezi). Ankara: Gazi Üniversitesi SBE.

Aon Risk Solutions. (2016). Politik risk haritası. Global Brokerlik Merkezi, 12.08.2017. http://www.Aon.Com/Turkey/Tr/Attachments/Politikriskharitasibolgeseldegerlendirmeler.Pdf

Aslan, K. (2005). Bölgesel kalkınma farklılıklarının giderilmesinde etkin bir araç: Bölgesel planlama ve bölgesel kalkınma ajansları. *İstanbul Ticaret Üniversitesi Sosyal Bilimler Dergisi, 7*, 275–294.

Albuquerque, R., Loayza, N., & Serven, L. (2005). World market integration through the lensor foreign direct investors. *Journal of International Economics, 66*(2), 267–295.

Atasoy, F. (2005). *Küreselleşme ve milliyetçilik*. İstanbul: Ötüken Yayınları.

Bayraktutan, Y., & Özgür, M. T. (2016). Politik riskler, iki taraflı yatırım anlaşmaları ve uyuşmazlıklar bağlamında doğrudan yabancı yatırımlar. *Uluslararası Ekonomik Araştırmalar Dergisi, 2*(4), 87–104.

Bennet, R., & Payne, D. (2000). *Local and regional economic development: Renegotiating power under labour*. Aldershot: Ashgate.

Bennett, R. J. (1990). Decentralization and local economic development. In R. Bennett (Ed.), *Decentralization local government and markets towards a post-welfare agenda*. Oxford: Clarendon Press.

Boekel, V. G., & Logtestijn, V. M. (2002). *Applying the comprehensive LED approach: The case of Mozambique*. Geneva: Cooperative Branch International Labour Office.

Bonefeld, W. (2001). Küreselleşme siyaseti: ideoloji ve kritik, Çev. Ali Kaban. *Türkiye Günlüğü, 64*, 49–60.

Bozkurt, V. (2000). Küreselleşme: kavram, gelişim ve yaklaşımlar, Der. V. Bozkurt. *Küreselleşmenin İnsani Yüzü.* İstanbul: Alfa Yay.

Brenner, N. (1999). Beyond state-centrism? space, territoriality and geographical scale in globalization studies. *Theory and Society, 28*(1), 39–78.

Candemir, A. (2009). Doğrudan yabancı sermaye yatırımlarını etkileyen faktörler. *Ege Akademik Bakış, 9*(2), 659–675.

Casanova, F. (2004). *Local economic development, productive networks and training: Alternative approaches to training and work for young people.* Montevideo: Cinterfor.

Çetin, M. (2006). Yerel kalkınma ajansları. *Ege Academic Review, 6*(2), 127–139.

Çetin, M. (2007). Yerel ekonomik kalkınma yaklaşımı ve uluslararası organizasyonlar. *Yönetim ve Ekonomi, 14*(1), 153–170.

Darıcı, B. (2007). Yerel kalkınmada küresel yaklaşımlar ve Türkiye'nin konumu. *Selçuk Üniversitesi Karaman İİBF Dergisi Özel Sayısı,* pp. 215–221.

Das, D. K. (2004). *The economic dimension of globalization.* London: Palgrave Macmillan.

De Montricher, N. (1995). Country report: Decentralization in France. *Governance: An International Journal of Policy and Administration, 8*(3), 405–418.

De Moura, D. F., Ferrari, M. A., Coelho, M., & Pedro, I. (2011). An analysis of the political risks environment in American developing countries. *International Journal of Academic Research, 3* (4), 287–291.

Demirci, F., & Önder, Ö. (2015). Bürokrasi. In H. Çetin (Ed.), *Siyaset bilimi* (pp. 559–617). Ankara: Orion kitabevi.

Dulupçu, M. A., & Özgür, H. (2006). Yerel ekonomik gelişmede yerel yönetimlerin rolü. In H. Özgür & B. Parlak (Eds.), *Avrupa Perspektifinde Yerel Yönetimler* (pp. 171–202). İstanbul: Alfa Aktüel Yayınları.

ECOTEC. (2002). *Thematic evaluation of the territorial employment pacts.* Final Report to Directorate General Regional Policy, Ecotec Research and Consulting Limited.

Eraydın, A. (2001). Küreselleşme-yerelleşme ve işlevleri farklılaşan kentler, Prof. Dr. Cevat Geray'a Armağan (pp. 363–392). Ankara: Mülkiyeliler Birliği Yayını.

Garrett, G. (2000). The causes of globalization. *Comparative Political Studies, 33,* 941–991.

Genç, N., & Erdoğan, Ü. (2013). Yerel demokrasi ve kalkınma bağlaminda sivil toplum kuruluşlarinin rolü: Aydin örneği. In B. Özer & G. Şeker (Eds.), *Yerel ve Bölgesel Kalkınma: Küresel ve Yerel Bakış Açıları* (pp. 249–263). Manisa: Celal Bayar Üniversitesi Matbaa Birimi.

Gibbs, D. (2002). *Local economic development & the environment.* New York: Routledge.

Giddens, A. (2000). *Elimizden kaçıp giden dünya.* Çev. Osman Akınhay. İstanbul: Alfa Yayınları.

Harvey, D. (2000). Globalization in questions. In J. Schmidt & J. Hersh (Eds.), *Globalization and social change.* London: Routledge.

Hazman, G. G. (2011). *Türkiye'de yerel düzeyde kalkınma hedefi ve belediyeler.* Ankara: Seçkin Yayınevi.

Helmsing, A. H. J. (2001). Local economic development, new generations of actors, policies and instruments. *Draft papers for the Cape Town symposium,* 15.07.2017. http://www.meso-nrw. de/helmsing.pdf

James, P. (2005). Arguing globalizations: Propositions towards an investigation of global formation. *Globalizations, 2*(2), 193–209.

Karabağ, S. (2002). *Mekanın siyasallaşması.* Ankara: Nobel yayınları.

Kaya, E. (2007). Modern kent yönetimi-III. *Yerel Siyaset, 2* (22).

Keleş, C. (2007). *Siyasal riskin finansal yansımaları üzerine bir çalışma* (yayınlanmamış doktora tezi), Ankara Üniversitesi, Sosyal Bilimler Enstitüsü, Ankara.

Kennedy, C. R. (1987). *Political risk management.* New York: Quorum Books.

Kobrin, S. J. (1979). Political risk: A review and reconsideration. *Journal of International Business Studies, 10*(1), 67–80.

Mayer, M. (1995). Post-Fordist city politics. In A. Amin (Ed.), *Post-Fordism: A Reader* (pp. 315–330). Cambridge: Blackwell.

McGrew, A. (2005). The logics of globalization. In J. Ravenhill (Ed.), *Global political economy*. Oxford: Oxford University Press.

Nagy, P. J. (1984). *Country risk*. London: Euromoney.

Pasquier, R. (2005). Cognitive Europeanization and the territorial effects of multilevel policy transfer: Local development in French and Spanish regions. *Regional and Federal Studies, 15* (3), 295–310.

Perraton, J. (2006). Küreselleşen bir dünyada ekonomik aktivite. In N. Demirci (Çev.) & K. Bülbül (Ed.), *Küreselleşme okumaları*. Ankara: Kadim yayınları.

Robertson, R. (1999). *Küreselleşme, toplum kuramı ve küresel kültür*, Çev. Ü. Hüsrev Yolsal. Ankara: Bilim ve Sanat Yayınları.

Robock, S. H. (1971). Political risk: Identification and assessment. *Columbia Journal of World Business, 6*(4), 1–20.

Rodriguez-Pose, A. (2001). *The role of the ILO in implementing local economic development strategies in a globalized world*. Working Papers, 20.07.2017. http://www.ilo.org/wcmsp5/ groups/public/---ed_emp/---emp_ent/led/documents/publication/wcms_111545.pdf

Steger, M. B. (2006). *Küreselleşme*, Çev. A. Ersoy. Ankara: Dost Kitabevi.

Taş, C. (2011). *Kalkınmaya giden yol ajanslardan mı geçer?*, 29.08.2017. http://www. ekonomikyorumlar.com.tr/dergiler/gundem/Gundem_1_Sayi_523.pdf

T.C. Ekonomi Bakanlığı. (2016). *Uluslararası doğrudan yatırımlar 2015 yılı raporu*.

Tekeoğlu, M., & Ildırar, M. (2012). Küreselleşme sürecinde kent ekonomileri: Gaziantep örneği. Türkiye Ekonomi Kurumu, 01.09.2017. http://www.tek.org.tr/dosyalar/gaziantep6.pdf

Tunalı, P. (2012). *Doğrudan yabanci sermaye yatirimlarinda politik risk ve Türk ilaç sektöründe politik riskin değerlendirilmesi* (Yayımlanmamış Yüksek Lisans tezi). İstanbul Üniversitesi SBE.

Tutar, F., & Demiral, M. (2007). Yerel ekonomiilerin yerel aktörleri: Bölge kalkınma ajansları. *Eskişehir Osmangazi Üniversitesi İİBF Dergisi, 2*(1), 65–83.

UNCTAD. (2016). Investor nationality: Policy challenges. World Investment Report, 12.09.2017. http://unctad.org/en/PublicationsLibrary/wir2016_en.pdf

UNCTAD. (2017). *Investment and digital economy*. World Investment Report, 11.09.2017. http:// Unctad.Org/En/Publicationslibrary/Wir2017_En.Pdf

Ünsal, E. (2007). *İktisadi büyüme*. Ankara: İmaj Yayınevi.

Van der Wusten, H. (1998). Globalization and geography. *Geojournal, 45*, 1–3.

Work, R. (2001). Decentralization, governance, and sustainable regional development. In W. Sthor (Ed.), *New regional development paradigms*. Westport, CT: Greenwood.

World Bank. (2001). Decentralization in the transition economies: Challenges and the road ahead, poverty reduction and economic management unit Europe and Central Asia, 20.08.2017. http:// www1.worldbank.org/publicsector/LearningProgram/Decentralization/wetzel.pdf

World Bank. (2014). *World investment on political risk 2013*. Washington, DC: MIGA, World Bank Group.

Zengin, E., & Öztaş, C. (2008). Kamu yönetiminde çağdaş gelişmeler ve Türkiye. *Alatoo Academıc Studies, 3*(1), 85–91.

The Unique Investment Risks of the Emerging Financial Markets

Arif Orçun Söylemez

Abstract The significance of the Emerging Financial Markets (EFMs) is on a steady rise. They offer significant advantages for international investors such as high yields and broader chance of global portfolio diversification. However, there exist unique risks of investments in EFMs that should be carefully observed. This article is a summary those risks such as the risk of survival bias, non-normality of returns, the peso problem, contagion issues, commodity and natural resource curse among other problems that investors should pay attention to in EFMs. At the end, a top-down analysis approach is recommended in this article to those investors who will invest in EFMs.

1 Introduction

Emerging economies are more significant for the global economy than ever before since the Great Recession in 2008.[1] Furthermore, their significance is set to expand. According to the IMF's World Economic Outlook data, emerging economies are

---

[1] "Emerging markets" is a term that The International Finance Corporation (IFC), a World Bank Group affiliate, began using in 1981 to describe a set of countries. Sometimes the term is used interchangeably with "emerging economies". Although so close, emerging markets puts more emphasis on financial markets. When the term was first introduced into usage in early 1980s, The informal criterion for a developing country to be called as an emerging market economy was to have 30–50 listed companies with a market capitalization of $1 billion or more and an annual trading of $100 million or more. However, the two terms melted together over the years to become an inseparable alloy today. Influenced by the characterization of emerging economies by Julien Vercueil, today, it is widely believed that emerging economies share three common characteristics: (i) higher than less developed, less than developed economies per-capita income figures, (ii) high growth performance, (iii) economic liberalization and institutional transition. The big 10 emerging economies, as identified by Jeffrey E. Garten in 1998, a former Dean of the Yale

A. O. Söylemez (✉)
Marmara University, Istanbul, Turkey
e-mail: orcun.soylemez@marmara.edu.tr

© Springer International Publishing AG, part of Springer Nature 2018
H. Dincer et al. (eds.), *Strategic Design and Innovative Thinking in Business Operations*, Contributions to Management Science,
https://doi.org/10.1007/978-3-319-77622-4_19

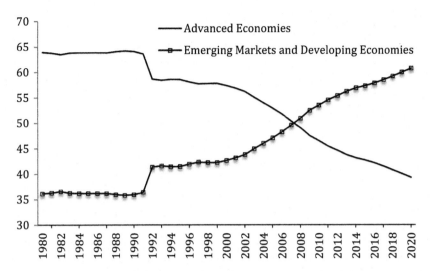

Fig. 1 The PPP-based GDP shares in the global economy (%). Source: IMF, April 2017 World Economic Outlook Data, (relevant data are updated according to the IMF's January 2018 revision)

projected to post 5.2% average growth rate annually in the next 3 years until 2020, while in the same period the advanced economies are projected to grow only at 2.2% annually. As a result, emerging markets and developing countries are likely to account for slightly more than 60% of the total purchasing power in the global economy by 2020 (Fig. 1).

Under those circumstances, it would be truly difficult for international investors not to consider the potential in emerging market assets. Still, it is worth noting that emerging markets pose their very unique and complex risks for investors.

The purpose of this study is to provide a survey of the various self-similar risk factors that are presented to investors by the emerging financial markets. The study is organized as follows. In Sect. 2, the possible risks that are associated with emerging markets are summarized. In Sect. 3, the usefulness of sovereign ratings are discussed. Concluding remarks are presented in Sect. 4.

School of Management and a former US Under Secretary of Commerce for International Trade, are Argentina, Brazil, China, India, Indonesia, Mexico, Poland, South Africa, South Korea and Turkey. IMF additionally classifies Bangladesh, Bulgaria, Chile, Colombia, Hungary, Malaysia, Pakistan, Peru, Philippines, Romania, Russia, Thailand, Ukraine and Venezuela as emerging economies.

2 A Summary of the Unique and Complex Risks of Emerging Financial Markets

The following table taken from Harvey's 1995 book illustrates the average of 1-year returns on International Finance Corporation (IFC) global stock indexes for 20 emerging financial markets (EFMs) from 1976 to 1992, and compares that average return figure with the performance of MSCI—World index (Table 1).

As the table indicates, EFMs present significantly higher return over the period. According to the modern portfolio theory, high-return assets typically bear high risks. That is why the higher return figure in the table unsurprisingly matches with the higher standard deviation figure. However, standard deviation cannot serve as the appropriate risk measure for broadly diversified portfolios. Capital Asset Pricing Model (CAPM) states that if investors can diversify the idiosyncratic risks of every individual asset, what matters is not the standard deviations of the assets but their correlation with the broader portfolio index. When we consider the correlation of EFMs with the broader index of MSCI, we see EFMs indeed come with high return and low correlation. That means, although emerging market assets may be risky individually, investors trying to create a well-diversified international equity portfolio should consider adding them to their portfolios since by doing so they could improve portfolio returns and mitigate overall risks at the same time. Although that sounds fabulous, several other problems arise with the EFM data on a closer examination. For instance one such problem common in emerging markets is known as the survival bias.

2.1 Survival Bias

Survival bias is the problem we would confront with whenever we look back in time at a sample that disproportionately represents investments that have survived over time, and filters out many that have disappeared from the market. Hence when we consider the historical performances of funds, indices or markets that exist today in EFMs, we may be taking into consideration a select group of those that have succeeded throughout the period. Thus whenever we are to study the EFM performances, we must keep in mind that probably we are dealing with a group from which submerged representatives are omitted. If that is truly the case, the empirical return

Table 1 20 EFMs versus MSCI value-weighted world index (from 1976 to 1992)

	20 EFMs (%)	MSCI (%)
Mean annual return	20.4	13.9
Standard deviation	24.9	14.4
Correlation with MSCI	0.16	1.00
Auto-correlation	0.15	0.01

Source: Harvey (1995)

distributions of emerging markets would be truncated from below causing the observed return figures to be artificially high and observed variance figures to be artificially low.

2.2 Non-normal Distributions of Returns

Second, the EFM instruments are highly dependent on the success of the countries' liberalization experiments. Especially, in the early phases of economic development the returns of EFM instruments present a win or lose character. This property of long-run outcomes on EFM instruments violate a basic assumption of the Capital Assets Pricing Model (CAPM), that is the normality of long-run returns. Hence, we cannot use CAPM safely for EFM assets.

The non-normal distributions of returns do not only impair the pricing ability of well-known models but also present issues in modeling the left-hand tail events in EFMs. Using daily returns from six Southeast European (SEE) stock markets, Totić and Božović (2015) report that when doing risk analysis in these six SEE countries, applying conditional extreme value theory (EVT) improves the predictive performance of value-at-risk (VaR) and expected shortfall (ES) calculations compared against several alternatives, such as historical simulation and analytical approach based on GARCH with a single conditional distribution. Their backtesting data indicates that EVT-based models provide more reliable VaR and ES forecasts than the alternative models in all of the six markets. According to Totić and Božović, their findings emphasize the importance of extreme events in SEE markets and indicates that the ability of a model to capture volatility clustering accurately is not sufficient for a correct assessment of risk in these markets. As a matter of fact, taking the possibility of extreme events into consideration is always a good idea when dealing with EFMs since many EFMs have thicker return distributions in various asset classes on the leftside.

2.3 The Peso Problem

Some events with low probability of occurrence may have unproportionately high effect on asset prices in EFMs. This is what the financial economists call "the peso problem", a term attributed by many to Milton Friedman. Throughout most of the twentieth century the Mexican peso remained more stable than many other currencies in Latin America since Mexican economy did not experience periods of hyperinflation, a problem common to many other countries in the region. Yet, constant interest rate differentials were observed between the Peso deposits and comparable US Dollar deposits in the 1970s after the Mexican government pegged Peso to the US Dollar. This was an anomaly because since the two currencies were pegged, the stubborn interest rate differential was serving as an everlasting arbitrage opportunity. Friedman then argued that the difference between the Mexican and US interest rates under such circumstance had to be reflecting an underlying concern of investors that the Peso should at some point in time be devalued. The long-lasting existence of such an arbitrage opportunity in the marketplace could be rationalized by a sudden and large devaluation expectation of Peso could.

The difficulty (and even impossibility sometimes) of predicting such tail events causes severe problems for modeling.[2] Although, the Peso problem is not used in mainstream asset pricing models yet, keeping it in mind while dealing with the EFMs may be helpful to explain unreasonably large risk premiums in equity returns,[3] unreasonably large forward discounts in inflationary currencies,[4] and apparent distortions in the term structure of interest rates.[5]

2.4   Contagion Problem

Another important problem regarding the EFMs is the "contagion" pattern. On the daily observations the EFM securities are not highly correlated across countries; but when a financial crisis happens in one country, it sometimes leaps from one country to another like a contagious disease. So the possible risk factors in one emerging market may put threat on some other emerging economies, too (Fig. 2).

Contagion may progress through trade partnership. If a country's currency collapses, its imports from another country may become prohibitively expensive, damaging the exporting country's real economy should the importing country be an important trade partner of the exporting country. Argentina used to sell a substantial part of its exports to Brazil, so when Brazilian real collapsed in early 1999, Argentina's exports contracted.

Alternatively, contagion may progress through trade by competition effect as well. If one country's currency collapses, it may become a serious export competitor to the other countries. In 1997 when Thai baht collapsed, this put competitive pressure on Indonesia, Malaysia, and the Philippines, triggering collapses on their currencies.

Thirdly, investors are often poorly informed about the precise details about emerging countries. When one country suffers from a crisis, they may begin feeling worried about the other, somehow similar, countries—for example countries in the same region or same trading bloc etc.—although these other countries have nothing to worry about. This type of negative "gut" feelings of investors may provoke sales

---

[2]Sill, Keith, 2000, "Understanding Asset Values: Stock Prices, Exchange Rates, And the Peso Problem", Federal Reserve Bank of Philadelphia Research Publication.

[3]Rietz T.A., 1988, "The Equity Risk Premium: A Solution", Journal of Monetary Economics.

[4]Krasker W.S., 1980, "The 'Peso Problem' in Testing the Efficiency of Forward Exchange Markets", Journal of Monetary Economics, 2, 269–276.

[5]Lewis K. K., 1991, "Was There a 'Peso Problem' in the Term Structure of US Interest Rates: 1979–1982?", International Economics, 32, 159–173.

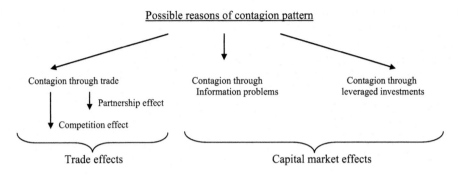

Fig. 2 Possible reasons of contagion

of other "seemingly" similar countries' securities. In 1997, with the Asian crisis, Taiwan's currency and security values initially fell but soon recovered on better standing of the country.

Lastly, some investors in EFM securities, like hedge funds and banks, are leveraged and when they confront with a loss on some part of their portfolios they may rush to get rid of same kind of risky assets in order to remain capable of paying their debt obligations back. The losses in Russia's 1998 collapse caused declines in other EFM securities.

2.5   The Resource/Commodity Curse

Economic wealth in some of the emerging economies depends extensively on a natural resource or commodity. The typical examples for such economies are the oil-dependent countries of the Middle East. However, natural gas, gold and diamond are also other important commodities for some Central Asian and African countries and Russia. It is so interesting that the very countries that suffer severely from lack of economic diversification usually suffer from major problems such as weak economic growth, insufficient democracy, high gender inequality as well. This observed association between economic dependency and various social and economic problems is known as the resource or commodity curse. Probable reasons for the curse are worth questioning since these reasons are likely to posit some of the unique risks of emerging countries.

2.5.1   Dutch Disease

The first probable reason for the natural resource or commodity curse is a monetary difficulty that firstly came into prominence in early 1960s when Holland discovered a fertile natural gas field in Groningen in late 1950s. When country began exporting the natural gas from that field to the rest of the world, Dutch currency started to appreciate as a result of the influx of foreign currencies to the country. Because natural gas market was growing at the time and also because natural gas was a highly demand inelastic product, the currency appreciation could not be corrected by the market forces and in return the long-lasting appreciation of Dutch currency crippled Holland's capacity to export other products other than the natural gas. Although the problem begins as a monetary issue at first, long lasting appreciation of a domestic currency may harm the domestic labor market as well resulting in unemployment problems and degradation in the level of human capital and capacity in manufacturing sectors. These issues are observable since cheaper imports in various industries would create demand insufficiency for labor and skills in tradable sectors other than the one sector which is the very natural resource or commodity sector itself.

2.5.2   Volatility in Government Finances

The prices of primary commodities, including the prices of fuel and other energy resources, are known to be highly volatile. The following two charts from the IMF provide an opportunity for eyeballing this phenomena (Figs. 3 and 4).

Hence, in case that a nation's revenues and wealth are overly dependent on a commodity or a natural resource, the country becomes prone to suffering from higher volatility in its revenues. Such volatility may therefore hinder the country from pursuing long standing social programs or from engaging itself in development-enhancing public spendings for a decade or so. In sum, backwardness becomes hard to fight against when a country does not have the stable resources to fight against it.

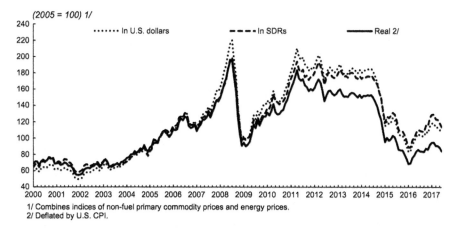

Fig. 3 Indices of primary commodity prices. Source: The IMF. The Primary Commodity Price data are updated monthly. Charts are from IMF's web page on the following URL: http://www.imf.org/external/np/res/commod/Charts.pdf

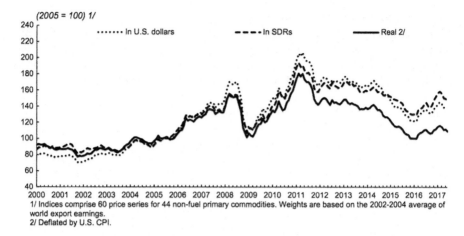

1/ Indices comprise 60 price series for 44 non-fuel primary commodities. Weights are based on the 2002-2004 average of world export earnings.
2/ Deflated by U.S. CPI.

Fig. 4 Indices of non-fuel primary commodity prices. Source: The IMF. The Primary Commodity Price data are updated monthly. Charts are from IMF's web page on the following URL: http://www.imf.org/external/np/res/commod/Charts.pdf

2.5.3 Rent-Seeking Behaviour Causing Political and Social Instability

The lucrative gains from the commodity or natural resource sectors may cause political or social struggles. This may serve as a risk, which is lessening the strength of the social harmony and the level of social capital in such emerging countries. As a result, political instability and abrupt regime switches are real dangers for international capital market investors in the EFMs.

All these said, the natural resource or commodity curses are not unavoidable. Countries may easily escape from these so-called curses should they have true determination for escape. For example, if a country suffers from the Dutch disease, it may transfer its extensive export earnings into a sovereign fund and seek international investment opportunities. Such a move could dampen the appreciation pressure on the national currency while helping to contain domestic inflation. Plus, the dividends from the international investments could be used to stabilize the markets in the adversity of volatile primary commodity prices. As for finding the compromise between the need for financing long-standing development projects and volatile government finances due to price fluctuations, emerging markets—if they are willing to do that of course—can always choose to tap the funds from international development agencies such as the World Bank Group, the European Bank for Reconstruction and Development, Asian Development Bank, InterAmerican Development Bank etc. as long as they submit development projects making economic sense to these development agencies. In case we insist on a domestic solution to the problem, again a development fund can be instituted using the excessive gains from the exports when the prices are high. Hence, it is worth repeating once again that the natural resource or commodity curses are not unavoidable.

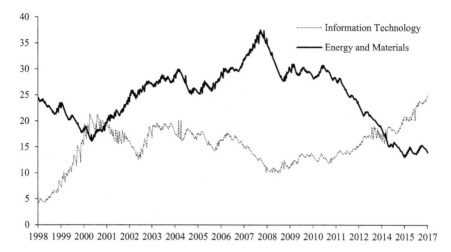

Fig. 5 Sector weights in MSCI EM equities index (%). Source: Primary source is MSCI. The above graph is taken from a related Financial Times article written by Wheatley (2017)

Nevertheless, as aforementioned, natural resource or commodity curse can truly harm the capacities of human and social capitals in emerging economies and cripple the power of such economies to diversify their economic output if not addressed properly. These are real top-down issues that should be considered before pouring money into an economy. But again, natural resource or commodity curse can be healed as long as there exist political and social will to heal it. Besides, the natural resources and commodities are becoming less and less important for many emerging economies. Since November 2014, technology stocks have more weight in the benchmark MSCI EM Equities Index than the weight of energy and materials (commodities) stocks. Only a decade ago, energy and materials stocks were on a dramatic rise and were making up more than one third of the whole MSCI EM index alone. Today, their weight is less than half of what it was in 2008 and stays 10% below the weight of IT stocks (Fig. 5).

Of course, this is not to claim that the importance of natural resource or commodity sectors diminished at the same degree in all the emerging markets. In Russia, GazProm, a big producer of natural gas, still exerts big multiplier effect on the economy. Likewise, Petrobras, an oil giant, and Vale, a mining giant, maintain their key role for Brazil. Saudi Arabia's most valuable asset without doubt is still Saudi Aramco, the largest oil/energy company in the world. However, especially in Asian countries such as South Korea, China and Taiwan high MCAP technology stocks are gaining considerable importance like Baidu and Alibaba of China, Samsung of South Korea and Hon Hai and TSMC of Taiwan among others. In sum, EFMs are not all the same and they need to be checked individually for their reliance on specific sectors. If a handful of sectors lead an economy, it is likely that this situation would cause monetary problems, capacity problems, human capital and social capital problems and political instabilities there. These are all important factors that need to be considered and hedged by the international investors, especially if they are planning to undertake long-term investments rather than making short-term money market trips. However, even an emerging market's being cursed need not serve as a deal breaker for the international investors since emerging economies can easily cope with such curse only if there is political and social will to heal the adverse effects of the curse. Hence, another advice for the international investors is they should always focus and understand the political and social dynamics in emerging economics. Because what the natural resource or commodity curse teaches us about the emerging economies is that reasonable ways of curing any anomaly in the emerging markets can be found. But is there will to cure? This is the real question for which international investors should seek an answer. Finally, some EFMs, especially the ones in Asia Pacific region seem to have gone a long way in diversifying their economies. In the overall, each EFM is an individual case and probably the best strategy for investors is to scrutinize each one of these markets individually and thoroughly.

2.6   Foreign Exchange Risks

Foreign exchange (FX) risks are always and everywhere material risks for international investors. The very first risk in the FX market is related with the FX rate determination problem. FX rate determination problem was first introduced by Meese and Rogoff in 1983 and it simply means that there does not exist any structural model that explains the movements in the exchange rates better than a driftless random walk model. As well known, after the collapse of the Bretton Woods system in 1971, the developed countries had started to switch from fixed and pegged type controlled FX rate regimes to more liberalized floating FX rate regimes during the 1970s. As of 1983, there was a set of structural models in the literature trying to explain how freely floating exchange rates would move in the FX market. Meese and Rogoff in 1983 found that a simple random walk model was a better out-of-sample predictor of future exchange rates than all the structural models at the date. A random walk model simply predicts that the exchange rates tomorrow would be the same with today's closing value plus a white-noise disturbance distributed around zero with time independent variance of one. That means if we are ever to rely on random walk modeling for forecasting future exchange rates, we can only conclude exchange rates tomorrow would be either the same with today or higher or less. As you can see this is rubbish and hence random walk cannot serve as a valid prediction model for exchange rates. Unfortunately, Meese and Rogoff's gloomy finding about the exchange rates still stands. Empirical findings in the following quarter century until the present time did not produce any meaningful improvement in our understanding of how we can predict exchange rates. That is why it would be no mistake to conclude in plain English that exchange rates are still unpredictable and hence any international investor migrating his or her money to a foreign land should be aware of the fact that exchange rate risk is always there. As such this is not a unique risk of EFMs but it is more general. Before the investment, all the hedging options and their costs should be properly included in the feasibility and sensitivity analyses. Before entering EFMs, properly planned scenario analyses should be considered and stop-loss decisions should be taken.

Secondly, in a world with perfect capital mobility, the exchange rate movements should be in accordance with the interest rate differentials between the two currencies. That is the outcome of a simple no-arbitrage condition in financial markets and known as the interest parity condition. There are two distinct interest parity conditions according to the forward exchange rate's being covered or uncovered. Uncovered (or unhedged) condition states that the high interest currencies should depreciate against the low interest currencies. Otherwise, there would be room for profitable interest arbitrage between two countries. Nevertheless, in reality, the contrary happens on a large scale. Under normal circumstances, countries offering higher yields attract international capital and hence their currencies appreciate. That is why borrowing in low interest currencies to invest in financial assets denominated in high interest currencies usually pays excess profits. This investment strategy is known as the carry trade. Because it is based on arbitrage and also because this arbitrage opportunity lives long, many investors tend to believe that carry trade is a high return strategy with low risks. Therefore, carry trade is so popular among currency traders and hedge fund managers. However, it is indeed subject to gigantic risks. First of all, the arbitrage is between interest rates or yields denominated in two different currencies and hence exchange rate risk is inherent. Common failure of the uncovered interest parity is no true hedge against the exchange rate risk. It is only a brave bet. Exchange rates may fail to move in accordance with the interest differentials most of the times but that does not mean that they always fail. The recent literature documents that carry trades may be prone to big losses during high volatility times. Menkhoff et al. (2012) report significantly negative co-movement of high interest currencies with volatility innovations in the global FX market, whereas low interest currencies provide a hedge against unexpected volatility changes. In this respect, the following excerpt from a chapter on foreign exchange rates in the 2008 annual report of the Bank for International Settlements (BIS) is quite illustrative for the volatility dependence in the FX market.

> Foreign exchange markets experienced a substantial increase in volatility in August 2007... Prior to August, historically low volatility and large interest rate differentials had underpinned cross-border capital flows that put downward pressure on funding currencies, ..., and supported high-yielding currencies. (As a result of the heightened volatility) there was a substantial reassessment... as the... problems in financial markets became more apparent. In this environment, (other) factors... which have an important bearing on the future path of monetary policy, became more of a focal point for market sentiment than the prevailing level of interest rates.
> Bank for International Settlements (BIS), 78th Annual Report, July 2008, p. 75.

In these lines, the BIS reporters obviously claim interest rate differentials to be the dominant factor for the determination of the foreign exchange rate returns during periods of less volatile market conditions, while other factors may take a more important role in high volatility periods. As a result, carry trade, which is based on the failure of uncovered interest parity condition, may be rewarding when everything is calm and when investors have appetite to assume risk. However, seeing 99 white swans is no proper guarantee for the color of the 100th swan that one will see in future. Just as that, international investors with carry trade positioning should be aware of the fact that they can always face a black swan one day. Some of the most popular high interest currencies used by carry traders are emerging country currencies such as Turkish Lira and Brazil Real. Hence investors who do not want to risk themselves as a result of possible exchange rate downturns in emerging markets should always hedge themselves and as aforesaid there is unfortunately no proper structural model in economics that can help them to predict the movement of exchange rates in short-term. In brief, exchange rate risks are always serious issues to consider and international investors lured by EFM returns should not forget that.

2.7   Less Liquidity and Depth Along with Some Other Issues

Menkhoff et al. (2012) further show that liquidity risk also matters for the cross-section of currency returns. In fact it is well known today that in many asset classes in emerging countries, investors have long positions exceeding in market value the total FX reserves in those countries. As Hawkins and Turner (2000) state countries can face liquidity problems not only because of the foreign assets and liabilities of the government and central bank, but also because of the foreign currency liabilities of the banks and even the corporate sector. Although authorities can provide virtually unlimited domestic currency liquidity, they are often tightly constrained in their provision of foreign currency liquidity. This has led to consideration of a broad concept of "national liquidity".[6] One of the things that international investors should focus on in EFMs is hence the FX liquidity since no one would like to be trapped in an emerging market during a market downturn because of not being able to convert their assets into the their home currencies.

Market depth is important as well since a shallow financial market can be manipulated with more ease. Hence, emerging market investors should also be concerned about the depth of markets in EFMs. Loose control on insider-trading activities and regulation risks (i.e. such as changing the rules of the game in an abrupt manner) are also important risk factors.

---

[6]For further discussion about the concept of national liquidity, see Hawkins and Turner (2000) on https://www.bis.org/publ/plcy08a.pdf

3   The Issues with Sovereign Ratings and Can Investors Use Them Confidently?

In conclusion, there are surely many tricks one has to consider while investing in the EFMs. According to many, the variations in the risk premium of EFM stocks and debts are often guided by sudden changes in perceptions about the long-term viability of the core institutions within EFM countries, since financial markets' risks are closely related to the health of the financial system and the government's fiscal balance. Calomaris and Beim (2001) therefore argue that the openness of financial market, privatization of state-owned enterprises, legal system reforms, development of new information, accounting and corporate governance systems, structuring of government finances and exchange rate policy, and prudential regulation of the banking system are important dimensions affecting investors. They say, when assessing the risks of EFM stocks or bonds, credit rating agencies are important. As seen until now the primary risk of EFM bonds or stocks or any other asset we are talking about are not the risks of the issuer companies but the sovereign risk of the countries themselves. If an EFM gets into a crisis, few of its companies can escape. But what exactly does sovereign credit analysis entail? What must be measured and what is being measured?

A study by Cantor and Packer (1996) finds that the best variables for explaining cross-country differences in sovereign ratings include the amount of debt outstanding, GDP per capita, GDP growth, inflation, and debt repayment history.[7] In another study, Erb et al. (1997) report that sovereign ratings are themselves mostly governed by the risk of institutional experiments in economic liberalization,[8] that is the steps taken forward to achieve financial market opening, the privatization of state-owned enterprises, the legal system reforms, the development of new information, accounting, and corporate governance systems, the structuring of government finances and exchange rate policy, and the prudential regulation of the banking system. On the other hand, are the ratings themselves that much reliable? In 1995 Korea was rated A1 by Standard and Poor's Corporation (S&P) and was upgraded from A+ to AA– by Moody's Investors Services (Moody's); Thailand was rated A2 by Moody's and A by S&P; the Czech Republic was rated Baa2 by Moody's and BBB+ by S&P. Two years later all three were on the brick of default. If ratings are governed by the macro variables like inflation, growth, and fiscal discipline of countries, then those ratings can be understood but must be seen that the macro variables are not sufficient for sovereign ratings. If it is mostly the political and institutional events that matter, then again we cannot rely on these ratings so safely, given that by July, 2002 S&P was rating Thailand A2 for short-term local currency and A3 for short-term foreign currency and outlook was declared to be stable for both rates, while Turkey was

---

[7]Cantor R., Packer F., 1996, "Determinants and Impact Sovereign Credit Ratings", FRBNY Economic Policy Review, 37–53.

[8]Erb C.B., Harvey C.R., Viskanta T.E., 1997, "Political Risk, Economic Risk and Financial Risk", Financial Analysts Journal, 29–46.

getting a C for both with a negative outlook. In the following few months a Coup came into being in Thailand but not in Turkey.

Although I chose the examples from late 1990s to refer to the Asian Crisis of 1998, which negatively affected the poster boy emerging countries of East and Southeast Asia at the date, credit rating agencies came under intense scrutiny in the wake of the Global Recession in 2008. In the US, at the height of the global financial crisis in 2008, the big three rating agencies, namely the S&P, Moody's and Fitch, were all accused of distorting the true risks associated with mortgage-related securities and hence criticisms did not focus on sovereign ratings. But in Europe, the sovereign debt ratings were at the heart of the debate again. European Union governments and European Central Bank officials accused the big three rating agencies of being too aggressive in rating eurozone countries' creditworthiness and thus exacerbating the financial crisis. They argued that the unjustifiably negative evaluations of the rating agencies made the Eurozone Debt Crisis worse. "S&P's April 2010 decision to downgrade Greece's debt to junk status weakened investor confidence, raised the cost of borrowing, and made a financial rescue package in May 2010 all but inevitable."[9]

The problem with the rating agencies in the US before the 2008 global financial meltdown was they for years overlooked the pricing problem in the housing market and did not include the possibility of price falls in housing market to their models. In Europe, their problem was they overlooked the growing current account imbalances within the Eurozone. In a monetary union with no central fiscal authority, growing current account imbalances should have never been underestimated. Hence, their pre-2008 ratings were at best too optimistic while their post-2008 ratings were probably too dismal.

Both the US and the EU took measures to regulate the big three rating agencies aiming to ensure better transparency and further competitiveness in the rating market. The Dodd-Frank Wall Street Reform and Consumer Protection Act that came into effect in the US in 2010 and the European Securities and Markets Authority (ESMA), that was created in 2011, both sought to hold agencies accountable for their ratings and protect investors. However, the OECD in 2010 reported that the industry's main problem still remains intact. The issuers of financial assets are known to be more willing to pay for having their assets rated than investors do. That is why, the rating industry since 1970s began to work on a "issuer pays" system rather than "subscriber pays" system. However, this system may be prone to creating conflict-of-interest problems. As long as this is the central pay system, there should not be any reason to expect that rating agencies' ratings are radically better today than they were before the Asian Crisis or the Global Recession.

---

[9]For a good explanation about the post-2008 criticisms regarding the rating agencies on the two sides of the Atlantic, see Council on Foreign Relations article on https://www.cfr.org/backgrounder/credit-rating-controversy

4   Concluding Remarks

As this study puts, EFMs pose their unique and complex risks to international investors. First of all, the global availability of loanable funds are important for determining the future economic performance of many emerging countries since access to international capital is still vital for ensuring economic growth in major part of the developing world. Use for example the following graph taken from Söylemez and Demirci (2013) to observe the strong relationship between the quarterly economic growth rates and the international capital flows in Turkey (Fig. 6).

As you can see, the co-movement tendency between the inflowing international capital and Turkish economic growth performance is striking. That is why, before investing in a country like that, international investors should definitely concentrate on the availability of external funds for the country.

Then the emerging countries, as we aforesaid in the second part of this study, suffer quite extensively from crisis contagions. Hence, investors should understand the situation of the trading partners and competitors of the emerging countries.

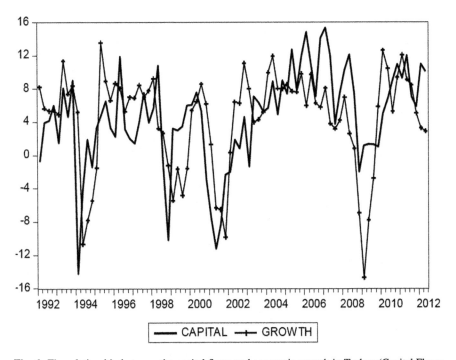

Fig. 6 The relationship between the capital flows and economic growth in Turkey (Capital Flows indicate net inflows to Turkey and include net portfolio liabilities, net FDI liabilities, Other liabilities and Net Errors and Omissions. Economic growth rates are YoY quarterly growth figures). Source: Primary source is the Central Bank of Turkey. The above graph is taken from Söylemez and Demirci (2013)

Thirdly, the regulatory capacity, the political landscape, the social cohesion etc. are third level issues to consider.

Then, the national economy, and the liquidity and depth of markets etc. should be considered and proper hedging options should be used.

This is to say a serious top-down analysis is most necessary before entering an emerging country. Sovereign ratings can be used as additional sources of information since most of the market will react to those ratings. Even so, investors should be wise enough to remember at all times the fact that the historical accounts quite persuasively show the poor strength of ratings to serve as leading indicators before the market downturns. Plus, investors should never forget that ratings provided by rating agencies may be suffering from conflict-of-interest problems to certain degrees.

Probably the worst thing that can happen to investors is being lured by the high rewards offered by many EFMs. EFMs can help to mitigate the overall risks in an international portfolio if the investors understand and properly add them to their portfolios. However, EFMs can dramatically increase the risks of international portfolios as well, especially when investors do not thoroughly understand them.

References

BIS 78th Annual Report. Bank for International Settlements. (2008).

Calomaris, C. W., & Beim, D. O. (2001). *Emerging financial markets*. New York: McGraw Hill-Irwin.

Cantor, R., & Packer, F. (1996). Determinants and impact sovereign credit ratings. *FRBNY Economic Policy Review, 2*, 37–53.

Council on Foreign Relations Web Article. (2015). *The credit rating controversy*. Retrieved August 2017, from https://www.cfr.org/backgrounder/credit-rating-controversy

Erb, C. B., Harvey, C. R., & Viskanta, T. E. (1997). Political risk, economic risk and financial risk. *Financial Anaylsts Journal, 52*, 29–46.

Garten, J. E. (1998). *The big ten: The big emerging markets and how they will change our lives*. New York: Basic Books (Reprinted Edition in April 1998).

Harvey, C. R. (1995). Predictable risk and returns in emerging markets. *The Review of Financial Studies, 8*(3), 773–816.

Hawkins, J., & Turner, P. (2000). *Managing foreign debt and liquidity risks in emerging economies: An overview*. Managing Foreign Debt and Liquidity Risks: BIS Policy Papers No. 8, 3–59.

IMF Primary Commodity Price Indices. Retrieved August 2017., from http://www.imf.org/external/np/res/commod/Charts.pdf

Krasker, W. S. (1980). The 'Peso Problem' in testing the efficiency of forward exchange markets. *Journal of Monetary Economics*, (2), 269–276.

Lewis, K. K. (1991). Was there a 'Peso Problem' in the term structure of US interest rates: 1979–1982? *International Economics, 32*, 159–173.

Meese, R., & Rogoff, K. (1983). Empirical exchange rate models of the seventies: Do they fit out of sample? *Journal of International Economics, 14*, 3–24.

Menkhoff, L., Sarno, L., Schmeling, M., & Schrimpf, A. (2012). Carry trades and global foreign exchange volatility. *The Journal of Finance, 67*(2), 681–718.

Rietz, T. A. (1988). The equity risk premium: A solution. *Journal of Monetary Economics, 22*, 117–131.

Sill, K. (2000). *Understanding asset values: Stock prices, exchange rates, and the peso problem.* Federal Reserve Bank of Philadelphia Research Publication.

Söylemez, A. O., & Demirci, S. (2013). The nonlinear causality between the international capital flows and economic growth in Turkey. *Finansal Araştırmalar ve Çalışmalar Dergisi, 4*(8), 99–110.

Totić, S., & Božović, M. (2015). Tail risk in emerging markets of Southeastern Europe. *Applied Economics, 48,* 1785–1798.

Vercueil, J. (2012). *Les Pays Emergents. Brésil – Russie – Inde – Chine. . . Mutations Economiques et Nouveaux Défis* (3rd edn., 232 p.). Paris: Bréal.

Wheatley, J. (2017, July 26). Emerging market assets are trapped by An outdated Cliché. *Financial Times.*

A Framework for Robust Estimation of Beta Using Information Fusion Approach

Mutlu Gürsoy

Abstract In terms of financial management, the precise estimation of the beta of a financial asset is of vital importance. Beta is the measure of the relationship between the return of an asset or a portfolio and the market return and means the systematic risk within the scope of the Capital Asset Pricing Model. In general, it is known that the distribution of returns is significantly non-normal with thick-tail and skewness features. The ordinary least square (OLS) estimator that focuses on the centre of a distribution loses its effectiveness in such cases as the divergence of the distribution from normality, the presence of outliers, and heteroscedasticity. Quantile regression (QR), which is regarded as a non-parametric method, shows robustness against the specified phenomena. QR reveals the information carried by the distribution in tails as the returns focus on the whole of distribution. This means different beta for each percentile requiring investigation, and causes the problem of fusion of this information. Ordered Weighted Averaging (OWA) operators can merge the information coming from different percentiles at a required orness level depending on the attitude of the investor towards the risk. This study also suggests the use of OWA operators in addition to different quantile combination techniques used in the literature. As a result of the analysis performed based on Borsa Istanbul (Istanbul Stock Exchange) data, it was shown that OWA operators have a performance that is comparable to OLS and quantile combination techniques.

1 Introduction

Companies would like to know the capital cost and return of an investment beforehand in terms of financial management when evaluating long-term investment projects. Since the expected return of a financial asset is the most basic input in portfolio management, the estimation of the expected return becomes important for the

M. Gürsoy (✉)
Istanbul Medipol University, Istanbul, Turkey
e-mail: mgursoy@medipol.edu.tr

investor for the evaluation of the asset. Normally, the realized returns of financial
assets are different from one another. Therefore, studies aimed at understanding why
we observe different financial assets with different expected return rates have an
important place among financial studies (Ferson and Jagannathan 1996, p. 1). The
output of these studies is the pricing models for capital assets. On the other hand, the
question of *"To what extent can the past history of a common stock's price be used to
make meaningful predictions concerning the future price of the stock?"* (Fama 1965,
p. 34) discussed in financial environments is not insignificant.

In contrast with the word price in the names of pricing models, financial studies
are generally interested in the return of an asset or an index, rather than its price. The
reason for this is that return series have more attractive statistical features such as
stability and ergodicity, and the idea that the size of the investment will not influence
price changes under full competition conditions (Campbell et al. 1997, p. 9).

Pricing models for capital assets explain the relationship between the expected
return and risk factors (or factors, in short). When the expected return for the ith
security among N securities that are present in the market is shown as $E(R_{it})$, it can be
expressed with a pricing model (1) equation in general.

$$E(R_{it}) = f(F_j) \quad i = 1, 2, \ldots, N \tag{1}$$

where (R_{it}) = one-period return of security i, and
F_j = risk factors ($j = 1, 2, \ldots, K$).

The Capital Asset Pricing Model (CAPM), the first model for explaining how the
prices of capital assets are formed, was developed by Sharpe (1964), Lintner (1965),
and Mossin (1966). The CAPM is a pricing model built on the concepts of the mean-
variance efficient portfolio of Markowitz and the Efficient Market Hypothesis
(EMH).

The EMH was developed by Fama (1965, 1970) and Samuelson (1965), independently of one another, in 1960. Although the authors address the subject on
different bases, they achieved the same results. The state in which any information
related with the price formation is fully reflected to the prices formed in a capital
market is named as "efficient market" by Fama (1970, p. 383). Here, the term "full
reflection" means that the investor rapidly takes, analyses, reviews the expectations
of new information, and buys or sells an asset accordingly. According to the EHM,
security markets are quite efficient in reflecting the information of a particular stock
or the market as a whole. As per the accepted view, the news is distributed rapidly
when the information emerges, and it is added to the price of the capital asset soon.

If the information flow is not prevented, and the information is directly reflected
in stock prices, past information will not influence future behaviours of the investor.
In other words, the future price change will reflect the information of the future, and
it is independent of today's price changes. It is equal to saying that return series have
martingale features. Since the future information cannot be predicted, the price
change that will occur cannot be predicted, and it is random. In this case, making
a prediction about future prices with the technical analysis of past price information,
or choosing under-valued stocks by examining the financial information of

companies with the fundamental analysis will not provide a higher profit than a randomly created portfolio to the investor (Malkiel 2003, p. 59).

Then, the EMH is related to the "random walk" theory. The random walk is a term used in finance literature for expressing a price series in which all consecutive price changes randomly emerge from previous prices. The random walk model for stock returns was first suggested by French mathematician Louis Bachelier (1870–1946) in 1900. The claim that the price movements of stocks exhibit random walk gained formality with Osborne (1964). Osborne suggests a model that is similar to moving particles within a liquid for price changes in stock markets. This model is the Brownian Motion (BM) model.

The random walk theory of stock prices includes two basic assumptions. Consecutive price changes for each stock are independent, and conform to a probability distribution (Fama 1965, pp. 40–41). This means that independence takes a more important place because it does not give a particular definition for the shape of the distribution, and it is sufficient that the process that produces price changes is characterized correctly. However, the theory becomes invalid if there is no independence. The shape of the distribution is also important for the investor since the shape of the distribution is the main element in determining the riskiness of the investment. For example; two different distributions can give the same expected value for price changes, but the probability of huge changes may be higher in one distribution than the other.

Elton et al. (2003, p. 402) find the assumption of the EMH that the investor will be in the urge of buy-sell until the information is fully reflected in prices very grave. According to them, this assumption takes the cost of obtaining the information and making transactions in the market as zero. In this case, investors cannot be expected to show homogenous behaviour as the costs in question will be positive.

Peters (1991, p. 61) says that the fact that the information is internalized irregularly by an investor and the other with different investment terms may cause the biased random walk. The biased random walk was first investigated by Hurst in the 1940s, and then re-addressed by Mandelbrot in the 1960s and 1970s. The phenomenon that is named the Fractal (Structured) Brown Movement by Mandelbrot is named the Fractal Time Series by Peters (1991, 1994).

The empirical findings for the distribution of stock price changes are fat-tail, leptokurtic and skewness (Reiss and Thomas 2007, p. 374). The most frequently encountered explanation for fat-tail is that the information shows itself in the form of sparse accumulation, rather than being regular and constant. Therefore, the reaction of the market to these sparse information accumulations leads to the fat-tail because the distribution of price changes is leptokurtic since the information distribution is leptokurtic. Peters (1991, pp. 36–37) attributes the sparseness of the information and its leading to fat-tail to the non-linear reaction of the investor to the information. Indeed, if the information is sparse, it is still necessary to be immediately internalized by the investor, show a reaction, and be reflected in prices. The situation that leads to accumulation is that the investor keeps the information until the trend is favourable and then reacts cumulatively. This means that the investor shows a non-linear approach towards the information. In other words, when the accumulated information reaches a critical level, investors will form a reaction towards the information that they have ignored so far. This result leads to the situation that today is affected by the past, and it is a clear violation of the EMH.

Nowadays, one of the basic tendencies of the financial economy is to form a trade-off between the risk and the expected return. The martingale hypothesis set bounds to the expected return but does not say anything about the risk. If the expected price change of a financial asset is positive, its prize may attract the investor, and the risk can be endured. Therefore, the martingale hypothesis does not include the risk avoidance and risk-taking behaviours that are effective in the price formation of the investor (LeRoy 1973, p. 444).

A period when the return of the investment was focused on, rather than the risk, ended with the study of Markowitz (1952), that provides a trade-off mechanism between risk and return. Markowitz thinks that a precise portfolio that ensures the expected level of return that is desired by the investor among all security alternatives in which different choices can be made can be created. What is necessary for this is to know the covariances or correlation matrices of all possible security combinations, i.e., that the investor possesses full information. In this case, the portfolio created by the investor is effective, and it will dominate all other portfolio combinations. Then, Markowitz defined the return of the investment portfolio for the expected level of income with the expected return and defined the risk with the standard deviation (or variance) of the return. The variance or standard deviation of the return, which means the total risk, can be divided into two groups as systematic risk and non-systematic risk. The non-systematic risk is peculiar to the security, and it can be eliminated through portfolio diversification. The risk that is created by the overall market and economic conditions, and the investor cannot eliminate through portfolio diversification means the systematic risk. Therefore, the total risk is reduced to the systematic risk.

It is common to put forth assumptions on the behaviours of the actors in the market in the process of creating economic models. This can be compared to the assumption of the frictionless environment in the creation of models in the science of physics. The model is a structure that contains mathematical expressions and logical relations that define how to calculate the output values based on the given input values. In order to be beneficial, the model should contain two necessarily contrasting features: reality and simplicity. On the one hand, the model should contain many important features of the real system and provide sufficient similarity, while not having a complexity that is impossible to understand and manipulate. It should be noted that containing more details by a model will reflect the reality better while adding details will increase the complexity and make the analysis hard. It may be more realistic to evaluate the effectiveness of a model with the high correlation between the prediction of the model and the behaviour of the real system, rather than its representing the system with all its aspects (Rubinstein 1981, p. 5).

Some of the assumptions are made on consumers and investors. In a clearer manner, they make up the expenditure and investment behaviours of consumers or the investors' ways of decision-making in the process choosing which financial assets to include in a portfolio. The main basis for the creation of assumptions is the utility theory. Kahneman and Tversky (1979) put forth that the investment decisions of investors under uncertainty do not match the presumptions of theoretical financial models in the framework of the utility theory. This claim that is put forth based on various models is compatible with the claims of economists such as Adam Smith and John M. Keynes that the psychology of investors affects security prices. Behavioural finance that takes the psychological state of the investor into consideration and can be classified within the descriptive decision theory claims that investors make mistakes since they rely on decisions taken by the rule of thumb, and therefore, their markets are affected by mistakes and decision frames. This includes the term heuristics that emphasises the rule of thumb strategies reducing the duration of decision-making. Heuristics causes cognitive bias, i.e., systematic bias.

2 Estimation of Beta and Testing the CAPM

The standard CAPM, which is a single-factor pricing model, attributes the systematic risk to the phenomenon of the market and creates a relation between the market return and the return of a security or portfolio. This relationship is the beta (β) of an security i or portfolio, and is given with Eq. (2).

$$\beta_i = \frac{Cov(R_{it}, R_{mt})}{Var(R_{mt})} \tag{2}$$

Here, R_m is the return of the market. According to Fama (1970), the market return is the return of the portfolio created by all financial assets in the market. At which rate to keep each asset in this portfolio is determined by the proportion of the asset's value in its market to the total market value of all the assets in the portfolio. For the market portfolio, market indices such as S&P 500 or BIST 100 are taken as proxy.

According to the CAPM, the expected return of an asset is a positive linear function of the systematic risk measured with the beta. Therefore, it measures the systematic risk, and it becomes the only measure of risk. This means that the beta of any mean-variance efficient portfolio to be created among a cluster that includes all stocks with a beta that is higher than a β^* value will also be higher than β^*. Therefore, diversification does not reduce the beta. It reduces the total risk.

The CAPM refers to a risk-free interest rate. The reason for this is that it is possible to get a return (R_f) even when there is no risk. Short-term treasury bills are generally taken as a reference for risk-free interest rates. Then, what is important for the investor is to get an excess profit above the non-risk return. The CAPM correlates the excess return on a specific stock directly with the beta of the stock, and says that the expected excess return is correlated with the excess return in the subsequent period. This results from the fact that the CAPM has one period. No matter which period is used, the CAPM takes into consideration only the expectations of the subsequent period. In this case, Eq. (1) becomes Eq. (3).

$$E(R_{it}) = (Risk - Free\ return) + Excess\ Return$$
$$= R_{ft} + \beta_i[E(R_{mt}) - R_{ft}] \tag{3}$$

The CAPM is a theoretical model, and related to ex-ante returns. Therefore, if we know the expected returns of securities, we can empirically test the theory, for example, the presence of the linear relationship between the return and the beta, through observation. However, we do not know them since the incident has not taken place. Since it is not possible to perform the statistical tests on incidents that have not taken place yet, it is obligatory to follow the historical behaviour of security returns and the market and the type of relationship between them. Therefore, we can predict future behaviours by looking at the behaviours in the past. We can find a suitable regression line for past data, or find another way for modelling, but we may not know the future apart from the expectation. The two-pass cross-sectional regression approach is generally applied for the estimation of the beta and the test of its precision. According to this approach, a simple linear regression model is created in the first-pass stage using the past returns of stocks and the market, just as any estimation-based market model.

$$R_{it} - R_{ft} = \alpha_i + \beta_i[R_{mt} - R_{ft}] + e_{it} \tag{4}$$

where $\alpha_i =$ intercept term, and
$e_{it} =$ errorm term.

Second-pass is across-sectional regression. At this stage, a simple linear regression relationship is built between the betas estimated at the first-pass and the mean excess returns of stocks $(\bar{R}_{it} - \bar{R}_{ft})$.

$$\bar{R}_{it} - \bar{R}_{ft} = \gamma_1 + \gamma_2\beta_i + e_{it} \tag{5}$$

The fact that the γ_1 intercept term is not statistically significantly different from zero, γ_2 regression slope is equal to the observed excess return of the market $(R_{mt} - R_{ft})$, and lastly, the presence of a linear relationship between the beta and $\bar{R}_{it} - \bar{R}_{ft}$ are required within the scope of the CAPM model, as of the results of the cross-sectional regression.

In cross-sectional regression, beta is used as an explanatory variable. Since beta is estimated with an error in the first-pass regression, it leads to the well-known errors-in-variables (EIV) problem in cross-sectional regression. The presence of an incorrectly estimated explanatory variable in simple linear regression leads to the inconsistent estimation of the regression coefficients (γ_1, γ_2). This leads to the attenuation of γ_2 coefficient, and therefore, it's getting close to zero. On the other hand, it may cause the γ_1 intercept term, which is supposed to be zero, to move away from zero. A big sample in first-pass regression, i.e., in case the security return series cover a wide period, the EIV problem that occurs in second-pass may vanish since the estimation of the beta will be consistent. Another solution is to create a portfolio instead of an individual security. Nevertheless, the betas may exhibit dispersion in case the portfolio is created randomly. The importance of the estimation of beta results from the fact that the CAPM is regarded as reasonable for many practices, and it provides quite beneficial information. The beta value is important for the investor since it will give an idea on the relative volatility of a security. However, a high beta value requires the high expected return, but the fact that a security has a high beta value does not require that security also has high variance, and therefore, high volatility. The CAPM is on future, and logically says that the more an investor carries systematic risk, the higher the expected return will be. All investors try to eliminate the unnecessary risk, but the risk they would take will differ since their attitudes towards risk will be at different levels. Therefore, the idea suggesting that it is good when beta is neither low nor high is incorrect. For example, while a conservative investor chooses a portfolio with low beta among two well-diversified portfolios, the more aggressive one may be interested in the one with a higher beta. Then, a beta estimation that is as close to the true beta as possible is important in terms of financial econometrics. In addition to this, a good estimation of the beta should be considered in the context of the CAPM. In other words, the discussion of the validity of the CAPM model is a separate subject.

The CAPM starts modelling by creating a world in which tax, commission and transaction costs do not exist. This frictionless environment actually prevents the entrance of the real behaviours of individuals into the model as a restriction and simplifies the mathematical structure of the model. In reality, people take into consideration the taxes when making an investment and pay commission. The CAPM is a one-period model, but many people look beyond a period. The CAPM says that an investor cannot be effective on the price alone, but especially large-scale organizations can affect the market. According to the CAPM, the beta is stationary, but the studies carried out by the researchers showed that the beta changes in time. Accordingly, when we divide a sufficiently long period into two parts, the beta of the first part and the beta of the second part will be different from one another.

Many researchers have developed and are developing alternative models to the CAPM. One of the important objections is that the CAPM explains the fluctuations in price with a single factor. Fama and French (1992) developed the Fama-French Three-Factor model by saying that the contribution of beta to the explanation of the expected return is low, and emphasising the explanation power of the variables of firm size, price/book ratio and price/earning ratio. Liu (2006) strengthened the CAPM by addressing liquidity as a factor.

The modelling of financial time series is a complex problem. This complexity does not only result from the diversity of the series to be used (stocks, exchange rates, etc.) or the importance of the observation frequency (daily, weekly, monthly, etc.). The main reason for complexity is that there are certain common statistical regularities (Stylized Facts) that do not vary much from one market to the other, and it is not possible to produce these structures again with the help of stochastic models (Francq and Zakoian 2010, p.7).

The stylized facts were first revealed by Mandelbrot (1963), and they have been documented by revealing them in different structures with many empirical studies since then. These structures may be observed in a low or highly open way depending on the nature and observation frequency of the time series. Although the fluctuations in the price series of a stock are not stationary (Hsu et al. 1974, p. 108), it is accepted that the return series almost have zero mean and are weak stationary (Gavrishchaka and Banerjee 2006, p. 148).

The fluctuations of the time series generally do not show a significantly (linear) autocorrelation, but this shows the closeness to white noise. The lack of significant autocorrelation in returns leads to considering the returns as random variables in terms of the random walk model of the price series. Reference is frequently made to support the efficient market hypothesis in the absence of the meaningful autocorrelation in price movements and returns. However, the lack of autocorrelation does not require the independence of the increments. It is also necessary for the non-linear functions of the returns not to contain autocorrelation. Empirical findings have shown that the return series do not fulfil this feature. In other words, the absolute values and squares of the returns contain positive autocorrelation. This points to the well-known volatility clustering or long-range dependence or persistency. In a clearer way, price changes are most probably followed by major price changes (Cont 2001, pp. 229–230).

Many distributions were tried, and many new distributions were discovered in the process of investigating satisfactory descriptive models for economic data. Certain distributions that fit the data well without requiring any change (for example, Pareto distribution) were not widely accepted probably since the standard statistical analysis cannot be applied to such distributions (Rachev et al. 1999, p. 24).

There are at least three competitive hypotheses for the distribution of the realized return of stocks. The first alternative is the stable distribution with infinite variance suggested by Mandelbrot (1963) and Fama (1965). Another alternative is the mix of normal distributions with different means, and lastly, the student-t distribution that says that the returns measured at a time interval that is higher than one day will converge to normal distribution and has more than two degrees of freedom (Hagerman 1978, pp. 1214–1215).

Mandelbrot (1960, 1963) showed that the return in capital markets follows a distribution family that he called stable Paretian. Stable distributions that are also called Mandelbrot-Lévy, Lévy stable, L-stable, Stable-Paretian and Pareto-Lévy distributions (Mulligan 2004, p. 155) allow thick-tail and skewness. In addition to this, either the variance in these distributions is infinite, or it is not defined (Peters 1994, p. 217).

The most widely used method for the estimation of beta is ordinary least square (OLS). OLS assumes that the distribution of returns is normal, and it is interested in the average effect of the independent variable on the dependent variable. It focuses on the centre of the distribution in the framework of the central limit theory. Mandelbrot's (2003, p. 6) expression *"the substance of the so-called ordinary central limit theorem would be better understood if it is relabeled as the center limit theorem. Indeed, that theorem concerns the center of the distribution, while the anomalies concern the tails."* is meaningful.

3 Quantile Regression and Fusion Problem

The fact that the observatory data obtained with scientific studies vary requires the determination of the central tendency of the distribution. For example; the most basic model for a random variable of an stock i, such as R_t return series, is the model that represents the distribution with its central tendency. The determination of a real number (ζ) that can be the measure of a central tendency requires the minimization of $(e_t = R_t - \zeta)$, that we can define as the error of the model, according to certain criteria. With a more mathematical expression, solving the optimization problem defined as $\min\limits_{\zeta \in \Re} \sum_{t=1}^{T} l(e_t)$ is required.

Here, $l(\cdot)$ is the loss function, and in case it is quadratic, the sample mean, which is the least square estimator of the unconditional population mean is obtained. When ζ is expressed as the parametric function (for example $\zeta = \beta_0 + \beta_1 R_{mt}$), what is found is the OLS regression, and its solution gives an estimation of the conditional expectation function of returns. When the absolute value function is used instead of the quadratic function, the median absolute deviation (MAD) estimator becomes in question as the minimization process will regulate the number of negative and positive errors as equal, i.e., will give equal weight to negative and positive errors.

Quantile regression that is formulated by Koenker and Basset (1978) is simply the use of $\rho_\tau(\cdot)$ check function as the loss function (Fig. 1). In a way, it is the function that has turned the MAD estimator that weighs negative and positive errors symmetrically into asymmetric.

Then, the quantile regression,

$$\sum_{t \in R_{it} - \alpha_\tau - \beta_\tau R_{mt} \geq 0} \tau |R_{it} - \alpha_\tau - \beta_\tau R_{mt}| + \sum_{t \in R_{it} - \alpha_\tau - \beta_\tau R_{mt} < 0} (1 - \tau)|R_{it} - \alpha_\tau - \beta_\tau R_{mt}|$$

can be expressed as the minimization of the objective function defined as above. Thereby, an estimation of the conditional median function of the return series is obtained for example for $\tau = 0.5$. The percentiles (or in a more way, quantiles) are the separation of the data set into sections, and a median is the 50th percentile. In this case, the estimation of different conditional quantile functions becomes into question depending on the values that τ will take at the interval of $(0,1)$. In other words, the

Fig. 1 Check function

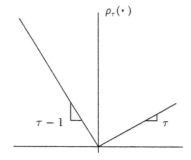

effect of the market on different return regions in the return distribution of an asset can be examined with the values of τ at the interval of $(0,1)$.

Methodologically, quantile regression can be regarded as a statistical tool to understand and test the way of the relationship between a response variable such as security returns and a conditioning variable such as market return. The use of the OLS estimator in the estimation of the beta will reduce the reliability of the estimated beta in the presence of atypical data. As the process of taking an absolute value will punish the deviant observations less than the process of taking a square, the quantile regression is more robust than the OLS regression. In many cases, one cannot have any information about the distribution of a time series. Quantile regression, which is a non-parametric method, does not require a specific distribution assumption. From another point-of-view, it becomes a good alternative to OLS, of which effectiveness decreases as we move away from the assumption of normality. On the other hand, while quantile regression is not regarded as a robust estimator in the modelling of the time series that contain heteroscedasticity, it can be used in revealing the presence and nature of heteroscedasticity (Koenker 1982).

Value at Risk (VaR) is regarded as a standard measure used by financial institutions to measure the market risk. Simply, Quantile Regression is regarded as a natural tool in the estimation of VaR, that we can define as a specific quantile value of distribution (return series). Nowadays, models that are based directly on the quantile estimation without the requirement of a complex model gradually gain importance. Although they actually do not estimate volatility directly, these models are used in volatility estimations as a result of their success in explaining the behaviour of the prices.

So far, it has been emphasised that the quantile regression is quite a useful tool in examining the distribution as a whole. The problem of merging the information obtained from the different percentiles of distribution is still evident. The term information fusion that is also used as decision fusion, information combination or information aggregation in the literature is used synonymously with the term data fusion most of the time. Information is the processed data, such as obtaining the beta by processing the market data based on a model. Therefore, the term information fusion is used in the context of the subject. Since fusion is the aggregation of the information from different sources (different quantiles), the fusion process should provide improved information (Castanedo 2013). In other words, it should be a good estimation of the true beta. Thus, the EIV problem that occurs in cross-sectional regression can be reduced, even if it cannot be eliminated.

An aggregation operator is an f function that turns a $\beta = (\beta_1, \beta_2, \ldots, \beta_n)$ input with n elements and real value at a closed interval into a real number such as $\widehat{\beta}$, and it is shown as $f(\beta) = \widehat{\beta}$. Actually, while the aggregation function term is mathematically more precise, it is observed that it is used simultaneously with the terms of function and operator in the literature.

There are basic characteristics of aggregation functions. When an input with n elements such as $\beta = (a, a, a, \ldots, a)$ is given for an $[a, b]$ interval, $f(\beta)$ should be equal to a, and similarly, when a $\beta = (b, b, b, \ldots, b)$ input with n elements is given,

$f(\beta)$ should be equal to b. This feature is the preservation of the bounds feature of the aggregation function. If $\beta_i^1 \leq \beta_i^2$ for all i values of two inputs such as β^1 and β^2, it should be $f(\beta^1) \leq f(\beta^2)$. This feature is the non-decreasing monotonicity condition. For example; when $\beta^1 = (0.7, 0.9, 1.0, 1.2)$ and $\beta^2 = (0.7, 0.9, 1.1, 1.2)$ are given, all elements apart from the third elements are equal, and it should be $\beta^1 < \beta^2$ as $1.0 < 1.1$.

How to determine the aggregation function varies from the subject addressed to the attitude of the decision-maker. If we do not attribute importance to the magnitude of the values of the betas, in other words, if we consider that each quantile is of equal importance, then it can be a choice that is suitable for the arithmetic mean. In this case, the following relationship is valid:

$$\min\beta \leq \widehat{\beta} = \frac{1}{n}\sum_{i=1}^{n}\beta_i \leq \max\beta$$

In other words, when we wish that low beta values pull all betas down, the aggregation function should exhibit a conjunctive behaviour. Mathematically, as an aggregation function that shows the

$$f(\beta) \leq \min\beta$$

relationship

$$f(\beta) = \frac{1}{\sum\beta_i}\prod_{i=1}^{n}\beta_i$$

can be given. In the opposite case, i.e., when high beta values try to pull all betas up, they exhibit a disjunctive behaviour. The disjunctive aggregation acts as follows;

$$f(\beta) \geq \max\beta$$

As an example;

$$f(\beta) = 1 - \frac{1}{\sum\beta_i}\prod_{i=1}^{n}(1 - \beta_i)$$

function can be given. When we pay attention, conjunctive and disjunctive behaviours correspond to risk-averse and risk-seeking behaviours, respectively. Whether the beta is big or small is a fuzzy term. If a point that can separate high or low beta values can be determined, an aggregation function can be obtained showing a conjunctive behaviour for the low ones, and a disjunctive behaviour for the high ones. This means that different attitudes can be shown for the quantiles that show the low beta effect and the quantiles that show the high beta effect. Consequently, we can basically classify the aggregation functions as averaging, conjunctive, disjunctive and mixed (Beliakov et al. 2007, p. 9).

The permutation of input elements (betas) is important to be able to determine certain features of aggregation functions, such as symmetry. The expression $\beta_p = (\beta_{(1)}, \beta_{(2)}, \ldots, \beta_{(n)})$ means one of the permutations of $\beta = (\beta_1, \beta_2, \ldots, \beta_n)$ possible number of $n!$. Accordingly, an aggregation function is symmetrical if each input (β) fulfills the condition $f(\beta) = f(\beta_p)$ for each permutation (β_p). A special case of the permutation means the ordering of the input at a determined order (non-decreasing or non-increasing). In this case $\beta\nearrow$ and $\beta\searrow$, respectively, show that the order is non-decreasing and non-increasing. For example; for $\beta = (1.1, 1.3, 0.8)$, $\beta\nearrow = (0.8, 1.1, 1.3)$ and $\beta\searrow = (1.3, 1.1, 0.8)$; and $\beta_{(1)}$ shows the smallest element in the first case, and the biggest element in the second case. The relationships between betas are $\beta_{(1)} \leq \beta_{(2)} \leq , \ldots, \leq \beta_{(n)}$ in the first case, and $\beta_{(1)} \geq \beta_{(2)} \geq , \ldots, \geq \beta_{(n)}$ in the second.

The Ordered Weighted Averaging (OWA) functions are aggregation functions developed by Yager (1988) and are based on the principle of weighting the input elements by their value. This means that, for example, betas are weighted according to the magnitude of the beta values formed in quantiles, and not by the quantiles themselves. This is its difference from the weighted arithmetic mean (WAM). The WAM gives the input element weight. For example; while it gives particular weight to the beta value for $\tau = 0.75$, OWA gives weight by the magnitude of the beta value. For a given w weighting vector, the OWA function is defined for the non-increasing order in a standard way. Therefore, only β is used instead of $\beta\searrow$ in the notation, and it is defined as follows:

$$OWA(\beta) = w_1\beta_{(1)} + w_2\beta_{(2)} + \ldots + w_n\beta_{(n)}$$

Here; it is $w_1 + w_2 + \ldots + w_n = 1$, and for each i $0 \leq w_i \leq 1$. For example; for $w = (0.7, 0.2, 0.1)$ and $\beta = (1.4, 0.5, 1.9)$; $OWA(\beta)$ is calculated as $1.9 \times 0.7 + 1.4 \times 0.2 + 0.5 \times 0.1 = 1.66$. For $\beta\nearrow$, the OWA function is called reverse OWA and it is obtained by regulating the weight vector as $w = (w_n, w_{n-1}, \ldots, w_1)$. While OWA is a symmetric function as of its definition, WAM is not symmetrical (as long as all weights are not equal). In case all weights are equal and $(1/n)$, OWA and arithmetic mean are equivalent. Choosing the weights as $w = (1, 0, 0, \ldots, 0)$ and $w = (0, 0, 0, \ldots, 1)$ makes the OWA function equivalent to $max\beta$ and $min\beta$, respectively. What gives the OWA function conjunctive (andlike), disjunctive (orlike) or mixed behaviour is the orness measure (Liu 2008). In other words, it reflects the attitudinal character of an investor. The orness measure of a weight vector is given by the following expression:

$$Orness(w) = \sum_{i=1}^{n} \frac{n-i}{n-1} w_i$$

In this case, the orness level for max, min and arithmetic mean is calculated as $1, 0$ and 0.5, respectively. Orness takes a value at the interval of $[0,1]$, and a w weighting vector can be found in such a way that the $Orness(w) = \alpha$ for an α level. An alpha value that is close to 1 points the relevant OWA function to "orlike" behaviour, and therefore, an optimistic investor. An alpha value that is close to 0 takes the related OWA function closer to "andlike" situation, therefore, it is the reason for preference for a pessimistic investor. Hence, the selection level at the interval of [0,1] is equivalent to a stance between optimism and pessimism. An important result found here is that the relationship between two weight vectors as w^1 and w^2 overlaps with the relationship between the OWA functions. So that, if orness $(w^1) \geq$ orness (w^2), then it should be; $OWA_{w^1}(\beta) \geq OWA_{w^2}(\beta)$.

The weight vector can be considered as the discrete probability distribution function of the betas in the OWA function. In this case, the uniform distribution level of the weights can be determined by the dispersion or the entropy measure.

Dispersion is given by the following expression; n being ≥ 2,

$$Disp(w) = -\sum_{i=1}^{n} w_i \ln w_i$$

Its value ranges between the interval of $0 \leq Disp(w) \leq \ln(n)$. Dispersion gets the values of 0, 0 and $\ln(n)$, respectively, for *max*, *min* and arithmetic mean. The fact that the dispersion is high guarantees that the number of null values in weight is reduced. In this case, it becomes a measure of the extent that all the information in the quantiles is used. In case of weighting that exhibits the maximum dispersion, OWA is named as Maximum Entropy OWA (MEOWA). The following two determinations are possible in the light of what is given. First, if no orness level has been determined, maximum dispersion is achieved such that w_i is 0.5. This is the arithmetic mean. Secondly, the maximum dispersions are equal for OWA and Reverse OWA. The determination of the weight vector making sure that all the information is reflected on the result, and at a required orness level is an optimization problem.

$$\min \sum_{i=1}^{n} w_i \ln w_i$$

$$s.t. \quad \sum_{i=1}^{n} w_i = 1$$

$$\sum_{i=1}^{n} \frac{n-i}{n-1} w_i = \alpha$$

$$w_i \geq 0, \quad i = 1, 2, \ldots, n$$

Upon investigating the literature, the most widely used quantile aggregation operators are Trimmed Regression Quantile, Gaswirth and Tukey's trimean estimators that we will code as TRQ, GAS and TRM. These estimators are defined as follows:

$$\widehat{\beta}_\alpha = \frac{1}{1 - 2\alpha} \int\limits_\alpha^{1-\alpha} \beta(\tau)d\tau \ , \ \ 0 < \alpha < 0.5 \quad (TRQ)$$

$$\widehat{\beta}_{GAS} = 0.3\beta\left(\frac{1}{3}\right) + 0.4\beta\left(\frac{1}{2}\right) + 0.3\beta\left(\frac{2}{3}\right) \quad (GAS)$$

$$\widehat{\beta}_{TRM} = 0.25\beta\left(\frac{1}{4}\right) + 0.5\beta\left(\frac{1}{2}\right) + 0.25\beta\left(\frac{3}{4}\right) \quad (TRM)$$

(α) used in the TRQ calculation is a parameter for the trimming level, and it should not be mistaken with the level of orness used in determining the OWA weights. Different symbols were not used in order to stick to the notations used in the literature.

4 Objective of the Chapter

For the correct estimation of beta, creating a sensor network positioned from one tail to the other of the distribution, for example, on different percentiles, and evaluating the information from each sensor may ensure that we have true information about the whole distribution. Hereby, we can see how the effect of the independent variable (market) on the dependent variable (security or portfolio) occurs in different regions (percentiles). Quantile regression gives us what kind of an effect the market will have on the security in different percentiles.

Each percentile means different beta. This means obtaining more than one beta rather than a beta value that can be obtained with OLS. This causes the problem of the fusion of different information (betas).

In the study they carried out with simulated and actual data, Chan and Lakonishok (1992) showed that the estimators based on quantile regression exhibit better performance than OLS. TRQ, GAS and TRM were used in the study in question as a robust estimator. A similar study was carried out by Jiang (2011), and similar results were obtained.

The aim of this part is to contribute to the literature by adding the use of OWA operators to the successfully used fusion techniques in the literature, in addition to emphasising the use of the increasingly common quantile regression. We know that this distribution is only to cause a discussion.

5 Data and Methodology

The daily closing prices of Borsa Istanbul for the period of 02/01/2013–19/09/2017 were used to evaluate the performance of OWA operators. AKBNK, BJKAS and BRISA stocks showing noticeably skewness and thick-tail features were chosen, and

Table 1 Descriptive statistics

	AKBNK	BJKAS	BRISA	BIST100
Mean	0.008511	−0.025658	0.0271253	0.023280
Median	0	0	0	0.062030
Maximum	9.252337	18.129644	9.493289	6.237859
Minimum	−9.867153	−98.875951	−12.467486	−11.063794
Std. Dev.	2.066965	4.206273	1.757013	1.429384
Skewness	0.066553	−10.890175	−0.285413	−0.611043
Kurtosis	4.250981	261.599929	8.038039	8.216396
Jarque-Bera	78.078356	3322516.466	1268.245397	1416.077589
Probability	0	0	0	0

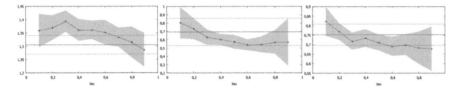

Fig. 2 Beta values across quantiles and OLS for stocks (AKBNK, BJKAS and BRISA)

BIST100 index return was used as a market return. The return series were calculated as percentage logarithmic return by using the following formula:

$$R_t = 100 \times \ln \frac{P_t}{P_{t-1}}$$

When the descriptive statistics values of the returns are examined (Table 1), the average return of the stocks other than BRISA is below the average return of the market. While AKBNK shows a slightly right-skewed distribution, others are left-skewed. BJKAS shows an excessively thick-tailed and skewed distribution.

Figure 2 shows the beta values between quantiles and OLS beta values for AKBNK, BJKAS and BRISA from left to right. The horizontal straight line shows the beta behaviour of the OLS estimator, while dashed lines show the confidence interval of the beta (95%). The piecewise lines show the beta effects in different quantiles, while shaded regions show the confidence interval that belongs to them. The vertical axis belongs to the regressor, i.e., the market return. Therefore, while the beta effect of the market on stocks can be steadily estimated by OLS along the distribution, the presence of quite different effects is observed when we look at different quantile values of the quantile regression.

It was taken as $\alpha = 0.20$ for the TQR estimation of the beta. Expression (4) was used for OLS and quantile regression estimations. $\beta = [\beta(0.1), \beta(02), \beta(0.3), \beta(0.4),$ $\beta(0.5), \beta(0.6), \beta(0.7), \beta(0.8), \beta(0.9)]$ vector was created for the OWA estimation, and w weight vectors for $\alpha = (0.3, 0.4, 0.5, 0.6, 0.7)$ orness levels were found by using the MEOWA optimization. Therefore, $\widehat{\beta}$ values were calculated for each orness level.

The Root Mean Square Error (RMSE) and Mean Absolute Error (MAE) statistics were calculated for 9 beta estimations in total together with the OLS, TQR, GAS and TRM estimations by placing them in the expression (4) for the stocks AKBNK, BJKAS and BRISA. The formulas used for RMSE and MAE are defined as follows (R_t = observed returns, $\widehat{R}_t$ = estimated returns and N = number of observations).

$$RMSE = \sqrt{\frac{1}{N} \sum_{t=1}^{N} \left(R_t - \widehat{R}_t\right)^2}$$

$$MAE = \frac{1}{N} \sum_{t=1}^{N} \left|R_t - \widehat{R}_t\right|$$

To measure the performance of the betas estimated in the modelling of the returns of the stocks, the RMSE and MAE statistics were calculated for four different regions of the distribution.

(I) The whole distribution,
(II) The region of the distribution that falls within one standard deviation interval,
(III) The region that falls outside the one standard deviation interval of the distribution and,
(IV) The region that falls outside the two standard deviation interval of the distribution.

Therefore, the performance values in 4 different regions were obtained for nine different beta estimations of each stock.

6   Results and Discussions

Tables 2 and 3 show the results and bold values indicate the best scores and hence the best estimator for each stocks. Table 2 presents the RMSE results. In general, OWA and other quantile regression based estimators are successful. Success stands out more in excessively skewed and fat-tailed examples such as BJKAS and BRISA. The OLS estimator has remained quite weak in (III) and (IV) regions of the distributions. OWA generally remains close to the best score even in places where it cannot have the best score. This closeness seems to increase further sometimes when the orness level is <0.3 and sometimes >0.7. OWA and OLS have the same scores for BRISA stock in (I) region. The effectiveness of OLS became weak and it could not be in the best state since there was no normal distribution for all the stocks in this region. Unlike OLS; the OWA, GAS and TRQ estimators better modelled the data at the interval within one standard deviation of the centre. OLS is in no case the estimator with the best score for tail regions. The OWA estimator is in the state of the estimator with the best score three times, TRQ three times, and GAS once. In the RMSE scores, TRM and GAS generally yielded close results. These two estimators generally remain close to TRQ. In general, the RMSE results show us that the

Table 2 Performance scores based on RMSE

RMSE	TRQ	OLS	GAS	TRM	0.3	0.4	0.5	0.6	0.7
(I)									
AKBNK	1.1017	**0.8893**	1.3638	1.3707	0.8899	0.8906	0.8914	0.8923	0.8933
BJKAS	**4.0860**	4.0863	4.0924	4.0922	4.0897	4.0887	4.0877	4.0869	4.0864
BRISA	1.3897	**1.3895**	1.4562	1.4569	1.3915	1.3907	1.3901	1.3897	**1.3895**
(II)									
AKBNK	1.1992	1.2161	1.9152	1.9270	1.2071	1.2041	1.2018	1.1999	**1.1985**
BJKAS	11.7021	11.7204	**11.6740**	11.6747	11.7624	11.755	11.7467	11.7376	11.7275
BRISA	**2.3115**	2.4513	2.3229	2.3227	2.4901	2.4816	2.4725	2.4628	2.4520
(III)									
AKBNK	**0.7133**	0.7253	1.079	1.083	0.7321	0.7351	0.7379	0.7406	0.7432
BJKAS	1.5464	1.5666	1.6243	1.6231	**1.5392**	1.5427	1.5473	1.5531	1.5606
BRISA	0.8301	0.8588	1.0781	1.0794	**0.8297**	0.8355	0.8421	0.8495	0.8581
(IV)									
AKBNK	2.7709	1.5027	3.087	3.1084	**1.4995**	1.4998	1.5009	1.5027	1.5051
BJKAS	22.3789	22.3987	**22.3224**	22.3237	22.462	22.4512	22.4388	22.4251	22.4097
BRISA	**3.5318**	3.8571	3.5596	3.5586	3.928	3.9127	3.8963	3.8784	3.8585

Bold values show the best scores and hence the best estimator for each stocks

Table 3 Performance scores based on MAE

MAE	TRQ	OLS	GAS	TRM	0.3	0.4	0.5	0.6	0.7
(I)									
AKBNK	0.7739	0.6863	0.9608	0.9654	0.6845	0.6841	0.6837	**0.6836**	0.6838
BJKAS	**1.8522**	1.8644	1.8906	1.8900	1.8580	1.8582	1.8588	1.8601	1.8623
BRISA	0.9651	0.9622	1.0386	1.0393	**0.9609**	0.9610	0.9612	0.9616	0.9621
(II)									
AKBNK	0.9811	1.0104	1.3035	1.3121	0.9912	0.9838	0.9773	0.9718	**0.9670**
BJKAS	**7.3514**	7.5055	7.3651	7.3673	7.6182	7.5995	7.5779	7.5535	7.5257
BRISA	1.8622	1.9840	1.7885	**1.7882**	2.0463	2.0331	2.0186	2.0029	1.9853
(III)									
AKBNK	0.7802	**0.5616**	0.8289	0.8319	0.5665	0.5687	0.5708	0.5727	0.5748
BJKAS	1.1839	1.1986	1.2444	1.2435	**1.1781**	1.1805	1.1837	1.1881	1.1938
BRISA	0.6629	0.6632	0.8192	0.8202	**0.6434**	0.6474	0.6519	0.6569	0.6628
(IV)									
AKBNK	1.2719	1.2678	2.1802	2.1991	1.2389	1.2279	1.2178	1.2096	**1.2026**
BJKAS	14.7489	14.9200	**14.7266**	14.7286	15.0968	15.0674	15.0335	14.9953	14.9517
BRISA	**3.0253**	3.4876	3.0275	3.0261	3.5925	3.5706	3.5465	3.5199	3.4899

Bold values show the best scores and hence the best estimator for each stocks

estimators based on quantile regression, and specifically the OWA operator model the distribution well. It can be concluded that the information in tail regions of the distributions showing excessively skewed and thick-tail features such as BJKAS and BRISA is better reflected by quantile regression-based methods.

Table 3 presents the MAE results. When we look at the results, the phenomenon that stands out first is that the OLS estimator has the best score only in (III) region and for AKBNK stock. Although OLS has the best score for this example, the OWA scores seem close to the OLS score for all orness levels. Among the other best 11 scores, OWA is in the state of the best score six times. The distribution of the remaining five best scores is as TRQ 3, TRM 1 and GAS 1. While the two best estimators by the MAE scores are OWA and TRQ, in general, quantile regression based estimators are at a better state than OLS. In addition to this fact, it can be said that what best aggregates the quantiles is OWA. The TRM and GAS estimators remain close to one another in terms of the MAE scores, just as in RMSE.

Consequently, quantile regression shows the information of different regions of the distribution. It can be said that OWA is the function that fuses the information of different regions by improving it. While it is impossible to generalize the findings of Borsa Istanbul and three stocks, they are the adequate reason to give weight to testing the performance of OWA operators in beta estimation.

7 Concluding Remarks

The pricing models of financial assets are generally of vital importance for the investor in terms of risk management. The CAPM as an asset pricing model is based on assumptions just as almost any economic model. It is known that most of these assumptions contradict with daily life. These models ignore the friction partly due to mathematical tractability. Phenomena such as the presence of taxes, the fact that the transaction costs are not zero, more than one period are taken into consideration in the investment rather than one period, the presence of asymmetrical information, and maybe the most important, the attitude of the investor towards risk create friction. As the friction force will have different effects on different surfaces, a homogenous investor and therefore, return series may not be expected to exhibit a normal behaviour. As friction will have different effects on different regions of distribution, the information that tails will carry should be taken into consideration, in addition to the centre.

Quantile regression enables focusing on the different percentiles of distribution, and therefore, modelling the heterogeneous distribution of the effect of the market on a security or portfolio. If the effect is not the same, then different betas are in question. Taking into consideration the magnitude of the information carried by each beta is possible with the help of OWA operators. At which weight to consider the information depends on the investor in terms of behavioural finance. The investor can create the OWA operator weights for an orness level to be determined.

In this study, the fusion problem of the beta of different quantiles, i.e., information was addressed while drawing the attention to the known advantages of quantile regression. It was shown that OWA operators should be taken into consideration as an alternative to aggregation approaches such as TQR, GAS and TRM that are widely used in the literature. In the example of Borsa Istanbul, it has been shown that OWA operators exhibit a comparable performance both to the traditional OLS and GAS, TRM and TQR.

References

Beliakov, G., Pradera, A., & Calvo, T. (2007). *Aggregation functions: A guide for practitioners.* Berlin: Springer-Verlag.

Campbell, J. Y., Lo, A. W., & MacKinlay, A. C. (1997). *The econometrics of financial markets.* Princeton, NJ: Princeton University Press.

Castanedo, F. (2013). A review of data fusion techniques. *The Scientific World Journal.* Hindawi Publishing Corporation. https://doi.org/10.1155/2013/704504

Chan, L., & Lakonishok, J. (1992). Robust measurement of beta risk. *The Journal of Financial and Quantitative Analysis, 27*(2), 265–282.

Cont, R. (2001). Emprical properties of asset returns: Stylized facts and statistical issues. *Quantitative Finance, 1,* 223–236.

Elton, E. J., Gruber, M. J., Brown, S. J., & Goetzmann, W. N. (2003). *Modern portfolio theory and investment analysis* (6th ed.). New York: Wiley.

Fama, E. F. (1965). The behavior of stock-market prices. *The Journal of Business, 38*(1), 34–105.

Fama, E. F. (1970). Efficient capital markets: A review of theory and emprical work. *The Journal of Finance, 25*(2), 383–417.

Fama, E. F., & French, K. R. (1992). The cross-section of expected stock returns. *Journal of Finance, 47,* 427–465.

Ferson, W. E., & Jagannathan, R. (1996). Econometric evaluation of asset pricing models. In G.S. Maddala & C.R. Rao (Eds.), *Handbook of statistics 14: Statistical methods in finance* (pp. 1–34). https://doi.org/10.1016/S0169-7161(96)14003-7

Francq, C., & Zakoian, J.-M. (2010). *GARCH models: Structure, statistical inference and financial applications.* Chichester: Wiley.

Gavrishchaka, V. V., & Banerjee, S. (2006). Support vector machine as an efficient framework for stock market volatility forecasting. *Computational Management Science, 3,* 147–160.

Hagerman, R. L. (1978). More evidence on the disribution of security returns. *The Journal of Finance, 33*(4), 1213–1221.

Hsu, D.-A., Miller, R. B., & Wichern, D. W. (1974). On the stable paretian behavior of stock-market prices. *Journal of the American Statistical Association, 69*(345), 108–113.

Jiang, C. (2011). On the robustness of beta risk in the cross-sectional regressions of stock return. Accessed 10.08.2017, from https://www2.bc.edu/chuanliang-jiang/Working_Paper.pdf

Kahneman, D., & Tversky, A. (1979). Prospect theory: An analysis of decision under risk. *Econometrica, 47,* 236–291.

Koenker, R. (1982). Robust tests for heteroscedasticity based on regression quantiles. *Econometrica, 50*(1), 43–61.

Koenker, R., & Bassett, G. (1978). Regression quantiles. *Econometrica, 46,* 33–50.

LeRoy, S. F. (1973). Risk aversion and the martingale property of stock prices. *International Economic Review, 14*(2), 436–446.

Lintner, J. (1965). The valuation of risk assets and the selection of risky investments in stock portfolio and capital budgets. *Review of Economics and Statistics, 47*(1), 13–37.

Liu, W. (2006). A liquidity-augmented capital asset pricing model. *Journal of Financial Economics, 82*, 631–671.

Liu, X. (2008). A general model of parameterized OWA aggregation with given orness level. *International Journal of Approximate Reasoning, 48*, 598–627.

Malkiel, B. G. (2003). The efficient market hypothesis and its critics. *The Journal of Economic Perspectives, 17*(1), 59–82.

Mandelbrot, B. (1960). The Pareto-Lévy law and the distribution of income. *International Economic Review, 1*(2), 79–106.

Mandelbrot, B. (1963). The variation of certain speculative prices. *The Journal of Business, 36*(4), 394–419.

Mandelbrot, B. (2003). Heavy tails in finance for independent or multifractal price increments. In S. T. Rachev (Ed.), *Handbook of heavy tailed distributions in finance* (pp. 1–34). https://doi.org/10.1016/B978-044450896-6.50003-0

Markowitz, H. (1952). Portfolio selection. *The Journal of Finance, 7*(1), 77–91.

Mossin, J. (1966). Equilibrium in a capital asset market. *Econometrica, 34*, 768–783.

Mulligan, R. F. (2004). Fractal analysis of highly volatile markets: An application to technology equities. *The Quarterly Review of Economics and Finance, 44*, 155–179.

Osborne, M. F. M. (1964). Brownian motion in stock market. In P. Cootner (Ed.), *The random character of stock market prices* (pp. 100–128). Cambridge, MA: MIT Press.

Peters, E. E. (1991). *Chaos and order in the capital markets: A new view of cycles, prices, and market volatility*. New York: Wiley.

Peters, E. E. (1994). *Fractal market analysis: Applying chaos theory to investment and economics*. New York: Wiley.

Rachev, S. T., Weron, A., & Weron, R. (1999). CED model for asset returns and fractal market hypothesis. *Mathematical and Computer Modelling, 29*, 23–26.

Reiss, R.-D., & Thomas, M. (2007). *Statistical analysis of extreme values with applications to insurance, finance, hydrology and other fields* (3rd ed.). Basel: Birkhauser Verlag.

Rubinstein, R. Y. (1981). *Simulation and the Monte Carlo method*. New York: Wiley.

Samuelson, P. A. (1965). Proof that properly anticipated prices fluctuate randomly. *Industrial Management Review, 6*(2), 41–49.

Sharpe, W. F. (1964). Capital asset prices: A theory of market equilibrium under conditions of risk. *Journal of Finance, 19*, 425–442.

Yager, R. (1988). On ordered weighted averaging aggregation operators in multicriteria decision making. *IEEE Transaction on Systems, Man and Cybernetics, 18*, 183–190.

Documentary Risk in International Trade

Yurdagül Meral

Abstract International trade is more risky than domestic trade. First of all international trade is effected cross borders between two different countries. Different countries have their own law, and culture, and language. Customs clearance is required in both importer's and exporter's countries. Main difference between domestic and international trade is customs process, specific documentation is required in clearing goods from customs between international boundaries.

Documentary risk is so important that approximately 70% of documents were rejected due to non-compliance of presented documents to the required specifications of letter of credit and sales agreement. International trade is based on documentation agreed upon by seller and buyer as per sales contract and letter of credit which is mirror reflection of contract. Documentary risk is non-compliance of documents detailed in sales contract or documentary credit. Discrepant documents might result in non-payment or delay in payment.

This chapter is about documentary risk, defining documentary risk and how to avoid such risks for both importer and exporter.

1 Introduction

Whether international trade or domestic trade, main question for seller (exporter) is to receive payment and main question for buyer (importer) is to receive goods or services in good order as per contract.

This process might be easier in domestic trade and to solve potential problems in case of dispute as both buyer and seller are in same country and subject to same law. However this is not the case in international trade, where importer and buyer are in different countries, where different laws apply.

Y. Meral (✉)
İstanbul Medipol University, Istanbul, Turkey
e-mail: ymeral@medipol.edu.tr

© Springer International Publishing AG, part of Springer Nature 2018
H. Dincer et al. (eds.), *Strategic Design and Innovative Thinking in Business Operations*, Contributions to Management Science,
https://doi.org/10.1007/978-3-319-77622-4_21

413

How will importers and exporters even communicate with each other, not only with different laws with different cultures and languages. How will international trade among two different countries will be handled in case of a dispute, which rules will apply, with US$16.5 trillion of export volume.

The major difference of international trade from local trade is documentation because for customs clearance process documentation is compulsory for both importer and exporter. All risks involved in international trade are directly or indirectly related with the documentation. Documentation plays a key role in both goods delivery and payment in international trade.

Documentary risk in international trade is crucial for both parties in international trade. Being in two different countries, subject to different laws, both parties must be aware of international trade rules and standards in international trade. The standardized, international trade rules for uniform practice are set by international organizations and widely accepted all over the world and these uniform specifications apply to documentation as well.

Approximately three thousand documents are used in international trade. Therefore correct documentation is very important to enable exporter to receive money in time and for importer to receive goods without delay. In other words international trade is actually based on documentation, from the very beginning starting with sales contract to the end clearing goods from import customs. Furthermore correct documentation is very important to avoid potential risks in international trade.

Before defining documentation and documentation risk, the international trade volumes are presented below are from International Trade Center (ITC), Trade Map. The Trade Map (www.trademap.org)[1] provides statistics are based on 220 countries export performance, international trade indicators, markets and companies directories of import and export.

The ITC Trade Map covers 5300 products. In international trade products are coded under The Harmonized System (HS) or commonly named as HS Code, Customs Tariff, Harmonized Code which is like every product has an ID number. The standard UNICODE is defined by World Customs Organization (WCO).[2] The UNICODE of products makes it possible to be used in any language and especially in customs. The World Customs Organization (WCO), an independent intergovernmental institution, previously named as Customs Co-operation Council, established in 1952, with nearly two hundred member countries covering 98% of international trade. Harmonized System (HS) by using standard UNICODE are used for tariffs, statistical data, quota controls, rules of origin, price monitoring and for research as well.

The international trade volume, that is the total export volume was US$15.8 trillion and the import volume was US$16 trillion in 2016. International trade export

---

[1] www.trademap.org

[2] http://www.wcoomd.org/en/topics/nomenclature/overview/what-is-the-harmonized-system.aspx

Fig. 1 Total exports
volume of the world in 2016

Exporters	Exported value in 2016
World	15,862,397,780
China	2,097,637,172
United States of America	1,453,167,148
Germany	1,340,752,046
Japan	644,932,439
Netherlands	569,383,956
Hong Kong, China	516,588,131
Korea, Republic of	495,465,606
France	488,885,072
Italy	461,529,407
United Kingdom	415,856,497

Fig. 2 Total imports
volume of the world in 2016

Importers	Imported value in 2016
World	16,062,472,839
United States of America	2,249,660,890
China	1,587,920,688
Germany	1,060,672,017
United Kingdom	635,569,887
Japan	606,924,047
France	560,554,863
Hong Kong, China	547,124,448
Netherlands	504,185,169

volumes 2012–2016 are presented in Fig. 1 and the import volumes are presented in Fig. 2 (www.trademap.org).[3]

The difference in the Trade Map data of the total imports and exports volumes are mainly because exports are usually reported as FOB and imports are reported as CIF values. Furthermore, re-exports that is importing goods and exporting after processing are not sometimes reported. Some countries include free zones where else other countries may not include free zones.

---

[3] www.trademap.org

1.1 Exports

Total world export volume was US$15.8 trillion, China with US$2 trillion dollars was the leader in 2016, followed by the second largest, US with US$2 trillion dollars and the third Germany with US$1.4 trillion dollars export volume.

1.2 Imports

In 2016, total world import was US$16 trillion, of which U.S. with US$2.2 trillion is the leader, followed by China with US$1.6 and Germany with US$1 trillion dollars of import volumes.

1.3 Export Import Process

Export process starts with sales contract which is one of the most important step to avoid potential risks in future. As mentioned earlier, international organizations are trying to make international trade easier by standardizing the rules, documentation, payment etc. to increase international trade volume. One of the standard instruments used in international trade is the "Model Contract for the International Commercial Sale of Goods"[4] will be used in this chapter, to show the documentation and the potential documentation risk in international trade.

The uniform model contract is based on other institutions'[5] contracts and covers main rights and obligations of both parties. Furthermore, it covers most common, accepted points of other international contracts. Model Contract has two versions. Standard and short form version. Standard version covers lack of conformity, non-conformity notices etc. where else short version covers only most common clauses covering main rights and responsibilities of parties and mainly covering international trade practise.

The first part of the Model Contract covers articles of goods, that is delivery terms, pricing, payment and documentation. Remaining parts cover buyer's non-performance, i.e. not paying as per sales contract, non-performance of seller, i.e. not delivering goods as per contract or delivered goods are not in compliance

[4]www.intracen.org/itc/exporters/model-contracts/

[5]United Nations Convention on Contracts for the International Sale of Goods (CISG)
Uniform Law on the International Sale of Goods (ULIS)
Principles of International Commercial Contracts UNIDROIT
Principles of European Contract Law (PECL)
ITC Model Contract for the International Commercial Sale of Perishable Goods
ICC Model International Sale Contract—Manufactured Goods Intended for Resale.

with contract, or not delivering transport document to buyer to enable buyer to clear goods from customs with transport document, avoidance that is terminating contract, in case of dispute how to resolve disputes, of which law or ICC guiding principles are the contract is subject to, force majeure reasons of non-performance.

2 Sales Contract

As per Model Contract for the International Commercial Sale of Goods (short version) following parties (i.e. buyer and seller) details, contract clauses covering most common points are: Goods, delivery terms of goods, pricing details, payment conditions/terms details, non-payment of buyer as per the contract, non-delivery of the goods by the seller as per the contract, lack of conformity of the goods as per the contract, transfer of property of the goods (transportation document delivery to the buyer), termination (avoidance) of contract, force majeure reasons of non-performance for both parties, agreement, notices, in case of dispute the process of resolution and applicable law and guiding principles of sales contract.

Goods Risk in international trade can be summarized as follows:

- *Transit Risk/Loss (partial/total) or damage to shipment during transit (transportation)*: Goods might be damaged or lost during shipment/transportation. If goods are lost or damaged in transit, owner of goods at the time of such occurrence will have to cover loss via insurance. Both parties must be aware that that insurance obligation is upto sales contract and only in CIF and CIP incoterms, it is exporter's liability.
- *Non-delivery*: Goods may not be delivered because of fraud, however applicant may have to pay issuing bank as banks do not deal with goods and they deal only with documents and are not liable with fraud/fake documents.
- *Product faults/ Short shipment and shipment of inferior goods*: Products might be delivered but delivered goods may not be in compliance with goods. Goods may be shipped lesser than sales contract (i.e. a lesser quantity than ordered) or with inferior quality.
- *Late delivery*: Another risk is if goods are *received late* importer may not be unable to sell as timing might not be appropriate. The opposite might be the case, goods may be received *before the documents*, then buyer may have to get goods under a shipping guarantee, of which he might have to pay irrespective of any discrepancies in documents.

2.1 Goods Details in Sales Contract

Description: In addition to definition of goods, using the UNICODE of the "HS" system, harmonized system code might be great assistance to standardization and harmonization of customs and reducing costs.

Quantity Details: Total quantity, measurement, if delivery with installment details of installment, if tolerance is acceptable, whether plus or minus of percentage details must be given following description of goods as price details with the tolerance percentage might change total amount to be paid.

Inspection: Inspection details, when, by whom, and specifications required must be given as it is one of important documents which verifies specification of goods confirm with requirements given in sales contract, like name of inspection organization for inspecting quality, place of inspection, date of inspection and who will bear inspection costs.

Packaging: Packing details are important as it is one of the documentation required by insurance companies in case of partial loss during transit and through customs as well with weight list, showing weight of the goods and the packages.

Other specification: if any

2.2 Delivery of Goods

The most common rules of International Trade, namely INCOTERMS are issued by International Chamber of Commerce (ICC) (https://iccwbo.org/)[6] was founded after First World War, when there were no rules of international trade, finance or commercial relations.

INCOTERMS, has been issued by which is world's largest business organization with members of local chamber of commerce and companies all over world work for international trade standardization and international trade rules to increase international trade.

The 11 Incoterms (**International Commercial Trade Terms**) issued by ICC are not only for international use, they can be used in domestic trade as well.

Incoterms cover details delivery place, delivery date or period, name of carrier and other delivery terms (if any).

The parties must be aware that only CIP and CIF terms insurance is exporter's obligation, in remaining incoterms insurance is subject to sales contract, either party can make insurance transactions. For DAT, DAP and DDP terms exporter must be aware that responsibility is to deliver at delivery place therefore exporter must make sure that insurance policy is ready before loading even if importer is responsible to make insurance.

---

[6]https://iccwbo.org/

Furthermore, the FAS, FOB, CFR, CIF terms can only be used for sea/inland waterway transportation only, where else all other terms can be used for all modes of transport.

Although EXW seems like selling like local trade, because goods must be ready for shipping at agreed exporter's premises at shipping date, exporter must be aware of risk that goods are delivered to importer and bill of lading/transport document in other words title of goods/owner of goods might be name of importer.

2.3   Price

Goods price per unit/measurement, total price, total amount (in letters as well), currency and determining method of price (if appropriate).

2.4   Payment Terms

Payment conditions in international trade is one of the most boilerplate matter as international payment methods differ from domestic trade and has risk for both parties. Unlike domestic trade, importer and exporter, in two different countries, not knowing each other, not trusting each other, exporter wants to receive payment at once, importer wants to receive goods at once.

However advance payment is not even possible in domestic trade, although all sellers wish so but usually end up agreeing on open account terms like a month, 2 months or even 3 months following shipment date.

Payment conditions must be clarified and given in sales contract.
How payment will be made, i.e. bank transfer via swift, unlikely but cash, bank draft etc.
Account and bank details of seller/beneficiary must be given.
Payment time details must be given.

The parties must agree upon whether advance payment, documentary collection, documentary letter of credit or bank guaranteed payments of which a summary of most common payment processes are given below.

Advance Payment Method
Advance payment method is preferred by exporters because exporter wants to receive value of goods in advance and after receiving value of goods, wants to ship goods, without any risk.

Advance payment process;

1. Sales contract between exporter and importer.
2. Importer transfers goods amount via SWIFT[7] payment system, which is a standard, secure payment method used for bank transfers all over world.
3. Exporter ships goods.
4. Exporter sends shipping documents, transportation document issued to the order of importer and sends directly to importer, via special courier to importer.
5. Importer, receiving shipping documents and transportation document issued in his name, clears goods through customs upon arrival of goods.

Open Account Payment Method

Open account payment is opposite to advance payment, exporter takes all risk and importer takes minimum risk. It is a cheap method, comparing to other methods where banking charges apply.

Open account method is usually preferred among parties with long term business where both parties trust each other or where importer is more powerful than exporter and importer prefers open account payment method as this method enables importer to check goods before payment.

However this is not the case for exporter as there is no security for payment of goods. Open account payment method process is as follows:

1. Sales contract between exporter and importer.
2. Exporter ships goods.
3. Exporter sends shipping documents, including transportation document issued to the order of or endorsed to the importer via special courier to importer.
4. Importer having received shipping documents, including transportation document issued or endorsed in his name, clears goods through customs.
5. Importer transfers goods value via Swift payment system at agreed time.

Documentary Collection Payment Method (Cash Against Documents)

Documentary collection method is subject to latest version related publication[8] and comparing advance payment method might be preferable by importer as well because in this method importer does not have to pay in advance. The process is as follows:

1. Sales contract between exporter and importer.
2. Exporter ships goods.
3. Exporter sends shipping documents to importer's bank with transportation document issued to the order of importer's bank.
4. Importer's bank advises importer about documents.

---

[7]https://www.swift.com/about-us
[8]ICC current latest version publication for collections is Uniform Rules for Collections (URC 522).

5. The importer pays documents value for further payment to exporter's bank via SWIFT and in return receives bank endorsed bill of lading (transport document) and other documents to clear goods through customs with documents.

Documentary Credit/Letter of Credit Payment Method

Letter of credit method is considered as most secure for both parties, subject to related publication of ICC.[9]

Letter of credit conditions reflect sales contract conditions like a mirror.

Letter of credit payment method can be shortly defined as "conditional payment order", which means that if letter of credit documents required condition is accomplished, in other words if compliance documents as per letter of credit are submitted to issuing/confirming bank and if conditions of letter of credit (like latest date of shipment, presentation date etc.) are met payment will be effected to seller by issuing/confirming bank.

Confirming bank takes issuing bank's non-payment risk and country risk of importer.

Letter of Credit payment process is as follows:

1. Sales contract between exporter and importer.
2. Importer requests his bank to issue a letter of credit.
3. Importer's Bank (issuing bank) issues letter of credit as per buyer's instruction and sends letter of credit swift message to exporter's bank.
4. Exporter's bank advises and/or confirms letter of credit to exporter.
5. Exporter ships goods.
6. Exporter prepares documents required in letter of credit and submits documents to his bank.
7. Exporter bank

    a. if confirmed letter of credit, checks documents and pays if documents are in compliance with letter of credit and if letter of credit conditions are met and requests and receives funds from issuing bank.

       Sends documents to importer's (letter of credit issuing) bank.

       Importer bank checks documents and informs importer.

    b. If only advised letter of credit, sends documents directly to importer's bank, without checking documents. The importer's bank (issuing bank) checks documents, if in compliance with letter of credit, pays importer's bank. Advises importer about documents.

8. The importer pays bank documents value and in return receives documents including endorsed bill of lading/transport document and clears goods through customs.

---

[9]ICC current latest version publication for letter of credits is Uniform Customs and Practice for Documentary Credits (UCP 600).

Payment Backed by Bank Guarantee

Payment backed by guarantee is one of the most simple and secure payment method. It can be summarized as open account payment basis with payment guaranteed by (usually importer's bank) guarantee in case importer fails to make payment on agreed time in open account basis.

In this payment method importer's bank guarantees a certain amount of payment. The process is as follows:

1. Importer's bank issues a bank guarantee stating that if importer fails to make payment of delivered goods at maturity bank guarantees payment of goods.
2. Exporter, upon receipt of bank guarantee, ships goods.
3. Sends shipping documents directly to importer with transport document blank endorsed or to order of importer.
4. Importer, upon receipt of documents, clears goods through customs.
5. If importer fails to make payment at maturity, exporter requests payment under bank guarantee.

Acceptance Payment Method

If payment term requires a draft in documentation then it is called Acceptance Payment because unlike check, promissory note etc. which are issued/signed by debtor, draft is issued by beneficiary and accepted by debtor. Therefore payment methods which requires the document, 'draft or bill of exchange' as an instrument for payment are called acceptance payment methods.

There are two ways of this payment method.

1. *Trade acceptance*, is where only buyer accepts draft and pays value of draft at maturity date.
2. *Bank Acceptance, is where the draft is accepted by importer's bank or Avalized Draft (bill of exchange) payment* is trade acceptance added with aval. By avalizing accepted draft, importer's bank guarantees payment at maturity, in other words as per aval, bank guarantees payment at maturity date even if buyer does not pay, bank is obliged to pay.

Deferred Payment Method

Deferred payment method is also a payment term to be paid in an agreed future date like acceptance payment method, the only difference is there is no draft required in documentation is called deferred payment method.

2.5 Documents and Documentary Risk

International trade requires documentation because it is cross borders and both import and export process requires customs clearance of goods which is effected with documentation.

Documentation risk can be defined discrepant documents or documents not confirming with documentation requirement of sales contract or letter of credit. As mentioned in letter of credit payment, bank checks documents presented with documents required in letter of credit and if there is a discrepancy in one of documents, bank's obligation for payment under letter of credit is no more valid as document is not in compliance with letter of credit.

Therefore failure or not complaint document result delay or even not being able to receive payment for goods delivered or service rendered.

Parties must avoid using "shipping documents", "stale documents acceptable", "third party documents acceptable", "third party documents not acceptable", "exporting country", "shipping company" and "documents acceptable as presented" as they are not defined in UCP 600.

Shipping documents are not only transportation documents which show that goods are shipped, shipping documents cover other documents like invoice, insurance, weight and packing list, certificate of origin etc. accompanying transport documents.

Approximately 3000 documents are used in international trade.

As per sales contract documentation required must be agreed upon by both parties.

Main document, at the same time showing title of goods is transport document, of which original transport is required to be submitted for clearance of goods through customs.

Original insurance policy covering risk from import country to export country, place of delivery, covering clauses as per sales contract or documentary credit.

Commercial documents, showing description of goods as per sales contract or documentary credit and official documents are like certificate of origin, verified by export country usually chamber of commerce to be submitted to import customs for clearance.

Last group of documentation is financial document, like a draft or bill of exchange which is an instrument used for payment generally used at a maturity date (a few months) after delivery of goods.

If there is any ambiguous or not clear document/condition in sales contract for exporter of which exporter will not be able to commit, it must be clarified, deleted or amended before shipment of goods by mutual agreement.

The basic documents used in international trade are as follows;

Commercial Invoice
Commercial invoices may not be signed unless otherwise requested specifically. Definition of goods, unit price, total amount, total price details are given.

Packing List
Document providing packing information, usually giving weight information as well, used as packing and weight list. It is necessary for customs clearance however in case of loss on the way during transfer of goods, like an accident etc. insurance company calculates exact loss as per packing list.

Insurance Document
As per incoterms, if CIF or CIP incoterms are agreed upon then insurance policy must be provided by exporter. In all other incoterms it is subject to contract, in other

words either party might be responsible for insurance. However for delivery terms, as mentioned earlier, in DAT, DAP and DDP Incoterms, although it is subject to the contract, exporter might be volunteer to take the responsibility of insurance as in these terms, exporter's responsibility is to deliver goods at the named place, port or in DDP after customs duty paid in importer's country. To avoid potential risks in transit, during transportation goods from exporter's country to importer's country, of which exporter is obliged to, to be on the safe side, insurance must be made by exporter as well. As per international standard rules of ICC Publication No. 600, for insurance document requirements, insurance cover notes are not accepted, insurance document presented must be original and signed by an agent or by a proxy. Of signed by agent/proxy, whoever signs insurance document must clarify whether signed for or on behalf of insurance company or underwriter.

Certificate of Origin

Certificate of origin, usually issued by chamber of commerce of export country is a document showing origin of goods, required by customs, to enable to control if there is a quote applicable to that country or tax increase or decrease. Certificate of origin shows and certifies origin of product. It is one of major documents of customs clearance and is used for customs duties calculation in customs. At the same it helps customs for inspection and international trade statistics among countries.

Certificate of Inspection

Inspection certificate is another document used in international trade, which is issued by a third party, usually professional credible inspection companies about related goods, verifying specification of goods given in contract and reflected in letter of credit. If goods are not in conformity with required specifications given in letter of credit as well, importer's bank does not have to pay exporter as document submitted will not be in compliance with letter of credit. Therefore documents in compliance with letter of credit is top priority importance for exporter to receive payment without delay.

Customs Documents

Documents which enable importer to clear goods from customs, these documents are basically, the original invoice, the original bill of lading/transport document, the original insurance document, the original certificate of origin, the original packing and weight list accompanied with export or import declaration.

Other Documents

All other required documents in sales contract or letter of credit.

Transport Documents

The most important, basic documents showing that goods are shipped. Transport documents are at the same used as collateral by banks because transport document bill of lading used in sea or internal water way transportation are at the same showing title of goods. If used as collateral by banks, ownership of goods must be bank. Bill of lading must be issued endorsed to order of bank. This aspect of transport of document is so important that it might effect payment term agreement between parties. Payment method choice might change according to exporter's trust perception and credibility of buyer. If exporter does not trust importer, might insist on transport document (bill of lading) to be issued or endorsed to a bank. Banks who disburse credit for importers or exporters might use documentation as collateral as well. In such cases transport document might be issued or endorsed to banks too.

The most important, basic document is transportation document showing that goods are shipped.

Furthermore bill of lading for sea and inland water transportation at the same show title of goods, which means goods can be delivered to bonafide holder of blank order/or endorsed original bill of lading. Although in international trade legislation only bill of lading or in multi modal transport (the last delivery point) is via sea therefore bill of lading which shows the title of goods, in practice usually even if transport document is not a bill of lading say a CMR, truck driver does not deliver goods if CMR is issued in name of a bank. The driver requests to see bank's endorsement to deliver goods.

To be on the safe side, both parties starting with sales contract must clarify documentation required to enable them to clear goods through customs, especially bill of lading or transport document showing title of goods must be issued in name of a bank, usually importer's bank. With this practice exporter is relieved that unless importer pays documents amount to bank, title of goods belongs to exporter. In case importer does not pay documents value and in return receive documents, then exporter still has a chance either to resell it or worst scenario he will have to bear only transportation risk.

The ICC publication which aims to protect both parties about letter of credit payments, has a rule which requires original bill of lading/transport document submission for presentation of documents under letter of credit. Which means that ICC requires the original bill of lading to be presented for payment to protect for both parties.

Delivery Note, Delivery Order, Cargo Receipt, Forwarder's Certificate of Receipt, Forwarder's Certificate of Shipment, Forwarder's Certificate of Transport, Forwarder's Cargo Receipt and Mate's Receipt are not acceptable as transport documents as per ICC related articles of its (UCP 600) articles of 19-25.

As they are not accepted as transport documents, presentation period of 21 calendar days of 14-c requires original of transport document given in articles 19-25 of ICC, related publication exporter must be aware of risk that documents will not be in compliance with letter of credit terms, which are subject to ICC Publication of Uniform Customs and Practice for Documentary Credits (UCP) 600.[10]

Clean Transport Document
Buyer requests a clean transport document, which means a document with no clause or notation that expressly declares a defective condition of goods or its packaging, that is 'clean on board' or the word 'clean' is not necessary. Unless transport

---

[10]ICC Uniform Customs and Practice for Documentary Credits (UCP 600).

document has a clause like 'box broken' etc. it is accepted as clean transport document.

Latest Date of Shipment
Latest date of shipment is another important matter which can be verified and controlled via transport document. Latest shipment date and estimated time of arrival of goods is another important aspect for both importer to receive goods as scheduled and exporter to be ready for shipment. Sales contract or letter of credit must clearly mention agreed latest date of shipment to enable exporter to be ready for shipment before that day and importer to be ready to clear goods through customs and receive goods.

Types of Transport Documents
Multimodal Transport Document
    As previously mentioned, INCOTERMS FOB, FAS, CFR and CIF terms can be only used by sea or inland water transportation, remaining terms can be used for all modes of transportation.
    However sometimes goods have to be transported by truck to port where has to be loaded to a vessel etc. in other words two modes of transport might be necessary. Transport document issued in such cases is called multimodal transport document. Although more than one mode of transport vehicle is used there is only one transport document namely multimodal transport document covering shipment of goods till delivery of goods to importer. The multimodal transport document, like other transport documents must be signed by carrier or an agent of a carrier or the master. Whoever signs as an agent must clarify on multimodal transport document as whose agent is he signing thereof i.e. agent for carrier or agent for master etc. It is cheaper and convenient for both parties to deal with one multimodal transport document then trying to deal shipment for different modes of transport.
    As mentioned earlier original bill of lading, that is transport document used for sea transportation, a negotiable document that is it is at the same time title of goods/ownership of goods and ownership can be transferred to a second party by endorsement and delivery of the original bill of lading in sea transportation. Same thing is applicable in multimodal transport document if the last delivery mode is sea transportation, which means the original multimodal transport document is also representing title of goods/ownership of goods and can be transferred by endorsement and delivery to another party. Banks might use it as collateral and might request multimodal transport document to be issued or to order of themselves to control goods ownership. Parties must be aware that original multimodal transport document can only be negotiable document, represent title of goods only if the last delivery transportation is done by sea transportation and that it will not represent goods/owner of goods if transportation is made by sea first than by truck, train or whatsoever other than sea transportation.
    Bills of Lading
    Main transport document, used in maritime, sea transportation of goods, representing title of goods/ownership of goods, can be transferred by endorsement and delivery to another party by endorsement (if issued to order of shipper) or to

order, which can be endorsed like other negotiable documents for example a cheque and by delivery exactly like a cheque the ownership of goods will be transferred to the new beneficiary. It must be signed by the carrier or on behalf of carrier. Banks might use them as collateral and request the original of bills of lading to be issued to order of banks in such cases. Carrier is authorized to deliver goods to (bona fide) holder of the original endorsed or issued to order bill of lading, whoever presents one original of bill of lading. If original bill of lading is issued to order of a bank, carrier delivers goods only upon endorsement of bank.

Non-negotiable Sea Waybills or Straight Consigned Transport Documents

If a sea waybill is not issued to the order of to order as detailed in bill of lading above and is issued like straight consigned to a specific named party, usually a bank, than it is a non-negotiable document and is not representing title of goods/ownership of goods. It enables a bank as a consignee, to enable bank to control goods. Delivery of goods are not effected against like original bill of lading in non-negotiable sea waybills, delivery can be made by only to the named consignee, original of nonnegotiable sea waybill is not necessary to be submitted for goods delivery.

Charter Party Bills of Lading

Charter party bill of ladings are not accepted by banks unless specifically letter of credit indicates that charter party bill of lading is accepted in letter of credit as article 19a of UCP600. Which means unless otherwise indicated, charter party bill of ladings are not accepted by bank. The parties must be aware of this risk as charter party contracts are different then other bill of lading contracts. Why are not charter party bill of ladings are not accepted, what are the risks involved compared to other bills of ladings?

First of all charter party bills of lading are different as they are subject to agreements between (charterer) and owner of vessel. Ship-owner has right to deliver whenever applicant wishes. The port of destination is not certain that is it might change on the way with approval of the charterer and buyer.

However if the charterer does not pay the fees for chartering vessel, ship-owner may take possession of goods in lieu of payment. Therefore banks avoid accepting charter party bill of ladings unless specifically instructed by buyer.

Charter party bill of lading are used for bulk goods transportation, like fertilizers, oil, sugar, steel. Charter party bill of lading is specifically issued for that specific transportation only. Charter party contracts are different from other seaway transportation i.e. negotiable or non negotiable bills of ladings. Parties must be aware of risks mentioned above as banks avoid using collateral of goods transported by charter party bill of lading.

Air Transport Documents or Air Waybill or Air Consignment Note

Air transport documents are not like airway bills, they are not negotiable, they do not represent documents, title of goods/ownership of goods. Banks must request to be shown as consignee because original for shipper page of air transport document must be presented for delivery to consignee.

Road, Rail, Inland Waterway Transport Documents

Road (Road Transport Documents or Road Consignment Notes or Truck Waywills or CMR (Convention Merchandises Routiers),

Rail (Rail Transport Document or Rail Consignment Notes) or
Inland Waterway Transport documents

They do not represent documents, they are not negotiable transport documents representing title of goods/ownership of goods except inland waterway bill if issued as a bill of lading. Goods are delivered to address of consignee (receiver) on transport document.

Courier receipts, post receipts or certificates of posting

They are not negotiable documents and they do not represent title of goods/ownership of goods like bill of lading. They are receipts show that post office or special courier service has received a post for delivery. Goods are delivered to name and address given on receipt. Usually goods that are not heavy like product sample, software etc. are sent by this method.

3   Conclusion and Suggestions

Sellers and importers have conflict of interest in trade because seller wants to get maximum value of goods and or services he has provided, importers want to pay minimum for goods or services he has received. In such a competitive global market, both parties try to make best of it, try their best to avoid risks while trading.

International organizations are trying their best to increase global trade among countries, one of supporting international trade is standardization of practices. Even description of goods are standardized by World Custom Organization with the six digit (Harmonize System) digital code. Payment messages, and other international trade correspondence are standardized by SWIFT system. International Chamber of Commerce (ICC) has standardized international rules for uniform international trade practices. International trade rules have been accepted worldwide for standards of international trade documentation as well. As international trade increased, standardization has increased in international trade practices as well.

Both exporters and importers must be aware of the critical role of international trade documentation and documentation risk in international trade, which are also standardized under international trade rules accepted by worldwide as well.

After finding a reliable partner, parties must start with a reliable sales contract-that is with an appropriate incoterms covering transportation of goods, insurance, transportation risks, which party is responsible for costs, when and how will goods be delivered, latest shipment date, payment method, i.e. when and how is value of goods will be paid, documentation details required for customs clearance, inspection report details for goods quality, transportation document showing title of goods, i.e. ownership of goods will be transferred with transfer of bill of lading whom it will be issued to.

To avoid documentation risk, they must work with international trade specialists, specialized bank officers, specialized customs broker, specialized experts, specialized insurance and freight brokers.

Keywords Definitions

International (Foreign) Trade	International trade is contrary to domestic trade are between two different countries, cross borders, subject to customs clearance therefore requires documentation.
Documentary Risk	Documentary risk is the non-compliance of the documents to the specific documentation requirements under a sales contract or documentary credit. Discrepant documents might result in non-payment or delay in payment.
Compliance Documents	Compliance documents are the documents required in sales contract or in letter of credit which are in compliance with the conditions of the sales contract or documentary credit.
International Chamber of Commerce (ICC)	International Chamber of Commerce is the largest business organization, setting international rules voluntarily accepted by the traders, dispute resolutions services, working to make international trade easier and with standard rules and uniform practice.
International Trade Rules	i.e. **ICC-The Incoterms® rules** are an internationally recognized standard and are used worldwide in international and domestic contracts for the sale of goods. The rules have been developed and maintained by experts and practitioners brought together by ICC. They have become the standard in international business rules setting. Launched in mid-September 2010, Incoterms® 2010 came into effect on 1 January 2011. The trade terms help traders avoid costly misunderstandings by clarifying the tasks, costs and risks involved in the delivery of goods from sellers to buyers. Incoterms® rules are recognized by UNCITRAL as the global standard for the interpretation of the most common terms in foreign trade. Please note that all contracts made under INCOTERMS® 2000 before 2011 remain valid.

Definitions of International Trade Organizations (Abbreviation)

International trade organizations who take part in standardization of international trade, the abbreviations and definitions are given as follows as per their web pages:

WTO—The World Trade Organization	Deals with the global rules of trade between nations. Its main function is to ensure that trade flows as smoothly, predictably and freely as possible. It operates a global system of trade rules, it acts as a forum for negotiating trade agreements, its settles trade disputes between its members and it supports the needs of developing countries (https://www.wto.org/english/thewto_e/thewto_e.htm). UNCTAD is a permanent intergovernmental body established by the United Nations General Assembly in 1964. UNCTAD is

UNCTAD—the United Nations Conference on Trade and Development	part of the UN Secretariat, report to the UN General Assembly and the Economic and Social Council but have our own membership, leadership, and budget and are also part of the United Nations Development Group (http://unctad.org/en/Pages/aboutus.aspx).
UNCITRAL—United Nations Commission on International Trade Law	The core legal body of the United Nations system in the field of international trade law. A legal body with universal membership specializing in commercial law reform worldwide for over 50 years, UNCITRAL's business is the modernization and harmonization of rules on international business. Trade means faster growth, higher living standards, and new opportunities through commerce. In order to increase these opportunities worldwide, UNCITRAL is formulating modern, fair, and harmonized rules on commercial transactions (http://www.uncitral.org/uncitral/en/about_us.html).
ITC—the International Trade Centre	Formed in 1964, ITC has been the focal point within the United Nations system for trade related technical assistance (TRTA). In line with our joint mandate from the World Trade Organization (WTO) and the United Nations through the United Nations Conference on Trade and Development (UNCTAD), support their parent organizations' regulatory, research and policy strategies (http://www.intracen.org/itc/about/).
WCO—World Customs Organization	In 1952, the Convention formally establishing the CCC (Customs Co-operation Council) came into force. The Council is the governing body of the CCC and the inaugural Session of the Council was held in Brussels on 26 January 1953. Representatives of seventeen European countries attended the first Council Session of the CCC. After years of membership growth, in 1994 the Council adopted the working name World Customs Organization, to more clearly reflect its transition to a truly global intergovernmental institution. It is now the voice of 180 Customs administrations which operate on all continents and represent all stages of economic development. Today, WCO Members are responsible for processing more than 98% of all international trade (http://www.wcoomd.org/en/about-us/what-is-the-wco/au_history.aspx).
HS—The Harmonized System	The Harmonized Commodity Description and Coding System generally referred to as "Harmonized System" or simply "HS" is a multipurpose international product nomenclature developed by the World Customs Organization (WCO). It comprises about 5000 commodity groups; each identified by a six digit code, arranged in a legal and logical structure and is supported by well-defined rules to achieve uniform classification. The system is used by more than 200 countries and economies as a basis for their Customs tariffs and for the collection of international trade statistics. Over 98% of the merchandise in international trade is classified in terms of the HS. The HS contributes to the harmonization of Customs and trade procedures, and the non-documentary trade data interchange in connection with such procedures, thus reducing the costs related to international trade. It is also extensively used by governments, international organizations and the private sector for many other purposes such as internal taxes, trade policies, monitoring of controlled

	goods, rules of origin, freight tariffs, transport statistics, price monitoring, quota controls, compilation of national accounts, and economic research and analysis. The HS is thus a universal economic language and code for goods, and an indispensable tool for international trade http://www.wcoomd.org/en/topics/nomenclature/overview/what-is-the-harmonized-system.aspx.
SWIFT—Society for Worldwide Interbank Financial Telecommunication	SWIFT is a global member-owned cooperative and the world's leading provider of secure financial messaging services. Provide community with a platform for messaging, standards for communicating and offer products and services to facilitate access and integration; identification, analysis and regulatory compliance. International Messaging and Standards SWIFT's messaging services are used and trusted by more than 11,000 financial institutions in more than 200 countries and territories around the world. Together with our role in standardization, SWIFT enables secure, seamless and automated financial communication between users (https://www.swift.com/about-us).
The Trade Map	The Trade Map is free to use and provides trade statistics and market access information for export development. By transforming the large volume of primary trade data into an accessible, user-friendly, web-based format, the Trade Map provides indicators on export performance, international demand, alternative markets and the role of competitors. The Trade Map covers yearly trade data for 220 countries and territories and all 5300 products of the Harmonized System (http://www.trademap.org/Index.aspx).

References

www.iccwbo.org/
www.intracen.org/itc/exporters/model-contracts/
www.swift.com/about-us
www.trademap.org
www.wcoomd.org/en/topics/nomenclature/overview/what-is-the-harmonized-system.aspx

Evaluation of Internal Control in Turkish Banking Sector in the View of Turkey Legislations and International Internal Control Models

Mustafa Tevfik Kartal and Neşe Çoban Çelikdemir

Abstract Banks are significant financial intermediaries in Turkey and World. They finance most of the trade and economic activities. Taken into consideration banks' this function, banks have systemic importance in some countries like Turkey which has bank-based financial system. Possible problems, which could be seen in banks, would affect financial markets, macro economy and macroeconomic indicators of Turkey. For this reason, banks' auditing, controlling and supervision are a must.

Turkish Banking Sector has sustained growth from 2002. Sector's total asset size has reached TL 2.972 billion as of 2017 June. In addition to asset size, other financial figures of the sector have grown at a significant rate. When taking into consideration this financial volume, banks' efficient auditing is seen as a requirement.

There are some actions to have been taken by regulatory bodies in order to guarantee of banks' auditing efficiently after banking crises seen in Turkey. First of all, Banking Regulation and Supervision Authority were established in year 2000 for Turkish Banking Sector's efficient regulation and supervision. After banking crises seen in Turkey specifically in 2001, a new department was added to banks' organizational structure named as *Internal Control* while taking effect of Banks' Internal Audit and Risk Management System Charter by Banking Regulation and Supervision Authority in 2001. New Banking Law number 5411 came into force including articles about internal control in 2005. After that new charter named as Banks' Internal Systems came into force by Banking Regulation and Supervision Authority in 2006 containing articles about internal control.

Although internal control concept has been known for years in abroad, it can be said that the concept is relatively new for Turkey taking into consideration that it came to Turkey in 2001. However, there is a discussion about internal control in banking in Turkey whether it is compliant with abroad and why there is difference.

M. T. Kartal (✉)
Istanbul Stock Exchange, Istanbul, Turkey

N. Ç. Çelikdemir
Marmara University, Istanbul, Turkey
e-mail: ncoban@marmara.edu.tr

© Springer International Publishing AG, part of Springer Nature 2018
H. Dincer et al. (eds.), *Strategic Design and Innovative Thinking in Business Operations*, Contributions to Management Science,
https://doi.org/10.1007/978-3-319-77622-4_22

433

So, this paper was prepared in order to make a comprehensive evaluation about internal control in banking in Turkey in the view of Turkey legislations and international internal control models.

As a result of study, it was concluded that Turkey's legislation about internal control is not compliant with international internal control models. In order to make Turkey legislation compliant with abroad, it was recommended that changes be made in Banking Law and Charter of Banks' Internal Systems.

By this study, it was aimed at making participation to literature by handling internal control in Turkey in the view of Turkey legislations and international internal control models as comparatively.

1 Introduction

Financial systems can be categorized as either bank-based or market-based financial system (Targan 1996; Duman and Lee 2000; Onur 2012). In the world, there are two type of financial systems which are bank-based and market-based financial system (Targan 1996; Duman and Lee 2000; Onur 2012). Banks are the most important financial intermediaries in bank-based financial systems while investment funds and other capital markets actors are important in market-based financial systems (Altıntaş and Ayrıçay 2010). Type of the financial system takes important role in legislations due to having different characteristics. In general, there are much more legislations in bank-based economies with regard to market-based economics (Onur 2012). In addition to system structure, efficiency of financial markets is also important.

Turkey has bank-based financial system. Banks basically finance individuals and corporations. Banks do this by collecting deposits, giving credits and deploy other banking activities. In this context, there are so many banking products and services and lots of transactions.

Taken into consideration that Turkey is a bank-based financial system and banks are so much important to finance individuals, corporations and economic activities, legislations on banks have been made in order to sustain growth and stability in banking. After banking crises experienced in recent years specifically in 1994 and 1999 in Turkey, some important precautions were taken. One of the taken measures is to establishment of Banking Regulation and Supervision Authority (BRSA) in 2000. The other important taken precautions is that banks are required to establish internal control departments in order to enhance banks' efficient and effective audit in 2001 after experiencing banking crisis of 2001.

Establishment of internal control departments was ruled in 2001 for the first time by regulation made by BRSA of which Banks' Internal Audit and Risk Management System Charter. Afterwards, main regulation was made in new Banking Law number 5411 in 2005. Also, new charter named as Charter of Banks' Internal Systems came into effect in 2006 also contains articles about internal control department. When making a general evaluation of regulatory framework in Turkey, it can be seen that all banks operate in Turkey have to establish internal control as a separate unit reporting to Audit Committee (AC) and Board of Directors (BoD) of banks.

Although establishment of internal control departments in banks is a required by BRSA, internal control practices in abroad is differ by Turkey. In other words, although there is a concept of internal control in Turkey and in abroad, there is a difference in practice. As far as it is known, there is no special and separate unit for internal control in abroad because of the fact that internal control is all personnel's responsibility not for only internal control staff. This the main difference in practice of Turkey and other countries.

This paper was prepared to make a comprehensive evaluation about internal control in Turkish Banking Sector (TBS). By this study, it was aimed at making participation to literature by handling internal control in Turkey in the view of Turkey legislations and international internal control models as comparatively and determining differences between Turkey and other countries. Hence, the authors will be able to make recommendation in order to remove difference in Turkey as against other countries. Hence, Turkey practice will be compliant with international practices after making necessary in regulatory framework in Turkey.

The study consists of five parts. After introduction part, studies about internal control in abroad and in Turkey were examined in Part II within the context of literature review. Information about internal control was shared in Part III. In Part IV, first of all, regulations in abroad and in Turkey related with internal control was considered. Secondly, taking into consideration Turkey legislations and international internal control models, a comparison was made. Thirdly, difference between Turkey and others were stated and recommendations that should be applied to provide harmony of Turkey legislations with international internal control models were considered. Finally, an evaluation is made in Part V.

2 Literature Review

In literature, there are studies related with internal control. Within the context of literature review, some of selected studies in abroad were included in Table 1.

Besides studies in abroad, there are also some studies related with internal control in Turkey. Some of selected studies in Turkey were included in Table 2.

3 Internal Control

Control in business management is one of the core functions of management and it covers all functions of entities such as supply, production and marketing, personnel, accounting and financing and encompasses all of its fields of activity (Çetin 2001).

The types of control in entities can be grouped into three (Doyrangöl 2002):

• Control of activities described as business functions such as production, marketing, accounting and financing and personnel,

Table 1 Some selected studies in abroad

Author	Year	Country	Results
Palfi	1986	Romania	It was determined that banks' internal control system should be organized taking into consideration all of significant risks
Higgins	2012	China	Principles of internal control were discussed
Chen et al.	2013	USA	It was stated that internal control makes financial reporting much more trustworthy for investors
Gündoğdu et al.	2013	Germany	They reached a conclusion that banks adopt internal control activities which are compliant with international standards. Also there are effective control procedures in the banking system
Rameli et al.	2013	Malaysia	They stated that in order to prevent fraud occurrence, internal control does not take important roles in Malaysian banking sector
Gamage et al.	2014	Sri Lanka	They determined that organizations face numerous problems and risks if internal control system is not proper and practicing
Shi and Wang	2014	China	They came to a conclusion that internal control deficiencies produces internal control risk in banks' accounting
Cho and Chung	2016	USA	It was stated that banks that take remedial actions of internal control weaknesses cease to stack unnecessary loan loss reserves
Donelson et al.	2016	USA	They determined that there is significant association statistically and economically between material internal control weaknesses and the future revelation of fraud
Du et al.	2016	China	It was determined that corporate governance has an important influence on quality of internal control
Frazer	2016	USA	It was stated that small companies are faced with challenges to implement internal control systems because of various limitations such as costs, few employees and other constraints
Sun	2016	USA	It was reached that firm which have unqualified opinion in internal control takes higher investments than firms which have adverse opinions in internal control by auditors
Akwaa and Gené	2017	Spain	They reached a conclusion that because of the fact that objectives of compliance and operational performance are achieved, there exist effective internal control systems among banks
Ji et al.	2017	Australia	It was stated that control of non-accounting related internal control weaknesses is critical for enterprise risk management
Rae et al.	2017	Australia	It was stated that control environment is associated with three dimensions of information and communication which are information accuracy, information openness, communication and learning

Source: Authors

Table 2 Some selected studies in Turkey

Author	Year	Results
Yavuz	2002	Internal control and internal audit are different from each other
Kiracı	2003	Efficiency and effectiveness internal control makes activities of businesses efficient and effective
Elitaş and Özdemir	2006	It was determined that efficient and functioning internal control system is a need in order to minimize risks in banks
Yurtsever	2008	Some information about internal control was shared
Dabbağoğlu	2009	Efficiency and reliability of internal control system is important for independent audit
Akyel	2010a	There are some problems in deployment of internal control in Turkey. Internal control should also be deployed in areas out of the financial management besides financial management
Akyel	2010b	Understanding and establishment of internal control correctly, and deploying internal control efficiently are important for successful management
Uyar	2010	It was determined that five components of internal control are affected by IFRS at every stage and IFRS directs internal control activities
Usul et al.	2011	They stated that efficiency of internal control system depends on efficiency or completeness of sub-systems
Yüksel and Demir	2011	Deficiency of internal control in banks causes financial crisis in Turkey
Acar and Akçakanat	2012	They reached a conclusion that internal control systems in universities' accounting departments are not satisfactory
Atmaca	2012	Weak internal control structure causes accounting scandals, financial losses, frauds and misstatements
Bakkal and Kasımoğlu	2012	COSO (Committee of Sponsoring Organizations of the Treadway Commission) is world-wide and basic internal control model with regard to CoCo (The criteria of control) model
İbiş and Çatıkkaş	2012	Perspectives of internal control have been continuously improved in the view of needs
Özten and Karğın	2012	They stated that internal control systems have to be worked well to increase efficiency of credit activities in banks
Sevim and Gül	2012	They determined that corporations should have best organizational structure in order to be able to established internal control systems
Türedi	2012	Corporations could bring synergy by establishing internal control system
Kızılboğa and Özşahin	2013	Senior management should fulfill its internal control system responsibilities
Elmaz and Kurnaz	2013	It was determined that department manager in factoring companies has high perception level regarding internal control, however practices is at the level desired
Ertuğrul	2013	Components of internal control is strictly related and interacted with people, in other words with culture, in organizations
Topçu	2013	It was seen that internal control system in Turkish public administration is not inclusive

(continued)

Table 2 (continued)

Author	Year	Results
Baskıcı	2015	Implementation of internal control system deployed by workers and managers affects success of the corporate governance in corporations
Doğan and Burgazlıoğlu	2015	They determined that losses which result in errors and frauds are decreased, accuracy and reliability are provided in financial statements and reliable information flow are provided by establishing efficient internal control structure in hospitals
Engin	2015	It was stated that designing, shaping and continuously auditing control environment is necessary for procurement and payment process
Gül and Kaban	2015	Internal control and internal audit are in semi-coordination with each other
Tüm and Reyhanoğlu	2015	They stated that effects of internal control should be taken into consideration in effect of organizational culture to performance, job satisfaction and organizational commitment
Türedi and Karakaya	2015	Each components of internal control is dependent to each other and any of them could be alone and independent
Türedi et al.	2015	COSO internal control model is much more comprehensive with regard to CoCo model and Turnbull report
Uysal	2015	Internal control system has positive effects on controlling costs and determining pricing policies in accommodation companies
Cömert	2016	Internal control and internal audit are different from each other and unfortunately internal control is not well understood due to misunderstanding in Turkey
Durmuş et al.	2016	Corporations should deploy COSO internal control framework and the three lines of defense model in order to provide reliability, efficiency, effectiveness and economy in corporate governance, internal control and risk management systems
Ergin et al.	2016	They stated that internal control activities and internal audit activities are not integrated to international degrees in public economic enterprises in Turkey
Karakaya	2016	Internal control utilizes fraud audit and in some cases it prevents frauds
Özbilgin	2016	It was determined that internal control system should be updated in order to make it compliant with international standards in intermediary firms
Türedi and Koban	2016	They stated that establishment of efficient internal control structure has to be mandatory in all corporations
Arıkan and Benk	2017	Efficient internal control makes contribution in preventing corruption and managing risky areas
Cengiz and Aslanoğlu	2017	Internal control transparency is associated with number of BoD, independence of BoD, women number in BoD, number of AC member
Hasanefendioğlu and Uzel	2017	COSO based internal control system is an indicator of a corporation's level of internal control system
Özkardeş	2017	Companies, which show importance to risk management, also show importance to internal control

Source: Authors

- Control of business manager,
- Control of departments/units of enterprise such as branches, departments and units.

A good operating control environment refers to an environment where the objectives, roles and responsibilities of the organization are clearly defined, the organizational chart shows the reporting and hierarchical relationships, human resources practices are based on objective rules, the management and personnel adopt ethical values, the training and equipment required by personnel to increase the competence are provided and where managers comply with the controls and thus, set an example to employees (Kamu İç Kontrol Rehberi 2014).

When the definition of internal control is considered in general, it means all business policies adopted as a whole to provide that the company's operations of are applied regularly and efficiently in line with the objectives for delivering compliance with the policies set by the management, the protection of assets, the prevention of wrong and fraudulent activities, complete and accurate records in accounting and preparation of financial information timely (Doyrangöl 2002).

In Auditing Standard No. 78 published by the Auditing Standards Board (ASB) of the American Institute of Certified Public Accountants (AICPA), internal control is described that "*a process, effected by an entity's board of directors, managers and other personnel, designed to provide reasonable assurance regarding the achievement of certain objectives*".

Although there are different models for internal control system across the globe, framework models prepared by COSO are the most effective and common models. COSO defines internal control as "*a process, effected by an entity's board of directors, managers and other personnel, designed to provide reasonable assurance regarding the achievement of objectives regarding operations, reporting and compliance*" (TİDE 2016). As it can be seen from definitions, COSO's internal control description is so similar to AICPA's.

Internal control and internal audit are concepts which are generally confused. These two concepts complement each other. Control is a business activity that should be considered thoroughly before the audit. Control is carried out at the same time when activities are carried out, i.e. simultaneously with the activities. Audit is a function that is carried out after the activities have been carried out and which examines a certain period in the past (Özten and Karğın 2012).

The objectives of COSO internal control model are summarized under three headings. These are effectiveness and efficiency of operations, reliability of financial reporting and compliance with applicable laws and regulations (TİDE 2016). Operation objectives include effectiveness and efficiency of operations and protection of assets belonging to the entity against loss and damage. Reporting objectives include reliability, timeliness and transparency principles of internal and external financial and non-financial reporting. Compliance objectives are related with organizations' compliance of with the laws and regulations of which organizations are subject to and have to be compliant (TİDE 2016).

Internal control is a wide dynamic process that involves many processes (TİDE 2016). The internal control structure can only be implemented in an entity at an adequate level through internal control components (Türedi and Koban 2016).

According to COSO internal control model, internal control consists of five components which are control environment, risk assessment, control activities, information and communication and monitoring.

Control Environment

The control environment consists of business management and behavior and attitudes of its personnel related to its internal control structure, management principles, and organizational structure of the entity, rules and methods to be followed in the distribution of authorities and responsibilities and personnel policies. This element covers every aspect of the internal control environment. The control environment comprises of corporate history, corporate culture and management philosophy. This includes the management style of the entity, the control methods of the management, personnel policies, the distribution of functions, authorities and responsibilities of the board of directors and the supervisory committee, and the role of internal audit in this organization (Türedi and Koban 2016).

The control environment, which is one of the fundamental components of internal control structure, is influenced by various internal and external factors such as corporate history, code of conduct, integrity, market in which it operates competitive conditions and statutory regulations (Türedi et al. 2014).

Risk Assessment

Entities use the resources allocated to them to achieve their goals and objectives. The decisions made for the use of these resources, the operations, processes and projects carried out entail risks. Risk management is a tool that helps entities to achieve their goals and objectives. Risk management includes defining the risk strategy, identifying and evaluating the risks, determining responses to such risks, reviewing the risks, monitoring and reporting the risks (Türedi and Koban 2016).

There is no method in practice to set the risk to zero. Management must determine how much risk is to be prudently accepted, strive to maintain risk within these levels, and understand how much tolerance it has for exceeding its target risk levels (TİDE 2016). The risk tolerance to be determined in the risk assessment process and the basics concerning how to manage the risks are established. At this stage, the prerequisite is to ensure that the executive management defines risks that may be faced in association with operations, reporting and compliance-related objectives for employees at all levels of entity and set well-defined criteria for their analyses that are consistent with the current facts of entity (Hasanefendioğlu and Uzel 2017).

Control Activities

Control activities are a mechanism that enables the achievement of objectives of an entity (TİDE 2016). Control activities are actions aimed at reducing the likelihood and/or impact of a predicted risk, thus increasing the chances of the entity to achieve its goals and objectives. The determination of control activities depends on the completion of the risk assessment. The management must plan, arrange and direct control activities based on risk management in order to obtain reasonable assurance that roles and objectives will be achieved. Control activities include both financial and non-financial controls and should be designed and implemented as a whole for all operations of the entity (Türedi and Koban 2016).

Information and Communication
Information and Communication enable the relationship among control environment, risk assessment, control activities and monitoring through information sharing and communication. Information and communication encompasses the information, communication and registration system that enables the necessary information to be communicated to the person, personnel and manager who needs such information in a certain format and within a time frame that allows them to fulfill their internal control and other responsibilities (Kamu İç Kontrol Rehberi 2014).

Useful information must be reliable, accessible, complete and appropriate and timely. This can only be achieved with high quality communication. Lack of appropriate control procedures for information systems, inadequate physical and electronic security arrangements and back-up systems of information systems equipment can result in damages due to internal control vulnerability (Ertuğrul 2013).

Information is a requirement for the organization to complete its internal control responsibilities in a manner to help them achieve their goals. Communication is the continual, iterative process of providing, sharing and obtaining necessary information. Internal communication is the tools by which information is disseminated throughout the organization, flowing up, down and across the entity. It enables personnel to receive clear messages from management that control responsibilities must be handled seriously. On the other hand, external communication consists two subparts. External communication enables inbound communication of relevant information. Besides this external communication provides information to external parties in response to requirements and expectations (TİDE 2016).

Monitoring
Monitoring is close monitoring by the management directly or indirectly through the supervisory committee or auditors of issues such as internal control, financial reporting procedures, internal conflicts of interest, fraudulent and immoral transactions, information technology systems and accounting information systems. While in some cultures, the manager may choose to apply direct monitoring, the manager may choose to monitor such issues with the help of an auditor in some cultures (Ertuğrul 2013).

Continuous assessments, separate assessments or assessments based on their combination are used to determine whether each of the five components of the internal control is available and operational, including controls on the principles within each internal control component. Continuous assessments built into business processes at different levels of the organization provide information in a timely manner. Separate assessments carried out periodically vary in scope and frequency depending on the assessment of risks, the effectiveness of continuous assessments and other assessments of the management.

Findings are evaluated according to the criteria set by the regulatory authorities, standard setting bodies or the management and the board of directors of organization, and deficiencies are reported to the management and board of directors accordingly.

4 An Evaluation Upon Internal Control in Turkish Banking Sector in the View of Turkey Legislations and International Models

After reviewing internal control and components in previous subunit, firstly Turkey's regulations and international internal control models were examined in this subunit. Secondly, a comparison was made considering legislations and internal control. In the last subunit, difference between Turkey legislation and international internal control models were examined.

Turkey Legislations

Banks, which operate in Turkey, are subject to Banking Law in terms of legislation (Banking Law 2005). Besides this, banks are subject to BRSA's regulations. So, internal control in banks in Turkey should be handled in terms of these aspects.

When the subject is handled in terms of Banking Law, it is obvious that there are articles related with internal control. According to article 29 and 30, banks have to establish internal systems and internal control is one of the internal systems. In this context, establishing a separate internal control departments and employing internal control staff in the department are a regulatory requirement (Banking Law 2005).

Besides Banking Law, there is also a charter issued by BRSA named as *Charter about Banks' Internal Systems and Internal Capital Adequacy Assessment Process* (shortly BRSA Charter) in 2014 (charter issued in 2001 and updated in 2006). Articles from 4 to 8 in the charter include general directions for banks. The Charter contains special articles from 9 to 20 about internal control in banks. These are as follows (BDDK 2014):

- Article 9: Aim and scope of internal control system,
- Article 10: Functional segregation of duties,
- Article 11: Establishment of information systems,
- Article 12: Establishment of communication channels and communication structure,
- Article 13: Management and plan of business continuity,
- Article 14: Internal control activities,
- Article 15: Control of transaction about activities,
- Article 16: Control of communication channels and information systems,
- Article 17: Control of financial reporting,
- Article 18: Control of compliance
- Article 19: Department of internal control

- Article 20: Duty and authority of internal control staff.

BRSA also put into enforce another charter named as *Charter about Banks' Corporate Governance Principles* (shortly BRSA Corporate Governance Charter) in 2006. Articles 5 and 6 in the Charter include general directions for banks. These are as follows (BDDK 2006):

- Principle 5: Banks' senior management should understand importance of internal control. Senior management should also use findings of internal control staff on time and should provide that necessary actions be taken by management.
- Principle 6: Wages and benefits of head and staff of internal control should be determined without taking into consideration of departments which are audited, supervised or controlled by internal control.

When evaluating Banking Law and BRSA charters together, it can be concluded that establishment of a separate internal control department and organization, employment of internal control staffs in these departments is a statutory and regulatory requirement in Turkey.

International Internal Control Models
Although Turkey made some regulations, there are some international models, best practices and advices about internal control. In this subunit, relevant international internal control models were examined.

COSO Internal Control Framework
The most important and basic international structure for internal control is *Internal Control-Integrated Framework* issued by COSO. The first model was published in 1992 and it was updated in 2013. COSO defines that *"internal control is a process, effected by an entity's BoD, management and other personnel, designed to provide reasonable assurance regarding the achievement of objectives relating to operations, reporting and compliance"* (TİDE 2016).

COSO internal control model aims achievement of three types of objectives. These can be stated as *"effectiveness and efficiency of operations, reliability of financial reporting, compliance with applicable laws and regulations"* (TİDE 2016).

COSO internal control model consists of five components and each component has principles. There are total 17 principles in 5 components. Control environment component has five principles which are as *"demonstrate commitment to integrity and ethical values; ensure that board exercises oversight responsibility; establish structures, reporting lines, authorities and responsibilities; demonstrate commitment to a competent workforce; hold people accountable"* (TİDE 2016).

Risk assessment component has four principles that are as *"specify appropriate objectives; identify and analyze risks; evaluate fraud risks; identify and analyze changes that could significantly affect internal controls"* (TİDE 2016).

Control activities component has three principles that are as *"select and develop control activities that mitigate risks; select and develop technology controls; deploy control activities through policies and procedures"* (TİDE 2016).

Information and communication component has three principles which are *"use relevant, quality information to support the internal control function; communicate internal control information internally; communicate internal control information externally"* (TİDE 2016).

Monitoring component has two principles that are as *"perform ongoing or periodic evaluations of internal controls (or a combination of the two); communicate internal control deficiencies"* (TİDE 2016).

When evaluating internal control framework model of COSO, taken into consideration definition, components and principles of internal control together, it can be said that internal control is a process owned by all organizational units and personnel. So, internal control cannot be addressed to separate department such as internal control department according to COSO internal control framework.

CoCo Guidance on Internal Control

Similar to COSO internal control model, there is also another model named as CoCo Guidance on Internal Control issued by The Canadian Institute of Chartered Accountants (the CICA). The model was issued in 1995 based on COSO model.

CoCo defines that *"control needs to be understood in a broad context. Control comprises those elements of an organization (including its resources, systems, processes, culture, structure and tasks) that, taken together, support people in the achievement of the organization's objectives"* (Accounting and Financial Tax 2017).

CoCo guidance on internal control aims objectives which are categorized as three types. That are summarized as *"effectiveness and efficiency of operations; reliability of internal and external reporting; compliance with applicable laws and regulations and internal policies"* (Qfinance 2017).

CoCo guidance on internal control consists of four components and each component has principles. There are total 20 principles in 4 components. Purpose component has five principles which are as *"objectives should be established and communicated; the significant internal and external risks faced by an organization in the achievement of its objectives should be identified and assessed; policies designed to support the achievement of an organization's objectives and the management of its risks should be established, communicated, and practiced so that people understand what is expected of them and the scope of their freedom to act; plans to guide efforts in achieving the organization's objectives should be established and communicated; objectives and related plans should include measurable performance targets and indicators"* (KPMG 1999).

Commitment component has four principles that are as *"shared ethical values, including integrity, should be established, communicated and practiced throughout the organization; human resource policies and practices should be consistent with an organization's ethical values and with the achievement of its objectives; authority, responsibility, and accountability should be clearly defined and consistent with an organization's objectives so that decisions and actions are taken by the appropriate people; an atmosphere of mutual trust should be fostered to support the flow of information between people and their effective performance toward achieving the organization's objectives"* (KPMG 1999).

Capability component has five principles which are as "*people should have the necessary knowledge, skills, and tools to support the achievement of the organization's objectives; communication processes should support the organization's values and achievement of its objectives; sufficient and relevant information should be identified and communicated in a timely manner to enable people to perform their assigned responsibilities; the decisions and actions of different parts of the organization should be coordinated; control activities should be designed as an integral part of the organization, taking into consideration its objectives, the risks to their achievement, and the inter-relatedness of the control elements*" (KPMG 1999).

Monitoring and learning component has six principles that are as "*external and internal environments should be monitored to obtain information that may signal a need to re-evaluate the organization's objectives or control; performance should be monitored against the targets and indicators identified in the organization's objectives and plans; the assumptions behind an organization's objectives should be periodically challenged; information needs and related information systems should be reassessed as objectives change or reporting deficiencies are identified; follow-up procedures should be established and performed to ensure appropriate change or action occurs; management should periodically assess the effectiveness of control in its organization and communicate the results to those to whom it is accountable*" (KPMG 1999).

When evaluating guidance on internal control of CoCo, taken into consideration definition, components and principles of internal control together, it can be said that internal control is addressed to all organizational units and personnel. So, similar to COSO, internal control cannot be addressed to separate department such as internal control department according to CoCo guidance on internal control.

Turnbull Report (Guidance for Directors on the Combined Code)
Turnbull Report is another international structure for internal control. It was published in 1999 and it was updated in 2005. It was defined in Turnbull Report that "*internal control facilitates the effectiveness and efficiency of operations, helps ensure the reliability of internal and external reporting and assists compliance with laws and regulations*" (The Institute of Chartered Accountants in England and Wales (The ICA), 1999).

Turnbull Report is intended "*to reflect sound business practice whereby internal control is embedded in the business processes by which a company pursues its objectives; remain relevant over time in the continually evolving business environment; enable each company to apply it in a manner which takes account of its particular circumstances*" (The ICA 1999).

Turnbull Report consists of four components and each component has some questions. There are total 19 questions in 4 components. Risk assessment component has three questions that are as "*does the company have clear objectives and have they been communicated so as to provide effective direction to employees on risk assessment and control issues; are the significant internal and external operational, financial, compliance and other risks identified and assessed on an ongoing basis; is there a clear understanding by management and others within the company of what risks are acceptable to the board*" (The ICA 1999).

Control environment and control activities component has seven questions which are as "*does the board have clear strategies for dealing with the significant risks that have been identified? Is there a policy on how to manage these risks; do the company's culture, code of conduct, human resource policies and performance reward systems support the business objectives and risk management and internal control system; does senior management demonstrate, through its actions as well as its policies, the necessary commitment to competence, integrity and fostering a climate of trust within the company; are authority, responsibility and accountability defined clearly such that decisions are made and actions taken by the appropriate people? are the decisions and actions of different parts of the company appropriately coordinated; does the company communicate to its employees what is expected of them and the scope of their freedom to act; do people in the company have the knowledge, skills and tools to support the achievement of the company's objectives and to manage effectively risks to their achievement; how are processes/ controls adjusted to reflect new or changing risks, or operational deficiencies*" (The ICA 1999).

Information and communication component has 4 questions that are as "*do management and the board receive timely, relevant and reliable reports on progress against business objectives and the related risks that provide them with the information, from inside and outside the company, needed for decision-making and management review purposes; are information needs and related information systems reassessed as objectives and related risks change or as reporting deficiencies are identified; are periodic reporting procedures, including half-yearly and annual reporting, effective in communicating a balanced and understandable account of the company's position and prospects; are there established channels of communication for individuals to report suspected breaches of laws or regulations or other improprieties*" (The ICA 1999).

Monitoring component has five questions that are as "*are there ongoing processes embedded within the company's overall business operations, and addressed by senior management, which monitor the effective application of the policies, processes and activities related to internal control and risk management; do these processes monitor the company's ability to re-evaluate risks and adjust controls effectively in response to changes in its objectives, its business, and its external environment; are there effective follow-up procedures to ensure that appropriate change or action occurs in response to changes in risk and control assessments; is there appropriate communication to the board on the effectiveness of the ongoing monitoring processes on risk and control matters; are there specific arrangements for management monitoring and reporting to the board on risk and control matters of particular importance*" (The ICA 1999).

When evaluating Turnbull Report, taken into consideration definition, components and principles of internal control together, it can be said that internal control is addressed to all organizational units and personnel. So, similar to COSO and CoCo, internal control cannot be addressed to separate department such as internal control department according to Turnbull Report (Guidance for Directors on the Combined Code).

Basle Committee's Framework for Internal Control Systems in Banking Organizations

One of the another important international structure for internal control is *Framework for Internal Control Systems in Banking Organizations* issued by Basle Committee on Banking Supervision (shortly Basle Committee) in Bank for International Settlements in 1998. Similar to COSO, Basle Committee defines that *"internal control is a process effected by the BoD, senior management, and all levels of personnel"* (BIS 1998).

Basle Committee categorizes objectives of internal control as three categories similar to COSO. These can be stated as *"efficiency and effectiveness of activities (performance objectives); reliability, completeness and timeliness of financial and management information (information objective); compliance with applicable laws and regulations (compliance objectives)"* (BIS 1998):

Basle Committee's framework for internal control systems in banking organizations consists of five components and each component has some principles. There are total 12 principles in 5 components and there is also 1 principle for regulatory bodies. Management oversight and the control culture component has three principles that are as *"BoD should have responsibility for approving and periodically reviewing the overall business strategies and significant policies of the bank and BoD is ultimately responsible for ensuring that an adequate and effective system of internal controls is established and maintained; senior management should have responsibility for implementing strategies and policies approved by the board and should set appropriate internal control policies; monitoring the adequacy and effectiveness of the internal control system; all personnel at a banking organization need to understand their role in the internal controls process and be fully engaged in the process"* (BIS 1998).

Risk recognition and assessment component has one principle which is as *"an effective internal control system requires that the material risks that could adversely affect the achievement of the bank's goals are being recognized and continually assessed and internal controls may need to be revised to appropriately address any new or previously uncontrolled risks"* (BIS 1998).

Control activities and segregation of duties component has two principles that are as *"control activities should be an integral part of the daily activities of a bank. An effective internal control system requires that an appropriate control structure is set up, with control activities defined at every business level; an effective internal control system requires appropriate segregation of duties and personnel not to having conflicting responsibilities"* (BIS 1998).

Information and communication component has three principles which are as *"an effective internal control system requires that there are adequate and comprehensive internal financial, operational and compliance data, as well as external market information about events and conditions that are relevant to decision making; an effective internal control system requires that there are reliable information systems in place that cover all significant activities of the bank; an effective internal control system requires effective channels of communication to ensure that all staff fully understand and adhere to policies and procedures affecting their duties and responsibilities and that other relevant information is reaching the appropriate personnel"* (BIS 1998).

Monitoring activities and correcting deficiencies component has three principles that are as *"overall effectiveness of the bank's internal controls should be monitored on an ongoing basis; there should be an effective and comprehensive internal audit of the internal control system carried out by operationally independent, appropriately trained and competent staff; internal control deficiencies, whether identified by business line, internal audit, or other control personnel, should be reported in a timely manner to the appropriate management level and addressed promptly"* (BIS 1998).

There is also one principle for regulatory bodies. According to Basle Committee's framework for internal control systems in banking organizations *"supervisors should require that all banks, regardless of size, have an effective system of internal controls that is consistent with the nature, complexity, and risk inherent in their on- and off-balance-sheet activities and that responds to changes in the bank's environment and conditions. In those instances where supervisors determine that a bank's internal control system is not adequate or effective for that bank's specific risk profile, they should take appropriate action"* (BIS 1998).

When evaluating Basle Committee's Framework for Internal Control Systems in Banking Organizations, taken into consideration principles of internal control, it can be said that internal control is a process owned by all organizational units and personnel of banks. So, similar to COSO, CoCo and Turnbull Report, internal control in banks cannot be addressed to separate department such as internal control department according to Basle Committee's Framework for Internal Control Systems in Banking Organizations.

International Internal Auditing Standards

In addition to internal control models and approaches mentioned above, international internal auditing standards also mention from internal control indirectly.

The Institute of Internal Auditors (The IIA) issue international internal auditing standards. There is a separate standard related with control. In standard 2130, it was stated that *"The internal audit activity must assist the organization in maintaining effective controls by evaluating their effectiveness and efficiency and by promoting continuous improvement"*.

In addition to standard 2130, concept of control is mentioned in other standards. In standard 1220, it is mentioned that control is a process (The IIA 2017). Similar to standard 1220, control is mentioned as a process in standard 2000, 2100, and 2210. On the other hand, control is defined as a framework in standard 2450.

When evaluating international internal auditing standards mentioned above, it can be said that internal control is a process and framework related with all organization. So, similar to other international internal control models, internal control cannot be addressed to separate department such as internal control department according to International Internal Auditing Standards.

Table 3 Summary of internal controls models

Content	Coso	CoCo	Turnbull
Publisher	American accounting association, American institute of certified public accounts, Financial executives international, Institute of management accountants, The IIA	The CICA	British financial reporting council
First publication year	1992	1995	1999
Update year	2013	Not applicable	2005
Focus	Internal control, components and dimensions	Behavioral values	Internal control responsibilities of members of BoD
Components	5 components and 17 principles	4 components and 20 principles	4 components
Details of components	Control environment, risk assessment, control activities, information and communication, monitoring	Purpose, commitment, capability, monitoring and learning	Control environment and control activities, risk assessment, information and communication, monitoring
Dimensions	3 dimensions	1 dimension	1 dimension
IT controls	Included	Not special unit exists	Not special unit exists
Is a practice guide for companies?	Yes	Limited	Limited

Source: Türedi et al. (2015)

A Summary of International Internal Control Models

Although there are a lot of approaches to internal control, COSO internal control framework, CoCo guidance on internal control and Turnbull report are basic models for internal control. A summary of relevant models are as follows:

As it can be understood from the Table 3, COSO internal control framework is the most acceptable and the best model for internal control and the other models are derived from COSO model. So, COSO internal control model is taken into consideration as benchmark point when an evaluation is made. Besides other models, COSO internal control framework will be taken into consideration to make comparison between Turkey legislations and international internal control models in coming subunit.

A Comparison between Turkey Legislations and International Internal Control Models

Turkey Parliament and BRSA evaluate and locate internal control different from international models in Turkey. Internal control is defined as a responsibility and addressed to internal control department in Turkey although internal control is defined as a system and addressed to all organization in international internal control models.

Depending on approach of Turkey Parliament and BRSA, all banks operating in Turkey established separate internal control due to fact that it is a mandatory and regulatory requirement.

Contrary to Turkey legislations, internal control is described as a process in international internal control models. So, it is impossible to address of internal control to a separate department such as internal control department.

When taking into consideration Turkey legislations and internal control models as a whole, it can be concluded that there is a strict difference between Turkey legislations and international internal control models.

Why is There Difference between Turkey Legislations and International Internal Control Models and What Should Be Done to Provide Harmony?

When evaluating Turkey legislation and international internal control models together, it can be concluded that there is a difference between them. But that is why?

A lot of banking crisis has been seen in Turkey. Some of banking crisis was seen in 1994, 1995, 2000 and 2001. Being seen banking crisis frequently affected point of view of regulatory authorities of Turkey. So, in order to prevent banking crisis, making new regulations was evaluated as compulsory. In this context, BRSA was established in 1999 and went into action in 2000 as an autonomous authority. Also banking law number 4389 was renewed with new banking law number 5411 in 2005. In addition to this, BRSA issues a charter related with banks' internal systems including internal control. According to Banking Law number 5411 and BRSA's Charter, it is a mandatory to establish a separate internal control department in banks.

As a result, it can be said that cause of difference between Turkey legislations and International Internal Control Models is banking crisis seen in Turkey. Because of this crisis, internal control departments are established as separate departments in banks to providing additional assurance.

Although internal control performs regular transactional controls in banks, it is inevitable that some assurance activities are performed repetitive due to fact that there are also internal audit departments in banks. So, founding separate internal control departments causes additional audit costs, repetitive assurance activities and audit fatigue on business departments. Therefore, internal control departments in banks should be disposed in order to be compliant with international internal control models. For this, related articles in Banking Law number 5411 and BRSA's Charter should be removed. Also, banks personnel's internal control responsibilities should be defined in mentioned regulation or another separate regulation if internal control related articles removed from Banking Law number 5411 and BRSA's Charter so as not to cause deficiency about internal control in banks.

5 Conclusion

Banks are most important financial intermediaries in Turkey. As a result of this condition, banks have systemically importance. For this reason, auditing, controlling and supervision of banks are so important.

There has been some banking crisis in Turkey seen in 1994, 1995, 2000 and 2001. In order to prevent another crisis resulting from banking, some precautions were taken. One of the most important precautions is establishment of BRSA in 1999. Another one is renovation of banking law in 2005. An important issue is foundation of internal control in banks. Turkey Parliament made regulation in Banking Law and BRSA made regulation in the Charter regarding internal control department. Hence, all banks operating in Turkey founded separate internal control department.

Establishment of internal control department in Turkey result from a think that additional assurance activities to be performed by internal control department besides internal audit department could be beneficial to banks and be prevented bank-based financial crisis. However, when internal control issue is handled in the view of international internal control models, it could be seen that internal control is responsibility of everyone in the banks, in other words, responsibility of all personnel of banks from BoD to staff and clerks. For this reason, it is inappropriate to establish a separate internal control department and address internal control responsibility to this department.

As a summary, it was concluded that Turkey's national legislation is incompliant with international internal control models. In order to be in harmony with international internal control models, Turkey should change its national legislations regarding internal control. In this context, articles related with separate internal control departments in Banking Law and BRSA Charter should be removed from legislations. Hence, Turkey legislations would be compliant with international internal control models.

References

Acar, D., & Akçakanat, Ö. (2012). Özel Bütçeli İdarelerden Üniversitelerin Muhasebe Birimlerinin İç Kontrol Uygulamalarına Yönelik Bir Araştırma. *Muhasebe ve Denetime Bakış*, (Eylül), 25–46.

Akwaa-Sekyi, E. K., & Gené, J. M. (2017). Internal controls and credit risk relationship among banks in Europe. *Intangible Capital, 13*(1), 25–50.

Akyel, R. (2010a). Günümüzde İç Kontrol Anlayışı ve Türkiye'ye Yansıması. *Amme İdaresi Dergisi, 43*(4), 167–191.

Akyel, R. (2010b). Türkiye'de İç Kontrol Kavramı, Unsurları ve Etkinliğinin Değerlendirilmesi. *Yönetim ve Ekonomi: Celal Bayar Üniversitesi İktisadi ve İdari Bilimler Fakültesi Dergisi, 17* (1), 83–97.

Altıntaş, H., & Ayrıçay, Y. (2010). Türkiye'de Finansal Gelişme ve Ekonomik Büyüme İlişkisinin Sınır Testi Yaklaşımıyla Analizi: 1987–2007. *Anadolu Üniversitesi Sosyal Bilimler Dergisi, 10* (2), 71–98.

Arıkan, M., & Benk, S. (2017). Kamu Sektöründe Yolsuzluk Riskini Önleyici Bir Araç Olarak İç Kontrol Sistemi. *İnönü Üniversitesi Uluslararası Sosyal Bilimler Dergisi, 6*(1), 41–56.

Atmaca, M. (2012). Muhasebe Skandallarının Önlenmesinde İç Kontrol Sisteminin Etkinleştirilmesi. *Afyon Kocatepe İİBF Dergisi, 14*(1), 191–205.

Bakkal, H., & Kasımoğlu, A. (2012). İç Kontrol Sistemine Karşılaştırmalı Bir Bakış: COSO ve CoCo Modeli. *Mevzuat Dergisi, 15*(178), 1–14.

Banking Law. (2005). 5411 sayılı, 01.11.2005 tarih ve 25983 sayılı Resmi Gazete.

Baskıcı, Ç. (2015). Kurumsal Yönetim Uygulamalarında İç Kontrol Sisteminin Önemi: Borsa İstanbul Şirketleri Üzerine Bir Araştırma. *Uluslararası Yönetim İktisat ve İşletme Dergisi, 11* (25), 163–180.

BDDK. (2006). Bankaların Kurumsal Yönetim İlkelerine İlişkin Yönetmelik, 01.11.2006 tarihli ve 26333 sayılı Resmi Gazete.

BDDK. (2014). Bankaların İç Sistemleri ve İçsel Sermaye Yeterliliği Değerlendirme Süreci Hakkında Yönetmelik, 11.07.2014 tarihli ve 29057 sayılı Resmi Gazete.

BIS. (1998). Framework for internal control systems in banking organizations. Retrieved September 16, 2017, from http://www.bis.org/publ/bcbs40.pdf

Cengiz, S., & Aslanoğlu, S. (2017). İç Kontrol Sisteminin Şeffaflığı ve Kurumsal Yönetim Uygulamaları Arasındaki İlişkinin İncelenmesi: Borsa İstanbul'da Bir Uygulama. *Gümüşhane Üniversitesi Sosyal Bilimler Enstitüsü Elektronik Dergisi, 8*(20), 40–60.

Çetin, C. (2001). Toplam Kalite Yönetimi ve Kalite Güvence Sistemi (ISO 9000-2000 Revizyonu), İlke Süreç, Uygulama. 2.Baskı. Beta Basım Yayım. İstanbul.

Chen, H., Dong, W., Han, H., & Zhou, N. (2013). A comprehensive and quantitative internal control index: Construction, validation and impact. *Review of Quantitative Finance and Accounting, 49*(2), 337–377.

Cho, M., & Chung, K.-H. (2016). The effect of commercial banks' internal control weaknesses on loan loss reserves and provisions. *Journal of Contemporary Accounting & Economics, 12*(1), 61–72.

Cömert, N. (2016). İşletmelerde Kontrol ve Denetim Kavramlarının Doğru Kullanılması Amacına Yönelik Kavramsal Bir İnceleme. *Marmara Business Review, 1*(1), 1–20.

Dabbağoğlu, K. (2009). İç Kontrol Sistemi. *Kafkas Üniversitesi Dergisi, 26,* 109–115.

Doğan, S., & Burgazlıoğlu, E. (2015). İç Kontrol Sistemi ve Özel Bir Hastanede Uygulaması. *Kırklareli Üniversitesi İİBF Dergisi, 4*(1), 18–33.

Donelson, D. C., Ege, M. S., & McInnis, J. M. (2016). Internal control weaknesses and financial reporting fraud. *Auditing: A Journal of Practice & Theory, 36*(3), 45–69.

Doyrangöl, N. (2002). *Sermaye Piyasası Aracı Kurumlarında Etkili Bir İç Kontrol Sistemi ve Denetim Fonksiyonu.* İstanbul: Lebib Yalkın Matbaası.

Du, H., Li, J., & Lei, L. (2016). Research on the relationship between internal control quality and company investment efficiency based on data mining. *Revista Iberica de Sistemas e Tecnologias de Informacao, 6*(8), 15–28.

Duman, A., & Lee, K. (2000). Financial system, financial liberalization and crises. A tale of two countries: Turkey and Korea. Retrieved September 13, 2017, from https://view.officeapps.live.com/op/view.aspx?src=http%3A%2F%2Fwww.ritsumei.ac.jp%2F~leekk%2Fstudy%2Fkotur.doc

Durmuş, C. N., Uzel, M. N., & Hasanefendioğlu, B. (2016). 3'lü Savunma Hattının COSO İç Kontrol Sisteminin Etkinliğinin Arttırılmasında Kaldıraç Etkisi. *Mali Çözüm Dergisi, 136,* 199–212.

Elitaş, C., & Özdemir, Y. (2006). Bankalarda İç Kontrol Sistemi. *Ticaret ve Turizm Eğitim Fakültesi Dergisi, 2,* 155–177.

Elmas, B., & Kurnaz, E. (2013). Türkiye'deki Faktoring Şirketlerinin İç Kontrol Sistemlerinde Etkinlik Araştırması. *Kocaeli Üniversitesi Sosyal Bilimler Dergisi, 26,* 61–76.

Engin, A. (2015). İşletmelerde Satın Alma ve Ödeme Süreçlerine Özgü Hile Riskleri ve Uygun İç Kontrol Ortamının Oluşturulması. *Mali Çözüm Dergisi, 25*(130), 101–119.

Ergin, H., Selimoğlu, S. K., & Tolkun, A. (2016). KİT'lerde Kurumsal Yönetim Etkinliğinin Arttırılmasında İç Kontrol ve İç Denetim Faaliyetlerinin Rolü: Bir Araştırma. *Sosyal Bilimler Dergisi, 49,* 1–28.

Ertuğrul, A. N. (2013). İç Kontrol İle Kurum Kültürü İlişkisi ve Anadolu Üniversitesi Araştırması. *Muhasebe ve Vergi Uygulamaları Dergisi, 1,* 63–100.

Frazer, L. (2016). Internal control: Is it a benefit or fad to small companies? A literature dependency perspective. *Journal of Accounting and Finance, 16*(4), 149–161.

Gamage, C. T., Lock, K. L., & Fernando, A. A. J. (2014). A proposed research framework: Effectiveness of internal control system in state commercial banks in Sri Lanka. *International Journal of Scientific Research and Innovative Technology*, 25–44.

Gül, M., & Kaban, İ. (2015). Bankalarda İç Kontrol-İç Denetim İlişkisi ve Bir Uygulama. *Muhasebe ve Denetime Bakış, 15*(45), 89–111.

Gündoğdu Aysel, Dinç Yusuf, Hayali Ayşe, Sarılı Selin, Dizman Arzu Seçil. (2013). The importance of internal control system in banking sector-evidence from Turkey. *Finance and Economics Conference 2013*, Lupcon Center for Business Research, Frankfurt Am Main, July 4–6.

Hasanefendioğlu, B., & Uzel, M. (2017). COSO Alaaddin'in Sihirli Lambası mı? (Tüm yönleriyle COSO Bazlı İç Kontrol Sistemi). *Mali Çözüm, 141*, 209–226.

Higgins, H. N. (2012). Learning internal controls from a fraud case at bank of China. *Issues in Accounting Education, 27*(4), 1171–1192.

İbiş, C., & Çatıkkaş, Ö. (2012). İşletmelerde İç Kontrol Sistemine Genel Bakış. *Sayıştay Dergisi, 85*, 95–121.

Ji, X.-d., Lu, W., & Qu, W. (2017). Voluntary disclosure of internal control weakness and earnings quality: Evidence from China. *The International Journal of Accounting, 52*(1), 27–44.

Kamu İç Kontrol Rehberi. (2014). Retrieved September 30, 2017, from http://www.pergen.gov.tr/icerik/pdf/8227_kamuickontrolrehberi1versiyon12.pdf

Karakaya, G. (2016). Çalışan Hileleri ve İç Kontrol İlişkisi. *Vergi Sorunları Dergisi, 330*, 159–172.

Kiracı, M. (2003). Faaliyet Denetimi ile İç Kontrol İlişkisi. *Eskişehir Osmangazi Üniversitesi Sosyal Bilimler Dergisi, 4*(2), 67–78.

Kızılboğa, R., & Özşahin, F. (2013). Etkin Bir İç Kontrol Sisteminin İç Denetim Faaliyetine ve İç Denetçilere Katkısı. *Ömer Halisdemir Üniversitesi İktisadi ve İdari Bilimler Fakültesi Dergisi, 6*(2), 220–236.

KPMG. (1999). Internal control: A practical guide. Retrieved September 22, 2017, from http://www.ecgi.org/codes/documents/kpmg_internal_control_practical_guide.pdf

Onur, S. (2012). Finansal Liberalizasyon ve GSMH Büyümesi Arasındaki İlişki. *Uluslararası Yönetim İktisat ve İşletme Dergisi, 1*(1), 127–152.

Özbilgin, İ. G. (2016). Aracı Kurumların İç Kontrol Sistemi ve İlgili Düzenlemenin Değerlendirilmesi. *Gazi Üniversitesi İİBF Dergisi, 12*(2), 219–242.

Özkardeş, L. (2017). Kurumsal Firmaların İç Kontrol, İç Denetim ve Riske Yaklaşımları. *Yaşar Üniversitesi Dergisi, 12*(47), 191–200.

Özten, S., & Karğın, S. (2012). Bankacılıkta İç Kontrol Faaliyetleri Kapsamında Krediler Kontrolü ve Muhasebeleştirme Süreci. *Afyon Kocatepe Üniversitesi İİBF Dergisi, 19*(2), 143–154.

Qfinance. (2017). Internal control frameworks: COSO, CoCo, and the UK Corporate Governance Code. Retrieved September 23, 2017, from http://www.financepractitioner.com/contentFiles/QF02/hnrfm9bx/13/4/internal-control-frameworks-coso-coco-and-the-uk-corporate-governance-code.pdf

Rae, K., Sands, J., & Subramaniam, N. (2017). Associations among the five components within COSO internal control-integrated framework as the underpinning of quality corporate governance. *Australasian Accounting Business & Finance Journal, 11*(1), 28–54.

Rameli, M. N. F., Mohd-Sanusi, Z., Mat-Isa, Y., Omar, N. (2013). Fraud occurrences in bank branches: The importance of internal control and risk management. *The 5th International Conference on Financial Criminology (ICFC)*. Retrieved September 17, 2017, from http://mak.trunojoyo.ac.id/wp-content/uploads/2014/04/P05_Internal-Control-Fraud-Occurence-in-Bank_Mohd-Nor-Firdaus-Rameli1.pdf

Sevim, A., & Gül, M. (2012). Elektronik İşletmelerde (e-İşletmelerde) Satın Alma İşlemleri ve İç Kontrol İlişkisi. *Afyon Kocatepe Üniversitesi İİBF Dergisi, 14*(2), 91–118.

Shi, X., & Wang, S. (2014). The application of information technology in bank accounting internal control risk. *In Applied Mechanics and Materials, 631*, 1291–1294.

Sun, Y. (2016). Internal control weakness disclosure and firm investment. *Journal of Accounting, Auditing & Finance, 31*(2), 277–307.

Targan, Ü. (1996). Finans Kesiminin Reel Sektöre Kaynak Yaratma Kapasitesi. *İstanbul Ticaret Odası Yayını, 31.*

The ICA. (1999). Internal control-guidance for directors on the combined code. Retrieved September 22, 2017, from http://www.ecgi.org/codes/documents/turnbul.pdf

The IIA. (2017). Uluslararası İç Denetim Standartları, Uluslararası Mesleki Uygulama Çerçevesi, ABD.

TİDE. (2016). Çerçeve ve Ekler. COSO İç Kontrol-Bütünleşik Çerçeve, *TİDE Yayınları,* Yayın No. 11.

Topçu, M. K. (2013). Kamuda İç Kontrol Sisteminin Coso Modeli Bağlamında Taşrada Uygulanabilirliği: İhalelerde Uygulanmasına Yönelik İki Vaka Analizi. *Sayıştay Dergisi, 91,* 5–31.

Tüm, K., & Reyhanoğlu, M. (2015). İç Kontrol Sisteminin Örgüt Kültürünü Belirlemesindeki Rolü. *Mustafa Kemal Üniversitesi Sosyal Bilimler Enstitüsü Dergisi, 12*(31), 395–422.

Türedi, S. (2012). İç Kontrol Sistemi ve Toplam Kalite Yönetimi İlişkisi. *Uluslararası Alanya İşletme Fakültesi Dergisi, 4*(14), 27–37.

Türedi, H., & Karakaya, G. (2015). COSO İç Kontrol Modeli ve Kontrol Ortamı. *Finans Politik & Ekonomik Yorumlar Dergisi, 52*(602), 67–76.

Türedi, H., & Koban, A. O. (2016). COSO İç Kontrol Modelinde Risk Değerlendirme Faaliyetleri. *Marmara Üniversitesi Öneri Dergisi, 12*(46), 155–177.

Türedi, H., Gürbüz, F., & Alıcı, Ü. (2014). COSO Modeli: İç Kontrol Yapısı. *Marmara Üniversitesi Öneri Dergisi, 11*(42), 141–155.

Türedi, H., Koban, A. O., & Karakaya, G. (2015). COSO İç Kontrol (ABD) Modeli İle İngiliz (TURNBULL) ve Kanada (CoCo) Modellerinin Karşılaştırılması. *Sayıştay Dergisi, 99,* 95–119.

Usul, H., Titiz, İ., & Ateş, B. A. (2011). İç Kontrol Sisteminin Kurumsal Yönetimin Oluşumundaki Etkinliği: Marmara Bölgesi Belediye İşletmelerine Yönelik Bir Uygulama. *Muhasebe ve Finansman Dergisi, 49,* 48–54.

Uyar, S. (2010). UFRS Uygulamalarında İç Kontrol Sisteminin Etkisi ve Önemi. *Alanya İşletme Fakültesi Dergisi, 2*(2), 38–62.

Uysal, T. U. (2015). Yiyecek-İçecek Hizmeti Veren Konaklama İşletmelerinde Maliyet Kontrol Sistemlerinin Etkinliği Açısından İç Kontrol. *Muhasebe ve Vergi Uygulamaları Dergisi, 8*(1), 53–65.

Yavuz, S. T. (2002). İç Kontrol Fonksiyonunun Bileşenleri. *Bankacılar Dergisi, 13*(42), 39–56.

Yüksel, A., & Demir, V. (2011). Bankalarda Denetim ve İç Kontrol Yapısı Eksikliğinin Sonucu: Finansal Kriz. *Mali Çözüm Dergisi, 55,* 1–10.

Yurtsever, G. (2008). *Bankacılığımızda İç Kontrol.* İstanbul: *Türkiye Bankalar Birliği (TBB) Yayını.*

A Non-compensative Index for Country Risk in OECD Countries

Enrico Ivaldi, Carolina Bruzzi, and Riccardo Soliani

Abstract In the last few years a fast growth of international lending and foreign investment has been happening. As a consequence of the large flow of capital going towards new developing countries, the risk exposure of the lenders and investors is rising, and country risk analysis becomes more and more important for the international financial operators. In the present paper we propose a non-compensatory index to reckon the country risk (since now, Country Risk) in OECD countries: the Mazziotta Pareto Index (MPI). It assumes the "non-substitutability" of the dimensions, all of them being considered of the same importance, without any compensation possible among them. The indicator classifies the Ocse with OECD into six main groups, according to their high or low country risk. Although based on a small number of variables, the MPI can to assess quite correctly the pre-figurative "latent dimensions" of the Country Risk in the short run. The proposed index sheds light particularly on the risk linked to political-economical events and decisions, and on the public finance. The Country Risk Index proposed allows to asses international country risk ratings comparatively, and to single out the relevance of economic, financial and political risk as components of a general risk rating.

E. Ivaldi (✉)
Department of Political Science, University of Genova, Genova, Italy

Centro de Investigaciones en Econometrìa, Universidad de Buenos Aires (UBA), Buenos Aires, Argentina
e-mail: enrico.ivaldi@unige.it

C. Bruzzi · R. Soliani
Department of Political Science, University of Genova, Genova, Italy
e-mail: riccardo.soliani@unige.it

© Springer International Publishing AG, part of Springer Nature 2018   455
H. Dincer et al. (eds.), *Strategic Design and Innovative Thinking in Business Operations*, Contributions to Management Science,
https://doi.org/10.1007/978-3-319-77622-4_23

1 Introduction

As the international debt of less developed countries grew rapidly in the 1970s and the incidence of debt rescheduling increased in the early 1980s, the international financial community has been concerned with country risk, which reflects the ability and willingness of a country to meet its financial obligations (Cosset and Roy 1991; Cosset et al. 1992) and international rating agencies have begun to measure the credit risk involving sovereign countries (Hoti and McAleer 2004). Nowadays "country risk" has become topical once again. The first and the most obvious reason for this is the intensifying process of globalization, which created a new economic and political setting (San-Martín-Albizuri and Rodríguez-Castellanos 2011). One more reason for the renewed interest is the recent sovereign and private debt crises in many of the European countries (both EU and not EU member states), including some of those that are part of the Euro zone (Eijffinger 2012). Furthermore, the aftermaths of the financial crisis spread all around the world (San-Martín-Albizuri and Rodríguez-Castellanos 2017). Finally, governments too are involved in this process, since their actions can often impact country risk directly. Increased country risk often translates into less foreign investment in the country, and leads to lower economic growth and potential political turmoil, which in turn may cause and increase in country risk (Bouchet et al. 2003; Erb et al. 1996; San-Martín-Albizuri and Rodríguez-Castellanos 2015; Aboura and Chevallier 2015).

Country Risk covers a mix of risks, which may reveal unsustainable, that emerge when investments or financial or commercial exchange flows arise, are made in a foreign country (Ivaldi 2013). Such an ample definition adapts to different investment strategies and includes all the areas at risk coming up outside one's own country. Country Risk assessment is extremely complex. In order to get it, one must collect and elaborate widespread information and quantitative data (Agliardi et al. 2012). In doing that, the "subjective" judgement is inevitably relevant (San-Martín-Albizuri and Rodríguez-Castellanos 2017).

The results of a country risk analysis can be employed as tools to make both pre-lending and post lending decisions (Hoti 2005). Before lending, the measured risk is the base to decide whether or not to lend, how much to lend, and how much risk premium to charge. After lending, the periodic country risk check is a monitoring action and provides a pre-warning system (Nath 2008).

In the studies on country crises throughout time, the methods applied are different: e. g., the variable selections through the principal component analysis (PCA), which allows the reduction of variables to include in the index in a new mix of "latent" variable rundowns, (Levy and Yoon 1996); the MHDIS (Multi-group Hierarchical Discrimination) analysis by Doumpos and Zopounidis (2002), which compares different analysis methods for developing countries; the creation of a Country Risk index on the level of geographical areas (Carment 2001); the two different models by Hammer et al. (2004, 2006): the first one based on multiple linear reversion, and the second that uses a logical analysis of data technique (LAD); Hybrid neural networks, logit models, discriminant analysis and cluster techniques used by Yim and Mitchell (2005); Factor DCC-model used by Aboura and Chevallier (2015).

In the 1960s and 1970s Country Risk was calculate only on qualitative types of studies (Avramovic et al. 1964; Frank Jr and Cline 1971) but from the 1980s the studies have become markedly quantitative, to forecast default danger or financial crisis. However, also sophisticated quantitative approaches can be incapable to account for phenomena not precisely described by numbers (Ivaldi and Di Gennaro 2011). Indeed, the Country Risk must be interpreted on the basis of a multidimensional approach, considering both well-known risks, such as macroeconomic fragility and geopolitical risks (Meldrum 2000). Nath (2008) argues for the necessity to enlarge the field of analysis, create more fitting models, and face new challenges, Cukier and Mayer-Schoenberger (2013) underline the new researchers' ability of using "big data".

In the present paper authors propose a non-compensatory index to reckon the country risk in OECD countries: the Mazziotta Pareto Index (MPI). It assumes the "non-substitutability" of the dimensions, all of them being considered of the same importance, without any compensation possible among them. Not only does it consider quantitative variables, but also qualitative elements, which play there a key role. Although based on a small number of variables, the MPI can to assess quite correctly the pre-figurative "latent dimensions" of the Country Risk in the short run. Finally, authors provide some additional considerations about the year of analysis.

2   Variables Selection

Literature is divided about which algorithms are to be used to select the variables to include in the analysis, taking into account that the choice is trained also by the obtainability of data. This impacts on the choice and, therefore, on the composition of the indicator itself (Ivaldi et al. 2016a, b), and by the purposes of the indicator (Soliani et al. 2011a, b; Testi and Ivaldi 2009; Carstairs 2000; Gordon and Pantazis 1997; Carstairs and Morris 1991; Jarman 1983). In general, the study must avoid the risk of considering separately dimensions that are really similar, incurring in overlaps.

It's useful to make an index based on currently available data, which do not require ad hoc surveys, basing decisions on transparent data and coming directly from certified sources (Gordon and Pantazis 1997; Jarman 1983, 1984; Forrest and Gordon 1993; Townsend 1987).

To define the field of research, a first test on data supplied by official research bodies and statistical institutions was made (Ivaldi and Testi 2010; Burlando et al. 2016). The study concentrated on a mix of variables dependable with the choices of most of literature (Carment 2001; Doumpos et al. 2001; Hammer et al. 2004; Doumpos and Zopounidis 2002; Levy and Yoon 1996; Ivaldi and Di Gennaro 2011) (Table 1).

3   Method

To select indicators principal component analysis (PCA) has been used. With PCA, it's possible to partition the total variance by first finding the linear combination of the variables that accounts for the maximum amount of variance:

$$y_1 = a_{11}x_1 + a_{12}x_2 + \ldots + a_{1p}p$$

Table 1 Variable selected

1. Government deficit/Surplus[a]
2. Employment to population ratio, 15+, total (%)[a]
3. Central Government Debt as a % of GDP)[a]
4. Population Growth Rate Annual[a]
5. Total reserves (includes gold, current US$) (% GDP)[a]
6. Exports of goods and services (% of GDP)[a]
7. Net Migration (% pop tot)[a]
8. GDP growth (annual %)[a]
9. GiniIndex[a]
10. Inflation, consumer prices (annual %)[a]
11. PoliticalRisk[b]
12. Human Development Index (HDI)[a]
13. Population 15–64 (%of total)[a]
14. Imports of goods and services (% of GDP)[a]

Sources of variables: [a]World Bank, [b]Marsh 2015

Where y_1 is the first principal component (Johnson and Wichern 2002). The method proceeds by finding a second linear combination, not correlated with the first component, such that it explains the next largest quantity of variance in the system, after the variance referred to the first component has been removed (Dillon and Goldstein 1984). The equation of the second component is:

$$y_2 = a_{21}x_1 + a_{22}x_2 + \ldots + a_{2p}p$$

The procedure goes on in this way. Thus, the use of principal components allows creating a set of uncorrelated variables (the components) by transforming a set of correlated variables. It means that the Pearson correlation between the components is equal to 0 (Pituch and Stevens 2016; Stevens 1986).

In order to better explain one single common factor it's possible to find a rotation solution (Johnson and Wichern 2002). A number of analytic rotation methods have been developed, (Krzanowski and Marriott 1995; Fabrigar et al. 1999) that explain solution in which factors are correlated or uncorrelated (Gorsuch 1983; Abdi 2003). In this case different rotation algorithm tests revealed the stability of the components extracted as well as the particular effectiveness of the Varimax rotation method (Kaiser 1958).

Once extraction and rotation have been carried out, it is important to select which factors, i.e. variables, are to be used in the indicator. This has been done taking simultaneously into consideration three selection criteria:

1. Kaiser criterion: is necessary to retain all factors extracted which have an eigenvalue superior than one (Kaiser 1960).
2. Explained variance criterion: the basis for the selection is the cumulative explained variance with a level of explained variance about 70% (Stevens 2002).
3. Scree test: this method aims to give a graphical representation of the factors to be taken into consideration. According to the Cattell method, the choice of factors should be limited where there is a levelling in the slope of the line (Cattel 1966).

Although it is desirable to assign different weights to the various factors considered, no reliable basis for doing this exists Once having selected the variables it is possible to aggregate them with the aim of getting an index which singles out Country Risk Index (CRI).

In this case it's possible to assign the same weights to the variables considered because there is no reliable basis to assign different weights (Myer and Jencks 1989; Testi and Ivaldi 2009; Nardo et al. 2005).

The selected methods to aggregate the four indicators in an index is Mazziotta Pareto Index (MPI) (Mazziotta and Pareto 2012; De Muro et al. 2007) MPI assumes the "non-substitutability" of the dimensions: equal importance is attributed to the dimensions and no compensation between them is allowed (Munda and Nardo (2005).

The MPI has been applied in the last decade to discuss the Millennium Development Goals (MDG) (De Muro et al. 2007), to measure the Italian health infrastructure endowment (Mazziotta and Pareto 2011), to identify social inequality in Italian regions (Mazziotta et al. 2010a, b), to assess the quality of life in the Italian provinces (Mazziotta and Pareto 2012) and to measure political utilization in Italian regions (Ivaldi et al. 2016b).

Therefore the MPI method require the standardization of the indicator and the aggregation of them by arithmetic algorithm with penalty function based on horizontal variability, measured by the coefficient of variation (CV), ensures that the score of the units which have a higher imbalance between the values of the indicators are penalized (Landi et al. 2017). Finally, by using the standardized deviation to calculate the synthetic index it is possible to obtain a measure which is robust and not very sensitive to the removal of a single elementary indicator (Mazziotta and Pareto 2012). The normalization process is carried out as follows:

$$z_{i,j} = 100 + \frac{\left(x_{i,j} - \mu_j \right)}{\sigma_j} 10$$

where $z_{i,j}$ is the standardized value of each j-th indicator of each i-th Country. $x_{i,j}$ is the original value of each j-th variable of each Country. μ_j is the mean of each j-th indicator. σ_j is the standard deviation of each j-th indicator (Ivaldi et al. 2017).

For each Country is calculated the average z-scores sum, the standard deviation and the Coefficient of variation (CV)

$$\mu_{z_i} = \frac{\sum_{j=1}^4 z_{i,j}}{4} \qquad \sigma_{z_i} = \sqrt{\frac{\sum_{j=1}^4 \left(z_{i,j} - \mu_{z_i} \right)}{4}} \qquad CV_{z_i} = \frac{\sigma_{z_i}}{\mu_{z_i}}$$

Then the index is calculated as:

$$MPI_i = \mu_{z_i} - \sigma_{z_i} cv_{z_i}$$

where MPI_i is the value of the index for each country.

In this methodology there is a function that attributes a penalty to the units with unbalanced values of the partial composite indices. The penalty is based on the CV and is zero if all values are equal. The aim is to give an advantage to areas that, mean being equal, have a greater balance among the different dimensions of deprivation (Mazziotta and Pareto 2012).

Therefore, MPI is construct with the aggregation of the indicators of each dimension and with the sum of the partial composite indices.

To complete the analysis, it's useful to divide countries in classes in order to make the comparison between the two indices easier. In this paper authors apply a cluster analysis since it can be applied to group the information on countries (Nardo et al. 2005).

As Berkhin (2006) points out: "clustering is a division of data into groups of similar objects; they are similar between themselves, but are dissimilar to the elements of other groups. Each group, called cluster, consists of objects that are similar between themselves and dissimilar to objects of other groups." Clustering techniques are divided in partitioning and hierarchical and in this case it's better to apply the second since this dataset is quite small, otherwise this technique would be very sub-optimal. There are two categories of hierarchical clustering methods: agglomerative (bottom-up) and divisive (top-down). If subsets of points are to be merged or split rather than individual points, one needs to generalise the distance between individual points to the distance between subsets. Such derived proximity measure is called a linkage metric. Hierarchical algorithms are significantly affected by the type of linkage metric used, since the latter reflects a particular concept of closeness and connectivity (Berkhin 2006).

In this work it's possible to use Ward's method, according to which the distance between two clusters, 1 and 2, is given by the increase of the sum of squares obtained merging them. With hierarchical clustering, the sum of squares starts out at zero and then increases as clusters are merged. In the method of Ward it's keep to limit this growth as much as possible (Ward 1963).

4 Results

Beginning from the variables listed in Table 2, authors use principal component analysis to evaluate which variables should be left, following the three criteria already highlighted above: Kaiser's method, scree test and explained variance criterion.

Figure 1 shows scree plot and Table 3 shows values of explained variance. Since the second component explains just 62% of the variance it's possible to take into account all the three components and do not exclude any variable, as suggested also by the other two methods.

Following what is shown in the method, the index has been calculated with MPI.

The final step consists in grouping the values of indexes into different categories in order to identify the areas with similar socio-economic conditions. Applying cluster analysis to CR Index it's possible to obtain six classes in which grouping the Countries. Table 4 and Fig. 2 show the resulted dendrograms from this analysis.

The index places a 107.50 for Switzerland, which shows the lowest Country Risk and at 90.28 from the Greece, which shows the highest Country Risk.

Table 2 Rotated component matrix(a)

	Component				
	1	2	3	4	5
Government deficit/Surplus OECD	0.801	0.151	0.008	0.241	0.122
Employment to population ratio, 15+, total (%) (modeled ILO estimate)	0.794	0.130	0.146	−0.305	−0.012
Central Government Debt total %GDP	0.732	0.105	−0.124	0.396	0.121
Total reserves (includes gold, current US$) (% GDP)	0.535	−0.125	0.081	−0.055	−0.342
Imports of goods and services (% of GDP)	0.142	−0.865	0.053	0.078	0.001
Net Migration (% pop tot)	0.358	0.794	0.138	0.179	−0.146
Population Growth Rate	0.500	0.649	−0.270	−0.130	0.345
GiniIndex	0.132	−0.020	0.818	0.115	0.045
Inflation, consumer prices (annual %) 02/08/2017	−0.320	−0.180	0.712	−0.154	−0.039
Political Risk	0.468	0.316	0.666	−0.233	0.013
Human Development Index (HDI)	0.159	0.011	0.084	−0.804	0.058
Population 15-64 (%of total)	0.254	−0.014	0.029	0.791	0.095
GDP growth (annual %)	−0.006	−0.078	−0.049	−0.069	0.902
Exports of goods and services (% of GDP)	0.094	0.087	0.418	0.414	0.610

Extraction Method: Principal Component Analysis
Rotation Method: Varimax with Kaiser Normalization
Rotation converged in eight iterations

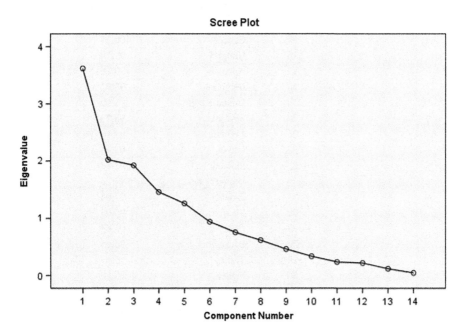

Fig. 1 Scree plot

Table 3 Total variance explained

Component	Rotation sums of squared loadings		
	Total	% of Variance	Cumulative %
1	2.930	20.930	20.930
2	2.014	14.384	35.314
3	1.943	13.875	49.189
4	1.906	13.616	62.805
5	1.488	10.627	73.432

Extraction Method: Principal Component Analysis.

Table 4 Country risk index (CRI)

n	Country	MPI (CRI)	Class
1	Switzerland	107.53	1
2	Luxembourg	106.75	1
3	Iceland	105.11	2
4	Norway	104.39	2
5	Czech Republic	103.49	2
6	Sweden	103.17	2
7	Estonia	101.68	3
8	Denmark	101.32	3
9	Korea. Rep.	101.02	3
10	Slovak Republic	100.93	3
11	Germany	100.63	3
12	Ireland	100.55	3
13	Austria	100.50	3
14	New Zealand	100.50	3
15	Canada	100.37	3
16	Hungary	99.50	4
17	Australia	99.16	4
18	Belgium	98.92	4
19	United Kingdom	98.40	4
20	Slovenia	98.28	4
21	Netherlands	98.10	4
22	Latvia	97.45	4
23	Finland	97.42	4
24	United States	97.23	4
25	Israel	97.04	4
26	Mexico	96.93	4
27	Chile	96.43	5
28	Portugal	96.05	5
29	Turkey	95.63	5
30	France	95.56	5
31	Poland	95.53	5
32	Japan	95.23	5
33	Spain	95.21	5
34	Italy	93.61	5
35	Greece	90.27	6

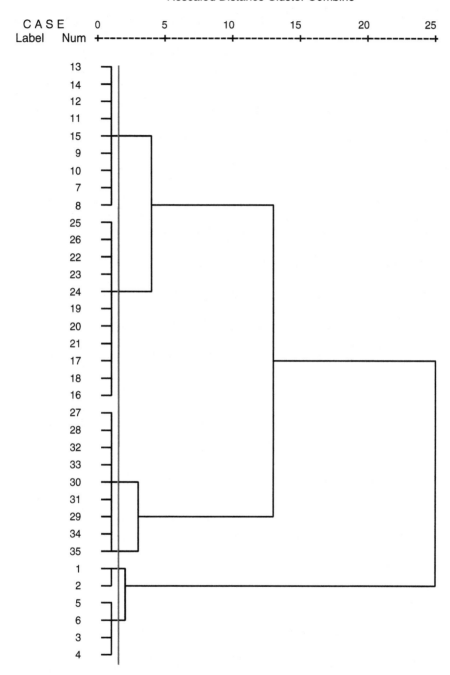

Fig. 2 Hierarchical cluster analysis—Dendrogram using Ward methods

The global financial crisis had significant implications on the trade's and financial's dynamics worldwide, so trying to make a measure of the country risk using different variables can show results unexpected compared to historical tendencies or single criterion of rating.

Switzerland and Luxembourg are in the first class. The two small countries are historically characterized by efficient markets and stable economies, high standards of living and widespread good socioeconomic conditions.

Switzerland has high standard of living, industrial productivity and quality of education and health care systems and its GDP per capita is among the highest in Europe. Luxembourg's economy is characterized by the catching taxation system and the high level of international openness. The financial sector is the main driving resource. It supports the Grand Duchy's economy, representing about 36% of the country's GDP, but also industry and export are important components.

The following class includes countries not very affected by the financial crisis. Iceland can exploit renewable energy sources and exports fishery products, so its economic outlook is positive: this country has a small budget surplus, public debt is falling (although remains above its pre-crisis levels) and, in 2015, was able to pay back the loan that was granted by the International Monetary Fund in 2008.

Another emergent country is Czech Republic, whose economy, based almost exclusively on automobile industry and tourism, is one of the most developed in Central and Eastern Europe. The country presents a very dynamic economy, with low rate of unemployment and growing wages; from 2015 its economy grows, thanks principally to domestic consumption and public investment. In the second class there are also Norway and Sweden, a couple of highly developed post-industrial societies: both of them have very high GDP per capita, and among the highest level of taxation in the world, coupled with outstanding welfare state. However, Norwegian economy is dependent on the revenue generated by the North Sea oil, and Sweden is sensitive to external shocks due to its dependence on export. Therefore, both of them contracted during the global financial crisis, which hit heavily also the Eurozone.

In the third class we have emerging countries and well-established economic powers. The European countries defined Ex Transition Countries (Slovak Republic and Estonia), became dynamic market economy in the 2000s. Emerging countries South Korea and Ireland participate well to the international trade with their specific production: high-tech goods and integrated circuits respectively. Furthermore, in recent years Slovak Republic and Ireland implemented a light taxation system that gave them important competitive advantages.

Rich countries like Germany, Austria, Canada suffered the global economic crisis and the shrinking European demand, which affected their economy performance.

In particular, Germany, whose external trade is about 84% of the GDP, exports cars, car components, drugs, and this gets it highly sensitive to the external shocks, namely the fall of European demand.

Now Austria, after a period of stagnation, has a recovery in terms of GDP growth, but its rate of unemployment increases, offering an impressive, extreme example of jobless recovery.

Danish economy is very open and financialized; but, in spite of its high GDP per capita and almost negligible social inequality, it suffers from low productivity.

Out of Europe, New Zealand's economy is based on tourism and agriculture. It has been damaged by the milk price decline on the international market, since New Zealand is the world's largest exporter of milk. It has restarted growing only in 2016. Canada, leader in the export of zinc, uranium, and other commodities, with a foreign trade representing about the 65% of the GDP, suffers the consequences of the low oil price.

In the fourth class, there is strong heterogeneity. We can find both countries heavily affected by the global financial crisis, and countries that in the last years have been able to invest their resources to gain higher level of competitiveness. The United Kingdom was hit by the crisis particularly in its financial market, but now it is recovering, even if remains the high public deficit and the significant rate of young unemployment remain, together with the aftermath of the Brexit, which are partly unpredictable today. The Netherlands have a very open economy, are the sixth largest economic power in the Eurozone and the fifth largest exporter of goods; but its strength transformed in weakness, because the Eurozone slump, contracted the demand for export. Finland is one of the leading countries in the new technologies, but it is also the country in the Eurozone much hit by the crisis. It suffers from increasing unemployment and inequality, despite its high living standard.

The big economy of the United States is growing, thanks to the fiscal and monetary stimulus package. On the other hand, the ratio public debt/GDP is growing as well, industrial exports slump and inequality is deepening.

Hungary, Slovenia, Latvia (ex-Transition Country) and Mexico, are developing countries, with open economies, characterized by deep inequality and widespread poverty. Hungary is the host country to several R&D division or headquarters of international companies, thanks to its light fiscal policy; furthermore, an effective policy against unemployment has been realized, therefore the rate of unemployment falls. Slovenia completed its economic transition successfully, following and consolidating its long tradition of economic integration with neighboring countries, particularly Germany, Austria and Italy, and drawing benefit from a skilled and productive labor force; therefore, it has a comparatively low unemployment rate. Due to its strategical geographic position, in Latvian economy logistics, especially transport of oil and raw materials between CIS and Europe, is the most important sector. Mexico has an export-oriented economy, strictly dependent on the USA economic cycle, and it is also an emerging financial market. Its per capita income is the highest in Latin America, but its deep inequality is witnessed by the amazing percentage of people living behind the line of poverty (45%).

In Australian economy, international trade is about the 41% of GDP (2015), mainly with China. The country has raw materials, parks and natural reserves, and its economic structure is based on export of commodities, tourism and services. Australia is the only OECD country that did not fall in recession during the financial crisis.

Belgium, after 2013, have had a slow recovery, thanks to its policies, but it suffers for high young unemployment.

Israel's financial market becomes more and more important, and it has a high level of investment in research and development. In recent years the unemployment rate has declined dramatically, but the social and economic integration of Arab and Haredi (ultra-Orthodox Jewish) minorities remains the great challenge to face.

The fifth group includes European country ravaged by the financial crisis, with unemployment and economic uncertainty; and developing countries that are building their economic structures.

In Portugal there are decline in investment, particularly in construction, and slowdown in private consumption and export. However, there are feeble signals of recovery in the medium-long run, e. g. the small decrease of the rate of unemployment.

France is one of the most important world export powers and has accused the decline of the foreign demand. Its unemployment has increased very much, as well as its public debt.

Spanish economy, based on tourism and financial services, after 6 years of recession has recovered from 2016 when, supported by domestic demand, the economy has begun to grow, also reducing the level of unemployment. It is the European country where the state integrity is most at risk.

Italy's points of weakness are public debt, young unemployment, stagnation and political instability. Another long-lasting question is territorial inequality, between the quite modern North, and the backward South, where the organized crime is a secular plague.

Poland is the only EU country that has maintained positive growth throughout the global economic crisis, and saw a significant growth that made it an important player in the European market. But it is still characterized by high inequality and unemployment, and territorial unbalances.

Chile, one of South America's most prosperous nations, must fight now against the widespread socioeconomic inequalities. The recent policy of investment in renewable energy should guarantee energy sufficient to cover the 20% of requirements in coming years.

Turkey suffers the political instability and the low level of household consumption, due also to inequality. A significant contribute to the national income comes from construction and from the public investment in infrastructure projects. Despite these positive points, the high level of unemployment, very low wages and large informal sector are persistent difficulties in Turkey.

Japan has a strong dependence on import of petroleum and raw material and on export of manufactures, then it is exposed to external shocks. Further concerns that Japan will have to address in the near future are the aging of the population and the political tensions with South Korea and China.

In the last class, Greece has a very precarious economy, that has been experiencing many years of recession, increasing levels of unemployment and also environmental crisis (a problem which receive less attention). The Greek crisis, since 2010, when the country neared bankruptcy, engendered the rise of the debt with Europe and IMF, which created political and economic tensions and the concrete risk of Grexit from UE.

5 Conclusions

Most large corporations make it a priority to understand, analyse and incorporate country risk, as their success in a global market is increasingly dependent upon growth in foreign markets (Brown et al. 2015; Stiglitz 2000).

Nowadays it is possible to question the accuracy of any risk rating agency in determining any or all of these measures (Cavallo et al. 2013; Alsakka and Ap Gwilym 2013). The proposed index can help to find out earlier, on the basis of a limited number of variables, the existence of potential risks for the operators. Operators will thus be allowed to formulate a better estimate of the ongoing events over a short period. With regard to this, there is no doubt that prompt insight can play a role of great importance, especially with regard to the events currently taking place and evolving (Aizenman et al. 2013).

Therefore, advance insight represents added value, which moreover needs further analysis to compare and complete with the opinions emerging from the procedure "consensus-building" put in place by experts from the top agencies and evaluators of the risk assessment institutions (Nordhal 2001).

In general, it is appropriate to consider that, besides the emerging risks from trading exchange, which can be partially covered by insurance, there are others scarcely safeguarded, or even without any protection at all (San-Martín-Albizuri and Rodríguez-Castellanos 2012). They are, e.g., the risks dependent on geopolitical events, or deriving from insolvency at the level of sovereign debt, from constraints and restrictions such as the financial and currency hindrances, from excessive variations of price, interest rate, and foreign exchange up-and-down (Kaminsky and Schmukler 2002; Gapen et al. 2008; Hilscher and Nosbusch 2010).

Country Risk Index classifies the Ocse with OECD into six main groups, according to their high or low country risk. Looking at the entire classification, authors have results partly foregone, but partly in contrast with historical tendencies or the rating based on a single criterion.

In the first class there is a couple of countries with high standards of living and efficient and stable markets. The second class includes countries scarcely affected by the financial crisis. Iceland, which exploits renewable energy sources and exports fishery products, has a positive economic outlook. The growth of Czech Republic, based on automotive industry and tourism, is largely due to domestic consumption and public investment. Norway and Sweden are post-industrial countries, with high GDP per capita, heavy taxation and, perhaps, the best welfare state in OECD countries. Nevertheless, both of them contracted during the global crisis.

In the third class there are emerging countries (Slovak Republic and Estonia, a couple of Ex Transition Countries, and South Korea and Ireland) and solid rich states, like Germany, Austria, Denmark, and, out of Europe, New Zealand and Canada, which have been affected by the crisis and have reduced their export. Also the fourth group is heterogeneous. There are the United Kingdom, hit by the financial crisis, and the Netherlands, which have a very open economy, suffering from the drop of export. Finland is leader in the new technologies, but has been greatly damaged by the crisis. Also the Country Risk of the US is quite high, perhaps unexpectedly. This is due to their growing public debt/GDP ratio, the slump of export and the growing inequality. Widespread poverty and deep inequality characterise also a group of countries, partly Ex Transition countries: Hungary, Slovenia, Latvia and Mexico. High young unemployment and political risk. Belgium and Israel, respectively; also them are part of the fourth class, together with Australia.

In the fifth class there are big countries of the UE (France, Spain, Italy), together with Poland and Portugal, and, out of Europe, Chile, Turkey and Japan. Political instability, crime, social and territorial inequality, public debt, unemployment, slump in household consumption affect more or less all of them. Japan due its poor score to the openness of its economy, which expose it to external shocks. Furthermore, the average age of population is high, and it is developing political tension with China and South Korea. Finally, Greece is at the last level. It has been experiencing recession and unemployment and also environmental crisis (a problem which receive less attention). In 2010, when the country neared bankruptcy, the debt with Europe and IMF soared, triggering internal political tension and the concrete risk of Grexit from UE.

The Country Risk Index proposed in this paper allows to asses international country risk ratings comparatively, and to single out the relevance of economic, financial and political risk as components of a general risk rating. The proposed index sheds light particularly on the risk linked to political-economical events and decisions, and on the public finance although observing that the process of measuring the Country Risk is a continuous *work in progress*.

References

Abdi, H. (2003). *Factor rotations in factor analyses. Encyclopedia for Research Methods for the Social Sciences* (pp. 792–795). Thousand Oaks, CA: Sage.

Aboura, S., & Chevallier, J. (2015). A cross-volatility index for hedging the country risk. *Journal of International Financial Markets, Institutions and Money, 38*, 25–41.

Agliardi, E., Agliardi, R., Pinar, M., Stengos, T., & Topaloglou, N. (2012). A new country risk index for emerging markets: A stochastic dominance approach. *Journal of Empirical Finance, 19*(5), 741–761.

Aizenman, J., Binici, M., & Hutchison, M. (2013). Credit ratings and the pricing of sovereign debt during the euro crisis. *Oxford Review of Economic Policy, 29*(3), 582–609.

Alsakka, R., & Ap Gwilym, O. (2013). Rating agencies' signals during the European sovereign debt crisis: Market impact and spillovers. *Journal of Economic Behavior and Organization, 85*(1), 144–162.

Avramovic, D., Husain, S. S., de Weille, J., Froland, J., Hayes, J. P., & Wyss, H. (1964). *Economic growth and external debt*. Washington, DC: The World Bank.

Berkhin, P. (2006). A survey of clustering data mining techniques. In J. Kogan, C. Nicholas, & M. Teboulle (Eds.), *Grouping multidimensional data: Recent advance in clustering* (p. 25). New York: Springer.

Bouchet, M. H., Clark, E., & Groslambert, B. (2003). *Country risk assessment: A guide to global investment strategy*. Chichester, England: John Wiley & Sons Ltd.

Brown Christopher L. Cavusgil Tamer, Lord A. Wayne (2015) Country-risk measurement and analysis: A new conceptualization and managerial tool. International Business Review 24, 2, 246-265

Burlando, C., Ivaldi, E., & Musso, E. (2016). An indicator for measuring the perceived quality of local public transport: Relationship with use and satisfaction with the ticket price. *International Journal of Transport Economics, 43*(4), 451–473.

Carment D. (2001); "Assessment country risk: Creating and index of severity"; Discussion Paper prepared for CIFP Risk Assessment Template. May 2001.

Carstairs, V. (2000). Socio-economic factors at area level and their relationship with health. In P. Elliott, J. Wakefield, N. Best, & D. Briggs (Eds.), *Spatial Epidemiology methods and applications* (pp. 51–68). Oxford University Press.

Carstairs, V., & Morris, R. (1991). *Deprivation and health in Scotland*. Aberdeen University Press.

Cattel, R. (1966). The scree test for the number of factors. *Multivariate Behavioural Research, 1*(2), 245–276.

Cavallo, E., Powell, A., & Rigobon, R. (2013). Do credit rating agencies add value? Evidence from the sovereign rating business. *International Journal of Finance and Economics, 18*(3), 240–265.

Cosset, J. C., & Roy, J. (1991). The determinants of country risk ratings. *Journal of International Business Studies, 22*(1), 135–142.

Cosset, J.-C., Siskos, Y., & Zopounidis, C. (1992). Evaluating country risk: A decision support approach. *Global Finance Journal, 3*(1), 79–95.

Cukier, K., & Mayer-Schoenberger, V. (2013). The rise of big data: How it's changing the way we think about the world. *Foreign Affairs, 92*, 28–40.

De Muro, P., Mazziotta, M., & Pareto, A. (2007). Composite indices for multidimensional development and poverty: An application to MDG indicators. In *Wye City Group Meeting. Held in Rome, Italy: June*. http://www.fao. org/es/ess/rural/wye_city_group.

Dillon, W., & Goldstein, M. (1984). *Multivariate analysis method and application*. New York: Wiley.

Doumpos, M., Pentaraki, K., Zopounidis, C., & Agorastos, C. (2001). Assessing country risk using a multi-group discrimination method: A comparative analysis. *Managerial Finance, 27*(8), 16–34.

Doumpos, M., & Zopounidis, C. (2002). On the use of a multi-criteria hierarchical discrimination approach for country risk assessment. *Journal of Multi-Criteria Decision Analysis, 11*(4-5), 279–289.

Erb, C. B., Harvey, C. R., & Viskanta, T. E. (1996). Political risk, economic risk, and financial risk. *Financial Analysts Journal, 52*(6), 29–46.

Eijffinger, S. C. (2012). Rating agencies: Role and influence of their sovereign credit risk assessment in the eurozone. *Journal of Common Market Studies, 50*(6), 912–921.

Fabrigar, L., Wegener, D., MacCallum, R., & Strahan, E. (1999). Evaluating the use of exploratory factor analysis in psychological research. *Psychological Methods, 4*(3), 272–299.

Forrest, R., & Gordon, D. (1993). *People and places: A 1991 census atlas of England*. SAUS: University of Bristol.

Frank, C. R., Jr., & Cline, W. R. (1971). Measurement of debt servicing capacity: An application of discriminant analysis. *Journal of International Economics, 1*(3), 327–344.

Gapen, M., Gray, D., Lim, C. H., & Xiao, Y. (2008). Measuring and analyzing sovereign risk with contingent claims. *IMF Staff Papers, 55*(1), 109–148.

Gordon, D., & Pantazis, C. (1997). *Breadline Britain in the 1990s*. Ashgate Publishing Limited: Ashgate.

Gorsuch, R. (1983). *Factor analysis* (2nd ed.). Hillsdale, NJ: Lawrence Erlbaum Associates.

Hammer, P. L., Kogan, A., & Lejeune, M. A. (2006). Modeling country risk ratings using partial orders (2006). *European Journal of Operational Research, 175*(2), 836–859.

Hammer P. L., Kogan A., Lejeune M.A. (2004), *Country risk ratings: Statistical and combinatorial non-recursive Models*, Rutcor Research Report 8-2004.

Hilscher, J., & Nosbusch, Y. (2010). Determinants of sovereign risk: Macroeconomic fundamentals and the pricing of sovereign debt. *Review of Finance, 14*(2), 235–262.

Hoti, S., & McAleer, M. (2004). An Empirical Assessment of Country Risk Ratings and Asso-
    ciated Models. *Journal of Economic Survey, 18*(4), 539–588.
Hoti, S. (2005). Modelling country spillover effects in country risk ratings. *Emerging Markets Review,*
    6(4), 324–345.
Ivaldi, E. (2013). A proposal of a country risk index based on a factoral analysis: An application to
    South Mediterranean and Central-East European Countries. *International Economics, 66*(2),
    231–249.
Ivaldi, E., Bonatti, G., & Soliani, R. (2016a). The construction of a synthetic index comparing
    multidimensional well-being in the European Union. *Social Indicators Research, 125*(2),
    397–430. https://doi.org/10.1007/s11205-014-0855-8.
Ivaldi, E., Bonatti, G., & Soliani, R. (2016b). An indicator for the measurement of political parti-
    cipation: the case of Italy. *Social Indicator Research.* online. https://doi.org/10.1007/s11205-
    016-1303-8.
Ivaldi, E., Bonatti, G., & Soliani, R. (2017). An indicator for the measurement of political parti-
    cipation: The case of Italy. *Social Indicators Research, 132*(2), 605–620.
Ivaldi E., Di Gennaro A. (2011) Il rischio paese e la sua misurazione: una proposta di indicatore,
    Collana Percorsi di Scienze Economiche e Sociali n.7 Impressioni Grafiche, Acqui Terme.
    ISBN 978-88-6195-105.
Ivaldi, E., & Testi, A. (2010) Genoa Index of Deprivation (GDI): An index of material deprivation
    for geographical areas. In C. M. Baird, (Ed.), *Social indicators: statistics, trends and policy*
    development. New York: Nova Publisher. isbn:978-1-61122-841-0.
Jarman, B. (1983). Identification of underprivileged areas. *British Medical Journal, 286,*
    1705–1709.
Jarman, B. (1984). Underprivileged areas: validation and distribution of scores. *British Medical*
    Journal, 289, 1587–1592.
Johnson, R.A., Wichern, D.W. (2002). *Applied multivariate statistical analysis.* (5th Ed. pp. 767).
    Englewood Cliffs: Prentice-Hall. isbn:0131219731.
Kaiser, H. F. (1958). The varimax criterion for analytic rotation in factor analysis. *Psychometrika,*
    23, 187–200.
Kaiser, H. (1960). The application of electronic computers to factor analysis. *Educational and Psycho-*
    logical Measurement, 20, 141–151.
Kaminsky, G., & Schmukler, S. L. (2002). Emerging market instability: Do sovereign ratings affect
    country risk and stock returns? *World Bank Economic Review, 16*(2), 171–195.
Krzanowski A., Marriott F. (1995), *Classification, covariance, structures and repeated measure-*
    ments, part 2 Kendall's Library of Statistics 2, Multivariate Analysis.
Landi, S., Ivaldi, E., & Testi, A. (2017). Measuring change over time in socio-economic deprivation
    and health in an Urban Context: The case study of Genoa. *Social Indicator Research.* https://doi.
    org/10.1007/s11205-017-1720-3.
Levy J.B., Yoon E (1996). "Methods of Country Risk Assessment for International Market – Entry
    Decision"; University of Massachusetts Lowell ISBM Report 11 – 1996.
Mazziotta, C., Mazziotta, M., Pareto, A., & Vidoli, F. (2010a). La sintesi di indicatori territoriali di
    dotazione infrastrutturale: metodi di costruzione e procedure di ponderazione a confronto.
    Rivista di economia e statistica del territorio, 1, 1–33.
Mazziotta, M., Pareto, A., & Talucci, V. (2010b). *La costruzione di indicatori di disuguaglianza*
    sociale: il caso delle regioni italiane. XXXI Conferenza italiana di scienze regionali. http://
    www.grupposervizioambiente.it/aisre_sito/doc/papers/Mazziotta_Pareto_Talucci_AISRE.pdf
Mazziotta, M., & Pareto, A. (2011). Un indice sintetico non compensativo per la misura della
    dotazione infrastrutturale: un'applicazione in ambito sanitario. *Rivista di statisticauffíciale,*
    13(1), 63–79.
Mazziotta, M., & Pareto, A. (2012). A non-compensatory approach for the measurement of the
    quality of life. In F. Maggino & G. Nuvolati (Eds.), *Quality of life in Italy, Social Indicator*
    Research Series (Vol. 48, pp. 27–40). Netherlands: Springer.
Meldrum D.H. (2000, July 34) Country risk and foreign direct investment, *Business Economics.*
    30–7.

Munda, G., &Nardo, M. (2005). Constructing consistent composite indicators: the issue of weights. EUR 21834 EN., EuropeanCommission.

Myer, S., & Jencks, C. (1989). Poverty and the distribution of material hardship. *Journal of Human Resources, 24*, 88–114.

Nath H.K. (2008) Country risk analysis: A survey of the quantitative methods, Working Paper Series, Sam Houstan State University, Huntsville, TX, pp. 1–31

Nardo, M., Saisana, M., Tarantola, S., Hoffman, A., & Giovannini, E. (2005). *Handbook on constricting composite indicators: methodology and user guide*. N° 2005/3. Paris: OECD Publishing.

Nordal, K. B. (2001). Country risk, country risk indices and valuation of FDI: A real options approach. *Emerging Markets Review, 2*(3), 197–217.

Pituch, K., & Stevens, J. (2016). *Applied multivariate statistics for the social sciences*. New York: Routledge.

San-Martín-Albizuri, N., & Rodríguez-Castellanos, A. (2017). *Measuring country risk: A topic of renewed interest*. In R.-D. Leon (Ed.), *Managerial strategies for business sustainability during turbulent timeseds*. Hershey, PA: Business Science Reference.

San-Martín-Albizuri, N., & Rodríguez-Castellanos, A. (2015). Country risk index and sovereign ratings: Do they foresee financial crises? *Journal of Risk Model Validation, 9*(1), 33–55.

San-Martín-Albizuri, N., & Rodríguez-Castellanos, A. (2012). Globalisation and the unpredictability of crisis episodes: An empirical analysis of country risk indexes. *Investigaciones Europeas de Direccion y Economia de la Empresa, 18*(2), 148–155.

San-Martín-Albizuri, N., Rodríguez-Castellanos, A. (2011) The unpredictability of the crisis: An empirical analysis of country risk indexes | [La imprevisibilidad de las crisis: Un análisis empírico sobre los índices de riesgo país] *Innovar* 21(39), pp. 161-178

Soliani R., Di Gennaro A., Ivaldi E. (2011a) How deprivation affects life expectancy in France and Italy: Comparative evidence from a factorial analysis, in Socioeconomic Status and Health Implications eds. Reibert S. and Jannings A. Nova, New York isbn: 978-1-62100-675-6

Soliani R., Di Gennaro A., Ivaldi E. (2011b) An Index of the quality of life for European Country: evidence of deprivation from EU-Silc data – *Proceeding of the Vienna 2011 Conference on Schumpeter's Heritage: the evolution of the Theory of Evolution, 27–30 October 2011*

Stevens, J. (1986). *Applied multivariate statistics for the social sciences*. Hillsdale: Lawrence Erlbaum A.

Stevens, J. (2002). *Applied multivariate statistics for the social sciences* (4th ed.). NJ Lawrence Erlbaum Associates: Mahwah.

Stiglitz, J. E. (2000). Capital market liberalization, economic growth, and instability. *World Development, 28*(6), 1075–1086.

Testi, A., & Ivaldi, E. (2009). Material versus social deprivation and health: A case study of an urban area. *The European Journal of Health Economics, 10*(3), 323–328.

Townsend, P. (1987). Deprivation. *Journal of Social Policy, 2*, 125–146.

Yim, J., & Mitchell, H. (2005). Comparison of country risk models: Hybrid neural networks, logit models, discriminant analysis and cluster techniques. *Expert Systems with Applications, 28*(1), 137–148.

Ward, J. (1963). Hierarchical grouping to optimize an objective function. *Journal of the American Statistical Association, 58*(301), 236–244.

Printed by Printforce, the Netherlands